COMMUNICATION
in Our Lives

Julia T Wood

LINEBERGER DISTINGUISHED PROFESSOR OF HUMANITIES EMERITA

THE UNIVERSITY OF NORTH CAROLINA AT CHAPEL HILL

CENGAGE
Learning

Australia • Brazil • Canada • Mexico • Singapore • Spain • United Kingdom • United States

**Communication in Our Lives,
Seventh Edition**
Julia T. Wood

Product Director: Monica Eckman

Senior Product Manager: Nicole Morinon

Content Coordinator: Alicia Landsberg

Product Assistant: Colin Solan

Media Developer: Jessica Badiner

Marketing Brand Manager: Lydia LeStar

Content Project Manager: Dan Saabye

Art Director: Linda May

Manufacturing Planner: Doug Bertke

Rights Acquisition Specialist: Ann Hoffman

Production Service: PreMediaGlobal

Text and Cover Designer: Rokusek Design

Cover Image: Courtesy of David April/ Fine
  Art America

Compositor: PreMediaGlobal

For product information and technology assistance, contact us at
Cengage Learning Customer & Sales Support, 1-800-354-9706

For permission to use material from this text or product,
submit all requests online at **www.cengage.com/permissions.**
Further permissions questions can be emailed to
permissionrequest@cengage.com.

Library of Congress Control Number: 2013944603

ISBN-13: 978-1-285-07597-6

ISBN-10: 1-285-07597-8

Cengage Learning
200 First Stamford Place, 4th Floor
Stamford, CT 06902
USA

Cengage Learning is a leading provider of customized learning solutions with office locations around the globe, including Singapore, the United Kingdom, Australia, Mexico, Brazil, and Japan. Locate your local office at: **international.cengage.com/region**

Cengage Learning products are represented in Canada by Nelson Education, Ltd.

For your course and learning solutions, visit **www.cengage.com.**

Purchase any of our products at your local college store or at our preferred online store **www.cengagebrain.com.**

Instructors: Please visit **login.cengage.com** and log in to access instructor-specific resources.

Printed in Canada
1 2 3 4 5 6 7 17 16 15 14 13

Brief Contents

Contents

PART II: INTERPERSONAL AND GROUP COMMUNICATION AND MEDIA LITERACY

16 PERSUASIVE SPEAKING   344

CLOSING: PULLING IDEAS TOGETHER   372

APPENDIX A   ANNOTATED SAMPLE SPEECHES   376

List of Boxes

SHARPEN YOUR SKILL

Preface

When I was an undergraduate student, I fell in love with the field of communication. In my first communication course, I discovered that communication was more central to my life than anything else I could study. That feeling grew stronger with each communication course I took during my undergraduate and graduate studies.

I wrote *Communication in Our Lives* to share with students my passion for communication and my belief that it is critically important in our everyday lives. Because I want this book to engage students, I've tried to make it as interesting and substantive as communication itself. I use a conversational style of writing and all chapters include examples, reflections from students, and applications that invite students to engage material personally. To help students develop their practical competence as communicators, I emphasize concrete skills and hands-on exercises.

DISTINGUISHING FEATURES OF COMMUNICATION IN OUR LIVES

Communication in Our Lives has three distinct conceptual emphases. In addition, it includes a number of pedagogical features designed to highlight the relevance of communication to students' everyday lives and experiences. Some of these features have been retained from the sixth edition, and some are new to this seventh edition.

Conceptual Emphases

Three conceptual goals guided my writing of this book: (a) to emphasize theories and research developed by scholars of communication, (b) to integrate coverage of social diversity as it relates to communication, and (c) to respond to student and faculty feedback about previous editions.

Emphasis on Communication Theory, Research, and Skills *Communication in Our Lives* highlights theories, research, and skills developed by scholars of communication. For example, Chapter 9 provides coverage of relational dialectics, a theory primarily developed by Leslie Baxter, a professor of communication at the University of Iowa. Chapter 11 relies on research by scholars of social media to sharpen understanding of how various digital technologies are making our lives ever more connected. Chapters 12 through 16 draw on communication scholars' knowledge of effective public communication. For instance, Clella

Jaffe (2013) has identified the wave pattern as a way of organizing speeches that is more common in ethnic groups with strong oral traditions, and James McCroskey and Jason Teven (1999) have shown that speakers who demonstrate goodwill toward listeners tend to have higher credibility than those who don't. I emphasize the work of communication scholars both because their research is valuable and because I want students to appreciate the intellectual richness of the communication field. Although I emphasize the work of communication scholars, I also include relevant research conducted by scholars in fields such as sociology, psychology, and anthropology. Thus, this book draws on research and theories in these and other related disciplines.

Communication scholars have long recognized the profoundly ethical dimensions of human communication. I incorporate this tradition in communication scholarship by calling attention to ethical issues and choices in communication. In addition to identifying ethical aspects of communication in each chapter, I include one question at the end of each chapter, flagged with an icon, that focuses on ethics.

Integrated Attention to Social Diversity I have woven discussion of social diversity into the basic framework of this book. I do not do this to be "politically correct." Instead, I provide integrated attention to social diversity because it is one of the most significant features of contemporary life in the United States. Our culture includes people of different ethnicities, ages, genders, physical and mental abilities, sexual orientations, economic classes, and religious and spiritual commitments.

Communication in Our Lives encourages students to appreciate social diversity as a fact of cultural life that has important implications for our communication with others. Because social diversity affects our communication in all contexts, I incorporate discussion of diverse cultures and communication practices into all chapters of this book. For example, in discussing personal identity in Chapter 3, I point out how social views of race, economic class, gender, and sexual orientation affect self-concept. In Chapters 12–16, I note that effective speaking requires adapting to diverse audiences with varied experiences, backgrounds, and values.

In addition to weaving social diversity into all chapters, Chapter 7 is devoted exclusively to communication and culture. This chapter provides a sustained and focused exploration of the reciprocal relationship between culture and communication.

Changes in This Edition Like communication, books are dynamic—they evolve and change over time. This edition of *Communication in Our Lives* attempts to retain the strengths of previous editions while also making changes in response to feedback. Before beginning work on this edition, I read feedback from hundreds of faculty members and students who used previous editions. Their suggestions and comments led me to make a number of changes in this new edition.

One significant change in this edition is its **shorter length**. Many faculty have said that they can't cover 18 chapters in a single academic semester or quarter. In response to this feedback, I've condensed previous editions' two chapters on interpersonal communication into a single chapter (Chapter 8), and I've condensed previous editions' two chapters on group discussion into a single chapter (Chapter 9). I've also further streamlined all chapters to make them more concise. Overall, this edition is 17% shorter than its predecessor.

A second change in this edition is **greater coverage of health communication**. Like other communication faculty, I've witnessed the growth of health communication as an important area of study and teaching and as a career choice for increasing numbers of students. This edition of *Communication in Our Lives* takes note of the importance of health communication by highlighting connections between communication and issues relevant to health. Every chapter includes one or more Health Communication feature that calls attention to the many ways that communication functions in health care settings.

A third change in this edition is greater **attention to social media**. Today, students (and everyone) rely on social media to build and navigate relationships and to stay connected. Posting on Facebook, texting, and tweeting are primary ways that people communicate with one another. The increased prominence of social media in our lives is reflected in this edition's Chapter 11 (media) as well as in examples and research presented in other chapters.

Finally, this edition of *Communication in Our Lives* also reflects changes in scholarship. Those familiar with the sixth edition of this book will notice that the current edition includes **more than 130 new references**.

Pedagogical Features

In addition to the conceptually distinctive aspects of this book and its thorough integration of and emphasis on social diversity, several other features are designed to make it interesting and valuable to students.

First, I adopt a *conversational style of writing* rather than the more distant and formal style often used by textbook authors. I share with students some of my experiences in communicating with others, and I invite them to think with me about important issues and difficult challenges surrounding communication in our everyday lives. The accessible, informal writing style encourages students to personally engage the ideas I present.

A second feature of this book is *student commentaries*. Every chapter is enriched by reflections written by students in my classes and other classes around the country who adopted previous editions of this book. The questions, thoughts, and concerns expressed by diverse students invite readers to reflect on their own experiences as communicators. I welcome ideas from students around the country, so students in your class may wish to send their insights to me for inclusion in future editions of this book.

Communication in Our Lives also includes pedagogical features that promote learning and skill development. At the end of each chapter I provide two *Sharpen Your Skill* exercises to encourage students to apply concepts and develop skills discussed in the text. Many of these exercises end with a prompt to the book's online resources, which offer additional opportunities for skill application. Each chapter also includes *Communication Highlights*, which call attention to interesting communication research and examples of communication issues in everyday life, and *Health Communication*, which focuses on connections between communication and health.

Another feature, *Beyond the Classroom*, appears at the end of chapters in Parts I and II. This feature offers suggestions for taking the material in the chapter beyond the classroom in three ways: considering the chapter's relevance in the workplace, probing ethical issues raised in the chapter, and connecting chapter material to civic and social engagement with the broader world.

To show students how research by communication scholars applies to the "real world," I've written summaries of six research articles relevant to issues in students' lives. These appear in *Research in Our Lives*, which is available on CourseMate.

Case studies are another feature that encourages students to engage ideas actively. These brief scenarios and speeches appear at the end of each chapter to bring to life the ideas and principles presented. Rather than using generic case studies, I wrote the ones used in this book so that they would directly reflect chapter content and provide students with representative examples of communication theories and skills—this edition features a new case study on groups and teams for Chapter 10. In addition to their presentation in the book, the case studies are featured on the CourseMate for *Communication in Our Lives* as short interactive video activities that include questions for discussion and analysis. (See the section on student resources for details about CourseMate.) With the multimedia enactments of the scenarios, instructors and students can analyze not only verbal messages but also nonverbal communication. Appendix A provides a collection of *annotated speeches* for student analysis.

Each chapter concludes with the **Communication in Our Lives Online** section, which provides both an introduction to the text's many online resources and the print version of the text's learning aids—a list of **definitions of key concepts**, the Sharpen Your Skills exercises, and then a series of For Further Reflection and Discussion questions that encourage students to reflect on and discuss the chapter's material. Each set of these questions includes at least one question that focused on **ethics**. Finally, as I discussed earlier, at the very end of each chapter in Part III, Public Communication, I suggest a related **Speech Builder Express** or Speech Studio activity.

RESOURCES FOR INSTRUCTORS

Katrina Bodey and I have written an *Instructor's Resource Manual* that describes approaches to teaching the basic course, provides a wealth of class-tested exercises, including new teaching resources for the public speaking segment of your course, and provides suggested journal topics and sample test items.

The password-protected Instructor Companion Website includes Computerized Testing via Cognero®, ready-to-use PowerPoint® presentations (with text, images, that can be customized to suit your course needs), Join In for Turning Point Clicker questions, and an electronic version of the Instructor's Manual.

The Teaching Assistant's Guide to the Basic Course by Katherine G. Hendrix is also available to adopters of this text. Designed specifically for the new communication teacher and based on leading teacher-training programs in communication, this guide includes general teaching and course management topics and specific strategies, such as giving performance feedback, managing sensitive class discussions, and conducting mock interviews.

Cengage Learning's extensive video library includes the *Student Speeches for Critique and Analysis* and *Communication Scenarios for Critique and Analysis*, which include sample student speeches and the interpersonal and group communication scenarios featured as case studies in this text. These videos provide realistic examples of communication that allow students and teachers to identify specific communication principles, skills, and practices, and to analyze how they work in actual interaction.

With Cengage's **Flex-Text Customization Program**, you can create a text as unique as your course: quickly, simply, and affordably. As part of our flex-text program you can add your personal touch to *Communication in Our Lives* with a course-specific cover and up to 32 pages of your own content, at no additional cost.

I encourage you to contact your local Cengage Learning representative or http://www.cengage.com/highered/ for more information, user names and passwords, examination copies, or a demonstration of these ancillary products. Available to qualified adopters.

RESOURCES FOR STUDENTS

If you want your students to have access to the online resources for *Communication in Our Lives*, please be sure to order them for your course. These resources can be bundled with every new copy of the text or ordered separately. If you do not order them, your students will not have access to these online resources. *Contact your local Wadsworth Cengage Learning sales representative for more details.*

MindTap from Cengage Learning represents a new approach to a highly personalized, online learning platform. A fully online learning solution, MindTap combines all of a student's learning tools—readings, multimedia, activities and assessments—into a singular Learning Path that guides the student through the curriculum. Educators personalize the experience by customizing the presentation of these learning tools to their students; even seamlessly introducing their own content into the Learning Path via "apps" that integrate into the MindTap platform. MindTap can also be deeply integrated into an institution's Learning Management System (LMS) through a service called MindLinks.

The *Communication in Our Lives* interactive video activities feature videos of the sample speeches and interpersonal and group communication scenarios featured in the book's case studies. This multimedia tool allows students to evaluate the speeches and scenarios, compare their evaluation with mine, and, if requested, submit their response electronically to their instructor.

The Speech **Communication CourseMate** brings course concepts to life with online interactive learning, study, and exam preparation tools like the interactive eBook, flashcards, Communication Highlight Activities and Sharpen Your Skills Activities that support the printed textbook. Watch comprehension soar as your class works with the printed textbook and the textbook-specific website. The Speech Communication CourseMate for *Communication in Our Lives* goes beyond the book to deliver what you need!

The **student companion workbook**, co-authored by Stacey Macchi of Western Illinois University and me, is available online through CourseMate for *Communication in Our Lives* and provides practical exercises and inventories that guide students in applying concepts and developing skills discussed in the book. It includes chapter outlines, class-tested activities, and self-tests.

Many Cengage Learning texts are available through **CengageBrain**, our textbook rental program or also available as an eBook where you can buy by the chapter. Keep CengageBrain in mind for your next Cengage Learning purchase. Visit http://cengagebrain.com for details.

A *Guide to the Basic Course for ESL Students* by Esther Yook of Mary Washington College is an aid for nonnative speakers. This guide includes strategies for accent management and overcoming speech apprehension, in addition to helpful Web addresses and answers to frequently asked questions.

Finally, *The Art and Strategy of Service Learning Presentations* by Rick Isaacson and Jeff Saperstein is an invaluable resource for students in the basic course that integrates or will soon integrate a service learning component. This handbook provides guidelines for connecting service learning work with classroom concepts and advice for working effectively with agencies and organizations. It also provides model forms and reports and a directory of online resources.

ACKNOWLEDGMENTS

All books reflect the efforts of many people, and *Communication in Our Lives* is no exception. A number of people have helped this book evolve from an early vision to the final form you hold in your hands. My greatest debts are to my editor, Monica Eckman, and my development editor, Julie Martinez. From start to finish, they have been active partners in the project. This book reflects their many insights and their generous support.

Other people at Wadsworth Cengage Learning have been remarkable in their creativity, attention to detail, and unflagging insistence on quality. I am grateful to Elm Street Publishing Services, for thoughtful copyediting.

I am also grateful to the people who reviewed previous editions of this book, who have been most generous in offering suggestions for improving the book.

Reviewers who worked with me in developing this edition, and to whom I am especially grateful, are

Karen Engels, Alverno College

Lisa Peterson, Boise State University

Terri Russ, Saint Mary's College

Kurt Lindemann, San Diego State University

LaKresha Graham, Rockhurst University

Brent Northup, Carroll College of Montana

Amie Kincaid, University of Illinois Springfield

I could not have written this book without the undergraduate students in my classes. They allow me to experiment with new approaches to teaching communication and help me refine ideas and activities that appear in this book. Invariably, my students teach me at least as much as I teach them, and for that I am deeply grateful.

I also thank my friends who are sources of personal support, insight, challenges, and experience—all of which find their way into what I write. Finally, and always, I acknowledge my partner Robbie (Robert) Cox. Like everything else I do, this book has benefited from his presence in my life. Being married to him for 39 years has enriched my appreciation of the possibilities for love, growth, kindness, understanding, and magic between people. In addition to being the great love of my life, Robbie is my most demanding critic and my greatest fan. Both his criticism and support have shaped the final form of this book.

Julia T. Wood
May 2013
Chapel Hill, NC

About the Author

Julia T. Wood is Lineberger Distinguished Professor of Humanities Emerita at the University of North Carolina at Chapel Hill. Since completing her Ph.D. (Pennsylvania State University) at age 24, she has taught classes, conducted research, and written extensively about communication in personal relationships and about gender, communication, and culture. In addition to publishing more than 70 articles and chapters, she has authored or co-authored 17 books and edited or co-edited 9 others. The recipient of 12 awards for outstanding teaching and 15 awards for distinguished scholarship, Professor Wood divides her professional energies among research, writing, and teaching.

Professor Wood lives with her partner, Robert (Robbie) Cox, who is Professor Emeritus at the University of North Carolina and who is on the board of directors of the national Sierra Club. Completing their family is their dog, Cassidy, and two cats, Rowdy and Rigby. When not writing and teaching, Professor Wood enjoys tutoring in reading, and spending time with students, friends, and family.

For Carolyn

For so many reasons

Introduction

FOCUS QUESTIONS

- A friend comes to you with a problem, and you want to show that you support him.
- A group you belong to is working on recycling programs for the campus, and you're frustrated by the group's inefficiency. You want to make meetings more productive.
- At the end of the term, the person you've been seeing will graduate and take a job in a city 1,000 miles away, and you wonder how to stay connected across the distance.
- You met an interesting person on Facebook. At first, you enjoyed interacting with him, but lately he's been texting you incessantly, and you feel he's intrusive.
- The major project in one of your courses is an oral research report, so your grade depends on your public speaking ability.

Situations like these illustrate the importance of communication in our lives. Unlike some of the subjects you study, communication is relevant to every aspect of your life. We communicate with ourselves when we work through ideas, psych ourselves up to meet challenges, and rehearse ways to approach someone about a difficult issue. We communicate with others to build and sustain personal relationships, to perform our jobs and advance our careers, to connect with friends and meet new people online, and to participate in social and civic activities. Every facet of life involves communication.

Although we communicate all the time, we don't always communicate effectively. People who have inadequate communication knowledge and skills are hampered in their efforts to achieve personal, professional, and social goals. On the other hand, people who communicate well have a keen advantage in accomplishing their objectives. This suggests that learning about communication and learning how to communicate are keys to effective living.

Communication in Our Lives is designed to help you understand how communication works in your personal, professional, and social life. To open the book, I'll introduce myself and describe the basic approach and special features of *Communication in Our Lives*.

INTRODUCTION TO THE AUTHOR

As an undergraduate, I enrolled in a course much like the one you're taking now. In that course, I began a love affair with the field of communication that has endured for more than 40 years. Communication is the basis of cultural life, and it is a primary tool for personal, social, and professional satisfaction and growth. It is a field that is both theoretically rich and exceptionally practical. I know of no discipline that offers more valuable insights, skills, and knowledge.

Because you will be reading this book, you should know something about the person who wrote it. I am a middle-aged, middle-class, Caucasian heterosexual woman. As is true for all of us, who I am affects what I know and how I think, act, interact, and write. My race, gender, social-economic class, and sexual orientation have given me certain kinds of insight and obscured others. As a woman, I understand discrimination based on sex because I've experienced it personally. I do not have personal knowledge of racial discrimination because Western culture confers privilege on European Americans. Being middle class has shielded me from personal experience with hunger, poverty, and class bias; and my heterosexuality has spared me from being a direct target of homophobic prejudice. Who you are also influences your experiences, knowledge, and ways of communicating.

Although identity limits our personal knowledge and experiences, it doesn't completely prevent insight into people and situations different from our own. From conversations with others and from reading, we can gain some understanding of people and circumstances different from our own. What we learn by studying and interacting with a range of people expands our appreciation of the richness and complexity of humanity. In addition, learning about people different from ourselves enlarges our personal repertoire of communication skills and our appreciation of the range of ways to communicate.

INTRODUCTION TO THE BOOK

The aim of *Communication in Our Lives* is to introduce you to many forms and functions of communication in modern life. The title reflects my belief that communication is an important part of our everyday lives. Each chapter focuses on a specific kind of communication or a particular context in which we communicate.

Coverage

Because communication is a continuous part of life, we need to understand how it works—or doesn't—in a range of situations. Therefore, this book covers a broad spectrum of communication encounters, including communication with yourself, interaction with friends and romantic partners, work in groups and teams, interaction in organizations, mass and social media, interaction between people with diverse cultural backgrounds, and public speaking. The breadth of communication issues and skills presented in this book can be adapted to the interests and preferences of individual classes and instructors.

Students

Communication in Our Lives is written for anyone interested in human communication. If you are a communication major, this book and the course it accompanies will provide you with a firm foundation for more advanced study. If you are majoring in another discipline, this book and the course you are taking will give you a sound basic understanding of communication and opportunities to strengthen your skills as a communicator.

Learning should be a joy, not a chore. I've written this book in an informal, personal style; for instance, I refer to myself as *I* rather than *the author*, and I use contractions (*can't* and *you're* instead of the more formal *cannot* and *you are*), as we do in normal conversation. I also punctuate chapters with concrete examples and insights from students at campuses around the country.

Theory and Practice

Years ago, renowned scholar Kurt Lewin said, "There is nothing so practical as a good theory." His words remain true today. In this book, I've blended theory and practice so that each draws on and enriches the other. Effective practice is theoretically informed: It is based on knowledge of how and why the communication process works and what is likely to result from different kinds of communication. At the same time, effective theories have pragmatic value: They help us understand experiences and events in our everyday lives. Each chapter in this book is informed by the theories and research generated by scholars of communication.

FEATURES

Ten key features accent this book:

Integrated Attention to Cultural Diversity

Diversity is woven into the fabric of this book. Awareness of diversity is integral to how we communicate and think about communication; it is not an afterthought. I integrate cultural diversity into the text in several ways. First, each chapter includes research on diverse people and highlights our commonalities and differences. Second, the photos I chose for this book include people of different races, ages, religions, and so forth. Likewise, each chapter includes examples from a range of people, walks of life, and orientations.

In addition to incorporating diversity into the book as a whole, in Chapter 7 I focus exclusively on communication and culture. There you will learn about cultures and social communities (distinct groups within a single society) and the ways cultural values and norms shape how we view and practice communication. Just as important, Chapter 7 will heighten your awareness of the power of communication to shape and change cultures. In addition, it will enhance your ability to participate effectively in a culturally diverse world.

To talk about social groups is to risk stereotyping. For instance, a substantial amount of research shows that women, in general, are more emotionally expressive than men, in general. A good deal of research also reports that blacks, in general, speak with greater animation and force than whites, in general. Yet, not all women are emotionally expressive, not all men are emotionally inexpressive, not all blacks communicate forcefully, and not all whites communicate blandly. Throughout this book, I try to provide you with reliable information on social groups while avoiding stereotyping. I rely on qualifying terms, such as *most* and *in general*, to remind us that there are exceptions to generalizations.

Student Commentaries

Communication in Our Lives also features commentaries from students. In my classes, students teach me and each other by sharing their insights, experiences, and questions. Because I've witnessed how much students learn from one another, I've included reflections written by students at my university and other campuses. As you read the student commentaries, you'll probably identify with some, disagree with others, and be puzzled by still others. Whether you agree, disagree, or are perplexed, I think you'll find that the student commentaries valuably expand the text by adding to the voices and views it represents. In the students' words, you will find much insight and much to spark thought and discussion in your classes and elsewhere. You may have insights about material covered in this book. If so, I invite you to send me your commentaries so that I might include them in the next edition of this book.

Health Communication

Each chapter includes one or more "Health Communication" features. These highlight the connections between communication principles and practices and health care. This feature will enlarge your understanding of the role of communication in shaping health care organizations, the importance of good communication between patients and clinicians, the usefulness of persuasive campaigns to encourage healthy behaviors, and relationships between communication skills and personal health.

Communication Highlights

"Communication Highlights" call your attention to especially interesting findings from communication research and news reports involving communication in everyday life. The "Communication Highlights" offer springboards for class discussions.

Experiencing Communication in Our Lives

Following each chapter is a case study, "Experiencing Communication in Our Lives." With each one, I invite you to think about how principles and skills we discuss in that chapter show up in everyday life. I ask a few questions about the case study that allow you to apply what you have learned in a chapter to analyzing real-life communication and developing strategies for improving interaction. You can access videos that depict each case study via the Online Resources for *Communication in Our Lives*.

Beyond the Classroom

Following chapters in Parts I and II is a "Beyond the Classroom" feature. It asks you to take the material in the chapter and extend it in three ways: asking how it applies to the workplace, how it involves ethical issues and choices, and how it applies to civic and social life. By thinking through these three issues for each chapter, you will actively engage the material and understand it more deeply.

Sharpen Your Skill

At the end of each chapter you will find two "Sharpen Your Skill" exercises. These bring to life the concepts we discuss by showing you how material in the text pertains to your daily life. They invite you to apply communication principles and skills as you interact with others. Some of the "Sharpen Your Skill" features suggest ways to practice particular communication skills. Others encourage you to notice how a specific communication principle or theory shows up in your interactions. If you do the "Sharpen Your Skill" exercises, you will increase your insight into communication in general and your own communication in particular.

Critical Thinking

Communication in Our Lives strongly emphasizes critical thinking. Competent communication demands critical thinking: distinguishing logical arguments from illogical ones, drawing sound conclusions from evidence, and applying concepts from one context to a different context. Each chapter calls attention to critical thinking by pointing out specific topics and issues that require critical thought.

Ethics

Because ethical issues are entwined with all forms of communication, I've integrated ethics into all chapters. As you read the chapter, you'll notice that I point out particular ethical questions and considerations. Also, I've included one question focused on ethics at the end of each chapter and an ethical extension is part of each "Beyond the Classroom" feature.

Research in Our Lives

A final feature, "Research in Our Lives," is available on your CourseMate. This feature answers a question that students often raise: What does academic research have to do with the "real world"? To show you that research conducted by communication scholars has important impact on real life, I offer short summaries of six research studies that are relevant to issues in today's world and your own life.

I hope you enjoy reading this book as much as I've enjoyed writing it. I also hope that this book and the class it accompanies will help you develop the skills needed for communication in your life. If so, then both of us will have spent our time well.

Julia T Wood

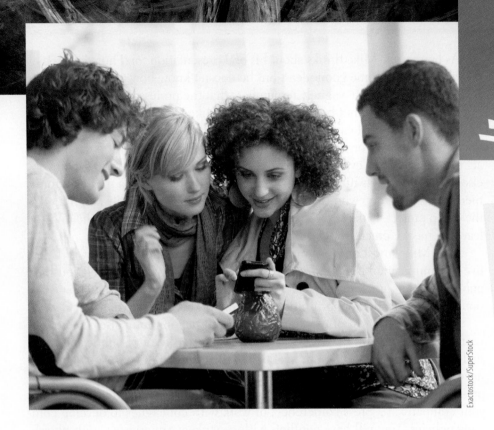

> The way we communicate with others and with ourselves ultimately determines the quality of our lives.
>
> **Anthony Robbins**

The World of Communication

MindTap

Review the chapter **Learning Objectives** and **Start** with a quick warm up activity.

Mike closes his iPhone and shakes his head; staying in touch with Chris is awkward now that they live 800 miles apart. They were buddies in high school but drifted apart after they went to different universities. They text frequently and visit each other's Facebook pages, but it's not the same as hanging out together. Shrugging, he turns on the TV while he finishes dressing for dinner with Coreen. The top news story is about another school shooting. He grimaces, thinking that the world has become a pretty mean place. Turning his thoughts back to Coreen, Mike hopes she won't want to talk about their relationship again tonight. He can't see the point of analyzing and discussing their relationship unless something is wrong, but she likes to talk about it when everything is fine.

SHARPEN YOUR SKILL

At the end of this chapter, refer to the Sharpen Your Skill features, Giving a Speech of Self-Introduction and Your Mediated World, to apply concepts from Chapter 1.

As he dresses, Mike thinks about his oral presentation for Thursday's sociology class. He has some good ideas, but he doesn't know how to turn them into an effective speech. He vaguely remembers that the professor talked about how to organize a speech, but he wasn't listening. Mike also wishes he knew how to deal with a group that can't get on track. He and six other students have worked for three months to organize a student book co-op, but the group can't get its act together. By now everyone is really frustrated, and nobody listens to anyone else. His phone alerts him to a new text message and he reads a message from a member of the group who is angry that nobody seems to be really committed to the co-op project. Mike saves the message for a later reply, turns off the TV, and leaves to meet Coreen.

Like Mike, most of us communicate continually in our daily lives. Effective communication is vital to long-distance friendships, romantic relationships, public speaking, interviewing, classroom learning, and productive group discussion. Communication opportunities and demands fill our everyday lives.

Mike—and the rest of us—relies on communication long after the college years. Even if you don't pursue a career that requires a lot of public speaking, such as teaching or law, communication will be essential in your work. You may need to talk with clients or patients, make progress reports, work on teams, and present proposals. You may persuade your boss you deserve a raise, represent your company at a press conference, or work with colleagues to develop company policies. You will have conflicts with coworkers, supervisors, and subordinates. You may need to have challenging discussions with superiors and peers who e-mail inappropriate content or with whom you simply disagree. Beyond your career, you'll communicate with family members, friends, neighbors, and social acquaintances in a range of settings, each of which will call for communication skills.

WHY STUDY COMMUNICATION?

Communication is the seventh most popular field of undergraduate study (McKinney, 2006). One reason for this popularity is that formal study can improve skill. Some people have a natural aptitude for playing basketball. They become even more effective, however, if they study theories of offensive and defensive play and if they practice skills. Likewise, even if you communicate well now, learning about communication and practicing communication skills can make you more effective (Hargie, 2006).

Another reason to study communication is that theories and principles help us make sense of what happens in our lives, and they help us have personal impact. For instance, if Mike learned about different gender communities, he might understand why Coreen, like many women, enjoys talking about relationships even when there is no problem. If Mike had better insight into the communication that sustains long-distance relationships, he might be able to enrich his friendship with Chris despite the miles between them. If he knew how to develop an agenda, he might be able to get his group on track. Studying public speaking could help Mike design a good presentation for his class report. Learning to listen better would help Mike retain information like his professor's tips on organizing oral reports. Communication theory and skills would help Mike maximize his effectiveness in all spheres of his life.

Communication in Our Lives will help you become a more confident and competent communicator. Part One clarifies how communication works (or doesn't work) and explains how perception, personal identity, language, nonverbal communication, listening, and cultural factors affect the overall communication process. In Part Two, we'll look at communication in four contexts: personal relationships, small groups, organizations, and mediated environments. Part Three focuses on public speaking.

This chapter lays a foundation for your study of communication. We'll first define communication. Next we'll discuss the values of communication in many spheres of your life. Then we'll examine some models of communication to clarify how the process works. In the third section of the chapter, we'll describe the breadth of the communication field and careers for communication specialists.

DEFINING COMMUNICATION

 MindTap™

Read, highlight and take notes online.

Communication* is a systemic process in which people interact with and through symbols to create and interpret meanings. Let's elaborate the key parts of this definition.

The first important feature of this definition is **process**. Communication is a process, which means it is ongoing and always in motion, moving ever forward and changing continually. It's hard to tell when communication starts and stops because what happened long before we talk with someone may influence interaction, and what occurs in a particular encounter may have repercussions in the future. We cannot freeze communication at any one moment.

Communication is also systemic because it occurs within a **system** of interrelated parts that affect one another. In family communication, for instance, each member of the family is part of the system (Galvin, Dickson, & Marrow, 2006). In addition, the physical environment and the time of day are elements of the system that affect interaction. People interact differently in a formal living room

• • • • • • • • • • • • • • • • •

*Boldfaced terms are defined in the glossary at the end of the book.

and on a beach, and we may be more alert at certain times of day than at others. If a family has a history of listening sensitively and working out problems constructively, and then when one family member says, "There's something we need to talk about," it's unlikely to cause defensiveness. On the other hand, if the family has a record of nasty conflicts, then the same comment might arouse strong defensiveness. A lingering kiss might be an appropriate way to show affection in a private setting, but the same action would raise eyebrows in an office. To interpret communication, we have to consider the system in which it takes place.

Our definition of communication also emphasizes **symbols**, which include all language and many nonverbal behaviors, as well as art and music. Anything that abstractly signifies something else can be a symbol. We might symbolize love by giving a ring, by saying "I love you," or by embracing. Later in this chapter, we'll have more to say about symbols. For now, just remember that human communication involves interaction with and through symbols.

Finally, our definition focuses on meanings, which are the heart of communication. Meanings are the significance we bestow on phenomena—what they signify to us. Meanings are not in phenomena. Instead, meaning grows out of our interaction with symbols; that is how we interpret words and nonverbal communication.

There are two levels of meaning in communication. The **content level of meaning** is the literal message. For example, if someone says to you, "Get lost!" the content level of meaning is that you should get lost. The **relationship level of meaning** expresses the relationship between communicators. In our example, if the person who says, "Get lost!" is a friend and is smiling, then you would probably interpret the relationship level of meaning as indicating that the person likes you and is kidding around. On the other hand, if the person who says, "Get lost!" is your supervisor, and he or she is responding to your request for a raise, then you might interpret the relationship level of meaning as indicating that your supervisor regards you as inferior and dislikes your work.

VALUES OF COMMUNICATION

Now that we have a working definition of communication, let's consider its value in our lives. We spend a great deal of time communicating. We talk, listen, have dialogues with ourselves, participate in group discussions, present oral reports, watch and listen to mass communication, and so forth. From birth to death, communication shapes our personal, professional, civic, and social lives as well as the culture in which we live.

Personal Identity and Health

George Herbert Mead (1934)[†] said that humans are "talked into" humanity. He meant that we gain personal identity as we communicate with others. In the earliest years of our lives, family members tell us who we are: "You're smart."

....

[†]I am using the American Psychological Association's (APA) method of citation. If you see "Mead (1934)," I am referring to a work by Mead that was written in 1934. If you see "Mead (1934, p. 10)" or "(Mead, 1934, p. 10)," I am specifically citing page 10 of Mead's 1934 work. The full bibliographic citations for all works may be found in the References section at the end of the book.

"You're strong." "You're a clown." Later, we interact with teachers, friends, romantic partners, and coworkers who communicate their views of us. Thus, how we see ourselves reflects the views of us that others communicate.

The profound connection between identity and communication is dramatically evident in children who have been deprived of human contact. Case studies of children who were isolated from others for long periods of time reveal that they lack a firm, healthy self-concept, and their mental and psychological development is severely hindered by lack of language (Shattuck, 1980).

A large body of research shows that communicating with others promotes health, whereas social isolation is linked to stress, disease, and early death (Fackelmann, 2006; Kupfer, First, & Regier, 2002). College students who are in committed relationships have fewer mental health problems and are less likely to be obese (Braithwaite, Delevi, & Fincham, 2010). People who have close friends have lower levels of anxiety and depression than people who do not have close friends (Lane, 2000; Ornish, 1999; Segrin, 1998). After reviewing scores of studies that trace the relationship between health and interaction with others, researchers (Holt-Lunstad, Smith, & Layton, 2010) conclude that social isolation is as dangerous to health as high blood pressure, smoking, obesity, alcoholism, or high cholesterol.

Life-threatening medical problems are also affected by healthy interaction with others. Heart disease is more common among people who lack strong interpersonal relationships (Holt-Lunstad et al., 2010; Ornish, 1998). Heart patients who feel the least loved have 50% more arterial damage than those who feel the most loved, and those who live alone are twice as likely to die within a year of having a heart attack (Crowley, 1998). Clearly, healthy interaction with others is important to our physical and mental well-being.

Communication skills are also essential to effective health care. Doctors, nurses, dentists, and others involved in health care need to be able to listen to patients and to communicate in ways patients understand. Equally important, patients need to be able to communicate clearly with health care professionals to explain their concerns and symptoms.

Relationship Values

Daniel Goleman, author of *Social Intelligence* (2007), says humans are "wired to connect" (p. 4). And communication is the primary way that we connect with others. Marriage counselors have long emphasized the importance of communication for healthy, enduring relationships (Gottman, 1994a, 1994b; Gottman & Carrère, 1994). They point out that the failure of some marriages is not caused primarily by troubles and problems or even by conflict because all marriages encounter challenges and conflict. A major distinction between relationships that endure and those that collapse is effective communication. In fact, results of a national poll showed that a majority of Americans perceive communication problems as the number one reason marriages fail—far surpassing other reasons such as sexual difficulties, money problems, and interference from family members (http://www.natcom.org/research/Poll/how_americans_ communicate.htm).

Communication is important for more than solving problems or making disclosures. For most of us, everyday talk and nonverbal interaction are the very essence of relationships (Duck & McMahon, 2012; Goleman, 2011; Wood &

Duck, 2006). Unremarkable, everyday interaction sustains intimacy more than the big moments, such as declarations of love. By sharing news about mutual acquaintances and discussing ordinary topics, partners keep up the steady pulse of their relationship (Duck, 2006; Schmidt & Uecker, 2007; Wood, 2006a, 2006b). For this reason, one of the biggest challenges of long-distance relationships is not being able to share small talk.

MYCA   *Last year, I did study abroad, and it was really hard to stay connected with my friends and family. I was in the Philippines so it was night here when it was day there—forget texting back and forth or even IMs. Plus, the Internet was spotty so sometimes I couldn't get on to share something cool that was happening in the moment. That was the hardest part—not being able to share the little things when they happened.*

Professional Values

One reason that communication is among the most popular majors is that communication skills are closely linked to professional success. The importance of communication is obvious in professions such as patient care, teaching, business, law, sales, and counseling, in which talking and listening are primary.

In other fields, the importance of communication is less obvious but nonetheless present. Leaders at organizations such as the *New York Times*, FedEx, and GlaxoSmithKline list communication as vital to their organizations' success (O'Hair & Eadie, 2009). Healthcare professionals must communicate effectively to explain medical problems to patients, describe courses of treatment, and gain information and cooperation from patients and their families (Beckman, 2003; Levine, 2004). Doctors who do not listen well are less effective in treating patients, and they're more likely to be sued than doctors who do listen well (Levine, 2004; Milia, 2003). The pivotal role of communication in health care makes it unsurprising that an increasing number of medical schools base admissions, in part, on applicants' communication skills, especially their ability to communicate empathy to patients (Rosenbaum, 2011). Even such

HEALTH COMMUNICATION

Communication and Health

Humans have a basic need to interact with and feel connected to others (Lane, 2000). After years of studying healthy and sick people, Dr. Dean Ornish (1998) concluded that one consistent difference between them is satisfying communication in their relationships. In an interview with *Newsweek* reporters, Dr. Ornish stated, "Love and intimacy are at the root of what makes us sick and what makes us well. I am not aware of any other factor in medicine—not diet, not smoking, not exercise—that has a greater impact" (Hager & Springen, 1998, p. 54).

HEALTH COMMUNICATION

Poor Communication = Preventable Death

As many as 98,000 preventable deaths each year have been traced to poor communication among doctors, nurses, and other members of health care teams (Harris, 2011). This disturbing fact has made effective team work a priority in training health care providers (Salas & Frush, 2012).

As a result, number of medical schools, including those at Stanford, Los Angeles, and Cincinnati, now base admissions to medical school not only on academic record but also on the ability to collaborate with others. In addition, they require students to take courses in teamwork.

highly technical jobs as computer programming, engineering, and systems design require communication skills (Darling & Dannels, 2003). Specialists must be able to listen carefully, work in groups and teams, and explain technical ideas to people who lack their expert knowledge.

In a recent survey, 89% of employers said colleges should focus on teaching students to communicate effectively to increase job success (Rhodes, 2010). The costs of poor communication in professional life are great. Executives in large companies report that 14% of each work week is wasted because of poor communication (Thomas, 1999). In the workplace, poor communication means that errors and misunderstandings occur, messages must be repeated, productivity suffers, and—sometimes—people lose jobs. No matter what your career goals are, developing strong communication skills will enhance your professional success.

Cultural Values

Communication skills are important to the health of our society. To be effective, citizens in a democracy must be able to express ideas and evaluate the ideas of others. One event typical of presidential election years is a debate between or among candidates. To make informed judgments, viewers need to listen critically to candidates' arguments and their responses to criticism and questions. We also need listening skills to grasp and evaluate opposing points of view on issues such as abortion, environmental policies, and health care reform. To be a good community member, you need skills in expressing your point of view and responding to those of others.

A recent survey shows that nearly half of first-year students at colleges and universities think that learning about other cultures is essential or very important (Hoover, 2010). In addition, there is great value in interacting with and learning from people from different cultures. The number of international students who enroll in U.S. colleges and universities is at an all-time high: 723,277 (McMurtrie, 2011). U.S.-born students appreciate the presence of peers from around the globe. In fact, exposure to students from a range of backgrounds is one of the best predictors of whether first-year college students return for a second year (Berrett, 2011).

JANET   *There are so many people from different cultures on this campus that you can't get by without knowing how to communicate in a whole lot of ways. In my classes and my dorm, there are lots of Asian students and some Hispanic ones, and they communicate differently than people raised in the United States. If I don't learn about their communication styles, I can't get to know them or learn about what they think.*

Janet is right. When she was a student in one of my courses, she and I talked several times about the concern she expresses in her commentary. Janet realized she needed to learn to interact with people who differ from her if she is to participate fully in today's world. She has learned a lot about communicating with diverse people, and no doubt she will learn more in the years ahead. Like Janet, you can improve your ability to communicate effectively with the variety of people who make up our society.

Communication, then, is important for personal, relationship, professional, and cultural reasons. Because communication is a cornerstone of human life, your choice to study it will serve you well. To understand what's involved in communication, let's now define the process.

MODELS OF COMMUNICATION

Over the years, scholars in communication have developed a number of models, which reflect increasingly sophisticated understandings of the communication process.

Linear Models

One of the first models (Laswell, 1948) described communication as a linear, or one-way, process in which one person acted on another person. This model consisted of five questions that described early views of how communication worked:

Who?
Says what?
In what channel?
To whom?
With what effect?

A year later, Claude Shannon and Warren Weaver (1949) advanced a model that included **noise**, which is anything that can interfere with the intended message. Figure 1.1 shows two versions of the Shannon and Weaver's model. Although linear models were useful starting points,

michaeljung/shutterstock.com

Verbal and nonverbal communication reflect cultural backgrounds and understandings.

COMMUNICATION HIGHLIGHT

U.S. Demographics in the Twenty-First Century

Demographics in the United States are changing rapidly. Currently, one in three U.S. residents is a minority. The latest Census shows that minorities increased 1.9% to 114.1 million, or 36.6% of the total U.S. population. The latest Census also reports that for the first time ever, there are more births of minorities in the United States (Yen, 2012). The following table shows demographic shifts from 2010 to projections for 2050 ("Demographics," 2009; Roberts, 2008; Yen, 2012):

	2010 (Percentage)	2050
African Americans	13	13
Asians	4	8
White, not Hispanic	64	46
Hispanics or Latino/a	16	30
Other	3	5

All figures are rounded off.

More and more people are convinced that a key function of higher education is to prepare people to function effectively and comfortably in a diverse society. Two-thirds of Americans polled by the Ford Foundation (1998) say it is very important for colleges and universities to prepare students to live and work in a society marked by diversity. Fully 94% of Americans polled say it is more important now than ever before for all of us to understand people who are different from us, and the majority of respondents believe that every college student should be required to study different cultures and social groups to graduate.

Learn more about diverse groups and their impact on the United States by visiting **WebLink 1.1** via MindTap for *Communication in Our Lives*. (To learn how to get started with your MindTap, see the inside front and back covers of this book.)

they were too simplistic to capture the complexity of most kinds of human communication.

Interactive Models

The major shortcoming of linear models was that they portrayed communication as flowing in only one direction, from a sender to a receiver. This suggests that speakers only speak and never listen and that listeners only listen and never send messages.

Realizing that receivers respond to senders and senders attend to receivers led communication theorists (Schramm, 1955) to adapt models to include **feedback**. Feedback may be verbal, nonverbal, or both, and it may be intentional or unintentional. Research has confirmed Schramm's insight that feedback is important. Supervisors report that communication accuracy and on-the-job productivity rise when they encourage their subordinates to give feedback: ask questions, comment on supervisors' messages, and respond to supervisory communication (Deal & Kennedy, 1999).

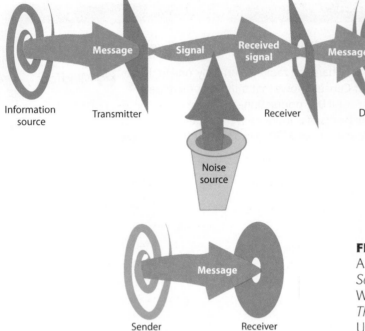

FIGURE 1.1
A Linear Model of Communication
Source: Adapted from Shannon, C., &
Weaver, W. (1949). *The Mathematical
Theory of Communication.* Urbana:
University of Illinois Press.

The interactive model also shows that communicators create and interpret messages within personal fields of experience. Adding fields of experience and feedback allowed Schramm and other communication scholars to develop models of communication as an interactive process in which both senders and receivers participate actively (Figure 1.2).

Transactional Models

A serious limitation of interactive models is that they don't acknowledge that everyone involved in communication both sends and receives messages, often simultaneously. While giving a press release, a speaker watches reporters to see whether they seem interested; both the speaker and the reporters are "listening," and both are "speaking."

Interactive models also fail to capture the dynamism of communication. To do this, a model would need to show that communication changes over time as a

FIGURE 1.2
An Interactive Model
of Communication
Source: Adapted
from Schramm, W.
(1955). *The Process
and Effects of Mass
Communication.*
Urbana: University
of Illinois Press.

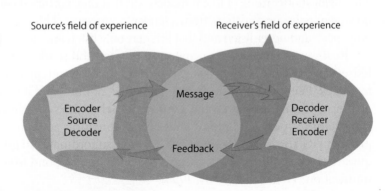

result of what happens between people. For example, Mike and Coreen communicated in more reserved and formal ways on their first date than after months of seeing each other. What they talk about and how they talk have changed as a result of interacting. An accurate model would include the feature of time and would depict features of communication as dynamically varying rather than constant. Figure 1.3 is a transactional model of communication that highlights these features and others we have discussed.

The transactional model includes **noise,** which is anything that has the potential to interfere with the intended communication. This includes sounds like a lawn mower or people nearby talking on smart phones, as well as "noise" within communicators, such as fatigue and preoccupation. In addition, our model shows that communication is a continuous, constantly changing process.

The outer lines on our model emphasize that communication occurs within systems that themselves affect communication and meanings. Those systems include contexts that both communicators share (e.g., a common campus, town, and culture) as well as each person's personal systems (e.g., family, religious associations, and friends). Also notice that our model, unlike previous ones, portrays each person's field of experience and the shared field of experience between communicators as changing over time. As we encounter new people and grow personally, our field of experience expands.

NISHA   *I lived in India until I was 14, and my family is still very Indian culturally. I am always surprised by how much U.S. college students disregard their parents' wishes. My parents insist that I marry an Indian so they do not want me to date Americans or other non-Indians. My friends say it is not my parents business who I date. They don't care if their parents don't approve of their boyfriends and girlfriends.*

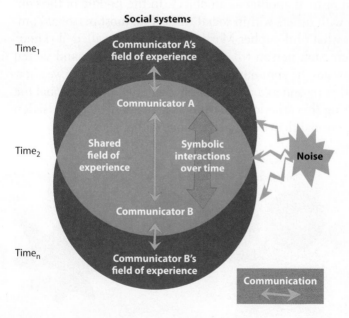

FIGURE 1.3
A Transactional Model of Communication
Source: Adapted from Wood, J. T. (2010). *Interpersonal Communication: Everyday Encounters* (6th ed.). Belmont, CA: Wadsworth.

Finally, our model doesn't label one person a "sender" and the other a "receiver." Instead, both people are defined as communicators who participate actively in the communication process. This means that, at a given moment in communication, you may be sending a message, receiving a message, or doing both at the same time (interpreting what someone says while nodding to show you are interested).

THE BREADTH OF THE COMMUNICATION FIELD

The discipline of communication dates back more than 2,000 years. Originally, the field focused almost exclusively on public communication. Aristotle, a famous Greek philosopher, believed that effective public speaking was essential to citizens' participation in civic life (Borchers, 2006). He taught his students how to develop and present persuasive speeches to influence public affairs.

Although public speaking remains a vital skill, it is no longer the only focus of the communication field. The modern discipline includes seven major areas of research and teaching: interpersonal communication, group communication, organizational communication, public communication, health communication, mass communication and social media, and intercultural communication.

Interpersonal Communication

A second major emphasis in the field of communication is **interpersonal communication**, which deals with communication between people. In one sense, everything except intrapersonal communication is interpersonal. But such a broad definition doesn't create useful boundaries for the area of study.

Interpersonal communication exists on a continuum from impersonal to highly personal. The most impersonal kind of communication occurs when we ignore another person or treat another as an object. In the middle of the continuum is interaction with others within social roles. The most personal communication occurs in what philosopher Martin Buber (1970) called "I–Thou" relationships, in which each person treats the other as a unique and sacred person. Figure 1.4 illustrates the communication continuum. The more we know and interact with another person as a distinct individual, the more personal the communication is. Using this criterion, we would say that a deep conversation with a friend is more personal than a casual exchange with a sales clerk.

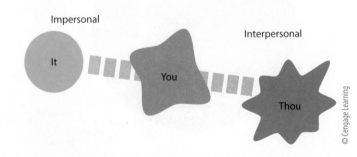

FIGURE 1.4
The Communication
Continuum

Interpersonal communication scholars study how communication creates and sustains relationships and how partners communicate to deal with the normal and extraordinary challenges of maintaining intimacy over time (Duck & McMahon, 2012; Wood & Duck, 2006).

Research indicates that communication is the lifeblood of close friendships and romantic relationships. Communication is the primary way people develop intimacy and continuously refashion relationships to meet their changing needs and identities. Intimates who learn how to listen sensitively and talk with each other have the greatest chance of enduring over time.

Group Communication

A third important branch of communication study is small-group communication, including therapeutic groups, social groups, decision-making committees, and work teams. Small-group communication scholars study leadership, member participation, agendas for decision making, and disruptive and constructive conflict. Chapters 10 and 11 will help us understand how communication affects each of these aspects of group life and how we can participate effectively in groups.

Group communication scholars also study teams, which are special types of groups that pull together people with diverse skills and experiences and which develop especially strong cohesion. Learning to communicate effectively in teams has become a criterion for success and advancement in careers.

Organizational Communication

Communication in organizations is another growing area of interest. Communication scholars have identified communication skills that enhance professional success, and they have traced the impact of various kinds of communication on morale, productivity, and commitment to organizations.

Many organizational communication scholars study **organizational culture**, which is the understandings about identity and codes of thought and action shared by members of an organization (Nicotera, Clinkscales, & Walker, 2002). From this understanding emerge rules for interaction and perspectives on work.

> **MADISON**   *I've had a number of part-time jobs, and I've noticed one interesting gender differences in my bosses. Men who are in charge tend to tell staff what to do—not like in a mean way, but it's very firm, like "Get that done right away." Women bosses tend to ask, like, saying "Would you do this?" or "Could you get this to me?" The bottom line is the same: We know to do whatever the boss says. But it feels more inclusive when a boss asks you instead of telling you.*

Health Communication

Health communication is one of the fastest-growing areas in the contemporary field of communication. Health communication is a very broad area that includes patient-clinician interaction, communication on health care teams, organizational dynamics in health care settings, marketing and advocacy of healthy practices for individuals and communities, and policy making (Kreps, 2010; Schiavo, 2007).

Effective communication is essential to successful public health practice in contexts that range from homes to doctor's offices and workplaces. Health communication includes not only face-to-face interaction but also interaction on health websites such as Web MD, online support groups, web portals, and mobile devices that monitor patients and send them messages. The broad range of health communication is one reason that many people plan careers in this area.

Mass Communication and Social Media

For some time, communication scholars have studied mass communication media such as film, radio, newspapers, books, magazines, and television. Their research has given us insight into how mass media work and how they represent and influence cultural values. For instance, the cultural value place on youth is reflected in, and perpetuated by featuring young, attractive models in ads and as news reporters and anchors.

A more recent focus of media scholars is social media. How do iPods, tablets, cell phones, and other social media influence our thinking, working, and relating? Do they increase social contact and productivity? Are we becoming less attentive because we're so often multitasking? Are we becoming more efficient because we multitask? Do they make us more connected with others?

Clearly, the verdict on the effects of social media will not be in for some time. Meanwhile, technologies of communication pervade many aspects of our lives. Skyping allows people who are separated by many miles to talk with and see each other. Many public presentations now include PowerPoint slides and clips from the Internet.

Public Communication

Even though not everyone will enter careers that call for extensive formal speaking, most of us will have opportunities to speak publically. When we join new groups, we may be asked to "say a few words about yourself," and others' first impressions of us will be based on our self-introductions.

In addition, we all will be in situations where speaking up is a responsibility. My editor speaks to her sales representatives to explain what her books are about and how to point out important features to faculty. I recently coached my doctor in public speaking so she could address

Joel Sartore/National Geographic

New technologies allow us to interact with people we've never met in person.

Public speaking is part of most people's lives, and, when done well, it's a powerful way to communicate information, beliefs, and ideas to foster understanding, build commitment, and motivate action.

her colleagues on a development in the treatment of kidney disease. My plumber presents workshops to his staff to update them on new plumbing products and to teach them how to communicate effectively with customers. My editor, doctor, and plumber don't consider themselves public speakers, but public speaking is a part of their lives, and doing it effectively is important to their success.

Scholars of public communication focus on critical evaluation of speeches and on principles for speaking effectively. Scholars of public communication also study principles of effective public speaking so we know a lot about what makes speakers seem credible to listeners and how credibility affects persuasion. Research has also enlightened us about the kinds of argument, methods of organizing ideas, and forms of proof that listeners find effective. If Mike studied this research, he could glean useful guidelines for his oral report in class.

Intercultural Communication

Intercultural communication is an increasingly important focus of research, teaching, and training. The United States has always been made up of many peoples with diverse cultural backgrounds and styles of communicating.

Scholars of intercultural communication increase awareness of different cultures' communication practices. For example, a Taiwanese woman in one of my classes seldom spoke up and wouldn't enter the heated debates that characterize graduate classes. One day after class, I encouraged Mei-Ling to argue for her ideas when others challenged them. She replied that that would be impolite. Her culture considers it disrespectful to argue or assert oneself and even more disrespectful to contradict others. Understood in terms of the communication values of her culture, Mei-Ling's deference did not mean she lacked confidence.

MEIKKO   *What I find most odd about Americans is their focus on themselves. Here, everyone wants to be an individual who is so strong and stands out from everyone else. In Japan, it is not like that. We see ourselves as parts of families and communities, not as individuals. Here I and my are the most common words, but they are not often said in Japan.*

A particularly important recent trend in the study of intercultural communication is research on different social communities within a single society. Cultural differences are obvious in communication between a Saudi Arabian and a Canadian. Less obvious are cultural differences in communication between people who speak the "same" language. Within the United States, there are distinct social communities based on race, gender, sexual orientation, and other factors. Intercultural communication scholars (Samovar, Porter, & McDaniel, 2011) have identified distinctive styles of communication used by women, men, blacks, whites, certain American Indian tribes, people with disabilities, and other groups. For example, women, more than men, tend to disclose personal information and to engage in emotionally expressive talk in their friendships (Wood, 1994a, 1994d, 2013). Many blacks are socialized in a culture that encourages dynamic talk, verbal duels, and other communication routines that have no equivalents in white speech communities (Houston & Wood, 1996). Participating effectively in a pluralistic society requires us to recognize and respect the communication practices of distinct social communities.

UNIFYING THEMES IN THE FIELD

After reading about the major branches of the modern field of communication, you might think that the field is a collection of separate, unrelated areas of interest. Actually, the field of communication is unified by a pervasive interest in symbols, meaning, critical thinking, and ethics.

Symbolic Activities

Symbols are the basis of language, thinking, and much nonverbal behavior. A wedding band is a symbol of marriage in Western culture; your name is a symbol for you; and a smile is a symbol of friendliness. Because symbols are abstract, they allow us to lift experiences and ourselves out of the present concrete world in order to reflect on past experiences and imagine future ones. Because symbols let us represent ideas and feelings, we can share experiences with others, even if they have not had those experiences themselves.

Whether we are interested in intrapersonal, interpersonal, mass, group, public, or intercultural communication, symbols are central to what happens. Thus, symbols and the mental activities they enable are a unifying focus of study and teaching about all forms of communication.

Meaning

Closely related to interest in symbols is the communication field's pervasive concern with meaning. The human world is one of meaning. We don't simply exist, eat, drink, sleep, and go through motions. Instead, we imbue every aspect of our lives with significance or meaning. When I feed my dog, Cassie, she eats her food and then returns to her canine adventures. For her, eating is a necessary and enjoyable activity. Unlike Cassie, we humans layer food and eating with significance. For example, kosher products reflect commitment to Jewish heritage, turkey is commonly associated with commemorating the first Thanksgiving in the United States (although vegetarians symbolize their commitment by *not* eating turkey), eggnog is a Christmas tradition, candles are part of Kwanzaa, and birthday cakes celebrate an individual.

To study communication, then, is to study how we use symbols to create meaning in our lives. Communication scholars see romantic bonds, friendships, families, teams, organizations, and cultures as growing out of human communication.

> **BENITA**   *It's funny how important a word can be. Nick and I had been going out for a long time, and we really liked each other, but I didn't know if this was going to be long term. Then we said we loved each other, and that changed how we saw each other and the relationship. Just using the word love transformed who we are.*

Critical Thinking

A third enduring concern in the communication field is **critical thinking**. To be competent communicators, we must examine ideas carefully to decide what to believe, think, and do in particular situations. Someone who thinks critically weighs ideas thoughtfully, considers evidence carefully, asks about alternative conclusions and courses of action, and connects principles and concepts across multiple contexts. Table 1.1 identifies key skills of critical thinking that affect communication competence.

Critical thinking is important in all aspects of our lives. The skills of critical thinking can enhance communication in friendships, romantic relationships, and family relationships. Critical thinking is also important to your success as a student. In class discussions and exams, you are asked to compare and contrast different policies or historical eras and to apply theories to particular situations—doing so requires critical thinking. Likewise, critical thinking is important in professional life. People who score low on measures of critical thinking are more likely to be unemployed than people who score highly (9.6% vs. 3.1%) (Berrett, 2012).

Table 1.1	Critical Thinking Skills for Effective Communication

- Identify assumptions behind statements, claims, and arguments.
- Distinguish between logical and illogical reasoning.
- Separate facts from inferences.
- Evaluate evidence to determine its reliability, relevance, and value.
- Connect new information and ideas to familiar knowledge; apply concepts learned in one context to other contexts; recognize when and where specific principles are and are not appropriate.
- Distinguish between personal experiences, attitudes, behaviors, and generalizations about human beings.
- Identify and consider alternative views on issues, solutions to problems, and courses of action.
- Define problems and questions clearly and precisely.
- Draw reasonable conclusions about the implications of information and argument for thought and action.
- Determine how to find answers to important questions by considering what needs to be known and what sources might provide relevant knowledge.

Learn more by accessing **WebLink 1.2** via MindTap for *Communication in Our Lives* to visit the website of the Foundation for Critical Thinking. (To learn how to get started with MindTap, see the inside front and back covers of this book.)

Ethics and Communication

A final theme that unifies research and teaching is ethical communication and interpretation of others' communication. Because all forms of communication involve ethical issues, this theme infuses all areas of the discipline. For instance, ethical dimensions of intrapersonal communication include the influence of stereotypes on our judgments of others. Ethical issues in the realm of interpersonal communication include honesty, compassion, and fairness in relationships. Pressures to conform that sometimes operate in groups are an ethical concern in group communication. Ethical issues also surface in public communication. For example, speakers who misrepresent facts or deliberately lie are violating an ethical principle.

Another ethical issue relevant to a range of communication contexts concerns attitudes and actions that encourage or hinder freedom of speech: Are all members of organizations equally empowered to speak? What does it mean when audiences shout down a speaker with unpopular views? How does the balance of power between relationship partners affect each person's freedom to express himself or herself? Because ethical issues infuse all forms of communication, we will discuss ethical themes in each chapter of this book.

Ethics

In the questions at the end of each chapter, the ethics icon will call your attention to a question focused on ethics of communication.

COMMUNICATION HIGHLIGHT

Thinking Critically About Language and Social Groups

It's especially important to think critically when using, listening to, or reading generalizations about social groups. The value of generalizations is that they allow us to recognize general patterns that can be useful starting points in understanding others. We can't learn about Koreans, blacks, whites, or Buddhists if we cannot use group labels such as *Korean* and *black*. At the same time, generalizations do not necessarily apply to particular individuals. For instance, it is true that Koreans in general are more communal than native-born Americans, particularly whites, in general, but a particular Korean may be very individualistic, and a particular native-born American may be very communal.

In this book, you will read many generalizations about various social groups. These generalizations are based on research, usually including research conducted by members of the social group being discussed. That doesn't mean that a generalization about men or whites is true about all men or all whites. You may well be a living exception to some of the generalizations about groups to which you belong.

To prevent ourselves from mistaking generalizations for absolute truths, it's important to use qualifying words such as *usually, in general, typically,* and *in most cases*. These remind us that there are exceptions to generalizations. As you read this book, notice how I qualify generalizations so we don't mistake them for universal truths. Notice also whether generalizations are appropriately qualified on television, in newspaper stories, in magazine articles, and in everyday conversations.

To explore your own experience with a generalization you applied to someone that turned out to be inaccurate or misleading, complete the Communication Highlight Activity for Chapter 1 via MindTap for *Communication in Our Lives*. (To learn how to get started with MindTap, see the inside front and back covers of this book.)

HEALTH COMMUNICATION

Careers in Health Communication

A strong background in communication prepares people for success in an amazing array of careers, including health communication. In addition to career choices such as doctor, nurse, or dentist, there are other interesting options in health care. Consider William Ellwood. Once a professor, Ellwood is now the OppNet Facilitator for the Office of Behavioral and Social Sciences Research at the National Institutes of Health. Or consider Marsha Vanderford who is the director of the Emergency Communication Center for the National Center for Health Marketing, which is part of the Centers for Disease Control. Or James Stiff, who owns and is a consultant at Trial Analysts (Kellerman, 2011). To learn more about careers of communication professionals, click **WebLink 1.3.**

CAREERS IN COMMUNICATION

As we've seen, communication skills are essential to success in most fields. In addition, people who major in communication are particularly sought after in a number of occupations.

Research

Communication research is a vital and growing field of work. A great deal of study is conducted by academics who combine teaching and research in faculty careers. In addition to academic research, communication specialists do media research on everything from message production to marketing. Companies want to know how people respond to different kinds of advertisements, logos, and labels for products. Before a new cereal or beer is named, various names are test marketed to test how customers will respond to different names. In addition, hospitals and other health care organizations need communication specialists to develop media campaigns for new products and services.

Education

Teachers are needed for communication curricula in secondary schools, junior colleges, colleges, universities, technical schools, and community colleges. The level at which a person is qualified to teach depends on how extensively he or she has studied communication. Generally, a bachelor's degree in communication education and certification by the board of education are required of teachers in elementary and secondary schools. A master's degree in communication qualifies a person to teach at community colleges, technical schools, and some junior colleges and colleges. The doctoral degree (Ph.D.) in communication is usually required for a career in university education, although some universities offer short-term positions to people with master's degrees.

Although generalists are preferred for many teaching jobs, university faculty often teach in specialized areas of communication. For instance, my research and teaching focus on interpersonal communication and gender and communication. Another faculty member specializes in environmental advocacy. Other college faculty concentrate on oral traditions, intercultural communication, family communication, organizational dynamics, and mass media on cultural values.

Communication educators are not limited to communication departments. People with advanced degrees in communication hold positions in other areas. Because communication is essential for doctors and businesspeople, increasing numbers of medical and business schools are creating permanent positions for communication specialists.

Media Production, Analysis, and Criticism

Increasingly, students are attracted to careers in mass communication and technologies of communication. There are many careers paths in media production, all of which demand good communication skills (Gregory, Healy, & Mazierkska, 2007). News reporters need skill not only in presenting information clearly but also in conducting interviews and fostering trust so that people will open up to them. To be effective, broadcasters must speak clearly and engagingly, and they must communicate credibly. Script writing and directing also require solid understanding of human communication.

Because our society is media saturated, we rely on media critics to help us understand what media are doing: Are they representing information fairly? Are they biased? Are they offering messages that are healthy for us?

Training and Consulting

Consulting is another field that welcomes people with backgrounds in communication. Organizations have programs to train employees in effective group communication skills, interview techniques, and group and team work. Some large hospitals and major corporations, such as IBM,

Study of communication prepares people to be media critics.

have entire departments devoted to training and development. People with communication backgrounds often join these departments and work with the corporation to design and teach courses or workshops that enhance employees' communication skills.

Communication specialists may also join or form consulting firms that provide particular kinds of communication training to government and organizations. One of my colleagues consults with organizations to help them develop work teams that interact effectively. Another advises a hospital on communication training program for members of health care teams. Other communication specialists work with politicians to improve their presentation styles and sometimes to write their speeches. I consult with attorneys on cases involving charges of sexual harassment and sex discrimination: I help them understand how particular communication patterns create hostile, harassing environments, and I collaborate with them to develop trial strategy. Other communication consultants work with attorneys on jury selection and advise attorneys on courtroom communication strategies.

Human Relations and Management

Because communication is the foundation of human relations, it's no surprise that many communication specialists build careers in public relations, human resources, grievance management, negotiations, customer relations, and development and fund-raising. In each of these areas, communication skills are essential.

Communication degrees also open the door to careers in management. The most important qualifications for management are not technical skills but the ability to interact with others and communicate effectively. Good managers are skilled in listening, expressing their ideas, building consensus, creating supportive work environments, and balancing task and interpersonal concerns in dealing with others.

BEYOND THE
CLASSROOM   🌐 MindTap™

Each chapter in this book concludes with suggestions for taking the material in the chapter beyond the classroom. We'll focus on three extensions: considering the chapter's relevance in the workplace, probing ethical issues raised in the chapter, and connecting chapter material to civic and social engagement with the broader world. For his first chapter, you'll learn what the National Communication Association (NCA) and the International Communication Association (ICA) have to offer relevant to all three of those foci. NCA's home page is available by clicking **WebLink 1.4**. Click **WebLink 1.5** to go to ICA's welcome page. I suggest more specific links that will allow you to become familiar with the impressive scope of the organization and the discipline it represents.

1. **Workplace.** Click **WebLink 1.4** to go to NCA's page on communication in the workplace. Follow links there to learn about multiple ways that communication intersects the workplace.

2. **Ethics.** Click **WebLink 1.6** to read NCA's Credo for Ethical Communication, a document that members voted to endorse in 1999. Click **WebLink 1.7** to access ICA's statement on ethics. Carefully consider what the documents advocate and condemn. Do you agree with the ethical principles identified in the documents?

3. **Engagement.** Click **WebLink 1.8** to learn about NCA's "Communicating Common Ground" program that was launched in 1999 to encourage faculty, students, and practitioners in the field of communication to work actively in their communities to reduce prejudice and hateful acts based on racial, ethnic, religious, and other human differences.

CHAPTER SUMMARY

 Practice and review the content in this chapter.

In this chapter, we took a first look at human communication. First, we defined communication, and then we discussed its value in our lives. Next we considered a series of models, the most accurate of which is transactional. The transactional model emphasizes that communication is a systemic process in which people interact to create and share meanings.

Like most fields of study, communication has developed over the years. Today, communication scholars and teachers are interested in a range of communication activities. This broad range of areas is held together by abiding interests in symbolic activities, meanings, critical thinking, and ethics, which together form the foundation of personal, interpersonal, and social life.

In the final section of this chapter, we considered some career opportunities open to people who specialize in communication. The modern field of communication offers an array of exciting career paths for people who enjoy interacting with others and who want the opportunity to be part of a dynamic discipline that evolves to meet changing needs and issues in our world.

APPLYING COMMUNICATION IN OUR LIVES

Communication in Our Lives is supported by MindTap, a new online learning platform that delivers content, assignments, and a tailored presentation of the course curriculum created by your instructor. MindTap combines all of your learning tools–readings, multimedia, activities and assessments–into a singular learning unit that guides you through the course. Practice and Present, a unique tool within MindTap, allows you to upload your speech video files for practice or for a grade, comment on your peer's speeches and review your grades. MindTap also includes Speech Builder Express, a powerful tool that guides you through the speech outline and preparation process. For more information or to access MindTap, visit cengagebrain.com.

DEFINITIONS OF KEY CONCEPTS

 MindTap Review your **Flashcards**.

communication A systemic process in which people interact with and through symbols to create and interpret meanings.

content level of meaning One of two levels of meaning in communication. The content level of meaning is the literal, or denotative, information in a message.

critical thinking Examining ideas reflectively and carefully to decide what you should believe, think, or do.

feedback Response to a message; may be verbal, nonverbal, or both. In communication theory, the concept of feedback appeared first in interactive models of communication.

interpersonal communication Communication between people, usually in close relationships such as friendship and romance.

noise Anything that has potential to interfere with intended communication.

organizational culture Ways of thinking, acting, and understanding work that are shared by members of an organization and that reflect an organization's distinct identity.

process Something that is ongoing and continuously in motion, the beginnings and endings of which are difficult to identify. Communication is a process.

relationship level of meaning One of two levels of meaning in communication; expresses the relationship between communicators.

symbol An arbitrary, ambiguous, and abstract representation of a phenomenon. Symbols are the basis of language, much nonverbal behavior, and human thought.

system A group of interrelated elements that affect one another. Communication is systemic.

FOR FURTHER REFLECTION AND DISCUSSION   MindTap™

1. Using each of the models discussed in this chapter, describe communication in your family. What does each model highlight and obscure? Which model best describes and explains communication in your family?

2. Interview a professional in the field you plan to enter to discover what kinds of communication skills he or she thinks are most important for success. Which of those skills do you already have? Which skills do you need to develop or improve? How can you use this book and the course it accompanies to develop the skills you will need to be effective in your career?

3. Think critically about the impact of digital technologies of communication. In what ways do you think these technologies might improve professional, personal, and social communication? In what ways might they be counterproductive?

4. Check out the NCA's online magazine, *Communication Currents*, which was launched in November 2006. To read it, click **WebLink 1.9**.

SHARPEN YOUR SKILL MindTap™

1. Giving a Speech of Self-Introduction

This exercise serves two purposes: It gives you a first experience in public speaking, and it allows you to introduce yourself to your classmates. You may choose to develop your speech on your own, or you may use criteria specified by your instructor. If you want a basic blueprint for your speech, try this:

Reflect on yourself and your life. Identify one interesting or unusual aspect of your identity of your life, and use that as the focus of your speech. Possible foci for your speech are experience living in another country, the origin of an unusual name, a unique event in your life, or an interesting hobby or skill. Use the following basic structure for your speech:

I.   My name is
     I want to tell you this about myself:
     _____

II. Describe the interesting or unusual aspects of yourself or your life. _____
     _____

III. Conclude by restating your main idea. _____
     _____

You may want to review the sample speech of introduction at the end of this chapter and via Mindtap for *Communication in Our Lives*. (To learn how to get started with MindTap, see the inside front of this book.)

2. Your Mediated World

How do social media affect your interactions? If you use the Internet, how are your electronic exchanges different from face-to-face interactions? Have you made any acquaintances or friends through social media? Did those relationships develop differently from ones formed through face-to-face contact? Do you feel differently about people you have never seen and those you see?

EXPERIENCING COMMUNICATION IN OUR LIVES   MindTap™

CASE STUDY: *A Model Speech of Self-Introduction*

The following speech is featured in your Chapter 1 MindTap for *Communication in Our Lives.* Select "Speech of Self-Introduction" to watch the video of Mona Bradsher's speech. Improve your own communication skills by reading, watching, and evaluating this sample speech.

© Cengage Learning

Speech of Self-Introduction

My name is Mona Bradsher. I'm a junior, although I'm older than most juniors at our school. In my speech, I want to introduce you to a very persuasive 6-year-old. Through her, you'll learn why I have come back to finish my college degree after a 10-year break from school.

When I was 18, I started college like many of you. But unlike most of you, I dropped out when I was 20—in the middle of my sophomore year. I left school because I wanted to get married to a man named Jason. I'd met him the summer before, and we had fallen in love. Jason and I did get married, and we had a daughter, Sasha.

In my case, the fairy tales were wrong: Jason and I didn't live happily ever after. We divorced just before our fifth wedding anniversary. So there I was: a 25-year-old single mom with a child to raise. My income was pretty low because I didn't have enough education to get a job that paid well. It was hard to get by on what I could make and the small amount of child support that Jason paid each month. We didn't go out for dinners or movies, but we did eat healthy meals at home. We didn't have money for a nice car, so we used the bus system. When Sasha was sick, I'd have to work extra hours to pay the doctor's bill and the cost of prescriptions. So it was tough, and I worried that as my daughter got older, I wouldn't be able to support her on what I made. I felt really trapped.

Last year, Sasha started school. One day, she came home and told me her teacher had taught them about the importance of education. Sasha's teacher had put up a chart showing the difference between what high school graduates and college graduates make. Her teacher also talked about how education helps every person fulfill his or her individual potential and lead a fuller life. The teacher told all the children that education was the most important gift they could give themselves. So Sasha said to me, "Mommy, now that I'm going to school, why don't you go too?"

At first, I told Sasha that Mommy had to work to pay for our apartment and food, but Sasha would have none of that. She insisted that I should go to school. I don't know how many of you have tried to argue with a very insistent 6-year-old, but take my word for it: You can't win! Because my daughter was so persistent, I checked around and found out there is an educational loan program specifically for older students who want to return to school and complete their education. I qualified, and I'll keep getting the loan as long as I maintain a B average. So far, my average is above that because Sasha and I have a deal: We study together for 3 hours every night.

And that's why I'm here now. That's why I've come back to finish my degree after a 10-year break. I'm here because my daughter reminded me of the importance of education. If I can learn an important lesson from a 6-year-old, then I can learn other important lessons from the teachers at our university.

QUESTIONS FOR ANALYSIS AND DISCUSSION   MindTap

You can also answer these questions and see my responses to them online via MindTap for Chapter 1.

1. Does Mona's speech give you a sense of who she is?

2. Did Mona's introduction catch your attention and give you a road map of what she covers in her speech?

3. How did Mona create identification between herself and listeners?

4. How did examples add to the speech?

5. Was the quotation from Sasha effective?

6. Did Mona's conclusion create closure by returning to the theme of her introduction?

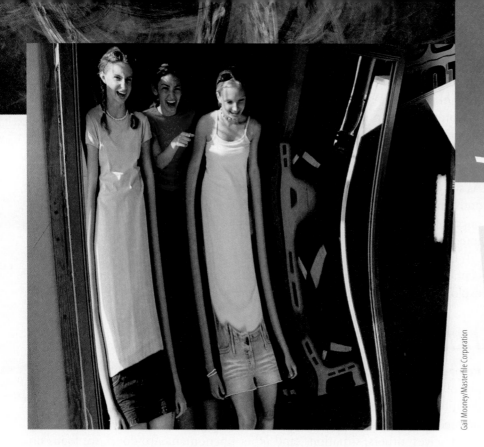

Gail Mooney/Masterfile Corporation

We see the world as "we" are, not as "it" is; because it is the "I" behind the "eye" that does the seeing.

Anaïs Nin

Perception and Communication

One of my research projects involved interviewing inmates in a medium-security prison. On the first day of interviewing, I arrived at the security station through which all visitors must pass. The guard looked at me and asked me to remove my necklace, a simple gold chain. "The inmates could use that to choke you," he explained. He then checked my purse, a standard procedure for visitors. He found my key ring, which is a two-inch piece of metal shaped like a cat's head with pointed ears. Pointing to the ears of the cat, he said, "This could be a weapon—they could put out your eyes." For the same reason, the guard confiscated my nail clipper and file. The guard also suggested that on future visits I should not wear a belt.

The guard's experience with prisoners led him to perceive dangers that I

MindTap

Review the chapter **Learning Objectives** and **Start** with a quick warm up activity.

SHARPEN YOUR SKILL

At the end of this chapter, refer to the Sharpen Your Skill features, Perceiving Others and Noticing Individualism, to apply concepts from Chapter 2.

didn't perceive. The necklace that I saw as a fashion accent he saw as a means of choking me. What I perceived as a key ring and manicure tools he saw as potential weapons. Our perceptions differed because we had different experiences and roles, which affected how we perceived necklaces, key chains, and nail files and clippers.

This chapter focuses on **perception,** which is the heart of communication. As we will see, perception shapes how we understand others' communication and how we ourselves communicate. At the same time, communication influences our perceptions of people and situations. The two processes are intricately intertwined.

In the first part of this chapter, we elaborate the three-part process of perception. Next, we'll consider factors that affect our perceptions. Finally, we will explore ways to improve our abilities to perceive and communicate effectively.

Read, highlight and take notes online.

HUMAN PERCEPTION

Perception is the active process of selecting, organizing, and interpreting people, objects, events, situations, and activities. The first thing to notice about this definition is that perception is an active process. Phenomena do not have intrinsic meaning that we passively receive. Instead, we actively work to make sense of ourselves, others, situations, and other phenomena. To do so, we focus on only certain things, and then we organize and interpret what we have selectively noticed. What something means to us depends on which aspects of it we attend to and how we organize and interpret what we notice.

Perception consists of three processes: selecting, organizing, and interpreting. These processes are overlapping, so they blend into and influence one another. They are also interactive, so each affects the other two.

Selection

Stop for a moment and notice what is going on around you right now. Is there music in the background? Is the room warm or cold, messy or clean, large or small, light or dark? Is there laundry in the corner waiting to be washed? Can you smell anything—food cooking, traces of cologne? Is anyone else in the room? Do you hear other conversations or music? Can you hear muted sounds of activities outside? What about this book—what do you notice about it? On what kind of paper is the book printed? Is the type large, small, easy to read? Do you like the size of the book, the colors used, the design of the text? Now think about what's happening inside you: Are you alert, sleepy, hungry, comfortable? Do you have a headache or an itch anywhere?

You probably weren't conscious of most of these phenomena when you began reading the chapter. Instead, you focused on reading and understanding the material in the book. You narrowed your attention to what you defined as important in that moment, and you were unaware of many other things going on around you. This is typical of how we live our lives. We can't attend to everything in our environment because there is simply far too much there, and most of it isn't relevant to us at any particular time.

Which stimuli we notice depends on a number of factors. First, some qualities of external phenomena draw attention. For instance, we notice things that **STAND OUT** because they are immediate, relevant, or intense. We're more likely to hear a loud voice than a soft one and to notice a bright shirt than a drab one. Second, our perceptions are influenced by the acuity of our senses. For instance, if you have a good sense of smell, you're likely to be enticed by the smell of freshly baked bread. People whose vision or hearing is limited or nonexistent often develop greater sensitivity in their other senses.

Third, change or variation compels attention, which is why we may take for granted all the pleasant interactions with a friend and notice only the tense moments. Effective public speakers apply the principle that change compels notice to keep listeners focused on their speaking. For instance, they may raise or lower their voices or move to a different place in the room during a presentation.

Image Source / Jupiter Images

We notice things that stand out or differ from their surroundings.

Sometimes we deliberately call phenomena to our attention. Self-indication occurs when we point out certain things to ourselves. Right now you're learning to indicate to yourself that you perceive selectively, so in the future you will be more aware of the selectivity of your perceptions. People who want to eat healthy diets deliberately notice nutritional content of food items. Health care professionals notice aspects of appearance that are clues to a person's health.

What we select to notice is also influenced by who we are and what is going on inside us. Our motives and needs affect what we see and don't see. If you've just broken up with someone, you're more likely to notice attractive people than if you are in an established romantic relationship. People tend to perceive things they desire as more accessible than they really are. In one study, the researchers (Balcetis & Dunning, 2010) had people sit across the table from a full bottle of water and then had them either eat pretzels or drink water from a glass. The participants were then asked to estimate how close they were to the bottle of water. Consistently, the participants who were thirsty from eating pretzels perceived the water bottle as being closer than the other participants.

We are also more likely to perceive what we expect to perceive. This explains the phenomenon of the **self-fulfilling prophecy,** in which one acts in ways consistent with how one has learned to perceive oneself. Children who are told they are unlovable may perceive themselves that way and notice rejecting but not affirming communication from others. Recent research shows that lonely people tend to perceive others more negatively than non-lonely people (Tsai & Reis, 2009). The negative judgments may lead those judging to make less effort to engage others. In turn, this leads to unsatisfying interactions and perhaps alienates others so loneliness continues or increases. Click **WebLink 2.1** to learn more about self-fulfilling prophecies.

LEE TENG-HUI   *Before I came to school here, I was told that Americans are very pushy, loud, and selfish. For my first few months here, I saw that was true of Americans just as I had been told it would be. It took me longer to see also that Americans are friendly and helpful because I had not been taught to expect these qualities.*

Organization

We don't simply string together randomly what we've noticed. Instead, we organize what we've selectively noticed to make it meaningful to us. The most useful theory for explaining how we organize what we've attended to is **constructivism,** the theory that we organize and interpret experience by applying cognitive structures called **schemata** (singular: *schema*). Originally developed by George Kelly in 1955, constructivism has been elaborated by scholars in communication and psychology. We use four kinds of cognitive schemata to make sense of phenomena: prototypes, personal constructs, stereotypes, and scripts (Burleson & Rack, 2008; Fehr, 1993; Hewes, 1995).

Prototypes   A **prototype** is a knowledge structure that defines the best or most representative example of some category (Fehr, 1993). For example, you probably have prototypes of best teachers, friends, public speakers, and romantic partners. Each of these categories is exemplified by a person who is the ideal case; that's the prototype.

We use prototypes to define categories: Jane is the ideal friend; Luke is the ideal romantic partner; Robin is the ideal work associate. We may then consider how close a particular phenomenon is to our prototype for that category. As Alicia's commentary points out, our prototypes can be faulty, leading us to fail to perceive someone as belonging in the appropriate category because he or she does not match our prototype for the category.

ALICIA   *I was working with a male nurse. Every time he met a new patient, the patient would say, "Hi, doctor." Even when he told them he was a nurse, they treated him as a doctor. No one ever confused me with a doctor. Patients just assume that men in white are doctors and women in white are nurses.*

Personal Constructs   **Personal constructs** are bipolar mental yardsticks that allow us to position people and situations along dimensions of judgment. Examples of personal constructs are intelligent–not intelligent, responsible–not responsible, kind–not kind, and attractive–not attractive. To size up a person, we measure him or her by personal constructs that we use to think about people. How intelligent, responsible, kind, and attractive is this person? Whereas prototypes help us decide into which broad category a person or situation fits, personal constructs let us make more detailed assessments of particular qualities of phenomena we have selectively perceived. Our personal constructs shape our perceptions because we define something only in terms of how it compares to the constructs we use. Thus, we may not notice qualities of people that are outside the constructs we use to perceive them.

Stereotypes   **Stereotypes** are predictive generalizations about people and situations. Based on the category in which we place a phenomenon and how the phenomenon measures up to the personal constructs we apply, we predict what it will do. For instance, if you classify Meredith into the prototype of liberal, and you perceive her as compassionate, generous, and kind (personal constructs), you might predict that she is likely to support government-funded programs to help disadvantaged citizens.

Stereotypes may be accurate or inaccurate. They are generalizations, which are sometimes based on facts that are generally true of a group and sometimes on prejudice or assumptions. Even if we have accurate understandings of a group, generalizations may not apply to particular individuals in it. Although college students as a group are more liberal than the population as a whole, some college students are very conservative. A particular individual may not conform to what is typical of his or her group as a whole. Ethical communicators keep in mind that stereotypes are generalizations that can be both useful and misleading.

> **SCOTT**   *The stereotype that really ticks me off is "dumb jock." I'm a fullback on the team, and I'm big just like any good fullback. But I'm also a good student. I study, and I put a lot into papers and homework for classes. But a lot of the professors here and the students, too, assume I'm dumb just because I'm an athlete. Sometimes I say something in class, and you can just see surprise all over everyone's faces because I had a good idea. When you think about it, athletes have to be smart to do all of their schoolwork plus practice and work out about 30 hours a week.*

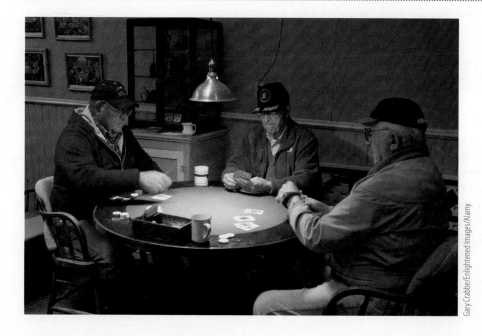

Gary Crabbe/Enlightened Images/Alamy

What stereotypes do you have of the men in this photograph.

Doctors' Stereotypes

In his book *How Doctors Think* (2007), Dr. Jerome Groopman points out that doctors' stereotypes may lead them to follow inappropriate scripts with patients. For instance, a doctor who perceives a patient as a homeless man might, based on that stereotype, diagnose the patient's stumbling as a symptom of intoxication and follow a script of letting the patient sober up rather than check for other causes of stumbling. If the doctor had perceived the patient as middle class, the doctor would be more likely to assume that stumbling indicated a medical problem and follow a script that included talking with the man and performing tests.

Scripts   To organize what we notice, we also use **scripts,** which are guides to action. A script consists of a sequence of activities that define what we and others are expected to do in specific situations.

Many of our daily activities are governed by scripts, although we're often unaware of them. You have a script for greeting casual acquaintances: "Hey, how ya doing?" "Fine. See ya around." You have scripts for checking in with friends online: hi. where r u? gotta go. brb. You also have scripts for managing conflict, talking with professors, interacting with superiors on the job, dealing with clerks, and relaxing with friends. Christine Bachen and Eva Illouz (1996) studied 184 people to learn about their views of romance. They found that most people agree on the scripts for appropriate sequences of events for first dates and romantic dinners. Similarly, Sandra Metts (2006b) has identified consistent scripts for heterosexual flirting.

Prototypes, personal constructs, stereotypes, and scripts are cognitive schemata that we use to organize the phenomena to which we selectively attend. They help us make sense of what we notice and help us anticipate how we and

Expectations and Perceptions

How we perceive others is influenced by past experiences and expectations. This has been demonstrated repeatedly in experiments (Bargh, 1997). In one study, two groups of research participants were asked to complete what was described as a language test. One group of participants worked with a list of words related to the personality, such as *honesty*. The other group of participants worked with a list of randomly selected words. Then both groups were asked to complete what they were told was a second, independent study, in which they read a short description of a person and then gave their impressions of the person. Participants who worked with the words related to honesty described the person they read about in the second study as more honest than did the participants who worked with words unrelated to honesty (Bargh, 1999).

others will act in particular situations. Our cognitive schemata are not entirely individualistic. Rather, they reflect our membership in a culture and in specific social groups. As we interact with others, we internalize their ways of classifying, measuring, and predicting interaction in various situations. Each of us has an ethical responsibility to assess social perspectives critically before relying on them to organize our perceptions and direct our activities.

Interpretation

To assign meaning, we must interpret what we have noticed and organized. **Interpretation** is the subjective process of explaining perceptions to assign meaning to them.

Attributions **Attributions** are explanations of why things happen and why people act as they do (Fehr, 1993; Fehr & Russell, 1991; Heider, 1958; Kelley, 1967). It's good to remind ourselves that the attributions we make aren't necessarily correct—they are our subjective ways of assigning meaning.

Attributions have four dimensions (Table 2.1). The first is *locus*, which attributes what a person does to either internal factors ("He's sick.") or external factors ("The traffic jam frustrated him."). The second dimension is *stability*, which explains actions as resulting either from stable factors that won't change ("She's a Type A person.") or from temporary, unstable factors ("She's irritable because she's just had a fight with the boss."). *Scope* (sometimes called *specificity*) is the third dimension, and it defines behavior as part of a global pattern ("He's a mean person.") or a specific instance ("He gets angry when he's tired."). Finally, the dimension of *responsibility* attributes behaviors either to factors people can control ("She doesn't try to control her outbursts.") or to ones they cannot ("She has a chemical imbalance that makes her moody.").

A student who was reading this book for a class at another university emailed me with a question about attributions. He and his classmates were debating whether scope and stability are really two different dimensions. This is a good question. Most global attributions are also stable. However, there are exceptions. For example, you might say that someone is always efficient at work but inefficient during leisure time. In this case, the attribution is stable and specific. If the person were efficient in all spheres of life, the attribution would be stable and global.

Investigations have shown that happy and unhappy couples have distinct attributional styles (Manusov & Harvey, 2001; Segrin, Hanzal, & Domschke, 2009; Tavris & Aronson, 2007). Happy couples make relationship-enhancing

Table 2.1	Dimensions of Interpersonal Attributions	
Locus:	Internal	External
Stability:	Stable	Unstable
Scope:	Global	Specific
Responsibility:	Within personal control	Beyond personal control

attributions. They attribute nice things a partner does to internal, stable, and global reasons that the partner controls: "She got the film because she is a good person who always does sweet things." They attribute unpleasant things a partner does to external, unstable, and specific factors and sometimes to influences beyond personal control: "He yelled at me because all the stress of the past few days made him irritable."

In contrast, unhappy couples make relationship-diminishing attributions. They explain nice actions as results of external, unstable, and specific factors: "She got the tape because she had some time to kill today." Negative actions are attributed to internal, stable, and global factors: "He yelled at me because he is a nasty person who never shows any consideration for anybody else." Thus, we should be mindful of our attributions because they influence how we experience our relationships.

The Self-Serving Bias   Research indicates that we tend to construct attributions that serve our personal interests (Hamachek, 1992; Manusov & Spitzberg, 2008; Sypher, 1984). Thus, we are inclined to make internal, stable, and global attributions for our positive actions and successes. We're also likely to claim that good results come about because of personal control we exerted. On the other hand, people tend to attribute negative actions and failures to external, unstable, and specific factors that are beyond personal control. In other words, we tend to attribute our misconduct and mistakes to outside forces that we can't help but attribute all the good we do to our personal qualities and effort. This **self-serving bias** can distort our perceptions, leading us to take excessive credit for what we do well and to abdicate responsibility for what we do poorly.

MARGARET   *Last summer, I worked at a day-care center for 4-to 6-year-olds. Whenever a fight started and I broke it up, each child would say the other one made them fight or the other one started it or they couldn't help hitting. They were classic cases of self-serving bias.*

We've seen that perception involves three interrelated processes. The first of these, selection, allows us to notice certain things and ignore others. The second process is organization, in which we use prototypes, personal constructs, stereotypes, and scripts to order what we have selectively noticed. Finally, we engage in interpretation by using attributions to explain what we have noticed and organized. Although we discussed these processes separately, in reality they interact continually.

INFLUENCES ON PERCEPTION

In opening this chapter, I mentioned an incident in which a prison guard's perceptions differed from mine. His experience and priorities as a guard who dealt with dangerous men led him to perceive that objects that I saw as harmless as potential weapons. Being unaccustomed to prison life, I didn't perceive the same

COMMUNICATION HIGHLIGHT

I'm Right; You're Wrong

When you are in conflict with a close friend or romantic partner, how do you see your role and the other person's? Do you often think you were being reasonable and the other person was being unreasonable? Do you tend to see yourself as having good intentions and the other person as having bad ones? If so, you're not alone. In 1999, Astrid Schütz separately asked husbands and wives to describe conflicts between them. Typically, each spouse described the problem as the other's fault. Each spouse saw his or her own behavior as justified and reasonable but described the partner's behavior as unfair, inconsiderate, inappropriate, or wrong. Participants also described their own intentions positively and their partners' intentions negatively—as unfair, irrational, mean-spirited, and so forth.

Schütz concluded that the self-serving bias is likely to affect how partners perceive themselves, each other, and conflicts between them. Resolution and positive feelings about each other are undermined when each partner perceives himself or herself as behaving well and the other as behaving wrongly.

In another experiment (Jaffe, 2004), peace proposals created by Israelis were labeled proposals created by Palestinians and proposals actually created by Palestinians were labeled proposals created by Israelis. Then Israeli citizens were asked to evaluate the proposals. The Israelis liked the proposal that was attributed to Israelis but actually authored by Palestinians better than they liked the proposal actually drafted by Israelis that was attributed to Palestinians. This displays how profoundly perceptions can be shaped by biases.

To explore your own experience with a conflict in which you were tempted to say "I'm right; you're wrong," complete the Communication Highlight Activity for Chapter 2 via MindTap for *Communication in Our Lives*.

---

things he did. Similarly, able-bodied people may not notice the lack of elevators or ramps in a building, but someone with a physical disability quickly perceives the building as inaccessible.

White students at predominantly white schools often don't notice that few people of color are in their classes, but the ethnic ratio is very obvious to students who are black, American Indian, Middle Eastern, Asian, and Hispanic. Let's consider some reasons why people differ in how they perceive situations and other people.

Physiology

The most obvious reason perceptions vary is that people differ in sensory abilities and physiologies. Music that one person finds deafening is barely audible to another. On a given day on my campus, students wear everything from shorts and sandals to jackets, indicating that they have different sensitivities to cold. Some people have better vision than others, and still others are color blind.

Our physiological states also influence perception. If you are tired, stressed, or sick, you're likely to perceive a comment from a coworker as critical of you, but the comment wouldn't bother you if you felt good. If you interact with someone who is sick, you might attribute his or her irritability to temporary factors rather than to enduring personality.

Age also influences our perceptions. The older we get, the more complex is our perspective on life and people. Many people 18–22 years old consider it normal to pay over $3 for a gallon of gas, but to a 60-year-old person who recalls when gas cost twenty cents a gallon, current prices seem high. The extent of discrimination still experienced by women and minorities understandably leads some young people to see inequities as unalterable. When I attended college, women weren't admitted on an equal basis with men, and almost all students of color attended minority colleges. The substantial progress made during my lifetime leads me to perceive remaining inequities as changeable.

Culture

A **culture** consists of beliefs, values, understandings, practices, and ways of interpreting experience that are shared by a number of people. It is a set of taken-for-granted assumptions that form the pattern of our lives and guide how we perceive as well as how we think, feel, and act.

Consider a few aspects of modern Western culture that influence our perceptions. One characteristic of our culture is an emphasis on technology and its offspring, speed. We expect things to happen fast—almost instantly. We fax or email PDFs of letters, jet across the country, engage in instant messaging and texting, and microwave our meals.

North America is also a fiercely individualistic culture in which personal initiative and independence are rewarded. When children become adults, they often move away from their parents, and older people are increasingly expected to take responsibility for themselves as they age. Some other cultures are more communal, and identity is defined in terms of one's family rather than as an individual quality. In communal cultures, children are looked after by the whole community instead of just their parents, and elders are given great respect and care.

In recent years, scholars have realized that we are affected not only by the culture as a whole but also by our particular location within the culture (Haraway, 1988; Harding, 1991; Wood 2005). **Standpoint theory** claims that a culture includes a number of social communities that have different degrees of

Calvin and Hobbes

social status and privilege. Each social community distinctively shapes the perceptions, identities, and opportunities of its members. If a member of a social group gains political insight into the group's social location, then he or she can develop a standpoint. For example, a Muslim has the social location of Muslims. If that person learns about ways in which Western society discriminates against Muslims, the person may develop a Muslim standpoint. Without that political awareness, however, the person cannot achieve a standpoint.

> **CARL** I'll admit that when Krista and I had a child, I expected Krista to stay home and take care of her. Actually, we both did, and that worked fine for 3 months. Then Krista got cancer, and she was in the hospital for weeks and then in and out for nearly a year for treatments. Even when she was home, she didn't have the energy to take care of little Jennie. I had to take over a lot of the child care. Doing that really changed me in basic ways. I had to learn to tolerate being interrupted when I was working. I had to tune into what Jennie needed and learn to read her. Before that experience, I thought women had a maternal instinct. What I learned is, anyone can develop a parental sensitivity.

Gendered locations explain the difference between the amount of effort women and men, in general, invest in communication that maintains relationships. Socialized into the role of "relationship expert," women are often expected by others and themselves to take care of relationships (Wood, 1994d, 2007a, 2013).

Social and Professional Roles

Our perceptions are also shaped by social roles that others communicate to us. Messages that tell us that we are expected to fulfill particular roles, as well as the actual demands of those roles, affect how we perceive and communicate.

Speakers are more likely than audience members to notice the acoustics of presentation rooms. Teachers often perceive classes in terms of whether the students are interested, whether they have read material, and whether they engage in class discussion. On the other hand, many students perceive classes in terms of the number and difficulty of tests, whether papers are required, and whether the professor is interesting.

The careers people choose influence what they notice and how they think and act. Doctors are trained to be highly observant of physical symptoms, and they may detect a physical problem before a person knows that he or she has it. For example, some years ago at a social gathering, a friend of mine who is a doctor asked me how long I had had a herniated disk. Surprised, I told him I didn't have one. "You do," he insisted, and sure enough, a few weeks later a magnetic resonance imaging examination confirmed a ruptured disk in my back. His medical training enabled him to perceive subtle changes in my posture and walk that I hadn't noticed.

Cognitive Abilities

In addition to physiological, cultural, and social influences, perception is shaped by our cognitive abilities. How elaborately we think about situations and people, and the extent of our personal knowledge of others, affects how we select, organize, and interpret experiences.

Cognitive Complexity   People differ in the number and types of knowledge schemata they use to organize and interpret people and situations. **Cognitive complexity** refers to the number of constructs used, how abstract they are, and how elaborately they interact to shape perceptions. Most children have fairly simple cognitive systems. They rely on few schemata, focus more on concrete categories (tall–not tall) than on abstract ones (introspective–not introspective), and often don't perceive relationships between different perceptions. For instance, infants may call every man Daddy because they haven't learned more complex ways to distinguish among men.

Adults also differ in cognitive complexity. If you perceive people only as nice or mean, you have a limited range for perceiving others. Similarly, people who focus exclusively on concrete data tend to have less sophisticated understandings than people who also perceive psychological data. For example, you might notice that a coworker is assertive, tells jokes, and contributes on task teams. These are concrete perceptions. At a more abstract, psychological level, you might infer that these concrete behaviors reflect a secure, self-confident personality. This is a more sophisticated cognition because it integrates three perceptions to develop an explanation of why the person acts as he or she does.

What if you later find out that the person is reserved in one-to-one conversations? Someone with low cognitive complexity would have difficulty integrating the new information into prior observations. Either the new information would be dismissed because it doesn't fit or the most recent information would alter the former perception, and the person would be redefined as shy. A more cognitively complex person would integrate all the information into a coherent account. Perhaps a cognitively complex thinker would conclude that the person is confident in social situations but less secure in more personal ones.

Cognitively complex people tend to be flexible in interpreting complicated phenomena and integrating new information into their thinking about people and situations. Less cognitively complex people are likely to ignore information that doesn't fit neatly with their impressions or to use it to replace the impressions they had formed (Delia, Clark, & Switzer, 1974). Either way, they fail to recognize some of the nuances and inconsistencies that are part of human life. The complexity of our cognitive systems affects the fullness and intricacy of our perceptions of people and interpersonal situations. Cognitively complex people also tend to communicate in more flexible and appropriate ways with a range of others. This probably results from their ability to recognize differences in people and to adapt their own communication accordingly.

Person-Centered Perception   **Person-centered perception** reflects cognitive complexity because it entails abstract thinking and a broad range of schemata. Person-centered perception is the ability to perceive another as a unique and distinct individual. Our ability to perceive others as unique depends both on the general ability to make cognitive distinctions and on our knowledge of particular others. As we get to know individuals, we gain insight into how they differ from others in their groups ("Rob's not like most campus politicos"; "Janet's more flexible than most managers."). The more we interact with one another and the greater variety of experiences we have together, the more insight we gain into other people. In long-term relationships, we fine-tune our perceptions throughout the life of relationships.

Person-centered perception is not the same as empathy. **Empathy** is the ability to feel with another person—to feel what he or she feels. Feeling with another is an emotional response. Because feelings are guided by our own experiences and emotions, it may be impossible to feel exactly and completely what another person feels. A more realistic goal is to try to recognize another's perspective and adapt your communication to how he or she perceives situations and people (Muehlhoff, 2006). With commitment and effort, we can learn a lot about how others see the world, even if that differs from how we see it.

HEALTH COMMUNICATION

MIA: Patients' Perspectives

Have you ever felt uncomfortable bringing up a medical issue to a doctor? Have you ever not questioned doctors because you didn't want them to think you were challenging them? If so, you're not alone. According to Dr. Pauline Chen (2012), despite increased effort to make health care patient friendly, often patients' perspectives are left out. A recent study showed that even normally assertive people feel shut down by physicians whom they perceive as not wanting to know their perspectives. Physicians, on the other hand, say they want to know what their patients think. Chen recommends changes in doctors' practices so that their communication is in line with their intent of partnering with patients. For instance, doctors should ask directly how patients perceive symptoms, how they feel about what's happening, and so forth.

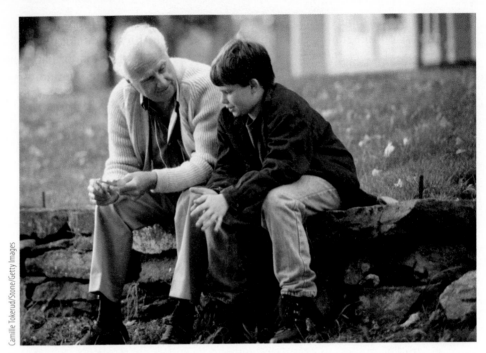

Camille Tokerud/Stone/Getty Images

Taking the perspective of others is a foundation of effective communication.

When we take others' perspectives, we try to grasp what something means to them and how they perceive things. We can't really understand someone else's perspective when we're judging whether it is right or wrong, sensible or crazy. Instead, we have to let go of our own perspective and perceptions long enough to enter the thoughts and feelings of another person. Doing this allows us to understand issues from the other person's point of view so we can communicate more effectively (Servaty-Seib & Burleson, 2007). You might learn why your boss thinks something is important that you've been disregarding. You might find out how a friend interprets your behavior in ways inconsistent with what you intend to communicate.

At a later point in interaction, we may choose to express our own perspective or to disagree with another's views. This is appropriate and important in honest communication, but voicing our own views is not a substitute for the equally important skill of recognizing another's perspective. In sum, differences based on physiology, culture, standpoint, social roles, and cognitive abilities affect what we perceive and how we interpret others and experiences. In the final section of the chapter, we consider ways to improve the accuracy of our perceptions.

ENHANCING COMMUNICATION COMPETENCE

To be a competent communicator, you need to realize how perception and communication affect each other. We'll elaborate on the connection between perception and communication and then discuss guidelines for enhancing communication competence.

Eye Witness Testimony: Fact or Fiction?

Many a defendant has been convicted because of eyewitness testimony. And many an *innocent* defendant has been convicted by eyewitness testimony. In recent years, a number of convicted felons have been given new trials because DNA evidence could now be introduced. Nearly 75% of cases in which DNA exonerated a person serving time involved eye-witness testimony that the imprisoned person was the person who committed the crime (Beil, 2011).

The eyewitnesses weren't lying, at least not intentionally. They simply misremembered. Researchers studying memory point out that most people perceive only a few details when an event happens. Later police questioning and line ups, coupled with repeating a false memory to themselves, make eyewitness very confident when they testify erroneously.

Perceptions, Communication, and Abstraction

Words crystallize perceptions. When we name feelings and thoughts, we create precise ways to describe and think about them. But just as words crystallize experiences, they can also freeze thought. Once we label our perceptions, we may respond to our own labels rather than to actual phenomena.

Consider this situation. You and five others form a study group, and a student named Andrea monopolizes the whole meeting with her questions and concerns. Leaving the meeting, one person says, "Gee, Andrea is so selfish and immature! I'll never work with her again." Another person responds, "She's not really selfish. She's insecure about her grades in this course, so she was hyper in the meeting." Chances are these two people will perceive and treat Andrea differently depending on whether they label her selfish or insecure. The point is that the two people respond not to Andrea herself but to how they selectively perceive and label her.

Communication is based on a process of abstracting from complex stimuli. Our perceptions are not equivalent to the complex reality on which they are based because we can never fully describe or even apprehend total reality. This means that what we perceive is a step removed from stimuli because perceptions are always partial and subjective. We move a second step from stimuli when we label a perception. We move even further from stimuli when we respond not to behaviors or our perceptions of them but to the judgments we associate with the label we have imposed. This process can be illustrated as a ladder of abstraction, as shown in Figure 2.1 (Korzybski, 1948). To learn more about the abstraction process, visit the general semantics site by clicking **WebLink 2.2.**

Guidelines for Enhancing Competence

Thinking of communication as a process of abstracting suggests ways to enhance competence in interaction. Five guidelines help us avoid the problems abstraction may invite.

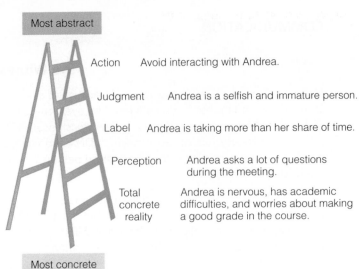

FIGURE 2.1
Perception, Communication, and Abstraction

Recognize That All Perceptions Are Subjective   Our perceptions are partial and subjective because each of us perceives from a unique perspective. A class you find exciting may put another student to sleep. Writing is a creative, enjoyable activity for some people and a tedious grind for others. There is no truth or falsity to perceptions; they represent what things mean to individuals based on their individual social roles, cultural backgrounds, cognitive abilities, standpoints, and physiology. Effective communicators realize that perceptions are subjective and don't assume that their own perceptions are the only valid ones.

Avoid Mind Reading   One of the most common problems in communication is **mind reading**—assuming we understand what another person thinks or perceives. When we mind read, we act as if we know what's on another's mind, and this can get us into trouble. Marriage counselors identify mind reading as one of the behaviors that contributes to interpersonal tension (Gottman, 1993). According to communication scholar Fran Dickson (1995), one exception may be mind reading between spouses in long-lasting marriages. After living together for a long time, partners may have sufficient person perception to mind read with great accuracy.

For the most part, however, mind reading is more likely to harm than help communication. Mind reading invites problems when we say things such as "I know why you're upset" or "You don't care about me." We also mind read when we tell ourselves we know how somebody else will feel or react or what they'll do. The truth is we don't really know—we're only guessing. When we mind read, we impose our perceptions on others, which can lead to resentment and misunderstandings.

SAWYER   *I learned my lesson about mind reading. A friend I'd known since childhood recently lost her mother to cancer. When I visited the friend, I said I was sorry for her sadness. She told me she wasn't sad at all; she said she was relieved. She had been sad to see her mother suffering so much. To her, death was a blessing.*

Check Perceptions With Others Because perceptions are subjective and mind reading is ineffective, we need to check our perceptions with others. Perception checking is an important communication skill because it helps people understand each other and their relationships. To check perceptions, you should first state what you have noticed. For example, a person might say, "Lately you've seemed less attentive to me." Second, the person should check to see whether the other perceives the same thing: "Do you feel you've been less attentive?" Third, it's appropriate to offer alternative explanations of your perceptions: "It might be that you're annoyed with me or that you're stressed out at work or that you're focused on other things." Finally, you may ask the other person to clarify how he or she perceives the behavior and the reasons for it: "What do you think is going on?" If the other person doesn't share your perceptions, ask him or her to explain the behaviors on which your perception is based: "Why have you wanted to be together less often lately?"

Speak tentatively when checking perceptions to minimize defensiveness and encourage open dialogue. Just let the other person know you've noticed something and would like him or her to clarify his or her perceptions of what is happening and what it means. It's also a good idea to check perceptions directly with the other person. It is more difficult to reach a shared understanding with another person when we ask someone else to act as a go-between or when we ask others whether they agree with our perceptions of a third person.

Distinguish Between Facts and Inferences Competent communicators know the difference between facts and inferences. A fact is a statement based on observation or other data. An inference involves an interpretation that goes beyond the facts. For example, it is a fact that my partner, Robbie, forgets a lot of things. Based on that fact, I might infer that he is thoughtless. Defining Robbie as thoughtless is an inference that goes beyond the facts. The "fact" of his forgetfulness could equally well be explained by preoccupation or general absentmindedness.

It's easy to confuse facts and inferences because we sometimes treat the latter as the former. When we say, "He is irresponsible," we make a statement that sounds factual, and we may then regard it that way ourselves. To avoid this tendency, substitute more tentative words for *is*. For instance, "Parker's behaviors seem thoughtless" is more tentative than "Parker is thoughtless." Tentative language helps us resist the tendency to treat inferences as facts.

Monitor the Self-Serving Bias The self-serving bias exemplifies humans' broad tendency to protect self-image (Tavris & Aronson, 2007). We want to be competent, good, smart, and right. If we make dumb decisions, we're inclined to deny or justify them. A primary means of doing this is to engage in

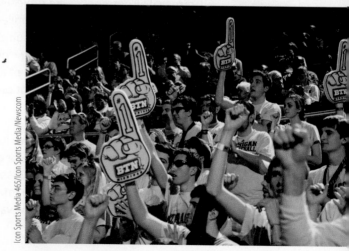

Icon Sports Media 465/Icon Sports Media/Newscom

The self-serving bias can distort fans' perceptions of their team.

the self-serving bias, which distorts our perceptions. Monitoring the self-serving bias also has implications for how we perceive others. Just as we tend to judge ourselves generously, we may also be inclined to judge others too harshly. Monitor your perceptions to see whether you attribute others' successes and admirable actions to external factors beyond their control and their shortcomings and blunders to internal factors they can (should) control. If you do this, substitute more generous explanations for others' behaviors, and notice how that affects your perceptions of them.

Perceiving accurately is a communication skill that can be developed. Following the five guidelines we have discussed will allow you to perceive more carefully and accurately.

BEYOND THE CLASSROOM

Let's take the material in this chapter beyond the classroom by thinking about how what you've learned about perception might apply to the workplace, ethical choices, and engagement with the broader world.

1. **Workplace.** This chapter discusses ways that culture and cultural values influence our perceptions. Think about how cultural values such as efficiency and individualism affect communication in your workplace or a former workplace. Continue this line of thinking by identifying other strong aspects of U.S. culture and tracing their impact on the workplace.

2. **Ethics.** This chapter presents five guidelines for enhancing competence in perceiving. Each guideline has ethical implications and assumptions. For example, the first guideline is to recognize that all perceptions are subjective. This assumes that there are multiple ways of perceiving any phenomena; in turn, this implies that there is no automatic validity to any particular perception. If you accept those assumptions, the implication is that we can't assume others are wrong if their perceptions differ from our own. Thus, the guideline implies that ethical communication requires awareness of and respect for others' perceptions. Now you analyze the ethical assumptions and implications of the other four guidelines for increasing competence in perceiving.

3. **Engagement.** Volunteer to work in a context that allows you to interact with a people you have not spent time with—for example, volunteer at a homeless shelter. Make a list of schemata (i.e., prototypes, personal constructs, stereotypes, and scripts) you have about these people before you interact with them. After spending time with them, review your list of schemata and evaluate how accurate they were.

CHAPTER SUMMARY

 Practice and review the content in this chapter.

In this chapter, we've explored human perception, which involves selecting, organizing, and interpreting experiences. These three processes are not separate in practice; they interact such that each one affects the others. What we selectively notice affects what we interpret and evaluate. In addition, our interpretations act as lenses that influence what we notice in the world around us. Selection, interpretation, and evaluation interact continuously in the process of perception.

Perception is shaped by many factors. Our physiological abilities and conditions affect what we notice and how astutely we recognize stimuli around us. In addition, our cultural backgrounds and social locations shape how we see and interact with the world. Social roles are another influence on perception. Thus, professional training and roles in families affect what we notice and how we organize and interpret it. Finally, perception is influenced by cognitive abilities, including cognitive complexity, person-centered perception, and perspective taking.

Thinking about communication as a process of abstracting helps us understand how perception works. We discussed five guidelines for avoiding the problems abstraction sometimes causes. First, realize that all perceptions are subjective, so there is no absolutely correct or best understanding of a situation or a person. Second, because people perceive differently, we should avoid mind reading or assuming we know what others perceive, think, and feel. Third, it's a good idea to check perceptions, which involves stating how you perceive something and asking how another person perceives it. A fourth guideline is to distinguish facts from inferences. Finally, avoiding the self-serving bias is important because it can lead us to perceive ourselves too charitably and others too harshly.

When we label our selective perceptions, we abstract or notice only some of the stimuli around us. Consequently, we can't see aspects of ourselves and others that our labels don't highlight. Realizing this encourages us to be more sensitive to the power of language and to make more considered choices about how we use it.

APPLYING COMMUNICATION IN OUR LIVES

Communication in Our Lives is supported by a MindTap, a new online learning platform that delivers content, assignments, and a tailored presentation of the course curriculum created by your instructor. MindTap combines all of your learning tools–readings, multimedia, activities and assessments–into a singular learning unit that guides you through the course. Practice

and Present, a unique tool within MindTap, allows you to upload your speech video files for practice or for a grade, comment on your peer's speeches and review your grades. MindTap also includes Speech Builder Express, a powerful tool that guides you through the speech outline and preparation process. For more information or to access MindTap, visit cengagebrain.com.

DEFINITIONS OF KEY CONCEPTS

 MindTap™ Review your **Flashcards**.

attribution A causal account that explains why a thing happened or why someone acted a certain way.

cognitive complexity The number of constructs used, how abstract they are, and how elaborately they interact to create perceptions.

constructivism Theory that claims we organize and interpret experience by applying cognitive structures called schemata.

culture Beliefs, understandings, practices, and ways of interpreting experience that are shared by a number of people.

empathy The ability to feel with another person or to feel what that person feels in a given situation.

interpretation The subjective process of evaluating and explaining perceptions.

mind reading Assuming that we understand what another person thinks or how another person perceives something.

perception The process of actively selecting, organizing, and interpreting people, objects, events, situations, and activities.

personal construct A bipolar mental yardstick that allows us to measure people and situations along specific dimensions of judgment.

person-centered perception The ability to perceive another as a unique and distinct individual apart from social roles and generalizations.

prototype A knowledge structure that defines the clearest or most representative example of some category.

schemata (singular: *schema*) Cognitive structures we use to organize and interpret experiences. Four types of schemata are prototypes, personal constructs, stereotypes, and scripts.

script One of four cognitive schemata. A script defines an expected or appropriate sequence of action in a particular setting.

self-fulfilling prophecy An expectation or judgment of ourselves brought about by our own actions.

self-serving bias The tendency to attribute our positive actions and successes to stable, global, internal influences that we control and to attribute negative actions and failures to unstable, specific, external influences beyond our control.

standpoint theory The theory that a culture includes a number of social groups that differently shape the knowledge, identities, and opportunities of members of those groups.

stereotype A predictive generalization about people and situations.

FOR FURTHER REFLECTION AND DISCUSSION

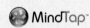 MindTap™

1. Identify an occasion when you engaged in the self-serving bias. Explain what you did, using the language of attributions.

2. Identify ethical issues involved in perceiving. What ethical choices do we make—perhaps unconsciously—as we selectively perceive, organize, and interpret others, particularly people whom we think are different from us in important ways?

3. Use the ladder of abstraction to analyze your perceptions and actions in a specific communication encounter. First, identify the concrete reality, what you perceived from the totality, the labels you assigned, and the resulting inferences and judgments. Second, return to the first level of perception and substitute different perceptions—other aspects of the total situation you might have perceived selectively. What labels, inferences, and judgments do the substitute perceptions invite? With others in the class, discuss the extent to which our perceptions and labels influence "reality."

1. Perceiving Others

Pay attention to the cognitive schemata you use the next time you meet a new person. First, notice how you classify the person. Do you categorize him or her as a potential friend, date, co-worker, or neighbor? Next, identify the personal constructs you use to assess the person. Do you focus on physical characteristics (attractive–not attractive), mental qualities (intelligent–not intelligent), psychological features (secure–not secure), or interpersonal qualities (available–not available)? Would different personal constructs be prominent if you used a different prototype to classify the person? Now note how you stereotype the person. What do you expect him or her to do, according to the prototype and personal constructs you've applied? Finally, identify your script: How do you expect interaction to unfold between the two of you?

2. Noticing Individualism

How do the individualistic values of our culture influence our perceptions and activities? Check it out by observing the following:

How is seating arranged in restaurants? Are there large, communal eating areas or private tables and booths for individuals, couples, and small groups?_____

How are living spaces arranged? How many people live in the average house?_____

Do families share homes? How many common spaces and individual spaces are there in homes?_____

How many people share a car in your family? How many cars are there in the United States?_____

How does the Western emphasis on individualism affect your day-to-day perceptions and activities?_____

CASE STUDY: *College Success*

A video of the conversation scripted here is featured in your Chapter 2 MindTap for *Communication in Our Lives*. Select "College Success" to watch the video of Jim's conversation with his dad. Improve your own communication skills by reading, watching, and evaluating this communication encounter.

Your friend Jim tells you about a problem he's having with his parents. According to Jim, his parents have unrealistic expectations of him. He tends to be an average student, usually making Cs, a few Bs, and an occasional D in his courses. His parents are angry that his grades aren't better. Jim tells you that when he went home last month, his father said this: "I'm not paying for you to go to school so you can party with your friends. I paid my own way and still made Phi Beta Kappa. You have a free ride, and you're still just pulling Cs. You just have to study harder."

Now Jim says to you, "I mean, I like to hang out with my friends, but that's got nothing to do with my grades. My dad's this brilliant guy,

Jason Harris/© 2001 Wadsworth

I mean, he just cruised through college, he thinks it's easy. I don't know how it was back then, but all my classes are hard. I mean, no matter how much studying I do, I'm not gonna get all As. What should I do? I mean, how do I convince them that I'm doing everything I can?"

QUESTIONS FOR ANALYSIS AND DISCUSSION

You can also answer these questions and see my responses to them online via MindTap for Chapter 2.

1. Both Jim and his parents make attributions to explain his grades. Describe the dimensions of Jim's attributions and those of his parents.

2. How might you assess the accuracy of Jim's attributions? What questions could you ask him to help you decide whether his perceptions are well founded or biased?

3. What constructs, prototypes, and scripts seem to operate in Jim's and his parents' thinking about college life?

4. What could you say to Jim to help him and his parents reach a shared perspective on his academic work?

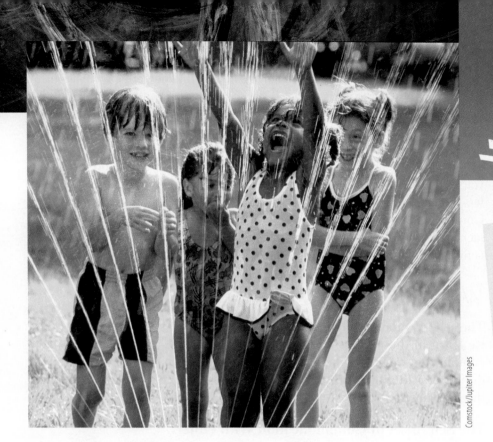

Comstock/Jupiter Images

Communication and Personal Identity

Kate is a 35-year-old physician's assistant. She is also a mother, an aunt, and a sister. Earlier in her life, Kate was a teenager, a student, and a fierce soccer player. One day, she may be retired and a grandmother. Like Kate, your identity changes over time. When you were 5 or 6, you probably defined yourself as your parents' son or daughter. In doing so, you implicitly recognized sex, race, and social class as parts of your identity. In high school, you may have described yourself in terms of academic abilities ("I'm better at math than at history"), athletic roles ("I'm a guard"), leadership positions ("I'm president of the Drama Club"), your social circle ("I hang out with Cindy and Mike"), or future plans ("I'm going to study hospital administration when I go to college").

If you entered college shortly after completing high school, you're probably

SHARPEN YOUR SKILL

At the end of this chapter, refer to the Sharpen Your Skill features, Reflecting on Your Identity Scripts and Your Looking-Glass Self, to apply concepts from Chapter 3.

🌐 **MindTap**™

Review the chapter **Learning Objectives** and **Start** with a quick warm up activity.

thinking of yourself in terms of a major, a career path, and perhaps a relationship you hope will span the years ahead. If you worked or committed to a relationship before starting or returning to college, you may already have a sense of yourself as a professional and a family member. By now, you've probably made some decisions about your spiritual beliefs and your political and social values.

As you think about the different ways you've defined yourself over the years, you'll realize that the self is not fixed firmly at one time and constant thereafter. Instead, the self is a process that evolves and changes throughout our lives. Communication with others is one of the greatest influences on our personal identities. In this chapter, we explore how the self develops continually through communication with others.

WHAT IS THE SELF?

MindTap

Read, highlight and take notes online.

The **self** is a process of internalizing and acting from social perspectives that we learn in the process of communication. At first, this may seem like a complicated way to define the self. As we will see, however, this definition directs our attention to some important insights into what is complicated: the human self.

The Self Arises in Communication With Others

The most basic insight into the self is that it isn't something we are born with. Instead, the self develops only as we communicate with others and participate in the social world. From the moment we are born, we interact with others. We learn how they see us, and we internalize many of their views of who we are and should be.

Communication With Family Members   For most of us, family members are the first important influence on how we see ourselves (Bergen & Braithwaite, 2009). Parents and other family members communicate who we are and what we are worth through *direct definition*, *identity scripts*, and *attachment styles*.

Direct definition, as the term implies, is communication that explicitly tells us who we are by labeling us and our behaviors. For instance, parents might say, "You're my little girl" or "You're a big boy" and thus communicate to the child what sex he or she is. Having been labeled *boy* or *girl*, the child then pays attention to how others talk about boys and girls to figure out what it means to be a certain sex. Parents' own gender stereotypes typically are communicated to children, so daughters may also be told, "Be nice to your friends" and "Don't mess up your clothes." Sons, on the other hand, are more likely to be told, "Stick up for yourself" and "Don't cry." As we hear these messages, we pick up our parents' and society's gender expectations. Direct definition also takes place as family members respond to children's behaviors. If a child is praised for dusting furniture, being helpful is reinforced as part of the child's self-concept. Positive labels enhance our self-esteem: "You are smart," "You're sweet," "You're great at baseball." Negative labels can damage children's self-esteem: "You're a trouble-maker," "You're stupid," and "You're impossible" are messages that can demolish a child's sense of self-worth.

Identity scripts are another way family members communicate who we are and should be. Psychologists define identity scripts as rules for how we are supposed to live and who we are supposed to be (Berne, 1964; Harris, 1969). Like the scripts for plays, identity scripts define our roles, how we are to play them, and basic elements in the plot we are supposed to have for our lives. Think back to your childhood to identify some of the principal scripts that operated in your family. Did you learn, "Always be prepared for emergencies," "We give back to our community," or "Live by God's word"? These are examples of identity scripts families teach us.

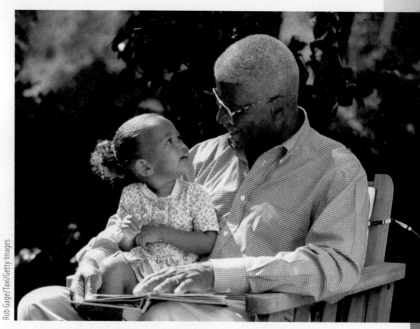

Family members' communication shapes personal identity.

Children seldom author, or even edit, initial identity scripts. In fact, children are generally not even conscious of learning identity scripts. As adults, however, we are no longer passive tablets on which others can define who we are. We have the capacity to review the identity scripts that were given to us and to challenge and change those that do not fit who we now choose to be.

Finally, parents communicate who we are through **attachment styles,** which are patterns of parenting that teach us who we and others are and how to relate to others. From extensive studies of interaction between parents and children, John Bowlby (1973, 1988) developed the theory that most of us learn attachment styles in our relationship with our first care givers—usually with parents. They communicate how they see us, others, and relationships. In turn, we are likely to internalize their views as our own. The first relationship is especially important because it shapes expectations for later relationships (Rhodewalt, 2007). Four distinct attachment styles have been identified (Figure 3.1).

A child is most likely to develop a *secure attachment style* when the primary caregiver interacts in a consistently attentive and loving way with the child. In response, the child develops a positive sense of self-worth ("I am lovable") and a positive view of others ("People are loving and can be trusted"). People with secure attachment styles tend to be outgoing, affectionate, and able to handle the normal challenges and disappointments of close relationships without losing self-esteem. Securely attached individuals tend to have more secure relationships (Rowe & Carnelley, 2005) than less securely attached individuals.

A child may develop a *fearful attachment style* if the primary caregiver communicates in negative, rejecting, or abusive ways to the child.

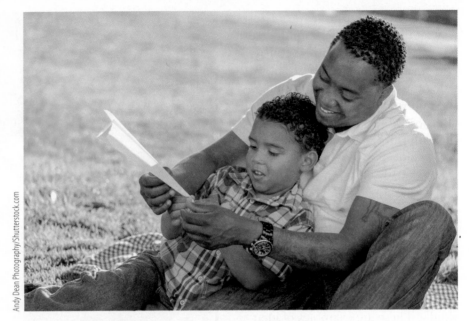

Andy Dean Photography/Shutterstock.com

Parents' communication is a major influence on identity.

Children who are treated unkindly often infer that they are unworthy of love and that others are not loving. Thus, they learn to see themselves as unlovable and others as rejecting. Although they may want close bonds with others, they fear that others will not love them and that they themselves are not lovable.

A caregiver who is disinterested, rejecting, or abusive may also lead a child to develop a *dismissive attachment style*, which makes the child tend to dismiss others as unworthy. People with dismissive attachment styles have a positive view of themselves and a low regard for others and relationships. This may lead them to regard relationships as unnecessary and undesirable.

FIGURE 3.1
Styles of Attachment

© Cengage Learning

AMELIA   *When I was in high school, I babysat to make money. One little girl I watched was very stand offish. No matter how hard I tried to play with Liza and be friends, she kept her distance. But sometimes I would see her looking at me almost longingly like she wanted to play with me. When her parents were around, they were focused on work or each other. If Liza needed something or spoke up, they acted as if she was interrupting them.*

Last is the *anxious/ambivalent attachment style,* which is the most complex of the four. Each of the other three styles results from a consistent pattern of treatment by a caregiver. However, the anxious/ambivalent style is fostered by *inconsistent* treatment from the caregiver. Sometimes the adult is loving and attentive, at other times indifferent or rejecting. The caregiver's communication is not only inconsistent but also unpredictable. He or she may respond positively to something a child does on Monday and react negatively to the same behavior on Tuesday. Naturally, this unpredictability creates anxiety in a child. Because children tend to assume that adults are right, they often believe they themselves are the source of any problem—that they are unlovable or deserve others' abuse. People who have high anxiety about attachments are likely to avoid or minimize attachments (Brenning, Soenens, Braet, & Bosmans, 2011).

In adult life, people who have anxious/ambivalent attachment styles know that others can be loving and affirming, but they also know that others can hurt them and be unloving. Reflecting the pattern displayed by the caregiver, people with anxious/ambivalent attachment styles often are inconsistent themselves. One day they invite affection; the next day they deny needing closeness. An interesting study by Tim Cole and Laura Leets (1999) found that people with anxious/ambivalent attachment styles often form relationships with television characters. It may feel safer to be in relationships with television characters than with real people.

Unless we consciously work to change the attachment styles we learned in our first close relationships, they tend to affect how we communicate in our adult relationships (Bornstein & Languirand, 2003; Bowlby, 1988; Guerrero, 1996). However, we can modify our attachment styles by challenging unconstructive views of us communicated in our early years and by forming relationships that foster secure connections today (Banse, 2004). To learn more about attachment theory, use MindTap for *Communication in Our Lives* to access **WebLink 3.1**.

MindTap

Communication With Peers   A second major influence on our self-concepts is communication with peers. From childhood playmates to work associates, friends, and romantic partners, we interact with peers throughout our lives. As we do, we gain further direct definitions that tell us how others see us. In turn, this affects how we see ourselves. As we interact with peers, we engage in **social comparison,** which involves comparing ourselves with others to gauge our talents, attractiveness, abilities, skills, and so forth (Stapel &

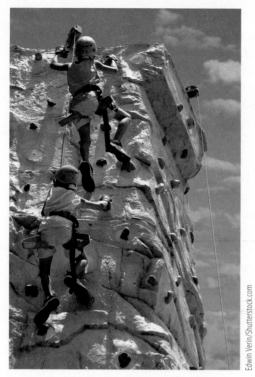

We measure our abilities against those of peers.

Blanton, 2006). We measure ourselves in relation to others in two ways. First, we compare ourselves with others to decide whether we are like them or different from them. Are we the same age, color, or religion? Do we have similar backgrounds and social and political beliefs?

Peers are particularly strong in commenting directly on conformity to expectations of gender. Some college-age men think drinking and sexual activity embody masculinity. Men who are not interested in drinking and hooking up may be ridiculed and excluded for not being "real men" (Cross, 2008; Kimmel, 2008). Women who don't wear popular brands of clothing or who weigh more than what is considered ideal may be belittled and excluded for being unfeminine (Adler, 2007; Barash, 2006).

Assessing similarity and difference allows us to decide with whom we fit. Research has shown that people generally are most comfortable with others who are like them, so we tend to gravitate toward those we regard as similar (Amodio & Showers, 2006; Chen, Luo, Yue, Xu, & Zhaoyang, 2009; Lutz-Zois, Bradley, Mihalik, & Moorman-Eavers, 2006). However, interacting only with people like us can impoverish our understandings of ourselves and the world.

We also use social comparison to measure ourselves in relation to others. Am I as good a goalie as Jenny? Am I as smart as Sam? We continuously refine our self-image by comparing ourselves to others on various criteria of judgment. This is normal and necessary if we are to develop realistic self-concepts. However, we should be wary of what psychologists call upward comparison, which is the tendency to compare ourselves to people who exceed us in what they have or can do (Tugend, 2011). For most of us, it isn't constructive to judge our attractiveness in relation to that of movie stars and models or our athletic ability in relation to that of professional athletes.

KEVIN *I learned more about myself and about being white when I was assigned to room with a black guy my freshman year. I'd never interacted much with blacks, and I'd never had a black friend, but I got really close with my roommate. Carl helped me see a lot of things I take for granted that he can't because of his skin. For example, people assume I'm here because I earned a good record in high school, but a lot of people think Carl got in just because he's black and the college had to meet its minority quota. His SAT was higher than mine and so are his grades, but people believe I'm smart and he's a quota admission.*

Communication With Society   A third influence on our self-concepts is interaction with society in general. As we observe and interact with others and media and as we participate in institutions, we learn how society regards each sex, race, sexual orientation, and socioeconomic class. We also learn broad cultural values.

Western society encourages people to perceive themselves as individuals and to form separate families in adulthood. In contrast, traditional Indian culture emphasizes collective identity, and households under the same roof often include grandparents, aunts, uncles, and cousins (Lustig & Koester, 1999). Western society also encourages competition, whereas many Asian societies teach children to place emphasis on cooperation and teamwork (Yum, 2000).

Media is a primary agent in teaching social perspectives. When we read popular magazines, watch films, and visit sites on the Web, we are inundated with messages about how women and men are supposed to look and act, who has status, and so forth. Media shape teens' views of sex and sexuality—what is appropriate and "cool" (Bodey & Wood, 2009; Wood, 2010).

HEALTH COMMUNICATION

Self-Help: A Healthier Self?

Do you love too much, too little, or the wrong people? Are you guilty of negative thinking? If so, there's a self-help book—or a dozen—for you. Don't want a book? No problem, buy self-help video and audio products, attend seminars, or hire a personal coach. You can join a support group with 12 steps or 7 principles. It's all part of the multibillion dollar self-help industry. And don't forget television programs such as *The* Swan (aired 2004), Extreme *Makeover* (aired 2002–2006) and *The Biggest Loser* (is being aired 2004–present), which also tell us to take charge of fixing ourselves with self-discipline perhaps along with multiple surgeries.

Although the self-help industry is wildly popular today, it's not exactly new. The first self-help book was published in 1859 by Samuel Smiles. Titled *Self-Help* and appropriately self-published, Smiles' book opened by telling readers "Heaven helps those who help themselves." Within a year of publication, the book sold 20,000 copies, extraordinary for that era. Another early self-help author was Dale Carnegie. After a short stint as a salesman, Carnegie failed as an actor and wound up broke, unemployed and living at the YMCA in New York. That's where he started teaching a public speaking course that formed the basis of *How to Win Friends and Influence People* (1936), which was a self-help manual for millions of readers.

Despite the popularity of self-help, caution may be wise. Steve Salerno, former editor of *Men's Health* magazine's books program, doesn't think much of self-help books. In *SHAM* (2005), a critique of the self-help industry, he writes that "self-help is an enterprise wherein people holding the thinnest of credentials diagnose in basically normal people symptoms of inflated or invented maladies, so that they may then implement remedies that have never been shown to work" (p. 1).

The institutions that organize our society further communicate social perspectives by the values they uphold. For example, our judicial system reminds us that as a society we value laws and punish those who break them. The number of schools and the levels of education in America inform us that our society values learning. At the same time, institutions reflect prevailing social prejudices. For instance, we may be a lawful society, but wealthy defendants often can buy better "justice" than poor ones. Similarly, although we claim to offer equal educational opportunities to all, students whose families have money and influence often can get into better schools than students whose families have fewer resources. These and other values are so thoroughly woven into the fabric of our culture that we learn them with little effort or awareness.

The Self-Fulfilling Prophecy   One particularly powerful way in which communication shapes the self is the self-fulfilling prophecy, which we discussed in Chapter 2. Self-fulfilling prophecies operate when we act in ways that bring about expectations or judgments of ourselves. If you have done poorly in classes in which teachers didn't seem to respect you and have done well with teachers who thought you were smart, then you know what a self-fulfilling prophecy is. The prophecies that we act to fulfill usually are first communicated to us by others' direct definitions, identity scripts, and attachment styles. Because we often internalize others' perspectives, we may label ourselves as they do and then act to fulfill our own labels.

TERRY   *I can really identify with the self-fulfilling prophecy idea. In the second grade, my family moved from our farm to a city where my dad could find work. The first week of class in my new school, we had show and tell. When it was my turn, as soon as I started talking the other kids started laughing at me. I had been raised on a farm in the rural South, and the other kids were from the city. They thought I talked funny, and they made fun of my accent—called me "hillbilly" and "redneck." From then on, I avoided public speaking like the plague. I thought I couldn't speak to others. Last year, I finally took a course in public speaking, and I made a B. It took me a long time to challenge the label that I was a bad public speaker.*

Many of us believe things about ourselves that are inaccurate. Sometimes labels that were once true aren't any longer, but we continue to believe them and act to fulfill them. In other cases, the labels were never valid, but we may believe them anyway. Unfortunately, children often are labeled "slow" or "stupid" when the real problem is that they have physiological difficulties such as impaired vision or hearing. Even when the true source of difficulty is discovered, the children may have already internalized a destructive self-fulfilling prophecy.

The Self Is Multidimensional

Although we use the word *self* as if it referred to a single entity, in reality the self has many dimensions. You have a physical self that includes your size, shape, skin, hair and eye colors, and so forth. In addition, you have a cognitive self that includes your intelligence, aptitudes, and education. You have an emotional self-concept. Are you interpersonally sensitive? Do you have a hot temper? Are you generally optimistic or pessimistic? You have a social self. Some people are extraverted, whereas others are more reserved. Our social selves also include our roles: daughter or son, student, worker, parent, volunteer, partner in a committed relationship. Each of us also has a moral self that is composed of ethical and spiritual principles we believe in and try to follow. As Carlyle points out, the different dimensions of ourselves sometimes seem at odds with one another.

> **CARLYLE**   *On my own, like with friends or family, I'm pretty quiet—even shy, you could say. But my job requires me to be real outgoing and sociable. I tend bar, and people expect me to kid around and talk with them and stuff. Believe me, if I were as quiet with my customers as I am with my friends, my tips would drop to nothing. It's like when I'm in my work role, I'm Mr. Hail-fellow-well-met, but away from work I'm pretty reserved.*

The Self Is a Process

The self develops over time; it is a process. A baby perceives no boundaries between its body and a nipple, a hand that tickles, or a breeze. As an infant has experiences and as others respond to him or her, the child gradually begins to develop **ego boundaries**, which define where the self stops and the rest of the world begins. This is the beginning of a self-concept: the realization that one is a separate entity.

As infants begin to differentiate themselves from the rest of the world, the self starts to develop. Infants and young children listen to and observe others to define themselves and to become competent in the identities others assign to them (Kohlberg, 1958; Piaget, 1932/1965). For instance, children work to figure out what it takes to be nice, tough, and responsible, and they strive to become competent at embodying those qualities. The ways we define ourselves vary as we mature. Struggling to be a good mud-cake maker at age 4 gives way to striving for popularity in high school and to succeeding in professional and family roles later in life.

Of course, we all enter the world with certain abilities and limits, which constrain the possibilities of who we can be. Someone without the genes to be tall and coordinated, for instance, probably is not going to be a star forward in basketball. Beyond genetic limits, however, we have considerable freedom to create who we will be.

We Internalize and Act From Social Perspectives

We've already noted that in developing a self, we internalize many of the perspectives of others. Let's now look more closely at how we internalize both the perspectives of individuals who are significant in our lives and the general perspective of our society.

Particular Others   We first encounter the perspectives of **particular others**. As the term implies, these are the viewpoints of specific people who are significant to us. Mothers, fathers, siblings, and often day-care providers are particular others who are significant to most infants. In addition, we may be very close to aunts, uncles, grandparents, godparents, and others. Children who grow up in large, extended families often have a great many particular others who affect how they come to see themselves.

SHENNOA   *My grandmother was the biggest influence on me. I lived with her while my mama worked, and she taught me to take myself seriously. She's the one who told me I should go to college and plan a career so that I wouldn't have to depend on somebody else. She's the one who told me to stand up for myself and not let others tell me what to do or believe in. But she did more than just tell me to be a strong person. That's how she was, and I learned just by watching her. A lot of who I am is modeled on my grandmother.*

The process of seeing ourselves through others' eyes is called **reflected appraisal**. It means that we see ourselves in terms of the appraisals reflected in others' eyes. The process has also been called the "looking-glass self" because others are mirrors who reflect who we are (Cooley, 1912). Reflected appraisals are not confined to childhood but continue throughout our lives. When a teacher communicates that a student is smart, the student may come to see himself or herself that way. In professional life, coworkers and supervisors reflect their appraisals of us when they communicate that we're on the fast track, average, or unsuited to our position. The appraisals that others communicate shape how we see ourselves. In turn, how we see ourselves affects how we communicate. Thus, if you see yourself as an interesting conversationalist, you're likely to communicate that confidence when you talk with others.

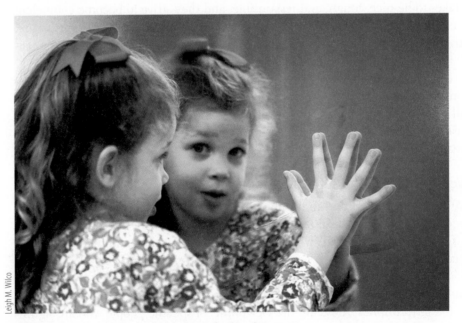

Leigh M. Wilco

We see ourselves in the looking glass of others' eyes.

The Generalized Other   The second social perspective that influences how we see ourselves is called the **perspective of the generalized other**. The generalized other is the collection of rules, roles, and attitudes endorsed by the specific culture in which we live (Mead, 1934). Modern Western culture emphasizes gender, race, sexual orientation, and economic class as central to personal identity (Andersen & Collins, 2006; Wood, 1995b, 2005). Each of these social groupings represents a standpoint, which we discussed in Chapter 2.

North American culture views race as a primary aspect of personal identity (González, Houston, & Chen, 2012). The white race historically has been privileged in the United States. In the early years of this country, it was considered normal and right for white men to own black women, men, and children and to require them to work for no wages and in poor conditions. Later, it was considered natural that white men could vote but black men could not. Clearly, racial prejudice has diminished substantially. Even so, the upper levels of government, education, and business are dominated by white men, whereas people of color continue to fight overt and covert discrimination in many spheres of society.

> **WEN-SHU**   *My family moved here when I was 9 years old. Because I look Asian, people make assumptions about me. They assume I am quiet (true), I am good at math (not true), and I defer to men and elders (true with regard to elders but not men). People also see all Asians as the same, but Taiwanese are as different from mainland Chinese as French Caucasians are from U.S. Caucasians. The first thing people notice about me is my race, and they make too many assumptions about what it means.*

Gender, another important facet of identity in Western culture, also is communicated through social practices and institutions (Martin & Finn, 2010). Historically, men—specifically, white men—have been seen as more

Jump Start reprinted by permission of United Feature Syndicate, Inc.

valuable than women and more entitled to privileges. In the 1800s, women weren't allowed to own property, attend college, or vote. Although there has been great progress in achieving equality between the sexes, in some respects women and men still are not considered equal or treated as such (Kaufman & Kimmel, 2011).

Western cultures have strong gender prescriptions. Girls and women are expected to be caring and cooperative, whereas boys and men are supposed to be independent and competitive. Consequently, women who are competitive and men who are gentle may receive social disapproval for violating gender prescriptions. Gender prescriptions also specify ideal body images—tall and muscular for men; slender or thin and not too tall for women.

A third aspect of identity that cultural communication establishes as salient is sexual orientation. Western culture's view that heterosexuality is normal and right is communicated not only directly but also through privileges given to heterosexuals but denied to gay men, lesbians, bisexuals, trans and gender non-conforming people. For example, a woman and man who love each other can be married, and their commitment can be recognized religiously and legally. Two men or two women who love each other are not allowed to marry in most states, although domestic partnerships are increasingly recognized. Heterosexual spouses can obtain insurance coverage for their partners and can will them money tax free, but people with other sexual orientations often cannot. By 2010, nearly 300 colleges had added gender identity and expression to their nondiscrimination policies, many have designated some bathrooms as available to everyone, and many have passed gender-neutral housing policies so that transgender students are not forced to live with people with whom they don't identify (Tilsley, 2010). Although biases against sexual orientation and gender identity are decreasing, they still very much affect how we are viewed and treated.

SANDI   *I've known I was lesbian since I was in high school, but only in the last year have I come out to others. As soon as I tell someone I'm lesbian, they see me differently. Even people who have known me a long time act like I've developed spots or something. Some of my girlfriends don't want to hug or touch me anymore, like they think I'm suddenly going to come on to them. Guys act as if I'm from another planet. It's really strange that sexual orientation makes so much difference in how others see you. I mean, relative to other things like character, personality, and intelligence, who you sleep with is pretty unimportant.*

A fourth dimension of identity, socioeconomic class, is also central to the generalized other's perspective in Western culture. Socioeconomic class isn't just the amount of money a person has. It's a basic part of how we understand our place in the world and how we think, feel, and act (Lawless, 2012). Socioeconomic class affects everything from the careers we pursue to the schools and lifestyles we see as possibilities for ourselves. Members of the middle and upper classes assume that they will attend college and enter good professions, whereas people from the working class may be directed toward vocational training regardless of their academic achievements. In such patterns, we see how the perspective of the generalized other shapes our identities and our concrete lives.

> **ROCHELLE**   *I got so mad in high school. I had a solid A average, and ever since I was 12 I had planned to go to college. But when the guidance counselor talked with me at the start of my senior year, she encouraged me to apply to a technical school that is near my home. When I said I thought my grades should get me into a good college, she did this double-take, like, "Your kind doesn't go to college." My parents both work in a mill and so do all my relatives, but does that mean that I can't have a different future? What really burned me was that a lot of girls who had average grades but came from "the right families" were told to apply to colleges.*

It's important to realize that social perspectives on race, sex, sexual orientation, and socioeconomic class interact. Race intersects gender, so women of color often experience double oppression and devaluation in our culture. Class and sexual orientation also interact: Homophobia tends to be pronounced among people in the working class, so a lesbian or gay person in a poor community may be socially ostracized. Socioeconomic class and gender are also interlinked; women are far more likely than men to live at the poverty level (Andersen & Collins, 2006; Kaufman & Kimmel, 2011). Intersections of race and class mean that minority members of the working class often are not treated as well as working-class whites (Rothenberg, 2006).

As we internalize the generalized other's perspective, we come to share many of the views and values of our society. Shared understandings are essential for collective life. If we all made up our own rules, there would be no shared standards and collective life would be chaotic. Yet, shared understandings are not carved in stone: People sometimes work to change how their society operates. Each of us has an ethical responsibility to think critically about which social views to accept and use as guides for our own behaviors, attitudes, and values. This suggests a fourth proposition about the self.

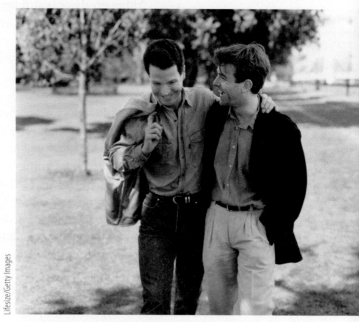

Lifesize/Getty Images

Social perspectives on same-sex relationships have changed over time.

Social Perspectives on the Self Are Constructed and Changeable

The generalized other's perspectives are not fixed. They are constructed and therefore can be changed if enough members of a society challenge them.

Constructed Social perspectives are created in particular cultures at specific times to support dominant ideologies, or the beliefs and comfort of those in power. When we reflect on social values, we realize that they are arbitrary and tend to serve the interests of those who benefit from prevailing values. The constructed nature of social values becomes especially obvious when we consider how greatly values differ between cultures and within particular cultures over time. For example, in Sweden, Denmark, and Norway, marriages between members of the same sex are given legal and social recognition.

Prescriptions for femininity and masculinity vary over time within a particular culture. In the 1700s and 1800s, women in the United States were defined as too delicate to engage in hard labor. During World Wars I and II, however, women were expected to do "men's work" while men were at war. When the men returned home, society once again decreed that women were too weak to perform labor, and they were reassigned to home and hearth.

Social prescriptions for men also have changed. The rugged he-man who was the ideal in the 1800s used his six-shooter to dispose of unsavory rustlers and relied on physical strength to farm. After the Industrial Revolution, physical strength and bravado gave way to business acumen, and money replaced muscle as a sign of manliness. As women, men, and families change, ideals of femininity and masculinity continue to evolve.

Although there is still prejudice against people who are not heterosexual, it is gradually diminishing. Laws have been enacted to protect lesbians and gays against housing and job discrimination. As social views of gender, race, class, and a range of sexualities evolve, individuals' views of others and their own self-concepts will also change.

Changeable Social perspectives are fluid. They change in response to individual and collective efforts to weave new meanings into the fabric of common life. Racial classifications in America have changed over time. In the country's earliest years, Irish immigrants were not considered white (Morning, 2011). In the 1960s, civil rights activism launched nationwide rethinking of actions and attitudes toward non-whites. The battle to recognize and respect gays and lesbians has begun to alter social perspectives. Changes in how we view sex, race, class, (dis)ability, and sexual orientation are negotiated in communication contexts ranging from one-to-one conversations to mass and social media. Each of us has an ethical responsibility to speak out against social perspectives that we perceive as wrong or harmful. By doing so, we participate in the ongoing process of refining social perspectives.

> **JANINE**   *My husband and I have really worked to share equally in our marriage. When we got married 8 years ago, we both believed women and men were equal and should have equal responsibilities for the home and family and equal power in making decisions that affect the family. But it's a lot harder to actually live that ideal than to believe in it. Both of us have struggled against our socialization that says I should cook and clean and take care of the kids and he should make big decisions about our lives. I think we've done a pretty good job of creating and living an egalitarian marriage. A lot of our friends see us as models.*

ENHANCING THE SELF

So far, we've explained how the self develops in the process of communicating with others. Building on that knowledge, we'll now explore guidelines for encouraging personal growth.

Make a Strong Commitment to Improve Yourself

The first principle for enhancing who you are is to make a firm commitment to personal growth. This isn't as easy as it might sound. A firm commitment involves more than saying, "I want to listen better" or "I want to be less judgmental." Saying these sentences is simple, but actually investing the effort to change is difficult. Changing ourselves takes persistent work. We have to be willing to invest ongoing effort. In addition, we must realize at the outset that there will be setbacks, and we can't let them derail our resolve.

Changing yourself is difficult because the self resists change. If you realize in advance that you may struggle against change, you'll be prepared for the tension that accompanies personal growth. Because change is a process and the self resists change, a firm and continuing commitment to growth is essential.

Gain Knowledge as a Basis for Personal Change

Commitment alone is insufficient to spur changes in who you are. In addition, you need several types of knowledge. First, you need to understand how the self is formed. In this chapter, we've discussed the influence of particular others and the generalized other. You may not want to accept all the views and values you were taught.

Second, you need to know how to develop goals you can achieve. Vague goals for self-improvement usually lead nowhere because they don't indicate concrete steps toward change. For instance, "I want to be better at intimate communication" is a very vague objective. You can't do anything to meet such an unclear goal until you know something about the talk that enhances and impedes intimacy. Books such as this one will help you pinpoint concrete skills that facilitate healthy intimate communication. For instance, Chapter 4 will help you develop

COMMUNICATION HIGHLIGHT

Failure on the Way to Success

Who was Babe Ruth? If you know baseball history, you probably think of him as having hit 714 home runs. He did, but he also struck out 1,330 times. R. H. Macy, who founded Macy's department store, failed in his first seven efforts to start a business. Superstar Michael Jordan was cut from his high school basketball team because he wasn't good enough. Early in his career, Walt Disney was fired from a newspaper job because his editor thought he had no good or creative ideas. The Beatles penned 59 songs before they had their first hit.

Most people who succeed fail along the way; sometimes they fail many times. If Babe Ruth had let his strikeouts defeat him, he would never have been a champion batter. The same is true of most of us. Failures and defeats are inevitable. Letting them define who we are is not inevitable.

To consider what your life would be like if you were completely unafraid of failing, complete the Communication Highlight Activity for Chapter 3 via MindTap for *Communication in Our Lives*.

listening skills, and Chapter 8 will explain how communication affects personal and social relationships.

Another important source of knowledge is other people. Perhaps you recall a time when you began a new job. If you were fortunate, you found a mentor who explained the ropes to you and gave you helpful feedback. In much the same way, others can also provide feedback on your progress in the process of change. In addition, others can serve as models. If you know someone you think is particularly skillful in supporting others, observe him or her carefully to identify concrete skills that you can tailor to suit your personal style.

Set Realistic Goals

Changing ourselves is most likely when we set realistic goals. If you are shy and want to be more extraverted, it is reasonable to try to speak up more often. On the other hand, it may not be reasonable to try to be the life of every party. Realistic goals are based on realistic standards. In a culture that emphasizes perfection, it's easy to be trapped into expecting more than is possible. A better method is to establish a series of realistic incremental goals. You might focus first on improving one communication skill. When you're satisfied with your ability at that skill, you can work on another one.

With regard to our discussion of social comparison, it's also important to select reasonable measuring sticks for yourself. It isn't realistic to compare your academic work with that of a certified genius. It isn't realistic to compare your public speaking skill with that of someone who has made public presentations for years. It is reasonable to measure your public speaking ability against that of others who have speaking experience similar to yours. Setting realistic goals and selecting appropriate standards of comparison are important in improving yourself.

> **MIKE**   *For a long time, I put myself down for not doing as well academically as a lot of my friends. They put mega-hours into studying and writing papers. I can't do that because I work 30 hours a week. Now I see that it's unfair to compare myself to them. When I compare myself to students who work as much as I do, my record is pretty good.*

Self-Disclose When Appropriate

Self-disclosure is the revelation of information about ourselves that others are unlikely to discover on their own. We self-disclose when we share private information about ourselves—our hopes, fears, feelings, thoughts, and experiences. Although we don't reveal our private selves to everyone and don't do it often even with intimates, self-disclosure is an important kind of communication.

Self-disclosure has notable values. First, sharing personal feelings, thoughts, and experiences often enhances closeness between people (Hendrick & Hendrick, 1996, 2006; Samp & Palevitz, 2009; Stafford, 2009). By extension, when others understand our private selves, they may respond to us more sensitively, as unique individuals. Self-disclosing also tends to invite others to self-disclose, so we may learn more about them. Finally, self-disclosure can affect what we know about ourselves and how we feel about who we are. For example, if we reveal a weakness or an incident of which we're ashamed, and another person accepts the disclosure without judging us negatively, we may find it easier to accept ourselves. As we reveal our hopes, fears, dreams, and feelings, we get responses from others that give us new perspectives on who we are.

Self-disclosure necessarily involves risk—the risk that others will not accept private information or that they might use it against us. Appropriate self-disclosure minimizes these risks by proceeding slowly and establishing trust. It's wise to test the waters gradually before plunging into major self-disclosures. Begin by revealing information that is personal but not highly intimate or able to damage you if exploited. Before disclosing further, observe how the other person responds to your communication and what he or she does with it. You might also pay attention to whether the other person reciprocates by disclosing personal information to you.

Accept That You Are in Process

Previously in this chapter, we saw that one characteristic of the human self is that it is continually in process. This implies that you need to accept who you are now as a starting point. You don't have to like or admire everything about yourself, but it is important to accept who you are today as a basis for going forward. The self that you are results from all the interactions and experiences in your life. Only by realizing and accepting who you are now can you move ahead.

Accepting yourself as being in process also implies that you realize you can change. Because you are in process, you are always changing and growing. Don't let yourself be hindered by defeating self-fulfilling prophecies or the fallacy of thinking that you can't change. You can change if you set realistic goals, make a genuine commitment, and then work for the changes you want. Just remember that you are not fixed as you are; you are always in the process of becoming.

Create a Supportive Context for Change

Just as it is easier to swim with the tide than against it, it is easier to change our views of ourselves when we have some support for our efforts. You can do a lot to create an environment that supports your growth by choosing contexts and people who help you realize your goals. First, think about settings. If you want to lose weight, it's better to go to restaurants that serve healthful foods and offer light choices than to go to cholesterol castles. If you want to become more extraverted, go to parties, not libraries. But libraries are a better context than parties if your goal is to improve academic performance.

JAN   *I never cared a lot about clothes until I joined a sorority where the labels on your clothes are a measure of your worth. The girls compete with each other to dress the best and have the newest styles. When one of the sisters wears something out of style, she gets a lot of teasing, but really it's pressure on her to measure up to the sorority image. At first, I adopted my sisters' values, and I spent more money than I could afford on clothes. For a while I even quit making contributions at church so that I could have more money for clothes. When I finally realized I was becoming somebody I didn't like, I tried to change, but my sisters made me feel bad anytime I wasn't dressed well. Finally, I moved out rather than face that pressure all the time. It just wasn't a good place for me to be myself.*

Because how others view us affects how we see ourselves, you can create a supportive context by consciously choosing to be around people who believe in you and encourage your personal growth without being dishonest about your limitations. It's also important to steer clear of people who put you down or say you can't change. In other words, people who reflect positive appraisals of us enhance our ability to improve who we are.

Others aren't the only ones whose communication affects our self-concepts. We also communicate with ourselves, and our own messages influence how we see ourselves. One of the most crippling kinds of self-talk we can engage in is **self-sabotage**—telling ourselves we are no good, we'll never learn something, there's no point in trying to change. We may be repeating others' judgments of us, or we may be inventing negative self-fulfilling prophecies. Either way, self-sabotage undermines belief in ourselves.

Distinguished therapist Albert Ellis wrote a book titled *How to Stubbornly Refuse to Make Yourself Miserable about Anything—Yes, Anything* (1988). In it, he asserted that most of our negative feelings about ourselves result from negative messages we communicate to ourselves. His advice is to challenge negative statements you make to yourself and to replace them with constructive intrapersonal communication. Self-sabotage is poisonous; it destroys our motivation to change and grow. We can be as critical of ourselves as others can; in fact, we probably can do more damage to our self-concepts than others can because we are most aware of our vulnerabilities and fears.

Following Ellis' advice, we can affirm our worth, encourage our growth, and fortify our sense of self-worth. Positive self-talk builds motivation and belief in yourself. It is also helpful to interrupt and challenge negative messages from yourself and others. The next time you hear yourself saying, "I can't do…," or someone else says, "You'll never change," challenge the self-defeating message with self-talk. Say out loud to yourself, "I can do it. I will change." Of course, you won't grow and improve if you listen only to praise, particularly if it is less than honest. Real friends can help us identify areas for growth without making us feel bad about ourselves.

In sum, to improve your self-concept, you should create contexts that support growth and change, and seek experiences and settings that foster belief in yourself and the changes you desire. Also, recognize uppers, downers, and vultures in yourself and others, and learn which people and which kinds of communication assist you in achieving your own goals for self-improvement.

If you'd like to try initiating changes in yourself related to the way you communicate interpersonally, complete the activity "Improving Self-Concept" via MindTap for *Communication in Our Lives*.

BEYOND THE CLASSROOM

MindTap

Let's take the material in this chapter beyond the classroom by thinking about how what you've learned about personal identity might apply to the workplace, ethical choices, and engagement with the broader world.

1. **Workplace.** We discussed direct definition and identity scripts as two ways that others define who we are and what we are worth during the early years of life. Extend this by asking how those two factors influence identity development on the job. Recall examples of supervisors and coworkers' direct definitions of you or other employees. For example, were you defined as "a good worker" or "a quick learner"? Consider identity scripts that you were given in a particular workplace. What did others tell you about the company or workplace's identity and about how employees in this particular job were supposed to think and act?

Ethics

2. **Ethics.** How does what you learned in this chapter affect ethical choices about parenting? Reflect on the ethical implications of knowing that parents affect children's self-concepts by their choices of direct definitions, identity scripts, and attachment styles. What ethical responsibilities, if any, do parents have regarding their impact on children's self-concepts and self-esteem?

3. **Engagement.** Not all children have the fortune of having parents who are able to nurture them lovingly and help them develop positive self-concepts. In 1964, the United States launched the Head Start Program to help children and their families who have limited resources. Click **WebLink 3.2** to access the National Head Start Program's Website. Spend some time reading this page and following links it provides. Can you identify ways that the program aims to enhance the self-concepts of underprivileged children and their families?

CHAPTER SUMMARY

 Practice and review the content in this chapter.

In this chapter, we explored the self as a process that evolves as we communicate with others over the course of our lives. As we interact with others, we learn and internalize social perspectives, both those of particular others and those of the generalized other, or society as a whole. Reflected appraisals, direct definitions, and social comparisons are key communication processes that shape how we see ourselves and how we change over time. The perspective of the generalized other includes social views of key aspects of identity, including gender, race, and sexual orientation. However, these are arbitrary social constructions that we may challenge and resist once we are adults. When we resist social views and values that we consider unethical, we promote change in both society and ourselves.

In the final section of the chapter, we focused on ways to enhance communication competence by improving self-concept. Guidelines include making a firm commitment to personal growth, gaining knowledge about desired changes and the skills they involve, setting realistic goals, accepting yourself as in process, and creating contexts that support the changes you seek. We can make amazing changes in who we are and how we feel about ourselves when we commit to doing so.

APPLYING COMMUNICATION IN OUR LIVES

Communication in Our Lives is supported by a MindTap, a new online learning platform that delivers content, assignments, and a tailored presentation of the course curriculum created by your instructor. MindTap combines all of your learning tools–readings, multimedia, activities and assessments–into a singular learning unit that guides you through the course. Practice and Present, a unique tool within MindTap, allows you to upload your speech video files for practice or for a grade, comment on your peer's speeches and review your grades. MindTap also includes Speech Builder Express, a powerful tool that guides you through the speech outline and preparation process. For more information or to access MindTap, visit cengagebrain.com.

DEFINITIONS OF KEY CONCEPTS

 Review your **Flashcards**.

attachment style Any of several patterns of attachment that result from particular parenting styles that teach children who they are, who others are, and how to approach relationships.

direct definition Communication that explicitly tells us who we are by specifically labeling us and reacting to our behaviors. Direct definition usually occurs first in families and then in interaction with peers and others.

ego boundaries A person's internal sense of where he or she stops and the rest of the world begins.

identity script A guide to action based on rules for living and identity. Initially communicated in families, identity scripts define our roles, how we are to play them, and basic elements in the plot of our lives.

particular others One source of social perspectives that people use to define themselves and guide how they think, act, and feel. The perspectives of particular others are the viewpoints of people who are significant to the self.

perspective of the generalized other The collection of rules, roles, and attitudes endorsed by the whole social community in which we live.

reflected appraisal Our perceptions of others' views of us.

self A multidimensional process in which the individual forms and acts from social perspectives that arise and evolve in communication with himself or herself.

self-disclosure Revelation of information about ourselves that others are unlikely to discover on their own.

self-sabotage Self-talk that communicates that we're no good, we can't do something, we can't change, and so forth. Undermines belief in ourselves and motivation to change and grow.

social comparison Comparing ourselves with others to form judgments of our own talents, abilities, qualities, and so forth.

FOR FURTHER REFLECTION AND DISCUSSION   MindTap™

1. Set one specific goal for personal growth as a communicator. Be sure to specify your goal in terms of clear behavioral changes and make it realistic. As you study different topics during the semester, apply what you learn to your personal goal.

2. What ethical issues do you perceive in the process of developing and continuously refining self-concepts, both your own and those of people around you? Is it as important to be ethical in communicating with yourself (self-talk, or intrapersonal communication) as in communicating with others?

Ethics

3. How do people you meet and get to know on the Internet affect your sense of who you are? Are they significant for you? Do they represent the generalized other to you? Is it useful to distinguish between the impact of face-to-face and online communication?

4. In what ways are your own experiences and your sense of identity consistent with generalizations about the effects on self-concept of race or ethnicity, economic class, sexual orientation, and sex? In what ways do your experiences and your sense of identity diverge from generalizations? What in your own life might account for the instances in which you do not fit generalizations?

5. Historically, India classified people according to caste, one of the most rigid systems of social class. To learn about how a person's caste affected his or her opportunities in life, click **WebLink 3.3**. MindTap™

SHARPEN YOUR SKILL   MindTap™

1. Reflecting on Your Identity Scripts

Recall identity scripts your parents communicated about who you were or were supposed to become. Can you hear them saying, "Our people do . . ." or "Our family doesn't . . ."? Can you recall messages that told you what and who they expected you to be? As a youngster, did you hear, "You'll go to college" or "You're going to be a doctor"?

Now review key identity scripts. Which ones make sense to you today? Are you still following any that are irrelevant to your present life or that are at odds with your personal values and goals? If so, then commit to changing scripts that aren't productive for you or that conflict with values you hold. You can rewrite identity scripts now that you're an adult.

For additional insight into identity scripts that were communicated to you, complete the activity "Identifying Your Identity Scripts" via MindTap for *Communication in Our Lives.*

2. Your Looking-Glass Self

Identify three people who have been or are particularly important to you. For each person, identify one self-perception you have that reflects the appraisal of you communicated by that person.

Now imagine that you'd never known each of the three people. Describe how you would be different. How would your self-image change?

For instance, Shennoa (see commentary, p.58) might think she would be less independent had her grandmother not influenced how she sees herself.

Trace the way you see yourself to the appraisals that particular others have reflected.

Prepare a 2-minute presentation in which you describe one of the people you've identified as a looking glass for yourself. Explain how this person has influenced the way you see yourself. You may want to look ahead to Part III of this book for guidelines on preparing a speech.

EXPERIENCING COMMUNICATION IN OUR LIVES

CASE STUDY: *Parental Teachings*

A video of the conversation scripted here is featured in your Chapter 3 MindTap for *Communication in Our Lives*. Select "Parental Teachings" to watch the video. Improve your own communication skills by reading, watching, and analyzing this communication encounter.

Kate McDonald is in the neighborhood park with her two children, 7-year-old Emma and 5-year-old Jeremy. The three of them walk into the park and approach the swing set.

© Cengage Learning

KATE: Jeremy, why don't you push Emma so she can swing? Emma, you hang on tight.

Jeremy begins pushing his sister, who squeals with delight. Jeremy gives an extra-hard push that lands him in the dirt in front of the swing set. Laughing, Emma jumps off, falling in the dirt beside her brother.

KATE: Come here, sweetie. You've got dirt all over your knees and your pretty new dress.

Kate brushes the dirt off Emma, who then runs over to the jungle gym set that Jeremy is now climbing. Kate smiles as she watches Jeremy climb fearlessly on the bars.

KATE: You're a brave little man, aren't you? How high can you go?

Encouraged by his mother, Jeremy climbs to the top bars and holds up a fist, screaming, "Look at me, Mom! I'm king of the hill! I climbed to the very top!"

Kate laughs and claps her hands to applaud him. Jealous of the attention Jeremy is getting, Emma runs over to the jungle gym and starts climbing. Kate calls out, "Careful, honey. Don't go any higher. You could fall and hurt yourself." When Emma ignores her mother and reaches for a higher bar, Kate walks over and pulls her off, saying, "Emma, I told you that is dangerous. Time to get down. Why don't you play on the swings some more?"

Once Kate puts Emma on the ground, the girl walks over to the swings and begins swaying.

QUESTIONS FOR ANALYSIS AND DISCUSSION) MindTap

You can answer these questions and see my responses to them online via MindTap for Chapter 3.

1. Identify examples of direct definition in this scenario. How does Kate define Emma and Jeremy?

2. Identify examples of reflected appraisal in this scenario. What appraisals of her son and daughter does Kate reflect to them?

3. What do Emma's and Jeremy's responses to Kate suggest about their acceptance of her views of them?

4. To what extent does Kate's communication with her children reflect conventional gender expectations in Western culture?

Jose Galvez/PhotoEdit

The best way to understand people is to listen to them.

Ralph Nichols

Listening Effectively

Do you have a minute to talk?" Joanne asks her friend Elly as she enters her dorm room.

"Sure," Elly agrees without looking up from her laptop where she is checking the latest status updates on Facebook.

"I'm worried about what's happening between Drew and me," Joanne begins. "He takes me for granted all the time. He never asks what I want to do or where I'd like to go. He just assumes I'll go along with whatever he wants."

"Yeah, I know that routine. Steve does it to me, too," Elly says with exasperation as she looks up from the laptop. "Last weekend, he insisted we go to this stupid war movie that I wouldn't have chosen to see in a million years. But what I wanted didn't make a lot of difference to him."

"That's exactly what I'm talking about," Joanne agrees. "I don't like it when Drew treats me that way, and I want to know how to get him to be more considerate."

"What I told Steve last weekend was that I'd had it, and from now on we

 MindTap

Review the chapter **Learning Objectives** and **Start** with a quick warm up activity.

decide together what we're doing, or we don't do it together," Elly says forcefully. "We've had this talk before, but this time I think I really got through to him that I was serious."

"So are you saying that's what I should do with Drew?"

"Sure. You have to stand up for your rights, or he'll walk all over you," Elly says while typing on the keyboard. "Take it from me, subtlety won't work. Remember last year when I was dating Larry? Well, he started this routine, and I tried to be subtle and hint that I'd like to be consulted about things. What I said to him went in one ear and out the other. If you're not firm, they'll run over you."

"But Drew's not like Larry or Steve. He's not trying to run over me. I think he just doesn't understand how I feel when he makes all the decisions," Joanne says.

"Well, I really don't think Steve's 'like that' either. He's just as good a guy as Drew," Elly snaps.

"That's not what I meant," Joanne says. "I just meant that I don't think I need to hit Drew over the head with a two-by-four."

"And I suppose you think Steve does need that?"

"I don't know. I'm just thinking that maybe our relationships are different," Joanne says.

How would you describe the communication between Elly and Joanne? Is Elly a good listener? Usually, when we think about communication, we focus on talking. Yet talking is not the only part—or even the greatest part—of communication. Effective communication also involves listening. As obvious as this is, few of us devote as much energy to listening as we do to talking.

Poor listening is evident in the conversation between Elly and Joanne. The first obstacle to effective listening is Elly's initial preoccupation with the email she's writing to her mother. If she really wants to listen to Joanne, she should postpone the email. A second problem is Elly's tendency to monopolize the conversation by focusing on her own problems and boyfriends instead of on Joanne's concerns about the relationship with Drew. Third, Elly listens defensively, taking offense when Joanne suggests that their relationships may differ. Like Elly, most of us often don't listen as well as we could. When we listen poorly, we are not communicating well.

You spend more time listening—or trying to—than talking. Studies of people from college students to professionals indicate that the average person spends 45% to 75% of waking time listening to others (Nichols, 2009; Steil, 1997; Wolvin, 2009). If we don't listen effectively, we're communicating poorly much of the time.

When people don't listen well on the job, they may miss information that can affect their professional effectiveness and advancement (Darling & Dannels, 2003; Deal & Kennedy, 1999; Gabric & McFadden, 2001; Landrum & Harrold, 2003). Skill in listening is also linked to resolving workplace conflicts (Van Styke, 1999). Doctors who don't listen fully to patients may misdiagnose or mistreat medical problems (Christensen, 2004; Scholz, 2005; Underwood & Adler, 2005). Ineffective listening in the classroom diminishes learning and performance on tests. In personal relationships, poor listening can hinder understanding of others, and listening ineffectively to public communication leaves us uninformed about civic issues. Learning to listen well enhances personal, academic, social, civic, and professional effectiveness.

Who Listens?

Dan Rather interviewed Mother Teresa shortly before her death (Bailey, 1998). She had this to say about listening.

Rather: "What do you say to God when you pray?"

Mother Teresa: "I listen."

Rather: "Well, what does God say?"

Mother Teresa: "He listens."

This chapter focuses on listening. First, we'll consider what's involved in listening, which is more than most of us realize. Next, we'll discuss obstacles to effective listening and how to minimize them. Third, we'll consider common forms of nonlistening. The fourth section of the chapter explains different types of listening and the skills needed for each. In our discussion, we'll identify principles for improving listening effectiveness.

THE LISTENING PROCESS

Read, highlight and take notes online.

Although we often use the words *listening* and *hearing* as if they were synonyms, actually they're not. **Hearing** is a physiological activity that occurs when sound waves hit our eardrums. Hearing is passive; we don't have to invest any energy to hear. Listening, on the other hand, is an active process that requires energy (International Listening Association, 1995). Listening involves more than just hearing or receiving messages through sight, as when we notice nonverbal behaviors or when people with hearing impairments read lips or receive messages in American Sign Language (ASL).

Listening is an active, complex process that includes being mindful, physically receiving messages, selecting and organizing information, interpreting communication, responding, and remembering. The complexity of listening is represented in the Chinese character for listening, which includes symbols for eyes, ears, and heart (Figure 4.1). As the character suggests, to listen effectively, we use not only our ears, but also our eyes and hearts.

Being Mindful

The first step in listening is deciding to be mindful. **Mindfulness** is being fully engaged in the moment. You focus on what is happening here and now. When you are mindful, you don't let your thoughts wander from what is happening in the present conversation. You don't think about what you did yesterday or about a friend you want to text, and you don't think about your own feelings and issues. Instead, when you listen mindfully, you tune in fully to another person and try to understand that person without imposing your own ideas, judgments, or feelings on the message. You may later express your thoughts and feelings, but when you listen mindfully, you attend to another fully.

Eyes

Ears

Heart

Listening

© Cengage Learning

FIGURE 4.1
The Chinese Character for
Listening

Mindfulness enhances communication in two ways. First, attending mindfully to others increases our understanding of how they feel and think about what they are saying. Second, when we listen mindfully, others tend to express themselves in greater depth.

Being mindful is a personal commitment to attend fully and without diversion to another person. No amount of skill will make you a good listener if you do not choose to attend mindfully to others. Thus, your own choice to be mindful or not is the foundation of how well you listen—or fail to.

Physically Receiving Messages

In addition to mindfulness, listening involves physically receiving messages. For many people, this happens through hearing. People who are deaf, however, receive messages by reading lips or by reading sign language. Regardless of our hearing acuity, most of us pay attention to nonverbal communication as part of any message. Our ability to receive messages may decline when we are fatigued or when we have to be attentive for extended periods without breaks. Physical reception of messages may also be impeded by background noises, such as a blaring television, others talking nearby, or by competing visual cues. Thus, it's a good idea to control distractions that hinder listening.

JIMMY   *It's impossible to listen well in my apartment. Four of us live there, and at least two different stereos are on all the time. Also, a TV is usually on, and there may be conversations or phone calls, too. It's crazy when we try to talk to each other in the middle of all the racket. We're always asking each other to repeat something or skipping over whatever we don't hear. If we go out to a bar or something, the noise there is just as bad. Sometimes I think we don't really want to talk with each other and all the distractions protect us from having to.*

Selecting and Organizing Material

The third part of listening is selecting and organizing material. As we noted in Chapter 2, we don't perceive everything around us. Instead, we selectively attend to some messages and elements of our environments and disregard others. What we select to attend to depends on many factors, including our physiology, interests, cognitive structures, and expectations.

We can compensate for our tendencies to attend selectively by remembering that we are more likely to notice stimuli that are intense, loud, or unusual. Thus, we may overlook communicators who speak softly. If we're aware of this tendency, we can guard against it. Once again, mindfulness comes into play. We can choose to listen fully even to communicators who are not especially dynamic.

Once we've selected what to notice, we organize what we've received. As you'll recall from Chapter 2, we use cognitive schemata to organize what we selectively notice. When others are talking, we make decisions—usually not consciously— about how to organize what they say: Does the communication fit the prototype of venting or problem solving or something else? We apply personal constructs to classify the message as rational or not rational, emotional or not emotional, and so forth. Based on how you construct what you are selectively attending to, you apply stereotypes to predict what the other person will do and expects you to do. Finally, based on the meanings you have constructed, you choose a script to follow in interaction.

When a friend is upset, you can reasonably predict that he or she may not want advice until he or she has first had a chance to express his feelings. On the other hand, when a coworker comes to you with a problem that must be solved quickly, you assume he or she might welcome concrete advice or collaboration. Your script for responding to the distraught friend might be to say, "Tell me more about what you're feeling" or "You sound really upset—let's talk." With a work team that is facing a deadline, you might adopt a more directive script and say, "Let's put our heads together and come up with a solution."

Interpreting Communication

The fourth part of listening is interpreting others' communication. When we interpret, we put together all that we have selected and organized to make sense of the overall situation. The most important principle in this process is to be person centered, which means trying to take the other person's perspective. Certainly, you won't always agree with other people and how they see themselves, others, issues, and situations. However, if you want to listen well, you have an ethical responsibility to make an earnest effort to understand others' perspectives. To interpret someone with respect for their perspective is one of the greatest gifts we can give.

MAGGIE   *Don and I didn't understand each other's perspective, and we didn't even understand that we didn't understand. Once I told him I was really upset about a friend of mine who needed money for an emergency. Don told me she had no right to expect me to bail her out, but that had nothing to do with what I was feeling. He saw the situation in terms of what rights my friend had, but to me it was about feeling concerned for someone I like. Only after we got counseling did we learn to really listen to each other instead of listening through ourselves.*

Responding

Effective listening includes responding, which is communicating attention and interest as well as voicing our own views when that is appropriate. Skillful listeners give outward signs that they are interested and involved not only when others finish speaking but throughout interaction. Indicators of engagement include attentive posture, head nods, eye contact, and vocal responses such as "um hmm," "okay," and "go on." When we respond with interest, we communicate that we care about the other person and what he or she is saying. This is what makes listening such an active process.

Remembering

The final part of effective listening is remembering, or retaining what you have heard. We remember less than half of a message immediately after we hear it. As time goes by, retention decreases further; we recall only about 35% of most messages 8 hours after we hear them (Adler, Towne, & Proctor II, 2010). Because we forget about two-thirds of what we hear, it's important to make sure we hang onto the most important third. Later in this chapter, we'll discuss strategies for increasing retention.

OBSTACLES TO EFFECTIVE LISTENING

There are two broad types of obstacles to good listening: those external to us and those inside us.

External Obstacles

There are many hindrances to effective listening in communication situations. Although we can't always control external obstacles, knowing what situational factors hinder listening can help us guard against them or compensate for the interference they create.

Message Overload   The sheer amount of communication in our lives makes it impossible to listen fully to all of it. When we're not talking face-to-face with someone, we're likely to be texting, talking on a cell, listening to podcasts, or watching YouTube videos. We simply aren't able to listen mindfully all of the time. Instead, we have to screen all of the communication directed at us to decide when to listen mindfully.

Message overload often occurs in academic settings. If you're taking four or five classes, you confront mountains of information. Message overload may also occur when communication takes place simultaneously in two channels. For instance, you might experience information overload if a professor presents information verbally while also clicking through PowerPoint slides with complex statistical data. It's difficult to know whether to focus your listening energy on the visual message or the verbal one.

Message Complexity   The more detailed and complicated ideas are, the harder it is to follow and retain them. Many jobs today are highly specialized;

hence much on-the-job communication is complex and increasingly rapid (Cooper, 1997; Hacker, Goss, & Townley, 1998). We need to guard against the tendency to tune out people who use technical vocabularies, provide lots of detail, and use complex sentences.

Environmental Distractions   Distractions in the environment can interfere with listening (Keizer, 2010). Perhaps you've been part of a crowd at a rally or a game. If so, you probably had trouble hearing the person next to you. Although most sounds aren't as overwhelming as the roar of crowds, there is always some noise in communication situations. Music, television in the background, side conversations in a class, or rings of smart phones can hinder communication.

Good listeners try to reduce environmental distractions. It's considerate to turn off televisions, phones, and laptops if someone wants to talk with you. In the example that opened this chapter, Elly should have signed off Facebook if she wanted to listen mindfully to Joanne. Even if we can't always eliminate distractions, we can usually reduce them or change our location to one more conducive to good communication.

Cognitive psychologists have found that email alerts, IMs, and notifications of text messages distract people and undermine their ability to listen to or focus mindfully (Begley, 2009). Interruptions fragment concentration so we have trouble resituating ourselves in whatever we were doing before the interruption. Attending to social media may have even more substantial costs: Since 2004, there has been a 200% increase in the number of pedestrians killed or

HEALTH COMMUNICATION

New Epidemic: Distracted Doctors

Would you want your neurosurgeon making personal calls during an operation on your spine? Would you want a surgical nurse checking competitive air fares while attending an operation? Would you want the technician texting while operating a bypass machine? Would you be comfortable knowing doctors and nurses were shopping online while you were on the operating table? Welcome to what some call "distracted doctoring" (Richtel, 2011). All of these examples are based on observations of real doctors, nurses, and technicians in surgery.

Surgery requires focus on the patient—his or her vital signs, detailed attention to incisions and procedures, and listening to other medical personnel in the operating room. In short, doctors need to control distractions. Dr. Peter Papadakos is an anesthesiologist who directs critical care at the University of Rochester Medical Center. He says, "My gut feeling is lives are in danger" (Richtel, 2011, p. A4). Dr. Papadakos's concern is illustrated by a patient who was partially paralyzed during an operation in which his neurosurgeon made personal and business calls—at least 10 of them!

injured while wearing headphones that prevented them from hearing traffic (Newsbeast, 2012).

Internal Obstacles

In addition to external interferences, listening may be hindered by four psychological obstacles.

Preoccupation   When we are preoccupied with our own thoughts and concerns, we can't focus on what someone else is saying. If you are preoccupied with a report you need to prepare, you may not listen effectively to what a colleague says.

> **ANDY**   *I've been really stressed about finding a job. I've had lots of first interviews, but no callbacks and no offers. Even when I'm not interviewing—like when I'm with friends or in class—getting a job is in the back of my mind. It just stays there so that it's hard for me to really focus on anything else happening around me.*

Prejudgments   Another obstacle to effective listening is prejudgment of others or ideas.

Sometimes we decide in advance that others have nothing to offer us, so we tune them out. If a coworker's ideas have not impressed you in the past, you might assume he or she will contribute nothing of value to a present conversation. The risk is that you might miss a good idea simply because you prejudged the other person. Research shows that, on average, doctors interrupt patients 23 seconds after patients have started explaining their medical situation or need (Levine, 2004). When doctors stop listening, they risk not getting information that could help them diagnose and treat patients. It's also important to keep an open mind when listening to communication regarding issues about which you already have opinions. You might miss important new information and perspectives if you don't put your prejudgments aside long enough to listen mindfully.

Another kind of prejudgment occurs when we assume we know

Rich Legg/E+/Getty Images

Attention to social media can interfere with mindful listening.

what another feels, thinks, and is going to say, and we then assimilate his or her message into our preconceptions. This is a form of mind reading that can lead us to misunderstand what the person means because we haven't really listened on his or her own terms.

> **KEITH**   *My parents need a course in listening! They are so quick to tell me what I think and feel, or should think and feel, that they never hear what I do feel or think. Last year I approached them with the idea of taking a year off from school. Before I could even explain why I wanted to do this, Dad was all over me about being responsible and getting ahead in a career. Mom jumped on me about looking for an easy out and not having the gumption to stick with my studies. The whole point was that I wanted to work as an intern to get some hands-on experience in media production, which is my major. It had nothing to do with wanting an easy out or not trying to get ahead, but they couldn't even hear me through their own ideas about what I felt.*

Lack of Effort   Because active listening takes so much effort, we're not always able or willing to do it well. Sometimes we make a decision not to listen fully, perhaps because the person or topic isn't important to us. There are also times when we really want to listen but have trouble marshaling the necessary energy. If you can't summon the effort to listen well, you might suggest postponing interaction until a time when you will be able to invest effort in listening. If you explain to the other that you want to defer communication because you really are interested and want to be able to listen well, he or she is likely to appreciate your honesty and commitment to listening.

Failure to Accommodate Diverse Listening Styles   A final internal obstacle to effective listening is not recognizing and adjusting to different listening styles that reflect diverse communities and cultures. The more we understand about different people's rules for listening, the more effectively we can signal our attention in ways they appreciate. For example, in the United States it is considered polite to make frequent but not continuous eye contact in conversation. Yet in some cultures, continuous eye contact is normative, and in others almost any eye contact is considered intrusive.

Even within the United States, there are differences in listening rules based on membership in racial, gender, and other social communities. For example, men generally provide fewer verbal and nonverbal clues than women to indicate they are interested in what another person is saying. They may also respond primarily to the content level of meaning and less to the relationship level of meaning. If you understand these general differences, you can adapt your listening style to particular people with whom you communicate. In addition, understanding diverse listening styles will improve your accuracy in interpreting what others mean by the ways they listen and signal interest.

LAVONDA   *My boyfriend is the worst listener ever. Whenever I try to tell him about some problem I have, he becomes Mr. Answer Man. He tells me what to do or how to handle a situation. That doesn't do anything to help me with my feelings or even to let me know he hears what I'm feeling.*

We have seen that there are many obstacles to effective listening. Obstacles inherent in messages and situations include message overload, message complexity, and environmental distractions. In addition, there are four potential interferences inside us: preoccupation, prejudgment, lack of effort, and failure to recognize and adapt to diverse expectations of listening.

FORMS OF NONLISTENING

Now that we've discussed obstacles to effective listening, let's consider some forms of nonlistening. As you read about these six types of nonlistening, they may seem familiar because you and others probably engage in them at times.

Pseudolistening

Pseudolistening is pretending to listen. When we pseudolisten, we appear to be attentive, but really our minds are elsewhere. Superficial talk in social situations and boring lectures are two communication situations in which we may consciously choose to pseudolisten so that we seem polite even though we really

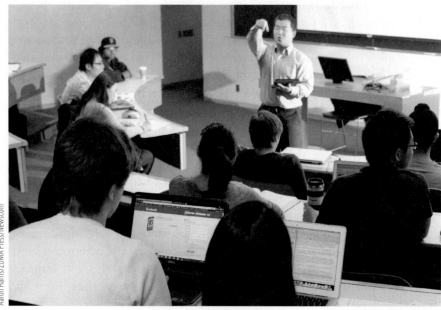

Aaron Harris/ZUMA Press/Newscom

Students sometimes pseudolisten in classes while also going online.

aren't involved. On the job, we often have to appear interested in what others say because of their positions.

> **SOURYANA**   *I do a lot of pseudolistening in classes where the teachers are boring. I pretend I'm taking notes on my laptop, but really I'm checking email or visiting my favorite blogs. Every now and then, I look up and nod at the teacher so I look like I'm listening.*

Monopolizing

Monopolizing is hogging the stage by continually focusing communication on ourselves instead of on the person talking. There are two primary forms of monopolizing. One is *conversational rerouting*, in which a person shifts the topic of talk to himself or herself. For example, if Harper tells Marla about a roommate problem, Marla might reroute the conversation by saying, "I know what you mean. My roommate is a real jerk." Then Marla goes off on an extended description of her own roommate problems. Rerouting takes the conversation away from the person who was talking.

Another form of monopolizing is *diversionary interrupting*, which is interrupting in ways that disrupt the person speaking. Often, this occurs in combination with rerouting, so that a person interrupts and then directs the conversation to a new topic. In other cases, monopolizers fire questions that break up a speaker's concentration and impel the speaker to answer the questions before continuing. Both rerouting and diversionary interrupting are techniques for monopolizing a conversation. They are the antithesis of good listening.

It's important to realize that not all interruptions are monopolizing tactics. We also interrupt to show interest, voice support, and ask for elaboration. This type of interrupting usually takes the form of minimal communication such as "umm," "go on," and "really?" that shows interest in the person who is speaking. Some research indicates that women tend to use interruptions to show interest and support (Anderson & Leaper, 1998; James & Clarke, 1993).

Selective Listening

Selective listening is focusing on only particular parts of messages. One form of selective listening is focusing only on aspects of communication that interest us or correspond with our values. Students often become highly attentive when teachers say, "This is important for the test." In the workplace, we may become more attentive when communication addresses topics such as raises, layoffs, and other matters that may affect us directly.

A second form of selective listening occurs when we reject communication that bores us or makes us uncomfortable. For instance, we may not listen when others praise accomplishments of public officials we don't like. Being mindful allows you to curb the tendency to tune out messages you find boring or uncomfortable.

Defensive Listening

Defensive listening involves perceiving personal attacks, criticisms, or hostility in communication when no offense is intended. When we listen defensively, we read unkind motives into whatever others say. Thus, an innocent remark such as "Have you finished your report yet?" may be perceived as suspicion that you aren't doing your work. Although defensive listening is often limited to particular moments, some people perceive insults and criticism in most communication (a global, stable attribution).

Ambushing

Ambushing is listening carefully for the purpose of attacking. Unlike the other kinds of nonlistening we've discussed, ambushing involves very careful listening, but it isn't motivated by interest in another. Instead, ambushers listen intently to gather ammunition, which they then use to attack a speaker. Political candidates routinely do this as do trial attorneys. Each person listens carefully to the other for the sole purpose of undercutting the adversary. Ambushing is not advisable when openness and connection are wanted.

> **ERIC** *One of the brothers at my house is a real ambusher. He's a pre-law major, and he loves to debate and win arguments. No matter what somebody talks about, this guy just listens long enough to mount a counterattack. He doesn't care about understanding others, just about beating them. I've quit talking when he's around.*

Literal Listening

The final form of nonlistening is **literal listening**, which is listening only to the content level of meaning and ignoring the relationship level of meaning. Literal listeners get the information in a message, but they miss the feelings and relationship dimension.

In summary, nonlistening comes in many forms, including pseudolistening, ambushing speakers, monopolizing the stage, responding defensively, attending selectively, and listening literally. Being aware of forms of nonlistening enables you to exercise control over how you listen and thus how fully and mindfully you participate in communication with others.

ADAPTING LISTENING TO COMMUNICATION GOALS

Effective listening is tailored to specific purposes. Informational listening, critical listening, and relational listening entail different listening styles and behaviors. We'll discuss the specific attitudes and skills that support each type of listening.

Informational and Critical Listening

Much of the time, we listen to gain information. We listen for information in classes, at political debates, in professional meetings, when important news stories are reported, and when we need guidance on everything from medical treatment to driving directions. In all of these cases, the goal of **informational listening** is to gain and understand information.

Closely related to informational listening is **critical listening**, in which we listen to form opinions, to make judgments, or to evaluate people and ideas. Critical listening goes beyond gaining information; it requires us to analyze and evaluate information and the people who express it. We decide whether a speaker is credible and ethical by judging the thoroughness of a presentation, the accuracy of evidence, and the carefulness of reasoning. In Chapter 13, we discuss ways to evaluate evidence. Both informational and critical listening require us to be mindful and to organize and retain information.

Be Mindful   Informational and critical listening begins with the decision to be mindful. Don't let your mind wander when information gets complicated or confusing. Instead, stay focused on gaining as much information as you can. Later, you may want to ask questions if material wasn't clear even though you listened mindfully.

Control Obstacles   Minimize distractions when listening for information or critically listening. You might shut a window to block out traffic noises and empty your mind of preoccupations and prejudgments that can interfere with attending fully.

Ask Questions   Asking speakers to clarify or elaborate on their messages allows you to understand information you didn't grasp at first and enhances insight into content that you did comprehend. Questions also compliment speakers because they indicate that you are interested and want to know more.

When listening critically, it's appropriate to ask probing questions of speakers: "What is the source of your statistics on the rate of unemployment?" "Have you talked with anyone who holds a point of view contrary to yours?" It's especially important and appropriate for non-native speakers to ask questions if they don't understand language, particularly colloquial terms (Lee, 1994, 2000). Sensitive communicators avoid or explain idioms when non-native speakers are present. If speakers don't offer explanations, listeners should request them.

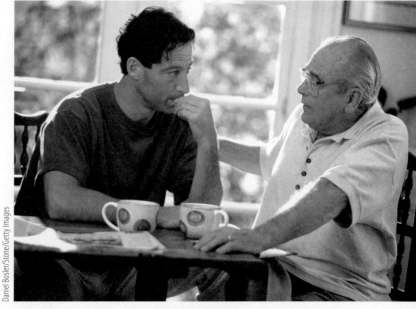

Daniel Bosler/Stone/Getty Images

Mindful listening is one of the greatest gifts we can give to another.

Between a Rock and a Hard Place

Most of us have had the experience of being frustrated by a speaker who used specialized language that we couldn't understand. That experience is common for people in the United States for whom English is a second language.

According to communication scholar Wen-Shu Lee (1994, 2000), phrases that often defy understanding for nonnative speakers include *miss the boat* (Where is the boat? I don't see a boat.), *kick the bucket* (Who's kicking what bucket?), *chew the fat* (Why would you want to chew fat?), *between a rock and a hard place* (Why is someone in such a position?), and *hit the road* (Why would anybody hit a road?).

To learn more about English slang and people for whom English is a second language, use your MindTap for *Communication in Our Lives* to access **WebLink 4.1**.

Use Aids to Recall   To understand and remember important information, we can apply the principles of perception we discussed in Chapter 2. For instance, we tend to notice and recall stimuli that are repeated. To use this principle to increase recall, repeat important ideas to yourself immediately after hearing them.

Another way to increase retention is to use mnemonic (pronounced "ne-monic," rhymes with *demonic*) devices, which are memory aids that create patterns for what you've heard. You probably already do this in studying. For instance, KIM is a mnemonic to remember that Kim (K) from Iowa (I) is going into medicine (M).

Organize Information   Another technique to increase retention is to organize information. For example, suppose a friend tells you he is confused about long-range goals, doesn't know what he can do with a math major, wants to locate in the Midwest, wonders whether graduate school is necessary, likes small towns, needs some internships to try out different options, and wants a family eventually. You could regroup this stream of concerns into two categories: academic information (careers for math majors, graduate school, internship opportunities) and lifestyle preferences (Midwest, small town, family). Remembering those two categories allows you to retain the essence of your friend's concerns, even if you forget many of the specifics.

Relational Listening

In some listening situations, we're as concerned or even more concerned with the relational level of meaning than the content level. We engage in **relational listening** when we listen to a friend's worries, counsel a coworker, or talk with a parent about health concerns. Whenever supporting a person and maintaining a relationship are key goals, we should engage in relational listening.

Be Mindful   The first requirement for effective relational listening is to be mindful. You'll recall that this was also the first step in informational and critical listening. When we're interested in relational meanings, however, a different kind of mindfulness is needed. Instead of focusing our minds on information, we need to concentrate on understanding feelings. Thus, mindful relational listening calls on us to pay attention to what lies "between the words," the subtle clues to feelings and perceptions.

Suspend Judgment   When listening to provide support, it's important to avoid highly judgmental responses. Although Western culture emphasizes evaluation, often we don't always need to judge others or what they feel, think, and do. When we judge what another says, we move away from that person and his or her feelings. To curb evaluative tendencies, ask whether you really need to pass judgment in the present moment.

Only if someone asks for our judgment should we offer it when we are listening to support. Even if our opinion is sought, we should express it in a way that doesn't devalue others. Sometimes people excuse strongly judgmental comments by saying, "You asked me to be honest" or "I mean this as constructive criticism." Too often, however, the judgments are not constructive and are harsher than candor requires. Good relational listening includes responses that support others.

> **JOSÉ**   *My best friend makes it so easy for me to tell whatever is on my mind. She never puts me down or makes me feel stupid or weird. Sometimes I ask her what she thinks, and she has this way of telling me without making me feel wrong if I think differently. What it boils down to is respect. She respects me and herself, so she doesn't have to prove anything by acting better than me.*

Understand the Other Person's Perspective   One of the most important principles for effective relational listening is to grasp the other person's perspective. We can't respond sensitively to others until we understand their perspective and meanings. This means we have to step outside of our own point of view, at least long enough to understand how another person sees things.

Paraphrasing is a method of clarifying another's meaning or needs by reflecting our interpretations of his or her communication back to him or her. For example, a friend might confide, "I'm really scared my kid brother is messing around with drugs." We could paraphrase this way: "It sounds as if you think your brother may be experimenting with drugs." This paraphrase allows us to clarify whether the friend has any evidence of the brother's drug involvement. The response might be, "No, I don't have any real reason to suspect him, but I just worry because drugs are so pervasive in high schools now." This tells us that the friend's worries are more the issue than any evidence that his or her brother is trying drugs.

Another skill to help you understand others is the use of **minimal encouragers**. These are responses that express interest in hearing more and thus gently invite another person to elaborate. Examples of minimal encouragers are "Tell me more," "Really?" "Go on," "I'm with you," "Then what happened?" "Yeah?" and "I see." We can also use nonverbal minimal encouragers, such as a raised eyebrow to show we're involved, a nod to indicate we understand, or widened eyes to indicate we're fascinated.

Minimal encouragers indicate that we are listening, following, and interested. They encourage others to keep talking so that we can more fully understand what they mean. Keep in mind that these are *minimal* encouragers. They are brief interjections that prompt, rather than interfere with, the flow of another's talk.

To enhance understanding of what another feels or wants from us we can ask questions. For instance, we might ask, "How do you feel about that?" or "Do you want to talk about how to handle the situation, or do you just want to air the issues?" Asking directly signals that we really want to help and allows others to tell us how we can best do that.

Express Support   Central to relational listening is communicating support. This doesn't necessarily require you to agree with another's perspective or ideas, but you should communicate support for the person. The following conversation between a father and son illustrates how we can support a person even if we don't agree another.

> SON: Dad, I'm changing my major from business to drama.
> FATHER: Oh.
> SON: Yeah, I've wanted to do it for some time, but I kept holding back because acting isn't as safe as accounting.
> FATHER: That's certainly true.
> SON: Yeah, but I've decided to do it anyway. What do you think about this?
> FATHER: It worries me. Starving actors are a dime a dozen. It just won't provide you with any economic security.
> SON: I understand acting isn't as secure as business, but it's what I really want to do.
> FATHER: Tell me what you feel about acting—why it matters so much to you.
> SON: It's the most creative, totally fulfilling thing I do. I've tried to get interested in business, but I just don't love that like I do acting. I feel like I have to give this a try, or I'll always wonder if I could have made it. If I don't get somewhere in 5 or 6 years, I'll rethink my career options.
> FATHER: Couldn't you finish your business degree and get a job and act on the side?
> SON: No. I've got to give acting a full shot—give it everything I have, to see if I can make it.
> FATHER: Well, I still have reservations, but I guess I can understand having to try something that matters this much to you. I'm just concerned that you'll lose years of your life to something that doesn't work out.

SON: Well, I'm kinda concerned about that too, but I'm more worried about wasting years of my life in a career that doesn't turn me on than about trying to make a go of the one that does.

FATHER: I can understand that. I wouldn't make the choice you're making, but I respect your decision and your guts for taking a big gamble.

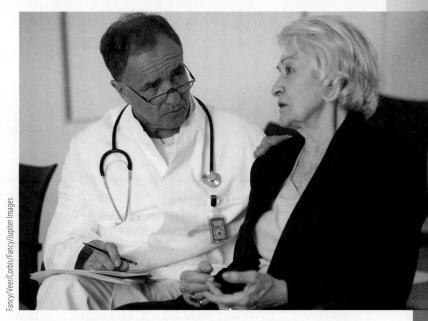

Listening to discriminate is vital when doctors communicate with patients.

This dialogue illustrates several principles of effective relational listening. First, notice that the father's first two comments are minimal encouragers that invite his son to elaborate thoughts and feelings. The father also encourages his son to explain how he feels. Later, the father suggests a compromise solution. When his son rejects that, the father respects the son's position. Importantly, the father makes his own position clear, but he separates his personal stance from his respect for his son's right to make his own choices. Sometimes it's difficult to listen openly and nonjudgmentally, particularly if we don't agree with the person speaking, as in the example. However, if your goal is to support another person, then sensitive, responsive involvement without evaluation is important to effective listening.

Other Purposes of Listening

Listening for information to evaluate critically and listening to support others are two major listening purposes. In addition, we will briefly discuss other listening goals.

Listening for Pleasure   Sometimes we listen for pleasure, as when we attend concerts or enjoy conversation with witty, funny people. When we listen for pleasure, we don't need to concentrate on organizing and remembering as much as when we listen for information, although retention is important if you want to be able to tell a joke to someone else later. Yet listening for pleasure does require mindfulness, hearing, and interpretation.

Listening to Discriminate   In some situations, we listen to make fine discriminations in sounds to draw valid conclusions and act appropriately in response. For example, doctors and nurses listen to discriminate when they use stethoscopes to diagnose heart functioning or chest congestion. Parents listen to discriminate among a baby's cries for attention, food, or a diaper change. Skilled mechanics can distinguish between engine sounds that most people cannot detect. Mindfulness and keen hearing abilities are particularly important when listening to discriminate.

BEYOND THE CLASSROOM

MindTap

Let's take the material in this chapter beyond the classroom by thinking about how what you've learned about listening might apply to the workplace, ethical choices, and engagement with the broader world.

1. **Workplace.** The chapter identified six forms of nonlistening. To what extent are any of these types of nonlistening evident in your current workplace or to what extent were they present in a former workplace? Reflect on particular instances of nonlistening in the workplace: Can you identify any causes or conditions that were common to them? Do you recognize any costs of the nonlistening in terms of productivity, relations among workers, and so forth? (You could apply this same analysis to a classroom or other campus location.)

2. **Ethics.** At the end of Chapter 1, I invited you to read NCA's Credo for Ethical Communication by clicking **WebLink 1.4**. Reread that now as **WebLink 4.2.** Using that credo as a guideline, develop a Credo for Ethical Listening that identifies both what listeners must do and what they cannot do if they wish to listen ethically.

3. **Engagement.** American Public Media developed a radio program called "The Story," which presents interviews with people who have interesting stories to tell about their lives. Most of the people interviewed are not celebrities; they aren't famous; and they aren't particularly heroic. In other words, many of them are regular people, but the interviewer uses excellent listening skills to bring the interviewees out and make their stories sing. Click **WebLink 4.3** to find the home page for "The Story." Listen to one podcast of a story. As you listen, pay particular attention to the interviewer: How does he demonstrate engagement with the interviewee? How does he encourage the interviewee to expand on points and to move along with the story?

CHAPTER SUMMARY

 Practice and review the content in this chapter.

According to Zeno of Citium, an ancient philosopher, "We have been given two ears but a single mouth, in order that we may hear more and talk less." Thousands of years later, we can still learn from his comment. Listening is a major and vital part of communication, yet too often we don't consider it as important as talking. In this chapter, we've explored the complex and demanding process of listening.

We began by distinguishing between hearing—physically receiving messages—and listening. The former is a straightforward physiological process that doesn't take effort on our part. Listening, in contrast, is a complicated and active process involving being mindful, hearing, selecting and organizing, interpreting, responding, and remembering. Listening well takes commitment and skill.

To understand what interferes with effective listening, we discussed obstacles in situations and messages and obstacles in us. Listening is hindered by message overload, complexity of material, and external noise in communication contexts. In addition, listening can be hampered by our preoccupations and prejudgments, lack of effort, and failure to recognize differences in listening styles. These obstacles to listening give rise to various types of nonlistening, including pseudolistening, monopolizing, selective listening, defensive listening, ambushing, and literal listening. Each of these forms of nonlistening signals that we aren't fully present in interaction.

We also discussed different purposes for listening and identified the skills and attitudes that advance each purpose. Informational listening and critical listening require us to adopt a mindful attitude and to think critically, organize and evaluate information, clarify understanding by asking questions, and develop aids to retention of complex material. Relational listening also requires mindfulness, but it calls for other, distinct listening skills. Suspending judgment, paraphrasing, giving minimal encouragers, and expressing support enhance the effectiveness of relational listening.

APPLYING COMMUNICATION IN OUR LIVES

Communication in Our Lives is supported by a MindTap, a new online learning platform that delivers content, assignments, and a tailored presentation of the course curriculum created by your instructor. MindTap combines all of your learning tools—readings, multimedia, activities and assessments—into a singular learning unit that guides you through the course. Practice and Present, a unique tool within MindTap, allows you to upload your speech video files for practice or for a grade, comment on your peer's speeches and review your grades. MindTap also includes Speech Builder Express, a powerful tool that guides you through the speech outline and preparation process. For more information or to access MindTap, visit cengagebrain.com.

DEFINITIONS OF KEY CONCEPTS

 MindTap™ Review your **Flashcards**.

ambushing Listening carefully in order to attack a speaker.

critical listening Attending to communication to analyze and evaluate the content of communication or the person speaking.

defensive listening Perceiving personal attacks, criticisms, or hostility in communication when no offense is intended.

hearing The physiological activity that occurs when sound waves hit our eardrums. Unlike listening, hearing is a passive process.

informational listening Listening to gain and understand information; tends to focus on the content level of meaning.

listening A complex process that consists of being mindful, physically receiving messages, selecting and organizing information, interpreting, responding, and remembering.

literal listening Listening only to the content level of meaning and ignoring the relational level of meaning.

mindfulness From Zen Buddhism, being fully present in the moment; the first step of listening and the foundation of all other steps.

minimal encouragers Communication that, by expressing interest in hearing more, gently invites another person to elaborate.

monopolizing Continually focusing communication on oneself instead of on the person who is talking.

paraphrasing A method of clarifying others' meaning by restating their communication.

pseudolistening Pretending to listen.

relational listening Listening to support another person or to understand another person's feelings and perceptions; focuses on the relational level of meaning as much as on the content level of meaning.

selective listening Focusing on only selected parts of communication. We listen selectively when we screen out parts of a message that don't interest us or with which we disagree and also when we rivet attention on parts of communication that do interest us or with which we agree.

FOR FURTHER REFLECTION AND DISCUSSION

 MindTap™

1. Select one type of nonlistening in which you engage, and work to minimize its occurrence.

2. How do you know whether someone is really listening to you when you are texting or talking on a cell? What signals mindful listening in these settings?

3. What ethical principles guide different listening purposes? What different ethical responsibilities accompany listening for information and listening relationally?

Ethics

4. Who is your prototype of an excellent listener? Describe what the person does that makes him or her effective. Do the person's listening behaviors fit with the guidelines offered in this chapter?

5. Dave Isay set out to make an oral history of the United States by listening to the stories of everyday people—not politicians, celebrities, or CEOs, but regular people. By January of 2009, StoryCorps had recorded more than 40,000 stories of ordinary Americans—what they value and how they understand life. Isay gathered a number of these stories into a book, which he titled *Listening as an Act of Love* (2008).

6. If you want to work on your listening skills, you might be interested in Madelyn Burley-Allen's book *Listening: The Forgotten Skill* (1995). She provides a self-teaching guide for improving listening effectiveness.

7. A Website that offers guidelines for listening better is available by clicking on **WebLink 4.4.**

SHARPEN **YOUR SKILL**   MindTap™

1. Improving Recall

Apply the principles we've discussed to enhance memory.

- The next time you meet someone, repeat his or her name to yourself three times after you are introduced. Do you remember the name?
- After your next class, take 15 minutes to review your notes in a quiet place. Read them aloud so that you hear as well as see the main ideas. Does this increase your retention of material?
- Invent mnemonics to create patterns that help you remember basic information in a message.
- Organize ideas into categories. To remember the main ideas of this chapter, you might use major subheadings to form categories: listening process, obstacles to listening, and listening goals. The mnemonic LOG (i.e., listening, obstacles, goals) could help you remember those topics.

2. Learn from the Pros

One way to improve your listening skills is to observe people who are experts at effective listening. Watch a television program that features interviews—Sunday morning news shows and programs such as *20/20* and *60 Minutes*. Select one interview to observe, and answer the following questions about it:

- How does the interviewer phrase questions to encourage the interviewee to talk? Are questions open or closed, biased or unbiased?
- How is the interviewer seated in relation to the interviewee—how close, at what angle?
- Does the interviewer paraphrase the interviewee's responses?
- Does the interviewer make minimal responses?
- How, if at all, does the interviewer show that he or she understands and respects the interviewee's perspective?
- How, if at all, does the interviewer demonstrate attentiveness?

EXPERIENCING COMMUNICATION IN OUR LIVES   MindTap™

CASE STUDY: *Family Hour*

A video of the conversation scripted here is featured in your Chapter 4 MindTap for *Communication in Our Lives*. Select "Family Hour" to watch the video. Improve your own communication skills by reading, watching, and evaluating this communication encounter.

    Over spring break, 20-year-old Josh visits his father. He wants to convince his family to support him in joining a fraternity that has given him a bid. On his second day home, after dinner Josh decides to broach the topic. His dad is watching the evening news on television when Josh walks into the living room. Josh sits down and opens the conversation.

© Cengage Learning

JOSH: Well, something pretty interesting has happened at school this semester.

DAD: I'll bet you found a girlfriend, right? I was about your age when your mother and I started dating, and that was the best part of college. I still remember how she looked on our first date. She was young, and then she was very slender and pretty. I saw her and thought she was the loveliest thing I'd ever seen. Before long, we were a regular item. Yep, it was about when I was 20, like you are now.

JOSH: Well, I haven't found a girlfriend, but I did get a bid from Sigma Chi.

DAD: Sigma Chi. What is that—a fraternity?

JOSH: Yeah, it's probably the coolest fraternity on campus. I attended some rush parties this semester—mainly out of curiosity, just to see what they were like.

DAD: Why'd you do that? Before you ever went to college, I told you to steer clear of fraternities. They cost a lot of money, and they distract you from your studies.

JOSH: Well, I know you told me to steer clear of fraternities, but I did check a few out. I'd be willing to take a job to help pay the membership fee and monthly dues. Besides, it's not that much more expensive when you figure I'd be eating at the house, and . . .

DAD: Do you realize how much it costs just for you to go to that school? I'm paying $14,000 a year! When I went to school, I had to go to state college because my parents couldn't afford to send me to the school of my choice. You have no idea how lucky you are to be going to the school you wanted to go to and have me footing all the bills.

JOSH: But we could work it out so that a fraternity wouldn't cost you anything. Like I said, I . . .

DAD: If you want to take a job, fine. I could use some help paying your tuition and fees. But you're not taking a job just so you can belong to a party house.

JOSH: I thought they were just party houses too, until I attended rush. Now, I went to several houses that were that way, but Sigma Chi isn't. I really liked the brothers at Sigma Chi. They're interesting and friendly and fun, so I was thrilled when . . .

DAD: I don't want to hear about it. You're not joining a fraternity. I told you what happened when I was in college. I joined one, and pretty soon my Dean's List grades dropped to Cs and Ds. When you live in a fraternity house, you can't study like you can in your dorm room or the library. I should know. I tried it and found out the hard way. There's no need for you to repeat my mistake.

JOSH: But, Dad, I'm not you. Joining a fraternity wouldn't necessarily mean that my grades . . .

DAD: What do you mean, you're not me? You think I wasn't a good student b
fraternity? You think you're so smart you can party all the time and still make goo
me tell you something, I thought that too, and, boy, was I ever wrong! As soon as I j
house, it was party time all the time. There was always music blaring and girls in the h
poker games—anything but studying. I wasn't stupid. It's just not an atmosphere that en
academic work.

JOSH: I'd like to give it a try. I really like these guys, and I think I can handle being in Sigma Ch
and still . . .

DAD: Well, you think wrong!

QUESTIONS FOR ANALYSIS AND DISCUSSION MindTap

You can also answer these questions and see my responses to them online via MindTap for Chapter 4.

1. What forms of ineffective listening are evident in this dialogue?

2. If you could advise Josh's father on listening effectively, what would you tell him to do differently?

3. Would you offer any advice to Josh on how he could listen to his father more effectively?

CTIVELY

efore I joined the
d grades? Let
oined the
ouse and
courages
.

95

Federico Fellini

©iStockphoto.com/Murillo

The Verbal Dimension of Communication

MindTap

Review the chapter **Learning Objectives** and **Start** with a quick warm up activity.

Perhaps you are familiar with the story of Helen Keller. As an infant, she contracted an illness that left her deaf and blind. Trapped in her silent world, Helen behaved more like an animal than a human infant. She reacted to whatever stimuli were in her immediate environment but did not show any ability to self-reflect, grasp meanings, or communicate with others. Later in life, she achieved remarkable things: She graduated with honors from Radcliffe, authored nearly a dozen books, met 12 U.S. presidents, learned to read and write four languages other than English, and lectured throughout the United States, Europe, and Asia.

What allowed Helen to move from reacting only to immediate stimuli to

SHARPEN YOUR SKILL

At the end of this chapter, refer to the Sharpen Your Skill features, Communication Rules and Assessing Your Stereotypes, to apply concepts from Chapter 5.

being an engaging, reflective person who connected with a wide range of people? Language. It was learning to use language that opened the human world of meaning for Helen. When Helen was 7, her life changed because Annie Sullivan became her teacher. Helen was smart, so Annie was able to teach her the manual alphabet quickly. In just a few weeks with Annie, Helen was able to use her hands to spell words, but she didn't understand what they meant. She didn't grasp that the actions of her or Annie's fingers were communicating meaning.

That changed in one electric moment. While one of Helen's hands was under the spout of a water pump, Annie spelled W-A-T-E-R into her other hand. Suddenly Helen got it; she understood that the actions of the fingers meant something; she realized she could actually communicate with others. Once Helen understood how to communicate, she was unstoppable and went on to accomplish amazing things in her life.

In this chapter, we take a close look at language. We begin by defining symbols, which are the basis of language. Second, we explore principles of verbal communication. Next, we consider what language allows us to do. The final section of the chapter focuses on guidelines for effective use of language.

Library of Congress Prints and Photographs Division [LC-USZ62-69879]

Learning to use language opened the human world of meaning for Helen Keller.

SYMBOLS AND MEANING

A **symbol** is a representation of a person, event, or other phenomenon. For instance, the word *house* is a symbol that stands for a type of building. *Emergency Room* is a verbal symbol that represents a hospital unit that deals with unscheduled medical problems. *Tweet* and *blog* are words we have coined to represent ways we use social media to communicate.

Language is symbolic. Much nonverbal communication—art, music, company, logos—is also symbolic. The key to understanding symbols is to realize that they are arbitrary, ambiguous, and abstract ways of representing things.

Read, highlight and take notes online.

Symbols Are Arbitrary

Symbols are **arbitrary,** which means they are not intrinsically connected to what they represent. For instance, the word *book* has no necessary or natural connection to what you are reading now. We could substitute a different word, as long as we agreed it would stand for what we now call a book. Certain words seem right because as a society we agree to use them in particular ways, but they have no natural correspondence to their referents.

Because language is arbitrary, we can create private communication codes. For example, most professions rely on specialized terms that are not understood

Business Buzz

The recession that began in 2008 had many consequences. One is new words coined to describe new experiences. Consider these (Stafford, 2012):

Mancession: occurs when men lose proportionately more jobs than women.

Furcation: time off because of mandated furlough from job.

Staycation: a vacation that takes place at home instead of one that involves traveling to another place. Staycations become popular when people have less discretionary money.

Permatemping: going from one temporary job to another without getting a full-time job with benefits.

Jobstoppers: characteristics that are usually physical and visible that may lead employers not to hire a person. Examples are piercings and tattoos.

by outsiders. Coded language also allows people to communicate confidential information. Two primary tasks of military intelligence are to invent secret, unbreakable codes and to break the secret codes of others. Click **WebLink 5.1** to learn about code talkers in the military during World War II.

Because language is arbitrary, we can create new words and terms. Today, many people work out of *virtual offices*, a term nobody had heard 20 years ago. The word *friend* was invariably a noun until people on social network sites such as Facebook began using it as a verb—one person *friends* another on the site.

Symbols Are Ambiguous

Symbols are also **ambiguous,** which means their meanings aren't fixed in an absolute way. The meanings of words vary based on the values and experiences of those who use them. *Government regulation* may mean positive assistance to citizens who are suffering from pollutants emitted by a chemical company. To owners of the chemical company, however, *government regulation* may mean complying with costly measures to reduce pollution. Although the words are the same, their meanings vary according to individuals' identities and experiences.

Although words don't mean exactly the same thing to everyone, many symbols have an agreed-on range of meanings within a culture. Thus, we all understand that *dog* means a four-footed creature, but each of us also has personal meanings for the word based on dogs we have known and our experiences with them. We've all experienced dynamic speakers, yet we may differ in our notions of what concrete behaviors would lead us to label a speaker *dynamic* (remember the abstraction ladder we discussed in Chapter 2).

The ambiguity of symbols explains why misunderstandings so often occur. At work, team members may have different meanings for the same words. Your supervisor tells you it's important to be "a team player," which you assume means you should cooperate with coworkers. However, your supervisor may mean that you are expected to initiate and participate in teams on the job. To minimize the likelihood of misunderstanding, we can offer clear, concrete translations of ambiguous words.

Symbols Are Abstract

Finally, symbols are **abstract,** which means not concrete or tangible. They stand for ideas, people, events, objects, feelings, and so forth, but they are not the things they represent. In Chapter 2, we discussed the abstraction ladder, whereby we move farther and farther away from concrete reality. The symbols we use vary in abstractness. *Managerial potential* is an abstract term. *Organizational and presentational skill* is less abstract. Even more concrete expressions are *experience in collaborating with others, speaking to large groups,* and *organizing project teams.*

> **ADIVA**   *My resident assistant told us we must observe "quiet hours" from 7 to 10 each night so that people can study. But everyone on my hall plays music and talks during quiet hours. My adviser told me I needed to take courses in social diversity, so I took a class in oral traditions of Asian cultures. Then my adviser told me that is a non-Western civilization course, not one in social diversity.*

To develop your ability to reduce the abstractness of language, complete the activity "Reducing the Abstractness of Language" via your Chapter 5 MindTap for *Communication in Our Lives.*

Because symbols are arbitrary, ambiguous, and abstract, they allow us to share complex ideas and feelings with others. At the same time, symbols have the potential to create misunderstandings. When we understand that symbols

COMMUNICATION HIGHLIGHT

Lost in Translation

Language doesn't always translate well across cultures. Consider these examples of English terms that turned out to mean something very different in other cultures (Leaper, 1999).

Don't say, "I'm a Pepper" in the United Kingdom. The manufacturer of the soft drink Dr. Pepper discovered that this didn't work because *pepper* is British slang for "prostitute" (Leaper, 1999).

When General Motors exported its Chevrolet Nova to South America, there were problems. In Spanish, *no va* means "does not go"—not a great advertisement for a car! (Leaper, 1999).

To avoid such cross-cultural blunders, many U.S. companies now hire consultants to develop names that will work for their products in other countries. In China, BMW is *Precious Horse*; Reebok shoes are *Quick Steps*; Coca-Cola is *Tasty Fun*; Marriott is *Wealthy Elites*; and Heineken is *Happiness Power* (Wines, 2011).

are ambiguous, arbitrary, and abstract, we can guard against their potential to hinder communication.

PRINCIPLES OF VERBAL COMMUNICATION

Three principles clarify how we use verbal communication and how it affects us.

Interpretation Creates Meaning

Because symbols are abstract, ambiguous, and arbitrary, their meanings aren't self-evident or absolute. Instead, we have to interpret the meaning of symbols.

If a work associate says, "Let's go to dinner after work," the comment could mean a variety of things. It could be an invitation to explore transforming the work relationship into a friendship. It could be a veiled request for a strategy session regarding some issue in the workplace. It might also indicate that the person issuing the invitation is interested in a romantic relationship. We invest effort to interpret words and assign meanings to them. By extension, effective communicators are alert to possible misunderstandings, and they check with others to see whether meanings match.

Communication Is Rule Guided

Verbal communication is patterned by unspoken but broadly understood rules (Argyle & Henderson, 1984; Shimanoff, 1980). **Communication rules** are shared understandings of what communication means and what kinds of communication are and are not appropriate in various situations. For the most part, rules aren't explicit or intentionally constructed; they often grow out of habits and norms. In the course of interacting with our families and others, we unconsciously absorb rules that guide how we communicate and how we interpret others' communication.

Two kinds of rules guide communication (Cronen, Pearce, & Snavely, 1979; Pearce, Cronen, & Conklin, 1979). **Regulative rules** specify when, how, where, and with whom to talk about certain things. For instance, we follow regulative rules for turn taking in conversation. In formal contexts, we usually know not to interrupt when someone else is speaking, but in more informal settings, interruptions may be appropriate. Talking during formal speeches is appropriate in some contexts, as in traditional black churches and public meetings. Patients sometimes think that they have to wait for questions from health care providers.

Regulative rules also define when, where, and with whom it's appropriate or necessary to communicate in particular ways. Some couples have the rule that it's okay to kiss in private but not in public. On the job, there are often unwritten regulative rules that specify that people with higher positions may interrupt subordinates but that subordinates may not interrupt organizational superiors.

> **JUDE**   *I can talk to Sam about politics all night long. Usually, we agree, but we also disagree on some issues and we enjoy arguing. I can't talk with Travis about politics. He totally disagrees with most of what I believe and he shuts down because he hates conflict. On the other hand, I can get into really deep discussions with Travis about religious stuff, and Sam has no interest in that.*

Constitutive rules define what communication means by telling us how to count certain kinds of communication. We learn that paying attention counts as showing respect, hugging counts as affection, and raising the middle finger counts as an insult. Social interactions tend to follow rules that are widely shared in a specific society.

Interaction between intimates also follows rules, but these may not be shared by the culture as a whole. Intimate partners negotiate private rules to guide how they communicate and what certain things mean. Couples craft personal rules that specify how to argue, express love, make decisions, and show support.

We may not realize that rules exist until one is broken and we become aware that we had an expectation. Becoming aware of communication rules empowers you to change those that don't promote healthy interaction and relationships.

Punctuation Affects Meaning

We punctuate communication to create meaning. In writing, we use periods to define where ideas stop and start. Similarly, in interpersonal communication, **punctuation** is the mental mark of the beginnings and endings of particular interactions (Watzlawick, Beavin, & Jackson, 1967). For example, when a teacher steps to the front of a classroom, that marks the beginning of the class. When the CEO enters a room, that marks the beginning of a meeting. When a speaker says, "Thank you for your attention" and folds notes, that marks the end of the formal speech.

When we don't agree on punctuation, problems may arise. A common instance of conflicting punctuation is the demand–withdraw pattern

Monkey Business Images/Shutterstock.com

What regulative and constitutive rules govern mealtime conversation in your family?

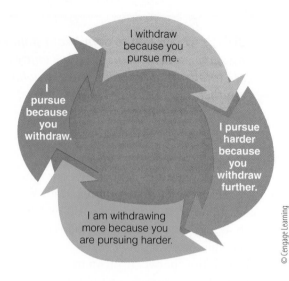

FIGURE 5.1
The Demand–Withdraw
Pattern

illustrated in Figure 5.1 (Bergner & Bergner, 1990; Caughlin & Vangelisti, 2000; Wegner, 2005). This occurs when one person tries to express closeness and the other strives to maintain autonomy by avoiding interaction. The more one partner pushes for personal talk, the more the other partner withdraws. Each partner punctuates the beginning of the interaction with the other's behavior. Thus, the demander thinks, "I pursue because you withdraw," and the withdrawer thinks, "I withdraw because you pursue."

Effective communicators realize that people don't always punctuate the same way. When they punctuate differently, they ascribe different meanings to what is happening between them. To break out of destructive cycles such as demand–withdraw, partners need to discuss how each of them is punctuating the experience. This reminds us of the importance of perspective taking. Steven's comment illustrates the demand–withdraw pattern and a lack of perspective taking between him and his parents.

STEVEN   *My parents say I am irresponsible if I don't tell them about something I do. So then they probe me and call more often to check up on me. I hate that kind of intrusion, so I don't return their calls and I sidestep questions. That makes them call more and ask more questions. That makes me clam up more. And we just keep going in circles.*

SYMBOLIC ABILITIES

Because we use symbols, we live in a world of ideas and meanings. Instead of just reacting to our concrete environments, we think about them and sometimes transform them. In much the same way, we don't simply accept ourselves as we are but continuously work to change and grow. Philosophers of language have identified five ways symbolic capacities affect our lives (Cassirer, 1944; Langer, 1953, 1979). As we discuss each, we'll consider how to realize the constructive power of symbols and minimize the problems they can generate.

Symbols Define

We use symbols to define experiences, people, relationships, feelings, and thoughts. As we saw in Chapter 2, the definitions we give to phenomena shape what they mean to us. When we label people, we focus attention on particular aspects of them, and we necessarily obscure other aspects of who they are. We might define a person as an environmentalist, a teacher, a gourmet cook, and a Republican. Each way of classifying the person directs our attention to certain, and not other, aspects of identity. We might discuss wilderness legislation with the environmentalist, talk about testing with the teacher, swap recipes with the cook, and discuss politics or not, depending on our own political stance, with the Republican. We tend to interact with people according to how we define and classify them.

Totalizing is using a single label to represent the totality of a person. We fixate on one symbol to define someone and fail to recognize many other aspects of who he or she is. Totalizing also occurs when we dismiss people by saying, "He's a liberal," "She's old," "She's preppy," or "He's a jock." When we totalize others, we negate most of who they are by spotlighting a single aspect of their identity.

NANYA *I'm Indian, and that's all a lot of people here see in me. They see that my skin is dark and I wear a sari, and they put me in the category "foreigner" or, if they are observant, "Indian." They mark me off as different, foreign, not like them, and they can't see anything else about me. How would they feel if I categorized them as "Americans" and didn't see their individual qualities?*

Symbols influence how we think and feel about experiences and people. In one study, colleagues and I asked romantic couples how they defined differences between them (Wood, Dendy, Dordek, Germany, & Varallo, 1994). We found that some people define differences as positive forces that energize a relationship. Others define differences as problems or barriers to closeness. There was a direct connection between how partners defined differences and how they dealt with them. Partners who labeled differences as constructive approached disagreements with curiosity and a belief that they would grow by discussing differences. On the other hand, partners who labeled differences as problems tended to deny differences or avoid talking about them.

Stewart Cohen/Blend Images/Getty Images

Wedding bands symbolize commitment.

COMMUNICATION HIGHLIGHT

What do you call yourself when language has no name that fits you? That didn't stump a young woman from San Diego whose mother was Mexican and whose father was African. She coined the term *Blaxican* to describe her ethnicity (Rodriguez, 2003). We're likely to see more creative language as multiracial children decide how to name themselves.

How we think about relationships directly affects what happens in them. People who dwell on negative thoughts about relationships heighten awareness of relationship flaws and diminish perceptions of strengths. Conversely, partners who focus on good facets of their relationships are more conscious of positive qualities of partners and relationships and less aware of imperfections (Seligman, 2002).

CHERYL   *About 3 years ago, my husband and I were seriously considering divorce. We decided to try marital counseling first, and that saved our marriage. The counselor helped us see that we noticed problems, aggravations, and faults in each other and didn't see all of the good qualities in each other and our relationship. Now we have a "warts-and-all" philosophy, which means we accept each other, warts and all. Changing how we think about our marriage really has changed what it is for us.*

As Cheryl's commentary indicates, our definitions of relationships can create self-fulfilling prophecies. Once we select a label for relationships or other phenomena, we tend to see what our label spotlights and to overlook what it doesn't highlight. This suggests an ethical principle for using and interpreting language: We should consider what the language that we and others use includes as well as what it excludes.

Symbols Evaluate

Symbols are not neutral. They are laden with values. We tend to describe people we like with language that accents their good qualities and downplays their flaws. The reverse is generally true of descriptions of people we don't like. My friend is *casual*; someone I don't like is *sloppy*. Restaurants use language that is designed to heighten the attractiveness of menu items. "Tender lobster accented with drawn butter" sounds more appetizing than "crustacean murdered by being boiled alive and then drenched in saturated fat."

Of course, there are degrees of evaluation in language. We might describe people who speak their minds as *assertive, outspoken, straightforward, blunt,* or *rude.* Each word has a distinct connotation. In recent years, we have become more sensitive to how the evaluative nature of symbols can hurt people. Most people with disabilities prefer *person with disability* to *disabled person* because they perceive the latter as totalizing who they are (Braithwaite & Braithwaite, 1997). The term *African American* emphasizes cultural heritage, whereas *black* focuses on skin color. The word *Hispanic* emphasizes the Spanish language spoken in the home countries, whereas *Latino* and *Latina* highlight the geographic origin of Latin American men and women, respectively. People with roots in Spanish-speaking Caribbean countries tend to refer to themselves as *Latinos* and *Latinas* or to use more specific labels such as *Cubano, Peruvian,* and *Mexican* (Rodriguez, 2003). An ethical guideline for using language is to try to learn and respect others' preferences for describing their identities.

Loaded language consists of words that strongly slant perceptions and thus meanings. For example, conservative television and radio commentators sometimes disparage people with liberal social and political values as *knee-jerk liberals* and call environmentalists *tree-huggers*. At the same time, liberal commentators sometimes describe people with conservative social and political values as *country club fat cats* and describe people who oppose environmental regulations as *maiming nature*. Loaded language also fosters negative views of older citizens. Terms such as *geezer* and *old fogey* incline us to regard older people with contempt or pity. Alternatives such as *senior citizen* and *elderly person* are more respectful.

Symbols Organize Perceptions

We use symbols to organize our perceptions. As we saw in Chapter 2, we rely on cognitive schemata to classify and evaluate experiences. How we organize experiences affects what they mean to us. For example, your prototype of a good friend affects how you judge particular friends. When we place someone in the category of friend, the category influences how we interpret that person's communication. An insult is likely to be viewed as teasing if made by someone we define as a friend but a call to battle if made by someone we classify as an enemy. The words don't change, but their meaning varies, depending on how we classify the person uttering them.

COMMUNICATION HIGHLIGHT

Language Shapes Our Realities

Language shapes our perceptions in ways that reflect a culture's values (Whorf, 1956). In one part of Australia, people speak Guugu Timithirr, a language that does not include the terms *right* and *left*. In Guugu Timithirr, special locations are described in relation to a compass. Thus, a person speaking this language might ask to have the pepper passed north (Monastersky, 2002). People recall colors more clearly if their language provides distinct terms, so English speakers do not remember shades of blue (light blue, dark blue) as precisely as Russian speakers who have different words for light blue (*goluboy*) and dark blue (*sinly*) (Gentner & Boroditsky, 2009).

To explore your own experience with how the language you speak influences your reality, complete the Communication Highlight Activity for Chapter 5 via MindTap for *Communication in Our Lives*.

Because symbols organize thought, they allow us to think about abstract concepts such as the work ethic, democracy, morality, good citizenship, and healthy family life. We use broad concepts to transcend specific, concrete activities and to enter the world of conceptual thought and ideals. Thinking abstractly relieves us of having to consider every specific object and experience individually.

Our capacity to abstract can also distort thinking. A primary way this occurs is in stereotyping—thinking in broad generalizations about a whole class of people or experiences. Examples of stereotypes are "Sorority women are yuppies," "Ph.D.s are smart," and "Democrats tax and spend." Notice that stereotypes can be positive or negative.

REGGIE *People say racism no longer exists, but I know it does. If I'm out walking at night, white girls cross the street because they think I'll mug them. They don't cross the street if they see a white guy. One of the guys on my hall asked me whether I thought the Bridge Program was helpful. I didn't go through it because I had a good high school record. Does he think every black needs special help?*

Clearly, we have to generalize. We can't think about each thing in our lives as a specific instance. However, stereotypes can discourage us from recognizing important differences among the phenomena we lump together. Thus, we have an ethical responsibility to stay alert to differences among the things and people that we place in a single category. To view a humorous video with a serious message about stereotyping, click **WebLink 5.2** (http://www.youtube.com /watch?v=qSElmEmEjb4).

Symbols Allow Hypothetical Thought

Who was your best friend when you were 5 years old? What would you do if you won the lottery? To answer these questions, you must think hypothetically, which means thinking about experiences and ideas that are not part of your concrete, present situation. Because we can think hypothetically, we can plan, dream, remember, fantasize, set goals, and weigh alternative courses of action.

Hypothetical thought is possible because we use symbols. When we symbolize, we name ideas so that we can hold them in our minds and reflect on them. We can contemplate things that currently have no real existence, and we can remember ourselves in the past and project ourselves into the future. Our ability to live simultaneously in all three dimensions of time explains why we can set goals and work toward them even though there is nothing tangible about them in the moment (Dixson & Duck, 1993). For example, you've invested many hours in studying and writing papers because you imagine having a college degree. The degree is not real now, nor is the self that you will become once you have the degree. Yet the idea is sufficiently real to motivate you to work hard for many years.

Close relationships rely on ideas of history and future. One of the strongest glues for intimacy is a history of shared experiences (Bruess & Hoefs, 2006; Cockburn-Wootten & Zorn, 2006; Wood, 2006a). Just knowing that they have weathered rough times in the past helps partners get through current trials.

Wireless Monitoring for Health

Monitoring patients' symptoms and responses to treatment is critical in medical care, yet it's difficult or impossible to monitor patients outside of an office or hospital. That persistent problem in health care may be solved if the FCC (Federal Communications Commission) allows a portion of the spectrum to be dedicated to Medical Body Area Networks (MBANs).

For years, patients who require monitoring have been attached by wires to monitoring device, which made it difficult for them to move and increased the chance of infection.

Wireless monitoring would solve those problems. MBANs would allow patients to use inexpensive sensors that attach wirelessly to their bodies. As a result, medical personnel could monitor more patients and know more quickly if intervention were needed.

Belief in a future also sustains intimacy. We interact differently with people we don't expect to see again and people who are continuing parts of our lives. Talking about the future also enhances intimacy because it suggests that more lies ahead.

Symbols Allow Self-reflection

Just as we use symbols to reflect on what goes on outside of us, we also use them to reflect on ourselves. In an argument, you may want to hurl a biting insult at a coworker who has criticized you, but you censor that impulse. You remind yourself that it's impolite to put others down and that doing so might create future problems with that coworker.

The ability to self-reflect allows us to think about who we want to be and set goals for becoming the self we desire. We can feel shame, pride, and regret for our actions—emotions that are possible because we self-reflect. We can control what we do in the present by casting ourselves forward in time to consider how we might later feel about our actions.

Self-reflection also empowers us to monitor ourselves and our actions. For instance, while giving a speech, you might notice that quite a few members of the audience are looking around or slouching. You think to yourself, "They seem bored. Perhaps I've been using too many statistics. Maybe I could regain their interest by mentioning some personal examples." In this case, monitoring allowed you to gauge your speaking effectiveness and make adjustments.

StockLite/Shutterstock.com

Self-reflection allows us to manage the image we project to others.

Self-reflection also allows us to manage our image, or the identity we present to others. Because we reflect on ourselves from social perspectives, we are able to consider how we appear in others' eyes. Our ability to manage how we appear sometimes is called *facework* because it involves controlling the face we present to others. When talking with teachers, you may consciously present yourself as a respectful, attentive student. When communicating with someone you'd like to date, you may choose to be more attentive and social than you are in other circumstances. In work situations, you may do facework to create an image of yourself as responsible, ambitious, and dependable. Continuously, we adjust how we present ourselves so that we sculpt our image to fit particular situations and people.

Summing up, we use symbols to define, evaluate, and organize experiences, think hypothetically, and self-reflect. Each of these abilities helps us create meaning in our lives.

ENHANCING EFFECTIVENESS IN VERBAL COMMUNICATION

We've explored what symbols are and how they may be used differently in distinct social communities. Building on these understandings, we can now consider ways to improve the effectiveness of our verbal communication.

Engage in Dual Perspective

The single most important guideline for effective verbal communication is to engage in **dual perspective.** Dual perspective involves taking another person's point of view into account as you communicate. For instance, effective public

HEALTH COMMUNICATION

Medical Emergency: Communication Breakdowns

Doctor–patient communication is the heart of health care. But what if doctors think they've communicated more clearly than patients do? That's the troublesome finding from a study by two doctors, Douglas Olson and Donna Windish (2010).

- 18% of patients correctly identified the physician in charge of their care; 67% of physicians thought patients knew their names.
- 57% of patients could correctly state their diagnosis; 77% of physicians thought their patients understood their diagnosis.
- 25% of patients who were prescribed a new medication while in the hospital said that their physicians never told them they were receiving a new medication; 100% of physicians stated they at least inform patients of new medications.
- 9% of patients said their physicians discussed possible adverse effects of medications; 81% of physicians stated they describe adverse effects at least some of the time.

The Joint Commission on the Accreditation of Healthcare Organizations strongly emphasizes that patients are entitled to effective communication.

speakers take listeners' values into consideration when planning and presenting speeches. The same is true of friends who communicate well: They take each other's perspective into account.

We don't need to abandon our own perspectives to recognize those of others. In fact, it would be just as unethical to stifle your own views as to dismiss those of others. *Dual perspective*, as the term implies, consists of two perspectives. It entails understanding both our own and another's point of view and acknowledging each when we communicate. For example, you and your supervisor may disagree about a performance review. It's important that you un-

Dual perspective was critical to Hillary Clinton's success as Secretary of State.

derstand why your supervisor assigns the ratings he or she does, even if you don't share his or her perceptions. By understanding the supervisor's perceptions and ratings, you enhance your ability to have a good working relationship and to perform effectively on the job.

Own Your Feelings and Thoughts

We sometimes use language that obscures our responsibility for how we feel and what we think. For instance, people say, "You made me mad," "You made me feel inadequate about my job performance," or "You hurt me," as if what they feel is caused by someone else. On a more subtle level, we sometimes blame others for our responses to what they say. "You're too demanding" really means that you don't like what someone else wants or expects. The sense of feeling pressured by another's expectations is in you; it is not created by the other person. In reality, others seldom directly cause our feelings.

Our feelings and thoughts result from how we interpret others' communication, not from their communication itself. Others sometimes exert a great deal of influence on how we feel and how we see ourselves. Yet they do not directly cause our feelings. Although how we interpret what others say may lead us to feel certain ways, we can't hold them directly responsible for our feelings. In relationships with manipulative or hurtful people, you may find it useful either to communicate in ways that don't enable the other and that do preserve your integrity or to leave the relationship before it jeopardizes your own well-being.

Effective communicators take responsibility for themselves by using language that owns their thoughts and feelings. They own their feelings and do not blame others for what happens in themselves. To take responsibility for your own

Table 5.1	*You*-Language and *I*-Language

You-Language	*I*-Language
You hurt me.	I feel hurt when you ignore what I say.
You make me feel small.	I feel small when you tell me that I'm selfish.
My boss intimidates me.	When my boss criticizes my work, I feel intimidated.
You're really domineering.	When you shout at me, I feel dominated.
The speaker made me feel dumb.	I felt uninformed when the speaker discussed such complex information.
You humiliated me.	I felt humiliated when you mentioned my problems in front of our friends.

feelings, rely on *I*-language instead of *you*-language. Table 5.1 gives examples of the difference.

In my work with inmates who have violent histories, one of the key skills they learn is using *I*-language. At the outset, the inmates say things such as, "She made me hit her by what she did." Through instruction, exercises, and practice, they learn to change their *you*-language to *I*-language, saying, "I hit her because I didn't like how she was acting." The inmates tell me that learning *I*-language is empowering because it helps them see that they have more control over their actions than they had realized.

There are two differences between *I*-language and *you*-language. First, *I*-statements own responsibility, whereas *you*-statements project it onto another person. *You*-language is likely to arouse defensiveness, which doesn't facilitate healthy communication. Second, *I*-statements offer more description than *you*-statements. *You*-statements tend to be abstract accusations, which is one reason they're ineffective in promoting change. *I*-statements, on the other hand, provide concrete descriptions of behaviors and feelings without directly blaming another person for how we feel.

Some people feel awkward when they first start using *I*-language. This is natural because most of us are accustomed to using *you*-language. With commitment and practice, however, you can learn to communicate using *I*-language. Once you feel comfortable using it, you will find that *I*-language has many advantages. It is less likely than *you*-language to make others defensive, so *I*-language opens the doors for dialogue.

I-language is also more honest. We deceive ourselves when we say, "You made me feel . . . " because others don't control how we feel. Finally, *I*-language is more empowering than *you*-language. When we say, "You hurt me," or "You made me feel bad," we give control of our emotions to others. This reduces our personal sense of agency and, by extension, our motivation to change what is happening. Using *I*-language allows us to own our feelings while also explaining to others how we interpret their behaviors.

To practice using *I*-language, complete the activity "Learning to Use *I*-Language" via MindTap for *Communication in Our Lives*.

> **ROTH** *I never realized how often I use you-language. I'm always saying my girlfriend makes me feel happy or my father makes me feel like a failure. What I'm beginning to see is that they really don't control my feelings. I do.*

Respect What Others Say About Their Feelings and Ideas

Has anyone ever said to you, "You shouldn't feel that way"? If so, you know how infuriating it can be to be told that your feelings aren't valid, appropriate, or acceptable. It's equally destructive to be told our thoughts are wrong. When someone says, "How can you think something so stupid?" we feel devalued. Effective communicators don't disparage what others say about what they feel and think. Even if you don't feel or think the same way, you can still respect another person as the expert on her or his perspective.

We also disrespect others when we speak for them instead of letting them speak for themselves. In Chapter 2, we learned about mind reading, and it is relevant to this discussion too. As we have seen, our distinct experiences and ways of interpreting life make each of us unique. We seldom, if ever, completely grasp what another person feels or thinks. Although it is supportive to engage in dual perspective, it isn't supportive to presume that we fully understand someone else's feelings or thoughts, especially when he or she differs from us in important ways. It's particularly important not to assume we understand people from other cultures or social communities.

Respecting how others express their thoughts and feelings is a cornerstone of effective communication. We also grow when we open ourselves to perspectives, feelings, and thoughts that differ from our own. If you don't understand what others say, ask them to elaborate. This shows you are interested and respect their expertise and experience.

Strive for Accuracy and Clarity

Because symbols are arbitrary, abstract, and ambiguous, the potential for misunderstanding always exists. Although we cannot entirely eliminate misunderstandings, we can minimize them.

Be Aware of Levels of Abstraction Misunderstandings are most likely when language is very abstract. For instance, suppose a professor says, "Your papers should demonstrate a sophisticated conceptual grasp of the material and its pragmatic implications." Would you know how to write a paper to satisfy the professor? You might not, because the language is very abstract and unclear. Here's a more concrete description: "Your papers should include definitions of the concepts

Used by permission of Mischa Richter and Harold Bakken

"Well, then, if 'commandments' seems too harsh to me, and 'guidelines' seems too wishy-washy to you, how about 'the 10 Policy Statements'?"

and specific examples that show how they apply in real life." With this less abstract statement, you would have a better idea of what the professor expected.

Abstract language is not always inadvisable. As we have seen, abstract language allows us to generalize, which is necessary and useful. The goal is to use a level of abstraction that suits particular communication objectives and situations. Abstract words are appropriate when speakers and listeners have similar concrete knowledge about what is being discussed. For example, a couple who have been dating for a year might talk about "light movies" and "heavy movies" as shorthand ways to refer to two kinds of films. Because they have seen many movies together, they have shared referents for the abstract terms *light* and *heavy*, and misunderstanding is unlikely.

Abstract language is particularly likely to lead to misunderstandings when people talk about how they want one another to change. Concrete language and specific examples help people share understandings of which behaviors are unwelcome and which ones are wanted. For example, "I want you to be more responsible about your job" does not explain what would count as being more responsible. Is it arriving on time, taking on extra assignments, or something else? It isn't clear what the speaker wants unless more concrete descriptions are supplied. Likewise, "I want to be closer" could mean the speaker wants to spend more time together, talk about the relationship, do things together, or anything else. Vague abstractions promote misunderstanding if people don't share concrete referents.

Qualify Language   Another way to increase the clarity of communication is to qualify language. Two types of language should be qualified. First, we should qualify generalizations so we don't mislead ourselves or others. "Politicians are crooked" is a false statement because it overgeneralizes. A more accurate statement would be, "A number of politicians have been shown to have accepted paybacks for favors." Qualifying reminds us of the limitations of what we say.

To develop your skill in using qualified language, complete the activity "Practicing Using Qualified Language" via MindTap for *Communication in Our Lives*.

We should also qualify language when describing and evaluating people. **Static evaluation** consists of assessments that suggest that something is unchanging or frozen in time. These are particularly troublesome when applied to people: "Ann is selfish," "Don is irresponsible," or "Bob is generous." Whenever we use the word *is*, we suggest that something is inherent and fixed. In reality, we aren't static but continuously changing. A person who is selfish at one time may not be at another. A person who is irresponsible on one occasion may be responsible in other situations.

To develop skill in avoiding static language, complete the activity "Guarding Against Static Language" via MindTap for *Communication in Our Lives*.

Indexing is a technique developed by early communication scholars that allows us to note that our statements reflect only specific times and circumstances (Korzybski, 1948). To index, we would say "Ann$_{\text{June 6, 1997}}$ acted selfishly," "Don$_{\text{on the task committee}}$ was irresponsible," Bob$_{\text{in college}}$ was generous." See how indexing ties description to a specific time and circumstance? Mental indexing reminds us that we and others are able to change in remarkable ways.

> **ROY**   *I had a couple of accidents right after I got my driver's license. Most teenagers do, right? But to hear my father, you'd think I am a bad driver today. Those accidents were 5 years ago, and I haven't even had a ticket since then. But he still talks about "reckless Roy."*

We've considered four principles for improving the effectiveness of verbal communication. Engaging in dual perspective is the first principle and a foundation for all others. A second guideline is to take responsibility for our own feelings and thoughts by using *I*-language. Third, we should respect others as the experts on what they feel and think and not speak for them or presume we know what they think and feel. The fourth principle is to strive for clarity by choosing appropriate degrees of abstraction, qualifying generalizations, and indexing evaluations, particularly ones applied to people.

BEYOND THE CLASSROOM

Let's take the material in this chapter beyond the classroom by thinking about how what you've learned about verbal communication might apply to the workplace, ethical choices, and engagement with the broader world.

1. **Workplace.** In this chapter, we discovered verbal interaction is guided by constitutive and regulative rules. Think about a place where you work or where you worked in the past. Identify two key rules of each type and analyze how they shaped communication in that work site.

2. **Ethics.** Articulate the ethical basis for the third guideline presented in this chapter: Respect what others say about their thoughts and feelings. Why might it be ethical to do so and unethical not to do so?

3. **Engagement.** Subordinate groups are often defined by others who have the power to name them. Yet subordinate groups may eventually challenge the names others confer on them. In the 1960s, blacks in the United States rejected names that had been applied to members of their race and advanced new names they chose for themselves: African American and Afro American. In the 1990s, people who are not heterosexual began resisting names that had been applied to them and using self-definitions. Thinking about these two examples, consider definitions others impose on groups that are currently subordinate in the United States. How do the labels define members of the group? If you want to extend this exercise, talk with members of these groups and ask how they would define themselves or what words they would like others to use when referring to them.

CHAPTER SUMMARY

 Practice and review the content in this chapter.

In this chapter, we've discussed the world of words and meaning, which make up the uniquely human universe of symbol users. Because symbols are arbitrary, ambiguous, and abstract, they have no inherent meanings. Instead, we actively construct meaning by interpreting symbols based on perspectives gleaned through interaction with others and our personal experiences. We also punctuate to create meaning in communication.

We use symbols to define, evaluate, and organize our experiences. In addition, we use symbols to think hypothetically so we can consider alternatives and inhabit all three dimensions of time. Finally, symbols allow us to self-reflect so we can monitor our own behaviors.

Because symbols are abstract, arbitrary, and ambiguous, misunderstandings can occur between communicators. We can reduce the likelihood of misunderstandings by being sensitive to levels of abstraction. In addition, we should engage in dual perspective, own our thoughts and feelings, respect what others say about how they think and feel, and monitor abstractness, generalizations, and static evaluations. In Chapter 6, we will continue our discussion of the world of human communication by exploring the fascinating realm of nonverbal behavior.

APPLYING COMMUNICATION IN OUR LIVES

Communication in Our Lives is supported by a MindTap, a new online learning platform that delivers content, assignments, and a tailored presentation of the course curriculum created by your instructor. MindTap combines all of your learning tools–readings, multimedia, activities and assessments–into a singular learning unit that guides you through the course. Practice and Present, a unique tool within MindTap, allows you to upload your speech video files for practice or for a grade, comment on your peer's speeches and review your grades. MindTap also includes Speech Builder Express, a powerful tool that guides you through the speech outline and preparation process. For more information or to access MindTap, visit cengagebrain.com.

DEFINITIONS OF KEY CONCEPTS

 MindTap™ Review your **Flashcards**.

abstract Removed from concrete reality. Symbols are abstract because they are inferences and generalizations derived from a total reality.

ambiguous Subject to more than one interpretation. Symbols are ambiguous because their meanings vary from person to person and context to context.

arbitrary Random; not determined by necessity. Symbols are arbitrary because there is no particular reason for any one symbol to stand for a certain referent.

communication rules Shared understandings of what communication means and what behaviors are appropriate in various situations.

constitutive rules Communication rules that define what communication means by specifying how certain communicative acts are to be counted.

dual perspective The ability to understand another person's perspective, beliefs, thoughts, or feelings.

hypothetical thought Cognitive awareness of experiences and ideas that are not part of the concrete, present situation.

indexing A technique of noting that statements reflect specific times and circumstances and may not apply to other times or circumstances.

loaded language An extreme form of evaluative language that relies on words that strongly slant perceptions and hence meanings.

punctuation Defining the beginning and ending of interaction or interaction episodes.

regulative rules Communication rules that regulate interaction by specifying when, how, where, and with whom to talk about certain things.

static evaluation Assessments that suggest something is unchanging or static. "Bob is impatient" is a static evaluation.

symbol An arbitrary, ambiguous, and abstract representation of a phenomenon. Symbols are the basis of language, much nonverbal behavior, and human thought.

totalizing Responding to people as if one aspect of them were the sum total of who they are.

FOR FURTHER REFLECTION AND DISCUSSION

 MindTap

1. Pay attention to *I-* and *you*-language in your own communication and that of others. What happens when you switch a *you*-statement to an *I*-statement? Does it change how you feel or what happens in interaction?

2. What is a good term for describing someone with whom you have a serious romance? *Boyfriend* and *girlfriend* no longer work for many people. Do you prefer *significant other, romantic partner, special friend,* or another term? Why?

 Ethics

3. What ethical responsibilities should accompany the right to free speech? Do you think individuals have an unqualified right to say whatever they want or are there limits to what people should be allowed to say?

4. Identify communication rules for online conversations. What counts as joking (how do you indicate you're joking)? What counts as flaming? How is interaction regulated with rules for turn taking and length of comment?

SHARPEN YOUR SKILL MindTap™

1. Communication Rules

Identify constitutive and regulative rules you follow when you are interacting on the job and when you are with your family.

Constitutive Rules

What counts as being attentive in a team meeting at work?
What counts as being attentive to a romantic partner?
What counts as being respectful of parents?
What counts as being responsible on the job?
What counts as showing affection to parents and stepparents?

Regulative Rules

When is it appropriate to interrupt parents, friends, or coworkers?

What topics are appropriate during family dinner conversation?
With which family members do you talk about personal issues?
With which family members do you talk about money problems?

2. Assessing Your Stereotypes

Identify a stereotype you use, and consider 10 people to whom you might apply it. Identify differences between the people. At first, this may be difficult because stereotypes gloss over differences. What do you discover as you look for individual variations in the people you lumped together under a single symbol?

EXPERIENCING COMMUNICATION IN OUR LIVES MindTap™

CASE STUDY: *The Roommates*

A video of the conversation scripted here is featured in your Chapter 5 MindTap for *Communication in Our Lives*. Select "The Roommates" to watch the video. Improve your own communication skills by reading, watching, and evaluating this communication encounter.

© Cengage Learning

Bernadette and Celia were assigned to be roommates a month ago when the school year began. Initially, both were pleased with the match because they discovered commonalities in their interests and backgrounds. They are both sophomores from small towns, they have similar tastes in music and television programs, and they both like to stay up late and sleep in.

Lately, however, Bernadette has been irritated by Celia's housekeeping or lack of it. Celia leaves her clothes lying all over the room. If they cook in, Celia often leaves the pans and dishes for hours, and then it's usually Bernadette who cleans them. Bernadette feels she has to talk to Celia about this problem, but she hasn't figured out how or when to talk. When Celia gets in from classes, Bernadette is sitting and reading a textbook on her bed.

CELIA: Hey Bernie, how's it going?

Celia drops her book bag in the middle of the floor, flops on the bed, and kicks her s[...] on the floor. As Bernadette watches, she feels her frustration peaking and decides now is th[...] to talk to Celia about the problem.

BERNADETTE: You shouldn't do that. You make me nuts the way you just throw your stuff all over the room.

CELIA: I don't "throw my stuff all over the room." I just took off my shoes and put my books down, like I do every day.

BERNADETTE: No, you didn't. You dropped your bag right in the middle of the room, and you kicked your shoes where they happen to fall without ever noticing how messy they look. And you're right—that is what you do every day.

CELIA: There's nothing wrong with wanting to be comfortable in my own room. Are we suddenly going for the Good Housekeeping Seal of Approval?

BERNADETTE: Comfortable is one thing. But you're so messy. Your mess makes me really miserable.

CELIA: Since when? This is the first I've heard about it.

BERNADETTE: Since we started rooming together, but I didn't want to say anything about how angry you make me. I just can't stand it any more. You shouldn't be so messy.

CELIA: Sounds to me like you've got a problem—you, not me.

BERNADETTE: Well it's you and your mess that are my problem. Do you have to be such a slob?

QUESTIONS FOR ANALYSIS AND DISCUSSION MindTap™

You can answer these questions and see my responses to them online via MindTap for Chapter 5.

1. Identify examples of *you*-language in this conversation. How would you change it to *I*-language?

2. Identify examples of loaded language and ambiguous language.

3. Do you agree with Celia that the problem is Bernadette's, not hers?

4. Do Celia and Bernadette seem to engage in dual perspective to understand each other?

...hoes off
...e time

What you do sp...
so loud that I cannot
hear what you say.

Ralph Waldo Emerson

Ryan McVay/Digital Vision/Getty Images

The Nonverbal Dimension of Communication

MindTap

Review the chapter **Learning Objectives** and **Start** with a quick warm up activity.

While a student at Yale, Kenta Koga interned with a Japanese company, hoping that would lead to a permanent position. It didn't. Kenta was criticized by his supervisors for speaking up and for crossing his arms in front of senior colleagues. A student from Brown University, also interning in a Japanese company, was told she could not be hired because she laughed too much (Tabuchi, 2012).

Maria noticed a nice-looking guy who was studying two tables away from her in the library. When he looked up at her, she lowered her eyes. After a

SHARPEN YOUR SKILL

At the end of this chapter, refer to the Sharpen Your Skill features, Communicating Closeness and Environmental Awareness, to apply concepts from Chapter 6.

moment, she looked back at him just for a second. A few minutes later he came over, sat down beside her, and introduced himself.

These examples illustrate the power of nonverbal communication. In the first case, the students interning in Japanese companies violated nonverbal norms of the host country. In the library scene, we see a gendered pattern of nonverbal communication. Maria follows feminine communication norms by indirectly signaling her interest and waiting for the man to initiate contact. In turn, he enacts the rules of masculine communication culture by gazing directly at her and moving to her table.

Gender, ethnicity, sexual orientation, and socioeconomic class are identities that we create and sustain by performing them day in and day out. Candice West and Don Zimmerman (1987) note that we "do gender" all the time by behaving in ways that announce that we are feminine or masculine. We also communicate nonverbally to perform, or "do," ethnicity, race, class, and sexual orientation. In this sense, nonverbal communication, like language, is a primary way in which we announce who we are. The intricate system of nonverbal communication helps us establish identity, negotiate relationships, and create environments we enjoy.

Nonverbal behavior is a major dimension of human communication. The nonverbal system accounts for 65% to 93% of the total meaning of communication (Birdwhistell, 1970; Hickson, Stacks, & Moore, 2003; Mehrabian, 1981). One reason for the impact of nonverbal communication is its breadth: It includes everything from dress and eye contact to body posture and vocal inflection.

In this chapter, we explore the fascinating realm of nonverbal interaction. We will identify principles of nonverbal communication and then discuss types of nonverbal behavior and ways to improve our effectiveness in nonverbal communication.

PRINCIPLES OF NONVERBAL COMMUNICATION

Nonverbal communication is all aspects of communication other than words themselves. It includes how we utter words (i.e., inflection, volume), features of environments that affect interaction (i.e., temperature, lighting), and objects that influence personal images and interaction patterns (i.e., dress, jewelry, furniture). Five key points highlight the nature and power of nonverbal communication to affect meaning.

MindTap
Read, highlight and take notes online.

Is Similar to and Different From Verbal Communication
Nonverbal communication and verbal communication are similar in some ways and different in others. We'll identify both the similarities and the differences.

Similarities   Like verbal communication, nonverbal behavior is symbolic, which means it is ambiguous, abstract, and arbitrary. Thus, we can't be sure what a smile or a gesture means, and we can't guarantee that others understand the meanings we intend to express with our own nonverbal behaviors. Second, like verbal communication, our nonverbal behavior and our interpretations of others' nonverbal behaviors are guided by constitutive and regulative rules.

A third similarity between the two communication systems is that both are culture bound. Our nonverbal communication reflects and reproduces values and norms of the particular culture and social communities to which we belong (Hickson et al., 2003). For instance, dress considered appropriate for women varies across cultures: Some women in the United States wear miniskirts; women in some other countries wear veils. Dress also reflects organizational identities: Bankers, attorneys, and many other professionals are expected to wear business suits or dresses; carpenters usually wear jeans; medical professionals typically wear white lab coats.

Last, both verbal and nonverbal communication may be either intentional or unintentional. Sometimes we carefully sculpt our appearance, just as we sometimes control our verbal communication. For instance, in a job interview we are highly conscious of our dress and posture as well as the words we use. At other times, our verbal and nonverbal communication may be unintentional. If an interviewer asks you a difficult question, your facial expression may reveal that you are caught off guard, or you may accidentally speak ungrammatically.

Different cultures prescribe different styles of dress.

Frans Lemmens/The Image Bank/Getty Images

Differences   There are also differences between the two systems of communication. First, nonverbal communication is perceived as more honest. If verbal and nonverbal behaviors are inconsistent, most people trust the nonverbal behavior. There is little evidence that nonverbal behavior actually is more trustworthy than verbal communication; after all, we often control it quite deliberately. Nonetheless, it tends to be *perceived* as more trustworthy (Andersen, 1999).

Second, unlike verbal communication, nonverbal communication is multichanneled. Verbal communication usually occurs within a single channel; oral verbal communication is received through hearing, and written verbal communication and sign language are received through sight. In contrast, nonverbal communication may be seen, felt, heard, smelled, and tasted. We often receive nonverbal communication simultaneously through two or more channels, as when we feel a hug while hearing a whispered "I love you."

Finally, verbal communication is discrete, whereas nonverbal is more continuous. Verbal symbols start and stop; we begin speaking at one moment and stop speaking at another moment. In contrast, nonverbal communication tends to flow continually. Before we speak, our facial expressions and posture express our feelings; as we speak, our body movements and appearance communicate; and after we speak, our posture changes, perhaps relaxing.

Supplements or Replaces Verbal Communication

Communication researchers have identified five ways that nonverbal behaviors interact with verbal communication (Andersen, 1999; Richmond & McCroskey, 1995b). First, nonverbal behaviors repeat verbal messages. For example, you might say "yes" while nodding your head. In making a public presentation, you might hold up one, then two, and then three fingers to signal to listeners that you are moving from the first to the second to the third points of your speech.

Second, nonverbal behaviors may highlight verbal communication, as when you use inflection to emphasize certain words ("This is the *most* serious consequence of the policy that I oppose"). Third, nonverbal behaviors may complement or add to words. When you see a friend, you might say, "I'm glad to see you" and underline the verbal message with a smile. Public speakers often emphasize verbal statements with forceful gestures and increases in volume and inflection. Fourth, nonverbal behaviors may contradict verbal messages, as when a group member says, "Nothing's wrong" in a hostile tone of voice. Finally, we

COMMUNICATION HIGHLIGHT

Cross-Cultural Nonverbal Clashes

Cross-cultural misunderstandings aren't limited to verbal communication, according to Siu Wa Tang, chair of the Department of Psychiatry at the University of California at Irvine (Emmons, 1998). When Tang and a colleague visited pharmaceutical plants in Changchun, China, Tang was well accepted, but his colleague was not. The Chinese took an immediate and strong dislike to the colleague. Tang says the problem was facial expressions. His U.S. colleague used facial expressions that Americans would interpret as showing honesty and directness but which the Chinese people interpreted as aggressive and rude.

Based on this experience, Tang conducted experiments to test the universality of facial expressions. He found that a few basic feelings and expressions were understood across cultures. Happiness and sadness, for example, were nonverbally expressed in similar ways. However, other facial expressions did not translate so well. Nine out of 10 Americans interpreted a photograph of a face as showing fear, yet 6 of 10 Japanese identified the same photograph as expressing surprise or sadness. A photo identified by 9 of 10 Americans as showing anger was interpreted by 75% of Japanese as expressing disgust or contempt. Another source of cross-cultural nonverbal misunderstandings is eye contact. Americans generally consider it polite to look another person in the eye when conversing, but Japanese look at each other's cheeks; to look another in the eyes is perceived as very aggressive.

Cross-cultural communication clashes may also occur over gift giving (Axtell, 2007). An American might offend a Chinese with the gift of a clock because in China clocks symbolize death. Giving a gift to an Arab on first meeting would be interpreted as a bribe. Bringing flowers to a dinner hosted by a person from Kenya would puzzle the host because in Kenya flowers are given only to express sympathy for a loss. And the Swiss consider even numbers of flowers bad luck, so giving a dozen is inappropriate, and the recipient would probably interpret the gift as reflecting ill will.

sometimes substitute nonverbal behaviors for verbal ones. For instance, you might roll your eyes to indicate that you are exasperated by something.

Regulates Interaction

You generally know when someone else has finished speaking, when a professor welcomes discussion from students, and when someone expects you to speak. But how do you know? There are no explicit, verbal cues to tell us when to speak and when to keep silent. Instead, conversations usually are regulated nonverbally (Guerrero & Floyd, 2006). We use our eyes and body posture to indicate that we want to enter conversations, and speakers step back from a podium to indicate that they have finished a speech. We invite people to speak by looking directly at them, often after asking a question (Knapp & Hall, 2006).

DARCY *I know one guy who dominates every conversation. I'd never noticed this until we studied how nonverbal behaviors regulate turn taking. This guy won't look at others when he's talking. He looks out into space, or sometimes he gives you a hard stare, but he never looks at anyone like he's saying, "Okay, your turn now."*

Establishes Relationship-Level Meanings

In Chapter 1, we noted that there are two levels of meaning in communication. To review: The content level of meaning concerns actual information or literal meaning; the relationship level of meaning defines communicators' identities and the relationship between them. Nonverbal communication is often more powerful than verbal language in conveying relationship-level meanings (Manusov & Patterson, 2006).

Nonverbal communication is used to convey three dimensions of relationship-level meanings: *responsiveness, liking,* and *power* (Mehrabian, 1981). Yet how we convey relationship meanings and what specific nonverbal behaviors mean depends on the communication rules we've learned in our particular cultures and social communities.

Responsiveness We use eye contact, facial expressions, and body posture to indicate interest in others, as Maria did in one of the examples that opened this chapter. We signal friendliness by laughing. But as the example with the interns in Japanese companies, laughter doesn't mean the same thing in all cultures. In cohesive groups in Western culture, there is typically a great deal of nonverbal communication indicating responsiveness. Less cohesive groups include fewer nonverbal indicators of engagement.

MARYAM *Americans do more than one thing at a time. In Nepal, when we talk with someone, we are with that person. We do not also write on paper or have the television on. We talk with the person. It is hard for me to accept the custom of giving only some attention to each other in conversation.*

As Maryam's observation indicates, different cultures teach members distinct rules for showing responsiveness. In the West, feminine speech communities emphasize sensitivity to others, so women generally are better than men at interpreting others' emotions (Burgoon & Le Poire, 1999). Decoding may be a survival strategy for people in subordinate standpoints. Their well-being and sometimes their physical safety depend on being able to decipher the feelings and intentions of those with greater power.

> **ELLEN** *Secretaries are the best decoders. They can read their bosses' moods in a heartbeat. I am a secretary, part time now that I'm taking courses, and I can tell exactly what my boss is thinking. Sometimes I know what he feels or will do before he does. I have to know when he can be interrupted, when he feels generous, and when not to cross his path.*

Liking   A second dimension of relationship-level meaning is liking. In Western societies, smiles and friendly touching usually indicate positive feelings, whereas frowns and belligerent postures express antagonism. Have you ever noticed how often political candidates shake hands, slap backs, and otherwise touch people whose votes they want? Similarly, in work settings, people who like one another often sit together, exchange eye contact, and smile at one another.

Power   The third aspect of relationship-level meanings is power, or control. We use nonverbal behaviors to assert dominance, express deference, and negotiate status and influence (Andersen, 1999; Remland, 2000). Powerful people, such as bosses, touch those with less power, such as secretaries, more than those with less power touch those with more power (Hall, Coats, & Smith-LeBeau, 2004). In general, men assume more space and use greater volume and more forceful gestures than women (Hall, 1987; Major, Schmidlin, & Williams, 1990).

> **RAMONA** *In my home, my father sits at the head of the table, and he has his chair in the family room and his workroom. My mother does not have her chair anywhere in the house, and she has no room of her own either.*

The connection between power and space is evident in the fact that CEOs usually have spacious offices, entry-level and mid-level professionals have smaller offices, and secretaries often have minuscule workstations, even though secretaries often store and manage more material than those higher in the organizational chain of command. Regulative communication rules also tacitly specify that people with status or power have the right to enter the space of people with less power, but the converse is not true. Space also reflects power differences in families. Adults usually have more space than children; like Ramona's father, men more

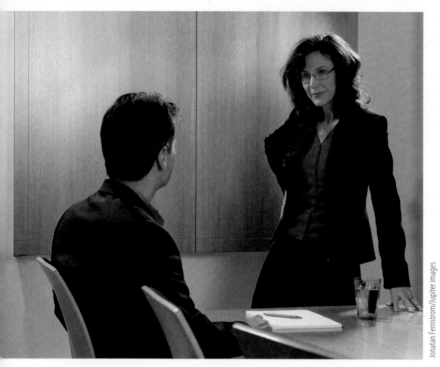

Jonatan Fernstrom/Jupiter Images

What nonverbal cues to power relations do you perceive in this photo?

often than women have their own rooms and sit at the head of the table. Men are also more likely than women to move into others' space, as the man in the library moved to Maria's table in the example at the beginning of this chapter.

Reflects Cultural Values

Like verbal communication, nonverbal patterns reflect communication rules of specific cultures and social communities (Manusov & Patterson, 2006). This implies that most nonverbal behavior isn't instinctual but learned in the process of socialization.

Have you ever seen the bumper sticker that says, "If you can read this, you're too close"? That slogan proclaims North Americans' fierce territoriality. We value our private spaces, and we resent—and sometimes fight—anyone who trespasses on what we consider our turf. We want private homes with rooms for each person and large lots. On the job, a reserved parking space and a private office with a door mark status; employees with lower status often park in satellite lots and share offices or have workstations without doors. In cultures where individuality is less valued, people are less territorial. For instance, Brazilians routinely stand close together in shops, buses, and elevators, and when they bump into each other, they don't apologize or draw back. Similarly, in countries such as Hong Kong, people are used to living and working in very close quarters, so territoriality is uncommon (Chan, 1999). In some cultures—Italy, for example—dramatic nonverbal displays of emotion are typical, but other cultures consider more reserved displays of emotion appropriate (Matsumoto, Franklin, Choi, Rogers, & Tatani, 2002).

SUCHENG   *In the United States, each person has so much room. Every individual has a separate room in which to sleep and sometimes another separate room in which to work. Also, I see that each family here lives in a separate house. People have much less space in China. Families live together, with sons bringing their families into their parents' home and all sharing the same space. At first when I came here it felt strange to have so much space, but now I sometimes feel very crowded when I go home.*

Patterns of eye contact also reflect cultural values. In the United States, frankness and assertion are valued, so meeting another's eyes is considered appropriate and a demonstration of personal honesty. Yet, as we've noted, in many

Asian and northern European countries, direct eye contact is considered abrasive and disrespectful (Axtell, 2007; Samovar, Porter, & McDaniel, 2009). On the other hand, in Brazil, eye contact often is so intense that people from the United States consider it rude staring.

Greeting behaviors also vary across cultures. In the United States and many other Western countries, the handshake is the most common way to greet. Arab men are more likely to kiss each other on both cheeks as a form of greeting. Embraces are typical greetings in Mexico. Bowing is the standard form of greeting in some Asian cultures (Samovar & Porter, 2009).

In sum, we've noted five important features of the nonverbal communication system. First, there are similarities and differences between nonverbal and verbal communication. Second, nonverbal behavior can supplement or replace verbal communication. Third, nonverbal behaviors regulate interaction. Fourth, nonverbal communication is often especially powerful in establishing and expressing relational meanings. Fifth, nonverbal behaviors reflect cultural values and are learned, not instinctive. We're now ready to explore the many types of behavior in the intricate nonverbal communication system.

TYPES OF NONVERBAL COMMUNICATION

In this section, we will consider nine forms of nonverbal behavior, noticing how we use each to communicate.

Kinesics

Kinesics is body position and body motions, including those of the face. Our bodies express a great deal about how we see ourselves. A speaker who stands erect and is relaxed announces self-confidence, whereas someone who slouches and shuffles may seem unsure of himself or herself. People whose nonverbal communication conveys vitality and assurance are less likely to be attacked than people whose nonverbal communication indicates less vigor (Gunns, Johnson, & Hudson, 2002).

How we position ourselves relative to others may express our feelings toward them. On work teams, friends and allies often sit together, and competitors typically maintain distance. We communicate dissatisfaction by moving away from others and by decreasing smiles and eye contact (Walker & Trimboli, 1989). Americans often cross their legs, but this is perceived as offensive in Ghana and Turkey (Samovar, Porter, & McDaniel, 2011).

Our faces are intricate messengers. Our eyes can shoot daggers of anger, issue challenges, express skepticism, or radiate love. With our faces, we can indicate disapproval (scowls), doubt (raised eyebrows), love (eye gazes), and challenge (stares). The face is particularly powerful in conveying responsiveness and liking (Gueguen & De Gail, 2003).

Our eyes communicate some of the most important and complex messages about how we feel. If you watch infants, you'll notice that they focus on others' eyes. As adults, we often look at eyes to judge emotions, honesty, interest, and self-confidence. Among Westerners, eye contact tends to increase feelings of closeness.

Haptics

Haptics is physical touch. Touch is the first of our senses to develop, and touching and being touched are essential to a healthy life (Whitman, White, O'Mara, & Goeke-Morey, 1999).

Touching also communicates power and status. Cultural views of women as more touchable than men are reflected in gendered patterns. Women tend to touch others to show liking and intimacy, whereas men more typically rely on touch to assert power and control (Andersen, 1999; Jhally & Katz, 2001).

YVETTE   *When I was pregnant, total strangers would walk up to me and touch my belly. It was amazing—and disturbing. They seemed to think they had a right to touch me or that the baby wasn't me, so they could touch him. Amazing!*

Physical Appearance

Western culture places an extremely high value on **physical appearance**. For this reason, most of us notice how others look, and we form initial evaluations based on their appearance. What we notice about others' appearance leads us to

Touch conveys emotions.

Crystal Kirk/Shutterstock.com

COMMUNICATION HIGHLIGHT

Kissing: Two Weeks of a Lifetime

Kissing is usually not considered a science, but hold on! Sheril Kirshenbaum's (2011) new book, *The science of kissing*, provides some facts about kissing.

- About two-thirds of people tilt their head to the right when kissing.

- The racing heart and elevated blood pressure that often accompanies kissing is caused by the neurotransmitter dopamine, which is related to pleasure and emotional responses.

- Passionate, smoldering kissing burns 6.4 calories a minute.

- Over a life time, the average person spends approximately 2 weeks kissing.

- Men tend to like sloppy, wet kisses more than women, perhaps because those kisses transfer men's saliva, which contains testosterone and may enhance women's interest in further intimacy.

- Closed-lip kisses require only 2 facial muscles whereas French kisses involve all 34 facial muscles.

- How many bacteria are exchanged in kissing? You don't want to know: millions—yes, millions!

form judgments of how attractive they are and to make inferences about their personalities. Although our judgments and inferences may be inaccurate, they can affect our decisions about friendships, dating, hiring, and promotion. In fact, economist Daniel Hamermesh (2011) reports that people who are above average in attractiveness are likely to make an average of 3% to 4% more than people who are below average in attractiveness. That could add up to well over $200,000 over the course of an average career.

Cultures stipulate ideals for physical form. Currently, cultural ideals in the West emphasize thinness and softness in women and muscularity and height in men (Davies-Popelka, 2011; Lamb & Brown, 2006; Levin & Kilbourne, 2008; Rhodes, 2010). In an effort to meet these ideals, some men engage in excessive body building or use steroids, and many people—particularly women—develop eating disorders. If you'd like to learn about eating disorders and ways to help people who have them, use your MindTap for *Communication in Our Lives* to access **WebLink 6.1** and visit the National Eating Disorders Association's website.

 MindTap

General Western standards for attractiveness are qualified by ethnic identity. African Americans generally admire fuller figures than European Americans, and this is especially true among African Americans who identify strongly with African American culture (Mernissi, 2004; Schooler, Ward, Merriwether, & Caruthers, 2004; Walker, 2007).

CASS   *I found out how much appearance matters when I was in an auto accident. It messed up my face so that I had scars all over one side and on my forehead. All of a sudden, nobody was asking me out. All these guys who had been so crazy about me before the accident lost interest. Some of my girlfriends seemed uneasy about being seen with me. When I first had the wreck, I was so glad to be alive that I didn't even think about plastic surgery. After a couple of months of seeing how others treated me, however, I had the surgery.*

Artifacts

Artifacts are personal objects with which we announce our identities and personalize our environments. We craft our image by how we dress, the jewelry we wear, and the objects we carry and use. George W. Bush insisted on formal dress—coat and tie—at all times in the Oval Office (Stolberg, 2009). When Barack Obama became president, he established a less formal working culture in the White House. He sometimes takes off his jacket while working in the Oval Office, and he often skips the tie on weekends. Like Bush and Obama, most of us dress according to our ideas of professionalism. To learn more about norms for professional dressing, use your MindTap to access **WebLink 6.2**.

 MindTap™

We also use artifacts to define settings and personal territories. At annual meetings of companies, the CEO usually speaks from a podium that bears the company logo. In much the same manner, we claim our private spaces by filling them with photos of family members and other objects that matter to us and reflect our experiences and values. Lovers of art adorn their homes with paintings and sculptures. Religious families display pictures of holy scenes and the *Bible*, the *Qur'an*, the *Vedas*, the *Koran*, or another sacred text.

NAOMI   *I've moved a lot since coming to college—dorm, apartment, another apartment, and another apartment. I never feel a place is home until I put a photograph of my grandmother holding me on my dresser. Then it's home.*

Artifacts can express personal identity. For instance, body piercing has become popular, particularly among people under 25. Because some people find it unattractive, however, restaurant chains such as Chili's have established policies to limit piercings that might offend customers: Ears are the only visible body part that employees may pierce ("Business Bulletin," 1996). Approximately one-third of Americans in the 25- to 29-year age range have at least one tattoo (Opfer, 2011). But many people who get tattoos later want to get rid of them. Enter people like Dr. Tattoff who have performed more than 110,000 tattoo removals (Opfer, 2011).

We also use artifacts to express ethnic identity. Kwanzaa is an African American holiday tradition that celebrates the centrality of home, family, and community. The kinara is a branched candleholder that holds seven candles, one of which is lit during each day of Kwanzaa (Bellamy, 1996; George, 1995). The Jewish holiday, Hanukkah, features the menorah that holds candles while Seder features an elaborate meal in which each item represents a part of Jewish history. The Christian tradition includes Christmas trees and Nativity scenes.

Artifacts chosen by others can communicate about relationships. We give gifts to say, "You matter to me." Artifacts such as engagement rings and wedding bands signify commitment. We also symbolize that we're connected to others by wearing their clothes, as when women wear male partners' shirts.

Proxemics

Proxemics is space and how we use it. Every culture has norms for using space and for how close people should be to one another (Samovar et al., 2011). In a classic study, Edward Hall (1966) found that in the United States, we interact with social acquaintances from a distance of 4 to 12 feet but are comfortable with 18 inches or less between us and close friends or romantic partners. In some cultures greater or lesser distances are considered comfortable.

Space also signals status; greater space is assumed by those of higher status. The prerogative of entering someone else's personal space is also linked to power; those with greater power are most likely to trespass into others' territory.

How space is arranged also tells us something about the expected form of interaction in the space. Formal businesses may have private offices with doors and little common space. In contrast, more casual businesses are likely to have fewer doors and more common space to encourage interaction between employees. Couples who are very interdependent tend to have greater amounts of common space and less individual space in their homes than do couples who are more independent (Werner, Altman, & Oxley, 1985). Families that enjoy interaction tend to arrange furniture to invite conversation and eye contact.

Environmental Factors

Environmental factors are elements of settings that affect how we feel and act. For instance, we respond to architecture, colors, room design, temperature, sounds, smells, and lighting. Rooms with comfortable chairs invite relaxation, whereas rooms with stiff chairs prompt formality. Research shows that students perceive professors as more credible and approachable if the professors have

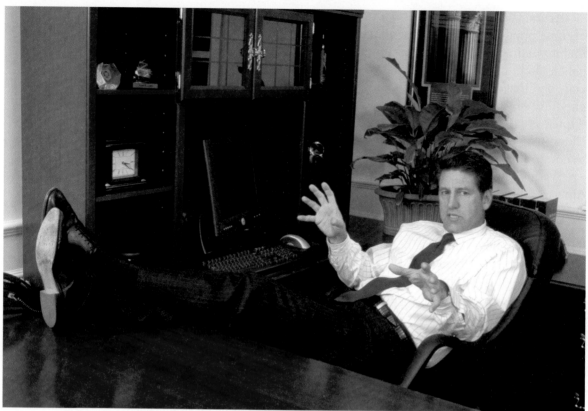

Brad Perks Lightscapes / Alamy

What does this executive's space convey about his power and openness to others?

attractively decorated offices (Taylor, Wiley, Kuo, & Sullivan, 1998). Dimly lit rooms can enhance romantic feelings, although dark rooms can be depressing.

Restaurants use environmental features to control how long people linger over meals. For example, low lights, comfortable chairs or booths, and soft music often are part of the environment in upscale restaurants where patrons tend to linger. On the other hand, fast-food eateries have hard plastic booths and bright lights, which encourage diners to eat and move on. To make a profit, inexpensive restaurants have to get people in and out as quickly as possible.

Ron Baker is an expert on classroom environments. He says that even when constructing new classroom buildings, planners are often "making the same kinds of stupid mistakes" (Bartlett, 2003, p. A36). What are those "stupid mistakes"? Lights that cause glare on laptop screens; chairs that are too small for some students; desks that won't accommodate a notebook, a laptop, and a textbook; and inadequate air-conditioning or heating. To learn more about Ron Baker's ideas on ideal classrooms, visit his Website by using your MindTap for *Communication in Our Lives* to access **WebLink 6.3**.

🌐 MindTap™

Chronemics

Chronemics is how we perceive and use time to define identities and interaction. Important people with high status can keep others waiting. Conversely, people with low status are expected to be punctual in Western society (Richmond &

Environmental Racism

According to Robert Cox (2013), president of the Sierra Club, the term *environmental racism* arose to describe a pattern whereby toxic waste dumps and hazardous industrial plants are located in low-income neighborhoods and communities of color. The pattern is clear: The space of minorities and poor people can be invaded and contaminated, but the territory of more affluent citizens cannot be.

To learn more about environmental racism (also called *environmental justice*), use your MindTap for *Communication in Our Lives* to access **WebLink 6.4.** This site provides information on the Environmental Protection Agency's strategies for preventing environmental racism.

McCroskey, 1995b). It is standard practice to have to wait, sometimes a long while, to see a doctor, even if you have an appointment. This carries the message that the doctor's time is more valuable than ours. Professors can be late to class, and students are expected to wait, but students sometimes are reprimanded if they arrive after a class begins. Subordinates are expected to report punctually to meetings, but bosses are allowed to be tardy.

Chronemics express cultural attitudes toward time. In Western societies, time is valuable, so speed is highly valued (Calero, 2005; Honoré, 2005). Thus, we replace our computers and cell phones as soon as faster models hit the market. We often try to do several things at once to get more done. Many everyday expressions reflect the cultural view that time is like money, a valuable and limited resource to be used wisely: "You're *wasting* my time." "This will *save* some time." "I don't *have* any time to *give* you." "That mistake *cost* me 3 hours." "I've *invested* a lot of time in this class, and now I'm *running out of time.*"

Many other cultures have far more relaxed attitudes toward time and punctuality. In many South American countries, it's not impolite to come late to meetings or classes, and it's not assumed that people will leave at the scheduled ending time. Whether time is treated casually, or closely watched and measured out, reflects larger cultural attitudes toward living.

The amount of time we spend with different people reflects our interpersonal priorities. A manager spends more time with a new employee who seems to have executive potential than with one who seems less impressive. A speaker spends more time responding to a question from a high-status member of the audience than to a person of lower status. We spend more time with people we like than with those we don't like or who bore us.

Paralanguage is vocal communication that does not involve words. It includes sounds, such as murmurs and gasps, and vocal qualities, such as volume, rhythm, pitch, and inflection. Our voices are versatile instruments that tell others how to interpret us and what we say. Vocal cues signal others to interpret what we say as a joke, threat, statement of fact, question, and so forth. Vocal cues

HEALTH COMMUNICATION

Sounding Like a (Wo)man

Deciding to transition from one sex to the other involves more than hormonal therapy and surgeries. It also requires retraining the voice to sound like that of the new sex. Richard Adler, Sandy Hirsch, and Michelle Mordaunt (2012) are clinicians who specialize in voice therapy for transgender people. From their work with transgender clients, they have developed evidence-based protocols for retraining the voice in the areas of pitch, intonation, volume, rate, articulation, language, resonance, and other facets of nonverbal communication.

Men who transition to women have to learn to use a higher pitch, more inflection, more pauses, and lower volume. They may also learn to cant their heads, hold more eye contact when speaking to others, and cross their legs knee over knee. For women who transition to men, the nonverbal challenges are to speak at a lower pitch, increase volume, decrease inflection, hold the head straight, use infrequent eye contact, and cross legs ankle over knee.

also express irritation. Effective public speakers know how to modulate inflection, volume, and rhythm to enhance their verbal messages.

We use our voices to communicate feelings. Whispering, for instance, often signals secrecy, and shouting conveys anger. Depending on the context, sighing may communicate empathy, boredom, or contentment. Research indicates that tone of voice is a powerful clue to feelings between marital partners. Negative vocal tones are among the most important symbols of marital dissatisfaction (Gottman, 1994b). Negative intonation may also signal dissatisfaction or disapproval in work settings. The reverse is also true: A warm voice conveys liking, and a playful lilt suggests friendliness.

We use our voices to communicate how we see ourselves and wish to be seen by others. For instance, we use a firm, confident voice in job interviews or when explaining why we deserve a raise. We also know how to make ourselves sound apologetic, seductive, or angry when it suits us. In addition to the ways we intentionally use our voices to project an image, vocal qualities we don't deliberately choose can affect how others perceive us. Pace of speaking may influence perceptions. For instance, research shows that people who speak at a slow to moderate rate are perceived as having greater control over interaction than people who speak rapidly (Tusing & Dillard, 2000).

RAYNA *When I first moved to the United States, I didn't understand many words and idioms. I did not understand that "A bird in the hand is worth two in the bush" meant it is smart to hold on to what is sure. I did not understand that "hang a right" meant to turn right. So when I did not understand, I would ask people to explain. Most times they would say the very same thing over, just louder and more slowly, like I was deaf or stupid. I felt like saying to them in a very loud, slow voice, "I am Indian, not stupid. You are stupid."*

Paralanguage also reflects our cultural heritage. For example, many African Americans' speech has more vocal range, inflection, and tonal quality than that of most European Americans (Garner, 1994). We also use paralanguage to perform gender. To perform masculinity, men use strong volume, low pitch, and limited inflection, all of which conform to cultural prescriptions for men to be assertive and emotionally controlled. To perform femininity, women tend to use higher pitch, softer volume, and more inflection. We also perform class by our pronunciation of words, our accents, and the complexity of our sentences.

Silence

A final type of nonverbal behavior is **silence,** which can communicate powerful

Antony Nagelmann/Taxi/Getty Images

Whispered secrets reflect special intimacy between people.

messages. The assertion "I'm not speaking to you" actually speaks volumes. We use silence to communicate different meanings. For instance, silence indicates contentment when intimates are so comfortable they don't need to talk. Silence can also communicate awkwardness, as you know if you've ever had trouble keeping conversation going with a new acquaintance. We feel pressured to fill the void.

Silence can also disconfirm others. In some families, children are disciplined by being ignored. No matter what the child says or does, parents refuse to acknowledge his or her existence. In later life, the silencing strategy may also surface. You know how disconfirming silence can be if you've ever said hello to someone and gotten no reply. Even if the other person didn't deliberately ignore you, you felt slighted. In some military academies, such as West Point, silencing is a recognized method of stripping a cadet of personhood if he or she is perceived as having broken the academy code. Whistle-blowers and union-busters are often shunned by peers. Similarly, the Catholic Church excommunicates people who violate its canons.

The complex system of nonverbal communication includes kinesics, haptics, physical appearance, artifacts, proxemics, environmental features, chronemics, paralanguage, and silence. We use these nonverbal behaviors to announce our identities and to communicate how we feel about relationships with others. To explore using nonverbal communication to project an identity for yourself in various situations, complete the activity "Sculpting Personal Image With Nonverbal Communication" via MindTap for *Communication in Our Lives.*

 MindTap™

In the final section of this chapter, we consider guidelines for improving the effectiveness of our nonverbal communication.

IMPROVING NONVERBAL COMMUNICATION

Nonverbal communication, like its verbal cousin, can be misinterpreted. You can reduce the likelihood of misunderstandings in nonverbal communication by following two guidelines.

Monitor Your Nonverbal Communication

The monitoring skills we have stressed in other chapters are also important for competent nonverbal communication. Think about the ways we use nonverbal behaviors to announce our identities. Are you projecting the image you desire? Do your facial and body movements represent how you see yourself and how you want others to perceive you? Do people ever tell you that you seem uninterested when they are talking to you? If so, you can monitor your nonverbal actions and modify them to more clearly communicate involvement and interest. You can also set up your spaces to invite the kind of interaction you prefer.

Interpret Others' Nonverbal Communication Tentatively

In this chapter, we've discussed findings about the meanings people tend to attach to nonverbal behaviors. It's important to realize that these are only generalizations about how we interpret nonverbal communication. We cannot state what any particular behavior means to specific people in a particular context. For instance, we've said that people who like each other tend to be physically closer when interacting. However, sometimes people prefer autonomy and want personal space. In addition, someone may maintain distance because she or he has a cold and doesn't want a partner to catch it. Also, the generalizations we've discussed may not apply to people from non-Western cultures. Ethical communicators qualify their interpretations of nonverbal behavior by considering personal and contextual considerations.

Personal Qualifications Nonverbal patterns that accurately describe most people may not apply to particular individuals. Although eye contact generally indicates responsiveness, some people close their eyes to concentrate when listening. In such cases, it would be inaccurate to conclude that a person who doesn't look at us isn't listening. Similarly, people who cross their arms and condense into a tight posture may be expressing hostility or lack of interest in interaction. However, the same behaviors might mean a person is cold. Most people use less inflection, fewer gestures, and a slack posture when they're not really interested in what they're talking about. However, fatigue can result in the same behaviors.

To avoid misinterpreting others' nonverbal communication, you can check perceptions and use *I*-language, not *you*-language, which we discussed in

Chapter 5. You can check perceptions to find out whether the way you interpret another's nonverbal behavior is what that other person means: "I sense that you're not really involved in this conversation; is that how you feel?" In addition, you can rely on *I*-language. *You*-language might lead us to inaccurately say of someone who doesn't look at us, "You're communicating lack of interest." A more responsible statement would use *I*-language to say, "When you don't look at me, I feel you're not interested in what I'm saying." Using *I*-language reminds us to take responsibility for our judgments and feelings. In addition, it reduces the likelihood that we will make others defensive by inaccurately interpreting their nonverbal behavior.

Contextual Qualifications   Like the meaning of verbal communication, the significance of nonverbal behaviors depends on the contexts in which they occur. Most people are more at ease on their own turf than on someone else's, so we tend to be more friendly and outgoing in our homes than in business meetings and public spaces. We also dress according to context. When I am on campus or in business meetings, I dress professionally, but at home, I usually wear jeans or running clothes.

In addition to our immediate settings, nonverbal communication reflects cultures. We are likely to misinterpret people from other cultures if we impose the norms and rules of our culture on them. An Arab who stands practically on top of others to talk with them is not being rude, according to his culture's standards, although Westerners might interpret him as such.

> **ELENI**   *I have been misinterpreted very much in this country. My first semester here, a professor told me he wanted me to be more assertive and to speak up in class. I could not do that, I told him. He said I should put myself forward, but I have been brought up not to do that. In Taiwan, that is very rude and ugly, and we are taught not to speak up to teachers. Now that I have been here for 3 years, I sometimes speak in classes, but I am still quieter than Americans. I know my professors think I am not so smart because I am quiet, but that is the teaching of my country.*

Even within a single culture, different social communities have distinct rules for nonverbal behavior. A man who doesn't make "listening noises" may be listening intently according to the rules of masculine speech communities. Similarly, when women nod and make listening noises while another is talking, men may misperceive them as agreeing. According to the rules typically learned in feminine social communities, ongoing feedback is a way of signaling interest, not necessarily agreement. We should adopt dual perspective when interpreting others, especially when they belong to cultures or communities that are different from ours.

BEYOND THE CLASSROOM

Let's take the material in this chapter beyond the classroom by thinking about how what you've learned about nonverbal communication might apply to the workplace, ethical choices, and engagement with the broader world.

1. **Workplace.** Visit a workplace of the type you imagine working in after you've completed your education. Analyze nonverbal communication and notice what it tells you about this particular workplace. How is space arranged? Are there individual offices or workstations that aren't isolated? If there are both, who gets the private offices? How do employees dress? How much do employees rely on nonverbal communication such as touch and eye contact to signal friendliness?

2. **Ethics.** Ethical issues surround space and who does and doesn't have access to particular spaces. Some managers of stores do not want homeless citizens in their places of business. They think that these citizens' presence would hurt business by discouraging other citizens from patronizing their stores. Yet advocates for homeless citizens say that businesses are places that are open to the public, and business owners and managers can't allow only some of the public to enter their establishments. What do you think is the most ethical way to address the issue of whether businesses should allow homeless citizens into their establishments?

3. **Engagement.** Attend a gathering of people from a culture different from yours. It might be a meeting at a Jewish temple if you're Christian, a black church if you are white, or a meeting of Asian students if you are Western. Observe nonverbal behaviors of the people there: How do they greet one another? How much eye contact accompanies interaction? How close to one another do people sit? Can you make inferences about cultural values based on nonverbal communication that you observe?

CHAPTER SUMMARY

 Practice and review the content in this chapter.

In this chapter, we've explored the world beyond words. We learned that there are similarities and differences between nonverbal communication and verbal communication. Next, we noted that nonverbal communication supplements or replaces verbal messages, regulates interaction, reflects and establishes relationship-level meanings, and expresses cultural membership.

We discussed nine types of nonverbal communication: kinesics, haptics, physical appearance, artifacts, proxemics, environmental features, chronemics, paralanguage, and silence. Each form of nonverbal communication reflects cultural understandings and values and also expresses our personal identities and feelings toward others.

Because nonverbal communication, like verbal communication, is symbolic, it has no inherent, universal meaning. Instead, we construct meaning as we notice, organize, and interpret nonverbal behaviors.

APPLYING COMMUNICATION IN OUR LIVES

Communication in Our Lives is supported by a MindTap, a new online learning platform that delivers content, assignments, and a tailored presentation of the course curriculum created by your instructor. MindTap combines all of your learning tools–readings, multimedia, activities and assessments–into a singular learning unit that guides you through the course. Practice and Present, a unique tool within MindTap, allows you to upload your speech video files for practice or for a grade, comment on your peer's speeches and review your grades. MindTap also includes Speech Builder Express, a powerful tool that guides you through the speech outline and preparation process. For more information or to access MindTap, visit cengagebrain.com.

DEFINITIONS OF KEY CONCEPTS   Review your **Flashcards**.

artifacts Personal objects we use to announce our identities and personalize our environments.

chronemics A type of nonverbal communication concerned with how we perceive and use time to define identities and interaction.

environmental factors Elements of settings that affect how we feel and act. Environmental factors are a type of nonverbal communication.

haptics Nonverbal communication that involves physical touch.

kinesics Body position and body motions, including those of the face.

nonverbal communication All forms of communication other than words themselves; includes inflection and other vocal qualities as well as several other behaviors.

paralanguage Vocal communication that does not include actual words; for example, sounds, vocal qualities, accents, and inflection.

physical appearance Physical features of people and the values attached to those features; a type of nonverbal communication.

proxemics A type of nonverbal communication that includes space and how we use it.

silence The lack of verbal communication or paralanguage. Silence is a type of nonverbal communication that can express powerful messages.

FOR FURTHER REFLECTION AND DISCUSSION

 MindTap

1. Attend a gathering of people who belong to a social community different from yours. Observe nonverbal behaviors of the people there: How do they greet one another, how much eye contact accompanies interaction, and how close to one another do people stand and sit?

2. Visit restaurants near your campus. Describe the kinds of seats, lighting, music (if any), and distance between tables. Do you find any connections between nonverbal patterns and expensiveness of restaurants?

3. Describe the spatial arrangements in the home of your family of origin. Was there a room in which family members interacted a good deal? How was furniture arranged in that room? Who had separate space and personal chairs in your family? What do the nonverbal patterns reflect about your family's communication style?

4. What ethical issues are entailed in interpreting others' nonverbal communication? What would be ethical and unethical interpretations?

 Ethics

SHARPEN YOUR SKILL

 MindTap

1. Communicating Closeness

What do nonverbal behaviors say about how intimate people are? To find out, observe (a) a couple who you know are very close, (b) a clerk and a shopper in a store, and (c) a teacher and student who are talking. How closely do the people sit or stand to each other? How do their postures differ? What facial expressions and eye contact do they use in each situation?

2. Environmental Awareness

Think of one place where you feel rushed and one where you linger. Describe the following about each place:

How is furniture arranged?
What kind of lighting is used?
What sort of music is played, and what other sounds are there?
How comfortable is the furniture for sitting or lounging?
What colors and art are there?
Based on your observations, can you make generalizations about environmental features that promote relaxation and ones that do not?

EXPERIENCING COMMUNICATION IN OUR LIVES

MindTap

CASE STUDY: *Nonverbal Cues*

A video of the conversation scripted here is featured in your Chapter 6 MindTap for *Communication in Our Lives*. Select "Nonverbal Cues" to watch the video. Improve your own communication skills by reading, watching, and evaluating this communication encounter.

A project team is meeting to discuss the most effective way to present its recommendations for implementing a flextime policy on a trial basis. Members of the team are Jason Brown, team leader; Erika Filene; Victoria Lawrence; Bill Williams; and Jensen Chen. They are seated around a rectangular table with Jason at the head.

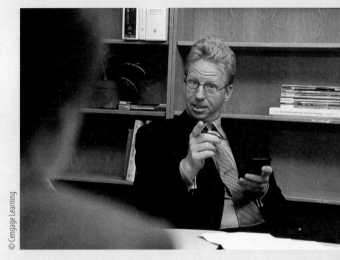
© Cengage Learning

JASON: So we've decided to recommend trying flextime for a 2-month period and with a number of procedures to make sure that people's new schedules don't interfere with productivity. There's a lot of information to communicate to employees, so how can we do that best?

VICTORIA: I think it would be good to use PowerPoint to highlight the key aspects of the new procedures. People always seem to remember better if they see something.

BILL: Oh, come on. PowerPoint is so overused. Everyone is tired of it by now. Can't we do something more creative?

VICTORIA: Well, I like it. It's a good teaching tool.

BILL: I didn't know we were teaching. I thought our job was to report recommendations.

VICTORIA: So what do you suggest, Bill? (*She nervously pulls on her bracelet as she speaks.*)

BILL: I don't have a suggestion. I'm just against PowerPoint. (*He doesn't look up as he speaks.*)

JASON: Okay, let's not bicker among ourselves. (*He pauses, gazes directly at Bill, then continues.*) Lots of people like PowerPoint, lots don't. Instead of arguing about its value, let's ask what it is we want to communicate to the employees here. Maybe talking about our goal first will help us decide on the best means of achieving it.

ERIKA: Good idea. I'd like us to focus first on getting everyone excited about the benefits of flextime. If they understand those, they'll be motivated to learn the procedures, even if there are a lot of them.

JENSEN: Erika is right. That's a good way to start. Maybe we could create a handout or PowerPoint slide—either would work—to summarize the benefits of flextime we've identified in our research.

JASON: Good, okay now we're cooking. Victoria, will you make notes on the ideas as we discuss them?

Victoria opens a notebook and begins writing notes. Noticing that Bill is typing into his PDA, Jason looks directly at Bill and speaks.

JASON: Are you with us on how we lead off in our presentation?

BILL: Sure, fine with me. (*He puts the PDA aside but keeps his eyes on it.*)

ERIKA: So maybe then we should say that the only way flextime can work is if we make sure that everyone agrees on procedures so that no division is ever missing more than one person during key production hours.

JENSEN: Very good. That would add to people's motivation to learn and follow the procedures we've found are effective in other companies like ours. I think it would be great if Erika could present that topic because she did most of the research on it. (*He smiles at Erika, and she pantomimes tipping her hat to him.*)

JASON: (*He looks at Erika with a raised brow, and she nods.*) Good. Okay, Erika's in charge of that. What's next?

VICTORIA: Then it's time to spell out the procedures and . . .

BILL: You can't just spell them out. You have to explain each one—give people a rationale for them—or they won't follow them.

    Victoria glares at Bill, then looks across the table at Erika, who shrugs as if to say, "I don't know what's bothering Bill today."

JASON: Bill, why don't you lead off, then, and tell us the first procedure we should mention and the rationale we should provide for it.

BILL: (*Looks up from his PDA, which he's been using again, and shrugs.*) Just spell out the rules, that's all.

VICTORIA: Would it be too much trouble for you to cut off your gadget and join us in this meeting, Bill?

BILL: Would it be too much trouble for you to quit hassling me?

JASON: (*He turns his chair to face Bill squarely.*) Look, I don't know what's eating you, but you're really being a jerk. If you've got a problem with this meeting or someone here, put it on the table. Otherwise, be a team player.

QUESTIONS FOR ANALYSIS AND DISCUSSION   MindTap™

You can answer these questions and see my responses to them online via MindTap for Chapter 6.

1. Identify nonverbal behaviors that regulate turn taking within the team.

2. Identify nonverbal behaviors that express relational-level meanings of communication. What aspects of team members' nonverbal communication express liking or disliking, responsiveness or lack of responsiveness, and power?

3. How do artifacts affect interaction between members of the team?

4. If you were the sixth member of this team, what kinds of communication might you enact to help relieve tension in the group?

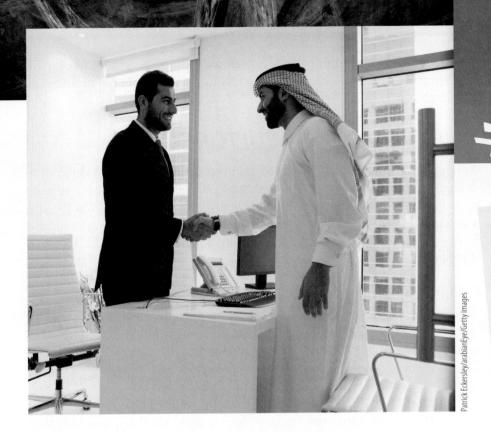

Patrick Eckersley/arabianEye/Getty Images

7

> Preservation of one's own culture does not require contempt or disrespect for other cultures.
>
> **César Chavez**

Communication and Culture

Today's world is one of global connectivity. More than ever in history, people from different cultures interact, work together, and live side by side. Further, events in one part of the world reverberate around the globe. The tsunami that devastated parts of Japan in 2011 was noticed in California in 2012 when debris from Japanese homes and lives washed ashore on the western shores of the United States. When Greece was on the brink of economic collapse in 2012, financial markets around the world quavered. Today, we all need to appreciate different cultures and the communication practices they cultivate.

In this chapter, we explore relationships between communication and culture. First, we'll define culture and discuss the intricate ways it

7 **MindTap**

Review the chapter **Learning Objectives** and **Start** with a quick warm up activity.

7 **SHARPEN YOUR SKILL**

At the end of this chapter, refer to the Sharpen Your Skill features, Communicating Culture and Your Culture's Sayings, to apply concepts from Chapter 7.

is entwined with communication. Then, we'll focus on guidelines for increasing the effectiveness of communication between people of different cultures.

UNDERSTANDING CULTURE

Although the word **culture** is part of our everyday vocabulary, it's difficult to define. Culture is part of everything we think, do, feel, and believe, yet we can't point to a thing that is culture. Most simply defined, culture is a way of life. It is a system of ideas, values, beliefs, structures, and practices that is communicated by one generation to the next and that sustains a particular way of life. To understand cultures more fully, we now consider four key premises about them.

Cultures Are Systems

The first premise about cultures is that they are systems. A culture is not a random collection of ideas, beliefs, values, and customs; rather, it is a coherent system of understandings, traditions, values, communication practices, and ways of living. As anthropologist Edward T. Hall noted years ago, "You touch a culture in one place and everything else is affected" (1977, p. 14).

Culture is one of the most important systems within which communication occurs. We are not born knowing how close to stand to others, how to express disagreement politely, or how much personal information to reveal to friends. We learn our culture's rules for these behaviors as we interact with others. For each of us, our culture directly shapes how we communicate, teaching us how much eye contact is polite, and whether argument and conflict are desirable in groups and personal relationships.

You'll recall from our previous discussion of systems that the parts of a system interact and affect one another. Because cultures are systems, aspects of a culture are interrelated and work together to create a whole. For example, one of the major changes in Western society was the Industrial Revolution. Before the mid-1800s, most families lived and worked together in one place. In agricultural regions, women, men, and children worked together to plant, tend, harvest, and store crops and to take care of livestock. In cities, family businesses were common. This preindustrial way of life promoted cooperative relationships and family togetherness. The invention of fuel-powered machines led to mass production in factories, where workers spent 8 or more hours each day. In turn, this activated competition among workers to produce and earn more, and on-the-job communication became more competitive and individualistic. As men were hired for industrial jobs, women assumed primary responsibilities in the home, and men's roles in family life diminished. Thus, a change in work life produced reverberations throughout the culture.

The technological revolution that began in the 1970s and continues today has also had multiple and interrelated repercussions in cultural life. The Internet and smart phones allow people to form and maintain relationships over great distances. Computer networking, virtual conferencing, and virtual offices allow many people to work at home. New technologies change how, where, and with whom we communicate, just as they change the boundaries we use to define work and personal life. Because cultures are holistic systems, no change is ever isolated from the overall system.

Cultures Vary on Five Dimensions

Geert Hofstede (1991, 2001; Hofstede et al., 2010), a Dutch anthropologist and social psychologist, provided insight into defining features of cultures. Before becoming a faculty member, Hofstede trained managers and supervised personnel research at IBM. In that job, Hofstede surveyed more than 100,000 IBM employees in countries all over the world. He noticed that there were clear differences among IBM employees in different cultures. Intrigued by his findings, Hofstede left IBM to study cultural differences. His program of research identified five key dimensions that vary among cultures.

Individualism/Collectivism   The dimension of **individualism/collectivism** refers to the extent to which members of a culture understand themselves as part of and connected to their families, groups, and cultures. In cultures high in collectivism (e.g., Pakistan, China), people's identity is deeply tied to their groups, families, and clans. In cultures high in individualism (e.g., United States, Australia), people tend to think of themselves as individuals who act relatively independently.

Communication scholar Stella Ting-Toomey has studied cultural differences in what she calls face, which includes individual and cultural facets of identity. For instance, individual facets of your identity include your major or profession and your tastes in music whereas cultural facets of identity include your membership in your family, your work and social networks, and your culture. Ting-Toomey (2005) reports that in collectivist cultures, group identity is more important than individual identity. In individualist cultures, individual facets of identity are more important than group facets.

Uncertainty Avoidance   **Uncertainty avoidance** refers to the extent to which people try to avoid ambiguity and vagueness. In some cultures (e.g., Poland, South Korea), people like to have everything spelled out very explicitly in order to avoid misunderstandings. Yet, in other cultures (e.g., Hong Kong, Sweden), uncertainty is more tolerated and expectations are more flexible.

Power Distance   The third dimension of culture is **power distance**, which refers to the size of the gap between people with high and low power and the extent to which that gap is regarded as normal. In some cultures (e.g., India, China), the distance between high and low power is great and is often inherited. Significant power differences that are passed on in families cultivate a society in which people respect the powerful, and there is low expectation of movement between classes, castes, or levels. In cultures where power distance is small (e.g., New Zealand, Norway), people tend to assume that those in power have earned it, rather than simply gaining power by virtue of being in powerful families.

Masculinity/Femininity   The fourth dimension of culture is **masculinity/femininity**. This dimension refers to the extent to which a culture values aggressiveness, competitiveness, looking out for yourself, and dominating others and nature (considered masculine orientations) versus gentleness, cooperation, and taking care of others and living in harmony with the natural world (considered feminine orientations). In cultures that are higher in femininity (e.g., Netherlands, Norway), men and women are more gentle, cooperative, and caring. In cultures that are higher in masculinity (e.g., Japan, Germany), however, men are more aggressive and competitive. In highly masculine cultures, women may also be competitive and assertive, but generally they are less so than men.

Long-Term/Short-Term Orientation   The final dimension was not included in Hofstede's original work, but he added it later when it became clear to him that cultures varied how long-term their orientations are. **Long-term/short-term orientation** refers to the extent to which members of a culture think about and long term (history and future) versus short term (present). Long-term planning, thrift, and industriousness and respect for elders and ancestors are valued in cultures with a long-term orientation (e.g., Japan, Korea). In contrast, living for the moment, not saving for a rainy day, and not having as much respect for elders and ancestors are more likely to be found in cultures with a short-term orientation (e.g., Australia, Germany). The long-term end of the continuum is associated with what are sometimes called Confucian values, although cultures not historically connected with this influence can also have a long-term orientation. This value is not just about future—it is also about respect for one's ancestors and plans and hopes for those who follow.

Cultures Are Dynamic

The third principle of cultures is that they are **dynamic**, which means they evolve and change over time. Scholars (Samovar et al., 2009, 2011) have identified four primary sources of change in cultural life. The first is *invention*, which is the creation of tools, ideas, and practices. The classic example of a tool is the wheel, which had far-reaching implications. Not only did its invention alter modes of transportation, but it is also the foundation of many machines and technologies. Other inventions that have changed cultural life are medical devices such as pacemakers, the computer, and the automobile.

Cultures also invent ideas that alter social life. For example, the United States was founded on the concept of *democracy*, which influenced laws, rights, and responsibilities. Another concept that has changed Western life is environmental awareness. Information about our planet's fragility has infused cultural consciousness. Terms such as *environmental responsibility* and *environmental ethics* have entered our everyday vocabularies, reshaping how we understand our relationship with the environment.

A second source of cultural change is *diffusion*, which involves borrowing from other cultures. What we call English includes a number of words imported from many cultures: *brocade*, *touché*, and *yin and yang*. U.S. businesses adopt best practices from businesses in other countries just as those countries adopt best practices developed in the United States.

A third source of cultural change is *calamity*, which is adversity that brings about change in a culture. For example, war may devastate a country, destroying land and people alike. Cultural calamity may also involve disasters such as hurricanes, volcanic eruptions, and plagues.

A fourth source of cultural change is *communication*. A primary way in which communication propels change is by naming things in ways that shape how we understand them. For instance, the term *date rape* was coined in the late 1980s. Although historically, many women had been forced to have sex by men they were dating, until recently there was no term that named what happened as a violent invasion and a criminal act (Wood, 1992). Similarly, the term *sexual harassment* names a practice that is certainly not new but only lately has been labeled and given social reality (Wood, 1994c). As a primary tool of social movements, communication impels significant changes in cultural life. Thirty years ago, the civil rights movement in the United States used communication to transform laws and views of blacks. Powerful leaders such as the Reverend Martin Luther King Jr., and Malcolm X raised blacks' pride in their identity and heritage and inspired them to demand their rights in United States. Simultaneously, black leaders used communication to persuade the nonblack citizens to rethink their attitudes and practices.

In addition to bringing about change directly, communication also accompanies other sources of cultural change. Inventions such as antibiotics had to be explained to medical practitioners and to a general public that believed infections were caused by fate and accident, not viruses and bacteria. Ideas and practices borrowed from other cultures similarly must be translated into the language and culture of a particular society. Cultural calamities, too, must be defined and explained: Did the volcano erupt because of pressure in the earth or because of the anger of the gods? Did we lose the war because we had a weak military or because our cause was wrong? The ways a culture defines and communicates about calamities establish what these events mean and imply for future social practices and social life.

Invention, diffusion, calamity, and community ensure that cultures are highly dynamic—always changing in subtle and not-so-subtle ways.

Multiple Social Communities Coexist Within a Single Culture

The fourth principle about cultures is that they may include multiple social communities. When we speak of different cultures, we often think of geographically distinct regions. For instance, India, South America, Africa, and Europe are separate cultures. Yet geographic separation isn't what defines a culture. Instead, a culture exists when a distinct way of life shapes what a group of people believes, values, and does. Even within a single country, there are numerous social communities with distinct ways of life.

Social communities are groups of people who live within a dominant culture yet also are members of another group or groups that are not dominant in a particular society. Social communities are distinct from dominant culture although not necessarily opposed to or entirely outside of it. Since the colonial days, mainstream Western culture has reflected the values and experiences of Western, heterosexual, young and middle-aged, middle- and upper-class,

COMMUNICATION HIGHLIGHT

Life on the Color Line

Gregory Howard Williams began life as the white son in a middle-class family in Virginia. At age 10, however, he became a black living in Muncie, Indiana. His father, James Anthony "Buster" Williams, was an olive-skinned man with some African ancestry. Buster wanted desperately to escape racism and gain the privileges that whites have as a birthright. His son, Gregory, has pale skin, thin lips, and straight hair, which allowed others to perceive him as White.

In his autobiography, *Life on the Color Line: The True Story of a White Boy Who Discovered He Was Black* (1995), Gregory Williams provides a stunning account of the differences in how he was treated when he was considered white and black.

able-bodied white men who are Christian, at least in heritage if not in actual practice.

Yet Western culture includes many groups that do not identify exclusively with the mainstream. Gay men, lesbians, intersexuals, transsexuals, transgendered people, and bisexuals experience difficulty in a society that defines them as marginal (Ekins & King, 2006). People who have disabilities encounter problems as they attempt to live and work in a society that is made for able-bodied people. Muslims in the United States grapple with a culture that, in many ways, doesn't accommodate or value their traditions.

Mainstream ideology is evident in nonverbal communication. For example, Western culture often conveys the message that people with disabilities don't matter. Notice how many buildings have no ramps and how many public presentations don't include signers for people with impaired hearing. Most campus and business buildings feature portraits of white men, leaving people of color and women unrepresented.

Mainstream values may be in tension with those of particular social communities. As Sabrina notes in her commentary, misunderstanding can erupt when values and communication practices of social communities and mainstream culture clash.

Collectivist cultures and social communities regard people as deeply connected to their families, groups, and communities. Thus, priority is given to harmony, group welfare, and interdependence (Jandt, 2009; Samovar, et al., 2011). Collectivist cultures and social communities tend to rely on a **high-context communication style**, which is

Members of some social communities may find it difficult to navigate mainstream culture.

©iStockphoto.com/abalcazar

HEALTH COMMUNICATION

Diagnosis: Cultural Miscommunication

If you plan a career in the field of health, learn all you can about different cultures. Patients' cultural beliefs and values affect how they perceive medical practitioners and how they can be most effectively treated. Consider a few examples of cultural misunderstandings (Galanti, 2000).

Some Asian cultures practice *coining*, in which a coin (often heated) is rubbed vigorously over a sick person's back to draw out the illness. The resulting red welts are perceived as evidence that the illness came out. However, on seeing red welts on children's backs, some American health professionals have had Asian parents investigated for child abuse.

American culture emphasizes autonomy and each person's right to information about herself or himself. As a result, physicians routinely share a poor prognosis directly with patients before discussing it with other family members. However, in places such as Mexico, China, Iran, and the Philippines, it is considered extremely insensitive to burden a person, particularly a sick person, with bad news. Instead, family members should be told and they, not the physician, decide when and how to tell the patient.

One hospital got a lesson in cultural values when it tried to assign a patient to Room 4. In the patient's home country, China, the character for 4 is pronounced almost identically to the character for the word *death*. The Chinese patient did not want to be in a room called death!

---

indirect and undetailed. Because it is assumed that people are deeply interconnected, people do not feel the need to spell everything out in explicit detail (Jandt, 2009).

Individualistic cultures and social communities regard each person as distinct from others; individuality is more prominent than membership in groups, families, and so forth. Priority is given to personal freedom, independence, and individual rights. Members of individualist cultures and social communities generally use a **low-context communication style**, which is explicit, detailed, and precise. The emphasis on individuality means that communicators cannot presume others share their meanings and values (Jandt, 2009).

> **SABRINA** *I get hassled by a lot of white girls on campus about being dependent on my family. They say I should grow up and leave the nest. They say I'm too close to my folks and my grandparents, aunts, uncles, and cousins. But what they mean by "too close" is that I'm closer with my family than most whites are. It's a white standard they're using, and it doesn't fit most blacks. Strong ties with family and the black community have always been our way.*

When people from different cultures and social communities interact, their different ways of communicating may cause misunderstandings. For instance, traditional Japanese people don't touch or shake hands to greet. Instead, they bow to preserve each person's personal space, which is very important in that culture. In Greece, however, touching is part of being friendly and sociable.

Gender as a Social Community   Of the many social communities that exist, gender has received particularly intense study. Because we know more about it than about other social communities, we'll explore gender to illustrate how a social community shapes members' communication.

You may have noticed that, despite many similarities, there are some fairly common differences in women's and men's communication. For instance, women's talk generally is more expressive and focused on feelings and relationships, whereas men's talk tends to be more instrumental and competitive (Wood, 1995a, 1996, 2005, 2013).

Another general difference lies in what each gender regards as the primary basis of relationships. Many men develop friendships by doing things together (i.e., working on cars, watching sports) and doing things for one another (i.e., trading favors) (Inman, 1996; Metts, 2006a; Swain, 1989; Wood & Inman, 1993). Women more often build relationships primarily by talking about feelings, personal issues, and daily life (Braithwaite & Kellas, 2006; Duck & Wood, 2006; Johnson, 1996; Metts, 2006a).

Given the differences between how women and men, in general, use communication, it's hardly surprising that the sexes often misunderstand one another. One clash between gendered communication styles occurs when women and men discuss problems. When women talk about something that is troubling them, they are often looking first for empathy and connection. Yet, masculine socialization teaches men to use communication instrumentally, so they often offer advice or solutions. Thus, women sometimes interpret men's

COMMUNICATION HIGHLIGHT

What's in a Name?

Long before the present era, some women resisted taking a man's name upon marriage. At the first Women's Rights Convention, held in 1848 at Seneca Falls, New York, Elizabeth Cady Stanton (Stanton, Anthony, & Gage, 1881/1969) said:

When a slave escapes from a Southern plantation, he at once takes a name as the first step in liberty—the first assertion of individual identity. A woman's dignity is equally involved in a life-long name, to mark her individuality. We cannot overestimate the demoralizing effect on woman herself, to say nothing of society at large, for her to consent thus to merge her existence so wholly in that of another.

If you are a woman, do you intend to keep or change your birth name if you marry? If you are a man who marries a woman, would you expect her to take your name?

Do the men in this photo appear to be communicating in ways consistent with research on masculine social communities?

advice as a lack of personal concern. On the other hand, men may feel frustrated when women offer empathy and support instead of advice for solving problems.

Perhaps the most common complication in communication between women and men occurs when a woman says, "Let's talk about us." To men, this often means trouble because they interpret the request as implying there is a problem in a relationship. For women, however, this is not the only—or even the main—reason to talk about a relationship. Within feminine social communities, talking is a primary way to celebrate and increase closeness. The instrumental focus of masculine social communities teaches that talking about a relationship is useful only if there is some problem to be resolved.

> **LARRY** *Finally, I see what happens between my girlfriend and me. She always wants to talk about us, which I think is stupid unless we have a problem. I like to go to a concert or do something together, but then she says that I don't want to be with her. We speak totally different languages.*

Other Social Communities Gender isn't the only social community, and communication between men and women is not the only kind of interaction that may be plagued by misunderstandings. Research indicates that communication patterns vary between social classes. For example, working-class people tend to stay closer to and rely more on extended family than do middle- and upper-class Americans (Bornstein & Bradley, 2003; Cancian, 1987). Working-class men also tend to see physical strength and practical skills as more central to masculinity than middle- and upper-class men (Mumby, 2006a).

Racial and ethnic social communities may also have distinct communication patterns. For example, research indicates that African Americans generally communicate more assertively than European Americans (Orbe & Harris, 2001). What some African Americans consider authentic, powerful exchanges may be perceived as antagonistic by people from different social communities. As a rule, African Americans also communicate more interactively than European Americans. This explains why some African Americans call out responses such as "Tell it," "That's right," and "Keep talking" during speeches, church sermons, and other public presentations. What many Caucasians regard as interruptions, some African Americans perceive as constructive participation in communication and community.

Notice that in discussing social communities and their communication patterns, I use qualifying words. For instance, I note that *most* women behave in certain ways and that *some* blacks *tend to* communicate more interactively than many whites. This is to remind us that not all members of a social community behave in the same way. Although generalizations are useful and informative, they should not mislead us into thinking that all members of any social community think, feel, and communicate alike. We engage in stereotyping and uncritical thinking when we fail to recognize differences between individual members of social groups.

In this section, we have discussed four key premises about cultures. First, cultures are systemic. Second, there are five dimensions that distinguish cultures: individualism/collectivism, uncertainty avoidance, power distance, masculinity/femininity, and long-term–short-term orientation. Third, we noted that cultures are dynamic, continuously changing as a result of invention, diffusion, calamity, and communication. Finally, we saw that multiple social communities with distinct norms, values, and practices may coexist within a single culture. With

COMMUNICATION HIGHLIGHT

Cybercommunities

Are groups that form and operate on the Web and the Internet cultures or social communities? To answer that question, we need to know whether cyber-communities have shared values, beliefs, practices, and languages that are not understood by people outside the groups. Many ongoing chat rooms and cybergroups do share values and unique practices and language that newcomers must learn in order to participate effectively (Swiss, 2001). They develop specialized abbreviations and phrases that cannot be understood by people who are not members. Does this make them cultures or social communities?

To learn more, use your MindTap for *Communication in Our Lives* to access **WebLink 7.1**.

these understandings of culture in mind, let's now elaborate the connections between cultures and communication.

COMMUNICATION'S RELATIONSHIP TO CULTURE AND SOCIAL COMMUNITIES

As our discussion so far suggests, communication and culture influence each other. Culture is reflected in communication practices; at the same time, communication practices shape cultural life. We'll discuss two principles that illuminate the intimate relationship between communication and social communities and cultures.

Communication Expresses and Sustains Cultures

Patterns of communication reflect cultural values and perspectives. For example, many Asian languages include numerous words to describe specific relationships (grandmother's brother, father's uncle, youngest son, oldest daughter). This reflects the cultural emphasis on family relationships (Ferrante, 2009). There are fewer English words to describe precise kinship bonds.

Understandings of family differ from culture to culture.

COMMUNICATION HIGHLIGHT

Proverbs Express Cultural Values

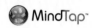

Here are examples of sayings that reflect the values of particular cultures (Gudykunst & Lee, 2002; Samovar & Porter, 2001).

- "It is the nail that sticks out that gets hammered down." This Japanese saying reflects the idea that a person should not stand out from others but instead should conform.

- "No need to know the person, only the family." This Chinese axiom reflects the belief that individuals are less important than families.

- "A zebra does not despise its stripes." Among the African Masai, this saying encourages acceptance of things and oneself as they are.

- "The child has no owner." "It takes a whole village to raise a child." These African adages express the cultural beliefs that children belong to whole communities and that rearing and caring for children are the responsibility of all members of those communities, not just the children's biological parents.

To learn proverbs in other countries such as Turkey and Palestine, use your MindTap for *Communication in Our Lives* to access **WebLink 7.2** and **WebLink 7.3**.

The respect of many Asian cultures for elderly people is reflected in language. "I will be 60 tomorrow" is an Asian saying that means, "I am old enough to deserve respect." In contrast, Western cultures tend to prize youth and to have many positive words for youthfulness (*young in spirit, fresh*) and negative words for seniority (*has-been, outdated, old-fashioned, over the hill*) (Ferrante, 2009).

Each time we express cultural values, we also perpetuate them. When some Asian Americans veil emotions in interaction, they fortify and express the value of self-restraint and the priority of reason over emotion. When Caucasians argue, emphasize their ideas, and compete in conversations, they uphold the values of individuality and assertiveness. Communication, then, is a mirror of a culture's values and a primary means of keeping them woven into the fabric of everyday life.

In the process of learning language, we also learn our culture's values. The importance that most Asian cultures attach to age is structured into Asian languages. For instance, the Korean language makes fine distinctions between different ages, and any remark to another person must acknowledge the other's age (Ferrante, 2009). Eastern cultures also tend to place greater emphasis on family and community than on individuals. It's unlikely that an Eastern text-book on human communication would even include a chapter on self, which is standard in Western textbooks. If I were a Korean, I would introduce myself as Wood Julia to communicate the greater value placed on familial than personal identity.

Calendars reflect cultural traditions and values by designating significant days as holidays that should be recognized and honored. In the United States, the Fourth of July commemorates the U.S. independence from Britain; Eastern societies have a day each year to honor the elderly people. In this way, calendars tell us who is in the mainstream in a given society and who is not.

RACHAEL   *It is hard to be Jewish in a Christian society, especially in terms of holidays. For me, Rosh Hashanah and Yom Kippur are high holy days, but they are not holidays on the calendar. Some of my teachers give me grief for missing classes on holy days, and my friends don't accept that I can't go out on Saturday, which is our sacred day. At my job, they act like I'm being a slouch and skipping work because my holidays aren't their holidays. They get Christmas and New Year's Day off, but I celebrate Hanukkah and Rosh Hashanah. And I don't have to tell you why making Easter a national holiday offends Jewish people.*

We Learn Culture in the Process of Communicating

We learn a culture's views and patterns in the process of communicating. As we interact with others, we come to understand the beliefs, values, norms, and language of our culture. By observing how others communicate, we learn language (*dog*) and what it means (i.e., a pest, a pet, a work animal, or food to eat). This allows us to participate in a social world of shared meanings.

From the moment of birth, we begin to learn the beliefs, values, norms, and language of our society. We learn our culture's values in a variety of communication contexts. We learn to respect our elders, or not to, by how we see others

Both verbal and nonverbal communication reflect cultural teachings. Here, an elder and a young boy wear traditional yarmulkes and partake of unleavened bread and wine as part of Passover Seder.

communicate with older people and by what we hear others say about elders. We learn what body shape is valued by what we see in media and how we hear others talk about people of various physical proportions. By the time we are old enough to appreciate the idea that culture is learned, our beliefs, values, languages, and practices are already thoroughly woven into who we are and are almost invisible to us.

In sum, we've seen that communication is a primary way in which cultures are expressed and sustained and that communication is a primary way that each of us learns our culture's codes so that we can participate effectively in it.

IMPROVING COMMUNICATION BETWEEN CULTURES AND SOCIAL COMMUNITIES

As long as we interact with others in our own culture and social communities, we can count on many shared rules for how to communicate and how to interpret others' communication. However, when we interact with people from other cultures and social communities, we can't count on shared rules of communication. Thus, misunderstandings often occur. Let's consider two principles for minimizing misunderstandings between members of different cultures and social communities.

Resist the Ethnocentric Bias

Most of us unreflectively use our home culture as the standard for judging other cultures. Some Japanese may regard many European Americans as rude for maintaining direct eye contact, whereas some European Americans may perceive some Japanese as evasive for averting their eyes (Jandt, 2009). Many Westerners' habitual self-references may appear egocentric to some Koreans, and many Koreans' unassuming style may seem passive to some Westerners. How we view others and their communication depends more on the perspective we use to interpret them than on what they say and do.

Although it is natural to use our own culture and social communities as the standard for judging other cultures, this tendency interferes with effective intercultural communication. **Ethnocentrism** is the use of one's own culture and its practices as the standard for interpreting the values, beliefs, norms, and communication of other cultures. Literally, ethnocentrism means to put our own ethnicity (*ethno*) at the center (*centrism*) of the universe. Ethnocentrism fosters negative judgments of anything that differs from our own ways. In extreme form, ethnocentrism can lead one group of people to think it has the right to dominate and exploit other groups and to engage in genocide.

To reduce our tendencies to be ethnocentric, we should first remind ourselves that culture is learned. What is considered normal and right varies between cultures. In place of ethnocentrism, we can adopt the perspective of **cultural relativism**, which recognizes that cultures vary in how they think, act, and behave as well as in what they believe and value. Cultural relativism reminds us that something that appears odd or even wrong to us may seem natural and right from the point of view of a different culture. That awareness facilitates understanding among people of different cultures and cocultures.

Recognize That Responding to Diversity Is a Process

We don't move suddenly from being unaware of how people in other cultures communicate to being totally comfortable and competent interacting with them. Dealing with diversity is a gradual process that takes time, experience with a variety of people, and a commitment to learning about a range of people and communication styles. We will discuss five responses to diversity, ranging from rejection to complete acceptance.

Resistance A common response to diversity is **resistance**, which occurs when we attack the cultural practices of others or proclaim that our own cultural traditions are superior. Without education or reflection, many people deal with diversity by resisting the practices of cultures and social communities different from their own. Some people think their judgments reflect universal truths about what is normal and right. They aren't aware that they are imposing the arbitrary yardstick of their own particular social communities and culture and ignoring the yardsticks of other cultures and social communities.

> **BRENDA** *I overheard three of my classmates complaining about all of the mess and noise in the building where we have a class. They were saying what an inconvenience it is. The construction is to install an elevator in the building so that students like me, who are in wheelchairs, can take classes in classrooms on the second and third floor. I don't think my classmates are mean, but I do think they've never put themselves in my shoes—or my wheelchair! Every semester they pick classes according to what they want to take and when they want to take it. My first criterion is finding classes that I can get to—either first floor or in buildings that are wheelchair accessible.*

Resistance may be expressed in many ways. It fuels racial slurs, anti-Semitic messages, and homophobic attitudes and actions. Resistance may also motivate members of a culture or social community to associate only with each other and to resist recognizing any commonalities with people from other cultures or social communities.

Members of a culture or social community may resist their own group practices in an effort to fit into the mainstream. **Assimilation** occurs when people give up their own ways and adopt those of the dominant culture. For many years, assimilation was the dominant response of immigrants who came to the United States. The idea of the United States as a "melting pot" encouraged newcomers to melt into the mainstream by abandoning anything that made them different from native-born Americans. More recently, Reverend Jesse Jackson used the metaphor of a family quilt, which portrays the United States as a country in which people's unique values and customs are visible, as are the individual squares in a quilt; at the same time, each group contributes to a larger whole, just as each square in a quilt contributes to its overall beauty.

Communicating with people who differ from us fosters personal growth.

Tolerance   A second response to diversity is **tolerance**, the acceptance of differences even though we may not approve of or even understand them. Tolerance involves respecting others' rights to their own ways even though we may think their ways are wrong or offensive. Judgment still exists, but it's not actively imposed on others. Tolerance accepts the existence of differences, but it does not necessarily respect the values of other cultures and social communities.

Understanding   A third response to diversity involves **understanding** that differences are rooted in cultural teachings and that no customs, traditions, or behaviors are intrinsically better than any others. This response grows out of cultural relativism, which we discussed previously. Rather than assuming that whatever differs from our ways is a deviation from a universally right standard (ours), we realize that diverse values, beliefs, norms, and communication styles are rooted in distinct cultural perspectives. A person who responds to diversity with understanding might notice that a Japanese doesn't hold eye contact, but he or she wouldn't assume that the Japanese was deceitful. Instead, he or she would try to learn what eye contact means in Japanese society to understand the behavior in its native cultural context. Curiosity, rather than judgment, dominates in this response to cultural diversity.

Respect   Once we move beyond judgment and begin to understand the cultural basis for practices that diverge from our own, we may come to **respect** differences. We can appreciate the value of placing family above self, of arranged marriage, and of feminine and masculine communication styles. We don't have to adopt others' ways to respect them on their own terms. Respect allows us to acknowledge differences yet remain personally anchored primarily in the values and customs of our own culture.

Participation   A final response to diversity is **participation**, in which we incorporate some of the practices and values of other groups into our own lives. More than other responses, participation encourages us to develop new skills and perspectives and to nurture a civic culture that celebrates both differences and commonalities.

Participation calls for us to be **multilingual**, which means we are able to speak and think in more than one language. Members of many social communities already are at least bilingual: Many blacks know how to operate in mainstream white society and in traditional black communities (Orbe & Harris, 2001). Most women know how to communicate in both feminine and masculine ways, and they adapt their style to the people with whom they interact. Bilingualism is also practiced by many Asian Americans, Hispanics, lesbians, gay men, and members of other groups that are simultaneously part of a dominant culture and minority communities.

My partner, Robbie, and I have learned how to communicate in both conventionally feminine and masculine styles. Like many men, he was socialized to be assertive, competitive, and instrumental in conversation, whereas I learned to be more cooperative, relational, and expressive. When we were first married, we often frustrated each other with our different ways of communicating. I perceived him as domineering and sometimes insensitive to feelings. He perceived me as being too focused on relationship issues and inefficient in moving from problems to solutions. Gradually, each of us learned to understand the other's

COMMUNICATION HIGHLIGHT

Learning Bias

Is racial bias still a problem in America? According to ABC News and *Washington Post* poll reported in January 2009, that depends on whom you ask. Twice as many blacks as whites think racism is still a problem, whereas twice as many whites as blacks think racial equality has been achieved (Blow, 2009).

What can explain the major discrepancy between blacks' and whites' views? One explanation is that most whites believe they are not racially biased but still hold implicit biases. That's the idea behind Project Implicit, a virtual lab managed by scholars at Harvard, the University of Virginia, and the University of Washington. After 6 years of testing people's biases, the findings are clear: 75% of whites have an implicit pro-white/anti-black bias. While some blacks also harbor implicit racial biases—some pro-black and some pro-white—blacks are the least likely of all races to have any racial bias (Blow, 2009).

Another question studied by scientists at Project Implicit is when racial prejudice starts. According to Mahzarin Banaji, a professor at Harvard, it starts at much earlier ages than most of us think. Banaji has devoted her career to studying hidden and often subtle biases and attitudes. According to Banaji's research, children as young as 3 years old have the same level of bias as adults (Fogg, 2008).

To explore, and perhaps better appreciate, differences between you and people from different groups in your own community, complete the activity "Appreciating Differences Among People" via your MindTap for *Communication in Our Lives.*

ways of communicating and to respect our differences without judging them by our own norms. Still later, we came to appreciate and participate in each other's style; now both of us are fluent in both ways of communicating. This not only has improved our relationship but also has made each of us a more competent communicator in a range of settings.

In the course of our lives, many of us move in and out of various responses as we interact with people from multiple cultures and social communities. Most of us will discover that our responses may change over time.

BEYOND THE CLASSROOM

Let's take the material in this chapter beyond the classroom by applying it to the workplace, ethical choices, and engagement with the broader world.

1. **Workplace.** Go to an office building (it could be one on your campus) and make note of the culture and social communities that it reflects. If there are portraits on the walls, what are the sexes, races, and nationalities of the subjects? How accessible is the building to people with mobility limitations?

2. **Ethics.** This chapter encourages people to resist the ethnocentric bias, but doesn't offer a specific plan or set of guidelines for reaching that ethical goal. Based on what you've learned in Chapters 1 through 7, as well as your life experiences, what can you suggest as concrete steps people can take to resist or at least reduce the tendency to judge other cultures by the norms and values of their home culture?

3. **Engagement.** Check your campus calendar for meetings of various groups and select an event sponsored by an ethnic group other than your own. Attend the event and pay attention not only to the event itself but to the verbal and nonverbal communication patterns, including protocols for greeting, parting, and introducing speakers (if there is one or more).

CHAPTER SUMMARY

 Practice and review the content in this chapter.

In this chapter, we've learned about the close connections between communication and cultures. Our communication reflects our culture's values and norms; at the same time, our communication sustains those values and norms and the perception that they are natural and right. We also discussed the importance of learning to communicate effectively in a multicultural society. Moving beyond ethnocentric judgments based on our own culture allows us to understand, respect, and sometimes participate in a diverse world and to enlarge ourselves in the process.

But differences between us are only part of the story. It would be a mistake to be so aware of differences that we overlook our commonalities. We all have feelings, dreams, ideas, hopes, fears, and values. Our common humanness transcends many of our differences.

APPLYING COMMUNICATION IN OUR LIVES

Communication in Our Lives is supported by a MindTap, a new online learning platform that delivers content, assignments, and a tailored presentation of the course curriculum created by your instructor. MindTap combines all of your learning tools—readings, multimedia, activities and assessments—into a singular learning unit that guides you through the course. Practice and Present, a unique tool within MindTap, allows you to upload your speech video files for practice or for a grade, comment on your peer's speeches and review your grades. MindTap also includes Speech Builder Express, a powerful tool that guides you through the speech outline and preparation process. For more information or to access MindTap, visit cengagebrain.com.

DEFINITIONS OF KEY CONCEPTS

 Review your **Flashcards**.

assimilation The giving up of one's own culture's ways for those of another culture.

cultural relativism The idea that cultures vary in how they think, act, and behave as well as in what they believe and value; not the same as moral relativism.

culture Beliefs, understandings, practices, and ways of interpreting experience that are shared by a number of people.

dynamic Evolving and changing over time.

ethnocentrism The tendency to regard ourselves and our way of life as superior to other people and other ways of life.

high-context communication style The indirect and undetailed communication favored in collectivist cultures.

individualism/collectivism One of five dimensions of variation among cultures, this refers to the extent to which members of a culture understand themselves as part of and connected to their families, groups, and cultures.

long-term/short-term orientation One of five dimensions of variation among cultures, this refers to the extent to which members of a culture think about and long term (history and future) versus short term (present).

low-context communication style The direct, precise, and detailed communication favored in individualistic cultures.

masculinity/femininity. One of five dimensions of variation among cultures, this refers to the extent to which a culture values aggressiveness, competitiveness, looking out for yourself, and dominating others and nature (considered masculine orientations) versus gentleness, cooperation, and taking care of others and living in harmony with the natural world (considered feminine orientations).

multilingual Able to speak and think in more than one language.

participation A response to cultural diversity in which people incorporate some practices, customs, and traditions of other groups into their own lives.

power distance One of five dimensions of variation among cultures, this refers to the size of the gap between people with high and low power and the extent to which that gap is regarded as normal.

resistance A response to cultural diversity in which the cultural practices of others are attacked or the superiority of one's own cultural traditions is proclaimed.

respect A response to cultural diversity in which one values others' customs, traditions, and values, even if one does not actively incorporate them into one's own life.

social communities Groups of people who live within a dominant culture yet who also have common distinctive experiences and patterns of communicating.

tolerance A response to diversity in which one accepts differences even though one may not approve of or even understand them.

uncertainty avoidance One of five dimensions of variation among cultures, this refers to the extent to which people try to avoid ambiguity and vagueness.

understanding A response to cultural diversity in which it is assumed that differences are rooted in cultural teachings and that no traditions, customs, and behaviors are intrinsically more valuable than others.

FOR FURTHER REFLECTION AND DISCUSSION

 MindTap

1. Some scholars claim that there are many distinct social communities in the United States. Examples are deaf people, people with disabilities, and elderly people. Do you agree that these groups qualify as distinct social communities? What is needed for a group to be considered a specific and distinctive social community?

2. Continue the exercise started on page 152 by listing common sayings or adages in your culture and social communities. Decide what each saying reflects about the beliefs, values, and concerns of your culture.

3. Are the different styles of communication typical of distinct social communities evident in online interaction? For instance, do you see patterned differences between messages written by women and men? If you see differences, are they consistent with the general-

izations about gendered social communities that we discussed in this chapter?

4. Think critically about how you do and do not fit generalizations about your racial or ethnic group. Identify three ways in which you reflect what is generally true of your group. Identify three ways in which you personally diverge from generalizations about your group. Extend this exercise by thinking critically about how people in racial or ethnic groups other than your own do and do not fit generalizations about their group.

5. Reflect on the different responses to diversity that we discussed in the last section of this chapter. What ethical values do you perceive in each response?

Ethics

SHARPEN YOUR SKILL

1. Communicating Culture

Locate a standard calendar and an academic calendar used on your campus. Check each calendar to determine which of the following holidays of different cultural groups are recognized on the calendars and which are declared as holidays by suspension of normal operations in communities and on campuses:

Christmas
Hanukkah
Kwanzaa
Elderly Day
Passover
Easter
Yom Kippur
Ramadan
Hegira

Rosh Hashanah
Saka
Martin Luther King Jr. Day

2. Your Culture's Sayings

What do common sayings and proverbs in the United States tell us about cultural values? What cultural values are expressed by the following sayings?

"You can't be too rich or too thin."
"A stitch in time saves nine."
"What goes around comes around."
"A watched pot never boils."
"Penny wise, pound foolish."
"You can't take it with you."
"You've made your bed, now you have to lie in it."

What other sayings can you think of that express key Western values?

EXPERIENCING COMMUNICATION IN OUR LIVES

CASE STUDY: *The Job Interview*

A video of the conversation scripted here is featured in your Chapter 7 MindTap for *Communication in Our Lives*. Select "The Job Interview" to watch the video. Improve your own communication skills by reading, watching, and evaluating this communication encounter.

Mei-ying Yung is a senior who has majored in computer programming. Mei-ying's aptitude for computer programming has earned her much attention at her college. She has developed and installed complex new programs to make advising more efficient and to reduce the frustration and errors in registration for courses. Although she has been in the United States for 6 years, in many ways Mei-ying reflects the Chinese culture into which she was born and in which she spent the first 15 years of her life. Today Mei-ying is interviewing for a position at New Thinking, a fast-growing tech company that specializes in developing programs tailored to the needs of individual companies. The interviewer, Barton Hingham, is 32 years old and a native of California, where New Thinking is based. As the scenario opens, Ms. Yung walks into the small room

© Cengage Learning

where Mr. Hingham is seated behind a desk. He rises to greet her and walks over with his hand stretched out to shake hers.

HINGHAM: Good morning, Ms. Yung. I've been looking forward to meeting you. Your résumé is most impressive.

Ms. Yung looks downward, smiles, and limply shakes Mr. Hingham's hand. He gestures to a chair, and she sits down in it.

HINGHAM: I hope this interview will allow us to get to know each other a bit and decide whether there is a good fit between you and New Thinking. I'll be asking you some questions about your background and interests. And you should feel free to ask me any questions you have. Okay?

YUNG: Yes.

HINGHAM: I see from your transcript that you majored in computer programming and did very well. I certainly didn't have this many As on my college transcript!

YUNG: Thank you. I am very fortunate to have good teachers.

HINGHAM: Tell me a little about your experience in writing original programs for business applications.

YUNG: I do not have great experience, but I have been grateful to help the college with some of its work.

HINGHAM: Tell me about how you've helped the college. I see you designed a program for advising. Can you explain to me what you did to develop that program?

YUNG: Not really so much. I could see that much of advising is based on rules, so I only need to write the rules into a program so advisors could do their jobs more better.

HINGHAM: Perhaps you're being too modest. I've done enough programming myself to know how difficult it is to develop a program for something with as many details as advising. There are so many majors, each with different requirements and regulations. How did you program all of that variation?

YUNG: I read the handbook on advising and the regulations on each major and then programmed decision trees into an advising template. Not so hard.

HINGHAM: Well that's exactly the kind of project we do at New Thinking. People come to us with problems in their jobs, and we write programs to solve them. Does that sound like the kind of thing you would enjoy doing?

YUNG: Yes. I very much like to solve problems to help others.

HINGHAM: What was your favorite course during college?

YUNG: They are all very valuable. I enjoy all.

HINGHAM: Did you have one course in which you did especially well?

YUNG: (*blushing, looking down*) I would not say that. I try to do well in all my courses, to learn from them.

Later, Barton Hingham and Molly Cannett, another interviewer for New Thinking, are discussing the day's interviews over dinner.

CANNETT: Did you find any good prospects today?

HINGHAM: Not really. I thought I was going to be bowled over by this one woman—name's Mei-ying Yung—who has done some incredibly intricate programming on her own while in college.

CANNETT: Sounds like just the kind of person we're looking for.

HINGHAM: I thought so too, until the interview. She just didn't seem to have the gusto we want. She showed no confidence or initiative in the interview. It was like the transcript and the person were totally different.

CANNETT: Hmmm, that's odd. Usually when we see someone who looks that good on paper, the interview is just a formality.

HINGHAM: Yeah, but I guess the formality is more important than we realized—Yung was a real dud in the interview. I still don't know what to make of it.

QUESTIONS FOR ANALYSIS AND DISCUSSION MindTap

You can answer these questions and see my responses to them online via MindTap for Chapter 7.

1. How does Mei-ying Yung's communication reflect her socialization in Chinese culture?

2. How could Mei-ying be more effective without abandoning the values of her native culture?

3. What could enhance Barton Hingham's ability to communicate effectively with people who were raised in non-Western cultures?

8

We love because
it's the only true
adventure.

Nikki Giovanni

Peter Arnold, Inc/Alamy

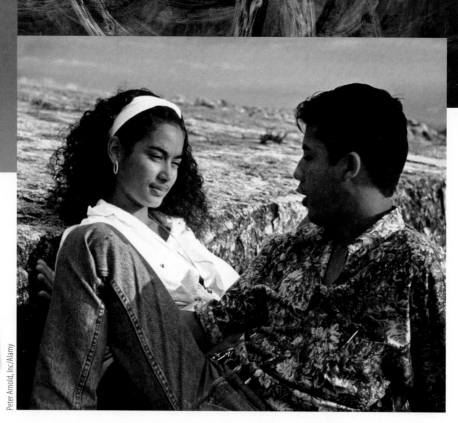

Communication in Personal Relationships

MindTap

Review the chapter
Learning Objectives
and **Start** with a quick
warm up activity.

Robin Dunbar (2012) studies the science of human love. As much as Dunbar tries to reduce love to scientific principles, he admits he is stumped by the intensity of human love. He can't explain why we yearn for the people we love or why thinking of a beloved makes us happy. Dunbar is one of the latest in a long line of scholars who have tried and failed to unravel the mysteries of human love and longing. While science has produced much useful knowledge about love relationships, it has not been able to fully explain them.

SHARPEN YOUR SKILL

At the end of this chapter,
refer to the Sharpen Your Skill
features, Faded Friendships
and Private Language, to apply
concepts from Chapter 8.

In this chapter, we focus on communication in two special types of personal relationships: friendships and romantic relationships. To launch the discussion, we'll define personal relationships. Next, we'll consider how communication guides the development of friendships and romances over time. Finally, we'll examine some of the special challenges to personal relationships in our era.

DEFINING PERSONAL RELATIONSHIPS

You have many relationships, but only a few are personal. **Personal relationships** are unique commitments between irreplaceable individuals who are influenced by rules, relational dialectics, and surrounding contexts. We'll discuss each part of this definition.

Uniqueness

Most of our relationships are social, not personal. In social relationships, participants adhere to social roles rather than interacting as unique individuals. For instance, you might exchange class notes with a classmate, play racquetball each week with a neighbor, and talk about politics with a coworker. In each case, the other person could be replaced by someone else taking the same role. The value of social relationships lies more in what participants do than in who they are because a variety of people could fulfill the same functions.

In personal relationships, however, the particular people—who they are and what they think, feel, and do—define the value of the connection. When one person in a personal relationship leaves the relationship or dies, that relationship ends. We may later have other intimates, but a new romantic partner or best friend will not replace the former one.

Commitment

For most of us, passion is what first springs to mind when we think about intimacy. **Passion** involves intensely positive feelings and desires for another person. The sparks and the emotional high of being in love or discovering a new friend stem from passion. It's why we feel "butterflies in the stomach" and fall "head over heels." Despite its excitement, passion isn't the primary building block of long-lasting personal relationships.

Passion is a feeling based on the rewards of involvement with a person. **Commitment,** in contrast, is a decision to remain in a relationship in spite of troubles, disappointments, sporadic boredom, and lulls in passion. The hallmark of commitment is the intention to share the future. Because a committed relationship assumes a future, partners are unlikely to bail out if the going gets rough. Instead, they weather bad times (Badiou, 2012; Le & Agnew, 2003; Lund, 1985).

Commitment grows out of **investments,** or that which we put into relationships that we could not retrieve if the relationship were to end. When we care about another person, we invest material things, such as money and possessions. Even more important, we invest time, energy, trust, and feelings. In doing this, we invest *ourselves*. We can't get back the feelings and energy and material investments. For good or ill, the more we invest in a relationship, the more difficult it is to end it (Dainton, 2006; Guerrero, Andersen, & Afifi, 2008).

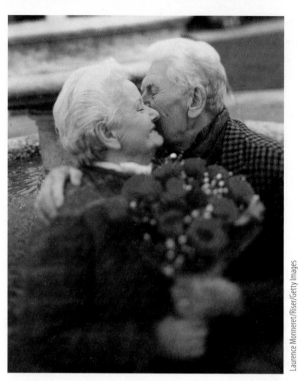

Partners in enduring, intimate relationships learn to negotiate dialectics.

Relationship Rules

All relationships have **rules** that guide how partners interact. As in other contexts, relationship rules define what is expected, what is not allowed, and when and how to do various things. As you may recall from our discussion in Chapter 5, two kinds of rules guide our communication. *Constitutive rules* define the meaning of various types of communication in personal relationships. For instance, women friends often count listening to problems as demonstrating care, whereas many men are more likely to count hanging out and doing things together as showing care (Metts, 2006; Wood, 1998, 2005). Couples work out constitutive rules to define what counts as loyalty, support, rudeness, love, joking, and so forth.

Regulative rules influence interaction by specifying when and with whom to engage in various kinds of communication. For example, some friends have a regulative rule that says it's okay to criticize each other in private but not okay to do so in front of others. Many men regard interrupting as a normal part of conversation between friends, whereas women sometimes interpret interruptions as rude (Wood, 1998, 2005). Some romantic partners limit physical displays of affection to private settings.

Affected by Contexts

Personal relationships are not isolated from the social world. Instead, the context of relationships influences interaction between partners (Dainton, 2006; Duck, 2007). Friendships and romances are affected by social circles, family units, and society as a whole. For instance, families may voice approval or disapproval of our choices of intimates or friends. Our social circles have categories for people who are cool and not cool and appropriate and not appropriate to socialize with. Our social circles also have norms for a range of activities such as recreation, community service, and spending.

KAYA   *I had never drunk much until I started going out with Steve. He was 10 years older than me. We usually spent time with his friends, who were also older and in business. All of them drank—not like a whole lot or anything, but several drinks a night. Pretty soon, I was doing that too—it was just part of the relationship with Steve.*

Changes in society and social norms go hand in hand with changes in the forms that relationships take. Compared to earlier eras, current Western society has increasing numbers of single parent families, gay and trans families, and blended families. Today, nearly 60% of couples live together before marrying (Stobbe, 2012), and 15% of new marriages are between people of different races (Jordan, 2012).

The growing number of dual-career couples is revising traditional expectations about how much each partner participates in earning income, homemaking, and child care (Galvin, 2006; Wood, 2011) and how much organizations are supposed to accommodate working parents (Wood & Dow, 2010). In all of these ways, our social circles and the larger society as well are contexts that influence the relationships we form and how we communicate within them.

Relational Dialectics

A final feature of personal relationships is **relational dialectics**—opposing and continual tensions that are normal in personal relationships. Scholars have identified three relational dialectics (Baxter, 1990, 1993; Baxter & Montgomery, 1996; Erbert, 2000).

Autonomy/Connection   In most close relationships there is frequent—sometimes continuous—friction arising from the contradictory impulses for autonomy and connection. Because we want to be deeply linked to intimates, we cherish the time with them and the sharing of experiences, thoughts, and feelings. At the same time, each of us needs some independence. We don't want our individuality to be swallowed up by relationships, so we sometimes seek distance, even from the people we love most. Friends and romantic partners may vacation together and be with each other almost all the time for a week or more. Yet the intense closeness leads them to crave time apart once the vacation ends. Both autonomy and closeness are natural human needs. The challenge is to preserve individuality while also creating intimacy.

> **STANLEY**   *For a long time, I've been stressed about my feelings. Sometimes I can't get enough of Annie, and then I feel crowded and don't want to see her at all. I never understood these switches, and I was afraid I was unstable or something. Now I see that I'm pretty normal after all.*

Novelty/Predictability   The second dialectic is the tension between wanting familiar routines and wanting novelty. We like a certain amount of routine to provide security and predictability in our lives. Friends often have standard times to get together, and they develop preferred interaction routines (Braithwaite & Kellas, 2006). Romantic couples develop preferred times and places for going out, and they establish patterns for interacting. Families have rituals to mark holidays (Bruess & Hoefs, 2006). Yet too much routine is boring, so friends occasionally explore a new restaurant, romantic couples periodically do something spontaneous to introduce variety into their customary routines, and families change established rituals.

Openness/Closedness   The third dialectic is the tension between a desire for openness and a desire for privacy. We want to share our inner selves with our intimates, yet there are times when we don't feel like sharing and topics that we don't want to talk about. All of us need some privacy, and our partners need to respect that (Petronio & Caughlin, 2006). Wanting some privacy doesn't indicate problems. It only means that we need both openness and closedness in our lives.

Managing Dialectics Leslie Baxter (1990) identifies four ways intimates deal with dialectical tensions. One response, called **neutralization,** negotiates a compromise in which each dialectical need is met to an extent but neither is fully satisfied. A couple might agree to be somewhat open but not intensely so. The **separation** response favors one need in a dialectic and ignores the other. For example, friends might agree to make novelty a priority and suppress their needs for routine. Separation also occurs when partners cycle between dialectical poles to favor each pole alternately. For example, a couple could spend weekends together and have little contact during the week.

A third way to manage dialectics is **segmentation** in which partners assign each need to certain spheres, issues, activities, or times. For instance, friends might be open about many topics but respect each other's privacy and not pry into one or two areas.

MARIANNE *Bart and I used to be spontaneous all the time. There was always room for something unexpected and unplanned. That changed when we had the twins last year. Now our home life is totally regulated, planned to the last nanosecond. If we get off schedule in getting the boys dressed and fed in the morning, then we're late getting to day care, which means we have to talk with the supervisor there, and then we're late getting to work. We try to have some spontaneity times when Bart's folks take the boys for a weekend, but it's a lot harder now that the boys are in our life.*

Novelty provides vitality to relationships.

The final method of dealing with dialectics is **reframing.** This is a complex strategy that redefines apparently contradictory needs as not really in opposition. My colleagues and I found examples of reframing in a study of romantic partners (Wood, Dendy, Dordek, Germany, & Varallo, 1994). Some of the couples said that their autonomy enhanced closeness because knowing they were separate in some ways allowed them to feel safer being connected. Instead of viewing autonomy and closeness as opposing, these partners transcended the apparent tension between the two to define the needs as mutually enhancing.

Research suggests that the least satisfying way of managing dialectical tension is separation in which only one need is fulfilled (Baxter, 1990). Separation is unsatisfying because repressing any natural human impulse diminishes us. The challenge is to find ways to honor and satisfy the variety of needs that humans have. Understanding that dialectics are natural and constructive allows us to accept and grow from the tensions they generate.

THE EVOLUTIONARY COURSE OF PERSONAL RELATIONSHIPS

Each relationship develops in unique ways. Yet there are commonalities in how personal relationships tend to progress. We'll explore typical patterns for the evolution of friendships and romances.

Friendships

Although friendships sometimes blaze to life quickly, usually they unfold through a series of fairly predictable stages (Rawlins, 1981, 1994). We meet a new person at work, in class, on an athletic team, in a club, or on Facebook. During initial face-to-face encounters, we rely on standard social rules and roles, and we tend to be careful about what we disclose. In the early stage of online relationships, people often venture into more personal, self-disclosing communication than they would at a similar stage of face-to-face acquaintance.

LEWIS *I met Stan over the Internet. We were both in the same chat room, and it was like we were on the same wavelength, so we started e-mailing each other privately. After a couple of months, it was like I knew Stan better than any of my close friends here, and he knew me, too—inside and out. It seemed safer or easier to open up online than in person. Maybe that's why we got so close so fast.*

If both people are interested, they communicate to learn whether they have shared interests and whether they enjoy interacting (Monsour, 2006). Riddick and Jason discover they share a passion for sci-fi films. As people discover shared interests, they generally spend more time together and are more relaxed. To signal that we're interested in being friends, we could introduce a more personal topic than any we've discussed so far. We also move toward friendship when we set up times to get together. Maria might ask Raul to go to lunch after class. People who have gotten to know each other online may arrange a face-to-face meeting. As people interact more personally, they begin to form a foundation for friendship.

At some point, people begin to think of themselves as friends or as becoming friends. When this happens, social norms and roles become less important, and friends begin to work out their own private ways of relating. When my friend Sue and I were in graduate school, we developed a ritual of calling each day between 5 and 6 o'clock to catch up while we cooked our dinners. Some friends settle into patterns of getting together for specific things (e.g., watching games, discussing books, walking, shopping).

When friends feel established in each other's lives, friendship stabilizes. Typically, stabilized friendships are integrated into the larger social contexts of the friends' lives so that they become part of an overall social network (Spenser & Pahl, 2006). Whereas in previous stages the friends didn't count on getting together unless they made a specific plan, stabilized friends assume they'll keep seeing each other. As trust and knowledge of each other expands, friends become more deeply woven into each other's life. Stabilized friendships may continue indefinitely.

While some friendships last for years or even lifetimes, not all do. Friendship withers when one or both people cease to be committed to it. Sometimes friends drift apart because each is pulled in a different direction by personal or career demands (Guerrero, Jones, & Boburka, 2006). In other cases, friendships deteriorate because they've become boring. Breaking relationship rules can also end friendships. Telling a friend's secrets to a third person or being dishonest may violate the rules of the friendship.

When friendships deteriorate, communication changes in predictable ways. Defensiveness and uncertainty rise, causing people to be more guarded and less open. Communication may also become more strategic as people try to protect themselves from further exposure and hurt. Even when serious violations occur between friends, relationships can sometimes be repaired. For this to happen, both friends must be committed to rebuilding trust and talking openly about their feelings and needs.

Romantic Relationships

Like friendships, romances also have a typical—but not a universal—evolutionary path. For most of us, romance progresses through the stages of escalation, navigation, and deterioration.

Escalation   Before a romantic relationship begins, there are individuals who have particular needs, goals, experiences, and qualities that affect what they want in others and relationships. Individuals have learned constitutive and regulative communication rules that affect how we interact with others and how we interpret their communication (Bachen & Illouz, 1996).

Romantic relationships usually start with predictable social interaction. The meaning of invitational communication is found on the relational level of meaning, not the content level. The content level of meaning of "Do you like jazz?" is unimportant. But on the relationship level of meaning, the comment says "I'm available and possibly interested. Are you?"

Out of all the people we meet, we are attracted romantically to only a few. The three greatest influences on initial attraction are self-concept, proximity, and similarity. Our self-concept affects our choices of candidates for romance. How we define our sexual orientation, for example, is a primary influence on our consideration of potential romantic partners, as are race and social class.

In addition to self-concept, proximity influences initial attraction. We can interact only with people we meet, whether in person or online. Consequently, the places in which we live, work, and socialize, as well as online communities in which we participate, constrain the possibilities for relationships. Some contexts, such as college campuses, promote meeting potential romantic partners, whereas other contexts are less conducive to meeting and dating.

Similarity is also important in romantic relationships. In the realm of romance, "birds of a feather flock together" seems truer than "opposites attract" (Samp & Palevitz, 2009). Most of us are attracted to people whose values, attitudes, and lifestyles are similar to ours and to people who are about as physically attractive as we are.

As in the early stages of friendship, potential romantic partners fish for common interests: "Do you like jazz?" "What's your family like?" "Do you follow politics?" As we continue to interact with others, both breadth and depth of disclosure increase. Self-disclosure tends to escalate intimacy (Duck & Wood, 2006) because we perceive it as a sign of trust.

If early interaction increases attraction, then we may increase the amount and intimacy of interaction. My students nicknamed this point in romance *euphoria* to emphasize the intensity and happiness it typically embodies. During this phase, partners spend more and more time together, and they rely less on external structures such as movies or parties. Instead, they immerse themselves in the budding relationship and may feel they can't be together enough. Additional and more personal disclosures are exchanged, and partners increasingly learn how the other feels and thinks. Increasingly, people develop relationships online. Compared to face-to-face relationships, online relationships tend to form more rapidly and tend to involve greater idealization in which partners have overly positive perceptions of one another.

At some point, partners consider whether they want the relationship to be permanent or at least extended. If so, they work through any problems and obstacles to long-term viability. In same-sex relationships, partners often have to resolve differences about openness regarding their sexual orientations and acceptance by families. Couples may also need to work out differences in religions and conflicts in locations and career goals.

KYLE *When Todd and I got together, I knew he was the one for me—the man I wanted to spend the rest of my life with. But we had a huge problem. He is totally out, and I'm not. If I came out at my job, I'd be off the fast track immediately, and I'd probably be fired. It was a huge issue between us because he wanted me to be as out as he is—like to take him with me to the holiday parties at my company. I can't do that. It's still a real tension between us.*

COMMUNICATION HIGHLIGHT

"How do I love thee? Let me count the ways." In opening one of her best-known poems with these lines, Elizabeth Barrett Browning foresaw what social scientists would later discover: that there are many ways of loving (Swidler, 2001). Just as people differ in their tastes in food and styles of dress, we differ in how we love. Researchers have identified six different styles of loving, each of which is valid in its own right, although not all styles are compatible with one another (Hendrick & Hendrick, 1996; Hendrick, Hendrick, Foote, & Slapion-Foote, 1984; Lee, 1973, 1988). See whether you can identify your style of loving in the descriptions given.

Eros is a style of loving that is passionate, intense, and fast moving. Not confined to sexual passion, eros may be expressed in spiritual, intellectual, or emotional ways.

How Do I Love Thee?

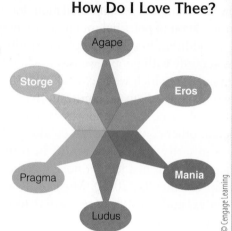

© Cengage Learning

FIGURE 8.1
The Colors of Love

Storge (pronounced "store-gay") is a comfortable, best-friends kind of love that grows gradually to create a stable and even-keeled companionship.

Ludus is a playful, sometimes manipulative style of loving. For ludic lovers, love is a challenge, a puzzle, a game to be relished but not one to lead to commitment.

Mania is a style of loving marked by emotional extremes. Manic lovers often are insecure about their value and their partners' commitment.

Agape is a selfless kind of love in which a beloved's happiness is more important than one's own. Agapic lovers are generous, unselfish, and devoted.

Pragma is a pragmatic and goal-oriented style of loving. Pragmas rely on reason and practical considerations to select people to love.

As you might expect, during this phase of romance, communication often involves negotiation and even conflict. Issues that weren't problems in a dating relationship may have to be resolved to allow a long-term future. Some couples find they cannot resolve problems. It is entirely possible to love a person with whom we don't want to share our life.

Commitment is a decision to stay with a relationship permanently. This decision transforms a romantic relationship from one based on past and present experiences and feelings into one with a future. Before making a commitment, partners don't view the relationship as continuing forever. With commitment, the relationship becomes a given around which they arrange other aspects of their lives.

Navigation   In lasting relationships, the longest span of time is navigation, which is the ongoing process of communicating to sustain intimacy in the face of changes in oneself, one's partner, the relationship, and surrounding contexts. Couples continuously work through new issues, revisit old ones, and accommodate changes in their individual and joint lives. To use an automotive analogy, navigating involves both preventive maintenance and periodic repairs (Stafford, 2009). Navigating communication aims to keep intimacy satisfying and healthy and to deal with problems and tensions. In her study of older couples who have stayed together, therapist Maggie Scarf (2008) found that the later years in very long-term marriages can be the happiest, in part because couples have learned to focus on what matters and not to sweat the small stuff. Other research (Parker-Pope, 2009b) confirms the finding that many couples find the "empty nest years" the happiest in their marriages because there are fewer stresses and more couple time.

The nucleus of intimacy is **relational culture**, a private world of rules, understandings, meanings, and patterns of interacting that partners

Bizarro

GROK LOOK AT CHONK, GROK FEEL DIZZY. GROK WANT CHONK STAY AT GROK'S CAVE ALWAYS. HERE PRETTY ROCK.

ORIGIN OF THE WEDDING RING

Bizarro(NEW) © 1998 Dan Piraro. King Features Syndicate

create for their relationship (Wood, 1982). Relational culture includes how a couple manages relational dialectics. Mei-Ling and Gregory may do a great many things together, whereas Lana and Kaya emphasize autonomy. Brent and Carmella may be open and expressive, whereas Marion and Nisha prefer more privacy. There aren't right and wrong ways to manage dialectics, because individuals and couples differ in what they need. Relational culture also includes communication rules, usually unspoken, about how to signal anger, love, sexual interest, and so forth. Especially important in navigation is small talk, through which partners weave together the fabric of their history and their current lives, experiences, and dreams.

Not all intimately bonded relationships endure. Despite popular belief that love is forever, often it isn't forever and may not even be for very long: Nearly half of first marriages end within 20 years (Tobbe, 2012). Tensions within a relationship, as well as pressures and problems in surrounding contexts, may contribute to the end of intimacy.

HEALTH COMMUNICATION

Marriage and Health

Does marriage make you healthier? For years, researchers believed that people who are married are healthier than those who are unmarried, leading them to dub this "the marriage advantage." Studies showed all kinds of health benefits for married people: lower risk of developing cancer, having heart attacks, getting dementia, and even being in car accidents.

New research, however, suggests the relationship between marriage and health is not as clear-cut as once believed. While people in happy, healthy marriages do seem to reap significant health benefits, those in troubled marriages may not. In fact, people in highly stressful marriages may be far less healthy than if they were single. A number of epidemiological studies suggest that unhappily married couples are more likely to suffer heart attacks, cardiovascular disease, and illnesses than happily married couples (Parker-Pope, 2010).

Deterioration   Deterioration often begins when one or both partners reflect and sometimes brood about dissatisfaction with the relationship. It's easy for intrapsychic processes to become self-fulfilling prophecies: As gloomy thoughts snowball and awareness of positive features of the relationship ebbs, partners may actually talk themselves into the failure of their relationship. There are some general sex and gender differences in what generates dissatisfaction (Duck & Wood, 2006). For women, unhappiness most often arises when communication declines in quality or quantity. Men are more likely to be dissatisfied by specific behaviors or the lack of valued behaviors or by having domestic responsibilities that they feel aren't a man's job. Because many women are socialized to be sensitive to interpersonal nuances, they are generally more likely than men to notice tensions and early symptoms of relationship problems.

If unchecked, dissatisfaction tends to lead to the breakdown of established patterns, understandings, and rules that have been part of the relationship. Partners may stop talking after dinner, no longer bother to call when they are running late, and in other ways depart from rules and patterns that have defined their relational culture. As the relational culture weakens, dissatisfaction mounts.

Conflict, which is normal in all enduring relationships, may escalate when a relationship is deteriorating. In addition, partners may feel less motivated to manage conflict constructively, so it can become increasingly hurtful and unproductive, which may accelerate relational decline. The following communication highlight identifies key aspects of conflict that can kill relationships.

Many people avoid talking about problems, refuse to return calls from partners, and in other ways evade confronting the difficulties. Although it is painful to talk about problems, avoiding discussion does nothing to resolve them and may make them worse. Whether a relationship survives at this juncture depends on how committed the partners are, on whether they perceive attractive alternatives to the relationship, and on whether they have the communication skills to work through problems constructively.

COMMUNICATION HIGHLIGHT

The Four Horsemen of the Apocalypse

Psychologist John Gottman has spent more than 20 years studying marriages and counseling couples (Gottman, 1994a, 1994b, 1999; Gottman & Silver, 1994). He concludes that there is no difference in the amount of conflict between happily married couples and couples who divorce or have unhappy marriages.

Healthy and unhealthy marriages do differ in two important respects. First, partners who are unhappy together and who often divorce tend to engage in what Gottman calls "corrosive communication patterns." Gottman views these destructive communication practices as "the four horsemen of the apocalypse":

   complaint and criticism

   defensiveness and denial of responsibility

   expressions of contempt

   stonewalling

These "four horsemen of the apocalypse" foster negative feelings: anger, fear, sadness, and dissatisfaction. Often these destructive communication patterns are evident in extensive nagging, which can profoundly sour marriages, according to Dr. Howard Markman, who directs the Center of Marital and Family Studies (Bernstein, 2012).

Gottman thinks the most corrosive of the four is **stonewalling**, which is refusing to discuss issues that are causing tension in a relationship. When people stonewall, they block the possibility of resolving conflicts. In addition, on the relationship level of meaning they communicate that problems in the relationship aren't worth dealing with.

The second major difference between marriages that succeed and those that fail is not bad moments but a predominance of good moments. Happy couples have as many conflicts and tensions as unhappy ones, but they have more enjoyable times together. Says Gottman, a positive balance is everything.

LUKE   *I'd been with Maggie for nearly a year when our relationship ended. Things had been a little rough, but I thought that was natural in long-distance relationships. I found out it was over when I saw her status update on Facebook!*

If partners lack commitment or the communication skills they need to restore intimacy, they often begin to tell others about problems in the relationship and to seek support from others. Friends and family members can provide support by being available and by listening. Partners may give self-serving accounts of the breakup to save face and secure sympathy from others. Although self-serving explanations of breakups are common, they aren't necessarily constructive. We have an ethical responsibility to monitor communication during this period so that we don't say things we'll later regret.

If partners decide they will definitely part ways, either separately or in collaboration, they decide how to explain their problems to friends, coworkers, children, family members, and social acquaintances. In addition, each partner works individually to make sense of the relationship: what it meant, why it failed, and how it affected him or her. Typically, partners mourn the failure to realize that which once seemed possible.

Yet mourning and sadness may be accompanied by other, more positive outcomes from breakups. Ty Tashiro and Patricia Frazier (2003) surveyed undergraduates who had recently broken up with their romantic partners. They found that people reported that breaking up gave them new insights into themselves, improved family relationships, and gave them more clear ideas about future partners. Once a relationship is declared over, each partner moves ahead to a future without the other.

Challenges in Personal Relationships

To sustain fulfilling personal relationships, partners rely on communication to deal with internal tensions between themselves and external pressures. The skill with which we manage these challenges is a major influence on the endurance and quality of personal relationships. We'll consider four specific challenges that many friends and romantic partners face.

Manage Distance   Geographic separation can be difficult for friends and romantic couples. One of the greatest problems for long-distance commitments is inability to share small talk face-to-face and to engage in daily routines is a major one. Unlimited calling plans are a great way to stay in touch about the day-to-day stuff in your lives.

A second common problem is unrealistic expectations for time together (Stafford, 2005). Because long-distance friends and partners have so little time together physically, they want every moment to be perfect. They may feel that there should be no conflict and that they should be with each other during all the time they have together. Yet this is an unrealistic expectation. Conflict and needs for autonomy are natural in all relationships. They may be even more pronounced in long-distance relationships because friends and partners are used to living alone and have established independent rhythms that may not mesh well. In fact, loss of autonomy is a key reason that some couples who have dated long-distance break up when they are reunited in the same place (Stafford, Merolla, & Castle, 2006).

A third common challenge in long-distance relationships is idealization. Because partners are apart much of the time, they are more likely than geographically close partners to idealize each other, and this tendency is not lessened by online contact or phone calls (Stafford & Merolla, 2007).

The good news is that these problems don't necessarily sabotage long-distance romance. Many people maintain satisfying commitments despite geographic separation. To learn more about long-distance relationships and ways to connect with people who are in them, use your MindTap for *Communication in Our Lives* to access **WebLink 8.1** and **WebLink 8.2.**

Create Equitable Romantic Relationships   On the job, we expect equity: to be treated the same as other employees at our level. If we are asked to do more work than our peers, we can appeal to a manager or supervisor. In romantic relationships, however, there is no supervisor to ensure equity. Researchers report that the happiest dating and married couples believe both partners invest equally (DeMaris, 2007). When we think we are investing more than our partner is, we tend to be resentful. When it seems our partner is investing more than we are, we may feel guilty (Guerrero, La Valley, & Farinelli, 2008).

Although few partners demand moment-to-moment equality, most of us want our relationships to be equitable over time (Wood, 2011). Equity has multiple dimensions. We may evaluate the fairness of financial, emotional, physical, and other contributions to a relationship. One area that strongly affects satisfaction of spouses and cohabiting partners is equity in housework and child care. Inequitable division of domestic obligations fuels dissatisfaction and resentment, both of which harm intimacy (Alberts, Tracy, & Trethewey, 2011; DeMaris, 2007).

How are domestic responsibilities managed in same-sex couples? Lesbian couples create more egalitarian relationships than either heterosexuals or gay men. More than any other type of couple, lesbians are likely to communicate collaboratively to make decisions about domestic work and parenting (Golberg & Perry-Jenkins, 2007). Consequently, lesbians are least likely to have negative feelings of inequity. In many gay couples, the man who makes more money has and uses more power, both in making decisions that affect the relationship and in avoiding housework (Huston & Schwartz, 1996).

As a rule, women assume **psychological responsibility** for relationships, which involves remembering, planning, and coordinating domestic activities (Hochschild with Machung, 2003). Parents may take turns driving children to the doctor, but it is often the mother who remembers when check-ups are

Equitable participation in domestic responsibilities enhances partners' satisfaction.

needed, makes appointments, and reminds the father to take the child. Both partners may sign birthday cards, but women typically remember birthdays and buy cards and gifts. Successful long-term relationships in our era require partners to communicate collaboratively to design equitable divisions of responsibility.

MOLLY   *It really isn't fair when both spouses work outside of the home but only one of them takes care of the home and kids. For years, that was how Sean's and my marriage worked, no matter how much I tried to talk with him about a more fair arrangement. Finally, I had just had it, so I quit doing everything. Groceries didn't get bought, laundry piled up and he didn't have clean shirts, he didn't remember his mother's birthday (and for the first time ever, I didn't remind him), and bills didn't get paid. After a while, he suggested we talk about a system we could both live with.*

Resist Violence and Abuse Between Intimates   Intimate partner violence is widespread and it cuts across lines of socioeconomic status, race, and ethnicity (Johnson, 2008; Spitzack & Cupach, 2009). Violence is high not only in heterosexual marriages but also in dating and cohabiting relationships (Johnson, 2006, 2008). In addition to physical abuse, verbal and emotional brutality poison altogether too many relationships. Although a majority of perpetrators of intimate partner violence are men (Johnson, 2006, 2008), the vast majority of men do not inflict violence on girlfriends and wives, and they would not consider doing so.

A rising form of intimate partner violence is stalking, which is repeated, intrusive behavior that is uninvited and unwanted, that seems obsessive, and that makes the target afraid or concerned for his or her safety. In studies conducted on college campuses (Bazar, 2007; Spitzack & Cupach, 2009), 13% to 21% of students report having been stalked—approximately the same percentage of the general population that reports being stalked (Spitzack & Cupach, 2009). Stalking is particularly easy on campuses because it isn't difficult to learn others' routines. Social networking sites such as Facebook give stalkers more ways to learn about (potential) victims' habits and patterns.

Intimate partner violence tends to follow a predictable cycle: Tension mounts in the abuser, the abuser explodes by being violent, the abuser then is remorseful and loving, the victim feels loved and reassured that the relationship is working, and then tension mounts anew and the cycle begins again. Too often, people don't leave abusive relationships because they feel trapped by economic pressures or by relatives and clergy who counsel them to stay (Foley, 2006; Jacobson & Gottman, 1998). Without intervention, the cycle of violence is unlikely to stop. Abusive relationships are unhealthy for everyone involved. They violate the trust that is a foundation of intimacy, and they jeopardize the comfort, health, and sometimes the lives of victims of violence.

Communication is related to intimate partner violence in two ways. Most obviously, patterns of communication between couples and the intrapersonal communication of abusers can fuel tendencies toward violence. Some partners deliberately annoy and taunt each other. Also, the language abusers use to describe physical assaults on partners includes denial, trivializing the harm, and

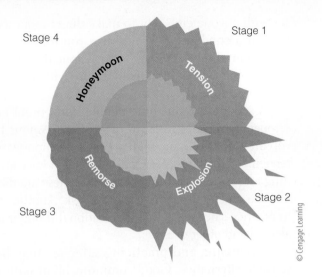

FIGURE 8.2
The Cycle of Abuse

blaming the partner or circumstances for "making me do it" (Johnson, 2006; Wood, 2001b). These intrapersonal communication patterns allow abusers to deny their offenses, justify violence, and cast responsibility outside themselves.

Intimate partner violence is also promoted by cultural communication practices that normalize violence, including violence against women (Herbert, 2009). From magazines to films to MTV, domination of women and violence against them are pervasive in media. News accounts that refer to "loving her too much" and "love that gets out of hand" camouflage the brutality and unloving nature of violence (Meyers, 1994, 1997).

Violent relationships are not the fault of victims. A person cannot earn battering, nor do victims encourage it. If you know or suspect that someone you care about is a victim of abuse, don't ignore the situation, and don't assume it's none of your business. It is an act of friendship to notice and offer to help. Victims of violence must make the ultimate decision about what to do, but the support and concern of friends can help them.

Negotiate Safer Sex   In our era, sexual activities pose serious, even deadly, threats to people of all sexual orientations. Each year in the United States, 18,000 people die of AIDS, and 56,000 people are diagnosed as HIV positive (Collins & Fauci, 2010). The cumulative numbers are grim: In the United States, more than one million people are living with HIV today, and over 500,000 people have died of HIV (Centers for Disease Control and Prevention, 2009, 2011).

HIV is not the only sexually transmitted disease (STD). Over 65 million Americans are currently living with one or more STDs, and 15 million new cases are diagnosed each year (Centers for Disease Control and Prevention, 2009). Because STDs often have no symptoms, they are often undiagnosed and untreated. The long-term effects of untreated STDs can be severe: infertility, blindness, liver cancer, increased vulnerability to HIV, and death.

Despite the real dangers of unsafe sex, many people find it awkward to ask partners direct questions (i.e., "Have you been tested for HIV?" "Are you having sex with anyone else?") or to make direct requests to partners (i.e., "I want you to wear a condom," "I would like you to be tested for STDs before we have sex"). Naturally, it's difficult to talk explicitly about sex and the dangers of STDs. However, it is far more difficult to live with a disease or the knowledge that you have infected someone else.

A second reason some people don't practice safer sex is that they hold erroneous and dangerous misperceptions. Among these are the assumptions that you are safe if you and your partner are monogamous, the belief that you can recognize "the kind of person" who might have an STD, and the idea that planning for sex destroys the spontaneity. These are dangerous, false beliefs that can put you and your partners at grave risk. Another reason people sometimes fail to practice safer sex is that their rational thought and control are debilitated by alcohol and other drugs.

Discussing and practicing safer sex may be awkward, but there is no sensible alternative. Good communication skills can help you negotiate safer sex. It is more constructive to say, "I feel unsafe having unprotected sex" than "Without a condom, you could give me AIDS." (Notice that the first statement uses *I*-language, whereas the second one relies on *you*-language.) A positive communication climate is fostered by using relational language, such as *we, us,* and *our relationship,* to talk about sex.

BEYOND THE CLASSROOM

Let's take the material in this chapter beyond the classroom by thinking about how what you've learned about communication in personal relationships might apply to the workplace, ethical choices, and engagement with the broader world.

1. **Workplace.** Apply the idea of investments and commitments to the employment context. Review the jobs that you have had in your life. Which ones did you invest most heavily in? Were you more committed to those jobs than ones in which you invested less?

2. **Ethics.** This chapter cites substantial research that shows equity between partners in romantic relationships is linked to satisfaction and relationship longevity. The chapter also notes that men and women in heterosexual relationships are not contributing equitably. Are inequitable relationships unethical? Is it right or fair for one partner to do more of the work required to keep a relationship going? If not, what ways can you think of to change the long-standing pattern whereby women do more of the work involved in maintaining relationships?

3. **Engagement.** Talk with someone who was raised in a culture different from the one in which you were raised. Ask him or her what he or she considers the most important qualities in a friend and in a romantic partner. Reflect on similarities and differences in his or her answers and the answers you would give.

CHAPTER SUMMARY

 Practice and review the content in this chapter.

In this chapter, we've explored communication in personal relationships, which are defined by uniqueness, commitment, relational dialectics, relationship rules, and interaction with surrounding contexts. We traced the typical evolutionary paths of friendships and romances by noting how partners communicate as relationships develop, stabilize, and sometimes decline.

In the final section of the chapter, we considered four challenges that friends and romantic partners face. The communication principles and skills we have discussed in this and previous chapters help us meet the challenges of sustaining intimacy across geographic distance, creating equitable relationships, resisting violence, and negotiating safer sex. Good communication skills enable us to meet these challenges so that our relationships survive and thrive over time.

APPLYING COMMUNICATION IN OUR LIVES

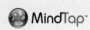

Communication in Our Lives is supported by a MindTap, a new online learning platform that delivers content, assignments, and a tailored presentation of the course curriculum created by your instructor. MindTap combines all of your learning tools–readings, multimedia, activities and assessments–into a singular learning unit that guides you through the course. Practice and Present, a unique tool within MindTap, allows you to upload your speech video files for practice or for a grade, comment on your peer's speeches and review your grades. MindTap also includes Speech Builder Express, a powerful tool that guides you through the speech outline and preparation process. For more information or to access MindTap, visit cengagebrain.com.

DEFINITIONS OF KEY CONCEPTS

 Review your **Flashcards**.

commitment A decision to remain with a relationship. One of three dimensions of enduring romantic relationships, commitment has more impact on relational continuity than does love alone.

investments Something put into a relationship that cannot be recovered should the relationship end. Investments, more than rewards and love, increase commitment.

neutralization One of four responses to relational dialectics; involves balancing or finding a compromise between two dialectical poles.

passion Intensely positive feelings and desires for another person. Passion is based on the rewards of involvement and is not equivalent to commitment.

personal relationship A relationship defined by uniqueness, rules, relational dialectics, and commitment and affected by contexts. Personal relationships, unlike social ones, are irreplaceable.

psychological responsibility The responsibility for remembering, planning, and coordinating domestic work and child care. In general, women assume the psychological responsibility for child care and housework even if both partners share in the actual tasks.

reframing One of four responses to relational dialectics. The reframing response transcends the apparent contradiction between two dialectical poles and reinterprets them as not in tension.

relational culture A private world of rules, understandings, and patterns of acting and interpreting that partners create to give meaning to their relationship; the nucleus of intimacy.

relational dialectics Opposing forces or tensions that are normal parts of all relationships. The three relational dialectics are autonomy/connectedness, novelty/predictability, and openness/closedness.

rules Patterned ways of behaving and interpreting behavior; all relationships develop rules.

segmentation One of four responses to relational dialectics. Segmentation responses

meet one dialectical need while ignoring or not satisfying the contradictory dialectical need.

separation One of four responses to relational dialectics, in which friends or romantic partners assign one pole of a dialectic to certain spheres of activities or topics and the contradictory dialectical pole to distinct spheres of activities or topics.

stonewalling Refusal to discuss issues that are creating tension in a relationship. Stonewalling is especially corrosive in relationships because it blocks the possibility of resolving conflicts.

FOR FURTHER REFLECTION AND DISCUSSION

Ethics

1. Think about the distinction between passion and commitment in personal relationships. Describe relationships in which commitment is present but passion is not. Describe relationships in which passion exists but not commitment. What can you conclude about the values of each?

2. Are you now or have you been involved in a long-distance personal relationship, either friendship or romance? How did you communicate to bridge the distance?

Do your experiences parallel the chapter's discussion of challenges in long-distance relationships?

3. Does a person who wants to end a serious romantic relationship have an ethical responsibility to talk with his or her partner about why he or she is no longer interested in maintaining the relationship? Under what conditions are we ethically obligated to help a partner through a breakup?

SHARPEN **YOUR SKILL**

1. Faded Friendships

Remember three friendships that were once very close but have faded away. Describe the reasons they ended. How did boredom, differences, external circumstances, or violations contribute to the decay of the friendships? How did communication patterns change as the friendships waned?

2. Private Language

Private language between intimates increases the sense of "we-ness," and heightens partners' sense

of themselves as a special couple. Partners make up words and nicknames for each other, and they develop ways to send private messages in public settings.

What are the special words and nonverbal codes in a close relationship of yours? Do you have a way to signal each other when you're bored at a party and ready to leave? Do you use nicknames and private words? Would you feel any loss if you had no private language in your relationship?

EXPERIENCING COMMUNICATION IN OUR LIVES | MindTap™

CASE STUDY: *Wedding Bells?*

A video of the conversation scripted here is featured in your Chapter 8 MindTap for *Communication in Our Lives*. Select "Wedding Bells?" to watch the video. Improve your own communication skills by reading, watching, and evaluating this communication encounter.

After meeting at a New Year's party in the winter of their senior year at Agora College, Trevor and Meg quickly developed an exclusive dating relationship. Now, 4 months later, they are trying to figure out what to do about their relationship.

TREVOR: Do you realize that half our friends are planning weddings? Maybe we should start thinking about ours.

MEG: Don't start this again. You know how I feel about that. It's just too soon. We need to know a lot more before we even think about marriage.

TREVOR: Why? I'm crazy in love with you, and you are with me, right?

MEG: (*Nods*)

TREVOR: So what's too soon? What else do we need to know?

MEG: First of all, I'll be starting law school in the fall, and that's a whole new thing for me. You haven't decided on a job yet. We don't even know if we'll be in the same city!

TREVOR: Sure we do. You'll be going to law school at State, and I can get a job near there. One good thing about being a business major is that I can get a job anywhere.

MEG: See, right there is a problem: I'm much more concerned about my career than you are about yours. Your whole attitude toward it is just so casual.

TREVOR: I am not casual about us. I love you enough to arrange the rest of my life around our relationship. So why aren't you willing to do the same?

MEG: 'Cause it's just too soon. Law school will be very demanding, and I don't want to try starting that and a marriage at the same time.

TREVOR (grinning): I'll help you study. Any other problems?

MEG: What about eating? We do okay now because we don't live together. But I'm a vegan, and you'll eat anything. I think we'd have problems if we lived together.

TREVOR: Just keep your tofu away from my chicken in the refrigerator, and we'll be fine.

MEG: I'm serious, Trevor.

TREVOR: So am I. I mean, just because we live together doesn't mean we have to eat the same things. That's not a problem.

MEG: You and I have different values and goals. You think I'm nuts to want a Mercedes, and I don't know how you can be happy with that old truck you drive. And you think I'm extravagant any time I buy anything for myself.

TREVOR: Okay, so we'll have separate accounts, and that way each of us can decide how to spend our own money. Next problem?

MEG: What about children?

TREVOR: What about children? I don't see any children. No problem there.

MEG: Quit kidding around, you know what I mean. You definitely want children; I don't know if I do. That's a big issue, one we should settle before we even think about marriage.

TREVOR: Meggie, if we wait until we've settled every issue, you know, solved every problem, we'll never get married. I totally love you, and I believe in us. I think that we can resolve any issue as it comes along. That's what love is.

MEG: I'm just not comfortable with that. I'd like a lot more of these issues settled before I marry anyone. Love is great, but it's not enough.

QUESTIONS FOR ANALYSIS AND DISCUSSION   MindTap

You can answer these questions and see my responses to them online via MindTap for Chapter 8.

1. Based on the scenario, which styles of loving do you think Meg and Trevor have? What communication by each of them leads you to perceive particular styles of loving?

2. Based on their conversation, what do you perceive to be Meg's and Trevor's levels of commitment to the relationship?

3. What aspects of context seem to influence Meg's and Trevor's preferences for how the relationship should proceed?

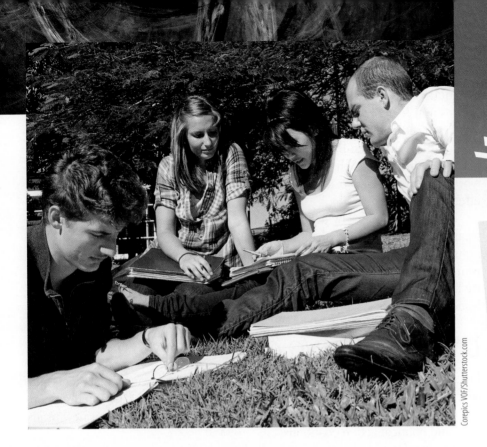

Corepics VOF/Shutterstock.com

> Never doubt that a small group of thoughtful committed citizens can change the world; indeed, it's the only thing that ever has.
>
> **Margaret Mead**

Communication in Groups and Teams

"Teams take too much time to decide anything."
"Working in groups increases creativity."
"Groups suppress individuality."
"Teams make better decisions than individuals."

With which of these statements do you agree? Actually, there's some truth to each statement. Groups generally do take more time to reach decisions than individuals, yet group decisions often are superior to those made by one person. Although group interaction stimulates creativity, it may also suppress individual opinions.

 MindTap™

Review the chapter **Learning Objectives** and **Start** with a quick warm up activity.

SHARPEN YOUR SKILL

At the end of this chapter, refer to the Sharpen Your Skill features, Group Creativity and Your Communication in Groups, to apply concepts from Chapter 9.

Communication is a major influence on whether groups and teams are productive and enjoyable or inefficient and unpleasant. Communication in groups and teams calls for many of the skills and understandings that we've discussed in previous chapters. For example, constructive group communication requires that members express themselves clearly, check perceptions, and listen mindfully. This chapter will increase your understanding of how groups work and enhance your ability to participate in and lead groups and teams effectively.

The chapter opens by defining groups and teams and identifying potential weaknesses and strengths of collective work. We then examine features of small groups. The third section of the chapter focuses on different types of group communication and considers how each affects collective climate and productivity leadership. As part of our discussion of group communication, we discuss leadership.

Read, highlight and take notes online.

UNDERSTANDING GROUPS AND TEAMS

Pick up any newspaper or surf the Internet and you will see announcements and advertisements for social groups, volunteer service committees, personal support groups, health teams, focus groups sought by companies trying out new products, and political action coalitions.

The tendency toward group work is especially pronounced in the workplace. Although groups and teams have gained increased prominence in today's organizations, they actually have a long history in the workforce. Miners, seafarers, and other laborers rely on groups to accomplish their jobs and often to survive harsh and dangerous working conditions (Hodson & Sullivan, 2002).

Today groups and teams are an even greater part of work life (Barge, 2009; Beebe & Masterson, 2011; Rothwell, 2009). Whether you are an attorney working with a litigation team, a health care professional who participates in health delivery teams, or a factory worker on a group assigned to find ways to reduce production time, working with others probably will be part of your career. In fact, some medical schools now include interviews in their admissions procedures specifically to weed out applicants who lack skill in teamwork (Harris, 2011).

HEALTH COMMUNICATION

Teamwork Lacking in the OR

Reports of errors in surgery are not uncommon. Have you ever wondered how a sponge could be left inside a patient or how surgery could be performed on the wrong knee? One contributor to surgical errors is poor teamwork among those working in the operating room. A survey of more than 2,100 surgeons, anesthesiologists, and nurses at 60 hospitals showed that many teams suffer from weak teamwork (Nagourney, 2006). Doctors' disregard for nurses' expertise was one of the most commonly cited dynamics that undermined effective teamwork.

What are groups and teams? Are six people standing together on a street corner waiting to cross the street a group? Are five people studying independently in a library a group? Are four students standing in line to buy books a group? The answer is *no* in each case. These are collections of individuals, but they are not groups.

For a group to exist, there must be interaction and interdependence between individuals, a common goal, and shared rules of conduct. Thus, we can define a **group** as three or more people who interact over time, depend on one another, and follow some shared rules of conduct to reach a common goal. To be a group, members must perceive themselves as interdependent—as somehow needing one another and counting on one another (Adams & Galanes, 2011; Harris & Sherblom, 2010; Lumsden & Lumsden, 2009).

HEALTH COMMUNICATION

Meet the Health Care Team

Years ago, a hospitalized patient looked to his or her doctor and nurse for most medical care. No longer is that the case. Today, most patients have health care teams (Apker, 2000) with members who continually communicate to coordinate patient care. Following are the typical components of health care teams.

Medical staff

An attending physician has overall responsibility for a patient's care. In some hospitals, particularly teaching hospitals, resident physicians and medical students may assist in a patient's care and may observe patients as part of their training.

Nursing staff

Registered nurses (RNs) administer medicines and treatments ordered by the attending physician. Nurse practitioners or clinical nurse specialists also may assist in care. Under the supervision of a registered nurse, licensed practical nurses (LPNs), nursing students and nursing assistants may assist in a patient's care.

Social services

Medical social workers provide counseling and information on resources following discharge to patients and their families. In some instances, social workers can provide limited assistance regarding financial matters related to health care.

Pastoral care

Most hospitals can contact a chaplain, rabbi, priest, or minister of particular faiths. In addition, most hospitals host interdenominational services for patients and their families.

Other health professionals

Depending on a patient's condition and needs, the health care team may also include specialists in areas such as physical therapy, psychology or psychiatry, laboratory technicians, dieticians, and respiratory care.

A **team** is a special kind of group that is characterized by different and complementary resources of members and a strong sense of collective identity. Like all groups, teams involve interaction, interdependence, shared rules, and common goals. Yet a team is distinct in two respects. First, teams consist of people with diverse skills and experience. Whereas group members may have similar backgrounds and abilities, a team consists of people who bring different resources to a common. Second, teams tend to develop greater interdependence and a stronger sense of collective identity than other groups (Lumsden & Lumsden, 2009).

Because groups consist of individuals who are interdependent and who interact over time, groups develop rules that members understand and follow. You'll recall from previous chapters that constitutive rules state what counts as what. For example, in some groups, disagreement counts as a positive sign of involvement, whereas other groups regard disagreement as negative. Regulative rules regulate how, when, and with whom we interact. For instance, a group might have regulative rules stipulating that members don't interrupt each other and that it's okay to be a few minutes late but more than 10 minutes is a sign of disregard for other group members. Groups generate rules over time in the process of interacting and figuring out what works for them.

Groups also have shared goals. Citizens form groups to accomplish political goals, establish social programs, protest zoning decisions, and protect the security of neighborhoods. Workers form teams to develop and market products, evaluate and refine company programs, and improve productivity. Other groups form around goals such as promoting personal growth (therapy groups), sharing a life (families), socializing (singles clubs), having fun and fitting in (peer groups), or participating in sports (intramural teams). As Mieko explains in her commentary, without a common goal, a group doesn't exist. Groups end if the common objective has been achieved or if it ceases to matter to members. To better understand small groups, we'll now consider their potential values and limits, features that affect participation, and the influence of culture on group communication.

Interaction between team members often heightens commitment to collective goals.

David K Purdy/Getty Images Sport/Getty Images

MIEKO *When I first came here to go to school, I felt very alone. I met some other students from Japan, and we formed a group to help us feel at home in the United States. For the first year, that group was most important to me and the others because we felt uprooted. The second year, it was good but not so important because we'd all started finding ways to fit in here, and we felt more at home. When we met the first time of the third year, we decided not to be a group anymore. The reason we wanted a group no longer existed.*

POTENTIAL LIMITATIONS AND STRENGTHS OF GROUPS

Researchers have compared individual and group decision making. As you might expect, the research identifies both potential weaknesses and potential strengths of groups.

Potential Limitations of Groups

Two significant disadvantages of group discussion are the time needed for the group process and the potential for pressure to conform; both can interfere with high-quality work from groups. A third potential problem is reduced individual responsibility.

Time From your own experience, you know that a group takes much longer to decide something than an individual does. Operating solo, an individual can think through ideas efficiently and choose the one she or he considers best. In group discussion, however, all members must have an opportunity to voice their ideas and to respond to the ideas others put forward. In addition, groups need time to deliberate about alternative courses of action. Thus, group discussion probably is not a wise choice for routine policy making and emergency tasks. When creativity and thoroughness are important, however, the values of groups may outweigh the disadvantage of time.

King Features Syndicate

Conformity Pressures   Groups also have the potential to suppress individuals and encourage conformity. This can happen in two ways. First, conformity pressure may exist when a majority of members has an opinion different from that of a minority of members or a single member. It's hard to hold out for your point of view when most of your peers have a different one.

Second, conformity pressures may arise when one member is extremely charismatic, powerful, or prestigious. Even if that person is all alone in a point of view, he or she may have sufficient status to sway others. Sometimes a high-status member doesn't intend to influence others and may not overtly exert pressure.

In effective groups, all members understand and resist conformity pressures. They realize that a high-status member isn't necessarily smarter than others, that the majority is sometimes wrong, and that the minority, even a minority of one, is sometimes right.

LANCE   *I used to belong to a creative writing group where all of us helped each other improve our writing. We were all equally vocal, and we had a lot of good discussions and even disagreements when the group first started. But then one member of the group got a story of hers accepted by a big magazine, and all of a sudden we thought of her as a better writer than any of us. She didn't act any different, but we saw her as more accomplished, so when she said something, everybody listened and nobody disagreed. It was like a wet blanket on our creativity because her opinion just carried too much weight once she got published.*

A third potential disadvantage of group work is the possibility of **social loafing**, which exists when members of a group exert less effort than they would if they worked alone (Hoon & Tan, 2008). If an individual is charged with a task and the task doesn't get done, the individual can be held accountable. When a group is charged with a task, however, members may have less of a sense of accountability for the end product.

Potential Strengths of Groups

In comparison to individuals, groups generally have greater resources, are more thorough and more creative, and generate greater commitment to decisions.

Greater Resources   A group obviously exceeds any individual member in the number of ideas, perspectives, experiences, and expertise it can bring to bear on solving a problem. The diversity on teams means that one member knows the technical aspects of a product, another understands market psychology, a third has expertise in cost analysis, and so forth.

Greater Thoroughness   Groups also tend to be more thorough than individuals, probably because members act as a check-and-balance system for each other (Rothwell, 2009). The parts of an issue one member doesn't understand, another person does; the details of a plan that bore one person interest another; and the holes in a proposal that one member overlooks are recognized by others.

COMMUNICATION HIGHLIGHT

Einstein's Mistakes

That's the title of a book by Hans Ohanian (2009). As brilliant as Einstein may have been, he didn't make his great discoveries alone. He is most famous for $E = mc^2$, the equation expressing the law of relativity. However, math wasn't Einstein's strong suit and his proof of the law contained a number of mathematical errors. Another physicist, Max Von Laue, worked out a complete and correct proof, at which point $E = mc^2$ was on scientifically solid ground.

The myth of the individual genius is popular in Western societies, in part because they place high value on individualism. However, great innovations, discoveries, and inventions usually reflect the work of many people (Rae-Dupree, 2008). In his book *Group Genius,* Keith Sawyer (2008) shows that most creativity is the product of groups and teams. One person may get the credit—the raise, the patent, or the Nobel Prize—but it takes many to do the work.

The greater thoroughness of groups isn't simply the result of more people. The discussion process promotes more critical and more careful analysis because members propel each other's thinking.

LAURA   *The first time I heard about brainstorming was on my job, when the supervisor said all of us in my department were to meet and brainstorm ways to cut costs for the company. I thought it was silly to take time to discuss cost saving when each person could just submit suggestions individually. But I was wrong. When my group started, each of us had 1 or 2 ideas—only that many. But the six of us came up with more than 25 ideas after we'd talked for an hour.*

Greater Creativity   The third value of groups is that they are generally more creative than individuals. Any individual eventually runs out of new ideas, but groups seem to have almost infinite generative ability. As members talk, they build on each other's ideas, refine proposals, see new possibilities in each other's comments, and so forth. Often, the result is a greater number of ideas and more creative final solutions.

Greater Commitment   Finally, an important strength of groups is their potential to generate stronger commitment to decisions. The greater commitment fostered by group discussion arises from two sources. First, participation in the decision-making process enhances commitment to decisions, which is especially important if members are to be involved in implementing the decision. Second, because groups have greater resources than an individual decision maker, their decisions are more likely to take into account the points of view of various people whose cooperation is needed to implement a decision.

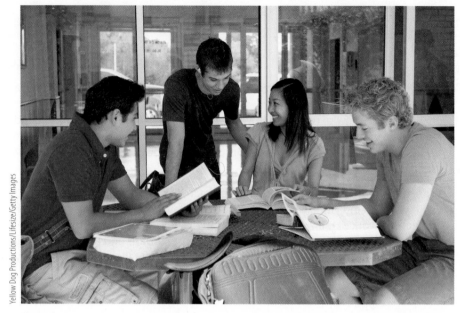

Effective communication in groups tends to generate commitment to group decisions.

This is critical because a decision can be sabotaged if the people it affects dislike it or believe their perspectives weren't considered.

Greater resources, thoroughness, creativity, and commitment to group goals are powerful values of group decision making. To realize these values, however, members must be aware of the trade-off of time needed for group discussion and must resist pressures to conform, or to induce others to conform, without critical thought.

FEATURES OF SMALL GROUPS

The group strengths we've identified are realized only if members participate effectively. Thus, we need to know what influences communication in small groups. We'll consider five features of small groups that directly affect participation.

Cohesion

Cohesion is the degree of closeness, esprit de corps, and group identity. In highly cohesive groups, members see themselves as linked tightly together and unified in their goals. This increases members' satisfaction with the group and, in turn, their productivity (Forsyth, 2009).

Communication can enhance cohesion in three ways. First, communication that emphasizes the group or team and the common objectives of all members builds cohesion. Second, cohesion is fostered by communication that highlights similarities between members. A third way to enhance cohesion is by talking in ways that allow all members to feel valued and part of the group.

Cohesion and participation influence each other reciprocally. Cohesion is promoted when all members participate. At the same time, because cohesion generates a feeling of identity and involvement, once established, it fosters participation. Encouraging all members to be involved and attending responsively to everyone's contributions generally foster cohesion and continued participation.

Although cohesion is important for effective group communication, too much cohesion can cause problems. When members are extremely close, they may be less critical of each other's ideas and less willing to engage in the analysis and arguments necessary for the best outcomes. When groups are too cohesive, they may engage in **groupthink**, a process in which members cease to think critically and independently about ideas generated by the group. Groupthink has occurred in such high-level groups as presidential advisory boards and national decision-making bodies (Janis, 1989; Young, Wood, Phillips, & Pedersen, 2001). Members perceive their group so positively that they share the illusion that it cannot make bad decisions. Consequently, they are less careful in evaluating ideas, which can result in inferior group outcomes.

Group Size

The sheer number of people in a group affects the amount of communication. The greater the number of people in a group, the fewer the contributions any individual may make. Because participation is linked to satisfaction and commitment, larger groups may generate less satisfaction and commitment to decisions than smaller ones. Groups with nine or more members may form cliques and may be less cohesive than smaller ones (Benenson, Gordon, & Roy, 2000).

Groups can be too small as well as too large. With too few members, a group has limited resources, which eliminates one of the primary advantages of groups. Also, in very small groups, members may be unwilling to disagree or criticize each other's ideas because alienating one person in a three- or four-person group would dramatically diminish the group. Five to seven members seems to be the ideal size for a small group (Lumsden & Lumsden, 2009).

YOLANDA *The worst group I was ever in had three members. We were supposed to have five, but two dropped out after the first meeting, so there were three of us to come up with proposals for artistic programs for the campus. Nobody would say anything against anybody else's ideas, even if we thought they were bad. For myself, I know I held back from criticizing a lot of times because I didn't want to offend either of the other two. We came up with some really bad ideas because we were so small we couldn't risk arguing.*

Power Structure

Power structure is a third feature that influences participation in small groups. **Power** is the ability to influence others (Rothwell, 2009; Young et al., 2001). There are different kinds of power, or ways of influencing others.

Power over is the ability to help or harm others. This form of power usually is expressed in ways that highlight the status and visibility of the person wielding influence. A group leader might exert positive *power over* a member by providing mentoring, positive reports to superiors, and visibility in the group. A leader could also exert negative *power over* a member by withholding these benefits, assigning unpleasant tasks, and responding negatively to the member's communication during group meetings.

Power to is the ability to empower others to reach their goals. *Power to* is expressed in creating opportunities for others, recognizing achievements and facilitating others in accomplishing their goals. Group members use *power to* foster a win–win group climate in which each member's success is seen as advancing collective work.

> **STANLEY**   *The different kinds of power we discussed make me think of my high school. The principal came over the intercom to make announcements or lecture us on improper behaviors and threaten us about what was going to happen if we misbehaved. The teachers were the ones with power to. Most of them worked to empower us. They were the ones who gave us encouragement and praise. They were the ones who helped us believe in ourselves and reach our goals.*

The power structure of a group refers to the distribution of power among various members. If all members of a group have equal power, the group has a *distributed power structure*. On the other hand, if one or more members have greater power than others, the group has a *hierarchical power structure*. In some cases, hierarchy takes the form of one person who is more powerful than all others, who are equal in power to each other. In other cases, hierarchy may be more complicated, with more than two levels of power. A leader might have the

COMMUNICATION HIGHLIGHT

Five Bases of Power

What is power? How does a person get it? There is more than one answer to each of these questions because there are different sources of power (Arnold & Feldman, 1986).

Reward power	The ability to give people things they value, such as attention, approval, public praise, promotions, and raises
Coercive power	The ability to punish others through demotions, firing, and undesirable assignments
Legitimate power	The organizational role, such as manager, supervisor, or CEO, that results in others' compliance
Expert power	Influence derived from expert knowledge or experience
Referent power	Influence based on personal charisma and personality

To explore your own preferences regarding power—your own and your supervisor's at work—complete the Communication Highlight Activity for Chapter 9 via MindTap for *Communication in Our Lives.*

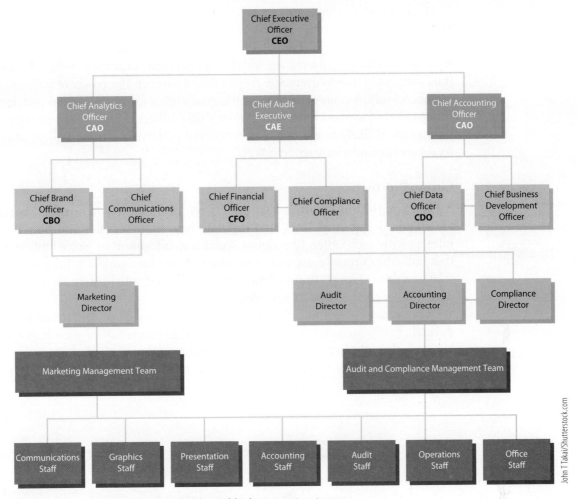

Corporate Hierarchy Structure

Individuals have unequal power in hierarchical power structures.

John T Takai/Shutterstock.com

greatest power, three others might have power equal to each other's but less than the leader's, and two other members might have little power.

How is power related to participation? First, members with high power tend to be the centers of group communication: They talk more, and others talk more to them. **Social climbing** is the attempt to increase personal status in a group by winning the approval of high-status members. If social climbing doesn't work to increase the status of the climber, he or she may become a marginal participant in the group. In addition, members with a great deal of power often have greater influence on group decisions. Not surprisingly, high-power members tend to find group discussion more satisfying than members with less power (Young et al., 2001). This makes sense because those with power get to participate more and get their way more often.

Power not only influences communication but also is influenced by communication. In other words, how members communicate can affect the power they acquire. People who demonstrate expertise in the group's task and who help build group cohesion tend to acquire power quickly.

Interaction Patterns

Another important influence on participation is the group's interaction patterns. Some groups are centralized; one or two people have key positions, and most or all communication is funneled through them (Figure 9.1). Other groups have decentralized patterns, in which communication is more balanced and thus more satisfying to everyone. As you might suspect, the power of individual members and the power structure of the group often affect interaction patterns. If one or two members have greater power than others, a centralized pattern of interaction is likely to emerge. Decentralized patterns are more typical when members have relatively equal power.

Group Norms

A final small-group feature that affects communication is **norms**. Norms are standardized guidelines that regulate how members act and how they interact with each other. Our definition of a small group, in fact, emphasizes that individuals must share understandings about their conduct. Like rules in relationships, a group's norms define what is allowed, what is not allowed, and what kind of participation is rewarded.

Group norms regulate all aspects of a group's life, from the trivial to the critical. Fairly inconsequential norms may regulate whether members take breaks and eat during meetings. More substantive norms govern how carefully members prepare for meetings, how critically they analyze ideas, how well they listen to one another, and how they deal with differences and conflict.

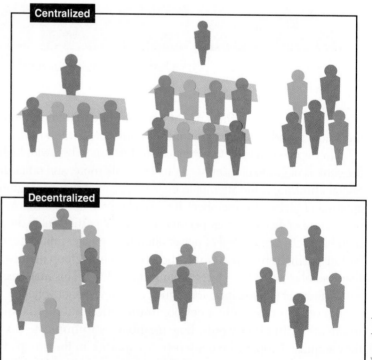

FIGURE 9.1
Group Interaction Patterns

© Cengage Learning

Norms grow directly out of interaction. For example, at a group's initial meeting, one person might dismiss another's idea as dumb, and several members might not pay attention when others are speaking. If this continues for long, a norm of disrespect will develop. On the other hand, when one member says an idea is dumb, another person might counter by saying, "I don't think so. I think we ought to consider the point." If others then do consider the idea, a norm of respectful communication may develop.

Because norms become entrenched, it's important to pay attention to them from the outset of a group's existence. By noticing patterns and tendencies, you can exert influence over the norms that take hold in groups.

COMMUNICATION IN SMALL GROUPS

We've seen that effective small group discussion entails knowing when groups are likely to be superior to individuals and understanding how group features affect participation. We're now ready to consider the variety of ways in which members communicate within groups and provide leadership to groups.

Forms of Group Communication

Because communication is the heart of all groups, the ways members communicate are extremely important to the effectiveness of group process. There are four kinds of communication in groups (Table 9.1). The first three— *task communication*, *procedural communication*, and *climate communication*—are

Table 9.1	Types of Communication in Groups
Task Communication	**Climate Communication**
Initiates ideas	Establishes and maintains healthy climate
Seeks information	Energizes group process
Gives information	Harmonizes ideas
Elaborates ideas	Recognizes others
Evaluates and offers critical analysis	Reconciles conflicts
	Builds enthusiasm for group
Procedural Communication	**Egocentric Communication**
Establishes agenda	Aggresses toward others
Provides orientation	Blocks ideas
Curbs digressions	Seeks personal recognition (brags)
Guides participation	Dominates interaction
Coordinates ideas	Pleads for special interests
Summarizes others' contributions	Confesses, self-discloses, and seeks personal help unrelated to the group's focus
Records group progress	Disrupts tasks
	Devalues others
	Trivializes group and its work

constructive because they foster good group processes and outcomes. The fourth kind of communication is *egocentric*, or *dysfunctional*, *communication*. It tends to detract from group cohesion and effective decision making.

Task Communication   **Task communication** focuses on the problems, issues, or information before a group. It provides ideas and information, ensures members' understanding, and uses reasoning to evaluate ideas and information. Task contributions may initiate ideas, respond to others' ideas, or provide critical evaluation of information before the group. Task contributions also include asking for ideas and evaluation from others. Task comments emphasize the content of a group's work.

Procedural Communication   If you've ever participated in a disorganized group, you understand the importance of **procedural communication**, which helps a group get organized and stay on track in its decision making. Procedural contributions establish an agenda, coordinate the comments of different members, and record group progress. In addition, procedural contributions may curb digressions and tangents, summarize progress, and regulate participation so that everyone has opportunities to speak and nobody dominates.

Climate Communication   A group is more than a task unit. It also includes people who are involved in a relationship that can be more or less pleasant and open. **Climate communication** focuses on creating and maintaining a constructive climate that encourages members to contribute cooperatively and evaluate ideas critically. Climate comments emphasize a group's strengths and progress, encourage cooperative interaction, recognize others' contributions, reconcile conflicts, and build enthusiasm for the group and its work.

Egocentric Communication   The final kind of group communication is not recommended but does sometimes surface in groups. **Egocentric communication**, or dysfunctional communication, is used to block others or to call attention to oneself. It detracts from group progress because it is self-centered rather than group centered. Examples of egocentric talk are devaluing another member's ideas, trivializing the group's efforts, aggressing toward other members, bragging about one's own accomplishments, dominating, disrupting group work, and pleading for special causes that aren't in a group's interest. Another form of egocentric communication is making cynical remarks that undermine group cohesion and enthusiasm.

Task, procedural, and climate communication work together to foster productive, organized, and comfortable group discussion. Egocentric communication, on the other hand, can sabotage a group's climate and hinder its progress. Communicating clearly that egocentric behavior will not be tolerated in your group fosters norms for effective interaction.

The following excerpt from a group discussion will give you concrete examples of each type of group communication. Each comment is coded as one of the four types of communication we have identified.

ED: We might start by discussing what we see as the goal of this group. *(procedural)*

JAN: That's a good idea. *(climate)*

BOB: I think our goal is to come up with a better meal plan for students on campus. *(task)*

ED: What do you mean by "better"? Do you mean cheaper or more varied or more tasteful? *(task)*

ANN: I think we need to consider all three. *(task)*

ED: Well, we probably do care about all three, but maybe we should talk about one at a time so that we can keep our discussion focused. *(procedural)*

BOB: Okay, I vote we focus first on taste—like it would be good if there were some taste to the food on campus! *(task and climate [humor])*

JAN: Do you mean taste itself or quality of food, which might also consider nutrition? *(task)*

BOB: Pure taste! When I'm hungry, I don't think about what's good for me, just what tastes good. *(task)*

JAN: Well, maybe that's a reason why we might want the food service to think about nutrition—because we don't. *(task)*

Effective teams have good climate communication, along with task and procedural communication.

BOB: If you're a health food nut, that's your problem. I don't think nutrition is something that's important in the food service on campus. *(task; possibly also egocentric if his tone toward Jan was snide)*

ED: Let's do this: Let's talk first about what we would like in terms of taste itself. *(procedural)* Before we meet next time, it might be a good idea for one of us to talk with the manager of the cafeteria to see whether they have to meet any nutritional guidelines in what they serve. *(task)*

ANN: I'll volunteer to do that. *(task)*

ED: Great. Thanks, Ann. *(climate)*

BOB: I'll volunteer to do taste testing! *(climate [humor])*

JAN: With your weight, you'd better not. *(egocentric)*

BOB: Yeah, like you have a right to criticize me. *(egocentric)*

ANN: Look, none of us is here to criticize anyone else. We're here because we want to improve the food service on campus. *(climate)* We've decided we want to focus first on taste *(procedural)*, so who has an idea of how we go about studying that? *(task)*

This dialogue includes all four kinds of communication that we've discussed. It's particularly noteworthy to recognize how skillfully Ann communicates to defuse tension between Bob and Jan before it disrupts the group. You might also notice that Ed provides the primary procedural leadership for the group, and Bob is effective in interjecting humor. Several members recognize contributions to the discussion.

In effective group discussion, communication meets the task, procedural, and climate demands of teamwork and avoids egocentrism that detracts from group progress and cohesion. By understanding how varied types of communication affect collective work, you can decide when to use each type of communication in your own participation in groups. Although you may not be proficient in all three valuable kinds of group communication right now, with commitment and practice you can develop the skill.

LEADERSHIP COMMUNICATION

For decades, it was assumed that leaders were born, not made. In following this assumption, researchers attempted to identify the traits of effective leaders. This line of study was unsuccessful in discovering any consistent traits that mark leaders (Northouse, 2006). However, the lack of identifiable leader traits led researchers to realize that **leadership** is not a person or a set of personal qualities. Instead, leadership is a set of communication functions that assists groups in accomplishing tasks efficiently and well while maintaining a good climate.

Whether there is one leader or shared leadership, the primary responsibilities are to organize discussion, ensure critical thinking, create a productive working climate, build group morale, promote effective communication between members, and discourage egocentric communication that detracts from group efforts. Even when an official leader exists, other members may contribute much of the communication that provides leadership.

KRYSTAL   *The most effective group I've ever been in had three leaders. I was the person who understood our task best, so I contributed the most to critical thinking about the issues. But Belinda was the one who kept us organized. She really knew how to see tangents and get us off of them, and she knew when it was time to move on from one stage of work to the next. She also pulled ideas together to coordinate our thinking. Kevin was the climate leader. He could always tell a joke if things got tense, and he was the best person I ever saw for recognizing others' contributions. I couldn't point to any one leader in that group, but we sure did have good leadership.*

Although leadership can't be reduced to a set of traits, it can be understood as an overall style of communication. The different styles of leadership communication differently impact group productivity and climate (Lewin, Lippitt, & White, 1939). Styles may be enacted by a single group leader or by several members. Researchers have identified three primary styles of leadership, each of which involves distinctive forms of communication and each of which has a unique impact on group climate and productivity.

Laissez-Faire Leadership

Laissez-faire is a French phrase that is roughly translated "do nothing." **Laissez-faire leadership** is laid-back and nondirective. The laissez-faire leader doesn't provide guidance or suggest directions in which the group should move. When a group consists of members who are mature, experienced, and self-directed, there may be little need for control by one or more leaders. Yet this is more the exception than the rule. Most groups need guidance, at least at times, to develop and sustain a good climate and to be productive.

Authoritarian Leadership

As the term suggests, **authoritarian leadership** is directive. This style of leadership tends to be used by a lone leader rather than by several members who share leadership. Authoritarian leaders may announce directions for discussion, assign specific tasks to members, make decisions without consulting others in the group, and otherwise exert control over the group process. Although groups with authoritarian leaders sometimes produce good decisions, this style of leadership seldom promotes satisfaction and cohesion among members. However, authoritarian leadership may be advisable when one member really has more expertise than other members and when a decision must be made quickly. In crisis situations, there often isn't time for the full participation of democratic leadership.

> **DOUG**   *It took me a while to learn that my boss doesn't want any of us to take initiative or state our ideas unless we agree with him. He is a classic authoritarian leader who tells us what to do as well as what answers and decisions he wants us to produce. He blasts anyone who doesn't play "yes man" to him. By now, none of us cares what happens in our project group. We don't even try to think of ways to improve our work. He's taught us not to take any initiative by penalizing us anytime we depart from his agenda and his prejudgments.*

Democratic Leadership

Democratic leadership provides direction and guidance but does not impose rigid authority. Democratic leadership, whether provided by one individual or by several members, fosters members' development by encouraging them to take responsibility within a group. This style of leadership tends to generate high participation and cohesion. Democratic leadership also tends to yield high-quality task outcomes that are generally more original and creative than those produced by groups with authoritarian or laissez-faire leadership (Blanchard, Carlos, & Randolph, 1998).

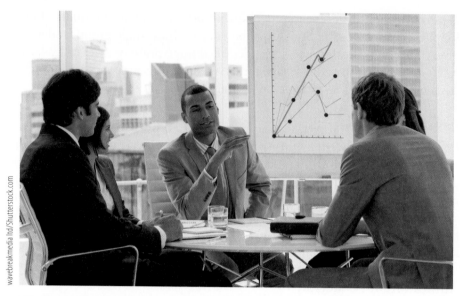

Effective leadership encourages all members to participate constructively.

Research that has found the democratic style of leadership is linked to good group climate and productivity was conducted in societies committed to democratic values. In societies that place higher value on authoritarian structures, an autocratic style of leadership might well be more acceptable and effective (Connerley & Pedersen, 2005). In other words, what counts as good leadership is influenced by cultural context.

In sum, whether provided by one member or several, effective leadership involves communication that advances a group's task, organizes deliberations, builds group morale, controls disruptions, and fosters a constructive climate.

COMMUNICATION HIGHLIGHT

Emotionally Intelligent Leadership

Psychologist Daniel Goleman (1995, 1998, 2007) asserts that standard IQ tests don't measure *emotional intelligence*, which is the ability to recognize which feelings are appropriate in which situations and the ability to communicate those feelings effectively.

Substantial research now indicates that emotionally intelligent people are more effective leaders (Ciarrochi & Mayer, 2007; Goleman, 1998; Goleman, McKee, & Boyatzis, 2002; Niedenthal, Krauth-Gruber, & Ric, 2006). They have keen awareness of their own feelings and can recognize and respond to the feelings of others. Thus, they are both self-confident and sensitive—a winning combination in leaders. Does this mean we have finally found a leadership "trait"? No. Goleman maintains that emotional intelligence is learned through commitment and practice.

BEYOND THE CLASSROOM

Let's take the material in this chapter beyond the classroom by thinking about how what you've learned about the foundations of group and team communication might apply to the workplace, ethical choices, and engagement with the broader world.

1. **Workplace.** Interview a professional in the field you hope to enter after college. Ask him or her to identify how various groups and teams discussed in this chapter are used on the job. If you are already employed in a career, reflect on your experiences with groups on the job.

2. **Ethics.** Ask several people who have lived in non-Western cultures whether the cultural values that affect group communication in the United States are present in the countries where they lived. In your conversation, explore how differences in cultural values affect group interaction.

3. **Engagement.** This chapter points out that groups exist within cultural contexts that affect how they operate. Talk with classmates or other students who were raised in a non-Western culture. Ask them what values of their home culture are reflected in the ways groups operate.

CHAPTER SUMMARY

 Practice and review the content in this chapter.

In this chapter, we've considered what small groups are and how they operate. We identified potential weaknesses and strengths of groups and discussed features of groups that affect group process. We also examined the nature of effective group communication, including leadership.

APPLYING COMMUNICATION IN OUR LIVES

Communication in Our Lives is supported by a MindTap, a new online learning platform that delivers content, assignments, and a tailored presentation of the course curriculum created by your instructor. MindTap combines all of your learning tools—readings, multimedia, activities and assessments—into a singular learning unit that guides you through the course. Practice and Present, a unique tool within MindTap, allows you to upload your speech video files for practice or for a grade, comment on your peer's speeches and review your grades. MindTap also includes Speech Builder Express, a powerful tool that guides you through the speech outline and preparation process. For more information or to access MindTap, visit cengagebrain.com.

DEFINITIONS OF KEY CONCEPTS

 Review your **Flashcards**.

authoritarian leadership Style of leading that is very directive.

climate communication One of three constructive forms of participation in group decision making. Climate communication focuses on creating and sustaining an open, engaged atmosphere for discussion.

cohesion Closeness among members of a group; esprit de corps.

democratic leadership Style of leading that provides direction and guidance but does not impose rigid authority.

egocentric communication An unconstructive form of group contribution that blocks others or calls attention to oneself.

group Three or more people who interact over time, are interdependent, and follow shared rules of conduct to reach a common goal. The team is one type of group.

groupthink The cessation of critical, independent thought on the part of a group's members about ideas generated by the group.

laissez-faire leadership Laid-back and nondirective style of leading.

leadership is a set of functions that assists groups in accomplishing tasks efficiently and well while maintaining a good climate.

norms Informal rules that guide how members of a group or culture think, feel, act, and interact. Norms define what is normal or appropriate in various situations.

power The ability to influence others; a feature of small groups that affects participation.

power over The ability to help or harm others. Power over others usually is communicated in ways that highlight the status and influence of the person using the power.

power to The ability to empower others to reach their goals. People who use power to help others generally do not highlight their own status and influence.

procedural communication One of three constructive ways of participating in group decision making. Procedural communication orders ideas and coordinates the contributions of members.

social climbing The attempt to increase personal status in a group by winning the approval of high-status members.

social loafing Exists when members of a group exert less effort than they would if they worked alone.

task communication One of three constructive forms of participation in group decision making; focuses on giving and analyzing information and ideas.

team A special kind of group characterized by different and complementary resources of members and a strong sense of collective identity. All teams are groups, but not all groups are teams.

FOR FURTHER REFLECTION AND DISCUSSION

 MindTap

1. Interview a professional in the field you hope to enter after college. Ask him or her to identify the different work groups and teams he or she has been part of in the past year. How many of the types of groups and teams described in this chapter do your interviewee name?

2. What ethical responsibilities accompany having power in a group? What are ethical and unethical uses of power in group and team situations?

   Ethics

3. Observe a group discussion on your campus or in your town. Record members'
contributions by classifying them as task, climate, procedural, or egocentric. Does the communication you observe explain the effectiveness or ineffectiveness of the group?

4. To learn more about groupthink, use your MindTap for *Communication in Our Lives* to access **WebLink 9.1**.

5. Click on **WebLink 9.2**, available among the book's online resources for this chapter, that will take you to an article on team cohesion among athletes.

SHARPEN YOUR SKILL

 MindTap

1. Group Creativity

Test the claim that groups tend to be more creative than individuals. Ask five students individually to write down all the ways they can think of to improve Facebook. When they have run out of ideas, ask them to form a group and generate as many improvements for Facebook as they can. Did the individuals or the group produce more ideas?

2. Your Communication in Groups

Draw on your own perceptions to answer the following four questions. After you have responded, ask one or two people who have worked with you in groups to answer these questions about your participation.

1. Observe yourself in a small group setting, and record the focus of your comments.

   _____

2. Do you specialize in task, procedural, or climate communication?

   _____

3. Which kinds of group communication do you do well? In which areas do you want to develop greater skill?

   _____

EXPERIENCING COMMUNICATION IN OUR LIVES MindTap

CASE STUDY: *The Class Gift*

A video of the conversation scripted here is featured in your Chapter 9 MindTap for *Communication in Our Lives*. Select "The Class Gift" to watch the video. Improve your own communication skills by reading, watching, and evaluating this communication encounter.

Andy, Erika, Camilla, Vernon, and Jenn are in charge of deciding what their graduating class will give to their university as the class gift. This is the second meeting of their group.

VERNON (*looking around at the other members*)**:** Hey, hey— good to see you all again.

CAMILLA: The most awesome group on campus!

ANDY: We're looking fine, for sure.

VERNON (*glances at watch*)**:** Okay, all of you fine-looking people (smiles at Andy), it's 10 minutes after. Has anyone heard from Jenn?

Erika, Camilla, and Andy shake their heads and shrug.

VERNON: Okay, well, let's get started and hope she joins us in a couple of minutes. I want to get rolling on this project!

ERIKA: Hear, hear! I'm really psyched about doing this. We have the coolest class ever, and I want us to come up with a gift that's as cool as we are.

ANDY: That would have to be waaaaaaaaaaaay cool!

The four slap hands, laugh, and chorus: Waaaaaaaaaaaaaay cool!!

VERNON: Okay, since we're so cool, what are our cool ideas for our class gift? Anybody have a suggestion?

CAMILLA: When we met last week, one idea we all kind of liked was giving a sculpture—you know, an outdoor one that could go in the main quad where everyone would see it.

ANDY: Yeah, I agree; that's the best idea we came up with.

CAMILLA: The image I have is a sculpture of a student studying—like maybe reading a book.

ERIKA: Hold on. Studying is not waaaaaaaaaaaay cool.

ANDY: Definitely not. Maybe we could have a sculpture of players on our basketball team. Now *that* would be cool!

ERIKA: Oh, please, that's even worse.

> Jenn walks in and pulls a chair into the circle with the others. Erika and Vernon smile at her as she joins them. Camilla gives her a quick hug.

ANDY: Hey, Jenn. Glad you made it.

JENN: Sorry I'm late. I was meeting with a study group for my Econ exam tomorrow.

CAMILLA (*smiling mischievously*)**:** I rest my case. Jenn was studying, which *is* what students do!

ERIKA: Yeah, but it's not waaaaaay cool.

VERNON: Wait a minute, let's give Camilla's idea a chance. A sculpture. I kind of like the idea of a sculpture.

JENN: That would be unique. I don't think any other class has given a sculpture.

ERIKA: I'm not against a sculpture. I just don't think a student studying is the most exciting thing.

VERNON: Maybe not the most exciting, but it really gets at what being at this school is about.

ANDY: I'm beginning to agree. I mean, the sculpture should celebrate this school and its values.

VERNON: What about you, Erika. Is this idea working for you yet?

ERIKA: Personally, I'm not wild about a sculpture of a student studying. But the most important thing is that we come up with something we can all support, and the other four of you seem to like this idea.

CAMILLA: I don't think any of us is settled on the idea yet. We may come up with a different kind of sculpture that we'd all love. Does anyone have a different idea for the sculpture?

> Erika, Vernon, and Andy shrug no.

JENN: How about a sculpture of a student in regalia—as if the student is graduating? Isn't that the goal of being here?

ERIKA: That's interesting—instead of symbolizing studying to get to the goal, we could symbolize achieving it.

ANDY: I don't know. Those regalia are pretty weird looking, and they're not what students wear, except for one day. I don't think students would identify with that as much as a sculpture of a student in regular dress, like we're wearing.

JENN: Good point. You could be right.

CAMILLA: Yeah, but we do identify with the goal that the regalia symbolize. I don't know that students wouldn't identify with a sculpture of a student wearing the regalia.

VERNON: I think they might.

ERIKA: I'm not convinced.

CAMILLA: We're just speculating and stating our own opinions. Let's do some research to find out what students think. Why don't we do a couple of sketches—one of a student studying and one of a student in regalia—and poll students as to which they like better?

JENN: Good idea, but let's not move to that just yet. We might come up with more ideas for the sculpture if we talk longer.

QUESTIONS FOR ANALYSIS AND DISCUSSION

 MindTap

You can answer these questions and see my responses to them online via MindTap for Chapter 9.

1. Apply material from this chapter to analyze the features of this small group.

2. How effective is the climate communication in this group?

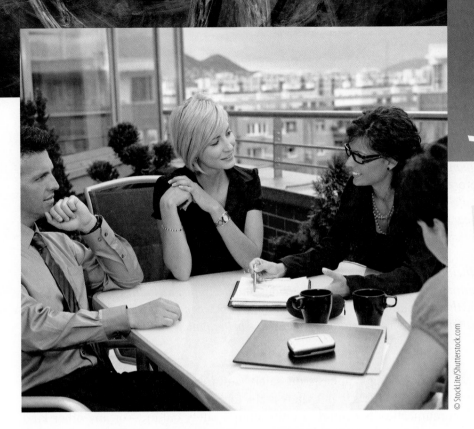

© StockLite/Shutterstock.com

Find a job you like
and you add five
days to every week.

H. Jackson Brown, Jr.

Communication in Organizations

*A patient dies after what should have been routine surgery. He is one of the
100,000 to 200,000 deaths that result from preventable medical errors in
U.S. hospitals each year (Gupta, 2012). As soon as the patient is pronounced dead,
the blame game begins. The doctor in charge of the case claims the nurse was not
monitoring vital signs. The nurse insists that she noted drops in the patient's blood
pressure on the chart, but the doctor didn't pay attention. The doctor says the nurse
should have told him about the drop, not
just made a note on the chart. The nurse
replies that the doctor has yelled at her
when she's called his attention to patient
information in the past. Both the nurse
and the doctor seem more interested in
defending themselves than figuring out
what went wrong. That's almost inevitable in a culture of blame.*

 MindTap™

Review the chapter
Learning Objectives
and **Start** with a quick
warm up activity.

SHARPEN YOUR SKILL

At the end of this chapter, refer
to the Sharpen Your Skill features,
Noticing Stories and the Work
They Do and Noticing Rituals
in Your Organization, to apply
concepts from Chapter 10.

When assigning blame is a priority, staff may hide errors rather than report them and protect themselves and their friends rather than talk honestly about what—not who—is the problem (Domrose, 2010; Palmieri, Peterson, Pesta, Flit, & Saettone, 2010). Evidence that a culture of blame can be counterproductive has convinced many health care organizations to cultivate a culture of safety to reduce risks and improve care for patients (Clancy, 2011). A safety culture exists when management and employees share a strong commitment to ensuring the safety of the work environment and to making safety of patients and employees paramount. In a safety culture, employees at all ranks feel free to report errors and near misses without fear of being reprimanded or punished. Open communication increases awareness of challenges to safety and enables teamwork in overcoming them.

To assess their culture, many hospitals rely on a survey that asks staff to rate their organization's emphasis on teamwork, openness in communicating about errors, and freedom to question actions and decisions, including those of staff with higher authority. Hospitals with more open communication have a stronger safety culture, which studies show means better patient care (Clancy, 2011).

T‍he increasing emphasis on safety culture in health care organizations follows similar efforts to put safety at the forefront in other high-risk workplaces. Communication is central to cultivating a safety culture—or any other kind of organizational culture. It is communication—upward, downward, lateral, internal, and external—that defines an organization's identity and how organizational members understand their roles and responsibilities.

HEALTH COMMUNICATION

Growing awareness of the links between communication and health has given rise to a number of organizations for health care professionals. If you plan a career in the health care field, check out these organizations.

The American Academy on Communication in Healthcare promotes research, education, and professional standards in patient–clinician communication.

The National Communication Association has a **Commission for Health Communication**, which supports research on communication and health.

The National Cancer Institute has five national **Centers of Excellence in Cancer Communication Research** (CECCRs), which are dedicated to advances in health communication research and application, as well as to training the next generation of health communication scholars.

The Centers for Disease Control and Prevention (CDC) is home to the **National Center for Health Marketing** (NCHM), which promotes health marketing and conducts communication research to support national health promotion efforts.

The Society for Participatory Medicine (SPM) promotes participatory medicine by and among patients, caregivers and their medical teams and to promote clinical transparency among patients and their physicians.

Communication in organizations is the topic of this chapter. In the first section, we'll identify key features of organizational communication. Next, we'll discuss the overall culture of the organization, which establishes the context for communication among members of the organization. As we will see, organizational culture is created and expressed in communication. Every organization has a distinct culture that consists of traditions, structures, and practices that reflect and reproduce a particular form of work life and on-the-job relationships. In the third section of the chapter, we'll discuss three guidelines for communicating in organizations in our era.

KEY FEATURES OF ORGANIZATIONAL COMMUNICATION

Read, highlight and take notes online.

Much of what you've learned in previous chapters applies to communication in organizations. For instance, effective communication on the job requires listening, verbal and nonverbal competence, appreciation of cultural differences, and the ability to work well on teams. To build on what you've already learned, we'll discuss three features of organizations: structure, communication networks, and links to external environments.

Structure

Structure is a patterned way of doing things. It is a set of procedures, relationships, and practices that provides predictability for members of an organization so that they understand roles, procedures, and expectations and so that work gets done.

Most modern organizations rely on a hierarchical structure, which assigns different levels of power and status to different members and specifies who is to communicate with whom about what. Rigidly hierarchical organizations have strict rules about following the chain of command. In more loosely structured organizations, members may communicate more openly with their own peers and with peers of their supervisors.

Communication Networks

A second characteristic of organizational communication is that it occurs in **communication networks**, which are formal and informal links between people. In most organizations, people belong to multiple networks (Modaff, Butler, & DeWine, 2011). For example, faculty belong to social networks that include colleagues; task networks consisting of people with whom they discuss teaching, research, and departmental and university issues; and ad hoc networks that arise irregularly in response to specific crises or issues. Overlaps among networks to which we belong ensure that we will interact with many people in any organization.

In addition to networks in physical places of work, an increasing number of workers are part of virtual networks. The growth in telecommuting is striking. Estimates suggest that over 50 million U.S. workers (about 40% of the working population) work from home at least part of the time, and 2.5 million employees (not including the self-employed) consider their home their primary place of business (Conley, 2009; Lister, 2009). In 2010, 67% of federal employees worked from home or other

AntonioDiaz/Shutterstock.com

Virtual networks are essential in professional life.

sites either 1–2 days a week or 3 or more days per week (Lister, 2009; Telework, 2010). Made possible by technologies, telecommuting allows millions of people to work from their homes or mobile offices. Using computers, email, cell phones, BlackBerrys, PDAs, and faxes, many telecommuters do their work and maintain contact with colleagues and clients without being at a central, physical workplace.

Links to External Environments

Like other communication systems, organizations are embedded in multiple contexts that affect how they work and whether they succeed or fail. In other words, an organization's operation cannot be understood simply by looking only within the organization. We must also look outside it to grasp how it is related to and affected by its contexts.

Consider the impact of recession that began in 2008 on a few U.S. organizations:

As companies' profits tumbled, they laid off workers.

Faced with unemployment, former workers scaled back spending. They drove less, which affected companies that sell and repair cars, sell gasoline, and host tourists.

As unemployment stretched from weeks to months and even years, homeowners could not pay mortgages, so homes were foreclosed.

As foreclosed homes flooded markets at bargain prices, fewer new homes were built, taking a bite out of companies that produce the raw material for construction.

As home building and tourist-oriented companies lost business, they laid off workers.

And on and on.

Although internal factors may have contributed to the sales losses and gains of these businesses, clearly many organizations suffered because of factors outside their organizational boundaries. When economic times are good, when war is not a threat, and when inflation is in check, even mediocre companies survive. When external conditions are bad, even good companies can be hurt or driven out of business.

ORGANIZATIONAL CULTURE

In Chapter 7, we noted that cultures are characterized by shared values, behaviors, practices, and communication forms. Extending the idea of culture to organizations, communication scholars focus on **organizational culture**, which consists of ways of thinking, acting, and understanding work that are shared by members of an organization and that reflect an organization's distinct identity.

Just as ethnic cultures consist of meanings shared by members of the ethnic groups, organizational cultures consist of meanings shared by members of organizations. Just as new members of ethnic cultures are socialized into preexisting meanings and traditions, new members of organizations are socialized into preexisting meanings and traditions (Goodall & Trethewey, 2009; Mumby, 2006a, 2006b; Pacanowsky, 1989; Pacanowsky & O'Donnell-Trujillo, 1983; Scott & Myers, 2005). Just as a culture's way of life continues even though particular people leave or die, an organization's culture persists despite the comings and goings of particular workers.

The relationship between communication and organizational culture is reciprocal: Communication between members of an organization creates, sustains, and sometimes alters the culture. At the same time, organizational culture influences patterns of communication between members. Four kinds of communication that are particularly important in developing, expressing, and sustaining organizational culture are vocabularies, stories, rites and rituals, and structures.

Vocabularies

Just as the language of an ethnic culture reflects and expresses its history, norms, values, and identity, the *vocabulary* of an organization reflects and expresses its history, norms, values, and identity.

Hierarchical Language   Many organizations and professions have vocabularies that distinguish levels of status among members. The military, for example, relies on language that continually acknowledges rank (i.e., *Yes, sir, chain of command*), which reflects the close ties between rank, power, and privilege. Salutes, as well as stripes and medals on uniforms, are part of the nonverbal vocabulary that emphasizes rank and honors.

Unequal terms of address also communicate rank. For instance, the CEO may use first names ("Good morning, Bob") when speaking to employees. Unless given permission to use the CEO's first name, however, lower-status

"I've never actually seen a corporate ladder before."

From The Wall Street Journal. Reprinted by permission of Cartoon Features Syndicate.

members of an organization typically use *Mr.*, *Ms.*, *Sir*, or *Ma'am* to address the CEO. Colleges and universities use titles to designate faculty members' rank and status: instructor, assistant professor, associate professor, full professor, and distinguished (or chaired) professor. Faculty generally use students' first names, whereas students tend to use titles to address their teachers: Dr. Armstrong or Professor Armstrong, for example.

Masculine Language   Because organizations historically have been run by men, and men have been the primary or exclusive members of them, it's not surprising that many organizations have developed and continue to use language more related to men's traditional interests and experiences than to women's (Ashcraft & Mumby, 2004; Mumby, 2006a, 2006b). Consider the number of phrases in the working world that are taken from sports (i.e., home run, ballpark estimate, touchdown, develop a game plan, be a team player, take a time out, the starting lineup), from military life (i.e., battle plan, mount a campaign, plan of attack, under fire, get the big guns, defensive move, offensive strike), from males (top man, king of the hill, man on the move, the man) and from male sexual parts and activities (i.e., a troublesome person is a *prick*; you can *hit* on a person, *screw* someone, or *stick it to* them; bold professionals have *balls*).

Less prevalent in most organizations is language that reflects traditionally feminine interests and experiences (i.e., put something on the back burner,

COMMUNICATION HIGHLIGHT

Language in Left Field

The prevalence of sports-related terms in U.S. business culture can pose challenges for international business conversations. Consider these foul balls that only Americans understood (Jones, 2007):

While at a global leadership meeting in Italy, William Mitchell, CEO of Arrow Electronics, wanted to change the agenda, so he said, "I'm calling an audible."

At a meeting with Indian executives, Alan Guarino, CEO of Cornell International, tried to change a contractual clause by demanding "a jump-ball scenario."

AFLAC CEO Dan Amos baffled Japanese executives when he told them that using the AFLAC duck for ads in Japan would be a "slam dunk."

percolate an idea, stir the pot, give birth to a plan, nurse an idea along). Whether intentional or not, language that reflects traditionally masculine experiences and interests can bind men together while prompting some women to feel excluded.

Similarly, many organizations in the United States reflect Caucasian and Christian values and experiences more than those of other ethnic and religious groups (Allen, 2006). For instance, most portraits are of white people; official holidays generally include Christmas but not Kwanzaa or Yom Kippur. This may be unconscious and unintended, but it can nonetheless make organizations feel more familiar and comfortable to Christians and whites than to other groups.

Stories

Scholars of organizational culture recognize that humans are storytellers by nature. We tell stories to weave coherent narratives out of experience and to create meaning in our lives. Furthermore, the stories we tell do some real work in establishing and sustaining organizational cultures. In a classic study, Michael Pacanowsky and Nick O'Donnell-Trujillo (1983) identified three kinds of stories within the organizational context.

Corporate Stories   Corporate stories convey the values, style, and history of an organization. Just as families have favorite stories about their histories and identities that they retell often, organizations have favorite stories that reflect their collective visions of themselves (Mumby, 2006a; Pacinowski & O'Donnello-Trujillo, 1983).

One important function of corporate stories is to socialize new members into the culture of an organization. Newcomers learn about the history and identity of an organization by listening to stories of its leaders as well as its trials and triumphs. For example, both Levi Strauss and Microsoft are known for their informal style of operation. Veteran employees regale new employees with tales about the laid-back founders of the companies. These stories socialize new employees into the cultures of the companies.

When retold among members of an organization, stories foster feelings of connection and vitalize organizational culture. As long-term members of organizations rehash pivotal events—crises, successes, and takeovers—in the organization's history, they cement bonds among them and their identification with the organization. Jed's commentary provides an example of how stories express and reinforce organizational culture.

> **JED**   *I sing with the Gospel Choir, and we have a good following in the Southeast. When I first joined the group, the other members talked to me. In our conversations, what I heard again and again was the idea that we exist to make music for God and about God, not to glorify ourselves. One of the choir members told me about a singer who had gotten on a personal ego trip because of all the bookings we were getting, and he started thinking he was more important than the music. That guy didn't last long with the group.*

Personal Stories Members of organizations also tell stories about themselves. Personal stories are accounts that announce how people see themselves and how they want to be seen by others (Cockburn-Wootten & Zorn, 2006). For example, if Sabra perceives herself as a supportive team player, she could simply tell new employees this "I am a person who believes in teamwork." On the other hand, she could define her image by telling a story: "When I first started working at this clinic, most folks were operating in isolation, and I thought a lot more could be accomplished if we collaborated. Let me tell you something I did to make that happen. After I'd been on staff for 3 months, I was assigned to work up a plan for downsizing our billing department. Instead of just developing a plan on my own, I talked with other managers, and then I met with people in accounting to get their ideas. The plan we came up with reflected all of our input." This narrative gives a concrete, coherent account of how Sabra sees herself and wants others to see her.

Collegial Stories The third type of organizational story is accounts of other members of the organization. When I first became a faculty member, a senior colleague took me out to lunch and told me anecdotes about people in the department and the university. At the time, I thought he was simply sharing some interesting stories. Later, however, I realized he had told me who the players were so that I could navigate my new context.

Collegial stories told by coworkers tell us what to expect from whom. "If you need help getting around the CEO, Jane's the one to see. A year ago, I couldn't finish a report by deadline, so Jane rearranged his calendar so he thought the report wasn't due for another week." "Roberts is a real stickler for rules. Once when I took an extra 20 minutes on my lunch break, he reamed me out." Whether positive or negative, collegial stories assert identities for others in an organization. They are part of the informal network that teaches new workers how to get along with others in the organization.

Rites and Rituals

Rites and rituals are verbal and nonverbal practices that express and reproduce organizational cultures. They do so by providing standardized ways of expressing organizational values and identity.

Rites Rites are dramatic, planned sets of activities that bring together aspects of an organization's culture in a single event. Harrison Trice and Janice Beyer (1984) identified six kinds of organizational rites. Rites of passage are used to mark membership in different levels or parts of organizations. For example, a retirement is often symbolized by a lunch or dinner, acknowledging the retiring employee's contributions. A desk plaque with a new employee's name and title is a rite that acknowledges a change in identity. *Rites of integration* affirm and enhance the sense of community in an organization. Examples are holiday parties, annual picnics, and retreats.

Organizational cultures also include rites that blame or praise people. Firings, demotions, and reprimands are common blaming rites—the counterpart of which are enhancement rites, which praise individuals and teams that embody the organization's goals and self-image. Campuses bestow awards on faculty who are especially gifted teachers and chaired professorships on outstanding scholars. Many sales companies give awards for productivity (i.e., most sales of the month, quarter, or year). Audrey describes an enhancement rite in her sorority.

> **AUDREY** *In my sorority, we recognize sisters who make the dean's list each semester by putting a rose on their dinner plates. That way everyone realizes who has done well academically, and we can also remind ourselves that scholarship is one of the qualities we all aspire to.*

Renewal rites aim to help organizations manage change. Training workshops serve this purpose, as do meetings at which new leaders are introduced and their visions are explained. Organizations also develop conflict resolution rites to deal with differences and discord. Examples are HR counseling, grievance, arbitration, collective bargaining, mediation, executive fiat, and ignoring or denying problems.

Rituals **Rituals** are forms of communication that occur regularly and that members of an organization perceive as familiar and routine parts of organizational life. Rituals differ from rites in that rituals don't necessarily bring together a number of aspects of organizational ideology into a single event. Rather, rituals are repeated communication performances that communicate a particular value or role definition.

Organizations have personal, task, and social rituals. *Personal rituals* are routine behaviors that individuals use to express their organizational identities. In their study of organizational cultures, Pacanowsky and O'Donnell-Trujillo (1983) noted that Lou Polito, the owner of a car company, opened all the company's mail every day. Whenever possible, Polito hand-delivered mail to the divisions of his company to communicate his openness and his involvement with the day-to-day business.

Social rituals are standardized performances that affirm relationships between members of organizations (Mokros, 2006; Mumby, 2006a). Some organizations have a company dining room to encourage socializing among employees. In the United Kingdom and Japan, many businesses have afternoon tea breaks. Many employees develop griping rituals in which the purpose is to complain about problems, not to solve them. Sharon provides an example of an office griping ritual.

> **SHARON** *Where I work, we have this ritual of spending the first half-hour or so at work every Monday complaining about what we have to get done that week. Even if we don't have a rough week ahead, we go through the motions of moaning and groaning. It's kind of like a bonding ceremony for us.*

Task rituals are repeated activities that help members of an organization perform their jobs. Common task rituals are forms and procedures that members of organizations are expected to use to do various things. These forms and

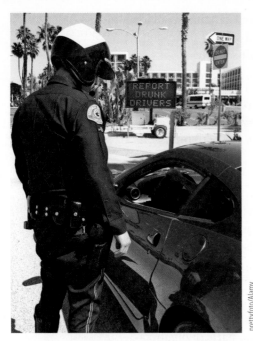

Law enforcement officers often follow rituals when talking with citizens whom they have stopped.

procedures standardize task performance in a manner consistent with the organization's view of itself and how it operates. In their study of a police unit, Pacanowsky and O'Donnell-Trujillo (1983) identified the routine that officers are trained to follow when they stop drivers for violations. The questions officers are taught to ask ("May I see your license, please?" "Do you know why I stopped you?" "Do you know how fast you were going?") allow them to size up traffic violators and decide whether to give them a break or a closer look.

Structures

Organizational cultures are also represented through structural aspects of organizational life. As the term implies, structures organize relationships and interaction between members of an organization. We'll consider four structures that express and uphold organizational culture: roles, rules, policies, and communication networks.

Roles   Roles are responsibilities and behaviors that are expected of people because of their specific positions in an organization. Most organizations formally define roles in job descriptions:

Training coordinator: Responsible for assessing needs and providing training to Northwest branches of the firm; supervises staff of 25 professional trainers; coordinates with director of human relations.

A role is not tied to any particular person. Rather, it is a set of functions and responsibilities that could be performed by any number of people who have particular talents, experiences, and other relevant qualifications. If one person quits or is fired, another can be found as a replacement. Regardless of who is in the role, the organization will continue with its structure intact. The different roles in an organization are a system, which means they are interrelated and interacting. Each role is connected to other roles within the system. Organizational charts portray who is responsible to whom and clarify the hierarchy of power among roles in the organization.

Rules   Rules, which we discussed in Chapter 5, are patterned ways of interacting. Rules are present in organizational contexts just as they are in other settings of interaction. As in other contexts, organizational rules may be formal (in the contract or organizational chart) or informal (norms for interaction).

Within organizations, constitutive rules specify what various kinds of communication symbolize. Some firms count working late as evidence of commitment. Socializing with colleagues after work may count as showing team spirit. Taking on extra assignments, attending training sessions, and dressing like upper management may communicate ambition. Lyle's commentary points out what counted as violating the chain of command in his company.

LYLE *I found out the hard way that a company I worked for was dead serious about the organizational chart. I had a problem with a coworker, so I talked with a guy in another department I was friends with. Somehow my supervisor found out, and he blew a gasket. He was furious that I had "gone outside of the chain of command" instead of coming straight to him.*

Regulative rules specify when, where, and with whom communication occurs. Organizational charts formalize regulative rules by showing who reports to whom. Other regulative rules may specify that problems should not be discussed with people outside the organization and that online communication with people outside the organization is (or is not) permitted during working hours. Some organizations have found that employees spend so much time online that productivity suffers, so rules regulating online time are instituted.

Policies   **Policies** are formal statements of practices that reflect and uphold the overall culture of an organization. Most organizations codify policies governing such aspects of work life as hiring, promotion, benefits, grievances, and medical leave. The content of policies in these areas differs among organizations in ways that reflect the distinct cultures of diverse work environments.

Organizational policies also reflect the larger society within which organizations are embedded. For example, as public awareness of sexual harassment has increased, most organizations have developed formal policies that prohibit sexual harassment and detail the procedure for making complaints. The prevalence of dual-career couples has prompted many organizations to create departments to help place the spouses of people they want to hire. The fact that many workers have children creates pressures on organizations to create family–friendly work contexts.

COMMUNICATION HIGHLIGHT

Balancing Work and Family

That's the challenge faced by more and more people today. The majority of adults—male and female—are in the paid labor force. At the same time, many of them have families, including young children and aging parents who need substantial time and help. What are organizations to do? In a survey of people who work in industry, academe, and nonprofits, 48% of women and 39% of men said the demands of work interfered with their personal lives too often (June, 2012). Some employees even put off child bearing because of work demands: Almost 40% of women and 27% of men said they had done this (June, 2012).

The cry for work–life balance often seems to pit employees against employers and sometimes even each other. Employees want more flexible work hours, longer and paid family leaves, and better insurance coverage for family members. Employers want reliable employees who are focused on their work. And employees who do not have family responsibilities or who keep those separate from their work lives may resent peers who expect accommodations (Wood & Dow, 2010).

These six people have different life situations, abilities, and goals that affect what they need and want to be effective on the job. Eileen and Denise need flexible working hours so that they can take care of family members. Eileen may also expect her employer to respect Rosh Hashanah, Yom Kippur, Hanukkah, and other holidays of her religion. Ned may need extended disability leave and a period of part-time work while he recuperates from his heart surgery. Javier may want to take family leave when his child is born, a benefit that wouldn't be valued by Frank or Sam. These six people are typical of the workforce today. They illustrate the diversity of people, life situations, and needs that characterize the modern workplace. The variety of workers is a major change, one that requires organizations to adapt.

Some organizations have a cafeteria-style benefits package that allows employees to select benefits from a range of options that includes family leave, flexible working hours, employer-paid education, telecommuting, onsite day care, dental insurance, and personal days. Other organizations have one-size-fits-all benefit plans in which some benefits are irrelevant to some employees.

The organizations that survive and thrive in an era of diversity will be those that adapt effectively to meet the expectations and needs of diverse workers. Flexible rules and policies, rather than one-size-fits-all formulas, will mark the successful workplaces of the future. By extension, the most competent, most effective professionals will be those who are comfortable with a stream of changes in people and ways of working. You might work closely with a colleague for several years and then see little of that person if he or she modifies working hours to accommodate changes in family life. If you choose to telecommute, you will need to develop new ways to stay involved in the informal network (which may operate largely on the Internet) and have the amount of social contact you enjoy. Managers will need to find ways to lead employees who work in different locations and at different hours.

Effective communication in today's and tomorrow's organizations requires interacting intensely with members of teams that may form and dissolve quickly. Whereas autonomous workers—single leaders, mavericks, and solo professionals—were prized in an earlier era, the team player is highly sought today. John, who returned to school in his mid-40s, describes the changes in his job over the past 13 years.

> **JOHN**   *My job is entirely different today than when I started it 13 years ago. When I came aboard, each of us had his own responsibilities, and management pretty much left us alone to do our work. I found authors and helped them develop their ideas, Andy took care of all art for the books, someone else was in charge of marketing, and so forth. Each of us did our job on a book and passed the book on to the next person. Now the big buzzword is team. Everything is done in teams. From the start of a new book project, the author and I are part of a team that includes the art editor, marketing director, manuscript designer, and so forth. Each of us has to coordinate with the others continually; nobody works as a lone operator. Although I had reservations about teams at first, by now I'm convinced that they are superior to individuals working independently. The books we're producing are more internally coherent, and they are developed far more efficiently when we collaborate.*

Tomorrow's Organizations

MindTap

Increasingly, work groups and teams will work virtually; their members will connect from different places and even different countries. Texting, skyping, and Webcasts allow groups to work across time and distance. In future years, we're sure to see additional technologies that further facilitate virtual group work.

One of the best ways to learn about social and organizational trends that are reshaping the world of work is to read online magazines. *Entrepreneurial Edge* discusses emerging trends and resources for entrepreneurs. Another savvy site is an idea café created by business owners, where you'll find advice on starting and running a business, using technologies, and networking. To check out *Entrepreneurial Edge* and the idea café online, use your MindTap for *Communication in Our Lives* to access **WebLink 10.1** and **WebLink 10.2**.

The skills we discussed in Part I of this book will help you adapt your communication to the diverse people on your teams. The challenge is to be able to adjust your style of communicating to the expectations and interaction styles of a variety of people and to the constraints of a range of situations. The greater your repertoire of communication skills, the more effectively you will be able to move in and out of teams on the job.

Manage Personal Relationships on the Job

A third challenge of organizational life involves relationships that are simultaneously personal and professional. You probably will be involved in a number of such relationships during your life. Although management has traditionally discouraged personal relationships, particularly romantic ones, between employees, they develop anyway. The goal, then, is to understand these relationships and manage them effectively.

Friendships between coworkers or supervisors and subordinates often enhance job commitment and satisfaction (Allen, 2006; Mokros, 2006; Mumby, 2006a). This is not surprising, as we're more likely to enjoy work when we work with people we like. Yet workplace friendships also have drawbacks. On-the-job friendships may involve tension between the role expectations for friends and for colleagues. A supervisor may have difficulty rendering a fair evaluation of a subordinate who is also a friend. The supervisor might err by overrating the subordinate–friend's

ANNA   *It's hard for me now that my best friend has been promoted over me. Part of it is envy, because I wanted the promotion too. But the hardest part is that I resent her power over me. When Billie gives me an assignment, I feel like as my friend she shouldn't dump extra work on me. But I also know that as the boss she has to give extra work to all of us sometimes. It just doesn't feel right for my best friend to tell me what to do and evaluate my work.*

strengths or might try to compensate for personal affection by being especially harsh in judging the friend–subordinate. Also, workplace friendships that deteriorate may create stress and job dissatisfaction (Sias, Heath, Perry, Silva, & Fix, 2004).

Romantic relationships betweenpeople who work together are also increasingly common. Most women and men work outside the home, sometimes spending more hours on the job than in the home. In Chapter 9, we learned that proximity is a key influence on the formation of romantic relationships. It's no surprise, then, that people who interact almost daily sometimes find themselves attracted to each other. Workplace romances involve many of the same tensions that operate in friendships between supervisors and subordinates. In addition, romantic relationships are especially likely to arouse coworkers' resentment and discomfort. Romantic breakups also tend to be more dramatic than breakups between friends. To learn more about personal relationships in the workplace, use your MindTap for *Communication in Our Lives* to access **WebLink 10.3**.

Stockbyte/Getty Images

Managing personal relationships in the workplace can be challenging.

EUGENE *Once, I got involved with a woman where I was working. We were assigned to the same team and really hit it off, and one thing led to another, and we were dating. I guess it affected our work some, since we spent a lot of time talking and stuff in the office. But the real problem came when we broke up. It's impossible to avoid seeing your "ex" when you work together in a small office, and everyone else acted like they were walking on eggshells around us. She finally quit, and you could just feel tension drain out of everyone else in our office.*

It's probably unrealistic to assume that we can avoid personal relationships with people on the job. The challenge is to manage those relationships so that the workplace doesn't interfere with the personal bond, and the intimacy doesn't jeopardize professionalism. Friends and romantic partners may need to adjust their expectations and styles of interacting so that personal and work roles do not conflict. It's also advisable to make sure that on-the-job communication doesn't reflect favoritism and privileges that could cause resentment in coworkers. It's important to invest extra effort to maintain an open communication climate with other coworkers.

BEYOND THE CLASSROOM

Let's take the material in this chapter beyond the classroom by thinking about how it might apply to the workplace, ethical choices, and engagement with the broader world.

1. **Workplace.** Think about the place where you work or a place you worked in the past. What stories—collegial, personal, and corporate—did you hear during the initial stage of your employment? How did those stories shape your early understandings of that workplace and your understandings of what was expected of you as an employee?

2. **Ethics.** In recent years, we've discovered instance after instance of egregiously unethical behavior by leaders of organizations. Between 2006 and 2008, loan officers in banks were told to sign people up for mortgages they didn't understand and couldn't afford. As a result, many of these people lost their homes to foreclosure. Bernie Madoff lied to thousands of people, taking their money in a giant Ponzi scheme that left many penniless. Incidents such as these have led some to recommend that ethical training of some sort be required for all professionals. Do you think it should be part of the curriculum in business and law schools?

3. **Engagement.** Watch the film *Remember the Titans*. It provides a dramatic account of a man who was assigned to coach a group of football players in a recently integrated high school. The players didn't work together well, largely because of ethnic differences and ethnocentric attitudes. This film provides rich insights into leadership and the development of a cohesive organizational culture for the team.

CHAPTER SUMMARY

 Practice and review the content in this chapter.

The culture of an organization is created, sustained, and altered in the process of communication between members of an organization. As they talk, interact, develop policies, and participate in the formal and informal networks, they continuously weave the fabric of their individual roles and collective life.

Organizations, like other contexts of communication, involve a number of challenges. To meet those challenges, we discussed three guidelines. One is to develop a large repertoire of communication skills so you can adapt effectively to diverse people, situations, and needs in the workplace. A second guideline is to be prepared to move in and out of teams rapidly, which is required in many modern organizations. Finally, we discussed ways to manage personal relationships in the workplace. It's likely that you and others will form friendships and perhaps romantic relationships with people in the workplace. The communication skills we've discussed throughout this book will help you navigate the tensions and challenges of close relationships on the job.

APPLYING COMMUNICATION IN OUR LIVES

Communication in Our Lives is supported by a MindTap, a new online learning platform that delivers content, assignments, and a tailored presentation of the course curriculum created by your instructor. MindTap combines all of your learning tools—readings, multimedia, activities and assessments—into a singular learning unit that guides you through the course. Practice and Present, a unique tool within MindTap, allows you to upload your speech video files for practice or for a grade, comment on your peer's speeches and review your grades. MindTap also includes Speech Builder Express, a powerful tool that guides you through the speech outline and preparation process. For more information or to access MindTap, visit cengagebrain.com.

DEFINITIONS OF KEY CONCEPTS

 MindTap Review your **Flashcards**.

communication networks Formal and informal links between members of organizations.

organizational culture Ways of thinking, acting, and understanding work that are shared by members of an organization and that reflect an organization's distinct identity.

policies Formal statements of an organizational practice. An organization's policies reflect and uphold the overall culture of the organization.

rites Dramatic, planned sets of activities that bring together aspects of an organization's culture in a single event.

rituals Forms of communication that occur regularly and that members of an organization perceive as a familiar and routine part of organizational life.

roles The collection of responsibilities and behaviors associated with and expected of a specific position in an organization.

structure In an organization, the set of procedures, relationships, and practices that provides predictability for members so that they understand roles, procedures, and expectations and so that work gets done.

FOR FURTHER REFLECTION AND DISCUSSION

 MindTap

1. Locate a copy of your college's policies governing students. From its policies concerning class attendance, drug use, and dishonorable conduct, what can you infer about the culture the college wants to promote? (Note how dishonorable conduct is defined; this differs among schools.)

 Ethics

2. Reflect on the corporate, personal, and collegial stories you heard during your first few weeks on a new job. What did these stories say about the organizational culture?

3. Think about a group to which you belong. It may be a work group or a social group, such as a fraternity or interest club. Describe some common rites and rituals in your group. What do these rites and rituals communicate about the group's culture?

4. How can organizational rites and rituals normalize discrimination against particular groups? Identify examples of organizational rites and rituals that encourage or allow unequal treatment based on factors such as race, sex, sexual orientation, or economic class. When, if ever, are such uses of rites and rituals ethical?

 SHARPEN YOUR SKILL — MindTap

1. Noticing Stories and the Work They Do

Think about an organization to which you belong, perhaps one in which you have worked or one that you have had many opportunities to observe. Identify corporate, personal, and collegial stories you were told when you first entered the organization. How did these stories shape your understandings of the organization?

Extend the concept of organizational stories to your family's culture. What family stories taught you your family's history and values? What personal stories did your parents tell you to define who they are and what they stand for? Did family members talk about others? If so, what collegial stories did you hear about other relatives? Do the stories told in your family form a coherent account of its identity?

2. Noticing Rituals in Your Organization

Think of an organization to which you belong. It could be your school or a more specific group such as a sports team, club, or workplace. Describe one ritual (i.e., personal, social, or task) and explain what it does for the organization and its members. What would be missing if this ritual were abandoned?

EXPERIENCING COMMUNICATION IN OUR LIVES

CASE STUDY: *Ed Misses the Banquet*

A video of the scenario featured here is included in your Chapter 10 MindTap for *Communication in Our Lives*. Select "Ed Misses the Banquet" to watch the video. Improve your own communication skills by reading, watching, and evaluating this communication encounter.

Ed recently began working at a new job. Although he's been in his new job only 5 weeks, he likes it a lot, and he's told you that he sees a real future for himself with this company. But last week, a problem arose. Along with all other employees, Ed was invited to the annual company banquet, at which everyone socializes and awards are given for outstanding performance. Ed's daughter was in a play the night of the banquet, so Ed chose to attend his daughter's play rather than the company event. The invitation to the banquet had stated only, "Hope to see you there" and contained no RSVP, so Ed didn't mention to anyone that he couldn't attend. When he arrived at work the next Monday morning, however, he discovered he should have rearranged his plans to attend or, at the very least, should have told his supervisor why he would not be at the event. That Monday, Ed talked with several coworkers who had been around a few years, and he discovered that top management sees the annual banquet as a "command performance" that signifies company unity and loyalty. Later in the day, Ed had the following exchange with his manager.

ED'S MANAGER: You skipped the banquet last Saturday. I had really thought you were committed to our company.

ED: My daughter was in a play that night.

ED'S MANAGER: I don't care why you didn't come. We notice who is really with us and who isn't.

QUESTIONS FOR ANALYSIS AND DISCUSSION

You can answer these questions and see my responses to them online via MindTap for Chapter 10.

1. How does the concept of constitutive rules, which we first discussed in Chapter 5, help explain the misunderstanding between Ed and his manager?

2. How might Ed use the informal network in his organization to learn the normative practices of the company and the meanings they have to others in the company?

3. How do the ambiguity and abstraction inherent in language explain the misunderstanding between Ed and his manager?

4. How would you suggest that Ed repair the damage done by his absence from the company banquet? What might he say to his manager? How could he use *I*-language, indexing, and dual perspective to guide his communication?

5. Do you think the banquet is a ritual? Why or why not?

11

RobinBeckham/Beepstock/Alamy

Television and the Internet are the most powerful socializing and enculturating forces in society.

Arthur Asa Berger

Media and Media Literacy

MindTap™

Review the chapter **Learning Objectives** and **Start** with a quick warm up activity.

Many Internet scholars believe that young people who grow up connected to the digital world will be nimble, analytic thinkers who connect easily with others.

Many Internet scholars say that the hyperconnectivity of today's youth will make them unable to think in depth and unskilled in face-to face relationships.

Which of these two predictions seems more likely to you? Are our ever-present, always-on devices making us smarter, more engaging, and more socially skilled or just the reverse? Whichever prediction you believe, you're in good company.

When the Pew Research Center recently polled people who are Internet experts, 55% said they believed that being electronically connected would make today's youth more capable than their predecessors of managing complex tasks and relating to others. On the other hand, 40% of the Internet experts believed that the extensive connectedness of young people would undermine their abilities for deep thinking and making meaningful relationships with others (Gregory, 2012). Despite their different overall predictions, the Internet experts did agree on one issue: Either you control your engagement with media, or the media will control you.

The goal of this chapter is to increase your control over the media you use so that they don't control you. In the most media-saturated and media-engaged era in history, we should think carefully about how our intense engagement with media affects our lives. How do we use media to develop and negotiate identity, participate in relationships, inform ourselves, and form opinions and perspectives? These are questions we'll consider in this chapter. We'll begin by defining and distinguishing between mass media and social media. Next, we'll explore how mass media and social media affect our lives. The last part of this chapter focuses on media literacy, a critical skill for living in today's world.

THE NATURE AND SCOPE OF MEDIA

Read, highlight and take notes online.

Media is a broad term that includes both mass media and social media. In this section, we define and distinguish between mass media and social media and explore how we interact with both.

Mass media

Mass media are electronic or mechanical channels of delivering one-to-many communication—in other words, they are means of transmitting messages to large audiences. Mass media broadcast messages to a large group of people who generally are not in direct contact with the sources of the messages. Mass media include television, newspapers, magazines, radios, books, and so forth. Television programs such as *Desperate Housewives, Dancing with the Stars*, and *Mad Men* attract millions of viewers; advertisements on TV and the Web and in magazines and newspapers reach millions of people each week; newspapers and the Web provide news updates to vast numbers of people. Each of these media reaches a mass audience.

Social media

Social media are means of connecting and interacting actively. Allison Fine (2006), author of *Momentum: Igniting Social Change in the Connected Age*, explains: "Combine the intimacy of the telephone with the reach of broadcast media and you have social media, the collection of tools used to connect people to one another" (p. xvi). Social media include smartphones and droids; email; iPads and iPods; MP3s; sites on the Web; and other tools that allow us to interact actively, collaborate, and participate in self-organizing, fluid communities. Social media are seamlessly integrated into our routines and identities (Bohil, Owen, Jeong, Alicea, & Bocca, 2009; Potter, 2009; Styer, 2012; Turkle, 2011).

COMMUNICATION HIGHLIGHT

Generations Online

Many people think that new technologies are favored far more by younger than older people. The latest survey, however, suggests the generational divide is not so great (Hill, 2011; Snider, 2012):

- People between the ages of 18 and 34 account for only 23% of the U.S. population, but make up 39% of smartphone owners and 33% of tablet owners.

- People between 35 and 49 years old compose 21% of the U.S. population and account for 30% of those using smartphones and 28% of those visiting social networks, blogs, and online videos.

- Both teens and people aged 18 to 32 go online for videos, games, virtual worlds, and music downloads.

- Baby boomers now represent about 20% of online daters.

- 67% of 33- to 44-year-olds bank online.

The primary difference between mass media and social media is digitalization. Three key implications of digitization are ease of manipulation, convergence, and nearly instant speed (Steele, 2009; Turow, 2008). Manipulation is not new; it was possible with analog film and video and film photography. For instance, a photo could be retouched and video could be edited. However, manipulating analog media took a high level of skill that few people had. In contrast, most people who have grown up using digital media know how to manipulate them—for instance, using Photoshop's clone stamping and despeckle filter allows a person to alter a photo. The line that divided production and consumption of media in the analog era is blurred, if not erased in the digital era.

Digital media also cultivate convergence. Just a few years ago, it was very difficult and expensive to have a voice-over Internet phone call. Today, soldiers in Iraq routinely skype with their families in the United States. This is possible because the technology for transmitting sound and the technology for transmitting visual images are both digital, and thus, they can be managed on a single network.

A third feature of digital media is nearly instant speed. With digital photography, you don't need to wait for photos to be developed. With texting, you are in immediate contact with another person or at least that person's smartphone. There's little, if any, pause between production of a message or photo and its consumption by others or us. That can lead to problems since we can't undo what we do in cyberspace. Anyone can do a screen capture of a photo you send on impulse and then share it with the world. Failbook is a blog Website that initially focused on screenshots of humorous actual status updates uploaded onto social networking sites such as Facebook and Twitter (Styer, 2012).

Interpersonal Mass

FIGURE 11.1
The Media Continuum

Telephone and Cell   IM   PDA   Email   Listservs   FaceBook   Blogs   YouTube   TV

© Cengage Learning

> **RICH** *Before I became a full-time student here, I took three online courses. It was great to be able to do the classes at home when I could make time. But the content of the class was only part of the experience. What I really loved was talking with other students who were also taking the class online. We set up discussion boards, and some of us put each other on our IM lists so we could talk even when we weren't on the course site. I really loved the interaction with other students.*

But the lines between social and mass media are not really clear cut. For instance, if you send a video to a friend who then posts it on YouTube, have you engaged in personal communication or mass communication or both? It is more appropriate to think of media as a continuum that ranges from clearly interpersonal, on one end, to clearly mass, on the other end, with a lot of mediated communication between those two ends (Figure 11.1).

UNDERSTANDING HOW MEDIA WORK

How do mass media and social media work? How do they affect our lives? In this section of the chapter, we'll first consider the ways we use mass media and ways they affect us.

Understanding Mass Media

Researchers have spent decades studying and theorizing about mass media. From their work, we can identify four key ways in which mass media influence—or *attempt* to influence—our lives.

Mass Media Provide Gratification   Think about the last time you watched a film. Did you choose it because the story mattered to you? Were you using the movie to escape from problems and worries? Did you watch because it featured stars you like? According to **uses and gratification theory**, we choose mass communication to gratify ourselves (Reinhard & Dervin, 2009). If you are bored and want excitement, you might watch an action film, whereas if you are stressed and want some lighthearted diversion, perhaps you choose a comedy or fantasy film. Uses and gratification theory says we use mass media to fulfill our needs and desires.

This theory assumes that people are active agents who deliberately choose media to gratify themselves. We use media to gain information, to alleviate loneliness, to divert us from problems, and so forth. As we look at the next theory, we'll see that not everyone agrees that people are active, deliberate consumers of mass communication.

Mass Media Set Agendas   Mass media spotlight some issues, events, and people and downplay others. This affects our perceptions of what is (and is not) happening in the world and what is (and is not) important. **Agenda setting** is selecting and calling to the public's attention ideas, events, people, and perspectives (Agee, Ault, & Emery, 1996; Bryant & Oliver, 2008; McCombs, Ghanem, & Chernov, 2009; Robinson, 2009).

Mass media exercise considerable control over the events, people, and issues that reach public consciousness (McCombs et al., 2009). For instance, television and newspaper reports make us aware of the sexual activities (real or rumored) of public figures. Historical accounts document the extramarital sexual activities of many past presidents, but at the time, those activities were not put on the public agenda. In our era, mass media call the sexual lives of public figures to our attention, making the public more aware of this issue than in previous times. Mass media also give prominence to celebrities; anyone who reads a newspaper or watches television or surfs the Web gets the latest updates on Lindsay Lohan's antics, real or suspected steroid use by athletes, and Justin Bieber's love life.

Within agenda-setting theory, the **gatekeeper** is a key concept. A gatekeeper is a person or group that decides which messages pass through the gates of media to reach consumers. Gatekeepers are people who manage mass media—producers, editors, Webmasters, and so forth. Gatekeepers screen messages, stories, and perspectives to create messages (i.e., programs, interviews, articles) and to shape our perceptions of what is happening and what is and is not significant. Which stories make the front page of a newspaper, which are placed on a back page of Section C, and which are not covered at all? Which stories are covered by online newspapers such as the *Huffington Post?* Which topics are cover headlines on *Elle* and *Men's Fitness?* When a controversial issue is covered, do spokespeople for all sides get opportunity to present their points of view, or are spokespeople for some points of view given more or all of the time and space? Each of these gatekeeping decisions shapes what we perceive to be significant and the information to which we do and do not have access. The media have many gatekeepers:

- Reporters and program hosts decide whose perspectives on a story to present and whose to ignore.

- Editors of newspapers, books, and magazines screen the information that gets to readers and decide where to place stories (cover, front page, back page).

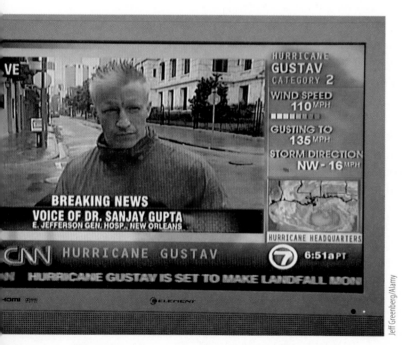

Mass media set agendas by highlighting some, and not other, issues and perspectives.

- Owners, executives, and producers filter information for radio and television programs.
- Government agencies may put pressure on the press and television and radio stations not to broadcast certain information.
- Advertisers and political groups may influence which messages get through.

There is evidence of racial bias in media accounts of crime stories. According to some media scholars (Devereux, 2007; Dixon, 2006), newspapers and television programs present minority citizens as violent criminals more often than they present European Americans as violent criminals and more often than they present minorities in positive stories. This pattern may lead us to inaccurate perceptions of the extent to which members of different races perpetrate violent crimes. Latino and Latina actors are underrepresented in commercial programming. When Latina and Latino actors do appear, they are often portrayed as low-level workers, criminals, or other undesirable characters. Latino and Latina actors who are presented positively usually appear to have assimilated into mainstream white culture, and their racial and ethnic heritage is underplayed or invisible.

Historically, gays and lesbians have been virtually invisible in mass media. One interesting change in commercial programming is the increased presence of gays, lesbians, and trans people who are portrayed positively on some prime-time shows and major films.

Mass Media Cultivate Worldviews **Cultivation theory** claims that television promotes a worldview that is inaccurate but that viewers nonetheless assume reflects real life. This theory is concerned exclusively with television, which it claims shapes heavy viewers' perspectives and beliefs about the world (Gerbner, 1990; Shanahan & Jones, 1999; Signorielli, 2009).

Cultivation is the cumulative process by which television shapes beliefs about social reality. According to this theory, television fosters particular and often unrealistic understandings of the world as more violent and dangerous than statistics on actual violence show it is. Thus, goes the reasoning, watching television promotes distorted views of life. The word *cumulative* is important to understanding cultivation. Researchers don't argue that a particular program has a significant effect on viewers' beliefs. However, they claim that watching a lot of television over a long period of time affects viewers' overall views of the world. By extension, the theory claims that the more television people watch, the more distorted their views of the world are likely to be. Simply put, the theory claims that television cumulatively cultivates a synthetic worldview that heavy viewers are likely to assume represents reality.

Cultivation theorists identify two means by which cultivation occurs: *mainstreaming* and *resonance*. **Mainstreaming** is a process by which mass communication stabilizes and homogenizes social perspectives. For example, if commercial programming consistently portrays Hispanics as unambitious, African Americans as criminals and uneducated, and European Americans as upstanding citizens, viewers may come to accept these representations as factual. If television programs, from Saturday morning cartoons to prime-time dramas, feature extensive violence, viewers may come to believe that violence is more common than it actually is.

The second explanation for television's capacity to cultivate worldviews is **resonance**, the extent to which media representations are congruent with personal experience. For instance, a person who has been robbed or assaulted is likely to identify with televised violence when watching shows that feature it. When media representations correspond with our personal experiences, we are more likely to assume that they accurately represent the world in general.

KELLY *I didn't think much about sex and violence on TV until my daughter was old enough to watch. When she was 4, I found her watching an MTV program that was absolutely pornographic. What does seeing that do to the mind of a 4-year-old girl? We don't let her watch TV now unless we can monitor what she sees.*

The high incidence of violence in news programming reflects in part the fact that the abnormal is more newsworthy than the normal. It isn't news that most couples either get along or work out their problems in nonviolent ways; it is news when one spouse kills another. Simply put, violence is news.

Perhaps you are thinking that few people confuse what they see on television with real life. Research indicates that this may not be the case. Investigations have shown that both males and females who watch sexually violent MTV are more likely to regard sexual violence as normal in relationships (Weimann, 2000). Children who watch a lot of violence on television tend to be less sensitive to actual violence than children who do watch less (Sparks, 2006). It's also the case that children who watch a lot of television violence score higher on measures of personal aggression than children who watch less television violence (Huesmann, Moise-Titus, Podolski, & Eron, 2003). To read a study of violence on children's TV, use your MindTap for *Communication in Our Lives* to access

MindTap™ **WebLink 11.1.**

KASHETA *To earn money, I babysit two little boys four days a week. One day they got into a fight, and I broke it up. When I told them that physical violence isn't a good way to solve problems, they reeled off a list of TV characters that beat up on each other. Another day, one of them referred to the little girl next door as a "ho." When I asked why he called her that, he started singing the lyrics from an MTV video he'd been watching. In that video women were called "hos." It's scary what kids absorb.*

Mass Media Exercise Ideological Influence Because individuals and groups that have benefited from the existing social structure tend to control mass media, they have a vested interest in promoting their own views and values. Thus, it's not surprising that mass media, where gatekeepers are largely those who have done well in the status quo, are more likely to portray whites and middle- and upper-class people good, powerful, and successful than they are to describe minority people or lower- and working-class people in those ways (Hesmondhaigh, 2007; Kendall, 2011).

We've considered four theories that offer insight into how mass media affect us. Probably each view has some validity. Surely, we make some fairly conscious choices about how to use mass media, as uses and gratification theory claims. At the same time, mass media probably influence us in ways we don't notice, as agenda setting and cultivation theories assert. And mass media clearly support dominant ideologies to a significant extent.

The prevalence of violence in mass media makes the world seem more dangerous than it actually is.

Understanding Social Media

Theories that emphasize mass media's ability to set agenda, cultivate worldviews, and maintain ideological control do not easily apply to social media. There is no mainstream view that dominates the Web; there is no single form of music or broadcast that people load onto iPods; there is not one privileged group that controls content on the Internet or blogs.

Yet one theory about mass media, uses and gratification theory, does seem applicable to social media. In fact, social media offer us considerably more options for gratifying ourselves than mass media do. With social media, we have nearly infinite choices for pleasure, information, conversation, collaboration, and the like. We can load our iPods with the songs and podcasts that we like, post and read friends' posts on Facebook, and participate in communities that gratify our various needs and desires.

> **SKINNYGIRL**   *Skinnygirl was the name I used when I belonged to a pro-ana blog. When I was anorexic I couldn't get any support or understanding from my family or ftf friends. It was only when I joined the pro-ana blog that I found people who were like me and who accepted me as I was. A lot of people say pro-ana sites are bad because they encourage girls to be unhealthy, but that's not true. The one I belonged to gave me support when I was anorexic and also when I decided I wanted to get better. It was a safe space to work out who I was and to evolve at my own pace.*

Four principles of social media help us understand how they fit into our lives and how they may change those lives.

Social Media Blur Production and Consumption   Unlike mass media, social media are increasingly produced and consumed by the same people, and most of them are not media executives. Rather, they are ordinary people who

Columbia Pictures/Everett Collection

HEALTH COMMUNICATION

Have App, Will Travel

Traveling through three different time zones is difficult for anyone, but imagine how much more difficult it is if you have a strict medication schedule. If it's 10 a.m. in Hanoi, it would be what time in Philadelphia? Add to the time problem the fact that travel often means different foods and eating schedules, which can affect blood sugar levels and other health matters.

The problem is greatly eased by mobile health apps. Phone apps such as Glucose Buddy and GluCoMo remind diabetic travelers to check blood sugar levels. RxmindMe, available for iPhones and iPods, reminds confused travelers when to take medicines. There's even an app to test blood pressure—a blood pressure cuff that attaches to a smartphone (Weed, 2012).

get to know social media by participating in their actual construction. Media scholar Henry Jenkins (2006, 2007) observes that production and consumption are not rigidly separated in social media. Rather, the lines between them have become blurred as people create personal blogs and podcasts, record their daily activities on LiveJournal, and post videos they've made on YouTube. Jenkins says that young people today figure out how social media work by "taking their culture apart and remixing it" (2007, p. B10).

Social Media Alter Conceptions of Space   Social media change how we create and participate in communities by redefining our sense of space. Prior to the invention of computers, we understood space as something that was abstract, an inert container—"an emptiness awaiting objects" (Nunes, 2006, p. 22). We viewed space as distinct from the people, objects, and events that happened within it. It was something we could enter, send messages through, and put things into. It was something that existed independent of our actions.

Prominent media scholars (Hillis, 2006; Nunes, 2006), however, say that's no longer how we understand space. They argue that cyberspace ushers in new understandings of space as a set of relations that is produced through the process of interacting. Rather than an empty container, cyberspace is a fluid, emergent process of connecting that grows out of interactions, not merely the context in which they occur. Cyberspace is social space in which

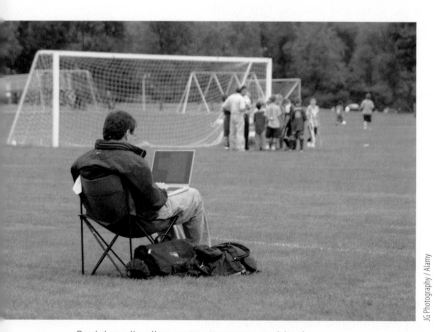

JG Photography / Alamy

Social media allow us to attempt to multitask.

dynamic actions and interactions actually constitute the environment. In other words, cyberspace is not something that exists prior to our interactions. It is not "out there" awaiting us. Instead, it comes into being only as a result of what we do. It is what we do in cyberspace that defines space—the space is produced by what we do.

Consider how we produce the spaces (and the possibilities of relations) in which we interact online. When you use Facebook, you enter into a set of relations, a community, that exists until and unless you friend and unfriend people. Once you do that, you produce a different community—a different space and new set of relations. The space that you are in is produced—brought into being—by what you do. As Nunes (2006) explains, "[C]yberspace is not where these relations take place, it is the *'where' enacted by these relations*" (p. 28).

Social Media Invite Supersaturation   Today's social media give us unprecedented access to information. We are saturated with information; at times we may feel overwhelmed and stressed by the information available to us, even as we increasingly believe Google should answer all of our questions (Hillis, Petit, & Jarrett, 2012).

COMMUNICATION HIGHLIGHT

What's Lost With Perpetual Connection?

We know what we get from being continuously connected, but do we know what we lose? Recent studies raise concerns about three potential losses.

One cost may be emotional health. Girls are particularly vulnerable because their emotional health tends to be established by age 12 whereas boys' emotional health develops over a longer span (Nass, 2012). Tween girls who spend a lot of time interacting socially online feel less normal than girls who spend less time interacting online (Nass, 2012). Research also shows that students who are the heaviest users of technology have the highest levels of anxiety and depression (Rice, 2011). Researchers think the reasons for this may be that online socializing is often done while also engaging in other activities so users are less attentive to relationship levels of meaning and that online interaction doesn't help us develop skill in responding immediately to others' emotions.

A second cost may be conversational skill. The Pew Internet and American Life Project reports that many people today prefer texting to phone calls and face-to-face contact. People whose main form of social engagement is texting may be less likely to make eye contact when they talk with others and may be less skillful in the give and take of conversation (Irvine, 2012). We also have more control over text and online interactions, which may mean we develop less skill in dealing with people and situations that are not within our control (Baron, 2010).

One more cost is sleep. Many young people sleep with their phones on and wake up to respond to texts. Many report they feel compelled to answer messages immediately. One study found that students lose an average of 45 minutes sleep each week because cell phones wake them. In addition, they may get less of the deep REM sleep that makes us feel rested (Rice, 2011).

But it's not just information that saturates us—it's also people. Social media allow us nearly instant contact with other people. At the same time, these media give others greater access to us than ever before. Although students are continuously engaged with digital media, they aren't wholly positive about it. A 2011 report (Levy, Nardick, Turner, & McWatters, 2011) noted that more than half of college students surveyed were concerned about being their immersed in technology. After college doesn't look much better: 62% of workers say they are so overloaded with information that it hampers the quality of their work (Schumpeter, 2011).

STELLA   *I totally count on iPhone to stay in touch with friends. We text all the time, like nonstop. As much as I love staying connected to everyone, I sometimes feel like it's not a choice anymore, like I can't cut off the phone. If I did, all my friends would be really upset and think I was mad or something. It's not okay to just want to be offline.*

Our 24/7 mobile means we can practically leave the physical world of face-to-face relationships and live in the virtual world of online contacts. In *Alone Together* (2011), MIT professor Sherry Turkle asserts that our ability to stay connected with many people all the time poses a paradox: It provides the illusion of intimacy without the responsibilities of intimacy. On the one hand, we can and do interact with more people more often. On the other hand, online connections allow us to control the amount and degree of closeness. Turkle calls this "connection made to measure," which is radically different from relationships in which we sometimes spend more time and deal with more intimacy than we like because the other person needs us and we're committed to her or him.

HEALTH COMMUNICATION

Using Social Media to Improve Health Care

What do social media have to do with health care? A lot, according to Ted Eytan, Benabio, Jeffrey Golla, Vince, Rahul Parikh, and Sara Stein. In a 2011 article, Eytan and his colleagues noted that in a patient-centered model of health care, health systems must use social media to reach today's patients. The authors point out these advantages of active participation in social media by health care systems:

- assisting patients in making healthy life choices
- assisting patients in managing chronic conditions
- providing timely information to patients in a medium they use
- allowing patients to provide timely information to health care providers about changes or needs
- facilitating online support groups
- recruiting new patients through twitter and other tools that accelerate dissemination of messages

S o c i a l   M e d i a   E n c o u r a g e Multitasking Multitasking is doing multiple tasks at the same time. During classes, students often take notes while also texting and checking favorite Websites. Many people play games while shopping and responding to texts.

Despite widespread use of the term *multitasking*, people do not really do multiple tasks at once. Neither do computers, for that matter—they do one task at a time; they just do each one very, very quickly. A slow computer can implement a million instructions in less than a second (Harmon, 2002), but it executes each one individually, in sequence.

What about humans? Can we multitask? Probably not. Neuroscientist Jordan Grafman says that people who try to do multiple tasks simultaneously tend to do all of them superficially (Aratani, 2007). Studies show that extensive use of computers (including smartphones, droids, and tablets) remaps our neural circuitry. For instance, people who spend a lot of time online are likely to skim, scroll, and focus on hypertexted words rather than to read material in

Dan Piraro/The Cartoonist Group

COMMUNICATION HIGHLIGHT

Do u txt whl drvng?

Perhaps the only thing more popular than cell phones is arguments about whether using them distracts drivers. At first, those who want to talk while driving argued that talking on a cell was no different than talking to a passenger. Once that argument was discredited, the new defense was that it was safe to drive and talk if you used a hands-free cell. Now that argument has also collapsed. Substantial research demonstrates that talking on phones—hands-free or not—while driving is dangerous. The problem isn't that "your hands aren't on the wheel. It's that your mind isn't on the road" (Parker-Pope, 2009a, p. D5). Researchers tested drivers' concentration when talking on a hands-free phone, talking with other passengers, and listening to radio or audio books. The results were clear-cut: Phone conversations are more distracting than any of the other activities. Accident statistics bear this out: Drivers talking on cells are four times as likely to have an accident as drivers who are not talking on cells. That's the same level of risk—four times—as driving while legally drunk.

But perhaps technology will save us from itself. Sebastian Thrun (2011), Google Fellow at Stanford, spends his time developing a self-driving car. According to Thrun, "Our cars use specialized lasers, radar, and cameras to analyze traffic at a speed faster than the human brain can process" (p. D4). His model self-driving cars have driven 200,000 miles and counting.

its entirety and with concentrated attention (Carr, 2011; Styer, 2012). This may explain why one former Microsoft and Apple executive refers to multitasking as "continuous partial attention" (Levy, 2006). There's also evidence that people who attempt to do several things at once make more mistakes and actually take longer than people who do one task at a time (Freeman, 2009; Jackson, 2009).

DEVELOPING MEDIA LITERACY

Because mass and social media pervade our lives, we need to be responsible and thoughtful about how we use them—and how they use us. This requires us to develop **media literacy**, which is the ability to understand the influence of mass media and to access, analyze, evaluate, and respond actively to mass media in informed, critical ways. Figure 11.2 shows the components of media literacy. Just as it takes effort to become literate in written and oral communication, it takes effort to develop literacy in interacting with media. How media literate you become depends on the extent to which you work to develop and apply critical skills.

Understand the Influence of Media

Media literacy begins with understanding the extent to which social and mass media influence us. Do they determine individual attitudes and social perspectives, or are they two of many influences on individual attitudes and social perspectives? The first view is both naive and overstated. It obscures the complex, multiple influences on how we think as individuals and how we organize social life. It also assumes that media are linear—that we passively receive whatever mass media's gatekeepers send us and that we don't exercise thought as we engage social media.

The second view represents a thoughtful, qualified assessment of the influence of media and our ability to exercise control over their effects. Media, individuals, and society interact in complex ways. We are not unthinking sponges that absorb whatever is poured on us. Instead, we can interact thoughtfully and critically with media to mediate how they affect our identities and what they encourage us to believe, think, feel, and do.

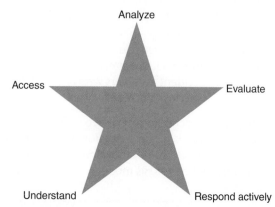

FIGURE 11.2
The Components of Media Literacy

© Cengage Learning

If we choose to interact thoughtfully with media to control their impact on us, then we embrace questions about access to media and deliberate choices of how to engage them.

Access to Media

Access is the capacity to own and use televisions, tablets, computers, smartphones, and so forth. You may be thinking that access is not an issue. After all, you probably have and regularly use four or more personal media as well as engaging with mass media. But not everyone does.

Democratic Access   The term **digital divide** refers to the gap between people and communities with access to media, especially social media, and people and communities with less or no access. Some media scholars (Doyle, 2008; McChesney, 2008) believe that an information elite already exists because access to media, especially social media, requires both knowledge and resources that not everyone has.

If access to technologies is limited to individuals and groups that are already privileged by their social, professional, and economic status, we will see an increasing chasm between the haves and the have-nots. In the short run, it would be expensive to provide access and training for people who cannot afford to purchase it for themselves. In the long run, however, it might be far less costly than the problems of a society in which a small technology elite is privileged and many citizens are excluded from full participation.

COMMUNICATION HIGHLIGHT

The Digital Divide

When communication technologies first gained widespread popularity, some critics and scholars worried about what they called "the digital divide," a term for the gap between people and communities that do and do not have access to technologies. As the costs of technologies and linking systems such as cable have declined, concern over the digital divide has lessened. Yet, recent data (Fox, 2011; Lubrano, 2012; Snider, 2012; Wayne, 2010) indicate that access is not uniform in the United States.

*   Smartphones: Whites own 61%, Hispanics own 17%, and African Americans own 12%.

*   Tablets: Whites own 60%, Hispanics own 15%, and African Americans own 11%.

*   Income affects access: Internet is accessed by 97% of Americans with income over $75,000 and only 62% of Americans with income under $30,000.

*   (Dis)ability affects access: Approximately 80% of all adults in America use the Internet, but only 54% of Americans with disabilities do.

*   94% of people with college degrees use the Internet, whereas only 43% of people without high school diplomas use the Internet.

People who can afford the newest technology will be the first to own multiple computerized devices, some of which will soon be connected to each other (e.g., when your computerized alarm clock rings, your computerized coffeemaker will start, and adjust the temperature in your home) and all of which will be linked to the Internet (e.g., the Internet will automatically reset your alarm clock and all other timing devices when you go on and off daylight savings time or after a power outage). If access is based on wealth, **convergence**—the integration of mass media, computers, and telecommunications—will increase the divide between haves and have-nots.

Expose Yourself to a Range of Media Sources   In addition to the issue of democratic access to mass communication, each of us faces a personal challenge in deciding what we attend. Many people access only media that support the views they already hold. For instance, if you are conservative politically, you might visit politically conservative blogs and sites, follow conservative commentators on twitter, and listen to conservative television programs. The problem with that is that you don't expose yourself to criticisms of conservative policies and stances, and you don't give yourself the opportunity to learn about more liberal policies and positions. The same is true if you are politically liberal—you cannot be fully informed if you engage only media that share your liberal leanings. To be truly informed about any issue, you must attend to multiple, and even conflicting, sources of information and perspective.

Analyze Media

When we are able to analyze something, we understand how it works. If you aren't aware of the grammatical structure and rules of the English language, you can't write, read, or speak English effectively. If you are unaware of the patterns that make up basketball, you will not be able to understand what happens in a game. In the same way, if you don't understand patterns in media, you can't understand fully how blogrings, advertising, programming, and so forth work.

James Potter (2009) points out that there are a few standard patterns that media use repeatedly. Most stories, whether in print, film, or television, open with some problem or conflict that progresses until it climaxes in final dramatic scenes. Romance stories typically follow a pattern in which we meet a main character who has suffered a bad relationship or has not had a serious relationship. The romance pattern progresses through meeting Mr. or Ms. Right, encountering complications or problems, resolving the problems, and living happily ever after.

Just as media follow a few standard patterns for entertainment, they rely on basic patterns for presenting news. There are three distinct but related features by which media construct the news.

- Selecting what gets covered: Only a minute portion of human activity is reported in the news. Gatekeepers in the media decide which people and events are newsworthy. By presenting stories on these events and people, the media make them newsworthy.

- Choosing the hook: Reporters and journalists choose how to focus a story, or how to "hook" people into a story. In so doing, they direct people's attention to certain aspects of the story. For example, in a story about a politician accused of sexual misconduct, the focus could be the charges made, the politician's denial, or the increase in sexual misconduct by public figures.

- Choosing how to tell the story: In the aforementioned story, media might tell it in a way that fosters sympathy for the person who claims to have been the target of sexual misconduct (i.e., interviews with the victim, references to other victims of sexual misconduct); or media might tell it in a way that inclines people to be sympathetic toward the politician (i.e., shots of the politician with his or her family, interviews with colleagues who proclaim the politician's innocence). Each way of telling the story encourages people to think and feel distinctly about the story.

Critically Evaluate Media Messages

When interacting with mass communication, you should think critically to assess what is presented. Rather than accepting news accounts unquestioningly, you should be thoughtful and skeptical. It's important to ask questions such as these:

- Why is this story getting so much attention? Whose interests are served, and whose are muted?

- What is the source of the statistics and other forms of evidence? Are the sources current? Do the sources have any interest in taking a specific position? (For example, tobacco companies have a vested interest in denying or minimizing the harms of smoking.)

- What's the hook for the story, and what alternative hooks might have been used?

- Are stories balanced so that a range of viewpoints are given voice? For example, in a report on environmental bills pending in Congress, do news reports include statements from the Sierra Club, industry leaders, environmental scientists, and so forth?

It's equally important to be critical in interpreting other kinds of mass communication, such as music, magazines, newspapers, and billboards. When listening to a piece of popular music, ask what view of society, relationships, and so forth it portrays, who and what it represents as normal, and what views of relationships it fosters. Raise the same questions about the images in magazines and on billboards. When considering an ad, ask whether it offers meaningful evidence or merely groundless claims for a product's superiority. Asking questions such as these allows you to be critical and careful in assessing what mass communication presents to you.

You should also keep a critical eye on claims that look or sound like facts. Tim Clydesdale (2009) says claims and reports grounded in fact appear side by side with opinions those that have no basis. Communication professor Rayford Steele (2009) extends this thinking one step further. He believes that newer media tempt people to rely on peer opinion rather than expert authority. In the online world, everyone may state opinions, make claims, and so on. The problem is that not everyone is equally qualified, and not every opinion is equally well grounded. When we don't think critically about sources and their qualifications, we impede our ability to make reasoned judgments about which opinions really are supported and good.

The popular online encyclopedia, Wikipedia, illustrates both the advantages and drawbacks of open-source architecture on the Internet. The good news is that anyone can add, delete, or edit entries in Wikipedia. The bad news is that anyone can add, delete, or edit entries in Wikipedia—yep, in this case, the bad news is the same as the good news. You or I can access Wikipedia and edit entries on cyberspace, baseball, or paragliding, regardless of whether we have any expertise on those topics. When anyone can contribute to a site, we need to exercise more than usual critical thinking about what we find on that site.

To practice thinking critically about what you watch on TV for entertainment, complete the activity "Critical Media Literacy" via your MindTap for *Communication in Our Lives*.

 MindTap™

Respond Actively

People may respond actively or passively to mass and social media. If we respond passively, we mindlessly consume messages and the values implicit in them. On the other hand, if we respond actively, we recognize that the worldviews presented in mass communication are not unvarnished truth but partial, subjective perspectives that serve the interests of some individuals and groups while disregarding or misrepresenting the interests of others. Responding actively to mass communication includes choosing consciously how and when to use it,

---

COMMUNICATION HIGHLIGHT

Puffery: The Very Best of Its Kind!

One of the most popular advertising strategies is **puffery,** superlative claims that seem factual but are actually meaningless. For instance, what does it mean to state that a particular juice has "the most natural flavor"? Most natural in comparison to what? Other juices? Other drink products? Who judged it to have the most natural flavor: The corporation that produces it? A random sample of juice drinkers? What does it mean to say a car is "the new benchmark"? Who decided this was the new benchmark? To what is this car being compared? It's not clear from the ad, which is only puffery.

Recently, researchers tested the advertising claims for dozens of fitness products such as sports drinks, oral supplements, footwear, and wrist bands. The researchers could not find valid scientific support for a single claim. In fact, the products that were carefully tested "appear to have no effect on strength, endurance, speed or reduced muscle fatigue" (Bakalar, 2012, p. D5). All of the claims are puffery. Media-literate people don't buy the claims or the products.

questioning what is presented, and involving yourself in controversies about media, particularly the newer technological forms. Responding actively to social media requires us to use our devices deliberately, choosing when to text and when to talk face-to-face, when to be online and when not to.

Participate in Decision Making About Media   Responding actively is not just looking out for ourselves personally. It also requires us to become involved in thinking about how media influence cultural life and how, if at all, media should be regulated. We've already discussed the escalation of violence in media and the digital divide. But there are other issues, particularly in the context of the Internet and the Web. What guidelines are reasonable? What guidelines infringe on freedom of speech and the press? We need to think carefully about what kinds of regulations we want and how to implement them.

Privacy is a key issue for those interested in regulation of social media. Many online advertisers rely on *cookies*, small electronic packets of information about users that the advertisers store in users' personal browsers. *Spyware* is a means by which a third party (neither you-the-user nor the site you are visiting) tracks your online activity and gains personal information about you. Because spyware is implanted on users' computers, it can monitor a range of online activities in which users engage. Should cookies, spyware, and similar tools be regulated? Should users have the right to control who monitors their online communication and with whom it is shared?

Much of the media, particularly social media, remains unregulated. We have an ethical responsibility to become involved in questions of whether regulations should be developed and, if so, who should develop and implement them.

COMMUNICATION HIGHLIGHT

Responding Actively

If you want to learn more about gender and media, or if you want to become active in working against media that foster views of violence as normal, girls and women as subordinate, and buying as the route to happiness, visit these Websites:

Action Coalition for Media Education: http://www.acmecoalition.org

Center for Media Literacy: http://www.medialit.org

Children Now: http://www.childrennow.org

Media Watch: http://www.mediawatch.com

National Association for Family and Community Education: http://www.nafce.org

TV Parental Guidelines Monitoring Board: http://www.tvguidelines.org

BEYOND THE
CLASSROOM

Let's take the material in this chapter beyond the classroom by thinking about how what you've learned about the media might apply to the workplace, ethical choices, and engagement with the broader world.

1. **Workplace.** How have technologies altered the operation of groups in the workplace? Reflect on your own experience or talk with others who have belonged to work groups that operate face-to-face and to work groups that operate virtually. Are the two types of groups equally effective? Do they cultivate equal commitment from group members? Are there particular advantages and disadvantages of each type?

Ethics

2. **Ethics.** Increasingly everything from attending school to communicating with coworkers to maintaining ties with friends and family depends on technologies of communication. Does the increasing importance of these technologies mean that we should ensure that everyone has equal access to them? Is there an ethical responsibility to prevent the digital divide?

3. **Engagement.** Technologies of communication have vastly increased our ability to learn about and even participate in cultures other than our own. Identify an issue that interests you—the election and voting process, a human rights issue, education—and use technologies such as PDA or computer to learn about that issue in the context of a specific culture other than your own.

CHAPTER SUMMARY

 Practice and review the content in this chapter.

In this chapter, we have examined mass and social media. We've explored ways in which these media influence our lives. They affect what we know and think about the world around us, and they affect how we think and act in our lives, both on- and offline.

The second section of the chapter focused on developing media literacy so that we can be informed, critical, and ethical citizens in a media-saturated world. To be responsible participants in social life, we need to think critically about what is included—and what is made invisible—in mass and social media.

Media-literate people do not accept media messages unthinkingly. Instead, they analyze and evaluate the messages and respond actively by participating thoughtfully in considerations about the extent of regulation of media and the people who should exercise that regulation.

Perhaps a good way to end this chapter is by returning to the opening observation that media, both mass and social, are not inherently good or bad. Michael Rich (2012), a pediatrician who directs the Center on Media and Child Health, reminds us, "It's what we do with the tools that decides how they affect us and those around us" (p. D5).

APPLYING COMMUNICATION IN OUR LIVES

Communication in Our Lives is supported by a MindTap, a new online learning platform that delivers content, assignments, and a tailored presentation of the course curriculum created by your instructor. MindTap combines all of your learning tools–readings, multimedia, activities and assessments–into a singular learning unit that guides you through the course. Practice and Present, a unique tool within MindTap, allows you to upload your speech video files for practice or for a grade, comment on your peer's speeches and review your grades. MindTap also includes Speech Builder Express, a powerful tool that guides you through the speech outline and preparation process. For more information or to access MindTap, visit cengagebrain.com.

DEFINITIONS OF KEY CONCEPTS

 Review your **Flashcards**.

agenda setting Mass media's ability to select and call to the public's attention ideas, events, and people.

convergence The integration of mass media, computers, and telecommunications.

cultivation The cumulative process by which television fosters beliefs about social reality.

cultivation theory The theory that television promotes an inaccurate worldview that viewers nonetheless assume reflects real life.

digital divide The gap between people and communities with access to media, especially social media, and people and communities with less or no access.

gatekeeper A person or group that decides which messages pass through the gates of media that control information flow to consumers.

mainstreaming The process by which mass communication stabilizes and homogenizes social perspectives; a concept in cultivation theory.

mass media Channels of mass communication, such as television and radio.

media literacy The ability to understand the influence of mass media and to access, analyze, evaluate, and respond to mass media in informed, critical ways.

puffery In advertising, superlative claims for a product that seem factual but are actually meaningless.

resonance The extent to which media representations are congruent with personal experience.

uses and gratification theory The theory that people choose to attend to mass communication in order to fulfill personal needs and preferences.

FOR FURTHER REFLECTION AND DISCUSSION

 MindTap

1. Would it be ethical to exercise control over the violence presented in media? Do you think viewers, especially children, are harmed by the prevalence of violence in media? If you think there should be some controls, what groups or individuals would you trust to exercise them?

2. Choose "PowerTrac" on your InfoTrac College Edition, then select "Key Word" in the search index. Type "Women and Weight and Magazine Covers." Read the article "Women and Weight: Gendered Messages on Magazine Covers" by Amy Malkin, Kimberlie Wornian, and Joan Chrisler, which was published in a 1999 issue of the journal *Sex Roles*. How well do the different theories of mass media that we've discussed explain their findings about the influence of magazine covers on women's feelings about weight?

3. Susan Crawford is a legal scholar with particular expertise on Internet law and issues of privacy, intellectual property, and advertising. Her blog gives her opinions on a range of legal issues entailed by cyberspace. To read her blog, use your MindTap *for Communication in Our Lives* to access **WebLink 11.2**.

Ethics

SHARPEN YOUR SKILL

 MindTap

1. Media Literacy in Action

In this chapter, you have learned about some of the ways that gatekeepers shape understanding, perspectives, and attitudes. Apply what you've learned by identifying ways that I, as the author of this chapter, shaped the information presented to you.

- *Gatekeeping*: Whose points of view do I emphasize in discussing mass communication and media literacy? Are there other involved groups that I neglect or ignore?
- *Agenda setting*: Which aspects of mass communication did I call to your attention? Which aspects of mass communication did I not emphasize or name?

2. Detecting Dominant Values in Media

Watch 2 hours of prime-time commercial television. Pay attention to the dominant ideology that is represented and normalized in the programming. Who are the good and bad characters? Which personal qualities are represented as admirable, and which are represented as objectionable? Who are the victims and victors, the heroes and villains? What goals and values are endorsed?

EXPERIENCING COMMUNICATION IN OUR LIVES   MindTap

CASE STUDY: *Social Media and Future Employers*

An audio recording of the scenario scripted here is featured in your Chapter 11 MindTap for *Communication in Our Lives*. Select "Social Media and Future Employers" to listen. Improve your own communication skills by reading, watching, and evaluating this communication encounter.

LEMOINE/BSIP/AGE Fotostock

Matthew Leone, a college senior, is a technology junkie who is currently looking for a job. After sending out several résumés but receiving no response, he texts his friend Anna.

As long as he could remember, Matthew Leone loved computers. When he was little, he'd had a Game Boy, and as he'd gotten older, his father had let him use his office computer so Matthew could download pictures of antique cars, one of his favorite things to do. Throughout college, Matthew not only texted and tweeted everyone in his life, but also had a Facebook page where he uploaded pictures of such diverse events as his sister's wedding and his dog's birthday party. It was clear that Matthew was one of those people who loved the ways social media entertained him and let him stay in touch with friends.

Matthew spent the month of February putting his résumé together and applying for jobs. He knew that his degree in economics and his 3.4 GPA would help him secure a good job, and he felt rather confident about his prospects after reading a glowing recommendation letter from one of his professors. Clearly, Matthew Leone was looking forward to a good-paying job with a great company.

Because Matthew's credentials are outstanding, he can't figure out why (it's now April) he hasn't been contacted for any interviews. He sent his résumé and cover letter to all sorts of companies—large and small, public and private—but never scored even one interview. He is confused and concerned, which is why he texted his best friend, Anna, to ask her what she thought.

Anna texted back that she was also surprised that Matthew hadn't been contacted for any interviews. Then she sent a second text that stopped Matthew in his tracks. She said that she'd read a newspaper article about how "controversial" material on Facebook had prevented a man in Florida from getting a job. Apparently, someone at the company the man had applied to had seen some damning pictures of him passed out in a bar. Matthew immediately thought of the pictures he'd put on his Website of his spring break vacation in Cancun, Mexico. He went immediately to his Facebook page and saw that, indeed, there were provocative pictures of him drinking—and drinking, and drinking. In one picture taken in a bar, his friend Damien was pouring beer down Matthew's throat.

Matthew sat motionless in front of his computer. He thought the pictures were harmless, and couldn't believe that someone would take them seriously. Certainly, Matthew thought, plenty of potential employers have been drunk and must know that these pictures were taken for fun. He no longer wondered why he wasn't being called for interviews. Over his lifetime, Matthew had been a huge fan of technology. But now this technology was influencing his life in ways he had never imagined.

QUESTIONS FOR ANALYSIS AND DISCUSSION

 MindTap

You can answer these questions and see my responses to them online via MindTap for Chapter 11.

1. According to the gratification theory, in what ways do you imagine Matthew was gratified by posting photos of himself on Facebook?

2. Matthew might initially appear to demonstrate media literacy because he uses lots of social media, but in what ways does Matthew not fully understand how media work?

3. How might Matthew's experiences with social media have altered his conception of space?

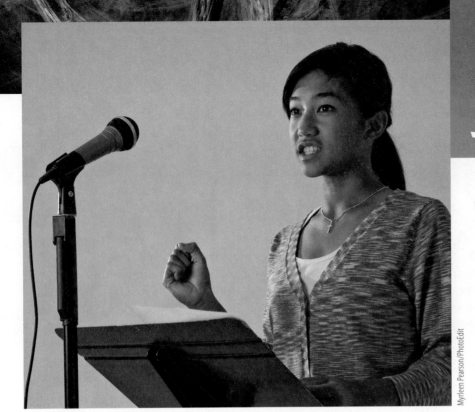

Myrleen Pearson/PhotoEdit

There are three things to aim at in public speaking: first, to get into your subject, then to get your subject into yourself, and lastly, to get your subject into the heart of your audience.

Alexander Gregg

Planning Public Speaking

- Hank is a commercial artist at a public relations firm. On Thursday, Hank's supervisor asks him to prepare a 10-minute presentation for a client whose million-dollar account the firm hopes to get.

- Bonnie belongs to a student group that opposes a tuition hike. At a meeting of the college president's advisory committee, a member of the committee turns to Bonnie's group and asks, "Can you explain why you oppose the tuition increase?" Bonnie realizes that someone in the group needs to present their reasons for opposing the increase, and she rises to speak.

- Miranda volunteers at the local animal protection society. The staff person who was scheduled to present an

MindTap

Review the chapter **Learning Objectives** and **Start** with a quick warm up activity.

SHARPEN YOUR SKILL

At the end of this chapter, refer to the Sharpen Your Skill features, Selecting and Narrowing Your Topic and Defining Your Purpose and Thesis Statement, to apply concepts from Chapter 12.

outreach program at a local high school calls in sick, and Miranda is asked to fill in.

- Juan is a software designer who has created a number of innovative programs. Today, he is giving a 20-minute talk about a new program to people who will be using the program on the job.

- At a public hearing on the location of a toxic waste dump, a representative of a chemical company claims that chemicals stored in the dump are safer than they really are. Noah feels compelled to speak up so that listeners know the truth about the danger of the chemicals.

Although these people aren't professional speakers, each of them is called on to speak in public. If you are competent at public speaking, you increase your opportunities for professional effectiveness and advancement and your influence in civic life. Expressing ideas freely is so basic to a democratic society that it is guaranteed by the First Amendment to the Constitution.

The role of public speaking in professional life is more obvious in some occupations than in others. If you plan to be an attorney, a politician, a salesperson, or an educator, it's easy to see that speaking in public will be a routine part of your life. The importance of public speaking is less obvious, yet also present, in other careers. If you intend to be an accountant, a city planner, a counselor, a doctor, or a businessperson, you will have many opportunities to speak to small and large groups. Whatever profession you enter, public speaking skills will be an asset.

The ability to present ideas effectively in public situations will also enhance your influence in civic, social, and political contexts. You'll have opportunities to voice your ideas at zoning meetings, neighborhood planning groups, and school boards. Public speaking is a basic communication skill that we all need if we want to have a voice in what happens in our workplaces, our communities, and our society.

Like other communication skills, effectiveness in public speaking can be developed with commitment and practice. Although some people may have more experience and perhaps more aptitude for public speaking than others, everyone can learn to make effective presentations. As we will see, many of the skills we've discussed in previous chapters are relevant to effective public communication.

This chapter and the four that follow lead you through the process of planning, developing, and presenting informative and persuasive speeches. In this

COMMUNICATION HIGHLIGHT

The First Amendment: Freedom of Religion, Speech, and Press

"Congress shall make no law respecting an establishment of religion, or prohibiting the free exercise thereof; or abridging the freedom of speech, or of the press; or the right of people peaceably to assemble, and to petition the Government for a redress of grievances."

—Amendment I, The Constitution of the United States

chapter, we'll first note similarities between public speaking and other kinds of communication we've studied. Next, we'll discuss foundations of effective public speaking: selecting and limiting topics, defining a general purpose and a specific purpose, and developing a thesis statement. The third section of the chapter emphasizes adapting speeches to particular speaking occasions and to particular listeners' orientations to topics and speakers.

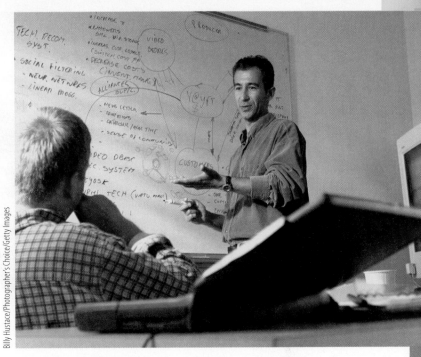

Billy Hustace/Photographer's Choice/Getty Images

The ability to speak effectively is critical to career success.

The next four chapters build on material presented in this one. Chapter 13 identifies types of support for public speeches and discusses methods of conducting research. In Chapter 14, we'll learn about ways to organize and present public speeches, and we'll discuss the widespread concern of communication anxiety and ways to manage it. If you feel anxious about giving a public speech, you may want to read that section of Chapter 15 now. Chapter 15 focuses on informative public speeches, and Chapter 16 focuses on persuasive public speeches. As we discuss these topics, I'll show you partial and complete sample speeches to illustrate how the principles we discuss apply in actual speaking situations. After reading these five chapters, you should be able to plan, develop, and present an effective speech.

PUBLIC SPEAKING AS ENLARGED CONVERSATION

Read, highlight and take notes online.

Years ago, James Winans (1938), a distinguished professor of communication, remarked that effective public speaking is really enlarged conversation. Winans meant that the skills of successful public speaking are not so different from those we use in everyday conversations. Furthermore, minor mistakes, such as stumbling over a phrase or forgetting a word, generally don't impair credibility (Motley, 1990). We make mistakes in everyday conversation and public speaking, and in neither case do they necessarily undercut our effectiveness.

Effective public communication uses and builds on skills and principles we've discussed in previous chapters. Whether we are talking with a couple of friends or speaking to an audience of 500, we need to consider listeners' perspectives, express our ideas clearly, organize what we say so that others can follow our thinking, explain and support our ideas, and present our thoughts in an engaging manner. In public speaking, as in everyday conversation, these are the skills of effective communication.

Effective public speaking is enlarged conversation.

David Young-Wolff/PhotoEdit

CHLOE *I had a great history teacher last year. We met twice a week for 75 minutes, so I was prepared for serious boredom. But it never seemed like he was "lecturing." It was more like he was talking with us—telling interesting stories and asking what we thought about stuff. The 75 minutes just flew by every time.*

CHOOSING AND REFINING A TOPIC

Effective speaking begins with planning. When people think of public speaking, they often focus on delivery. However, 90% of the creation of a speech happens before it is delivered. The choices you make in planning your speech give you great control over its effectiveness.

A well-crafted speech begins with a limited topic, a clear purpose, and a concise thesis statement that listeners can grasp quickly and retain.

Choosing Your Topic

The first step in preparing a public speech is to select a topic. If you don't already have a topic in mind, you might consult newspapers and news magazines, current events programs on TV, and online news sites. To visit online sites, use MindTap for *Communication in Our Lives to access* **WebLink 12.1**.

MindTap

Select a Topic That Matters to You   When you care about your topic, you have a head start in that you already know a fair amount about it. In addition, personal interest in the subject will make your delivery more engaging and more dynamic. Maybe you have strong beliefs about the death penalty, inner-city crime, or environmental responsibility. A speech is the ideal opportunity to influence how others feel and think about issues that matter to you.

Select a Topic Appropriate to the Speaking Occasion   You should also consider the expectations, demands, and constraints of particular speaking situations (Ferguson, 2008). Some contexts virtually dictate speech topics. For example, a rally for a political candidate demands speeches that praise the candidate, a ceremony honoring a person requires speakers to pay tribute to the person, or a speech at a professional conference should address issues of that profession.

> **PAT**   *When we had our Phi Beta Kappa induction last spring, we had a very well-known scholar give the speech. He began by talking about how great our basketball team is and how we may win the championship this year. He talked about the team for about 5 minutes before he said anything else. It's not like I'm against sports or anything. I mean, I go to games and I think our team is way cool. But Phi Beta Kappa is the highest academic honor society on campus. It didn't seem the right situation to be leading a rally for the team.*

Physical setting is also part of the speaking occasion. You know what your classroom is like and the time of day you will speak. In other speaking situations, it's appropriate to ask in advance about the physical setting. Is the room in which you will speak large or small? Is it well lit or dim? Are chairs comfortable or not? Will you present your speech at 10 A.M., after a heavy lunch, or in mid-afternoon? Will listeners have sat through a long day of meetings and speeches? Each of these factors influences listeners' ability to listen and pay attention.

If possible, check the room in advance. You might be able to control some possible hindrances, such as temperature or seating arrangement. If undesirable aspects of the setting are beyond your control (i.e., uncomfortable seating, speaking after listeners have had a big meal), you must do your best to compensate for them. A dynamic and engaging delivery can do much to surmount listeners' lethargy or discomfort.

Sometimes, you won't know the physical setting in advance or won't be able to control it. In that case, you must adapt as best you can on the spot. Once, my partner, Robbie, was asked to give a keynote speech after dinner at a meeting of the North Carolina Student Sierra Club. In the past, he had given many keynote speeches at Sierra Club meetings. Based on past events, Robbie assumed that the dinner would be in a banquet room and that people would be dressed somewhat formally. He prepared a 30-minute speech, which he planned to deliver from a speaking podium. He dressed in a good suit and tie. When he got to the meeting, he discovered that the dinner was a cookout—certainly appropriate for a Sierra Club group, but not what he was expecting!

Robbie quickly adapted his appearance by taking off his jacket and tie and rolling up his shirtsleeves. He then adapted the content of his speech and his delivery to the informal speaking situation in which he found himself. He decided to eliminate some of the quotations from environmental leaders

COMMUNICATION HIGHLIGHT

Connecting Yourself With Your Topic

One of the most powerful ways for speakers to enhance impact is to demonstrate personal involvement with their topics. Some good examples of speakers who show their personal involvement with topics come from acceptance speeches at Academy Awards ceremonies (Robinson, 2001). When Tom Hanks won the best actor award for his portrayal of an attorney with AIDS in *Philadelphia*, he used his speech to honor the millions of people who have died of HIV-related illnesses. He also paid tribute to a former teacher who was gay and who inspired his performance. That same year, Gerda Weisman Klein won an award for her documentary film about the Holocaust, *One Survivor Remembers*. Accepting the award, Weisman said, "I've been in a place for 6 incredible years where winning meant a crust of bread and to live another day" (p. 16).

because the light from the campfire would not be sufficient for him to read the quotations from note cards, and he didn't want to risk misquoting others. And he adapted his planned, forceful, podium delivery to a more conversational, storytelling style. Robbie would have been ineffective had he not adapted to the physical setting.

Select a Topic Appropriate to Your Audience   Effective speakers also select topics that will appeal to the needs, interests, and situations of listeners. A public speech is not primarily a chance to showcase yourself by showing how smart, clever, funny, or knowledgeable you are. Rather, it is first and foremost a chance to affect others—that's the reason for speaking. And if you want to affect others, you begin thinking about them in the first stages of planning a speech.

In selecting a topic, ask how topics that matter to you are or can be relevant to your listeners, what knowledge they have, and what experiences and concerns they are likely to share with you. Later in this chapter, we'll discuss in depth how you can take listeners into consideration.

Narrow Your Topic   Effective speakers limit their speeches to a manageable focus (McGuire, 1989). If you're interested in the general topic of health care reform, you might narrow that to reducing the costs of drugs or increasing preventive medicine (wellness). You can't cover the broad topic of health care reform in a single speech, but you can cover a particular aspect of it.

Another way to narrow your speaking purpose is to use a *mind map* (Jaffe, 2013). A **mind map** is a holistic record of information on a topic, which many visual thinkers prefer to an outline. You create a mind map by free-associating ideas in relation to a broad area of interest. For example, perhaps you want to speak on the general topic of the environment. To narrow that broad topic to a manageable focus for a single speech, you could brainstorm issues related to the topic. Figure 12.1 shows many specific issues that might occur to someone who creates a mind map on the topic of environment. If you would like to use a software program to map your ideas, use MindTap for *Communication in Our Lives* to access **WebLink 12.2**.

FIGURE 12.1
A Mind Map

Defining Your General and Specific Purposes in Speaking

The second step in designing an effective speech is to define your purpose for speaking. This involves two steps. First, decide whether your general purpose is to persuade, entertain, or inform listeners. Second, refine your general purpose into a specific purpose.

General Purposes of Speaking Traditionally, three general speaking purposes have been recognized: informing, persuading, and entertaining (Table 12.1). You probably realize that these purposes often overlap. For example, informative speeches routinely include humor or interesting comments that aim to entertain listeners. Persuasive speeches typically contain much information about issues and solutions. Speeches intended to inform may also persuade listeners to adopt new beliefs, attitudes, or actions. Although speeches often involve more than one purpose, usually one purpose is primary.

Table 12.1	Speaking Purpose	
General Purposes		
To Inform	**To Persuade**	**To Entertain**
Speaking to define, instruct, explain, clarify, demonstrate, teach, or train	Speaking to influence attitudes, beliefs, or actions; to convince, motivate to action, inspire, or sell	Speaking to create interest, amusement, warm feelings; to celebrate, remember, or acknowledge others or events; to create or fortify ties between people
Specific Purposes		
To help listeners understand the balloting procedure used in the 2000 presidential elections in Florida	To persuade listeners to sign a petition demanding new voting systems for all districts in the United States	To have listeners laugh at my jokes in the after dinner speech at the retreat

One speaking goal is to entertain. In **speeches to entertain**, the primary objective is to interest, amuse, or please listeners. You might think that speeches to entertain are presented only by accomplished comics and performers. Actually, in the course of our lives many of us will be involved in speaking to entertain. You might be asked to give an after-dinner speech, to present a toast at a friend's wedding, or to make remarks at a retirement party for a colleague. In each case, the primary goal is to entertain, although the speech might include information about the occasion, the couple being married, or the colleague who is retiring.

Even when your primary purpose in speaking is not to entertain, you'll want to interest listeners whom you intend to inform or persuade. If you want to include some entertainment in your speech, it's a good idea to test your jokes or amusing comments in advance. Don't assume that others will find humor in something you think is funny, and don't rely exclusively on close friends' judgment; after all, friends often think alike and have similar senses of humor.

Humor isn't the only means of entertaining. We also entertain by telling stories to share experiences, build community, pass on history, and teach lessons. Storytelling is prominent in cultures that emphasize oral, more than written, communication. In some countries and in some social communities in the United States, individual and collective histories are kept alive through storytelling (Einhorn, 2000; Fitch, 2000; Schram & Schwartz, 2000). In traditional West African culture, storytellers, who are called griots, tell stories that blend words, song, and dance, and audience members respond as a chorus (Cummings, 1993).

Speaking to inform is a second presentational goal. **Speeches to inform** have the primary goal of increasing listeners' understanding, awareness, or knowledge about some topic. When you speak to inform, your goal is to tell listeners something they don't already know.

Consider several purposes for informative speaking:

- to make listeners aware of a new way of thinking about a familiar topic
- to teach listeners how to do something new
- to correct listeners' misconceptions
- to make listeners aware of issues or problems
- to inform listeners about important events
- to describe a new procedure or policy
- to demonstrate how to do something

Speeches to persuade aim to change people's attitudes, beliefs, or behaviors or to motivate people to act. Persuasive goals are to influence attitudes, change practices, alter beliefs, and to motivate action. Rather than an entertainer or teacher, the persuasive speaker is an advocate who argues for a cause, issue, policy, attitude, or action. To persuade, a speech must do more than provide information, although information typically is part of persuasive speaking as well. Persuasive purposes include the following:

Storytelling is a powerful way to pass on history and strengthen community bonds. It plays a central role in oral cultures.

- to convince listeners to do something they are not currently doing
- to convince listeners to stop doing something they are currently doing
- to show listeners they should support a specific policy, law, or organization
- to convince listeners to buy a product
- to motivate listeners to vote for a candidate
- to inspire listeners to volunteer time or donate to a worthy cause

In one of my classes, a student named Chris gave a speech to persuade other students to donate blood. He began by telling us that he was a hemophiliac and that his life depended on blood donations. This self-disclosure increased his credibility with listeners. He then informed listeners about the procedures for donating blood (a subordinate informational purpose) so that they would not be deterred by fear of the unknown. Next, he described the cases of several people who died because adequate supplies of blood weren't available. In the 2 weeks after his speech, more than one-third of the students who had been in the audience donated blood!

Specific Purposes of Speaking   Once you have decided on your general speaking purpose, you will want to define a **specific purpose**, which is a behavioral objective or observable response that will indicate that you have been effective in achieving your communication goal. Here are some examples of specific speaking purposes:

- I want 25% of listeners to sign up to donate blood.
- I want listeners to be able to give correct answers to questions about how HIV is and is not spread.
- I want listeners to know this candidate's stand on free trade.

Developing a Thesis Statement

Once you have selected and narrowed your speaking topic and defined your general and specific purpose, you're ready to develop the thesis statement of your speech. A **thesis statement** is the main idea of an entire speech. It should capture the heart of your speech in a short, precise sentence that listeners can remember easily (Table 12.2).

A good thesis statement is one that listeners can grasp at the beginning of your talk and remember after you have finished. They may forget the specific details and evidence you present, but you want them to remember the main idea. When Chris gave his persuasive speech, his thesis statement was, "You should donate blood."

Speech Builder Express, which you can access via MindTap for *Communication in Our Lives*, includes a section on developing thesis statements that are appropriate and effective for the type of speech you're preparing.

In sum, the first steps in planning a public speech are to select and narrow a topic, define your general and specific speaking purposes, and develop a clear, concise thesis statement (Table 12.3). Now we're ready to consider the key process of adapting your speaking goals, content, and delivery to specific listeners and speaking contexts.

Table 12.2	Sample Thesis Statements
Ineffective	**Effective**
Think twice before you decide you're for gun control.	Gun control jeopardizes individuals' rights and safety.
Vegetarianism is a way of life.	Vegetarian diets are healthful and delicious.
Big business should get breaks.	Tax breaks for businesses are good for the economy.

Table 12.3	Steps in Planning Public Speaking
Step	**Example**
1. Identify the broad topic.	Education
2. Narrow the topic.	Continuing education
3. Define a general purpose.	To persuade
4. Determine a specific purpose.	To motivate listeners to take courses after graduating from college
5. Develop a thesis statement.	"Taking courses after you graduate can enrich your personal life and your professional success."

ANALYZING YOUR AUDIENCE

A student named Harold gave a persuasive speech to convince listeners to support affirmative action. He was personally compelling and dynamic in his delivery, and his ideas were well organized. The only problem was that his audience had little background on affirmative action, and he didn't explain exactly what it does and does not involve. He assumed listeners understood how affirmative action works, and he focused on its positive effects. His listeners weren't persuaded because Harold failed to give them information they needed. Harold's speech also illustrates the point that speeches often combine more than one speaking purpose; in this case, giving information was essential to Harold's primary goal of persuading listeners.

Another student named Christie spoke passionately about vegetarianism. She provided dramatic evidence of the cruelty animals suffer as they are raised and slaughtered. When we polled listeners after her speech, only 2 of 30 had been persuaded to consider vegetarianism. Why was Christie ineffective? Because she didn't recognize and address listeners' beliefs that vegetarian foods are unhealthy and tasteless. Christie's listeners weren't about to consider a diet that they thought was neither nutritious nor appetizing.

Christie and Harold made the mistake of not adapting to their audiences. Speakers need to know what listeners already know and believe as well as what reservations they might have about a topic (Coopman & Lull, 2013; Griffin, 2012; McGuire, 1989). To paraphrase the advice of an ancient Greek rhetorician, "The fool persuades me with his or her reasons, the wise person with my own." That is, effective speakers work with listeners' reasons, values, knowledge, and concerns.

Demographic Audience Analysis

Demographic audience analysis identifies general features common to a group of listeners. Demographic characteristics include age, sex, religion, cultural heritage, race, occupation, political allegiances, and educational level. Demographic information is useful in two ways.

First, demographic information can help you adapt your speech to your listeners. For example, if you know the age or age range of listeners, you know

COMMUNICATION HIGHLIGHT

What Do People Think About . . .?

Speakers often want to know what the general public thinks about issues related to their topics. Tracking down information on opinions about specific issues can be time consuming, but there's a shortcut. The People & the Press Website, sponsored by the Pew Charitable Trusts, presents the results of public opinion surveys on a variety of topics, such as the present administration, national health care, and biological warfare. To check it out, use MindTap for *Communication in Our Lives* to access **WebLink 12.3**.

MindTap

what experiences are likely to be part of their history. You could assume that 60-year-old listeners know a fair amount about the Vietnam War but that 20-year-olds might not. You can assume that 60-year-olds remember President John F. Kennedy and Martin Luther King Jr., but that 18-to-22-year-old listeners will not remember them. In planning a speech, references to events, people, music, and so forth should be appropriate to the ages of listeners. In many speaking situations, you will have listeners of different ages—sometimes of several generations. In those cases, you'll want either to restrict your references to ones that will be familiar to listeners of all ages or to explain any references that might not be understood by some listeners.

Age is also linked to persuadability. In general, as people age, they are less likely to change their attitudes, perhaps because they've held their attitudes longer than younger people or because they've acquired knowledge that supports their attitudes (Meyers, 1993). Thus, it's generally reasonable to expect to move older listeners less than younger listeners toward new beliefs, attitudes, or actions.

Other demographic information can also guide speakers in preparing presentations that will interest and involve particular listeners. Because we live in a multicultural world, effective speakers must be careful not to use examples that exclude some groups. For instance, the use of generic male language (*chairman*, the pronoun *he* to refer to a doctor) is likely to offend some listeners. Similarly, referring to the winter break from school as "the Christmas holiday" may be perceived as ignoring listeners who are not Christian.

Speakers also use demographic information to make inferences about listeners' likely beliefs, values, and attitudes. For example, assume you plan to give a speech on the general topic of health care reform. If your listeners' average age is 68, they are likely to be more interested in containment of drug costs and in

HEALTH COMMUNICATION

Adapting to Listeners

On Saturday, January 8, 2011, Representative Gabrielle Giffords of Arizona was shot in the head when Jared Lee Loughner opened fire during Giffords' meeting with constituents. Giffords was a popular congressperson, and many people anxiously awaited news about her injury and chances of recovery. Miraculously, she survived the head wound.

Her doctors held a press conference to inform the public of her status. In that public communication, Dr. Dong Kim, the Chair of Neurosurgery at UT Health where Giffords was treated, demonstrated how to adapt highly technical medical information to listeners without medical expertise. He told viewers that Giffords had mild hydrocephalus. Since many in his audience wouldn't know the term *hydrocephalus*, Dr. Kim translated it by saying, it's like "water in the head." He went on to explain that patients with brain injury often have difficulty absorbing fluid in the head, which he made easily understandable by adding that it's like "having a partially clogged drain." Again, Dr. Kim used something laypeople are familiar with (a clogged drain) to give them an understanding of Representative Giffords' situation. The entire press conference is available at http://www.youtube.com/watch?v=OuG6uV4cJ54.

reasonable options for long-term care of older adults than in preventive care and vaccines for children. Listeners with an average age of 21, on the other hand, would be likely to perceive preventive health care as more immediately relevant than ensuring reasonable options for long-term care.

Knowing something about the general characteristics of listeners may also suggest what type of evidence and which authorities will be effective. Statistics bore many listeners, especially if presented in a dull manner, but they might be interesting to an audience of economists or mathematicians. A quotation from Barack Obama is more likely to be effective with a Democratic audience than with a Republican one. Citing Justice Sonja Sotomayor might impress a group of women attorneys more than citing Clarence Thomas would. Although both are Supreme Court justices, they have different degrees of credibility with different groups.

Speakers may also draw on demographic information to create connections with their listeners. Politicians create points of identification with voters in diverse regions. In the South, a candidate might tell stories about growing up in Southern towns; in New England, the candidate might reminisce about college years at Harvard or Dartmouth; in the Midwest, the candidate might speak about friends and family who live there. It is unethical for a speaker to disguise or distort his or her background, ideas, or positions to build common ground with listeners. However, understanding the demographic characteristics of listeners helps a speaker decide which aspects of his or her life and interests to emphasize in a particular situation.

> **LAMONT**   *A big filmmaker came to talk to our class, and I figured he was in a world totally different from ours. I mean, the man makes multimillion-dollar movies and knows all the big stars. But he started his talk by telling us about when he was in college, and he talked about his favorite classes, about a bar he went to on Fridays, and about the special friends he'd made at college. I felt like he understood what my life is about, like he wasn't so different from me after all.*

Demographic analysis can provide useful general information about listeners. However, it's important to guard against stereotypes of groups of people. Although many college students are between 18 and 22 years old, some are older than 22. Thus, it would be inadvisable to design a speech to college students for an exclusively 18-to-22-year-old audience. Although many women work outside the home, not all do, so an audience of women should not be addressed as if no homemakers were present. Similarly, speakers shouldn't stereotype an audience of men as uninterested in child care because many men are involved parents.

Situational Audience Analysis

A second method of audience analysis is **situational audience analysis**, which seeks information about listeners that relates directly to the speaker's topic and purpose. Situational audience analysis allows a speaker to discover what listeners already know and believe about a topic, speaker, and occasion so that the speaker can adapt to his or her listeners.

Listeners' Orientation Toward the Topic   Effective speakers develop their speeches with attention to their listeners' interest, knowledge, and attitudes toward the speech topic. In many cases, listeners are already interested in the speech topic—that's why they attend. However, if listeners do not begin with interest in your topic, your job is to pique their interest. You might make them aware of how the topic relates to them: How does it, or how will it, affect them? What's at stake for them? Why should they care about what you have to say? Emma, a student of mine, began an informative speech about breast cancer this way: "Think about 8 women who matter to you. According to statistics, 1 of those 8 women will develop breast cancer."

You also want to analyze listeners' knowledge about your topic so that you can adapt appropriately. What do they already know about the topic? How much information (or misinformation) do they have? Once you have assessed listeners' knowledge about your topic, you can decide how much information to provide and how detailed and technical you can be.

Finally, in assessing your listeners' orientation toward your topic, you want to know what attitudes they hold. If they already favor something you are proposing, you don't need to persuade them to adopt a positive attitude. Instead, you may want to move them to action—to motivate them to act on what they already favor. On the other hand, if your listeners are against or indifferent to something you are proposing, your persuasive goal is to convince them to consider your point of view. You will need to provide more evidence than you will if they already favor your position.

Listeners' Orientation Toward the Speaker   Listeners' perceptions of a speaker shape how they respond to the message. The more credibility a speaker has with listeners, the more likely they are to believe what the speaker says and to consider her or his proposals. Do the listeners already know who the speaker is? Do they respect the speaker's expertise on the topic? Do listeners believe the speaker cares about what is good for them? If not, the speaker needs to give listeners reasons to trust him or her and to believe that he or she is interested in their welfare.

If you do not have credentials that establish you as an expert on a topic, you will want to demonstrate to listeners that you know what you are talking about. Explain how you learned about it. Describe your experiences with the topic. Include research that shows you are knowledgeable. Similarly, you will want to convince listeners that you care about what is good for them. Demonstrate that what you say is relevant to their health or success.

Because a speaker's credibility is critical to effectiveness, we'll return to this topic when we discuss using evidence (Chapter 13), building a strong introduction to a speech (Chapter 14), and increasing credibility (Chapter 16).

Listener's Orientation Toward the Speaking Occasion   In the fall of 2002, Paul Wellstone, a Democratic senator from Minnesota, was killed in a plane crash. In addition to grieving for his tragic loss, Democrats were worried about the elections coming up in just a month. Wellstone had seemed assured of reelection. His sudden death meant that the Republican candidate might win his seat in the United States Senate. After late-night strategy sessions, the Democrats announced that Walter Mondale, a former vice president from Minnesota, was the Democratic candidate and would carry on Wellstone's legacy.

The nationally televised memorial service for Senator Wellstone and those of his family who also died in the plane crash began with speeches honoring the fallen senator, as was expected on this occasion. However, after the opening speeches, the memorial service turned into a political rally for Mondale, the new Democratic candidate. Many viewers were shocked and offended by what they perceived as disrespect for Wellstone and his family and a blatant exploitation of a memorial service for political purposes. Mondale was defeated, and most political analysts cited the voting public's negative reaction to the memorial service as the key reason.

This example illustrates the importance of considering what listeners expect in a particular speaking situation and what they will consider appropriate and inappropriate. At a wedding reception I once attended, guests were toasting the newlyweds. One old friend of the groom got up to "say a few words" and then spoke for 15 minutes! That's much too long for a toast, and other guests were clearly unimpressed. A speech introducing a main speaker should be short. Listeners will be displeased if a speech of introduction drags on because they came to hear the main speaker. On the other hand, the main speaker generally speaks at length; listeners would be disappointed by a 6-minute speech from a featured speaker.

Occasion also influences the type of speech. In the example of the memorial service for Wellstone, the occasion demanded speeches honoring Wellstone. After-dinner speeches generally should include some entertainment—jokes, stories, and so forth—and should not be overly somber or information packed.

Whereas politicians and corporations can afford to conduct sophisticated polls to discover what people know, want, think, and believe, most of us don't have the resources to do that. So how do ordinary people engage in situational

Small Society © King Features Syndicate

audience analysis? One answer is, by observation. Often, a speaker has some experience with his or her listeners. Based on past interactions, a speaker may know a great deal about the knowledge, attitudes, and beliefs of listeners.

It's also appropriate to gather information about listeners through conversations, interviews, or surveys. You might conduct a survey to learn about your classmates' knowledge of and attitudes toward your thesis statement. The results of your survey should give you sufficient insight into the opinions of students on your campus to enable you to adapt your presentation to the students in your class.

Demographic and situational audience analysis provides you with direct knowledge of listeners and information from which you can draw additional inferences. Taking listeners into consideration allows you to build a speech that is adapted to your particular listeners and thus likely to have impact.

CHAPTER SUMMARY

 Practice and review the content in this chapter.

In this chapter, we considered the nature of public speaking and the first steps in designing effective presentations. We began by noting that, rather than differing radically from other kinds of communication, public speaking is enlarged conversation, in which a speaker interacts personally with listeners. To do this effectively, it's important to select and limit your topic, to define your general and specific purposes, and to develop a clear thesis statement. In addition, designing an effective presentation requires consideration of listeners. Effective speakers take into account what listeners know, believe, value, think, and feel about the topic, speaker, and occasion. When a speaker adapts to listeners, they are likely to be more receptive to the speaker's ideas.

In the next chapter, we'll discuss ways to conduct research and use research in public speaking. Building good arguments increases a speaker's credibility and enhances the power of ideas presented. Before proceeding to Chapter 13, complete the checklist to make sure you've done the preliminary work to create a strong foundation for your speech.

CHECKLIST FOR PLANNING A PUBLIC SPEECH   MindTap

If you prefer, you may complete this checklist online under your Chapter 12 MindTap for *Communication in Our Lives*.

In addition, you may want to use Speech Builder Express, which you can access through MindTap. At the end of this chapter, I've included a specific suggestion for using Speech Builder Express to begin planning your speech.

My speech topic is _____

_____

My general purpose is _____

_____

My specific purpose is _____

_____

My thesis statement is _____

_____

1. I know the following demographic information about the people who will listen to my speech:

   Age: _____

   Education: _____

Political position: _____

Sex ratio: _____

Ethnicities: _____

Other: _____

2. I know the following information about my particular listeners:

Listeners' interest in my topic: _____

_____

Listeners' knowledge about my topic: _____

_____

Listeners' personal experience with my topic: ___

_____

Listeners' beliefs about my topic: _____

_____

Listeners' attitudes about my thesis: _____

_____

Listeners' expectations of the speaking occasion:

_____

Listeners' orientation toward me as a speaker: ___

_____

APPLYING COMMUNICATION IN OUR LIVES   MindTap™

Communication in Our Lives is supported by a MindTap, a new online learning platform that delivers content, assignments, and a tailored presentation of the course curriculum created by your instructor. MindTap combines all of your learning tools–readings, multimedia, activities and assessments–into a singular learning unit that guides you through the course. Practice and Present, a unique tool within MindTap, allows you to upload your speech video files for practice or for a grade, comment on your peer's speeches and review your grades. MindTap also includes Speech Builder Express, a powerful tool that guides you through the speech outline and preparation process. For more information or to access MindTap, visit cengagebrain.com.

DEFINITIONS OF KEY CONCEPTS   MindTap™ Review your **Flashcards**.

demographic audience analysis A form of audience analysis that seeks information about the general features of a group of listeners.

mind map A holistic record of information on a topic. Mind mapping is a method that can be used to narrow speech topics or to keep track of information gathered during research.

situational audience analysis A method of audience analysis that seeks information about specific listeners that relates directly to a topic, speaker, and occasion.

specific purpose A behavioral objective or observable response that a speaker specifies as a gauge of effectiveness; reinforces a speaker's more general speaking goals.

speech to entertain A speech the primary goal of which is to amuse, interest, or engage listeners.

speech to inform A speech, the primary goal of which is to increase listeners' understanding, awareness, or knowledge of some topic.

speech to persuade A speech, the primary goal of which is to change listeners' attitudes, beliefs, or behaviors or to motivate listeners to action.

thesis statement The main idea of an entire speech. It should capture the key message in a concise sentence that listeners can remember easily.

1. Selecting and Narrowing Your Topic

Identify three broad topics or areas that you care about.

Topic 1: _____

Topic 2: _____

Topic 3: _____

Now list three subtopics for each one. The subtopics should be narrow enough to be covered well in a short speech.

Topic 1: 1. _____

2. _____

3. _____

Topic 2: 1. _____

2. _____

3. _____

Topic 3: 1. _____

2. _____

3. _____

Select one of the nine subtopics for your upcoming speech.

2. Defining Your Purpose and Thesis Statement

Write out the general purpose of your speech.
I want my speech to _____

_____

Define the specific purpose of your speech by specifying the observable response that will indicate you have succeeded:
At the end of my speech, I want listeners to_____

_____

Does your specific purpose require you to meet subordinate goals, such as including information in a persuasive speech?
To achieve my specific purpose I need to [entertain, inform, and/or persuade]. _____

_____

For additional practice in developing thesis statements, complete the activity "Developing Effective Thesis Statements" in your Chapter 12 MindTap for *Communication in Our Lives*.

FOR FURTHER REFLECTION AND DISCUSSION MindTap

Ethics

1. Think about one presentation that you recently attended—perhaps a lecture in a class or a speech at a campus event. To what extent did the speaker seem to take the audience into consideration? Identify specific factors that affect your perception of the speaker's knowledge of you and other listeners. Did this make a difference in the speaker's effectiveness?

2. In this chapter, we discussed the importance of adapting to particular listeners. What ethical considerations apply to the process of adapting speeches to particular listeners? Is it ethical for a speaker not to disclose certain experiences with a topic? Is it ethical for a speaker to leave out evidence that is contrary to his or her speaking goal?

3. Check two databases for sources on a topic that interests you. Track down two sources from each database to read in detail.

4. Use your MindTap for *Communication in Our Lives* to access **WebLink 12.4** to review commonly believed myths about public speaking.

EXPERIENCING COMMUNICATION IN OUR LIVES

© Cengage Learning

CASE STUDY: *A Model Speech of Introduction*

The following speech is featured in your Chapter 12 MindTap for *Communication in Our Lives*. Select "Speech of Introduction" to watch the video of Dan's speech. Improve your own public speaking skills by reading, watching, and evaluating this sample speech.

Dan's assignment was to present a speech of introduction in which he introduces his classmates to Dr. Evelyn Horton. Dr. Horton is a doctor who specializes in family medicine, the profession that Dan hopes to enter.

"If you don't listen to your patients, you'll never be able to provide them with good medical care." That was the first thing Dr. Evelyn Horton said to me when I asked her what kinds of communication are essential to her work. Last Monday, I interviewed her because I hope one day to be a doctor. I want to introduce you to Dr. Horton and to describe the role of communication in her work as a doctor. I'll focus on the importance of two communication skills that Dr. Horton emphasized: listening and building a supportive, trusting relationship.

The first communication skill that Dr. Horton emphasized is listening. She told me that one of the reasons she wanted to become a doctor is that she had encountered too many doctors who didn't listen to her when she was a patient. "How can a doctor treat you if he or she doesn't listen to you?" asked Dr. Horton. Dr. Horton isn't alone in feeling that many doctors don't listen. The *Journal of the American Medical Association* reported last year that patients' biggest dissatisfaction with doctors is that they don't listen.

I asked Dr. Horton to explain what was involved in effective listening. She said, and I quote, "To be a good listener, I have to let my patients know I really want to hear what's going on with them. I have to give them permission to tell me how they are feeling and if anything is bothering them." Some of the ways that Dr. Horton does this are to repeat what patients tell her so that they will elaborate, and to keep eye contact with them when they are speaking.

So focusing on patients and encouraging them to talk openly with her are the keys to effective listening in Dr. Horton's practice. The second communication skill that Dr. Horton emphasized is building a supportive, trusting relationship with her patients. She told me about one of her patients who had an eating disorder. Dr. Horton suspected the problem, but she couldn't do much to treat it until her patient, a 19-year-old woman, was willing to admit she had a problem.

How did Dr. Horton gain the patient's trust? She told me that she showed the patient she wasn't going to judge her—that it was okay to say anything, and it would be confidential. When the patient made a small disclosure about being afraid of gaining weight, Dr. Horton recalled, and I quote, "I told her many women have that fear, and there are healthy ways to control weight." Later, the patient told her that sometimes she skipped meals. Dr. Horton responded, and again I quote her, "That's an understandable thing to do when you're afraid of gaining weight, but there are healthier ways to maintain a good weight." As Dr. Horton responded without judgment to the patient, the young woman gradually opened up and told Dr. Horton about her excessive dieting and exercise. Together, they worked out a better plan for managing the patient's weight.

Being nonjudgmental, then, is a key to building a trusting doctor
you've met Dr. Evelyn Horton, a doctor who knows the importance of c
work. For her, listening and building a supportive, trusting relationship wit
to being a good doctor. Let me close with one last statement Dr. Horton mad
treat people, you have to communicate well with them."

QUESTIONS FOR ANALYSIS AND DISCUSSION MindTap

You can answer these questions and see my
responses to them online via your Online
Resources for Chapter 12.

1. Does Dan's speech give you a sense of who
   Dr. Horton is?

2. Did Dan's introduction catch your attention
   and give you a road map of what he would
   cover in his speech?

3. How did Dan move you from one part
   speech to the next?

4. How did quotes and examples from
   Dr. Horton add to the speech?

5. Was Dan's conclusion effective?

6. Which model of communication presented
   in Chapter 1 best describes Dr. Horton's
   communication with patients?

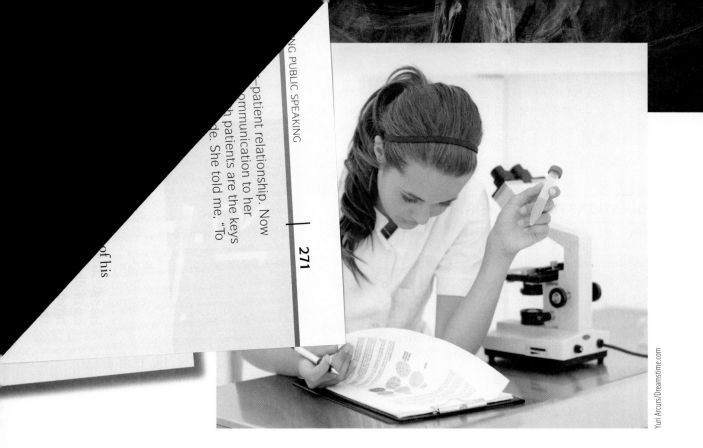

-patient relationship. Now
ommunication to her
h patients are the keys
e. She told me, "To

of his

Yuri Arcurs/Dreamstime.com

Researching and Developing Support for Public Speeches

Review the chapter
Learning Objectives
and **Start** with a quick
warm up activity.

A speaker's success is tied directly to whether listeners understand, believe, and accept what he or she says. In this chapter, you will learn how to conduct research and weave it into your speech so that listeners understand and believe in you and your message. Throughout the process of researching and building support for a speech, it's important to conduct research and select evidence adapted to particular listeners.

SHARPEN **YOUR SKILL**

At the end of this chapter, refer to the Sharpen Your Skill features, Background on Experts and Bringing Statistics Alive, to apply concepts from Chapter 13.

CONDUCTING RESEARCH

At the outset of developing a speech, you may already have a definite point of view and know a good deal about your topic. Research continues throughout the development of the speech. In the early stages of research, you may unearth information that leads you to modify your original thesis statement. As you continue, you may find evidence that convinces you to add additional points. We'll discuss four types of research that helps you develop informative and persuasive presentations: library and online research, personal knowledge, interviews, and surveys.

Library and Online Research

Libraries and online services hold a wealth of information that can help you develop and support the ideas in your speech. Begin your research by paying a visit to the reference librarian at your library. Describe your speech topic to your reference librarian, and ask for suggestions on relevant print and electronic sources of information.

COMMUNICATION HIGHLIGHT

Evaluating Online Sources for Speeches

Material found online is not necessarily trustworthy. Anyone can set up a Website, and anyone can make claims on the Internet. Because Internet content is unregulated, you should be especially critical when evaluating it. To assess information found on the Internet, begin by applying the five standard tests for evidence summarized in Table 13.4 on page 289. In addition, ask the following questions:

1. Can you verify the material independently (by checking another source or consulting an expert)?

2. Does the source have the experience, position, or other credentials to be an authority?

3. Does the source have any vested interest in making the claim or presenting the alleged information?

4. Does the source acknowledge other sources, including ones that advance different points of view?

If you decide the online material is sound, you should cite it in your bibliography as well as your text, using the following format:

Hulme, M. & Peters, S. (2001). *Me, my phone, and I: The role of the mobile phone.* Workshop: Mobile communications: Understanding users, adoption, and design, Seattle WA. Retrieved January 3, 2002, from http://www.cs.colorado.edu/~palen/chi_workshop.

Basic principles for evaluating material found on the Web, as well as links to multiple sites that discuss the credibility of web information, can be found at **WebLink 13.1.** You can access this link via MindTap for *Communication in Our Lives.*

The Internet   Although the Internet offers a lot of information, that information isn't necessarily credible or reliable. Most magazines and newspapers have fact checkers who check all information in articles before they go to press. In contrast, there is no systematic procedure for checking the accuracy of information posted on the Internet. People who create or contribute to sites may not have sound backing for their claims. They may have vested interests in particular viewpoints. Information you find online should be verified.

Indexes   Libraries have indexes, some of which are online, that summarize publications and backgrounds of individuals. Indexes of articles published in academic journals are important resources. *Psychological Abstracts*, for example, surveys articles published on psychological topics. If you want to know what research has been done on self-concept, simply look up "self-concept" in *Psychological Abstracts*, and you will find a list (probably a very long one) of published research on the topic. In addition, indexes of government documents summarize laws, policies, and regulations related to many topics.

There are several good sources of background information on experts you may cite in your speech. Some of the more popular ones are *Who's Who in America*, *Who's Who in American Women*, *Biography Index*, and *Directory of American Scholars*. You enhance your own credibility by citing the qualifications of sources in your speech.

Databases and Search Engines   Databases allow you to search a library's or service's holdings from a computer terminal. One widely used database is Dialog Information Retrieval Service (DIRS), which includes more than a million records from popular and academic publications and news services. Two other superior information retrieval systems are Bibliographic Retrieval Service (BRS) and Wilsonline.

Reference Works   Specialized references can save you hours of work by directing you to materials specific to your topic. The *Reader's Guide to Periodical Literature* summarizes articles published in popular magazines, including *Newsweek*, *Ebony*, and *Fortune*. The *Public Affairs Information Service Bulletin* indexes books, pamphlets, and other materials pertinent to public affairs. *American Demographics* is an amazing reservoir of information on Americans' patterns, behaviors, possessions, and so forth. It's the resource to check if you want to know how many televisions the average household has, how much sugar the average person consumes in a year, or how often most people eat out. *Facts on File* is a weekly publication that provides factual information and background on world news.

Personal Knowledge

Another source of information is yourself. What do you already know about your topic? How are you involved with it? What experiences have you had that qualify you to speak on the topic? Why does this topic matter to you? When you draw on your own experiences and knowledge, listeners are likely to perceive you as

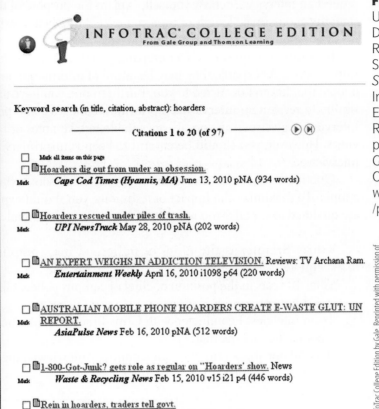

FIGURE 13.1

Using an Online Database to Research Your Speech Topic *Source:* From InfoTrac College Edition by Gale. Reprinted with permission of Gale a division of Cengage Learning. www.cengage.com /permissions

From InfoTrac College Edition by Gale. Reprinted with permission of Gale a division of Cengage Learning. www.cengage.com/permissions

more credible than someone who is not personally involved with the topic.

Interviews

Interviews allow you to gather information, to check the accuracy of ideas you have, and to understand the perspective of people who are experts or who have special experience with your topic. Many community organizations have experts who can provide you with a wealth of information on specific topics. Staff at your local parent–teacher association, animal protection society, Nature Conservancy, Habitat for Humanity, and Alcoholics Anonymous can provide current information in their respective areas.

You need to plan ahead for interviews. When you call or email to

Reprinted by permission of www.Virtual Library, http://vlib.org.

Online research includes sites such as the U.S. Census Bureau, which provides information on demographics and many facets of American life.

request an interview, identify yourself, explain the purpose of the interview, and state the approximate length of time you expect the interview to take. Prepare a list of questions in advance to ensure that you don't forget important questions.

In addition to questions you prepare, you'll want to invite interviewees to initiate ideas. As experts, they may be aware of information and dimensions of a topic that haven't occurred to you. Furthermore, you have an ethical responsibility to respect an interviewee's priorities, concerns, and perspectives. If an interviewee gives permission, it's acceptable to take notes or tape during interviews. However, you should be careful to keep your primary attention on the interviewee.

Quoting interviewees shows that you invested personal effort in researching a topic. To maximize the impact of testimony, you should explain why sources are qualified as experts. You may credit your sources in several ways:

> "Chris Brenner is the chief of police on our campus. He says, and I quote, . . ."
>
> "After 10 years in the position of chief of campus police, Chris Brenner says, and I quote, . . ."
>
> "In an interview I conducted with Chris Brenner, longtime chief of campus police, he told me that. . ."
>
> "To find out about crime on our campus, I interviewed the chief of campus police. According to Chief Brenner, . . ."

COLE *It was really effective when Joel told us he had interviewed police officers to find out their views about drivers who use cell phones. He had lots of good information from other sources, but what really impressed me was that he took the time to talk with police officers himself. I felt like that showed he cared enough to really learn about his topic in a personal way.*

Surveys

Survey research involves asking a number of people about their opinions, views, values, actions, or beliefs. Surveys are useful in two situations. First, sometimes there's no published research on something important to your speech. Yumiko, a student taking his first speaking course, was concerned that many of his peers at the university had misperceptions about Japanese people and their traditions. He decided to use his speech as an opportunity to correct misperceptions. After 2 weeks of research, he was discouraged because he couldn't find any studies of U.S. college students' views of Japanese people. We developed a short questionnaire on views of Japanese people that he handed out to 100 students on campus. This gave Yumiko some information about local students' perceptions (Table 13.1).

Second, sometimes you can directly survey your listeners. Although this isn't always feasible, when it is possible this helps you find out what listeners know. Based on what you learn, you can include information they don't have

Table 13.1	Guidelines for Constructing Surveys

The following guidelines will help you construct a survey that will provide you with solid information.

1. Respondents should be chosen to reflect the population (or larger group) whose opinions you seek to understand. (Students may reflect students' opinions. However, students generally would not reflect homeowners' opinions.)

2. Respondents should be qualified to answer the questions. (Only people who are informed about inflation and living expenses have the information to answer this question: "How much should the cost-of-living adjustment be for Social Security recipients?")

3. Questions should be worded to avoid bias. ("You favor gun control, don't you?" is a leading question that biases respondents toward answering affirmatively. The question "Do you favor gun control?" is not biased. You will get different responses if you ask people if they favor "helping the poor" and if they favor "welfare.")

4. Each question should focus on only one issue. ("Do you favor Medicare and Medicaid?" asks respondents' opinions on two distinct issues. This question should be split into two separate questions.)

5. Questions should allow for all possible responses. (It would not be accurate to ask respondents whether they are Democrats or Republicans because those two responses don't include other possible choices, such as Libertarians and Independents.)

6. Questions should rely on language that will be clear to respondents. (For years, the U.S. Bureau of the Census asked people whether they worked "full time," which the bureau defined as 35 hours a week or more. However, many respondents interpreted "full time" to mean 40 hours a week or more. The bureau revised the wording of the question to remove the ambiguity.)

7. Avoid negative language in survey items; it tends to be confusing. (Respondents are likely to misunderstand the question "Do you agree or disagree that the United States should not have socialized medicine?" The question is clearer when phrased this way: "Do you agree or disagree that the United States should have socialized medicine?")

For practice in determining effective survey strategies and questions, complete the activity "Survey Construction Guidelines" via your MindTap for *Communication in Our Lives*   MindTap™

© Cengage Learning

and avoid boring them by telling them what they already know. Surveys of listeners also allow you to discover what personal experience they have pertinent to your topic. Attitudes based on direct experience are more difficult to change (Wu & Shaffer, 1988).

If you plan to speak on gun control, you might want to know whether your listeners are aware of existing legislation, whether they hunt, and whether they or members of their families own firearms for protection. For a speech on family leave practices, it would be helpful to find out whether listeners understand the limits of the Family Medical Leave Act and whether they are aware that the United States is the only industrialized nation that doesn't have guaranteed family leave for all workers.

Audience surveys can also help you learn what attitudes your listeners hold. At a minimum, you'll want to know whether your listeners agree or disagree with your position and how strong their attitudes are. If you want to argue for more severe sentences for convicted felons, and your listeners are strongly against that, then you might choose to limit your persuasive goal to reducing the strength of listeners' resistance to stronger sentencing. On the other hand, if they already agree with your position, you might try to move them toward action by asking them to write letters to senators or to vote for candidates who share their attitudes. What you can achieve in a given speech depends to a large extent on the starting beliefs and knowledge of your listeners (Wu & Shaffer, 1988).

Now that we have discussed ways to conduct research, we're ready to consider specific forms of support, or evidence.

USING EVIDENCE TO SUPPORT IDEAS

Evidence is material used to support claims a speaker makes. Evidence serves a number of important functions in speeches. First, it can be used to make ideas clearer, more compelling, and more interesting. Second, evidence fortifies a speaker's opinions. Finally, evidence heightens a speaker's credibility. Speakers who use good evidence show that they are informed and prepared.

MARTEL   *We had a guest speaker in my econ class. He quoted Nobel Prize–winning economists and the findings of a report that was just done and hasn't even been published yet. All of us felt he was highly informed and credible.*

To decide when to use evidence in a speech, ask yourself, "Will my listeners understand and believe this claim on my say-so alone?" If not, then you'll want to include evidence Speech Builder Express, which you can access via MindTap for *Communication in Our Lives*, includes a section focused on selecting the amount and types of supporting material you may need, based on the main points of your speech.

The next decision you need to make is which type of evidence to use. Five forms of support are widely recognized. Before including any form of evidence in a speech, the speaker should check the accuracy of the material and the credibility of the source. When presenting evidence to listeners, speakers have an ethical responsibility to give credit to the source (an oral footnote).

Statistics

Statistics are numbers that summarize many individual cases or demonstrate relationships between phenomena. Including statistics can enhance speaker credibility (Crossen, 1997). For example, a speaker could demonstrate the prevalence of injuries caused by drivers who are under the influence of alcohol by stating, "According to the American Automobile Association, one in four people injured in traffic accidents is the victim of a driver who had been drinking." Statistics can also be used to document connections between two or more things. For

HEALTH COMMUNICATION

Evidence-Based Practice

More than 2,500 years ago, Hippocrates urged careful testing, monitoring and record keeping in treating the sick. Yet only in the 20th century did the idea of evidence-based practice infuse a full range of health fields including nursing, hospital care, psychology, and dentistry.

Evidence-based medicine uses techniques from science, engineering, and statistics to discover and apply the best evidence to clinical decision making relevant to treating individual patients and delivering health services (Straus, Glasziou, Richardson, & Haynes, 2010). Once considered the final word in health care, clinicians' judgment or beliefs are not considered dependable unless they are substantiated by good evidence.

Evidence-based practice is not a complete formula for health care. Reliable, valid evidence doesn't always address subjective issues such as patient preference and quality of life. What evidence-based practice does offer is an approach to those aspects of health care that can be decided based on scientific methods.

instance, a speaker could tell listeners, "According to the Highway Patrol, you are 50% more likely to have an accident if you drink before driving."

Statistics aren't boring, but they can be poorly presented. Effective speakers translate statistics into information that is meaningful to listeners. To describe a million homeless people in terms listeners will immediately understand, a student speaker said, "That's 50 times the number of students on our campus." Here's how another student speaker translated the statistic that one in four college-age women will be raped in her lifetime: "Of the seventeen women students in this room today, four will probably be raped sometime during their lives." With imagination and effort, you can make statistics interesting and powerful.

Cartoon by Signe Wilkinson. Reprinted by permission of Cartoonists & Writers Syndicate/cartoonweb.com

Table 13.2	Guidelines for Using Statistics Effectively

Used unimaginatively, statistics are likely to bore listeners. To avoid this fate when you are speaking, follow these guidelines for using statistics effectively.

- Limit the number of statistics you use in a speech. A few well-chosen numbers mixed with other kinds of support can be dramatic and persuasive, whereas a laundry list of statistics can be monotonous and ineffective.
- Round off numbers so that listeners can understand and retain them. We're more likely to remember that "approximately a million Americans are homeless" than that "987,422 Americans are homeless."
- Select statistics that are timely. Occasionally, an old statistic is still useful. For example, the number of people who died in the Great Plague is not likely to change over the years. In most cases, however, the most accurate statistics are recent. Remember that statistics are a numerical picture of something at a specific time. But things change, and speakers should get new snapshots when they do.
- Make statistics interesting to listeners by translating statistics into familiar and relevant information.

Examples

Examples are single instances used to make a point, dramatize an idea, or personalize information. There are four types of examples that have different uses for speakers.

Undetailed Examples When speakers want to make a point quickly, undetailed examples are useful. These are brief references that quickly recount specific instances of something. In this chapter, I've used a number of undetailed examples of student speeches to give you a concrete idea of conceptual points we're discussing. Undetailed examples may also be used to remind listeners of information with which they're already familiar. One student opened a speech on the costs of textbooks by saying, "Remember standing in the long lines at the bookstore and paying for more than your tuition at the start of this term?" His listeners immediately identified with the topic of the speech.

Detailed Examples Detailed examples provide more elaborate information than undetailed ones, so they are valuable when listeners aren't familiar with an idea. A student included this detailed example in her speech on environmental justice:

> *Most of you haven't lived near a toxic waste dump, so you may not understand what's involved. In one community, the incidence of cancer is 130% higher than in the country as a whole. The skin on one man's hands was eaten away when he touched the outside of a canister that stored toxic waste. His skin literally dissolved when it came in contact with the toxin.*

Detailed examples create vivid pictures that can be moving and memorable. However, they take time to present, so they should be used sparingly.

Hypothetical Examples   Sometimes a speaker has no real example that adequately makes a point. In such cases, a speaker can create a hypothetical example, which is not factual but can add clarity and depth to a speech. To be effective, hypothetical examples must be realistic illustrations of what you want to exemplify. Hypothetical examples often are used to portray average cases rather than to represent a single person or event. If you use a hypothetical example, you have an ethical responsibility to inform listeners that it is not a factual, real example.

Stories   A final kind of example is the story, or anecdote. Stories included in speeches often are based on personal experiences. Presidents routinely include personal stories in their speeches to personalize their ideas and create identification with listeners. Religions rely on stories—parables in Christianity, *teichos* in Buddhism—to teach values and persuade people to follow them. Attorneys rely on stories to persuade judges and jurors, taking all the known facts in a case and weaving them together in a way that makes sense and supports their clients' accounts of events. The attorneys with whom I consult tell me that the key challenge in trial court is to create a story that covers all the facts and is more believable than the story created by the opposing counsel.

Speakers often tell a story to put a human face on abstract issues. To help middle-class listeners understand the personal meaning of poverty, a student told this story of a woman he interviewed to prepare his speech:

> *To start her day, Annie pours half a glass of milk and mixes it half and half with water so that the quart she buys each week will last. If she finds day-old bread on sale at the market, she has toast, but she can't afford margarine. Annie coughs harshly and wishes this throat infection would pass. She can't afford to go to a doctor. Even if she could, the cost of drugs is beyond her budget. She shivers, thinking that winter is coming. That means long days in the malls so that she can be in heated places. It's hard on her and the kids, but the cost of heat is more than she can pay. Annie is only 28 years old, just a few years older than we are, but she looks well into her forties. Like you, Annie grew up expecting a pretty good life, but then her husband left her. He doesn't pay child support, and she can't afford a detective to trace him. Her children, both under 4, are too young to be left alone, so she can't work.*

The story about Annie puts a human face on poverty. A story that has depth takes time, so speakers have to consider whether the point they want to make justifies the time a story will take.

Comparisons

Comparisons are associations between two things that are similar in some important way or ways. **Similes** are explicit comparisons that typically use the words *like* or *as* to link two things: "A teacher is like a guide." "Service is like paying dues for membership in a community." **Metaphors** are implicit comparisons that suggest likeness between two things that have something in common: "A teacher is a guide," "Service is the dues you pay for belonging to a community."

COMMUNICATION HIGHLIGHT

The Typical American Family

John F. Kennedy was a powerful public speaker. He wove many kinds of support into his speeches to strengthen his credibility and increase the impact of his ideas.

On May 19, 1962, President John F. Kennedy used the following hypothetical example in his speech at the rally for the National Council of Senior Citizens at Madison Square Garden.

Diamond Images/Getty Images

> Let's consider the case of a typical American family—a family which might be found in any part of the United States. The husband has worked hard all of his life, and now he has retired. He might have been a clerk or a salesman or worked in a factory. He always insisted on paying his own way. This man, like most Americans, wants to care for himself. He has raised his own family, educated his children, and he and his wife are drawing Social Security now. Then his wife gets sick, not just for a week, but for a very long time. First the savings go. Next, he mortgages his home. Finally, he goes to his children, who are themselves heavily burdened. Then their savings begin to go. What is he to do now? Here is a typical American who has nowhere to turn, so he finally will have to sign a petition saying he's broke and needs welfare assistance.

Quotations

Quotations, or testimony, are exact citations of statements made by others. Speakers often use quotations to clarify ideas or to make them more credible. If someone has stated a point in an especially effective manner, then you may want to quote that person's words. In a speech on homeless citizens, a student quoted a metaphor used by a social worker: "Homelessness is a cancer that eats away at the decency of our society."

Quotations may also be used to substantiate ideas. Using an expert's testimony may be persuasive to listeners, but only if they respect the expert who is quoted. Thus, it's important to provide "oral footnotes" in which you identify the name, position, and qualifications of anyone you quote, as well as the date of the quoted statement. For example, in a speech advocating tougher laws for driving under the influence, you might say, "Speaking in 2008, our senior state senator, Ben Adams, observed that if we had enacted the proposed law 3 years ago, 23 people killed by drunk drivers would be alive today."

Whenever you quote another person, you are ethically obligated to give credit to that person, just as you credit the sources of all forms of evidence. This can be done by changing your tone of voice after stating an authority's name,

COMMUNICATION HIGHLIGHT

I Have a Dream

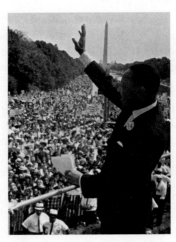

In 1963, Reverend Martin Luther King Jr. delivered his moving speech, "I Have A Dream" to more than 200,000 people gathered on the National Mall in front of the Lincoln Memorial. In it, he compared the unfulfilled promises of the United States to African American citizens to an unpaid check. He said that the nation's founders had guaranteed rights to citizens and that those rights were a check for which payment was due. Comparing promises due to all citizens to a check was a compelling metaphor.

To search for more information about Martin Luther King Jr.'s "I Have a Dream" speech, use MindTap for *Communication in Our Lives* to access **WebLink 13.2**.

Anonymous/AP Images

or by telling listeners, "This authority stated that...." It is also acceptable to say "quote" at the beginning of a quotation and "end quote" at the end of it, although this method of citing sources becomes boring if it is used repeatedly in a speech.

Effective and ethical quotations meet four criteria. First, as we've already noted, sources should be people whom listeners know and respect or whom they will respect once you identify the source's credentials.

A second criterion is that a quotation should come from someone who is qualified to speak on the issue (Cooper & Lull, 2013; Olson & Cal, 1984). Michael Phelps is an awesome athlete. However, his swimming skill has no relevance to Subway sandwiches, which he endorses in ads. Subway is counting on the **halo effect**, the tendency to assume that an expert in one area is also an expert in other areas. Although some people may fall prey to the halo effect, discerning listeners will not. Ethical speakers rely on authorities who are qualified, and they identify authorities' qualifications.

Ethical quotations must also meet the criterion of accuracy. For instance, you should respect the context in which

From the *Wall Street Journal*. Reprinted by permission of Cartoon Features Syndicate.

Pepper . . . and Salt

THE WALL STREET JOURNAL

YOU CAN DO IT! EASY SHOT CAN'T MISS!

"He's a great field dog, and is much in demand as a motivational speaker."

COMMUNICATION HIGHLIGHT

Avoiding Plagiarism

🌀 MindTap™

The word *plagiarism* comes from the Latin word *plagiare*, which means "to kidnap." Plagiarism is the unattributed use of the language or ideas of another person. If you use the actual words or ideas of someone else, you must give credit to that person. Also, if you only slightly modify another's words or ideas, you must attribute the words or ideas to that person.

There is a distinction between paraphrasing and plagiarism. Paraphrasing is putting another person's ideas in your own words. Paraphrasing does not mean changing a word or two in someone else's sentence, changing the sentence structure while maintaining the original words, or changing a few words to synonyms. If you are tempted to rearrange a sentence in any of these ways, you are writing too close to the original. That's plagiarizing, not paraphrasing.

In the academic world, plagiarism by students is a very serious academic offense that can result in punishments such as a failing grade on the particular assignment, a failing grade for the course, suspension, or even expulsion from school. To learn more about what plagiarism is and how to avoid it, use MindTap for *Communication in Our Lives* to access **WebLink 13.3**.

comments are made. It is unethical to take a statement out of context to make it better support your ideas. Also, it's unethical to alter a direct quotation by adding or deleting words. Sometimes, writers omit words and indicate the omission with ellipses: "Noted authority William West stated that 'there is no greater priority . . . than our children.'" In oral presentations, however, it is difficult to indicate omitted words smoothly. When using quotations, speakers have an ethical responsibility to be accurate and fair in representing others and their ideas.

Finally, quotations should come from unbiased sources. It's hardly convincing when scientists paid by the tobacco industry tell us cigarettes don't cause cancer. For the same reason, it's not persuasive when spokespeople for Microsoft assure us that it is not trying to create a monopoly. These two sources have a vested interest in a particular viewpoint.

Visual Aids

Support also is provided by **visual aids**, such as charts, graphs, photographs, transparencies, computer graphics, and physical objects. Visual aids can increase listeners' understanding and retention of ideas presented in a speech (Hamilton, 2008; Hamilton & Parker, 2001). Visual aids also tend to increase listeners' interest in a presentation because they add variety to the message (Hamilton, 2005; Hamilton & Parker, 2001).

Visual aids can be used either to reinforce ideas presented verbally or to provide information. For example, Figure 13.2 is a bar graph that could effectively strengthen statistics on juvenile reform. Pie charts can forcefully emphasize contrasts and proportions (Figure 13.3). You can also use technologies to create visual aids. You may want to use part of a film or create a videotape to dramatize a point in your speech. A student speaker showed parts of the Disney film

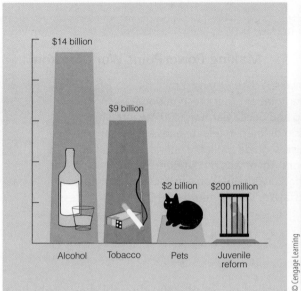

FIGURE 13.2
Bar Graphs Dramatize Statistics

FIGURE 13.3
Pie Charts Clarify Proportions

Pocahontas to support her claim that the main character was different from the historical figure.

Diagrams or models help speakers explain complex concepts and unfamiliar topics. Especially in speeches of demonstration, a model or physical diagram can be useful. One of my students prepared a diagram to show listeners how a nuclear reactor works.

Photographs can reinforce verbal messages, or they can be messages in their own right. To fortify her argument that development is eroding coastal land, a student showed enlarged pictures of an island community before development, when healthy sand dunes existed, and after development, when the dunes had eroded.

Handouts are also useful visual aids. Because listeners can take handouts with them, they are particularly valuable when a speaker wants information to remain with listeners. After a speech encouraging students to vote for a bill currently under consideration by the state legislature, a student gave every listener a handout with the names, addresses, and phone numbers of their representatives. Another student, who spoke on the topic of the dangers of drinking, concluded her speech by handing out a list of agencies and

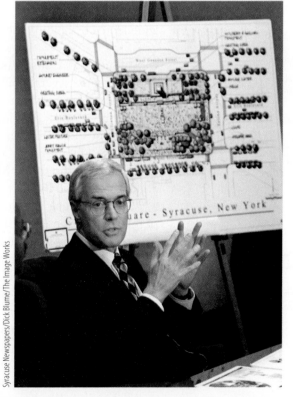

This speaker maintains eye contact with listeners while using a well-designed visual aid.

COMMUNICATION HIGHLIGHT

Making PowerPoint Work for You

Because computerized presentations can enhance speeches, many public speaking courses require students to learn PowerPoint or other presentational software. Communication scholars Joe Downing and Cecile Garmon (2001) wanted to know whether hands-on instruction and online learning differed in effectiveness. They had one group of students learn PowerPoint through a users' guide available online. A second group of students were taught PowerPoint in the classroom. There was no difference in the two groups of students' confidence and competence in using PowerPoint. You can access an online guide to using PowerPoint at **WebLink 13.4**. Use MindTap for *Communication in Our Lives* to access this link.

🌐 MindTap™

phone numbers that could be called by people who thought they might have problems with alcohol. In both cases, the handouts were passed to listeners at the end of the speeches. This was effective because it avoided breaking up a speech to pass out paper and listeners reading the handout while the speaker was talking.

Visual aids don't need to be complex to have impact. Even simple ones can be effective. For example, President Reagan often held up letters from which he read to audiences. He could have simply summarized what the letter said, but he added force by holding the actual sheet of paper (Spaeth, 1996).

Guidelines for Using Visual Aids   For visual aids to be effective, speakers should observe several guidelines (Williams, 1994). First, a visual aid should be large enough and clear enough to be seen clearly by all listeners. As obvious as this advice is, speakers routinely violate it by showing photographs, graphs, or PowerPoint slides that can be seen only by listeners in the front of the room. Make sure any numbers, words, or emblems can be seen clearly by listeners in the back of the room. Make sure that letters in major headings are at least 3 inches high and that letters in subpoints are at least 2 inches high.

Second, visuals should be simple and uncluttered. Visuals with a great deal of information are more likely to confuse than clarify. Especially if you are presenting a series of slides (computerized or not), simplicity is important. You can create effective slides by following the guidelines in Table 13.3. A good basic rule is to use visual aids to highlight key information and ideas, not to summarize all content.

Third, visual aids should be safe and nondistracting. Some visual aids are not appropriate for use in any circumstances. For example, a real, functional firearm is dangerous in public situations. In addition to the fact that "there's no such thing as an unloaded gun," firearms may frighten listeners, distracting them from listening to the speech. Other visual aids that are risky and should be avoided include live animals, illegal substances, and chemicals that could react with one another. It's also unwise to use visual aids that might seriously upset or

Table 13.3	Guidelines for Using Slides in a Speech

To create effective slides, including PowerPoint presentations for speeches, follow these guidelines:

1. Each slide should focus on a single concept or point and key information to support that concept or point (phrases or key words generally are preferable to whole sentences or lengthy text).
2. Fonts should be large enough to be read by listeners at the back of the speaking room. Generally, main points should appear in 36-point type, supporting ideas should appear in 24- or 28-point type, and text should appear in type no smaller than 18 points.
3. Typefaces should be clean and clear. Avoid script styles, *overuse of italics*, or TRENDY TYPEFACES. They are distracting and can detract from clarity.
4. Mix uppercase and lowercase lettering. ALL CAPITAL LETTERS CAN BE HARD TO READ.
5. Use art to provide visual relief from text and enhance interest. If using a computerized presentation program, consider using clip art or pictures imported from the Web.
6. Use one design consistently. Computerized programs such as PowerPoint have design templates. Stick with one design to provide visual continuity and transitions.
7. Select a color scheme that is visually strong but not overpowering. Especially if you are showing a series of slides, avoid glaring colors that can tire listeners. Occasionally, you may violate this guideline to adapt to your particular listeners. For instance, if you are speaking at the banquet of a company whose logo is teal and white, you might want a teal and white color scheme.
8. Use special effects sparingly. It may be effective to have text zoom in from the right with a blaring sound on one slide, but it would be tiring and ineffective for text to zoom in on slide after slide.
9. Use visual highlighting sparingly. It can be effective to **boldface** or highlight one particularly important idea. However, the impact of visual highlighting is lost when it is overdone.
10. Give credit to those who created material you use. Acknowledge authors of quotations or other material. You should also get permission to use any materials that are not in the public domain.
11. Don't sacrifice content for flashy visuals. Visual aids, including computerized ones, should enhance your content, not substitute for it.
12. Make slides bright enough that you do not have to darken the room fully.

disgust listeners. The purpose of visuals is to enhance your speech, not to be so sensational that they take attention away from your ideas.

Many visual aids are verbal texts—main ideas of a speech, major points in a policy, or steps to action. When visual texts are used, certain guidelines apply. As a general rule, a visual text should have no more than six lines of words, should use phrases more than sentences, and should use a simple typeface. Color and variations in type size can be used to add emphasis to visual texts. This applies to handouts, slides, and large visuals displayed at the front of a room. For practice identifying effective slides, complete the activity "Slide Construction Guidelines" via MindTap for *Communication in Our Lives.*

Although visual aids can be effective, it's possible to have too much of a good thing. When speakers use too many visuals or too much variation in type color and style, listeners may experience visual overload. As a guideline for deciding how many visuals to use in a speech, Cheryl Hamilton (2005) suggests this formula:

$$\frac{\text{Length of speech}}{2} + 1 = \text{Maximum number of visuals}$$

If you are preparing a 10-minute speech, you should include no more than 6 visual aids (10/2 + 1 = 6). Note that each slide in a series of slides counts as one visual aid.

There are also some mechanical guidelines for using visual aids effectively. First, remove or cover visual aids before and after you use them. A visual aid that's strong enough to be effective in supporting ideas will distract listeners'

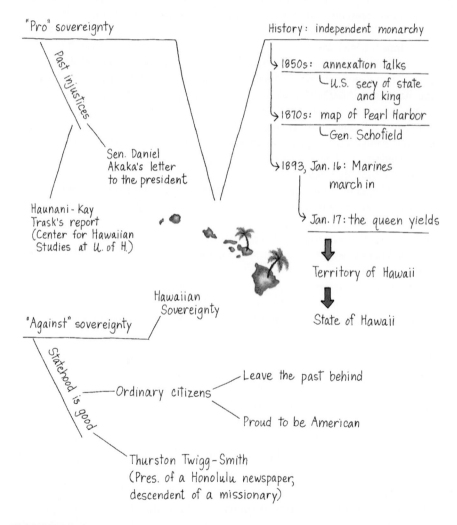

FIGURE 13.4
Mind Map of Evidence
Source: Jaffe, C. (2007). Public Speaking: Concepts and Skills for a Diverse Society, Fifth Edition, Belmont, CA: Wadsworth.

Table 13.4	Testing Evidence

Five questions help speakers test whether evidence is ethical and effective. Each question addresses a specific criterion for assessing the worth of evidence:

1. Is there enough evidence to support a claim? (sufficiency)
2. Is the evidence accurately presented—quotations are verbatim, nothing is taken out of context? (accuracy)
3. Does the evidence relate directly to the claim it is intended to support? (relevance)
4. Is the evidence appropriately timely—are statistics, quotations, examples, and comparisons current or appropriate for the time discussed? (timeliness)
5. Is the evidence free of biases such as vested interest? (impartiality)

attention from what you are saying if it is left in view when not in use. Also, maintain visual contact with listeners when using visual aids. Novice speakers often make the mistake of facing their charts or pictures when discussing them. This breaks the connection between speaker and listeners. Also, make sure that any visual aids you use do not eclipse content or compensate for the lack of careful development of ideas in your speech (Zukerman, 1999).

It's a good idea to keep an ongoing record of evidence you discover during the research process. There are two ways to do this. The traditional method is to write out each piece of evidence and save the file. A mind map is an alternative method of keeping track of information you find while you are researching a speech. In Chapter 12, we discussed mind maps as a way to narrow the focus of a broad topic. The same method can also help you record information. To construct a mind map for your speech, begin by writing the subject of your presentation in the center of a blank page. Then, draw a line from the center to each piece of evidence that you discover as you conduct your research. Once you have a complete record of information you've gathered, you can decide which evidence to include in your presentation. Figure 13.4 shows a mind map record of information for a speech on Hawaiian sovereignty.

Statistics, examples, comparisons, quotations, and visual aids support your ideas in different ways. Whereas evidence such as statistics, examples, and quotations can provide strong logical support, visual aids and analogies often are more powerful in adding clarity, interest, and emotional appeal to a speech. All forms of evidence, when carefully chosen and ethically used, tend to increase the credibility listeners confer on a speaker and the extent to which they retain the speaker's ideas (Table 13.4).

CHAPTER SUMMARY

 Practice and review the content in this chapter.

The process of researching a speech includes reviewing your personal experiences and knowledge about your topic, interviewing experts who can expand your insight into the subject, scouting libraries for evidence, and conducting surveys to find out about others' beliefs, practices, and knowledge relevant to your topic. It isn't unusual for speakers to revise the focus of a speech in the course of conducting research. This is appropriate when information you discover modifies or alters your knowledge or even your position.

Research for a speech provides speakers with different kinds of evidence that they can use to clarify, dramatize, and energize a speech.

The five types of evidence we discussed are statistics, examples, comparisons, quotations, and visual aids. These are effective forms of support when they are used thoughtfully and ethically and when they are adapted to the interests, knowledge, attitudes, and experiences of listeners.

Now that you've gone through the phases of planning, researching, and finding support for speeches, we're ready to consider the final steps in designing effective presentations. Chapter 14 explains how to organize and present public speeches. Before you move on to Chapter 14, take a moment to fill in this chapter's checklist for researching and supporting your speech.

CHECKLIST FOR RESEARCHING AND SUPPORTING A PUBLIC SPEECH   MindTap

If you prefer, you may complete this checklist online under your Chapter 13 MindTap for *Communication in Our Lives*.

1. I conducted the following research:
   A. Review of my personal experience showed that _____
   B. I interviewed (name/title): _____
   _____
   (name/title): _____
   (name/title): _____
   C. I checked these three indexes: _____
   _____
   D. I checked these three online sources: _____
   _____
   E. I surveyed on the following issues: _____
   _____

2. I found the following key evidence for my speech:

   A. Statistics: _____
   B. Authorities I will quote: _____
   C. Examples: _____
   D. Comparisons: _____
   E. Visual aids: _____

3. I have all the information to identify my sources appropriately and to explain why they are qualified and relevant to the ideas I will present.

If you have not completed all items on this checklist, do so now before moving on to Chapter 14. You may want to use Speech Builder Express to complete some of these tasks, which you can access through your Online Resources.

APPLYING COMMUNICATION IN OUR LIVES

Communication in Our Lives is supported by a MindTap, a new online learning platform that delivers content, assignments, and a tailored presentation of the course curriculum created by your instructor. MindTap combines all of your learning tools–readings, multimedia, activities and assessments–into a singular learning unit that guides you through the course. Practice and Present, a unique tool within MindTap, allows you to upload your speech video files for practice or for a grade, comment on your peer's speeches and review your grades. MindTap also includes Speech Builder Express, a powerful tool that guides you through the speech outline and preparation process. For more information or to access MindTap, visit cengagebrain.com.

DEFINITIONS OF KEY CONCEPTS Review your **Flashcards**.

comparisons Forms of evidence that use associations between two things that are similar in some important way.

evidence Material used to support claims. Types of evidence are statistics, examples, comparisons, and quotations. Visual aids may be used to represent evidence graphically.

examples Forms of evidence; a single instance that makes a point, dramatizes an idea, or personalizes information. The four types of examples are undetailed, detailed, hypothetical, and anecdotal.

halo effect The tendency to assume that an expert in one area is also an expert in other unrelated areas.

metaphors Implicit comparisons of two different things that have something in common.

quotations Forms of evidence that use exact citations of statements made by others. Also called *testimony*.

similes Direct comparisons that typically use the words *like* or *as* to link two things.

statistics A form of evidence that uses numbers to summarize a great many individual cases or to demonstrate relationships between phenomena.

survey research Research that involves asking a number of people about their opinions, preferences, actions, or beliefs relevant to a speaking topic.

visual aids Presentation of evidence by such visual means as charts, graphs, photographs, and physical objects to reinforce ideas presented verbally or to provide information.

FOR FURTHER REFLECTION AND DISCUSSION

1. After you've interviewed two experts on your topic, reflect on what you learned. What did they explain, reveal, or show you that added to your knowledge of the topic?

2. How did the process of researching your speech affect your understandings, beliefs, and speaking goal? Explain what changed and why.

3. Use an online database to find current evidence to support your speech. If you plan to speak on a health-related topic, use publications such as *World Health, Health News*, or *Healthfacts*. If you plan to speak on a public policy issue, check out publications such as *Public Welfare, Weekly Compilation of Presidential Documents*, and *Public Interest*. Type in the keywords relevant to your topic.

4. Pay attention to evidence in a speech on campus. Evaluate the effectiveness of evidence. Are visuals clear and uncluttered? Does the speaker explain the qualifications of sources cited, and are those sources adequately unbiased? What examples and

comparisons are presented, and how effective are they? Evaluate the ethical quality of the evidence used. Did the speaker provide enough information for you to assess the expertise of any sources cited? Did the speaker show that the sources were not biased?

5. Experiment with PowerPoint or other computerized software. Notice how different designs, colors, and special effects affect the clarity and impact of your slides.

SHARPEN YOUR SKILL   MindTap

1. Background on Experts

Research the credentials of three authorities you plan to cite in your speech. Below, write important information that contributes to their credibility.

1. _____holds the following titles: _____ and has the following experiences and qualifications:
_____

2. _____holds the following titles: _____ and has the following experiences and qualifications:
_____

3. _____holds the following titles: _____ and has the following experiences and qualifications:
_____

2. Bringing Statistics Alive

Practice translating statistics into interesting and meaningful information. Here's an example.

Statistic: Americans annually spend $14 billion on alcohol, $9 billion on tobacco, $2 billion on pets, and $200 million on juvenile reform.

Translation: For every $1 spent on juvenile reform in the United States, $70 are spent on alcohol, $45 on tobacco, and $10 on pets.

Statistic: Children under 10 watch television an average of 50 hours each week.

Translation: _____

Statistic: The Stealth bomber program cost $40 billion and produced a total of 20 aircraft.

Translation: _____

Statistic: The number of working poor, people who make $13,000 or less a year, rose from 12% of the workforce in 2000 to 18% in 2013.

Translation: _____

Now, apply what you've learned to your own speech. Select three statistics you could use in your speech, and translate them into meaningful, interesting terms.

Statistic 1: _____
can be translated this way _____
Statistic 2: _____
can be translated this way _____
Statistic 3: _____
can be translated this way _____

For additional practice in bringing statistics alive, complete the activity "Translating Statistics" in your Chapter 13 MindTap for *Communication in Our Lives.*

EXPERIENCING COMMUNICATION IN OUR LIVES   MindTap

CASE STUDY: *Understanding Hurricanes*

The following speech is featured in your Chapter 13 MindTap for *Communication in Our Lives*. Select "Understanding Hurricanes" to watch the video of speech titled "Understanding Hurricanes." Improve your own public speaking skills by reading, watching, and evaluating this sample speech.

© Cengage Learning

Think about a time you've been absolutely terrified—whether it was by a person, event, or situation, and all you wanted to do was go home and be with your family and friends.

Now imagine the feeling you might have if you were that afraid, but you had no idea if your home would even be there when you arrived. This is the reality for many people living on the coastlines of the United States. Hurricanes affect the lives of those living in their direct paths, but they can also affect the entire country.

I have lived about 45 minutes from the Gulf Coast of Texas my entire life and have seen and experienced the destruction caused by hurricanes first hand, especially in the past 3 years. (*Slide 1: Picture of hurricane that hit my hometown last year.*) This is a picture of my hometown when a hurricane hit it last year.

Today I'd like to speak with you about the way hurricanes work, the ways they affect our whole country and, most importantly, the toll they have on the people who live in their direct paths.

To begin, let's discuss how hurricanes form and the varying degrees of intensity of them so we can be better informed when we watch news broadcasts and read newspaper reports about them.

Several basic conditions must be present for a Hurricane to form. According to award-winning Discovery Communications Website, HowStuffWorks.com, hurricanes form "when an area of warm low-pressure air rises and cool, high pressure seizes the opportunity to move in underneath it." This causes a center to develop. This center may eventually turn into what is considered a hurricane. The warm and moist air from the ocean rises up into these pressure zones and begins to form storms. As this happens, the storm continues to draw up more warm moist air and a heat transfer occurs because of the cool air being heated causing the air to rise again. "The exchange of heat creates a pattern of wind that circulates around a center," (the eye of the storm), "like water going down a drain." The "rising air reinforces the air that is already" being pulled up from the surface of the ocean, "so the circulation and speeds of the wind increase."

Classifications of these types of storms help determine their intensity so we can prepare properly for them. Winds that are less than 38 miles per hour are considered tropical depressions. Tropical storms have winds that range from 39 to 73 miles per hour. And lastly, hurricanes are storms with wind speeds of 74 miles per hour and higher.

When storms become classified as a *hurricane*, they become part of another classification system that is displayed by the Saffir-Simpson Hurricane Scale. Hurricanes are labeled as categories 1-5 based on their wind intensity level or speed. (*Slide 2: Hurricane scale chart*) Hurricane Ike was labeled differently at different places. (*Slide 3: Map showing the different places Ike was labeled in the different categories*)

Knowing how and where hurricanes occur help us determine how our daily lives, even here in Kentucky, may be affected when one hits.

A hurricane can affect more than just those living in its direct path and these effects can actually be seen across the country in terms of the environment and the economy.

Hurricanes affect wildlife in negative ways. According to the Beaumont Enterprise on October 7, 2008, Christine Rappleye reported that the storm surge, which is basically a wall of water, Hurricane Ike brought in across some parts of Southeast Texas—about 14 feet in some places—swept dolphins inland with the surge and then, when the waters flowed back out to sea, dolphins were left stranded in the marsh. Some were rescued, but not all. This dolphin was rescued from a ditch. (*Slide 4: Dolphin being rescued*)

Hurricanes also affect the economy. Prices climb close to all time highs when hurricanes hit. According to economist Beth Ann Bovino, quoted in the September 29, 2005, issue of the *Washington Post*, gas prices skyrocket when a hurricane like Katrina, Rita, or Ike hits. Paul Davidson said, in a September 12, 2008, article in *USA Today*, that in the anticipation of Hurricane Ike, 12 refineries in Texas were shut down. "This is 17% of the U.S. refining capacity" he said. That's why even residents here in Lexington saw a dramatic spike in gas prices immediately following Ike's landfall.

Energy costs to heat and cool our homes also rise. When consumers have to pay more to heat and cool our homes, we also have less to spend eating out at restaurants. And we have less to spend on nonessentials at the mall. So, economically we all feel the ripple effect when hurricanes hit.

So, yes, we all feel the effects of hurricanes, but we should not overlook the dramatic ways in which people who live in the direct path of a hurricane are affected.

When a hurricane hits, many of these people become homeless, at least for a while, and suffer emotionally and financially as they evacuate to places all over the country, including Kentucky!

People who go through hurricanes suffer extreme emotional effects. Evacuation is stressful because people have to pack up what they can and have no way of knowing if their home will still be standing or inhabitable when they return (*Slides 5 and 6: Before and after pictures from Hurricane Ike*).

Even returning home is emotionally taxing because returning home means rebuilding homes, neighborhoods, and even memories. Though we try to get back to a "normal" life, it can never really be the same as it once was. Instead, it's what Silicon Valley venture capitalist and investor, Roger McNamee, calls the "new normal" in his book, *The New Normal: Great Opportunities in a Time of Great Risk*.

Because they have to rebuild their homes and lives, people also go through financial difficulties. People battle with insurance companies about whether a home has wind or water damage as they seek financial assistance. Insurance companies will often claim that it is the one (wind or water) the homeowner is uninsured for.

Price gouging is another financial challenge hurricane victims face. When families and businesses begin the process of rebuilding, people come from outside areas to help with labor and materials and will charge exorbitant fees. An example of this is when my father needed people to help remove two trees from our home in September 2005 after Hurricane Rita.

To close, I'd like to remind you that hurricanes affect victims who live in their direct path and the country as a whole. To understand some of these effects, we talked about how hurricanes work, how they affect our country and daily lives, and the impacts they have on the lives of people who live through them. Maybe knowing some of these facts will help each of us appreciate our homes and our families just a little bit more. (*Handout: Hurricane tracking charts*)

REFERENCES

Associated Press. (2008, October 8). Windstorm costs insurers $550M. *Newark Advocate*, p. x.

Bovino, B. A. (2005, September 29). Hurricanes impact national economy. *Washington Post*, Retrieved online at: http://washingtonpost.com/wp-dym/content/discussion/2005/09/28/D12005092801431.html

Davidson, P. (2008, September 12). Ike blows gasoline prices higher." *USA Today*, p. x.

Marshall, B., Freudenrich, C., & Lamb, R. How hurricanes work. Retrieved October 8, 2008, from: http://www.howstuffworks.com/hurricanes.htm

McNamee, R. (2004). *The new normal: Great opportunities in a time of great risk*. New York: Penguin.

Rappleye, C. (2008, October 7). Hurricane strands marine mammals, damages facility for the stranded. *Beaumont Enterprise*.

QUESTIONS FOR ANALYSIS AND DISCUSSION   MindTap

You can answer these questions and see my responses to them via MindTap for Chapter 13.

1. Identify the types of evidence that the speaker used to develop the point in this excerpt from a speech.

2. Was the evidence effective? Did it meet the five tests for evidence?

3. Was the evidence ethical?

14

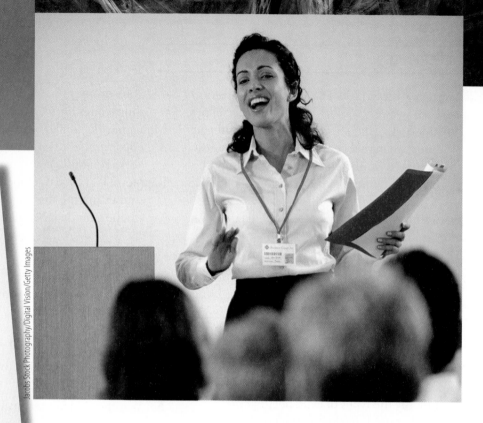

> As long as there are human rights to be defended; as long as there are great interests to be guarded; as long as the welfare of nations is a matter for discussion, so long will public speaking have its place.
>
> **William Jennings Bryan**

Jacobs Stock Photography/Digital Vision/Getty Images

Organizing and Presenting Public Speeches

Review the chapter **Learning Objectives** and **Start** with a quick warm up activity.

Millions of people have back problems in this country. It's hard to recover from back problems, particularly ruptures of discs. A lot of problems result from strains caused by lifting heavy objects. People could save themselves a lot of pain if they avoided doing things that hurt their backs. It's important to take care of your back because a disc rupture can immobilize you for up to 2 weeks. Another way discs rupture is from unhealthy everyday habits such as sitting too long in one position or not using chairs that provide good support.

SHARPEN **YOUR SKILL**

At the end of this chapter, refer to the Sharpen Your Skill features, Designing Your Introduction and Rehearsing Your Speech, to apply concepts from Chapter 14.

Millions of people in this country who suffer from back problems could save them-selves a lot of pain by avoiding the two primary causes of back injury. One major cause is excessive strain, for example, from lifting heavy objects. A second cause is unhealthy everyday habits, such as sitting too long in one position. Avoiding strain and unhealthy habits can save weeks of recuperation.

Which of these paragraphs was easier for you to understand and follow? Which one made more sense to you? If you're like most people, the second para-graph seemed more logical and coherent. The content of the two paragraphs is the same. What differs is how they are organized. In the first paragraph, the speaker doesn't tell us that he or she is going to focus on two causes of back prob-lems. Instead, the speaker wanders from discussing one cause (strain) of back problems, to noting the length of recuperation time, and then back to discussing a second cause (unhealthy habits) of back problems.

In contrast, in the second paragraph the speaker tells us that there are two primary causes of back problems, so we're prepared at the outset to learn about two causes. The speaker next explains both causes, and only then does the speaker discuss the recuperation time we're in for if we don't take care of our backs. The organization of the second paragraph makes it easier to follow and retain the information presented.

This chapter guides you through the process of organizing your speech and practicing your delivery. In the pages that follow, we'll consider alternative ways to organize ideas, styles of delivery, and ways to practice effectively.

ORGANIZING SPEECHES

Read, highlight and take notes online.

We've all sat through speeches in which speakers seemed disorganized. They rambled or moved from one idea to the next in a way that was hard to follow. Without strong organization, a speech will fail, no matter how good the ideas are and no matter how thoroughly they are researched and supported.

Organization increases speaking effectiveness for several reasons. First, people like structure, and they expect ideas to come to them in an orderly way. Second, orga-nization influences comprehension of ideas. Listeners can understand and remember a speech that is well organized because they grasp connections between ideas. Third, listeners find an organized speech more persuasive than a disorganized one. Finally, organization enhances a speaker's credibility, probably because a carefully structured speech reflects well on a speaker's preparation and respect for listeners.

Organizing an effective speech is not the same as organizing a good paper, although the two forms of communication benefit by some similar structural principles. Effective organization for oral communication differs from organiza-tion for written communication in three key ways:

1. **Oral communication requires more explicit organization.**
2. **Oral communication benefits from greater redundancy within the message.**
3. **Oral communication should rely on less complex sentence structures.**

Unlike readers, listeners can't refer back to a previous passage if they become confused or forget a previous point. To increase listeners' comprehension and retention, speakers should use simple sentences, provide signposts to highlight organization, and repeat key ideas (Woolfolk, 1987). Consistent with the need for redundancy in oral communication, good speeches follow the form of telling listeners what you're going to tell them, presenting your message, then reminding them of your main points. This translates into preparing an introduction, a body, and a conclusion for an oral presentation.

Effective organization begins with a good outline. We'll discuss different kinds of outlines and how each can help speakers organize their ideas. Next, we'll focus on organizing the body of a speech because that is the substance of a presentation. Finally, we'll discuss how to build an introduction and a conclusion and how to weave in transitions to move listeners from one point to another.

Outlining Speeches

An outline helps you organize your ideas and make sure that you have enough evidence to support your claims. An outline also provides you with a safety net in case you forget what you intend to say or are interrupted by a question or a disturbing noise. There are three kinds of outlines: working, formal, and key word.

The Working Outline

Speakers usually begin organizing their ideas by creating a **working outline** to give themselves a basic map of the speech. The working outline is just for the speaker; it is his or her sketch of the speech. In it, the speaker usually jots down main ideas to see how they fit together. Once the ideas are laid out in a basic structure, the speaker can tell where more evidence is needed, where ideas don't seem well connected, and so forth. Working outlines usually evolve through multiple drafts as speakers see ways to improve their speeches. Because working outlines aren't meant for others' eyes, they often include abbreviations and shorthand that make sense only to the speaker.

The Formal Outline   A **formal outline** includes all main points and subpoints, supporting materials, and transitions, along with a bibliography of sources. It should not be the whole speech unless you are giving a manuscript speech, which we will discuss later in this chapter.

An effective formal outline has main headings for the introduction, body, and conclusion. Under each main point are subpoints, references to supporting material, and abbreviated transitions. If your speech includes quotations, statistics, or other evidence that must be presented with absolute accuracy, you should write the evidence in full, either in your outline or on separate index cards. Your written evidence should include the source and date of the evidence so that you can provide oral footnotes to listeners. Full references should be listed as your bibliography, or **Works Cited**. Table 14.1 presents guidelines for constructing formal outlines. Figure 14.1 shows a sample formal outline prepared by a student.

Table 14.1	Principles for Preparing a Formal Outline

1. Use full sentences for each point.

2. Each point or subpoint in a speech should have only one idea.

3. Use standard symbols and indentation for outlines.

   I. Roman numerals are used for main points.

     A. Capital letters are used for subpoints that support main points.

       1. Arabic numbers are used for material that supports subpoints.

         a. Lowercase letters are used for material that amplifies supporting material.

4. A point, subpoint, or supporting material should never stand alone. If you have a point I, you must have a point II (and possibly III). If you have a subpoint A, there must be a subpoint B (and possibly C). Outlines show how ideas are developed and related. If there is only one subpoint, you don't need to outline it—it's the main point.

5. Strive for parallelism when wording main points and subpoints. This adds to the coherence of a speech and makes it easier for listeners to follow. Here's an example of parallel wording of main and subpoints in a speech:

   I. Poor advising diminishes students' academic experiences.

     A. Students lose out by taking courses that don't interest them.

     B. Students lose out by missing courses that would interest them.

   II. Poor advising delays students' graduation.

     A. Some students have to return for a fifth year to graduate.

     B. Some students have to take extension courses to graduate.

     C. Some students have to attend summer school to graduate.

6. Include all references in your outline. These should be written as full citations according to the guidelines of a standard style manual, such as those published by the Modern Language Association (MLA) or the American Psychological Association (APA), or *The Chicago Manual of Style*. Your instructor may specify the style guidelines that you should follow.

7. Cite sources using accepted style guidelines for research reports. Three widely used systems for citing sources in papers and speech outlines are APA, MLA, and Council of Biology Editors (CBE). You can learn how to cite your sources using each set of guidelines by visiting these Websites:

APA: http://owl.english.purdue.edu/handouts/research/r_apa.html

MLA: http://library.osu.edu/sites/guides/mlagd.php

CBE: http://library.osu.edu/sites/guides/cbegd.html

The Key Word Outline   Some speakers prefer a less detailed formal outline, called a **key word outline**. As the term implies, a key word outline includes only key words for each point. Like the working outline, a key word outline is intended for the speaker's use. Therefore, it may include abbreviations and shorthand that make sense only to the speaker. For instance, to prompt your memory of a quotation by Quincy Grady on the values of college sports, you might write this: "Grady—college sports." Although those three words might not make sense

I. Introduction
  A. **Attention:** Would you vote for a system in which half of us work only one job, the other half of us work two jobs, and everyone gets equal rewards? No? Well that's the system that most families in this country have today.
  B. **Thesis statement:** Women's double shift in the paid labor force and the home has negative effects on them personally and on marriages.
  C. **Preview:** In the next few minutes, I will show that the majority of married women work two jobs: one in the paid labor market and one when they get home. I will then trace the harmful effects of this inequitable division of labor.
II. Body
  A. The majority of married women today work two jobs: one in the paid labor market and a second one when they get home each day.
    1. Most families today have two wage earners.
      a. Only 17% of contemporary families have one earner.
      b. As married women have taken on full-time jobs outside of the home over the past three decades, husbands of working wives have increased the amount of housework and child care they do from 20% to 30%.
    2. Working wives do more "homework" than working husbands.
      a. Research shows that husbands tend to do the less routine chores while wives do most of the daily chores.

© Cengage Learning

FIGURE 14.1
A Formal Outline

continued

to anyone else, they would jog your memory of the quotation you want to share with listeners. Figure 14.2 (page 303) shows a key word outline for a student speech.

Organizing the Body of a Speech

The body of a speech develops and supports the central idea, or thesis statement, by organizing it into several points that are distinct yet related. In short speeches of 5 to 10 minutes, no more than three points can be developed well, and two are often adequate. In longer speeches of 11 to 20 minutes, more points can be developed.

We'll discuss eight organizational patterns. As we discuss each pattern, you'll have the opportunity to think about how you might use it in your speech. In Chapter 16, we'll discuss one additional pattern that can be especially effective for persuasive speaking.

b. Husbands' reasons for not doing more work in the home are that they are tired after work, they don't feel men should do many home chores, and their wives don't expect them to help out more.

3. Working wives tend to do more homemaking and child care chores, regardless of which spouse earns more in the job outside the home.

a. Consider Jeremy and Nancy. She earns 65% of the family's income, and she does 80% of the child care and home chores.

b. Sociologist Arlie Hochschild found that 2 out of 10 husbands in two-worker families do 50% of the work involved in homemaking and child care.

Transition: Now that we've seen what the double shift is, let's consider its effects.

B. The double shift harms women's health and creates marital stress.

1. The double shift harms women's physical and psychological health.

a. Research shows that women who work outside of the home and do most of the homemaking and child care suffer sleep deprivation, reduced immunity to infections, and increased susceptibility to illnesses.

b. A recent study by the American Medical Association found that working women who do the majority of "homework" are more stressed, depressed, and anxious.

2. The double shift also erodes marital satisfaction.

a. Women resent husbands who don't contribute a fair share to home life.

FIGURE 14.1 (*Continued*)

continued

The Time Pattern   Time patterns (also called temporal and chronological patterns) organize ideas on the basis of temporal relationships. Listeners find it easy to follow a time pattern because we often think in terms of temporal order: what follows what, what comes first, and what comes next.

Time patterns are useful for describing processes that take place over time, explaining historical events, and tracing sequences of action. Time patterns are also effective for presentations that create suspense and build to a climax. One student speaker led his listeners through the detective work of pharmaceutical research to develop a new drug for treating mood disorders. In an informative speech, a student described the history of immigration in the United States.

Thesis: Immigration has been part of America since the time of Columbus.

Main Point 1: Columbus is credited with having brought the first immigrants to America in 1492.

    b. Inequitable division of "homework" is linked to
        separations and divorces.
Transition: Let me now pull together what the double shift
is and how it harms women and marriages.
III. Conclusion
    A. **Summary:** I've shown you that the majority of wives
        today work a double shift while their husbands do not.
        This is not only unfair, it is also harmful to women's
        health and to marriages.
    B. **Final appeal:** Each of us who chooses to marry can
        create an equitable marriage. As I've shown you, the
        reward for making that choice is healthier wives and
        happier, more enduring marriages. That's a pretty good
        return on the investment of creating an equitable
        marriage.

FIGURE 14.1
A Formal Outline (*Continued*)

Main Point 2: In the 1700s and 1800s, people from Europe and Asia came to
America to make it their home.
Main Point 3: Today, the largest group of immigrants comes from South America.

The Spatial Pattern   Spatial patterns organize ideas according to physical
relationships. This structure is especially appropriate for speeches that describe
or explain layouts, geographic relationships, or connections between objects or
parts of a system.

Spatial patterns can be used to structure both informative and persuasive
speeches. Student speakers have successfully used spatial patterns to inform
listeners about the relationships between components of nuclear reactors, the
layout of a new library, and the four levels of forest vegetation. In persuasive
speeches, students have relied on spatial patterns to argue that solar energy is
sufficient to heat homes; that urban sprawl is increasing in the United States;

I. Introduction
   A. Half work one, half work two
   B. Effects—personal, on marriage
   C. Majority of married women; effects of inequity
II. Body
   A. Majority of married women—two jobs
      1. Two wage earners standard
         a. 17% single wage earner
         b. 10% increase in husbands' contribution
      2. 20% husbands assume half
      3. Pattern varies
         a. Class
            i. Jacob and Ina
            ii. John and Jennifer
         b. Education
      4. Women's double shift not tied to salary
         a. Jeremy and Nancy
         b. Hochschild study (see card 1)
   B. Effects
      1. Physical and psychological
         a. Sleep, illness, infection
         b. Stress unhappiness
      2. Marital satisfaction erodes
         a. Resentment
            i. Marion
            ii. Study (see card 2)
         b. Marital stability
            i. Divorce statistics (see card 3)
            ii. Therapist quote (see card 4)
III. Conclusion
   A. Unfair + health harms + marital stability and satisfaction
   B. Your choice—return on investment

© Cengage Learning

FIGURE 14.2
A Key Word Outline

that global climate change will have devastating effects on the Antarctic, Africa, and Asia; and that a campus is made up of different kinds of spaces.

> *Thesis*: Our campus includes spaces for learning, socializing, and living.
> *Main Point 1*: At the center of our campus are the classroom buildings.
> *Main Point 2*: Surrounding the classroom buildings are places for students to eat and socialize.
> *Main Point 3*: The south part of campus consists of dormitories and apartments for students with families.

The Topical Pattern   Topical patterns order a presentation into several categories, classes, or areas of discussion. The classification pattern is appropriate when your topic breaks down into two or three areas that aren't related temporally, spatially, causally, or otherwise. Although topical patterns don't have the organic power of structures that highlight relationships, they can effectively order points in a speech.

Topical patterns are appropriate for informative speeches on the three branches of government, the social and academic activities funded by student fees, and the contributions of students, faculty, and staff to campus life.

Topical patterns can also be effective for persuasive speeches. In a speech urging students to vote for a candidate, one student focused on the candidate's personal integrity, experience in public service, and commitment to the community. Another student designed a persuasive speech that extolled the benefits of student fees.

> *Thesis*: Student fees fund extracurricular, intellectual, and artistic activities on campus.
> *Main Point 1*: Fully 40% of student fees is devoted to extracurricular organizations.
> *Main Point 2*: Another 30% of student fees pays for lectures by distinguished speakers.
> *Main Point 3*: The final 30% of fees supports concerts and art exhibits.

The Star Pattern   The star pattern is a particularly organic variation on the topical structure, yet in which each point is linked to an overriding theme (Jaffe, 2013). A standard topical organization has two or three points that a speaker covers in the same order and to the same extent each time the speech is given. With a star pattern, however, a speaker might start with different points and give more or less attention to specific points when speaking to different audiences.

One of the more common uses of the star pattern is in political speeches. Most candidates for office have a standard stump speech that includes their key positions and proposals. The order in which a candidate presents points and the extent to which each point is developed vary from audience to audience. For example, a candidate's platform might include garnering strong support for the environment, enhancing the fiscal security of the United States, and ensuring adequate care for elderly citizens. When the candidate speaks to environmental activists, he or she would lead with the stand on the environment and elaborate it in detail. When the candidate speaks to older citizens, he or she would begin by emphasizing his or her commitment to their health and to shoring up Medicare and Medicaid. When the candidate speaks to young and middle-aged audiences, the first point would be ensuring the fiscal security of the United States so young people aren't strapped with debt. Using the star pattern, the candidate could adapt the order of points and the emphasis placed on each one. It would not be ethical to misrepresent positions to suit different audiences, but it is both ethical and effective to adapt the order and emphasis on different points.

Similarly, a star pattern could be used to describe the ways in which different groups contribute to campus life.

> *Thesis*: Our campus reflects contributions of administrators, faculty, students, and staff.

Main Point 1: Administrators are in charge of planning and coordinating all aspects of campus life.

Main Point 2: Faculty take the lead in charting the academic character of college life.

Main Point 3: Students are the primary designers of extracurricular life on campus.

Main Point 4: Staff make sure that the initiatives of administrators, faculty, and students are implemented consistently.

> **ANNE**   *I'm an orientation counselor, and I think I've been using the star pattern to talk to new students, but I didn't know you called it that. With each new group, I have to tell them about the campus and town and school policies and so forth. With first-year students, I start off by talking about school policies because not knowing them can get the kids in trouble. With junior transfers, I get to that last and just spend a little time on it. With out-of-state students, I spend more time talking about the town and even the region—how the South is, which some of them don't understand. I pretty much cover everything with each group, but how I do it varies a lot, depending on who is in the group.*

The Wave Pattern   Like waves in an ocean, the wave pattern consists of repetition. Each wave, or main idea, builds up from evidence and then crests in a main point. Then more evidence follows, leading to the crest of another wave (Jaffe, 2013; Zediker, 1993). Each crest repeats the main theme, using the same words or variations on them. Martin Luther King Jr., in his "I Have a Dream" speech, gave examples of injustices and then crested with the statement, "I have a dream." He then gave more examples, and crested again by repeating the key line. Between each crest in a speech using the wave pattern, speakers should present listeners with evidence: multiple undetailed examples, a few well-chosen detailed examples, statistics, quotations, and visual aids. The wave pattern moves organically, pulling listeners into its rhythm.

Thesis: The key mission of higher education is complete literacy.

Main Point 1: All students who graduate should be literate in speaking, reading, and writing.

Main Point 2: All students who graduate should be literate in communication technologies.

Main Point 3: All students who graduate should be literate in cultural life.

The Comparative Pattern   As the term suggests, comparative patterns compare two or more objects, people, situations, events, or other phenomena. This structure is also called *comparison/contrast* and *analogical organization*. It encourages listeners to be aware of similarities or differences between two or more things or to understand a new idea, process, or event in terms of one with which they're already familiar.

COMMUNICATION HIGHLIGHT

Creating a Sense of Time

Reverend Martin Luther King Jr. relied on a time pattern in his "I Have a Dream" speech (Cox, 1989). He opened with a reference to "today," then traced the history of African Americans in the United States. Next, he returned to the present to argue that the government's promises to African Americans should be kept. He concluded by quoting a Negro spiritual that envisioned a future when all people of all races would be free. Throughout the speech, he fortified the time structure by using words such as *now, today,* and *urgency* and by repeating the key phrase "Now is the time." Read the following excerpts from his speech to appreciate how King crafted his speech around a temporal theme.

I am happy to join with you today in what will go down in history as the greatest demonstration in the history of our nation. . . .

Five score years ago, a great American, in whose symbolic shadow we stand today, signed the Emancipation Proclamation. . . .

But one hundred years later, the Negro is still not free. One hundred years later, the life of the Negro is still sadly crippled by the manacles of segregation and the chains of discrimination. . . .

We have come to this hallowed spot to remind Americans of the fierce urgency of now. . . . Now is the time to make real the promises of Democracy. Now is the time to rise from the dark and desolate valley of segregation to the sunlight of racial justice. Now is the time to lift our nation from the quicksands of racial injustice to the solid rock of brotherhood. Now is the time to make justice a reality for all of God's children. . . .

Nineteen-sixty-three is not an end, but a beginning . . .

And as we walk, we must make a pledge that we shall always march ahead. We cannot turn back . . .

I say to you today, my friends, so even though we face the difficulties of today and tomorrow, I still have a dream. . . . I have a dream that one day this nation will rise up and live out the true meaning of its creed: "We hold these truths to be self-evident; that all men are created equal." This will be the day . . . This will be the day when all of God's children will be able to sing with new meaning, "My country 'tis of thee, sweet land of liberty, of thee I sing." . . .

We allow freedom to ring, when we let it ring from every village and every hamlet, from every state and every city, we will be able to speed up that day when all of God's children, black men and white men, Jews and Gentiles, Protestants and Catholics, will be able to join hands and sing in the words of the old Negro spiritual, "Free at last! Free at last! Thank God Almighty, we are free at last!"

Informative speeches using the comparative structure might explain how computers are like (or not like) human brains, how research for new drugs is like a detective's investigation, or how fission and fusion are different means of creating energy. Students giving persuasive speeches have used the comparative pattern to argue that socialized medicine is inferior to or superior to the U.S. system, that computer literacy is as important as oral and written literacy, and that undergraduate education is different from career preparation. In each case, the comparative structure invites listeners to perceive how two or more phenomena are alike or different.

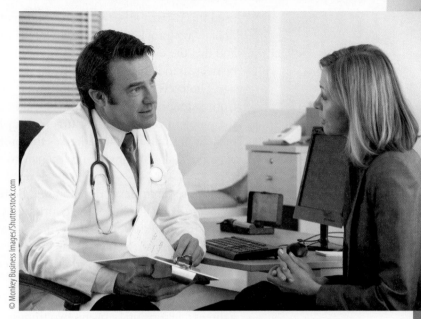

Medical professionals frequently present information to patients.

MAYUMI   *I selected comparative organization for my informative speech about American and Japanese marriages because I wanted the class to understand how people from my country think differently about marriage than Americans do. I divided my speech into courtship, division of household work, and meaning of divorce to show the difference between Americans and Japanese in each area.*

Thesis: Health maintenance organizations are inferior to private medical practices.

Main Point 1: Health maintenance organizations provide less individualized patient care than private practices do.

Main Point 2: Health maintenance organizations are less likely than private practices to authorize important diagnostic tests.

Main Point 3: Health maintenance organizations place less emphasis on preventive care than private medical practices do.

The Problem–Solution Pattern   This pattern divides a topic into two major areas: a problem and a solution. Usually, a speaker begins by describing a problem and its severity and then proposes a solution. Occasionally, this sequence is inverted when a speaker begins by discussing a solution and then explains the problem it solves. The problem–solution structure can be used for informative presentations with thesis statements, such as "The increased cost of running a university (problem) explains the rise in tuition costs (solution)" or "Deregulation (solution) is designed to prevent monopolies that are unfair to consumers (problem)."

The problem–solution pattern is also effective for persuasive speeches because it lends itself naturally to advocating policies, answers, and practices. Students have used this pattern effectively to persuade others that many people who are severely ill or dying (problem) could be helped if more people were organ donors (solution), and that the overcrowding of jails and the backlog of court cases (problems) could be decreased if all victimless crimes were made misdemeanors (solution).

The power of this pattern derives from the sequential involvement it invites from listeners. If they accept a speaker's description of a problem and believe the problem is important or urgent, they hunger for a solution. The speaker who presents a solution that addresses the problem they've already acknowledged has a good chance of convincing listeners to endorse the recommended proposal.

> *Thesis*: Victimless crimes should be reclassified as misdemeanors.
> *Main Point 1*: Currently, courts across the nation are overwhelmed by cases in which there is no victim.
> *Main Point 2*: Reclassifying victimless crimes as misdemeanors would dramatically ease the burden on our courts.

The Cause–Effect and Effect–Cause Patterns   This pattern is used to argue a direct relationship between two things: a cause and an effect. In some instances, speakers want to inform people that a situation, policy, or practice (effect) results from certain previous choices or events (causes). In other cases, speakers argue that a specific action (cause) will lead to an effect. Cause–effect and effect–cause patterns are appropriate for both informative and persuasive speeches.

You should be aware that it is extremely difficult to prove direct causation. Scientific researchers cannot conclusively verify that smoking causes lung cancer. They can show that smokers (or those who chew tobacco) are more likely to develop lung cancer, but that does not definitively prove that smoking causes lung cancer. Thus, although speakers can seldom, if ever, prove direct causation, they can demonstrate relationships, or correlations, between two things, and this is often persuasive to listeners.

> *Thesis*: Raising the minimum wage would be bad for our economy.
> *Main Point 1*: Raising the minimum wage would reduce worker productivity.
> *Main Point 2*: Raising the minimum wage would lead to greater unemployment.
> *Main Point 3*: Raising the minimum wage would decrease profits for businesses.

The eight patterns we've discussed represent different ways to organize public presentations. To structure your speech effectively, you should consider how each of the eight patterns might shape the content and impact of your presentation.

For practice in identifying organizational patterns for various speech topics and thesis statements, complete the activity "Identifying Clues to Organization" in MindTap for *Communication in Our Lives*.

Designing the Introduction

The introduction to a speech is the first thing listeners hear. A good introduction accomplishes four goals: (a) It captures listeners' attention and motivates them to listen; (b) it presents a clear thesis statement; (c) it enhances the speaker's credibility;

and (d) it previews how the speech will be developed. That's a lot to accomplish in a short time, so careful thought is required to design a strong introduction.

Capture Listeners' Attention and Motivate Them to Listen   The first objective of an introduction is to gain listeners' attention and give them a reason to listen. Often, speakers accomplish those objectives simultaneously because listeners are motivated to listen when something catches their attention.

There are many ways to gain listeners' attention and interest. You might begin with a dramatic piece of evidence, such as a stirring quotation, a striking visual aid, or a startling statistic or example. Each of these forms of evidence can capture listeners' interest and make them want to hear more.

You may also open with a question that invites listeners to become involved with the topic. "Do you know the biggest cause of death among college students?" "Would you like to know how to double your chances of getting a job offer?" Questions engage listeners personally at the outset of a speech.

There are other ways to capture listeners' attention. For example, speakers sometimes refer to current events or experiences of listeners that are related to the topic of a speech. A student who spoke on homelessness immediately after fall break opened this way: "If you're like me, you went home over the break and enjoyed good food, a clean bed, and a warm, comfortable house—all the comforts that a home provides. But not everyone has those comforts."

Another effective way to capture listeners' attention is to provide them with direct experience, which is a highly effective foundation for persuasion (Baron & Berne, 1994). For example, in a speech advocating a low-fat diet, a speaker began the presentation by passing out low-fat cookies he had baked. All the listeners then had an immediate experience with delicious and healthful food.

When appropriate to the speaking situation, humor can also be an effective way to open a speech—but only if it succeeds in amusing listeners. Thus, it's a good idea to try jokes out on people who are similar to your listeners.

Effective speakers capture listeners' attention at the outset of a speech.

Present a Clear Thesis Statement   The second function of an introduction is to state the main message of your speech, which is the thesis statement we discussed in Chapter 12. Your thesis should be a short, clear sentence that directly states the overall theme of your presentation.

- "I will describe problems with advising on our campus and ask your help in solving them."
- "Today, I want to persuade you that we should protect the Arctic National Wildlife Refuge from development."
- "I will inform you of your legal rights when interviewing for a job."
- "I will show you that the death penalty is ineffective and discriminatory."

Build Credibility   The third function of an introduction is to establish a speaker's credibility. Listeners regard a speaker as credible if he or she seems qualified to speak on a topic, shows goodwill toward them, and demonstrates dynamism.

To show that they are qualified to speak on a topic, speakers may mention their personal experience: "I've spent the last three summers working with inmates in a prison." "I am a hemophiliac." Speakers may also explain how they gained expertise on their topics. "For the past 2 years, I have volunteered at the homeless shelter here in town." If you do not have personal experience with a topic, let listeners know that you have gained knowledge in other ways. "I interviewed 10 people who work with abused children."

COMMUNICATION HIGHLIGHT

Gaining Listeners' Attention

Here are examples of ways in which students have captured audiences' initial attention:

Question to create suspense: "Have you ever wondered what life would be like if there were no deadly diseases?"

Startling evidence: "Nearly two-thirds of people over 60 who are poor are women."

Personal involvement: "Many of you have to work extra hours to make the money for your textbooks so that the student store can make its 35% profit—that's right, 35% profit just for selling you a book."

Inviting listeners' participation: "Imagine that you could design the undergraduate curriculum at this university. What would you recommend for all students who attend?"

Quotation: "Mahatma Gandhi said, 'You must be the change that you wish to see in the world.'"

Dramatic example: "My brother Jim and I grew up together, and we were best friends. He taught me to play basketball; I gave him advice on girls he was dating; we went to California together one summer. Jim would be 22 today if he had not been killed last summer by a drunk driver."

In addition to letting your listeners know that you are qualified to speak on your topic, you want to demonstrate that you have goodwill and are trustworthy. You might do this by explaining why you think your speech will help them. "What I'm going to tell you might save a life, perhaps your own." "My speech will give you information vital to making an informed choice when you vote next week."

Speakers confront a particular problem in establishing goodwill if they are advocating an unpopular position. They need to demonstrate that they respect listeners' possible objections. One way to do this is to show that you once held their attitudes. "Some of you may think homeless people are just lazy. I thought so, too, before I volunteered at the local shelter and got to know some of them."

Preview the Body   The final purpose of an introduction is to preview your major points so that listeners understand how you will develop ideas and can follow you. The preview announces the main points of your speech. Typically, a preview enumerates or lists the main points. Here are examples from student speeches:

- "I will show you that there has been a marked decrease in advisers' accessibility and helpfulness to students. Then I will ask you to sign a petition that asks our provost to hire more advisers and provide ongoing training to them."

- "In discussing the Arctic National Wildlife Refuge, I will describe the Coastal Plain, which is the biological heart of the refuge, and then tell you about the Porcupine caribou that come there each year to calve."

- "To convince you that the death penalty should be abolished, I will first provide evidence that it is not effective as a deterrent to crime. Second, I will demonstrate that the death penalty discriminates against minorities and people who are poor."

Craft the Conclusion

The next step in organizing a speech is to craft a conclusion. An effective conclusion summarizes content and provides a memorable final thought. As you may realize, these two functions are similar to the attention and preview in introductions. In repeating key ideas and leaving the audience with a compelling final thought, a speaker provides psychological closure on the speech. Like introductions, conclusions are short. Thus, you have to accomplish the two objectives of a conclusion very concisely.

To summarize the content of your speech, it's effective to restate your thesis and each major point. Here are examples from student speeches:

- "Today I've identified two key problems with advising: an insufficient number of advisers and inadequate training of advisers. Both of these problems can be solved if you will join me in urging our president to increase the number of advisers and the training they get."

- "If you believe, as I do, that Alaska's Arctic Wildlife Refuge should be protected from drilling, then please write or call your congressional representatives."
- "My speech has informed you of your legal rights in interviews and what you can do if an interviewer violates them."
- "I've shown you that the death penalty doesn't prevent crime and that it discriminates against minorities and the poor."

After reviewing main points, a conclusion should offer listeners a final idea, ideally something particularly memorable or strong or an ending that returns to the opening idea to provide satisfying closure. In a speech on environmental activism, the speaker began with "'One earth, one chance' is the Sierra Club motto" and ended with "We have one chance to keep our one earth. Let's not throw it away." This was effective because the ending returned to the opening words but gave them a slightly different twist. A student who argued that the death penalty should be abolished ended the speech with this statement: "We need to kill the death penalty before it kills anyone else." A third example, again from a student speaker, is this memorable closing: "I've given you logical reasons to be a blood donor, but let me close with something more personal: I am alive today because there was blood available for a massive transfusion when I had my automobile accident. Any one of us could need blood tomorrow." Effective conclusions are short and focused. They highlight central ideas one last time and offer listeners a powerful or compelling concluding thought.

Speech Builder Express, which you can access through MindTap for *Communication in Our Lives*, includes extensive prompts and a clear framework for organizing and outlining different types of speeches.

Build in Transitions

The final organizational issue is **transitions**—words and sentences that connect ideas and main points in a speech so that listeners can follow a speaker. Transitions signal listeners that you are through talking about one idea and are ready to connect it to the next one. Effective transitions are like signposts for listeners. They tell listeners where you have been, where you are, and where you are heading (Wilson & Arnold, 1974).

Transitions may be words, phrases, or entire sentences. Within the development of a single point, it's effective to use transitional words or phrases such as *therefore, and so, for this reason, as this evidence suggests,* and *consequently.* To make transitions from one point to another in a speech, phrases can be used to signal listeners that you are starting to discuss a new idea:

- "My second point is…"
- "Now that we have seen how many people immigrate to the United States, let's consider what they bring to us."
- "In addition to the point I just discussed, we need to think about…"

To move from one to another of the three major parts of a speech (i.e., introduction, body, and conclusion), you can signal your audience with statements that summarize what you've said in one part and point the way to the next. For example, here is an internal summary and a transition between the body of a speech and the conclusion:

"I've now explained in some detail why we need stronger educational and health programs for new immigrants. Let me close by reminding you of what's at stake."

Transitions also may be nonverbal. For example, you might hold up one, two, and three fingers to reinforce your movement from the first to the second to the third main point in the body of your speech. Changes in vocal intensity, eye contact, and inflection can effectively mark movement from one idea to the next. For instance, you could conclude the final point of the body of your speech with strong volume and then drop the volume to begin the conclusion. Silence is also effective in marking transitions. A pause after the introduction signals listeners that a speaker is going to a new place. Visual aids also help listeners move with a speaker.

Transitions are vital to effective speaking. If the introduction, body, and conclusion are the bones of a speech, the transitions are the sinews that hold the bones together.

COMMUNICATION APPREHENSION: NATURAL AND OFTEN HELPFUL

There are very few people who don't sometimes feel apprehensive about talking with others (Bostrom, 1988; Richmond & McCroskey, 1992). Virginia Richmond and James McCroskey (1995a) reported that almost 95% of Americans surveyed

COMMUNICATION HIGHLIGHT

I'd Rather Lose Than Have to Give a Speech

Bob Daemmrich / PhotoEdit

Have you ever seen an interview with pro golfer Annika Sorenstam? If so, you've probably noticed that she seems at ease speaking in public. That wasn't always the case. As a high school student, she was so afraid of speaking that she often deliberately played to win second place so that she wouldn't have to give the winner's speech (Morreale, 2003). Her confidence today reminds us that communication apprehension can be managed.

To explore any anxiety you may feel about public speaking, complete the Communication Highlight Activity for Chapter 14 via MindTap for *Communication in Our Lives.*

 MindTap

said they had some degree of anxiety about communicating in some situations. As you prepare to present your speech, it's important for you to understand **communication apprehension** and how to manage it so that it doesn't detract from your effectiveness.

A degree of anxiety may actually improve communication. It makes us more alert, largely because our bodies produce adrenaline and extra blood sugar, which increase energy. The energy produced in response to communication anxiety allows speakers to be more dynamic and interesting.

Although a degree of anxiety about speaking is natural, too much can interfere with effectiveness. Anxiety strong enough to hinder our ability to interact with others is communication apprehension.

Causes of Communication Apprehension

There are two types of communication apprehension: situational and chronic. For many of us, certain situations spark anxiety. For instance, if you are scheduled to speak to a group that is known to be hostile to you or your ideas, anxiety is to be expected. In other cases, we feel apprehensive because real or imagined features of a situation worry us. Before a performance review, it's natural to be a little anxious about what your supervisor might say about areas in which you need to improve.

Research indicates that five situational factors often generate apprehension. First, we tend to be more anxious when communicating with people who are unfamiliar to us or who we think are different from us. Apprehension is also likely to be present in new or unusual situations, such as your first job interview. A third situational cause of apprehension is being in the spotlight. When we are the center of attention, we tend to feel self-conscious and anxious that we might embarrass ourselves. Fourth, we may feel apprehensive when we're being evaluated.

A final situational reason for apprehension is a past failure or failures in a particular speaking situation. For example, my doctor called me one day to ask

HEALTH COMMUNICATION

People who are nearing the end of their lives often receive palliative care services, which do not cure or halt disease but do keep them as comfortable as possible during the final stage of life. Whether in hospitals, homes, or hospices, patients receiving palliative care often want to communicate with those around them. Nurses and aides are primary in palliative care so they are particularly likely to have opportunities to communicate with dying patients. Yet, some nurses, like many of us, are particularly apprehensive when facing end-of-life situations. A study (Fanning, Brewer, Parker, Reyna, & Weigel, 2007) found that nurses have a high level of apprehension in caring for dying patients, and male nurses have higher apprehension than female nurses. Based on these findings, the researchers recommended greater exposure and training for nurses who do or will provide care to patients at the end of life.

me to coach her for a speech she had to give to a medical society. Eleanor had last given a public speech 8 years ago in medical school. Just before the speech, her first patient had died, and she was badly shaken. As a result, she was disorganized, flustered, and generally ineffective. That single incident, which followed a history of successful speaking, was so traumatic that Eleanor developed acute speaking anxiety.

Communication apprehension is more difficult to manage when it is chronic. Rather than feeling anxious in specific situations, which is often appropriate, some people are generally apprehensive about communicating. People who have chronic communication anxiety learn to fear communication, just as some of us learn to fear heights or water (Beatty, Plax, & Kearney, 1985; DeFleur & Ball-Rokeach, 1989).

Reducing Communication Apprehension

Communication scholars have developed four methods of reducing communication apprehension. If you do not have significant communication apprehension, reading this section may help you understand people who do. If you have more communication apprehension than you would like, reading this section will give you ways to reduce your anxiety.

Systematic Desensitization   **Systematic desensitization** is a method of treating many fears, from fear of flying to fear of speaking. It focuses on reducing the tension that surrounds the feared event (Beatty & Behnke, 1991; Daly & McCroskey, 1984). Systematic desensitization teaches people how to relax and thereby reduce the physiological features of anxiety. The goal is to learn to associate feeling relaxed with images of oneself in communication situations.

Cognitive Restructuring   **Cognitive restructuring** is a method of helping people change how they think about speaking situations. According to this method, the problem is how we use irrational beliefs to interpret speaking situations. For example, if you think you must be perfect, totally engaging, and liked by everyone who hears you, then you've set yourself up for failure. You've created expectations that are impossible to meet, which might be why you feel emotionally uneasy about communicating. A key part of cognitive restructuring is teaching apprehensive people to identify and challenge negative self-statements, which we discussed in Chapter 3.

Positive Visualization   **Positive visualization** aims to reduce anxiety by guiding apprehensive speakers through imagined positive speaking experiences (Hamilton, 2008). Researchers report that positive visualization is especially effective in reducing chronic apprehension (Ayres & Hopf, 1990; Bourhis & Allen, 1992; Lau, 1989). In professional life, managers are coached to visualize successful negotiations and meetings. In the world of sports, athletes are taught to imagine playing well, and those who engage in positive visualization improve as much as athletes who physically practice their sport. To read about positive visualization and other ways of reducing speaking anxiety, use MindTap for *Communication in Our Lives* to access **Weblink 14.1**.

Skills Training   **Skills training** assumes that lack of speaking skills causes us to be apprehensive about speaking. This method focuses on teaching people skills such as how to start conversations, organize ideas, build introductions, and support claims.

Research that indicates that a combination of all three methods is more likely to relieve speaking anxiety than any single method (Allen, Hunter, & Donahue, 1989). If communication apprehension interferes with your ability to express your ideas, ask your instructor to direct you to professionals who can work with you.

PRESENTING PUBLIC SPEECHES

We turn now to the final aspect of public speaking. Delivery, or oral style, affects every aspect of speaking effectiveness, from listeners' interest to listeners' judgments of a speaker's credibility. We'll first discuss oral style, pointing out how it differs from written style. Then, we'll consider alternative styles of delivery.

Oral Style

Oral style refers to speakers' visual, vocal, and verbal communication with listeners. *Oral style includes everything from* gestures and movement during a presentation to her or his sentence structures, volume, inflection, and speaking rate.

A common mistake of speakers, both new and experienced, is to use written style rather than oral style. But a speech is not a spoken essay. There are three primary qualities of effective oral communication (Wilson & Arnold, 1974). First, it is usually more informal than written communication. Thus, speakers use contractions and sentence fragments that would be inappropriate in a formal written document. The informal character of oral style also means it's appropriate for speakers to use colloquial words in informal speaking contexts. However, speakers shouldn't use slang or jargon that might offend any listener or that might not be understood by some listeners.

Second, effective oral style also tends to be more personal than written style. It's generally effective for speakers to include personal stories and personal pronouns, referring to themselves as "I" rather than "the speaker." In addition, speakers should sustain eye contact with listeners and show that they are approachable. If you reflect on speakers you've found effective, you'll probably realize that they seemed personal and open to you.

Third, effective oral style tends to be more immediate and more active than written style. This is important because listeners must understand ideas immediately as they are spoken, whereas readers can take time to comprehend ideas. In oral presentations, simple sentences ("I have three points") and compound sentences ("I want to describe the current system of selling textbooks, and then I will propose a less costly alternative") are more appropriate than complex sentences ("There are many reasons to preserve the Arctic National Wildlife Refuge, some of which have to do with endangered species and others with the preservation of wilderness environment, yet our current Congress is not protecting this treasure").

Immediacy also involves moving quickly instead of gradually to develop ideas. Rhetorical questions, interjections, and redundancy also enhance the immediacy of a speech. Reread the excerpts from Martin Luther King Jr.'s speech on page 306, and notice his skill in repeating key phrases, such as, "Now is the time." Also note Dr. King's use of simple sentences and his emphasis on personal language (*I* and *we*).

Obama speaking.

Styles of Delivery

The style of delivery that's effective at a political rally is different from the style appropriate for an attorney's closing speech in a trial; delivering a toast at a wedding requires a style different from that required in testifying before Congress. There are four presentational styles.

Impromptu Style   **Impromptu speaking** involves little preparation. Speakers speak off the cuff, organizing ideas as they talk and working with evidence that is already familiar to them. You use an impromptu style when you make a comment in a class, answer a question you hadn't anticipated in an interview, or respond to a request to share your ideas on a topic. There is no time to prepare or rehearse, so you have to think on your feet.

Impromptu speaking is appropriate when you know a topic well enough to organize and support your ideas without a lot of advance preparation. For instance, the president of a company could speak off the cuff about the company's philosophy, goals, and recent activities. Impromptu speaking is not an effective style when speakers are not highly familiar with topics and at ease in speaking in public.

Table 14.2	Guidelines for Effective Delivery

1. Adapt your appearance to your listeners. It's often effective for speakers to look similar to their listeners, probably because this suggests common ground.

2. Adapt your appearance to the speaking situation. Formal dress is likely to be appropriate for a speech to executives that is given in an office or board room. However, if that same speech were given at a company retreat by the ocean, casual dress would be more appropriate.

3. Use gestures to enhance impact. Gestures can reinforce ideas and complement verbal messages. Moving your arm in an arc motion can suggest progression to reinforce a time pattern.

4. Adopt a confident posture. Stand erect, with your shoulders back and your feet slightly apart for optimum balance.

5. Use confident, dynamic body movement to communicate your enthusiasm and confidence. Walk to the speaking podium (or wherever you will speak) with assurance: head up, arms comfortably at your side, at a pace that is neither hurried nor halting. As you speak, move away from the podium to highlight key ideas or to provide verbal transitions from one point to the next.

6. Maintain good eye contact with listeners. Try to vary your visual zone so that you look at some listeners at one moment and then move your gaze to a different segment of listeners.

7. Use volume that is strong but not overpowering. The appropriate volume will vary, depending on the size of your audience. You need to speak louder to an audience of 200 than to an audience of 25. You also need to adapt your volume to the environment. If a noisy air conditioner is running, you'll need to increase your volume to be heard. Be careful not to let your volume drop off at the end of sentences, a common problem for beginning speakers. At the same time, avoid excessive volume; listeners don't appreciate feeling that a speaker is shouting at them.

8. Use your voice to enhance your message. Pitch, rate, volume, and articulation are vocal qualities that allow you to add emphasis to important ideas. As you practice your speech, decide which words and phrases you want to emphasize.

9. Use pauses for effect. It is often effective to pause for a second or two after stating an important point or presenting a dramatic example or statistic.

10. Do not let accent interfere with clarity. Most of us speak in ways that reflect our ethnic and regional heritage. For everyone but professional broadcasters, regional dialects are acceptable. However, your accent must be understandable to listeners.

11. Articulate clearly. Speakers lose credibility when they mispronounce words or when they add or delete syllables. Common instances of added syllables are *cohabitate* for *cohabit*, *orientated* for *oriented*, *preventative* for *preventive*, and *irregardless* for *regardless*.

Extemporaneous Style   Probably the most common presentational style today, **extemporaneous speaking** relies on preparation and practice, but actual words aren't memorized. Extemporaneous speaking (also called *extemp*) requires speakers to do research, organize ideas, select supporting evidence, prepare visual aids, outline the speech, and practice delivery. Yet the speech itself is not written out in full. Instead, speakers speak from an outline—usually a key word outline.

Effective extemporaneous speaking requires a fine balance between too little and too much practice. Not rehearsing enough may result in stumbling, forgetting key ideas, and not being at ease with the topic. On the other hand, too much practice tends to result in a speech that sounds canned. Extemporaneous speaking involves a conversational and interactive manner that is generally effective with listeners.

Manuscript Style   As the term suggests, **manuscript speaking** involves speaking from the complete manuscript of a speech. After planning, researching, organizing, and outlining a presentation, a speaker then writes the complete word-for-word text and practices the presentation using that text or text transferred to a teleprompter. One clear advantage of this style is that it provides security to speakers. Even if a speaker gets confused when standing before an audience, he or she can rely on the full text. A second advantage of manuscript speaking is that it ensures precise content, which is important in official ceremonies, diplomatic agreements, and formal press statements and legal proceedings.

There are also disadvantages to manuscript speaking. First, this style limits a speaker's ability to adapt on the spot to listeners. If someone looks puzzled, the extemporaneous speaker can elaborate an idea, but the manuscript speaker may be locked into the written text. This points to a second hazard of manuscript speaking: the tendency to read the speech. It's difficult to be animated and visually engaged with listeners when reading a manuscript.

BRAD   *Most of my professors are pretty good. They talk with us in classes, and they seem to be really involved in interacting with students. But I've had several professors who read their notes—like, I mean, every day. They'd just come in, open a file, and start reading. I had one professor who almost never looked at us. It didn't feel like a person was communicating with us. I'd rather have read his notes on my own.*

Memorized Style   The final presentational style is **memorized speaking**, which carries the manuscript style one step further. After going through all the stages of manuscript speaking (i.e., preparing, researching, organizing, outlining, writing out the full text, and practicing), a speaker commits the entire speech to memory and speaks from a manuscript that is in his or her head. The

A relaxed, friendly appearance enhances a speaker's appeal.

advantages of this style are the same as those for manuscript speaking: An exact text exists, so everything is prepared in advance and the speaker has security.

There are serious disadvantages to memorizing. Because memorized speaking is based on a full written speech, the presentation may reflect written rather than oral style. In addition, memorized speaking is risky because a speaker has no safety net in case of memory lapses. Speakers who forget a word or phrase may become rattled and unable to complete the presentation. Memorized style also can limit effective delivery. It is difficult for a speaker to sound spontaneous when she or he has memorized an entire speech. Because the speaker is preoccupied with remembering the speech, she or he can't interact fully with listeners. These drawbacks of memorized speaking explain why it isn't widely used or recommended.

Knowing the benefits and liabilities of each presentational style provides you with alternatives. For most speaking occasions, extemporaneous style is effective because it combines good preparation and practice with spontaneity. For additional tips for effective delivery, use MindTap for *Communication in Our Lives* to access **WebLink 14.2**.

Practice

For all styles except impromptu, practice is important. Ideally, you should begin practicing your speech several days before you plan to deliver it. During practice, you should rely on the outline you will use when you actually deliver the speech. This ensures that you will be familiar with its layout and will know where various materials are on the outline. You should also practice with visual aids and any other materials you plan to use in your speech so that you are comfortable working with them.

There are many ways to practice a speech. Usually, speakers prefer to practice alone initially so that they gain some confidence and comfort. You may find it helpful to practice in front of a mirror to see how you look and to keep your eyes focused away from the outline. Practicing before a mirror is especially helpful in experimenting with different nonverbal behaviors that can enhance your presentational impact.

You may want to tape yourself during practice so that you can see and hear yourself and make decisions about how to refine your delivery. If the videotape shows you not keeping eye contact, you can work to increase your eye contact when speaking. Take breaks between practices so that you don't wind up memorizing the speech inadvertently.

When you've rehearsed enough to feel comfortable with the speech, it's time to practice in front of others. Ask friends to listen, and invite their feedback on ways you can refine your presentation. Practice until you know your material well but haven't memorized it. Then stop! Rehearsing too much is just as inadvisable as not practicing enough. You want to preserve the spontaneity that is important in oral style.

CHAPTER SUMMARY

Practice and review the content in this chapter.

In this chapter, we focused on ways to organize and present public communication. We discussed different types of outlines that assist speakers in organizing material. Next, we considered eight patterns for ordering the ideas in a speech and explored how each pattern affects the residual message of a presentation. Which organizational structure is best depends on a variety of factors, including the topic, your speaking goal, and the listeners with whom you will communicate.

We also noted that communication apprehension is common, natural, and often helpful to speakers. If you understand why it occurs and how to manage any apprehension you have, you can be effective in making public presentations. We identified different presentational styles and saw that each one has potential advantages and liabilities. To make sure that you've thought through all important aspects of organizing, outlining, and delivery, review the checklist at the end of this chapter. Then you'll be ready to proceed to Chapter 15, in which we analyze the full text of a student speech to see how organization, evidence, and other facets of public speaking work in an actual presentation.

CHECKLIST FOR ORGANIZING AND PRESENTING A SPEECH

Complete this checklist to help you organize your next speech.

If you prefer, you can complete this checklist online via your Chapter 14 MindTap for *Communication in Our Lives.*

In addition, you can use Speech Builder Express to help you organize your speech. At the end of this chapter, I've included a suggestion for using Speech Builder Express to help you with your next speech.

1. How could you structure your speech using each of the organizational patterns we discussed? Write out a thesis statement for each pattern.
   A. time: _____
   B. spatial: _____
   C. topical: _____
   D. star: _____
   E. wave: _____
   F. comparative: _____
   G. problem–solution: _____
   H. cause–effect: _____
   I. effect–cause: _____

2. Which pattern have you decided to use?
   A. List the two or three main points into which you've divided your topic:
      _____, _____, and _____.

3. Describe the three parts of your introduction:
   A. I will gain attention by _____
      _____
   B. My thesis statement is _____
      _____
   C. My preview is _____
      _____

4. Describe the transitions you've developed to move listeners from idea to idea in your speech.
   A. My transition from introduction to the body of the speech is _____
   B. My transitions between major points in the body are _____
   C. My transition from the body to the conclusion of the speech is _____

5. Describe the two parts of your conclusion:
   A. Restatement of thesis and major points:
      _____
   B. Concluding emphasis: _____
      _____

6. The delivery style I will use is _____
   because _____
   _____

7. I've practiced my speech
   A. on my own
   B. in front of others
   C. in front of a mirror
   D. in the room where I will deliver it
   E. on video

APPLYING COMMUNICATION IN OUR LIVES MindTap

Communication in Our Lives is supported by a MindTap, a new online learning platform that delivers content, assignments, and a tailored presentation of the course curriculum created by your instructor. MindTap combines all of your learning tools–readings, multimedia, activities and assessments–into a singular learning unit that guides you through the course. Practice and Present, a unique tool within MindTap, allows you to upload your speech video files for practice or for a grade, comment on your peer's speeches and review your grades. MindTap also includes Speech Builder Express, a powerful tool that guides you through the speech outline and preparation process. For more information or to access MindTap, visit cengagebrain.com.

DEFINITIONS OF KEY CONCEPTS MindTap Review your **Flashcards**.

cognitive restructuring A method of reducing communication apprehension that involves teaching people to revise how they think about speaking situations.

communication apprehension Anxiety associated with real or anticipated communication encounters. Communication apprehension is common and can be constructive.

extemporaneous speaking A presentational style that includes preparation and practice but not memorization of words and nonverbal behaviors.

formal outline A complete outline of a speech, including the parts of a speech, main points, supporting material, transitions, and citations for sources.

impromptu speaking Public speaking that involves little preparation. Speakers think on their feet as they talk about ideas and positions with which they are familiar.

key word outline An abbreviated speaking outline that includes only key words for each point in a speech. The key words trigger the speaker's memory of the full point.

manuscript speaking A presentational style that involves speaking from the complete manuscript of a speech.

memorized speaking A presentational style in which a speech is memorized word for word in advance.

oral style The visual, vocal, and verbal aspects of the delivery of a public speech.

positive visualization A technique of reducing speaking anxiety; a person visualizes herself or himself communicating effectively in progressively challenging speaking situations.

skills training A method of reducing communication apprehension that assumes that anxiety is a result of lack of speaking skills and therefore can be reduced by learning skills.

systematic desensitization A method of reducing communication apprehension that teaches people how to relax physiologically and then helps them practice feeling relaxed as they imagine themselves in progressively difficult communication situations.

transitions Words and sentences that connect ideas and main points in a speech so that listeners can follow a speaker.

working outline A sketch of main ideas and their relationships; used by and intended only for the speaker.

works cited A list of sources used in preparing a speech.

FOR FURTHER REFLECTION AND DISCUSSION

 MindTap™

 Ethics

1. Does a speaker have an ethical responsibility to organize a speech well, or is organization strictly a strategic matter—something to help a speaker have impact? Does careful organization reflect ethical issues, such as respect for listeners?

2. Attend a public presentation and keep notes on how the speaker organizes the speech. What is the overall pattern of the presentation?

Did the speaker make a wise choice? Identify transitions in the speech, and evaluate their effectiveness. Do the introduction and conclusion serve the appropriate speaking goals?

3. Give a 1- to 2-minute impromptu speech on your favorite activity. Next, spend 2 days preparing an extemporaneous speech on the same topic. How do the two speeches differ in quality and effectiveness?

SHARPEN YOUR SKILL

 MindTap™

1. Designing Your Introduction

Apply the principles we've discussed to develop an introduction to a speech you plan to give. Using the following outline, fill in full sentences for each element of your introduction.

I. Introduction

    A. Attention and motivation: _____
    B. Thesis: _____
    C. Credibility: _____
    D. Preview: _____

    To further enlarge your awareness of the elements in a good introduction, view the sample speech by Mariah Morgan, "Hate Crimes," in your Chapter 14 MindTap for *Communication in Our Lives.*

2. Rehearsing Your Speech

You'll need three 20-minute periods at different times to complete this activity.

    a. After you have prepared the outline that you will use when you present your speech, find a quiet place where you will not be disturbed. Present the speech as you intend to deliver it to your class. As you rehearse, practice looking at different parts of the room as you will later engage in eye contact with classmates.

    b. Wait at least a few hours after your first practice to do the second one. This time, practice in the same room, but stand in front of a mirror; ideally it should be a full-length mirror so that you can see yourself as listeners will see you. Give your speech as you plan to deliver it to your classmates. As you speak, notice your posture and non-verbal communication. Are you using effective hand gestures, facial expressions, and changes in body posture and position?

    c. Wait at least a few hours after your second practice to do the third one. You may want to invite several friends or classmates to join you in this practice session so that you have an audience. For this rehearsal, go to your classroom or another classroom that is set up similarly to yours. Sit down in the room as you would sit in your class. Imagine the teacher announcing that it is your turn to speak. Get up from your seat, go to the podium or front of the classroom, and present your speech as you plan to deliver it to your classmates. Practice looking at different areas of the room or at your friends as you will later engage in eye contact with classmates. If you have access to a video camera, you may tape this third rehearsal and then analyze your presentation.

EXPERIENCING COMMUNICATION IN OUR LIVES

CASE STUDY: *Analyzing Delivery: Speech of Self-Introduction*

A video of the speech introduced here is featured in your Chapter 14 Online Resources for *Communication in Our Lives*. Select "Delivery" to watch the video of Adam Currier's speech of introduction. Improve your own public speaking skills by reading, watching, and evaluating this speech.

Every year since I've remembered, we've gone back to Iowa and spent a week of that summer just being with my dad's parents, my grandparents. And each year, as I grew, I grew closer and closer to my grandfather. And it got to the point where I no longer just knew him as a relative but I knew him as a human being. Sitting outside on his porch one day, right before he died, he told me about his life. We were talking about what he had done, being in World War II, being a dentist, being a community leader, all the things he had ever achieved in his life—and it all sounded so perfect. I said, "Grandfather, what do you regret most in your life?" He said, "Adam, I regret not seeing more sunsets."

A couple months later, he passed on, and I realized that I didn't enjoy every single minute with him as much as I could've, and I didn't have the time with him that I thought that I had. So I look at my wall now, and I see the quotes on it and see the stories on it and the pictures on it and I realize that everyone I've come into contact with, everyone I've ever met, everything I've done, has all contributed to shaping the person that I am.

QUESTIONS FOR ANALYSIS AND DISCUSSION

You can answer these questions and see my responses to them online via your Online Resources for Chapter 14.

1. Was the speaker dynamic—excited about the topic?

2. Was the speaker's language clear, immediate, and vivid?

3. Did the speaker use nonverbal communication to enhance effectiveness?

4. What style of speaking did the speaker use? Was this an appropriate choice for this speech, this occasion, and the particular listeners?

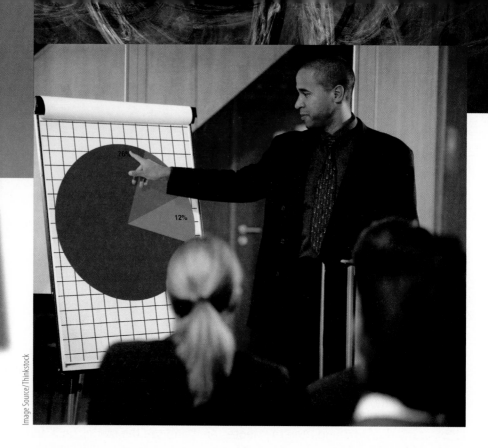

Image Source/Thinkstock

Informative Speaking

Review the chapter **Learning Objectives** and **Start** with a quick warm up activity.

Our era has been called "the information age." To live and work effectively in today's world, we need share information—in the workplace, in social situations, and in community and civic contexts. Skill at informative speaking is critical if you want to be effective personally, professionally, and socially. To learn more about the importance of informational speaking in professional life, use MindTap for *Communication in Our Lives* to access **WebLink 15.1.**

Building on what you've learned in Chapters 12, 13, and 14, this chapter will guide you through the process of developing and presenting an informative speech. We will first highlight the importance of informative speaking in everyday life and note how it differs from persuasive speaking, which we will cover in Chapter 16. Next, we'll discuss guidelines for effective informative speaking. At the end of the chapter, you'll find a sample informative speech.

SHARPEN YOUR SKILL

At the end of this chapter, refer to the Sharpen Your Skill features, Informative Speaking in Your Life and Organizing Your Informative Speech, to apply concepts from Chapter 15.

THE NATURE OF INFORMATIVE SPEAKING

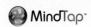

An **informative speech** is a presentation that aims to increase listeners' knowledge, understanding, or abilities. Competence in informative speaking is important if you plan to coach sports, to be part of neighborhood and civic groups, and to succeed in your profession (Morreale, Osborn, & Pearson, 2000).

Informative Speaking in Everyday Life

It's likely that you'll give a number of informative speeches in your life (see Table 15.1). Some will be short; some will be longer. Some will be formal; others will be informal. All of them will have the goal of conveying information to others. Consider these examples of everyday informative speaking:

- Explaining a medical procedure to a patient.
- Telling Boy Scouts how to start a fire without matches.
- Informing your neighbors about a community watch program that's decreased burglaries in other neighborhoods.
- Briefing stakeholders on the new strategic plan your firm is implementing.
- Describing a new offensive strategy to the Little League team you coach.
- Telling a civic group about traditions in your culture.
- Teaching a group of friends how to prepare a complicated dessert.
- Reporting to your coworkers on what you learned at a conference so that they understand new developments in your field.

Comparing Informative and Persuasive Speaking

Informative speaking and persuasive speaking differ, yet they also have much in common. Both require research, organization, supporting material, and delivery. There are also overlaps between informative and persuasive goals. For example, in an informative speech, you are trying to persuade listeners to attend to what you say and to care about learning. In persuasive speeches, you often need to inform listeners about certain issues to influence their values, attitudes, or behaviors.

Table 15.1	Types of Informative Speeches
Type	**Sample Specific Purpose**
Demonstration	To show listeners how to construct a speech outline
Instruction	To teach listeners how to perform CPR
Description	To describe the people and land of Nepal
Explanation	To explain why (or how) hurricanes form
Briefing	To summarize the results of a new marketing strategy
Reporting	To provide detailed information on the results of a new marketing strategy

Table 15.2	Informative Versus Persuasive Speaking
1. Persuasive speeches tend to have more controversial purposes.	
2. Persuasive speeches seek more powerful responses from listeners.	
3. Persuasive speeches need more and better proof.	
4. Persuasive speeches require the speaker to earn greater credibility.	

Four differences between informative and persuasive speaking are particularly important and are outlined in Table 15.2.

The Controversial Nature of the Purpose The purposes of informative speeches tend to be less controversial than the purposes of persuasive speeches. Something is controversial when it can be debated or argued—in other words, when not everyone is likely to agree. Typically, informative presentations aim to give listeners new information: to teach, explain, or describe a person, object, event, process, or relationship. Persuasive speeches, on the other hand, aim to change listeners' attitudes, beliefs, or behaviors.

Obviously, information can have persuasive impact, so it can be controversial. Yet the degree to which a purpose is controversial is much greater in persuasive speeches. An informative speech might have the specific purpose of describing the historical conditions that led to establishment of affirmative action policies. A persuasive speech on the same topic might have the specific purpose of persuading listeners to support or oppose affirmative action policies. Clearly, the latter purpose is more controversial than the former.

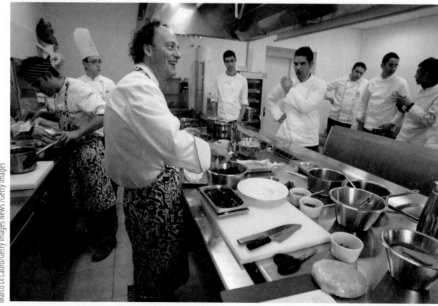

Marco Di Lauro/Getty Images News /Getty Images

This chef engages in informative speaking to instruct chef trainees in the preparation of food.

The Response Sought Related to their differing purposes are the responses informative and persuasive speeches seek from listeners. In the affirmative action example, the speaker giving an informative speech wants listeners to understand certain historical conditions. The speaker giving a persuasive speech wants listeners to believe that affirmative action is right or wrong, justified or not justified, beneficial or harmful. The persuasive speaker might even want to persuade listeners to take specific actions to oppose or support affirmative action at local, regional, or national levels. In seeking to change listeners in some way, persuasive speeches seek a more powerful response: change rather than acceptance of new information.

The Evidence Needed Because persuasive speeches tend to be more controversial and seek to convince listeners to change in some way, they generally need stronger supporting material than informative speeches do. This does not mean that informative speeches don't need proof; they do. However, an effective persuasive speech generally must include more supporting material. Why? Because listeners expect more evidence when they are asked to think, feel, or act differently than when they are asked only to understand something. Listeners will want convincing evidence not only that discrimination exists and is wrong but also that affirmative action policies are an effective response to the problem.

In persuasive speeches, speakers also have a responsibility to anticipate and address their listeners' reservations. To do this effectively requires evidence. Perhaps, in researching public opinions on affirmative action, you learn that the most common objection is based on the assumption that it lowers standards for admission to schools and professions. To persuade listeners to support affirmative

HEALTH COMMUNICATION

Information Gathering in Medical Interviews

Nurses, doctors, technicians, dentists, and other clinicians need skill in gathering information from patients since information is key to effective diagnosis and treatment. Doctors Judith Lyles, Francesca Dwamena, Catherine Levin, and Robert Smith (2001) call attention to communication skills that facilitate information gathering interviews:

• Nonverbal encouragement	head nods and smiles and saying "um hmm,"
• Reflecting or paraphrasing what the patient says	"What I think you're saying, is. . . ."
• Direct questions	"What do you eat for breakfast?"
• Open-ended questions	"Could you tell me more about what's happening on your job?"
• Helping patient name feelings	"You sound upset."
• Empathizing	"I'd be worried about that too."
• Understanding	"It makes sense that you're concerned."
• Respecting	"You've shown a lot of courage in dealing with this condition."
• Inviting partnership	"Together, we'll figure out what's going on."

action, you should present evidence that shows that standards have not declined in institutions that follow affirmative action policies.

VINCE   *Last week, I went to hear a speaker on capital punishment. He was trying to convince us that we should abolish it, but I wasn't convinced. What he mainly did was to inform us that there are cases where innocent people are convicted or even put to death. But he never showed us—or me, anyway—that abolishing capital punishment is the answer. Why can't we just reform it, like, require absolute proof of guilt before someone can be sentenced to die? And what about all the people who really are guilty of horrible things, like school killings or the Oklahoma bombing? Shouldn't they be sentenced to death? He never talked about that.*

The Importance of Credibility   Credibility is important to any speaker's effectiveness. As with evidence, however, the credibility a speaker needs varies with the speaking purpose. In general, a speaker who attempts to change people needs more credibility than a speaker who seeks only to inform them. Because credibility is so important in persuasive speaking, we will discuss it in depth in Chapter 16.

GUIDELINES FOR EFFECTIVE INFORMATIVE SPEAKING

Eight guidelines are particularly important for informative speeches.

Provide Listeners With a Clear Thesis Statement

Listeners want to know what they are supposed to get out of listening to an informative speech. Only then can they focus their listening. When giving an informative presentation, the speaker should state a simple, clear thesis that tells listeners what the speech will provide or do. The thesis should motivate listeners by alerting them that the information to come will be useful to them. As you'll recall from previous chapters, a good thesis is clear and direct: "At the end of my talk, you will understand the different citizen responsibilities and effects of three popular neighborhood watch programs used in our county." Upon hearing this thesis, listeners know exactly what the speaker plans to give them and what they should get out of listening.

Connect With Listeners' Values and Experiences

As with all communication, informative speeches should build connections with listeners. For instance, in a speech with the specific purpose of describing alternative neighborhood watch programs, a speaker might open by saying, "I know we share a concern for safety in our neighborhood. What I want to do is describe the three neighborhood watch programs in our county so that we can make an informed choice about what is right for our community." This opening establishes common ground between the speaker and listeners by noting that they "share a

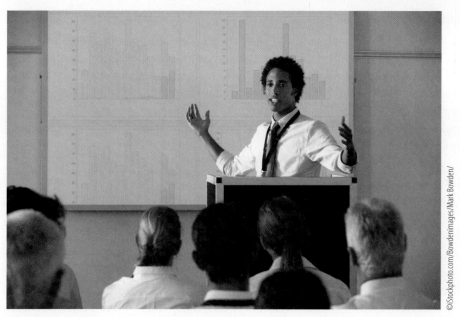

Effective nonverbal communication is important in public speaking.

concern" and by using *we* language: "our neighborhood," "we can make," "our community."

Motivate Listeners to Want Information

Information is so pervasive today that we screen much of it out. For an informative speech to be effective, listeners must be motivated to want what the speaker offers. In some cases, listeners are motivated for their own reasons. People who attend cardiopulmonary resuscitation (CPR) class want to learn how to perform CPR. They are already motivated.

In other cases, the speaker may need to motivate people to want information. For example, a supervisor may need to fuel employees' hunger for information on a new procedure the company wants them to follow. In this situation, the supervisor might say, "I know we all get tired of learning new procedures, but the one I'm going to explain today will make your jobs easier and increase your productivity." This statement motivates employees to listen, especially if their pay is based on their productivity. Notice that the statement also recognizes that listeners have been asked to learn numerous procedures and that it can get tiring.

MANDY   *I went to the placement office the other day for a workshop on interviewing. I wasn't really interested, but I thought I should go, so I was just kind of there but not really paying attention. Then the facilitator got us started. The first thing she said was that students who attend these workshops tended to get more and better job offers than students who don't. That definitely got my attention! From then on, I was listening very carefully and taking lots of notes.*

Build Credibility With Listeners

As we've noted, for a speaker to be effective, listeners must perceive him or her as credible. When giving an informative speech, you should demonstrate that you have some expertise relevant to your topic. You may show you have personal experience ("I took a CPR course"). You may also demonstrate to listeners that you have gained information in other ways ("To prepare to talk to you today, I spoke with emergency department doctors about people whose lives were saved by CPR").

You'll also want to show listeners that you care about them or that the information you are offering will help them in some way. You might say, "This information will come in handy when you start interviewing for jobs."

Adapt to Diverse Listeners

In our diverse society, few audiences are homogeneous. For the informative speaker, this implies that it is important to speak in ways that include and respect diverse experiences, values, and viewpoints. People whose homes have been burglarized have had a different experience from those whose homes have not been burglarized. People who believe in nonviolence as a way of life differ in key respects from people who believe that everyone has a right to use violence to protect themselves and their property. Citizens who were raised in highly communal cultures are likely to be more inclined toward communal efforts to protect a neighborhood than are people who were raised in highly individualistic cultures. Families without children may have different security concerns from families with children, especially young ones.

> **DIMITRI**   *I am looking for a new car, so I went to a dealership. I was looking at a model that Consumer Reports said has the highest safety rating. Then the salesman came over and started talking about the car I was looking at. His pitch was that it was cheap and fuel efficient. I asked him a couple of questions about safety issues, which are my primary concerns with cars, and he just brushed them back and kept telling me how economical it was. He lost that sale.*

Organize So Listeners Can Follow Easily

In Chapter 4, we learned that listening is hard work. When giving an informative talk, a speaker should do all that she or he can to reduce the amount of work listeners have to invest. Applying the principles we discussed in Chapter 14, this means that you should structure your speech clearly. As we learned, your introduction should capture listeners' attention ("Would you like to increase your productivity and paychecks by 10%?"), provide a clear thesis ("I'm going to explain a new procedure that will increase your efficiency and income"), and preview what will be covered ("I will demonstrate a new method of sorting and routing stock and show how much faster and more accurate it is than the method we've been using").

Table 15.3	Organizing Informative Speeches	
Specific Purpose	**Thesis**	**Organizational Patterns**
Listeners will learn how to recognize differences between poisonous and nonpoisonous plants.	I will teach you how to tell which plants are safe to eat.	Comparison/contrast
Team members will know management's response to our strategic plan.	I will summarize the feedback from management on our goals and implementation strategies.	Topical
To teach friends how I make crème brûlée.	I am going to take you through the steps involved in making a perfect crème brûlée.	Time
Employees will understand the reasons for a new procedure for sorting and routing stock.	I want to explain how the new procedure we're going to start using solves problems that have frustrated us for years.	Problem–solution

Transitions should be woven throughout the speech to assist listeners in following the flow of ideas. The conclusion should summarize key points ("I've shown you how to increase your paycheck") and end with a strong idea or punch ("In this case, what's good for the company is also good for you").

The body of an informative speech should also be organized clearly (see Table 15.3). Time and spatial patterns can be effective for speeches that aim to demonstrate, describe, explain, or teach ("In my speech, I will describe how interviews progress from opening stage to substance and closing stage"; "I will explain how leg and arm positions at the keyboard affect the back and neck"). Topical patterns are commonly used for reports and briefings that address several areas of a topic ("I will summarize developments in our sales and marketing divisions"). When introducing new or alternative ideas or procedures, the comparative pattern can be effective ("The new method of sorting and routing stock differs from our current method in two key ways").

Although they are less commonly used in informative presentations, problem–solution and cause–effect or effect–cause patterns can be good choices. For instance, an informative speech might explain how a new procedure for sorting and routing stock solves a problem. The same topic might be organized using a cause–effect pattern to show that the new procedure (cause) will increase productivity (effect).

Speech Builder Express, which you can access via MindTap for *Communication in Our Lives*, includes extensive prompts and a clear framework for organizing and developing speeches that incorporate a variety of informative strategies.

 MindTap

Design Your Speech to Enhance Learning and Retention

Much of the information we need to do our jobs and live our lives is not particularly interesting. This poses a challenge for you when you give an informative speech. The informative speaker is responsible for making material interesting to listeners. In addition, information can be complex and difficult to grasp, particularly in oral presentations. This creates a second challenge for informative speakers: You must do all you can to increase the clarity of the information. Five strategies can help you make your information interesting and clear.

Limit the Information You Present   By the time you are ready to give an informative speech, you know a great deal about the topic. It's your job to sort through all your knowledge to choose wisely the two or three points you want to make. You may think five points are important. If you try to present all five, however, you risk having listeners remember none or the less important ones.

If you must cover more than two or three points to inform listeners fully, then you have two choices. You may give multiple informative talks, separated by time to allow listeners to absorb and apply the information you've provided before they get more. A second option is to rely on other principles of increasing clarity and interest that we discuss later in this chapter.

Move From Familiar to Unfamiliar   It's normal to feel uneasy when you are asked to understand new information or learn a new process or skill. Speakers can reduce this anxiety by starting with what is familiar to listeners and moving to what is new. For instance, the supervisor in our example might open an informative speech by saying, "All of you know the sorting and routing procedure we've used for years. The new procedure extends what you already know. What you've done in the past is to sort incoming stock into three piles. From now on, you'll be sorting it into four. It's the same process—just one more pile." Upon hearing this, listeners realize that skills they already have will transfer to the new procedure.

Repeat Important Ideas   Repetition is a powerful way to increase retention (Thompson & Grundgenett, 1999). Have you ever been introduced to someone and not been able to remember the person's name 5 minutes later? That's because you heard it only once. The introduction probably was like this: "Pat, I'd like you to meet Leigh." If the person doing the introduction had wanted to help you remember Leigh's name, it would have been better to say this: "Pat, I'd like you to meet Leigh. Leigh and I go way back; we met in our sophomore year. We got together when Leigh and I were trying out for the chorus, and Leigh got a place when I didn't." In that short introduction, Leigh's name was mentioned four times. You'll probably remember it. You're more likely to remember something you hear four times than something you hear only once.

The same principle applies to informative speaking. As an illustration, let's return to our supervisor. It's important that employees retain the new classifications into which they will be sorting stock, so these bear repeating: "In the past you've sorted stock into new, returns, and used. As most of you know, the stock we've been putting in the return pile has really been of two types: stock that was missing something and stock that was defective. Now we're breaking returns into two separate piles: ones with missing parts and ones with defective parts. So we have missings and defects. The missing pile is for stock that is missing a part. We can fix these items by adding the missing part. The defect pile is for stock that has something wrong with it, usually a defective part. So missings and defects are the new piles we want to use." The repeated references to *missings* and *defects* increase listeners' ability to retain the new classifications for stock.

Highlight Key Material   Do you become more attentive in class when a teacher says, "This next point is really important" or "You're likely to see this on the test"? Probably you do. That's what the teacher intends. He or she is highlighting key material to get your attention. In this example, the teacher highlighted by framing. "This material is important" is a frame that calls your attention to important material.

"This material is important."

$$\boxed{\text{MATERIAL}}$$

There are other ways to highlight key material. You might say something direct, such as, "Listen up. This is important." Or you might say, "I hope you'll really tune in to this next point." You could also say, "If you remember only one thing from my talk, it should be this: . . ." All of these statements give verbal clues to listeners that you are presenting especially important material.

You can also provide nonverbal clues to highlight key material. Raising volume or changing inflection tends to capture interest, so listeners are likely to listen more carefully when a speaker alters volume or inflection. Gestures can also emphasize the importance of key ideas. You can change your position— move from behind a podium to in front of it, move from sitting to standing—to draw listeners' attention

Rely on Multiple Communication Channels   If a speaker says, "Red berries often are poisonous," you might get the point. You'd be more likely to get it and retain it if the speaker made that statement and also showed you pictures of red berries or gave you red berries. When we use multiple channels to communicate, we increase the likelihood that listeners will learn and retain new information.

When you're presenting a lot of information or complex information, handouts can greatly increase listeners' retention and ability to use new information. Listeners both hear the talk and see the notes summarizing key points. Visual aids can also highlight information. The supervisor in our example might develop a visual aid to show the two new classifications that grow out of the one former one (Figure 15.1). Showing this while also talking about the two new classifications lets listeners learn and retain through two senses: seeing and hearing. The visual aid would be especially effective if the two new classifications stood out visually. They might be larger or a different color font.

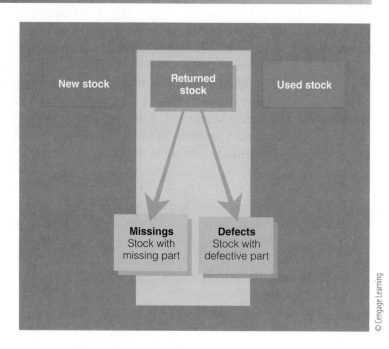

FIGURE 15.1
A Visual Aid to Illustrate a
New Procedure

© Cengage Learning

Involve Listeners

Have you ever been a passenger when someone else was driving and later been unsure how to get back to where the two of you went? If you drive yourself, there's a greater likelihood that you'll learn how to get to the place. This common experience reminds us that we learn best when we do something ourselves rather than just hear or see someone else do it. There are many ways to involve listeners in informative speeches. We'll highlight four of the most effective.

Call for Participation   You might give sticks to Boy Scouts and so they can rub them together as you demonstrate how to do this to start a fire (but only if fire codes allow this and if you can control possible danger). You might let people try a new procedure at a demonstration stand you set up. You might bring plants that are poisonous and nonpoisonous so that listeners can see, smell, and touch them as you describe how they differ.

Table 15.4	Generating a Sense of Listener Participation
Specific Informative Purpose: To Teach Listeners How to Recognize Poisonous Plants	
Method	**Example**
Direct participation	I want each of you to smell the berries I'm handing out.
Rhetorical question	If you were stranded on a camping trip, would you know how to survive?
Poll listeners	How many of you have ever pulled a ripe berry off a bush and wondered if it was safe to eat?
Refer to specific listeners	Jane, remember when you watched Tom Hanks in *Cast-away* and wondered how he knew what was safe to eat on the island?

Ask Rhetorical Questions You can also involve listeners by asking rhetorical questions. These are questions that a speaker doesn't actually expect listeners to answer. By asking them, however, a speaker invites listeners' mental participation: They are likely to answer rhetorical questions silently in their heads. "How many of you have ever wished you had an extra $100?" "What would you do if you made 20% more each week? Would you take a vacation, buy a new car, or pay some bills?"

Poll Listeners Another way to involve listeners is to poll them to find out what they think, feel, or want or what experiences they have had. "How many of you have ever left your home for a vacation and worried about whether someone was going to break into it?" "How many of you would like to earn $100 more a week?" Speakers can ask for audible responses ("If you have had this experience, say yes") or a show of hands ("Let me see the hands of everyone who has had this experience").

Refer to Specific Listeners You may also speak directly to or about particular members of your audience. Ethically, you must be careful not to speak to or about others in ways that could embarrass them or reveal information they consider private. Speaking to or about specific listeners generates a sense of participation and community. "Bill and Sally, we've all heard about the break-in at your house." "Just the other day, I overheard Ed talking about what he'd do if he won the lottery. Well, Ed, I've got good news for you: You may not win the lottery, but you can get more money."

To practice involving listeners for various speech topics, complete the activity "Involving Listeners" in MindTap for *Communication in Our Lives*.

 MindTap™

USE EFFECTIVE AND ETHICAL SUPPORTING MATERIALS

To be effective in informing listeners, speeches must include supporting material that is both effective and ethical. Effective supporting materials add interest, force, and clarity to a speech. Ethical supporting materials present accurate information fairly and without distortion (Lehman & DuFrene, 1999).

Returning to our previous example, the supervisor might take the average employee's salary and show how much it should go up using the new procedure. The speaker might develop a visual aid to show how that increase would multiply over a period of time (Figure 15.2).

To be ethical, supporting material should meet the criteria we discussed in Chapter 13 (see Table 13.4 on page 289). To review, supporting material should be:

- Sufficient to achieve the speaking purpose, such as teaching or describing (sufficiency).
- Accurate, correct and complete, with sources cited, presented in its original context (accuracy).
- Relevant to the topic and claims made (relevance).
- Timely, usually current or in some cases historically situated (timeliness).
- Free of biases, such as vested interests (impartiality).

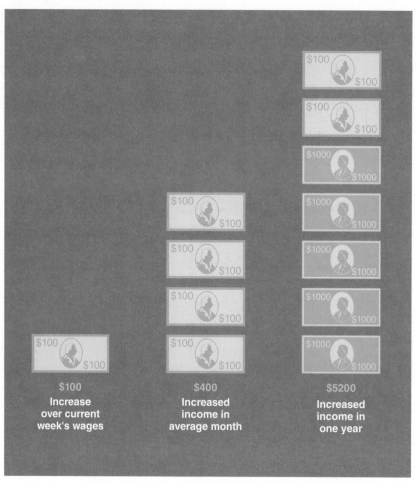

FIGURE 15.2
A Visual Aid to Motivate
Employees

Using these criteria, it would be ethical for the speaker to tell employees that their wages should increase an average of 20% only if the speaker had adequate data to support that claim (the criterion of accuracy). If only 25% of employees who have used the new procedure increase their productivity, it would not be ethical to state that they could expect to increase their wages because only one in four could reasonably expect that. If most employees do increase their productivity by 20% but only after 4 to 6 months of adjusting to the new procedure, the speaker would be ethically obligated to inform them of the time lag (the criterion of timeliness). If employees who use the new procedure at other plants have different working conditions and tools, the change in their productivity might not generalize to the listeners in this case (the criterion of relevance).

CHAPTER SUMMARY

 Practice and review the content in this chapter.

In this chapter, we described the many types of informative speeches and noted how informative speaking differs from persuasive speaking. We then highlighted eight guidelines for effective informative speaking. Because these guidelines are at the heart of the impact of your informative presentations, we summarize them here:

1. Provide listeners with a clear thesis statement.
2. Connect with listeners' values and experiences.
3. Motivate listeners to want information.
4. Build credibility with listeners.
5. Adapt to diverse listeners.
6. Organize so listeners can follow easily.
7. Design your speech to enhance learning and retention.
8. Involve listeners.

In following these eight guidelines, speakers should use effective and ethical supporting materials to develop their ideas.

APPLYING COMMUNICATION IN OUR LIVES

Communication in Our Lives is supported by a MindTap, a new online learning platform that delivers content, assignments, and a tailored presentation of the course curriculum created by your instructor. MindTap combines all of your learning tools–readings, multimedia, activities and assessments–into a singular learning unit that guides you through the course. Practice and Present, a unique tool within MindTap, allows you to upload your speech video files for practice or for a grade, comment on your peer's speeches and review your grades. MindTap also includes Speech Builder Express, a powerful tool that guides you through the speech outline and preparation process. For more information or to access MindTap, visit cengagebrain.com.

DEFINITIONS OF KEY CONCEPTS

 MindTap Review your **Flashcards**.

informative speech A presentation that aims to increase listeners' knowledge, understanding, or abilities.

FOR FURTHER REFLECTION AND DISCUSSION

 MindTap

1. Attend an informative speech. Identify the thesis and the organizational pattern. Evaluate the ethical and strategic quality of the speaker's evidence.
2. To find quotations that are relevant to your speech, use your Online Resources for *Communication in Our Lives* to access **WebLink 15.2** and visit the Quotations Home Page.
3. Use the evaluation form on page 341 to evaluate Michael Daniels's speech on black boxes.

Informative Speech Outline

General Purpose: _____

Specific Purpose: _____

Introduction
I.   Attention device _____
II.   Motivation for listening _____
III. Thesis statement _____
IV.   Preview of speech _____

Body
I.   First main point _____
      A. Supporting material _____
      B. Supporting material (You may have only two main points) _____
      C. Transition_____
II.   Second main point (You may have more than two kinds of supporting materials for main points)
      _____
      A. Supporting material _____
      B. Supporting material _____
      C. Transition _____
Transition to conclusion _____

Conclusion
I.   Summary of main points _____
II.   Strong closing statement _____

References_____

Evaluation Form for Informative Speeches
Speaker's Name: _____ Date: _____

Speech Topic: _____

_____

1. Did the speaker capture listeners' initial attention?_____
    _____

2. Did the speaker motivate listeners to want information?_____
    _____

3. Did the speaker state a clear thesis? _____
    _____

4. Did the speaker preview the body of the speech? _____
    _____

5. Was the speech structured clearly and appropriately? _____
    _____

6. Were strong transitions provided between parts of the speech and main points in the body of the
    speech? _____
    _____

7. Did the speaker provide effective supporting material? _____
    _____

8. Did the speaker use ethical supporting material? _____
    _____

Did the speaker involve listeners directly by polling them, asking rhetorical questions, or speaking to or about particular listeners? _____

_____

Did the speaker use strategies to enhance listeners' learning and retention? _____

_____

Did the speaker connect the topic to listeners' experiences and values? _____

_____

Did the conclusion summarize main points of the speech? _____

_____

Did the speech end on a strong note? _____

_____

SHARPEN YOUR SKILL   🔵 MindTap™

1. Informative Speaking in Your Life

How common is informative speaking in your everyday life? For the next week, keep a record of the informative speeches you hear (those given by others), grouped into the four categories listed here. Remember that an informative speech need not be long—it may be just a couple of minutes in which someone teaches you how to do something or explains a new procedure, describes a rule or policy, or tells you the background of an issue.

   a. Informative speaking in classes
   b. Informative speaking on the job
   c. Informative speaking with friends
   d. Other informative speaking

2. Organizing Your Informative Speech

Apply the principles of effective organization as you develop your informative speech. Provide the following information for your speech:

Introduction
   To capture listeners' attention and motivate them to listen, I will _____

   My thesis statement is _____
   To establish my initial credibility,
   I will _____
   To preview my speech, I will say _____
   My transition from the introduction to the body is _____

Body
   My organizational pattern is _____
   To provide transitions from one main point to the next, I will say
   A. Points one to two: _____
   B. Points two to three: _____
   C. Point three to conclusion: _____
   My transition from body to conclusion is

   _____

Conclusion
   I will summarize the key points in my speech by saying _____
   I will close with this strong statement:

   _____

EXPERIENCING COMMUNICATION IN OUR LIVES

 MindTap

CASE STUDY: *Informative Speech: Anytown USA*

A video of the speech described here is featured in your Chapter 15 Online Resources for *Communication in Our Lives*. Select "Informative Speech" to watch the video of Enriques Ruiz's speech. Improve your own public speaking skills by reading, watching, and evaluating this speech.

© Cengage Learning

I would not be the person I am today if it was not for Anytown. I would not be in this room if it was not for this organization. You're probably wondering what I'm talking about. What can so dramatically change someone's life?

Anytown is a summer leadership camp. Now there are thousands of summer leadership camps all around the world. You have science camps, young life camps, all kinds of camps—camps that change our lives in positive ways.

The summer before my junior year, I attended Anytown. Before camp, I was a deviant young man. After camp I was never the same. So what exactly is Anytown? What is its history and what goes on at camp that's so powerful? Today I'll discuss these three things with you.

According to the Website, Anytown Arizona is a youth development program that focuses on diversity awareness, social justice, and personal empowerment. Its mission is to be a catalyst and facilitator for social change. This camp brings together people from different backgrounds and different cultures.

The Anytown USA organization has several types of programs: Anytown Junior is for junior highers; Unitowns are for weekend programs; Beyond Anytown is for people who have attended Anytown; and Powertown focuses on parents and community members.

The weeklong camp is filled with activities geared toward understanding diversity through a great deal of educational activities that have emotional impact. Typically the counselors act out different levels of violence that are seen everywhere. They start with verbal violence—someone saying an inappropriate comment to somebody just because they are a different color. They continue to physical violence, ganging up and pummeling another counselor because they are a different color. They finish with genocide. Genocide consists of four or six counselors acting out being Jewish, killed by two counselors acting out being Nazis. This is only one of the activities and there are many others.

So where did Anytown come from? What's its history? According to the Anytown Website, Anytown began in 1957 known as the National Conference for Christians and Jews, now better known as the National Conference for Community and Justice. The goal then and now was to bring together a group of diverse young youth from a variety of different backgrounds, empower them to understand each other, and learn from each other.

In one cabin you will have a young man who has been very wealthy growing up and a young man who has had a very dysfunctional past. Together, throughout the week, they come together and they learn about each other and where they're from and what they've lived. Toward the end of the week they become kind of like brothers.

The staff, in a way, tests the students. They segregate them. Each day has a different theme, such as "know yourself," "know your friends," and "know your family." During the week in the end, when they become segregated they either continue to stay segregated or they desegregate themselves. These students never fail the test of desegregating themselves.

Each camp reacts differently to the segregation. Some break it and integrate to the camp. Some stay segregated until one specific student speaks up.

I hope you have learned a thing or two about this great organization that [...] for years. I'm sure that Anytown will be around for the future, helping our youth [...] diversity, and understand each other. Jared Cohan, an Anytown alumni, quotes, "[...] achieve wonders by helping one person—an individual. Then that individual passes t[...] to another and so on and so on." This is the power Anytown has, changing the world o[...] at a time.

QUESTIONS FOR ANALYSIS AND DISCUSSION   MindTap™

You can answer these questions and see my responses to them online via your Online Resources for Chapter 15.

1. Did Enriques Ruiz effectively capture your attention at the beginning of his speech?

2. Did the preview forecast coverage adequately?

3. Did he provide effective and ethical evidence to support his ideas?

4. Were there good transitions between main points?

5. Did the conclusion summarize main points in the speech?

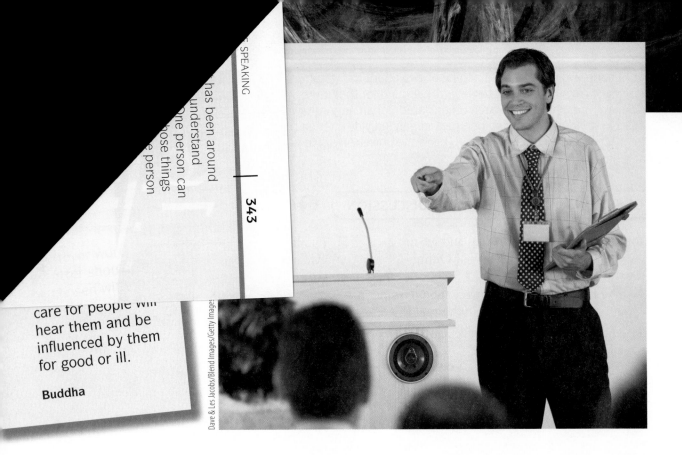

Dave & Les Jacobs/Blend Images/Getty Images

...has been around
...understand
...One person can
...hose things
...e person

care for people will hear them and be influenced by them for good or ill.

Buddha

Persuasive Speaking

- You need to persuade a group of medical students to practice active listening with patients.
- As the coach of a soccer team, you want to persuade the teenage players not to experiment with drugs.
- You want members of your fraternity to commit to a community service project.
- You want to convince the town council not to build a commercial center on the edge of your neighborhood.

MindTap

Review the chapter **Learning Objectives** and **Start** with a quick warm up activity.

Although most of us won't give persuasive speeches regularly, nearly all of us will do so at times. In some cases, we'll be asked to make persuasive presentations. For instance, your manager might want you to persuade a potential client that your firm can provide the best

SHARPEN **YOUR SKILL**

At the end of this chapter, refer to the Sharpen Your Skill features, Using the Motivated Sequence Pattern and Deciding Whether to Present One or Two Sides, to apply concepts from Chapter 16.

service. In other cases, your values and commitments will compel you to speak in an effort to persuade others to ideas or actions that you think are right or desirable.

This chapter focuses on persuasive speaking. As you'll discover, much of what you've learned in previous chapters applies to persuasive speaking. Building on that knowledge, in this chapter we'll begin by defining persuasive speaking. Second, we'll discuss three pillars of persuasion and ways to build your credibility as a speaker. Next, we'll identify organizational patterns that are particularly effective for persuasive speeches. Fourth, we'll identify guidelines for effective persuasive speaking.

UNDERSTANDING PERSUASIVE SPEAKING MindTap™

Read, highlight and take notes online.

Persuasive speeches aim to change others by prompting them to think, feel, believe, or act differently. You may want to change people's attitudes toward policies, candidates for office, or groups of people. You may want to alter the strength of others' attitudes for or against particular issues. You may want to convince others to use seat belts, donate blood, or volunteer for community service. In each case, your goal is persuasive: You aim to change the people with whom you speak.

HEALTH COMMUNICATION

The Persuasive Campaign for Designated Drivers

Have you ever been a designated driver? Have you ever been driven home by a designated driver? Today, most of us are familiar with the idea of a designated driver, but that wasn't always the case. In 1988, the Harvard School of Public Health launched the Harvard Alcohol Project, an intensive persuasive campaign to diffuse the concept of designated driver through American society. A pioneering venture, the Harvard Alcohol Project was the first time that a health organization partnered with mass media communication specialists (Harvard Alcohol, 2012).

The campaign began when Harvard convinced writers for top-rated television programs to weave references to "designated driver" into characters' dialogue, making them part of story lines. This was designed to influence viewers' perceptions of appropriate behavior and to model the specific behaviors of asking for and serving as a designated driver.

Simultaneous with the introduction of the term into prime-time television shows, Harvard asked ABC, CBS, and NBC to air public service announcements encouraging the use of designated drivers. This was another first: the first time the three major networks simultaneously aired a public service campaign's messages.

By 1991, the term *designated driver* was added to *Merriam-Webster's Collegiate Dictionary*, signaling its widespread usage. Also in 1991, a Roper poll showed that nine of ten respondents in the United States knew about the designated driver program and rated it favorably.

When Harvard launched the campaign in 1988, annual fatalities attributed to drivers under the influence of alcohol were 23,626. By 1994, annual fatalities were 16,580, a decline of 30% in 6 years.

In thinking about persuasive speaking, it's important to keep three characteristics in mind. First, like all other communication, persuasive speaking involves multiple communicators. The transactional model of communication we discussed in Chapter 1 is as relevant to persuasive speaking as it is to other kinds of communication. Effective persuasion is not something speakers do to listeners. Instead, it is engagement between a speaker and listeners. Although the speaker may be in the spotlight, the listeners are part of effective persuasive speaking, from planning to delivery. Speakers should consider listeners' experiences, expectations, values, and attitudes as they plan, research and present speeches.

Second, remember that persuasion is not coercion or force. The great rhetorical scholar Aristotle distinguished between what he called inartistic proofs and artistic proofs. An inartistic proof requires no art or skill on our part. We don't have to consider or respect others to get what we want using inartistic proofs. For instance, if you hold a gun to someone's head and say, "Give me your money or I'll shoot you," you may get the money. In that sense, you've been effective in getting the money (although you might wind up in jail). However, you haven't been artistic, and you haven't engaged in persuasion. To do that, you would need to use reasons and words to motivate, not force, the other person to do what you want. Persuasion relies on artistic, not inartistic, proofs.

Third, persuasive impact usually is gradual and incremental. Although people's positions occasionally change abruptly, usually we move gradually toward new ideas, attitudes, and actions. When we hear a persuasive speech, we compare its message with our experience and knowledge. If the speaker offers strong arguments, good evidence, and coherent organization, we may shift our attitudes or behaviors to some degree. If we later encounter additional persuasion, we may shift our attitudes further.

Because persuasion tends to happen gradually and incrementally, speakers should understand the attitudes and behaviors of listeners and adapt their persuasive goals accordingly. For example, assume you believe that the role of the electoral college in national elections should be abandoned, and you want to persuade others to your point of view. How would an effective persuasive speech differ if you knew in advance that listeners strongly favored the current electoral college system or if you knew that they already had reservations about it?

In the first case, it would be unrealistic and ineffective to try to persuade listeners to support abolition of the electoral college. A more realistic

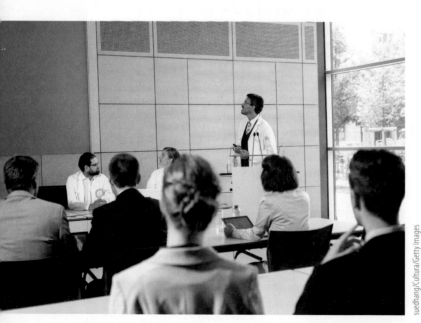

suedhang/Cultura/Getty Images

Most people engage in persuasive speaking during their lives.

speaking purpose would be to persuade listeners that there are some disadvantages to the current electoral system. In this instance, you would be effective if you could reduce the strength of their position favoring the electoral college. Because the second group of listeners already has reservations, you can build on those and lead them closer to supporting abolition of the electoral college.

THE THREE PILLARS OF PERSUASION

Teachers in ancient Greece and Rome understood that effective speaking, especially persuasive speaking, is essential to democratic societies. These ancient teachers recognized three pillars of persuasion, which are also called three forms of proof, or reasons people are persuaded: These are *ethos*, *pathos*, and *logos* (Kennedy, 1991). Although these three forms of proof are also important in other kinds of speaking, they assume special prominence when we engage in persuasion (Figure 16.1).

Ethos

Ethos refers to the perceived personal character of the speaker. We are more likely to believe the words of people whom we trust. We tend to attribute high ethos to people if we perceive that

- they have integrity
- they can be trusted
- they have goodwill toward us
- they know what they are talking about
- they are committed to the topic (show enthusiasm, dynamism)

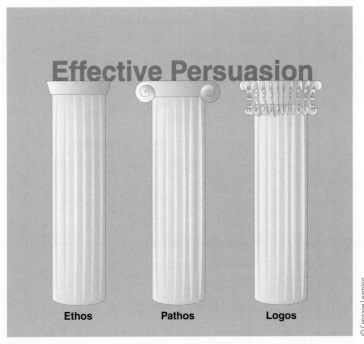

FIGURE 16.1
The Three Pillars of Persuasion.

Listeners will have confidence in you and your words if they think you care about their welfare, are trustworthy, have relevant expertise, care about your topic, and have good character (Stiff, 1994). Conversely, listeners are likely not to place confidence in speakers they think are uninformed, uninvolved with the topic, untrustworthy, manipulative, or otherwise of poor character.

CARL *Last year, I had a teacher who didn't know anything about the subject. She made a lot of really vague statements, and when we tried to pin her down on specifics, she would blow off hot air—saying nothing at all. Nobody in the class thought she had any credibility.*

Because ethos is critical to persuasive impact, you should do what you can to demonstrate to your listeners that you are of good character. Table 16.1 identifies specific ways that you can influence listeners' perceptions of your ethos.

Pathos

Pathos refers to emotional reasons for attitudes, beliefs, or actions. Logic is not the only thing that affects what we believe. We are also influenced by appeals to our passions, fears, love, compassion, and so forth. Emotional proofs address the more subjective reasons for our beliefs in people, ideas, causes, and courses of action.

In preparing your persuasive presentation, develop ways to help your listeners not just to understand your ideas but also to feel a certain way about

Table 16.1	**Demonstrating Ethos**
Dimensions of Ethos	**Ways to Demonstrate**
Goodwill	Identify common ground between you and listeners.
	Show respect for listeners' attitudes and experiences.
	Show that what you're saying will benefit them.
Expertise	Provide strong support for your claims.
	Document sources of support.
	Address concerns about or objections to your position.
	Demonstrate personal knowledge of the topic.
Trustworthiness	Use supporting materials ethically.
	Address other points of view fairly.
	Demonstrate that you care about your listeners.
Dynamism	Use appropriate volume and vocal emphasis.
	Assume a confident posture.
	Use gestures and kinesics to enhance forcefulness.
	Be energetic in presentation.

Table 16.2	Enhancing Pathos

Ways to Enhance Pathos in Persuasive Speaking	Example
Personalize the issue, problem, or topic.	Include detailed examples. Tell stories that give listeners a sense of being in situations, experiencing problems. Translate statistics to make them interesting and personal.
Appeal to listeners' needs and values.	Show how your position satisfies listeners' needs, is consistent with their values. Use examples familiar to listeners to tie your ideas to their values and experiences. Show listeners how doing or believing what you advocate helps them live up to their values. Include quotations from people whom listeners respect.
Bring material alive.	Use visual aids to give listeners a vivid, graphic understanding of your topic. Use striking quotes from people involved with your topic. Use active, concrete language to paint verbal pictures.

them. You may want them to feel outraged about an injustice, compelled to help others, or afraid of a policy or possibility. Appealing to feelings such as these may enhance the persuasive impact of your speech. Table 16.2 shows particular ways to enhance pathos.

> **MELANIE** *Last night, I saw an ad on television that asked viewers to help children who were starving in other countries. At first, I paid attention, but it just went over the top. The pictures were so heartbreaking that I just couldn't watch. I felt disgusted and guilty and mainly, what I really felt was turned off.*

As Melanie notes, appeals to emotions are powerful—and dangerous. They can easily alienate listeners instead of involving them. Fear and guilt are uncomfortable emotions, so speakers should be cautious in arousing them. You may want your listeners to fear what will happen if they don't do what you advocate, but you don't want them to be so overwhelmed by fear that they quit listening to you. Also, fear appeals can decrease a speaker's ethos if listeners are skeptical of the claimed dangers.

Generally, it's more effective to encourage listeners to do something they will feel good about (e.g., send money to help starving children overseas) than to berate them for what they are or aren't doing (e.g., living well themselves while others starve).

Logos

The third reason for belief is **logos,** which is rational or logical proof. In persuasive speeches, logical proofs are arguments, reasoning, and evidence to support claims.

Forms of Reasoning   Most reasoning can be classified as one or the other of two basic forms. **Inductive reasoning** begins with specific examples and uses them to draw a general conclusion (Faigley & Selzer, 2000). Suppose you want to present a speech arguing that climate change is damaging our environment. To reason inductively, you would start by citing specific places where global climate change has demonstrable impact and document the harm in each case. Then you would advance the general conclusion that global climate change threatens life on our planet.

Deductive reasoning begins with a broad claim that listeners accept. Following this, the speaker then offers a specific claim. The conclusion follows from the general claim combined with the specific claim. Reasoning deductively, you would start by stating a commonly accepted claim (i.e., "Climate change is having a negative impact on the world") and then advance a specific claim (i.e., "Our region is part of the world"). From these two claims, it naturally follows that "Climate change is having negative impact on our region" (your conclusion).

The Toulmin Model   Another way to think about reasoning was originated by philosopher Stephen Toulmin (1958; Toulmin, Rieke, & Janik, 1984). Toulmin said that logical reasoning consists of three primary components: claims, grounds for the claims, and warrants that connect the claims to the grounds for them. In addition to these three basic parts of logical reasoning, Toulmin's model includes qualifiers and rebuttals. Figure 16.2 shows the **Toulmin model of reasoning.**

The first component of Toulmin's model is the **claim,** which is an assertion. For instance, you might advance this claim: "The death penalty does not deter crime."

To give persuasive impact to a claim, you need to provide some *grounds* for believing it. **Grounds** are evidence or data that support the claim. For example, you might cite statistics showing that crime did not diminish when some states enacted the death penalty or that crime did not rise when other states repealed the death penalty.

Consider a second example. You assert, or claim, that global climate change is harming the planet. Grounds, or evidence, to support that claim might include statistics to document the occurrence of global climate change, detailed examples of people whose lives have been negatively affected by changes in the earth's temperature, the testimony of credible scientists, and photos that show changes over time. All these kinds of evidence support your claim that global climate change harms the planet.

Grounds are necessary to support claims. However, they aren't sufficient; the grounds must be justified. That justification is a **warrant**—an explanation of the relevance of the grounds to the claim. You've probably heard the word *warrant* in connection with law enforcement. If a police officer wants to search

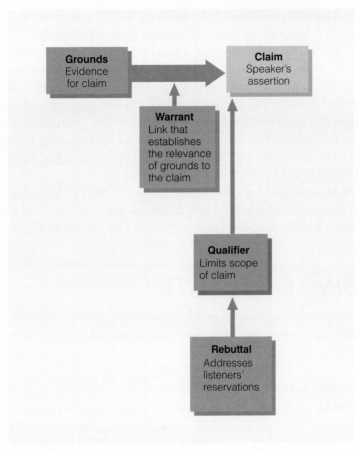

FIGURE 16.2
The Toulmin Model
of Reasoning

© Cengage Learning

the home of Pat Brown, the officer must obtain a search warrant from a judge. The officer shows the judge evidence suggesting that Brown has engaged in criminal activity. If the judge agrees that the evidence links Brown to criminal activity, a search warrant is issued. However, if the judge thinks the evidence is insufficient to link Brown to criminal activity, a warrant is not issued. Warrants operate the same way in persuasive speaking. If listeners perceive your evidence as relevant to and supportive of the claim, they're likely to believe your claim.

Let's return to a previous example. To support your claim that the death penalty does not deter crime, you provide statistics showing that crime rates did not increase when certain states repealed the death penalty. If the statistics were compiled by the Department of Justice, your listeners may perceive them as justifying the claim. On the other hand, if the statistics were compiled by an organization that opposes the death penalty, your listeners might perceive the source of the evidence as biased and therefore untrustworthy. In that case, listeners might decide that there was no warrant to justify linking the evidence to the claim.

A **qualifier** is a word or phrase that limits the scope of your claim. "Everyone can be rehabilitated" is a very broad claim—so broad that it is difficult to support. A more supportable claim would be qualified: "Some people who commit crimes can be rehabilitated." The qualified claim is more supportable.

Finally, Toulmin's model includes **rebuttal**, which anticipates and addresses reservations that listeners are likely to have about claims. Speakers demonstrate respect for listeners by acknowledging and addressing their reservations.

In our example, the speaker might realize that listeners could say to themselves, "The death penalty may not deter all crimes, but it deters serious crimes like homicide." If the speaker has reason to think listeners may resist the claim on this basis, the speaker would offer a rebuttal to the reservation. It would be effective for the speaker to cite the *New York Times* 2012 investigative report that shows that since 1976, states without the death penalty have had homicide rates no higher than those of states with the death penalty.

Careful reasoning and good evidence allow you to offer logical appeals that are sound, effective, and ethical. Later in this chapter, we'll discuss some of the most common kinds of logical fallacies so that you can avoid them when you make persuasive presentations.

BUILDING CREDIBILITY

We've already introduced the term *ethos* and noted its importance to effectiveness in persuasive speaking. Now, we want to consider ethos in more depth because of its critical role in persuasion.

Understanding Credibility

Another word for ethos is **credibility**, which a speaker earns by convincing listeners that he or she has integrity and goodwill toward them and can be trusted. Notice that credibility is tied to listeners' perceptions of a speaker. This means that credibility doesn't reside in the speaker. Instead, it is conferred or withheld by listeners.

COMMUNICATION HIGHLIGHT

Goodwill and Credibility

More than 2,000 years ago, the Greek rhetorician Aristotle wrote that a speaker's credibility depended on listeners' perceptions of the speaker's intelligence, character, and goodwill. Since Aristotle's time, research has established empirical support for strong links between credibility and perceived intelligence and character. But what about goodwill?

In a 1999 investigation, Jim McCroskey and Jason Teven found that perceived goodwill is positively linked to perceptions of likableness and believability. In other words, when listeners think a speaker cares about them and has ethical intentions toward them, they are likely to trust and like the speaker. The practical implication of this study is that speakers who want to be judged credible should establish goodwill toward listeners.

According to McCroskey and Teven (1999), goodwill tends to be established in three ways: showing understanding of listeners' ideas, feelings, and needs; demonstrating empathy, or identification, with listeners' feelings; and being responsive to listeners while speaking.

SOYANA   *The greatest teacher I ever had taught a class in government policies and practices. Before coming to campus, he had been an adviser to three presidents. He had held a lot of different offices in government, so what he was teaching us was backed up by personal experience. Everything he said had so much more weight than what I hear from professors who've never had any practical experience.*

Credibility arises from the three pillars of persuasion: ethos, pathos, and logos. Listeners are likely to find speakers credible if they demonstrate their personal integrity, establish emotional meaning for their topics, and present ideas logically and with good evidence.

Types of Credibility

Credibility is not static; it can change in the course of communication (Figure 16.3). Have you ever attended a public speech by someone you respected greatly and found the presentation disappointing? Did you think less of the speaker after the speech than before it? Have you ever gone to a presentation without knowing much about the speaker and found it so impressive that you changed an attitude or behavior? If so, then you know from personal experience that credibility can increase or decrease as a result of a speech.

Developing Credibility

Initial Credibility   Some speakers have high **initial credibility**, which is the expertise and trustworthiness recognized by listeners before a presentation begins. Initial credibility is based on titles, positions, experiences, or achievements that are known to listeners before they hear a speech. For example, most listeners would grant Secretary of State John Kerry high credibility on foreign affairs. A former inmate of a state prison would have high initial credibility in a speech on prison conditions.

Derived Credibility   In addition to initial credibility, speakers may also gain **derived credibility**, which is the expertise and trustworthiness that listeners

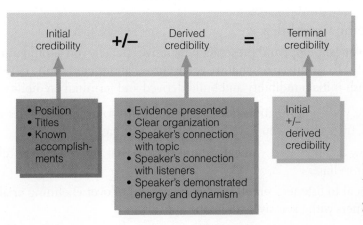

© Cengage Learning

FIGURE 16.3
Developing Credibility

A majority of Americans perceive Michelle Obama as highly credible on issues involving children.

confer on speakers as a result of how speakers communicate during presentations. Speakers earn derived credibility by organizing ideas clearly and logically, by including convincing and interesting evidence that connects with listeners, and by speaking dynamically. Speakers who are not well known tend not to have high initial credibility, so they must derive credibility from the quality of their presentations.

Terminal Credibility   The credibility of speaker at the end of a presentation is **terminal credibility**. It is the cumulative expertise, goodwill, and trustworthiness listeners attribute to a speaker—a combination of initial and derived credibility. Terminal credibility may be greater or less than initial credibility, depending on how effectively a speaker has communicated.

Enhancing Credibility

As you plan, develop, and present a persuasive speech, you should aim to earn credibility. To summarize what we've discussed about credibility, here are ways to establish initial credibility and build derived and terminal credibility:

- State your qualifications for speaking on this topic: experiences you have had, titles or jobs you have held, research you have done.
- Show listeners that you care about them—that your speech is relevant to their welfare.
- Appeal to listeners' emotions, but be careful of overwhelming or alienating listeners with excessively dramatic appeals.

- Reason carefully, and avoid reasoning fallacies.
- Use effective, ethical supporting materials.
- Communicate both verbally and nonverbally that you care about the topic and are involved with it.
- Respond to questions fairly and with an open mind.

ORGANIZING SPEECHES FOR PERSUASIVE IMPACT

In Chapter 14, we discussed ways to organize speeches. The principles you learned in that chapter apply to persuasive speaking:

- Your introduction should capture listeners' attention, provide a clear thesis statement, establish your credibility, and preview your speech.
- Your conclusion should summarize main points and end with a strong closing statement.
- You should provide internal summaries of main points.
- You should provide smooth transitions between the parts of your speech.
- The body of your speech should be organized to reinforce your thesis and show listeners how your ideas cohere.

To build on these general principles for organizing speeches, we want to focus on special organizational concerns relevant to persuasive speaking. We will discuss two topics: the motivated sequence pattern, which is particularly well adapted to persuasive goals, and the relative merits of one-sided and two-sided presentations.

The Motivated Sequence Pattern

Any of the organizational patterns that we discussed in Chapter 14 can be used to structure persuasive speeches. Table 16.3 shows how each of the eight patterns we discussed could support a persuasive thesis.

In addition to the eight patterns we have already discussed, there is a ninth structure that can be highly effective in persuasive speaking. In the 1930s, public speaking scholar Alan Monroe developed the **motivated sequence pattern** for organizing speeches (Monroe, 1935). It has proven quite effective in diverse communication situations (Gronbeck, McKerrow, Ehninger, & Monroe, 1994; Jaffe, 2007). The primary reason for the effectiveness of the motivated sequence pattern is that it follows a natural pattern of human thought by gaining listeners' attention, demonstrating a need, offering a solution, and then helping them visualize and act on the solution. This pattern progressively increases listeners' motivation and personal involvement with a problem and its solution. The motivated sequence pattern includes five sequential steps, summarized in Table 16.4.

In the first step, listeners' attention is drawn to the subject. Here, a speaker makes a dramatic opening statement (e.g., "Imagine this campus with no trees whatsoever"), shows the personal relevance of the topic (e.g., "The air you are

Table 16.3	Organizing for Persuasion

Lloyd Bennett works for a public relations firm that wants to convince Casual Cruise Lines to become a client. Lloyd could use any of the eight basic organizational patterns to structure his speech to persuade the cruise line to hire his firm.

Pattern	Thesis and Main Points
Time	Our firm can move Casual Cruise Lines into the future.
	I. Originally, Casual Cruise Lines attracted customers whose average age was 58.
	II. In recent years, that customer base has shrunk.
	III. To thrive in the years ahead, Casual Cruise Lines needs to appeal to younger customers.
Spatial	Our proposal focuses on redesigning the space on cruise ships to appeal to the 30-to 45-year-old market.
	I. In the staterooms, we propose replacing the conventional seafaring motif with abstract, modernistic art.
	II. In the public area of the lower deck, we propose replacing the current coffee shops with sushi and espresso bars and adding fitness rooms.
	III. On the upper deck, we propose building hot tubs beside the pool.
Topical	Our firm has the most experience advertising cruise lines and the most innovative staff.
	I. Our firm has increased revenues for three other cruise lines.
	II. Our firm has won more awards for innovation and creativity than the other firms Casual Cruise Lines is considering for this account.
Star	Let's consider how younger customers might be attracted if we revamped ship décor, activities, and cuisine.
	I. Younger customers like modern décor.
	II. Younger customers want youthful activities.
	III. Younger customers want trendy food.
Wave	The theme we propose is: "No shuffleboard and no kids—Casual Cruise Lines."
	I. If you're too young for shuffleboard, you're ready for Casual Cruise.
	II. If you're too old to babysit, you're ready for Casual Cruise.
Comparative	Casual Cruise Lines needs to adapt to younger customers whose needs and interests differ from those of older customers.
	I. We recommend 3-, 5-, and 7-day cruises because, although older people have the time for extended cruises, 30-to 45-year-olds can usually spare only a week or less at a time.

continued

	II. Casual Cruise Lines should get rid of bingo and shuffle-board and add dancing and nightclubs, which are favorite leisure activities of 30-to 45-year-olds.
	III. We recommend adding 24-hour espresso bars and onboard fitness rooms to meet the preferences of 30-to 45-year-olds.
Problem–solution	We have a solution to Casual Cruise Lines' inability to attract younger customers.
	I. Casual Cruise Lines hasn't been able to get a substantial share of the lucrative 30-to 45-year-old market.
	II. Our advertising campaign specifically targets this market.
Cause–effect	The advertising campaign we propose will attract young, affluent customers by appealing to their interests and lifestyles.
	I. Our proposal's emphasis on luxury features of the cruise caters to this market's appreciation of extravagance.
	II. Our proposal to feature adults-only cruises caters to this market's demonstrated preferences.
	III. Our proposal to offer 2-day to 4-day cruises meets this market's interest in long weekend getaways.

Table 16.4	The Motivated Sequence Pattern

1. **Attention:** Focus listeners' attention.
2. **Need:** Demonstrate that a real problem exists.
3. **Satisfaction:** Propose a solution to the demonstrated problem.
4. **Visualization:** Give listeners a vision of the impact of the solution.
5. **Action:** Ask listeners to think, feel, or act to bring the proposed solution into being.

breathing right now exists only because we have trees"), or otherwise captures listeners' attention.

The second step establishes need with evidence and reasoning that a real and serious problem exists (e.g., "Acid rain is slowly but surely destroying the trees of this planet"). Next is the satisfaction step, in which a speaker recommends a solution (e.g., "Stronger environmental regulations and individual efforts to use environmentally safe products can protect trees and thus the oxygen we breathe"). The fourth step, visualization, increases listeners' commitment to the solution identified in the satisfaction step by helping them imagine the results that would follow from adopting the recommended solution (e.g., "You will have ample air to breathe, and so will your grandchildren. Moreover, we'll all have the beauty of trees to enrich our lives").

Speech Builder Express, which you can access via your MindTap for *Communication in Our Lives*, includes extensive prompts and a clear framework for organizing and developing speeches that incorporate a variety of persuasive strategies.

 MindTap

Finally, speakers move to the action step, which involves a direct appeal for concrete action on the part of listeners (e.g., "Refuse to buy or use any aerosol products," "Sign this petition that I am sending to our senators in Washington, D.C."). The action step calls on listeners to take action to bring about the solution the speaker helped them visualize.

VELMA *I've heard a lot of speeches on discrimination, but the most effective I ever heard was Cindy's in class last week. Other speeches I've heard focused on the idea that discrimination is wrong, but that's something I already believe, so they weren't helpful. Cindy, on the other hand, told me how to do something about discrimination. She showed me how I could act on what I believe.*

Velma's commentary explains why the motivated sequence pattern is especially suited to persuasive speaking: It goes beyond identifying a problem and recommending a solution. In addition, it intensifies listeners' desire for a solution by helping them visualize what it would mean and gains their active commitment to being part of the solution. When listeners become personally involved with an idea and with taking action, they are more enduringly committed. To read tips and see a sample speech using the motivated sequence patterns, go to **WebLink 16.1**. http://www.sanjuan.edu/webpages/mikeberry/speech.cfm?subpage=66682

One-Sided and Two-Sided Presentations

Perhaps you are wondering whether it's more effective to present only your own point of view or both sides of an issue in a persuasive speech. That's an important question, and it's one that communication scholars have studied in depth.

Research conducted to discover whether one-sided or two-sided presentations are more effective tell us that it depends on the particular audience a speaker addresses, which reminds us again that audience analysis and adaptation are critical to effective public speaking. Specifically, deciding whether to present one or both sides of an issue depend on the particular listeners' expectations, attitudes, and knowledge.

Listeners' Expectations As we've noted before, effective speakers always try to learn what listeners expect so they don't fail to meet expectations. In educational settings, listeners are likely to expect speakers to discuss more than one side of an issue (Lasch, 1990). On the other hand, at campaign rallies, candidates are generally expected to present only their own views. Expectations may also be shaped by prespeech publicity. Imagine that you decide to attend a speech after seeing a flyer for a presentation on the pros and cons of requiring students to purchase computers. You might be irritated if the speaker presented only the pros or only the cons of the proposed requirement.

Listeners' Attitudes It makes a difference whether listeners are likely to be favorably disposed toward your ideas (Griffin, 2012). If they already favor your position, you may not need to discuss alternative positions in depth. However, if listeners favor a position different from yours, then it's essential to acknowledge and deal with their views. If your listeners oppose what you propose, it's unlikely that you will persuade them to abandon their position and adopt yours. With an audience hostile to your views, it's more reasonable to try to lessen their hostility to your ideas or to diminish the strength of their commitment to their present position (Trenholm, 1991).

Failure to consider listeners' opposing ideas diminishes a speaker's credibility because listeners may assume that the speaker either is uninformed about another side or is informed but trying to manipulate them by not discussing it. Either conclusion lessens credibility and the potential for impact on listeners. Speakers have an ethical responsibility to give respectful consideration to listeners' ideas and positions. Doing so encourages reciprocal respect from listeners for the ideas you present. R. J.'s commentary illustrates this.

> **R. J.**   *In my ROTC unit, there's a lot of bad will toward the idea of gays in the military. Some of the guys have really strong feelings against it, so I was interested in what would happen at a required seminar last week with a guest speaker who was arguing that gays should be allowed in the services. He was really good! He spent the first 10 minutes talking about all of the concerns, fears, and reasons why officers and enlisted personnel disapprove of having gays in the military, and he showed a lot of respect for those reasons. Then he presented his own ideas and showed how they answered most of the concerns people had. I won't say everyone was persuaded 100% that gays should be allowed in, but I will say he managed to get a full hearing with a group that I thought would just turn him off from the word go. Since he talked to us, I've heard some of the guys saying that maybe gays wouldn't be a problem.*

Listeners' Knowledge   What an audience already knows or believes about a topic should influence decisions on whether to present one or more sides of an issue. Listeners who are well informed about a topic are likely to be aware of more than one side, so your credibility will be enhanced if you include all sides in your presentation (Jackson & Allen, 1990). Also, highly educated listeners tend to realize that most issues have more than one side, so they may be suspicious of speakers who present only one point of view.

In some instances, speakers know that later on listeners will be exposed to *counterarguments*—arguments that oppose those of a speaker. In such cases, it's advisable to inoculate listeners. **Inoculation** in persuasion is similar to inoculation in medicine. Vaccines give us limited exposure to diseases so that we won't contract them later. Similarly, persuasive inoculation "immunizes" listeners in advance against opposing ideas and arguments they may encounter in the future. If listeners later hear the other side, they have some resistance to arguments that oppose your position (Kiesler & Kiesler, 1971). For example, in political campaigns, candidates often make statements such as this: "Now, my opponent will tell you that we don't need to raise taxes, but I want to show you why that's wrong." By identifying and dispelling the opposing candidate's ideas in advance, the speaker inoculates listeners against an opponent's ideas.

Research indicates that generally the most persuasive strategy is to present both sides and refute arguments for the other side (Allen et al., 1990).

There is no quick and easy formula for deciding whether to present one-sided or two-sided discussions of a topic. Like most aspects of public speaking, this decision involves judgment on the speaker's part. That judgment should be informed by ethical considerations of what listeners have a right to know and what content is necessary to represent the issues fairly. In addition, judgments of whether to present more than one side should take into account listeners' expectations, attitudes, and knowledge and the likelihood that listeners have been or will be exposed to opposing arguments.

GUIDELINES FOR EFFECTIVE PERSUASIVE SPEECHES

In this chapter, we've already discussed some guidelines for effective persuasive speaking. For instance, we discussed the importance of developing a speech that includes the three pillars of persuasion: ethos, pathos, and logos. We also emphasized the importance of speaker credibility, and we identified specific ways to build yours when you speak. We extended our previous discussion of organizing speeches to discuss the motivated sequence pattern and the merits of presenting one or two sides of arguments. In addition to these guidelines, three other principles are important for effective persuasive speaking.

Create Common Ground With Listeners

In any communication context, common ground is important. That general principle has heightened importance in persuasive speaking. A persuasive speaker tries to move listeners to a point of view or action. It makes sense that they will be more likely to move with the speaker if they perceive some common ground with him or her. Listeners may think, "If we share all of these values and concerns, then maybe I should rethink my position on this one issue we disagree on."

Kenneth Burke (1950), a distinguished theorist of language, believed that communication as the primary way that people transcend their divisions and enlarge what is common to them. Burke saw finding common ground as a process of **identification**, or recognizing and enlarging commonalities between communicators.

Effective persuasive speakers seek out similarities between themselves and their listeners and bring those similarities into listeners' awareness. A few years ago, a student of mine wanted to persuade his listeners that fraternities are positive influences on members' lives. From polling students on campus, Steve knew that many held negative stereotypes of "frat men." He reasoned that most of his listeners, who did not belong to Greek groups, would be likely to view him both negatively and as different from them. This is how he established common ground in opening his speech:

> You've probably heard a lot of stories about wild fraternity parties and "frat men" who spend most of their time drinking, partying, and harassing pledges. I confess, I've done all of that as a brother in Delta Sigma

Phi. I've also spent every Sunday for the last semester volunteering in the Big Brother Program that helps underprivileged kids in the city. And I've built friendships with brothers that will last my entire life. Like many of you, I felt a little lost when I first came to this campus. I wanted to find a place where I belonged at college. Like you, I want to know people and be involved with projects that help me grow as a person. For me, being in a fraternity has done that.

This is an effective opening. Steve began by showing listeners that he realized they might hold some negative views of fraternity men. He went further and acknowledged that he personally fit some of those stereotypes. But then Steve challenged the adequacy of the stereotypes by offering some information that didn't fit with them. Volunteering as a Big Brother isn't part of the "party guy" image. Having recognized and challenged stereotypes his listeners were likely to hold, Steve then began to create common ground. Most of his listeners could remember feeling lost when they first came to college. Most of them could identify with wanting to belong and to grow as people. Steve's opening successfully identified similarities between himself and his listeners, so they were open to considering his argument that fraternities are valuable.

Adapt to Listeners

A good persuasive speech is not designed for just anyone. Instead, it is adapted to specific listeners' knowledge, attitudes, motives, experiences, values, and expectations. The methods of audience analysis that we discussed in Chapter 12 should help you learn what your listeners know, believe, and expect in relation to your topic.

As a speaker, your job is to apply what you learn about your listeners as you develop and present your speech. In his speech on the values of fraternities, Steve adapted to his listeners by showing that he understood common stereotypes of "frat men" and that there was some truth to them. This enhanced Steve's credibility and his listeners' willingness to open their minds to what he had to say.

In 1998, Raymond W. Smith, chairperson of Bell Atlantic, spoke about hate speech on the Internet. Smith spoke at the Simon Wiesenthal Center, which is dedicated to human rights (Smith, 1998). Although Smith spoke against censoring hate speech on the Internet, he realized that his largely Jewish listeners had acute knowledge of the dangers of hate speech. In his opening remarks Smith said,

Neo-Nazis and extremists of every political stripe who once terrorized people in the dead of night with burning crosses and painted swastikas are now sneaking up on the public—especially our kids—through the World Wide Web.

Although Smith went on to argue against censorship, he let his listeners know that he was well aware of hate speech and the harms it can cause. Within his speech, Smith further adapted to his listeners by quoting Jewish leaders, who had high credibility with listeners.

Knowing that many of his listeners favored censorship, Smith presented a two-sided speech. He began by considering the arguments of those who favor censorship, treating them thoroughly and respectfully. He then turned to the other side (the one he favored): not censoring hate speech on the Internet. Smith argued that censorship will not get to the source of the problem, which is hate. Instead, he said the solution is to teach tolerance and respect. In making this argument, Smith adapted to his listeners at the Wiesenthal Center by saying,

> *While cyberhate cannot be mandated or censored out of existence, it can be countered by creating hundreds of chat lines, home pages, bulletin boards, and websites dedicated to social justice, tolerance, and equality for all people. . . . Moral leadership can have a tremendous impact. Quite simply, we need more Simon Wiesenthal Centers.*

To adapt to his listeners, Smith acknowledged their cultural history, quoted authorities they respected, and thoughtfully considered the argument for censorship. Therefore, his listeners were then willing to give an equally thoughtful hearing to Smith's argument against censorship.

Avoid Fallacious Reasoning

A **fallacy** is an error in reasoning. The word *fallacy* is derived from the Latin word *fallacia*, which means "deceit." Fallacies present false, or flawed, logic. Despite the original meaning, deceit, fallacies may be intentional or unintentional. Either way, they are not effective with educated or thoughtful audiences. They detract from a speaker's credibility because they suggest that the speaker is not ethical. To be effective and ethical, you should avoid using fallacies in your

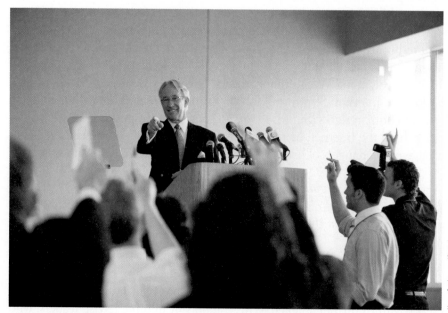

Dynamism enhances a speaker's credibility.

speeches. To be a critical listener, you should be able to recognize fallacies used by others. We'll discuss eight of the most common fallacies in reasoning.

***Ad Hominem* Arguments** In Latin, the word *ad* means "to," and *hominem* means "human being." Thus, ***ad hominem* arguments** are ones that go to the person instead of the idea. It is not ethical to argue for your point of view by attacking the integrity of someone who has taken a stand opposing yours.

"You can't trust what George Boxwood says about the importance of a strong military. After all, he never served a day in the military." Although it may be true that Boxwood didn't serve in the military, that doesn't necessarily discredit his argument about the importance of a strong military. Boxwood may have researched the topic vigorously, interviewed military personnel, and studied historical effects of strong and weak military forces. Boxwood's own service—or lack thereof—is not directly relevant to the quality of his argument for a strong military. Unethical speakers sometimes try to undercut people whose positions oppose their own by attacking the people, not the arguments. Critical listeners recognize this fallacy and distrust speakers who engage in it.

Post Hoc, Ergo Propter Hoc *Post hoc, ergo propter hoc* is a Latin phrase meaning "after this, therefore because of this." Sometimes when one thing follows another, we mistakenly think the first thing caused the second. Unethical speakers sometimes try to persuade us to think that a coincidental sequence is causal. For instance, the U.S. economy faltered and verged on recession after George W. Bush became president. Does that mean Bush and his administration caused the economic slowdown? Not necessarily. To support the claim that Bush caused the economic slowdown, a speaker would need to demonstrate that policies implemented by Bush hurt the economy.

The Bandwagon Appeal When I was a child, I often tried to persuade my parents that I should be allowed to do something because all of my friends were doing it. Invariably, my parents rejected that reason and replied, "If all of your friends jumped off the roof, would you do that?" At the time, that answer exasperated me. But my parents were right. They rejected the **bandwagon appeal**, which argues that because most people believe or act a particular way, you should too. Widely held attitudes are not necessarily correct, as Christopher Columbus and Galileo proved. Thoughtful listeners won't be persuaded to your point of view just because lots of other people have been. It's more ethical and more effective to give them good reasons why they should agree with you.

Slippery Slope The **slippery slope** fallacy claims that once we take the first step, more and more steps inevitably will follow until some unacceptable consequence results. For example, an unethical speaker who wanted to argue against a proposal to restrict logging in a protected environmental area might state, "Restricting logging is only the first step. Next, the environmentalists are likely to want to prohibit any timber cutting. Pretty soon, we won't be able to build homes or furniture." The idea that we won't have lumber to build homes and furniture is extreme. It has little to do with the question of whether we should restrict logging in one particular area.

Hasty Generalization   A **hasty generalization** is a broad claim based on too-limited evidence. It is unethical to assert a broad claim when you have only anecdotal or isolated evidence or instances. Consider two examples of hasty generalizations based on inadequate data:

- Three congressional representatives have had affairs. Therefore, members of Congress are adulterers.
- An environmental group illegally blocked loggers and workers at a nuclear plant. Therefore, environmentalists are radicals who take the law into their own hands.

In each case, the conclusion is based on limited evidence. In each case, the conclusion is hasty and fallacious.

Red Herring Argument   Years ago, fox hunters sometimes dragged a dead herring across the trail of a fox to see whether the dogs would be diverted in the wrong direction (Gass, 1999). They were trying to train the dogs not to let the smell of the herring deflect them from hunting the fox. Speakers who try to deflect listeners from relevant issues engage in **red herring arguments**. They say something that is irrelevant to their topic or that doesn't really respond to a listener's question. The point is to divert the listener from something the speaker can't or doesn't want to address.

Either–Or Logic   What is wrong with the following statement: "Either abolish fraternities on our campus or accept the fact that this is a party school where drinking is more important than learning." The fallacy in this statement is that it implies there are only two options: either get rid of fraternities altogether or allow partying to eclipse academics. Are there no other alternatives? Might it be possible to work with fraternities to establish policies limiting parties to weekends? Might it be possible to increase the quality of academics so that students are motivated to be more involved with learning? In most instances, **either–or logic** is simplistic and fallacious.

Reliance on the Halo Effect   The **halo effect** occurs when we generalize a person's authority or expertise in a particular area to other areas that are irrelevant to the person's experience and knowledge. It is fallacious to think that because a person is knowledgeable on particular topics, he or she is knowledgeable on all topics. William Shatner and Leonard Nimoy, who starred in *Star Trek*, encourage us to use priceline.com. Well-known people appear in the mustache advertisements promoting milk. Are any of these people experts on the products they are urging us to buy and use?

To be effective and ethical, persuasive speakers should avoid fallacies in reasoning (Table 16.5). Likewise, effective critical listeners should be able to detect fallacies in reasoning and to resist being persuaded by them.

To practice identifying fallacies in various statements, complete the activity "Recognizing Fallacies" in your MindTap for *Communication in Our Lives*.

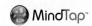 MindTap

Table 16.5	Fallacies in Reasoning
Ad hominem attack	You can't believe what Jane Smith says about voting because she doesn't vote.
Post hoc, ergo propter hoc	The new flextime policy is ineffective because more people have been late getting to work since it went into effect.
Bandwagon appeal	You should be in favor of the new campus meal plan because most students are.
Slippery slope	If we allow students to play a role in decisions about hiring and tenure of faculty, pretty soon students will be running the whole school.
Hasty generalization	People should not be allowed to own Rottweilers because there have been three instances of Rottweilers attacking children.
Either–or	Tenure should be either abolished or kept exactly as it is.
Red herring argument	People who own Rottweilers should own cats instead. Let me tell you why cats are ideal pets.
Reliance on the halo effect	World-famous actor Richard Connery says that we should not restrict people's right to own firearms.

CHAPTER SUMMARY

 Practice and review the content in this chapter.

This chapter focused on persuasive speaking. After noting the many situations in which persuasive speaking occurs, we identified ethos, pathos, and logos and the cornerstones of effective persuasion, and we highlighted ways in which speakers can incorporate each into presentations. Extending this, we discussed credibility, which is especially important in persuasive speaking. We identified three types of credibility—initial, derived, and terminal—and discussed ways in which speakers can build their credibility during the process of planning, developing, and presenting persuasive speeches. The next section of the chapter reviewed general organizational principles and highlighted organizational concerns that are particularly relevant to persuasive speaking.

We introduced the motivated sequence pattern, which can be powerful in moving listeners to accept and act on persuasive appeals. We also discussed the merits of one-sided and two-sided presentations, and we identified criteria for choosing the one that will be most effective in particular situations and with particular listeners.

The last section of the chapter provided guidelines for persuasive speaking. The first is to build common ground between a speaker and a listener. The second is to adapt to particular listeners by tailoring a persuasive speech to their expectations, knowledge, experiences, motives, values, and attitudes. The third is to avoid fallacies in reasoning, which are usually ineffective and always unethical.

APPLYING COMMUNICATION IN OUR LIVES

Communication in Our Lives is supported by a MindTap, a new online learning platform that delivers content, assignments, and a tailored presentation of the course curriculum created by your instructor. MindTap combines all of your learning tools—readings, multimedia, activities and assessments—into a singular learning unit that guides you through the course. Practice and Present, a unique tool within MindTap, allows you to upload your speech video files for practice or for a grade, comment on your peer's speeches and review your grades. MindTap also includes Speech Builder Express, a powerful tool that guides you through the speech outline and preparation process. For more information or to access MindTap, visit cengagebrain.com.

DEFINITIONS OF KEY CONCEPTS

 Review your **Flashcards**.

ad hominem **arguments** Latin for "to the man," arguments that attack the integrity of the person instead of the person's ideas.

bandwagon appeal The fallacious argument that because many people believe or act in a certain way, everyone should.

claim An assertion. A claim advanced in speaking requires grounds (evidence) and warrants (links between evidence and claims).

credibility The perception that a person is informed and trustworthy. Listeners confer it, or refuse to confer it, on speakers.

deductive reasoning A form of reasoning in which a general premise followed by a specific claim establishes a conclusion.

derived credibility The expertise and trustworthiness that listeners attribute to a speaker as a result of how the speaker communicates during a presentation.

either–or logic The fallacy of suggesting or assuming that only two options or courses of action exist when in fact there may be more.

ethos The perceived personal character of the speaker.

fallacy An error in reasoning.

grounds Evidence that supports claims in a speech.

halo effect The tendency to assume that an expert in one area is also an expert in other unrelated areas.

hasty generalization A broad claim based on too few examples or insufficient evidence.

identification The recognition and enlargement of common ground between communicators.

inductive reasoning A form of reasoning that begins with specific instances and forms general conclusions based on them.

initial credibility The expertise and trustworthiness that listeners attribute to a speaker before a presentation begins. Initial credibility is based on the speaker's titles, positions, experiences, or achievements known to listeners before they hear the speech.

inoculation "Immunization" of listeners to opposing ideas and arguments that they may later encounter.

logos Rational or logical proofs.

motivated sequence pattern A pattern for organizing persuasive speeches that consists of five steps: attention, need, satisfaction, visualization, and action.

pathos Emotional proofs for claims.

persuasive speech A presentation that aims to change listeners by prompting them to think, feel, or act differently.

post hoc, ergo propter hoc Latin phrase meaning "After this, therefore because of this." The fallacy of suggesting or assuming that because event B follows event A, event A has therefore caused event B.

qualifier A word or phrase that limits the scope of a claim. Common qualifiers are *most*, *usually*, and *in general*.

rebuttal A response to listeners' reservations about a claim made by a speaker.

red herring argument An argument that is irrelevant to the topic; an attempt to divert attention from something the arguer can't or doesn't want to address.

slippery slope The fallacy of suggesting or assuming that once a certain step is taken, other steps will inevitably follow that will lead to some unacceptable consequence.

terminal credibility The cumulative expertise and trustworthiness listeners attribute to a speaker as a result of the speaker's initial and derived credibility; may be greater or less than initial credibility, depending on how effectively a speaker communicates.

Toulmin model of reasoning A representation of effective reasoning that includes five components: claim, grounds (evidence), warrant (link between grounds and claim), qualifier, and rebuttal.

warrant A justification for grounds (evidence) and claims in persuasive speaking.

FOR FURTHER REFLECTION AND DISCUSSION

 MindTap

 Ethics

1. Reread this chapter's discussion of one-sided and two-sided persuasive speeches. When is it ethical to present only one side of a topic? When is it unethical? In answering this question, remember that ethical considerations are not necessarily the same as strategic ones. A speaker who uses unethical arguments or evidence might be effective in convincing listeners to think or do something.

2. To see and hear famous speeches, go to **WebLink 16.2**.

3. To read an article on the importance of skill in persuasive speaking for top-level positions in business, go to **WebLink 16.3**.

SHARPEN YOUR SKILL MindTap™

1. Using the Motivated Sequence Pattern

Think about how you might organize a speech using the motivated sequence pattern. Write a thesis and five main points for a motivated sequence appeal.

Thesis _____

1. Attention: _____
   _____

2. Need: _____
   _____

3. Satisfaction: _____
   _____

4. Visualization: _____
   _____

5. Action: _____
   _____

2. Deciding Whether to Present One or Two Sides

Apply what you have learned to decide whether you should present one or two sides in your persuasive speech.

1. Are your listeners likely to expect to hear more than one side of the issue?
   _____

   A. How much education do they have?
      _____

   B. Has there been any prespeech publicity?
      _____

   C. Is there any reason to think that listeners do or do not care about hearing both sides? _____

2. What are your listeners' attitudes toward your topic?
   _____

   A. Do they have a position on the topic? If so, is it the same as yours?
      _____

   B. How strongly do listeners hold their opinions on the topic?
      _____

3. What level of knowledge about the topic do your listeners have?
   _____

   A. Do they know about more than one side of the issues?
      _____

   B. How much information about the topic have they already gained?
      _____

4. Are your listeners likely to hear counterarguments after your speech?
   _____

EXPERIENCING COMMUNICATION IN OUR LIVES   MindTap™

CASE STUDY: *Persuasive Speech: No Child Left Behind: Addressing the School Dropout Rate Among Latinos*

© Cengage Learning

A video of the speech described here is featured in your Chapter 16 MindTap for *Communication in Our Lives*. Select "Persuasive Speech" to watch the video of Dana Barker's speech entitled "No Child Left Behind: Addressing the School Dropout Rate Among Latinos." Improve your own public speaking skills by reading, watching, and evaluating this speech.

Dana gave this speech in an introductory public speaking class. The assignment was to give a 4- to 6-minute speech, with a minimum of four sources cited. Students were also asked to create a preparation outline that included a Works Cited section.

I'll begin with a story from the *Santa Fe New Mexican* newspaper about a young woman named Mabel Arellanes. After becoming pregnant and dropping out of school at 16, Mabel has re-enrolled in high school and is now the junior class president. Although her dynamic change in attitude toward education has led her to the hope of becoming a lawyer, Mabel's story is not representative of the current trends among other Latinos. I have been conducting extensive research on trends in the socioeconomic status, graduation rates, and the population of Latinos in the United States. Today I will discuss the problem of the Latino dropout rate from high school and college, as well as provide a solution for addressing this intensifying issue. Let me begin by discussing the problem.

The dropout rate among Latinos in secondary schools and colleges must be addressed. Why? Because the dropout rate is simply excessive. Statistics and first-hand accounts attest to this fact. According to the *News and Observer*, one in twelve Latino students dropped out of high school in North Carolina during the 2003–2004 school year, but this statistic does not account for the 47.5% of Latino students who have not graduated in the four years since the beginning of the 1999–2000 academic year. Gamaliel Fuentes, who dropped out of school at age 15, said, "We have no money; that's why I dropped out of school. [My father] asked me [to stay in school], but I decided. Now, if I could go back in time, I would stay still in school." The tendency for Latinos to drop out is triggered by their generally low socioeconomic status and a lack of family support. The *Hispanic Outlook in Higher Education* explains that students coming from families of lower socioeconomic status are less likely to succeed in college because high schools do not prepare them well. In addition, Latino families expect their teens and young adults to contribute to the family's economic needs, and work schedules often conflict with studies.

Next, I will discuss the importance of addressing the Latino dropout rate. Addressing the dropout rate will keep Latinos from remaining at a generally low economic status. It is no secret that income is heavily dependent on education level. According to the *Daily Evergreen* newspaper, a person with a bachelor's degree is likely to earn almost one million dollars more over their course of their lifetime than someone with no college education. While a census report in the *San Antonio Express-News* found that Latinos earned merely 6.2% of bachelor's degrees awarded in 2001, the U.S. Census Bureau found that Latinos made up 12% of the national population in 2000 and 13.3% in 2002. In her essay, "Canto, Locura, y Poesia," Olivia Castellano, Latina professor at California State University, writes, "[Latinos] carry a deeply ingrained sense of inferiority, a firm conviction that they are not worthy of success." Ultimately, all who hold the belief that our country is the "land of opportunity" are affected by the Latino dropout rate. Again, referencing the 2001 findings of the U.S. Census Bureau, two out of every ten Hispanics live below the poverty line, while only one out of every four earned a yearly salary of $35,000 or more. Comparatively, around 50% of non-Hispanic whites earned $35,000 or more that year. These figures are far from exemplifying opportunity for Latinos.

What will happen if the problem is not solved? Since the percentage of Latinos in our population is still climbing, ignoring this issue will lead to a greater gap between the life of the typical American and the life of the Latino-American. As I proceed to discuss the solutions for this problem, are you beginning to sense the urgency of this situation?

To solve the problem of a high dropout rate, we must fund teacher sensitivity training programs that help Latinos succeed in education, and Latinos must change their perspective on the importance of education and their ability to succeed. Let me first address teacher sensitivity training. Programs that educate teachers about Latino culture and beliefs and that help Latino students succeed in education will have the most impact on the dropout rate. Properly educated teachers will become aware of how they are able to meet the needs of Latino students. For example, the *Santa Fe New Mexican* reported on the success of a program called AVID, which boasts a 95% college entrance rate among its Latino students. This solution, which can be implemented at the national, state, and local levels, is dependent on increased funding and the efforts of educators with experience in Latino culture. Increased funding will help reform educational budgets for Latino communities and fund college success programs like AVID. This solution also requires the collective efforts of highly knowledgeable professionals with experience in education and in Latino culture who can train other educators.

Given proper attention and execution, the plan to address the Latino dropout rate will help the dropout rate begin to fall and will instill pride in the Latino community. Although it will take at least a decade before results are fully apparent, perhaps even a generation, ideally the plan will result in an increase in Latinos earning bachelor's, master's, and doctoral degrees. The sense of accomplishment gained by furthering education will change the typical Latino mindset regarding education and instill an overall sense of pride in the U.S. Latino community.

In summary, today I have discussed the problem of high dropout rate among Latinos, and I have discussed a possible solution for addressing the issue. Hopefully, you can clearly see that the high Latino dropout rate is an issue of great concern, one that requires prompt and thorough attention.

QUESTIONS FOR ANALYSIS AND DISCUSSION   MindTap

You can answer these questions and see my responses to them online via MindTap for Chapter 16.

1. Did Dana provide a strong introduction with an attention device, a clear thesis, and a clear preview?

2. Are the sources of evidence credible? Why or why not? Is there any reason to suspect that the sources are biased?

3. What other kinds of evidence might Dana have used to strengthen the persuasive impact of her message?

4. Did Dana's speech reflect awareness of ethos, pathos, and logos?

5. How did Dana adapt the message to listeners who were 19-to 24-year-old college students? Can you think of additional ways she might have adapted this message to these particular listeners?

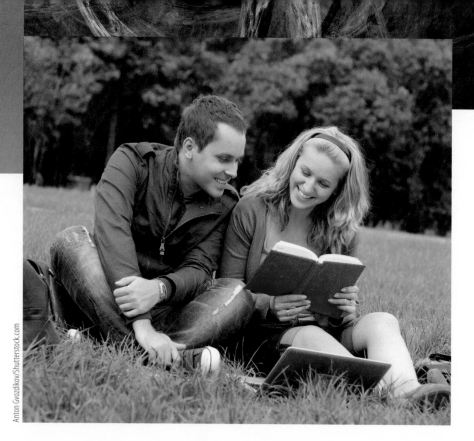

Anton Gvozdikov/Shutterstock.com

Closing: Pulling Ideas Together

Communication is an intricate tapestry woven from the threads of self, others, perceptions, relationships, contexts, culture, climate, listening, and verbal and nonverbal messages. Each thread has its own distinct character, and yet each thread is also woven into the complex, ever-changing tapestry of human communication. We've taken time to discuss each thread in its own right and then explored how it blends with other threads in particular communication situations.

Sometimes a particular thread stands out boldly, as individual threads sometimes do in woven fabric. For instance, the thread of delivery is quite prominent in public speaking, and the thread of listening is less visible. Yet, as we learned, to be effective, speakers must understand and adapt to their listeners because listeners decide how credible a speaker is and how effective public communication can be. Similarly, in personal relationships the thread of climate stands out as particularly important. Yet, the climate we create through our communication is also important in organizational communication and small group work. Thus, even when threads of communication are restrained in particular interactions, they are present and important.

At other times, an individual thread blends so completely with other threads that we don't perceive it as separate from the overall pattern of the tapestry. Organization, for example, is present in interaction between friends as they decide what to talk about and how to sequence the topics. Yet in friends' conversation, the thread of organization is muted, and other threads, such as sensitive listening, stand out. Similarly, the thread of delivery is subdued in casual conversations, yet our communication with friends is affected by how we articulate our ideas—by vocal force, volume, pace, and other aspects of delivery. The many threads that make up the tapestry of communication vary in intensity and prominence from one point in the tapestry to another, yet all are part of the whole.

To conclude our study of the communication tapestry, let's review what we've discussed and what it means for us. The overall goal of this book is to increase your insight into the ways in which communication is an integral part of our everyday lives.

We launched our journey in Chapter 1, which described the range of human communication and the modern academic field that bears its name. Chapter 2 allowed us to delve into the complicated process of perception so that we could understand how perception, thought, and communication interact. We learned that we seldom, if ever, perceive the full, raw reality around us. Instead, we perceive selectively, noticing only some things and overlooking others. The labels we use to name, classify, and evaluate our perceptions reverberate in our consciousness to shape what we perceive and what it means to us. In fact, most of the time, how we think, feel, and act are based less on objective realities in the external world than on how we label our selective perceptions of it. This is normal, yet it can cause us trouble if we forget that we are responding to our labels, not to the world itself. In Chapter 3 we explored the profound ways in which communication shapes personal identity and, in turn, the ways in which our identities shape how we communicate.

Chapters 4 through 6 focused on primary forms of communication: listening, verbal communication, and nonverbal behavior. As we considered each topic, we examined ways to improve our personal effectiveness as communicators. Particularly important to our understanding of these topics is the realization that people differ in their styles of listening and their verbal and nonverbal communication. Awareness of these differences helps us understand others on their terms. The principles and skills we discussed in these chapters should serve you well throughout your life as you seek to interact effectively and sensitively with others in personal, social, and professional contexts.

The elaborate and fascinating relationships between culture and communication were the focus of Chapter 7. There, we unmasked the subtle ways in which communication creates and sustains the beliefs, values, and practices that define cultures and social communities. Equally important, we saw that cultures shape the forms and content of communication by telling us what is and is not important and what are appropriate and inappropriate ways of interacting with others. Understanding differences between cultures and social communities allows us to appreciate the distinct character of each one and to enlarge our own repertoire of communication skills.

The second part of the book extended the first seven chapters by weaving basic communication concepts and skills into interpersonal, group, organizational, and mass communication. In Chapter 8, we explored interpersonal communication in general and as it occurs in friendships and romantic relationships. The intimate bonds that grace our lives are communicative achievements because we create and sustain them largely through interaction and the meanings we assign to it. Communication is the lifeblood of intimacy. In dramatic forms, such as declarations of love and disclosure of secrets, and in everyday small talk, it is communication that continually breathes life and meaning into our relationships with others.

We moved to quite a different context in Chapter 9, which examined communication in small groups. There, we learned what types of communication facilitate and hinder effective group discussion and what communication responsibilities accompany effective membership and leadership. We also studied the standard agenda for problem solving, which gives participants an effective method of organizing group discussion.

Chapter 10 focused on organizational communication, with particular emphasis on how interaction among members of an organization creates an overall culture for the organization. In Chapter 11, we explored mass communication and social media, which permeate our lives. Here we focused on ways to develop critical skills that enhance your media literacy.

Part III of this book concentrated on public speaking. From the early stages of planning presentations, to researching and developing evidence, and finally

Communication skills are a foundation for effectiveness in personal, professional, and social life.

to organizing, outlining, and practicing, public speaking involves skills that most of us already have and use in other communication situations. As is true for all interactions, good public speaking centers on others; the values, interests, knowledge, and beliefs of listeners guide what speakers can and cannot wisely say and how they develop and present their ideas. Effective public speaking, like effective everyday conversation, is a genuine interaction between people in which the views and values of all participants should be taken into account.

Throughout *Communication in Our Lives,* we've seen that people differ in their communication and in the meanings they attach to words and actions. The cornucopia of cultures and social communities in our world gives rise to a fascinating range of communication styles. No single way of communicating is inherently superior to any other; the differences result from diverse cultural heritages and practices.

Learning not to impose our own communication patterns and our culture's judgments on others allows us to enlarge and enrich who we are individually and collectively. Curiosity, appreciation, and openness to unfamiliar ways of communicating are vital to a healthy pluralistic society in which each of us preserves our own distinct identity while remaining part of and engaged with a larger whole.

If you have learned these principles and skills of human communication, then you have the foundation to be effective in personal, professional, and social settings. If you are committed to practicing and continually enlarging the principles and skills introduced in this book, then you can look forward to a life of personal growth, meaningful relationships, professional success, and social impact. What is more, you are on the threshold of a life filled with joy.

Julia T Wood

Annotated Sample Speeches

WATER

Brandon Perry

Specific Purpose: To commemorate the strength, flexibility, and beauty of water

Thesis Statement: I'm thankful for all that water's enduring strength, everlasting flexibility, and exciting beauty have done for us and given us.

 Are you ready to give a special occasion speech? Use the following speech as a model. Brandon gave this speech in an introductory public speaking class. The assignment was to give a three- to five-minute speech commemorating a special person, place, or thing in the speaker's life. In addition, use your CourseMate for Invitation to Public Speaking to access video clips of other commemorative speeches, such as Tara Flanagan's "My Grandfather, John Flanagan Sr."

Commentary

By asking a series of questions, Brandon piques his audience's curiosity and draws them in. He then reveals the topic of his speech.

In his introduction Brandon indicates how he appreciates his topic by describing some of water's virtues. In addition, by talking about water's "strength," "flexibility,"

It is in the sky. It is on the ground. It is in us. Do you know what IT is? Father Time has no control over it, weapons weep at its power, and like an architect, it chisels and creates. Do you what IT is? Water is what I speak of, and nowadays we view water passively—nothing more than a convenience—but it is more than that. Every day I see the strength of water in how it shapes the landscape of this earth. I see its flexibility in giving me the ability to shape snow to throw. And I see a beauty that competes with the most beautiful sunset.

Discovering the amazing strength of water doesn't require going halfway across the Earth. Think about the strange and mysterious creatures of the deep blue sea. Turn your head toward the purple majestic skyscrapers of the West. Listen to the sounds of a roaring old-man-winter blizzard in Colorado. Take a walk down the hallway, then a right, arrive at the fountain, and take a nice long relaxing cool drink. Water, like a lifelong friend, is the regenerator, the reviver, the reliever of your life that you can't live without.

Water is uniquely flexible to many contexts. Little kids throwing water balloons and running through sprinklers would be unheard of without water. College students, enjoying a day off from classes, throwing snowballs at each other and building snowmen, would be unimaginable without water. The clouds that crowd and bustle through our bright blue sky, giving inspiration to artists and kids alike, would be unthinkable without water. The water we use every day once quieted the cries of an early Earth, quenched the thirst of a dinosaur, and gave blood to the mighty trees of the past and present of our world.

Beauty, they say, is in the eye of the beholder. But for those who claim they cannot see water's beauty, they need to look again. The glistening songs of blooming flowers in a midday spring afternoon are water's beauty transformed. Stand by a remote mountain lake, and a perfect, clear reflection of the mighty trees and peaks in the crystal clear water might just say hello. What makes water's beauty more unique and special, though, than any other is its ability to pass it on. The mighty Amazon rainforest or slopes covered in twenty feet of snow are just a couple examples. This beauty also allows all of us to view ourselves in a different light, like a mirror—it tells no lies. So when you stop and stare into a reflection that water gives you, do you see just yourself, or can you see deeper things, deeper ideas, deeper emotions?

Water was here long before and will be here long past our deaths, on this planet or the next. Life without water's enduring strength, everlasting flexibility, and exciting beauty would be all but impossible for most living things on this Earth. Be thankful for all that water has done for us; it has given us ALL that we see before us, in one form or another.

and "beauty," he previews his main points.

He connects to his audience by inking his topic to human senses—he asks his audience to think about, move toward, and listen to the sounds of water.

The use of alliteration ("the regenerator, the reviver, the reliever") helps make the speech appealing to listeners.

Brandon includes an anecdote about playing in the snow to relate to his audience of college-aged students.

In using personification ("the clouds that crowd and bustle . . . . giving inspiration"), he helps bring life to his topic.

Notice the vivid imagery and rhythm Brandon uses in this paragraph to describe water's beauty.

In his conclusion. Brandon provides a short summary of the three virtues he admires most about water.

MARTIN LUTHER KING JR. REMEMBRANCE SPEECH: TRANSCRIPT OF 2010 SPEECH

Barack Obama

Abstract: President Obama honors Martin Luther King Jr.'s life and activism while also encouraging Americans that his work is not finished and that individual people must work hard and persevere to end discrimination of all kinds and make our country and world more stable and safe.

Full Text: Address by Barack Obama, 44th president of the United States, during his presidency at the Vermont Avenue Baptist Church in Washington, DC, delivered on January 17, 2010.

Barack Obama, Martin Luther King Jr. Remembrance Speech, delivered on January 17, 2010, at Vermont Avenue Baptist Church, Washington, DC.

Acknowledges and thanks audience and those who invited him.

Good morning. Praise be to God. Let me begin by thanking the entire Vermont Avenue Baptist Church family for welcoming our family here today. It feels like a family. Thank you for making us feel that way. To Pastor Wheeler, first lady Wheeler, thank you so much for welcoming us here today. Congratulations on Jordan Denice—aka Cornelia.

Uses humor to make a connection.

Michelle and I have been blessed with a new nephew this year as well—Austin Lucas Robinson. So maybe at the appropriate time we can make introductions. Now, if Jordan's father is like me, then that will be in about 30 years. That is a great blessing.

Michelle and Malia and Sasha and I are thrilled to be here today. And I know that sometimes you have to go through a little fuss to have me as a guest speaker. So let me apologize in advance for all the fuss.

Identifies the purpose of the speech: to honor Dr. Martin Luther King Jr.

We gather here, on a Sabbath, during a time of profound difficulty for our nation and for our world. In such a time, it soothes the soul to seek out the Divine in a spirit of prayer; to seek solace among a community of believers. But we are not here just to ask the Lord for His blessing. We aren't here just to interpret His Scripture. We're also here to call on the memory of one of His noble servants, the Reverend Dr. Martin Luther King, Jr.

Shows respect by honoring the history of the church at which he is speaking.

Now, it's fitting that we do so here, within the four walls of Vermont Avenue Baptist Church—here, in a church that rose like the phoenix from the ashes of the civil war; here in a church formed by freed slaves, whose founding pastor had worn the union blue; here in a church from whose pews congregants set out for marches and from whom choir anthems of freedom were heard; from whose sanctuary King himself would sermonize from time to time.

One of those times was Thursday, December 6, 1956. Pastor, you said you were a little older than me, so were you around at that point? You were three years old—okay. I wasn't born yet.

On Thursday, December 6, 1956. And before Dr. King had pointed us to the mountaintop, before he told us about his dream in front of the Lincoln Memorial, King came here, as a 27-year-old preacher, to speak on what he called "The Challenge of a New Age." "The Challenge of a New Age." It was a period of triumph, but also uncertainty, for Dr. King and his followers—because just weeks earlier, the Supreme Court had ordered the desegregation of Montgomery's buses, a hard-wrought, hard-fought victory that would put an end to the 381-day historic boycott down in Montgomery, Alabama.

Provides background information to inform the audience and build credibility.

And yet, as Dr. King rose to take that pulpit, the future still seemed daunting. It wasn't clear what would come next for the movement that Dr. King led. It wasn't clear how we were going to reach the Promised Land. Because segregation was still rife; lynchings still a fact. Yes, the Supreme Court had ruled not only on the Montgomery buses, but also on *Brown v. Board of Education*. And yet that ruling was defied throughout the South—by schools and by states; they ignored it with impunity. And here in the nation's capital, the federal government had yet to fully align itself with the laws on its books and the ideals of its founding.

Uses detailed imagery to help the audience imagine being at the church at a particular time.

So it's not hard for us, then, to imagine that moment. We can imagine folks coming to this church, happy about the boycott being over. We can also imagine them, though, coming here concerned about their future, sometimes second-guessing strategy, maybe fighting off some creeping doubts, perhaps despairing about whether the movement in which they had placed so many of their hopes—a movement in which they believed so deeply—could actually deliver on its promise.

Continued use of imagery.

So here we are, more than half a century later, once again facing the challenges of a new age. Here we are, once more marching toward an unknown future, what I call the Joshua generation to their Moses generation—the great inheritors of progress paid for with sweat and blood, and sometimes life itself.

Uses a transition to make a connection between the past and present.

We've inherited the progress of unjust laws that are now overturned. We take for granted the progress of a ballot being available to anybody who wants to take the time to actually vote. We enjoy the fruits of prejudice and bigotry being lifted—slowly, sometimes in fits and starts, but irrevocably—from human hearts. It's that progress that made it possible for me to be here today; for the good people of this country to elect an African American the 44th President of the United States of America.

Reverend Wheeler mentioned the inauguration, last year's election. You know, on the heels of that victory over a year ago, there were some who suggested that somehow we had entered into a post-racial America, all those problems would be solved. There were those who argued that because I spoke of a need for unity in this country that our nation was somehow entering into a period of post-partisanship. That didn't work out so well. There was a hope shared by many that life would be better from the moment that I swore that oath.

Addresses a popular counter-argument.

Thesis: the work Dr. King began is not finished.

Of course, as we meet here today, one year later, we know the promise of that moment has not yet been fully fulfilled. Because of an era of greed and irresponsibility that sowed the seeds of its own demise, because of persistent economic troubles unaddressed through the generations, because of a banking crisis that brought the financial system to the brink of catastrophe, we are being tested—in our own lives and as a nation—as few have been tested before.

Uses general statistical information to support the thesis.

Unemployment is at its highest level in more than a quarter of a century. Nowhere is it higher than the African American community. Poverty is on the rise. Home ownership is slipping. Beyond our shores, our sons and daughters are fighting two wars. Closer to home, our Haitian brothers and sisters are in desperate need. Bruised, battered, many people are legitimately feeling doubt, even despair, about the future. Like those who came to this church on that Thursday in 1956, folks are wondering, where do we go from here?

Identifies with audience to create a connection.

Uses and emotional appeal.

I understand those feelings. I understand the frustration and sometimes anger that so many folks feel as they struggle to stay afloat. I get letters from folks around the country every day; I read 10 a night out of the 40,000 that we receive. And there are stories of hardship and desperation, in some cases, pleading for help: I need a job. I'm about to lose my home. I don't have health care—it's about to cause my family to be bankrupt. Sometimes you get letters from children: My mama or my daddy have lost their jobs, is there something you can do to help? Ten letters like that a day we read.

Uses a metaphor to advance his point.

(metaphor continues)

So, yes, we're passing through a hard winter. It's the hardest in some time. But let's always remember that, as a people, the American people, we've weathered some hard winters before. This country was founded during some harsh winters. The fishermen, the laborers, the craftsmen who made camp at Valley Forge—they weathered a hard winter. The slaves and the freedmen who rode an underground railroad, seeking the light of justice under the cover of night—they weathered a hard winter. The seamstress whose feet were tired, the pastor whose voice echoes through the ages—they weathered some hard winters. It was for them, as it is for us, difficult, in the dead of winter, to sometimes see spring coming. They, too, sometimes felt their hopes deflate. And yet, each season, the frost melts, the cold recedes, the sun reappears. So it was for earlier generations and so it will be for us.

Uses more concrete language to suggest a solution to the problem addressed in the thesis.

What we need to do is to just ask what lessons we can learn from those earlier generations about how they sustained themselves during those hard winters, how they persevered and prevailed. Let us in this Joshua generation learn how that Moses generation overcame.

Continues to suggest specific actions for the identified problem.

Let me offer a few thoughts on this. First and foremost, they did so by remaining firm in their resolve. Despite being threatened by sniper fire or planted bombs, by shoving and punching and spitting and angry stares, they adhered to that sweet spirit of resistance, the principles of nonviolence that had accounted for their success.

Second, they understood that as much as our government and our political parties had betrayed them in the past—as much as our nation itself had betrayed its own ideals—government, if aligned with the interests of its people, can be—and must be—a force for good. So they stayed on the Justice Department. They went into the courts. They pressured Congress, they pressured their President. They didn't give up on this country. They didn't give up on government. They didn't somehow say government was the problem; they said, we're going to change government, we're going to make it better. Imperfect as it was, they continued to believe in the promise of democracy; in America's constant ability to remake itself, to perfect this union.

Continues to suggest specific actions for the identified problem.

Urges people to take action.

Third, our predecessors were never so consumed with theoretical debates that they couldn't see progress when it came. Sometimes I get a little frustrated when folks just don't want to see that even if we don't get everything, we're getting something. King understood that the desegregation of the Armed Forces didn't end the civil rights movement, because black and white soldiers still couldn't sit together at the same lunch counter when they came home. But he still insisted on the rightness of desegregating the Armed Forces. That was a good first step— even as he called for more. He didn't suggest that somehow by the signing of the Civil Rights that somehow all discrimination would end. But he also didn't think that we shouldn't sign the Civil Rights Act because it hasn't solved every problem. Let's take a victory, he said, and then keep on marching. Forward steps, large and small, were recognized for what they were—which was progress.

Uses specific historical examples to encourage the audience toward action in the present.

Fourth, at the core of King's success was an appeal to conscience that touched hearts and opened minds, a commitment to universal ideals—of freedom, of justice, of equality—that spoke to all people, not just some people. For King understood that without broad support, any movement for civil rights could not be sustained. That's why he marched with the white auto worker in Detroit. That's why he linked arm with the Mexican farm worker in California, and united people of all colors in the noble quest for freedom.

Continues to suggest specific actions for the identified problem.

Of course, King overcame in other ways as well. He remained strategically focused on gaining ground—his eyes on the prize constantly—understanding that change would not be easy, understanding that change wouldn't come overnight, understanding that there would be setbacks and false starts along the way, but understanding, as he said in 1956, that "we can walk and never get weary, because we know there is a great camp meeting in the promised land of freedom and justice."

Effective use of a quotation.

And it's because the Moses generation overcame that the trials we face today are very different from the ones that tested us in previous generations. Even after the worst recession in generations, life in America is not even close to being as brutal as it was back then for so many. That's the legacy of Dr. King and his movement. That's our inheritance. Having said that, let there be no doubt the challenges of our new age are serious in their own right, and we must face them as squarely as they faced the challenges they saw.

Summarizes the previous main points: To accomplish the task, people must persevere.

Uses general examples to encourage and bring a more positive tone.

I know it's been a hard road we've traveled this year to rescue the economy, but the economy is growing again. The job losses have finally slowed, and around the country, there's signs that businesses and families are beginning to rebound. We are making progress.

Uses repetition of a phrase (i.e., "I know it's been a hard road we've traveled . . .") to emphasize and engage.

Uses repetition again (e.g., "This will be a victory . . .").

I know it's been a hard road that we've traveled to reach this point on health reform. I promise you I know. But under the legislation I will sign into law, insurance companies won't be able to drop you when you get sick, and more than 30 million people—our fellow Americans—will finally have insurance. More than 30 million men and women and children, mothers and fathers, won't be worried about what might happen to them if they get sick. This will be a victory not for Democrats; this will be a victory for dignity and decency, for our common humanity. This will be a victory for the United States of America.

Uses repetition again ("Don't give up on . . .")

Uses an effective quotation that supports his point.

Let's work to change the political system, as imperfect as it is. I know people can feel down about the way things are going sometimes here in Washington. I know it's tempting to give up on the political process. But we've put in place tougher rules on lobbying and ethics and transparency—tougher rules than any administration in history. It's not enough, but it's progress. Progress is possible. Don't give up on voting. Don't give up on advocacy. Don't give up on activism. There are too many needs to be met, too much work to be done. Like Dr. King said, "We must accept finite disappointment but never lose infinite hope."

Briefly returns to the metaphor (of winter and spring) used before.

Let us broaden our coalition, building a confederation not of liberals or conservatives, not of red states or blue states, but of all Americans who are hurting today, and searching for a better tomorrow. The urgency of the hour demands that we make common cause with all of America's workers—white, black, brown—all of whom are being hammered by this recession, all of whom are yearning for that spring to come. It demands that we reach out to those who've been left out in the cold even when the economy is good, even when we're not in recession—the youth in the inner cities, the youth here in Washington, D.C., people in rural communities who haven't seen prosperity reach them for a very long time. It demands that we fight discrimination, whatever form it may come. That means we fight discrimination against gays and lesbians, and we make common cause to reform our immigration system.

Builds credibility by citing his own work toward the goals that he encourages his audience to work toward.

And finally, we have to recognize, as Dr. King did, that progress can't just come from without—it also has to come from within. And over the past year, for example, we've made meaningful improvements in the field of education. I've got a terrific Secretary of Education, Arne Duncan. He's been working hard with states and working hard with the D.C. school district, and we've insisted on reform, and we've insisted on accountability. We're putting in more money and we've provided more Pell Grants and more tuition tax credits and simpler financial aid forms. We've done all that, but parents still need to parent. Kids still need to own up to their responsibilities. We still have to set high expectations for our young people. Folks can't simply look to government for all the answers without also looking inside themselves, inside their own homes, for some of the answers.

Progress will only come if we're willing to promote that ethic of hard work, a sense of responsibility, in our own lives. I'm not talking, by the way, just to the African American community. Sometimes when I say these things people assume, well, he's just talking to black people about working hard. No, no, no, no. I'm talking to the American community. Because somewhere along the way, we, as a nation, began to lose touch with some of our core values. You know what I'm talking about. We became enraptured with the false prophets who prophesized an easy path to success, paved with credit cards and home equity loans and get-rich-quick schemes, and the most important thing was to be a celebrity; it doesn't matter what you do, as long as you get on TV. That's everybody.

Uses vivid, emotional language (i.e., "false prophets," Biblical language for those who pretend to be messengers of God) that will appeal to his audience (i.e., church members).

We forgot what made the bus boycott a success; what made the civil rights movement a success; what made the United States of America a success—that, in this country, there's no substitute for hard work, no substitute for a job well done, no substitute for being responsible stewards of God's blessings.

What we're called to do, then, is rebuild America from its foundation on up. To reinvest in the essentials that we've neglected for too long—like health care, like education, like a better energy policy, like basic infrastructure, like scientific research. Our generation is called to buckle down and get back to basics.

Personalizes his message by referring to specific individuals (i.e., his nephew and the pastor's daughter, who were mentioned at the start of the speech).

We must do so not only for ourselves, but also for our children, and their children. For Jordan and for Austin. That's a sacrifice that falls on us to make. It's a much smaller sacrifice than the Moses generation had to make, but it's still a sacrifice.

Yes, it's hard to transition to a clean energy economy. Sometimes it may be inconvenient, but it's a sacrifice that we have to make. It's hard to be fiscally responsible when we have all these human needs, and we're inheriting enormous deficits and debt, but that's a sacrifice that we're going to have to make. You know, it's easy, after a hard day's work, to just put your kid in front of the TV set—you're tired, don't want to fuss with them—instead of reading to them, but that's a sacrifice we must joyfully accept.

Connects with audience by acknowledging their circumstances.

Continues to connect with the audience by acknowledging their challenges.

Sometimes it's hard to be a good father and good mother. Sometimes it's hard to be a good neighbor, or a good citizen, to give up time in service of others, to give something of ourselves to a cause that's greater than ourselves—as Michelle and I are urging folks to do tomorrow to honor and celebrate Dr. King. But these are sacrifices that we are called to make. These are sacrifices that our faith calls us to make. Our faith in the future. Our faith in America. Our faith in God.

Suggests a way (i.e., faith) to meet the difficult challenge he has asked of them.

And on his sermon all those years ago, Dr. King quoted a poet's verse:
Truth forever on the scaffold
Wrong forever on the throne . . .
And behind the dim unknown stands God
Within the shadows keeping watch above his own.

Uses a quotation.

Even as Dr. King stood in this church, a victory in the past and uncertainty in the future, he trusted God. He trusted that God would make a way. A way for prayers to be answered. A way for our union to be perfected. A way for the arc of the moral universe, no matter how long, to slowly bend towards truth and bend towards freedom, to bend towards justice. He had faith that God would make a way out of no way.

You know, folks ask me sometimes why I look so calm. They say, all this stuff coming at you, how come you just seem calm? And I have a confession to make here. There are times where I'm not so calm. Reggie Love knows. My wife knows. There are times when progress seems too slow. There are times when the words that are spoken about me hurt. There are times when the barbs sting. There are times when it feels like all these efforts are for naught, and change is so painfully slow in coming, and I have to confront my own doubts.

Shares personal information and makes himself vulnerable to relate to the audience.

But let me tell you—during those times it's faith that keeps me calm. It's faith that gives me peace. The same faith that leads a single mother to work two jobs to put a roof over her head when she has doubts. The same faith that keeps an unemployed father to keep on submitting job applications even after he's been rejected a hundred times. The same faith that says to a teacher even if the first nine children she's teaching she can't reach, that that 10th one she's going to be able to reach. The same faith that breaks the silence of an earthquake's wake with the sound of prayers and hymns sung by a Haitian community. A faith in things not seen, in better days ahead, in Him who holds the future in the hollow of His hand. A faith that lets us mount up on wings like eagles; lets us run and not be weary; lets us walk and not faint.

Makes a Biblical reference to further emphasize the point (i.e., faith).

So let us hold fast to that faith, as Joshua held fast to the faith of his fathers, and together, we shall overcome the challenges of a new age. Together, we shall seize the promise of this moment. Together, we shall make a way through winter, and we're going to welcome the spring. Through God all things are possible.

May the memory of Dr. Martin Luther King continue to inspire us and ennoble our world and all who inhabit it. And may God bless the United States of America.

Thanks his audience.

Thank you very much, everybody. God bless you.

"THE DUN DUN DRUM"

Joshua Valentine

Josh gave this speech in an introductory public speaking class. The assignment was to give a 4- to 6-minute speech with visual aids. Students were also asked to create a preparation outline that indicated where in the speech the visual aids were to be displayed, that cited the sources of the visual aids, and that included a Works Cited section. As you watch Josh's speech, consider the effectiveness of his use of photographs and audio to illustrate and clarify points.

Imagine that your friend comes up to you and asks you what you did this weekend, and instead of using words, your friend simply beats a drum. You've probably never had this type of encounter. However, there are many cultures in the world where music is used for customs that we're really not accustomed to.

Webster's Dictionary defines language as "any system of symbols, sounds, or gestures used for the purpose of communication." Here in America we don't really have instrumental sounds that represent English words, but there are many cultures around the world where sounds do have meaning.

I've been playing percussion since junior high. I first learned about the *dun dun* drum while attending a percussion workshop two years ago. So, today I'll explain the origins of the *dun dun* drum, its uses as a linguistic tool, and its uses as a musical instrument.

The *dun dun* drum, also known as the Nigerian talking drum, actually does talk in the Yoruba language. *[Display photograph of* dun dun *drum downloaded and used with permission from http://media.dickinson.edu/gallery/Sect5 .html.]* The *dun dun* originated in the Oyo Empire of Yoruba-land during the fifteenth century A.D. for the purposes of communication, mainly for spiritual communication. As such, the Yoruba language is easily adaptable to the *dun dun* drum.

Now, the Yoruba language is a tonal language, which basically means it uses three basic tones, or pitches, with glides between them—this is an essential part of how words are pronounced. Listen to this sound clip and see if you can examine the three different glides. *[Play a sound clip downloaded for one-time use from the Internet.]* I'll play that again for you. If you have a sharp ear, you may also be able to pick out three glides that are essential to the pronunciation of the Yoruba language. Melody is the basis for the Yoruba language, since the same word pronounced with a different melody might mean something completely different.

Josh, a drummer, takes his topic from his interest in music. He catches his audience's attention by asking them to imagine using a musical instrument to communicate language, something people in the United States don't typically do.

In the second main point of his introduction, he introduces his topic. He adapts his topic to his audience by using a familiar source, *Webster's Dictionary*, to define what language is and then explain that although Americans don't use music as language, other cultures do.

He establishes his credibility by indicating that he is a musician and that he learned about his topic in a percussion workshop.

In the last point of his introduction, Josh previews the two main points of his speech.

Because his audience is unfamiliar with his topic, Josh uses his first main point to explain what the *dun dun* drum is, where it originated, and what it is used for.

By allowing his audience to see and hear a *dun dun* drum, Josh helps his audience better understand his topic. In particular, the audio clips let the audience hear what is complicated to explain in words alone.

He kept a careful record of where he obtained his visual and audio aids so he could cite his sources accurately in his speech. Note that he downloaded copyrighted material according to the terms of use posted by the Websites he accessed—he requested permission or agreed to use the material only for his speech in class.

The visual aid Josh used for subpoint D of his first main point clarifies how the drum works.

In his second main point, Josh explains how the drum is used to communicate. He continues to use his visual and audio aids to enhance and clarify the information in his speech.

In subpoint B, he provides details that his audience can relate to: "saying hi," "cracking jokes," "telling stories." Notice that he cites his sources simply but effectively.

Here Josh uses a specific example to explain how the Yoruba "talk" with the *dun dun* drum.

The Yoruba drum, the *dun dun*, functions mainly by using and changing the tension between two different skin heads. *[Point out the straps on the PowerPoint slide.]* By doing such, they can actually have a lot of control about how the *dun dun* operates and its use in communication. And, the *dun dun* was originally created for the purpose of communication.

The Yoruba are people of southwestern Nigeria who have used the *dun dun* drum for communication throughout their history. *[Show photo of carved drum downloaded from* www.hamillgallery.com . . .*YorubaDrum01.html.]* It was originally, of course, created first for spiritual communication. Since its inception, the drum has mainly been used to create religious songs and hymns of praise, and these songs are still recited today among the modern Yoruba people.

Here's an example of a very intense spiritual worship song done on talking drums. *[Play example downloaded for one-time use from* http://www.world-beats .com/instruments/dundun.htm.*]*

The Yoruba talking drum is also used heavily for day-to-day social communication. According to worldbeats.com, a master drummer can maintain a regular monologue while cracking jokes, saying hi to different people, even telling stories on the *dun dun* drum. Additionally, many *dun dun* drummers are known to say the names of friends and family on the *dun dun* drums as a sign of greeting and as a form of respect. So it's used very heavily in those senses, and it's very important—it's a huge part of the Yoruba culture.

And, additionally, the most obvious use of the *dun dun* drum, and its secondary use, really, is as a musical instrument. Now, we've already gone over the fact that the *dun dun* drum originally was used for spiritual communication. But since corporate worship in Yoruba is so prolific, people come together, and making music on the *dun dun* was born. That's essentially an example of how it's evolved. In fact, today, modern Yoruba people still use the *dun dun* for religious songs, although mainly for their musical purposes.

Everyday speech on the Yoruba drum becomes rhythmic when it's used. For example, the word *kabo*, which means "welcome" in the Yoruba language, is only a two-syllable word, so it's really not that exotic—it's not that interesting; it's not that musical. According to Drum Talk Limited, a more common phrase that someone might speak on the Yoruba talking drum is, "Welcome, we are happy that you arrived safely," because it's more musical. It has more of that flair to it. And even when a word spoken, or a phrase spoken, with regular words wouldn't be rhythmic, it is when the Yoruba people use the talking drum, because melody, as I said, is the basis of the talking drum.

The use of the Nigerian talking drum has spread far beyond Nigeria. In fact, next to the *djembe* drum, the *dun dun* is the most well-known and recognizable African drum used in America today. It's also very versatile. According to Francis Awe, a renowned African American musician, the *dun dun* drum fares well in jazz, blues, R&B, rock and roll, reggae, classical, even choral music. Here's one particular clip from renowned African American musician Francis Awe. *[Play sample clip downloaded from http://www.nitade.com/html/cd1.html.]*

So, in conclusion, whether the *dun dun* drum is used in language or in song, it always has a very unusual and beautiful sound. Today I've talked about the origins of the *dun dun* drum. I've also talked about its linguistic uses, and its uses as a musical instrument. So next time you hear music as simple as someone beating a drum, you might think to yourself that maybe that drummer, maybe that musician, is communicating much more than you first think.

Here he adapts to his audience by explaining how the *dun dun* drum is used in a way that is familiar to people in the United States, as a musical instrument.

Josh ends the body of his speech with an audio clip that reinforces his final sub-subpoint, that the *dun dun* drum is now an international instrument.

Josh begins his conclusion by reinforcing that the drum is used for both language and music. He then summarizes his main points.

He ends his speech with an intriguing statement that encourages his audience to remember what he's told them about a particular African drum.

Interviewing

You've probably participated in a number of interviews during your life. Perhaps you were interviewed by committees that appoint students to leadership positions at your school or award scholarships to students. You may have had interviews with members of groups you sought to join. Probably you have interviewed for part-time or full-time jobs.

You've probably been on the other side of the interviewing process, too; you may have interviewed people who were applying to join organizations to which you belong. You may have interviewed experts to gain information about a topic on which you were writing a paper or preparing a speech. Because interviews are common, learning to communicate effectively in interviews is important to your personal and professional success.

An **interview** is a communication transaction that emphasizes questions and answers. In this appendix, we will discuss interviewing and identify ways you can enhance your effectiveness as both interviewer and interviewee. First, we will identify a range of purposes or types of interviews. Second, we will discuss the typical structure and style of interviews. Third, we will describe different kinds of questions interviewers use. Then, we will identify challenges that are part of interviewing. We will focus on hiring interviews because those are particularly important to many college students. Our discussion will provide tips for preparing to interview and for dealing with inappropriate or illegal questions.

UNDERSTANDING COMMUNICATION IN INTERVIEWS

Types and Purposes of Interviews

Communication scholars have identified distinct types of interviews. Each interview is defined by its primary purpose, although many interviews have multiple, and sometimes conflicting, purposes. For example, an interviewer may want to gain objective information for a speech, yet may be biased about the topic that he or she wants to support. We'll discuss 11 types of interviews.

Information-Giving Interviews   In the first type of interview, the interviewer provides information to the interviewee. Doctors engage in **information-giving interviews** when they explain to patients how to prepare for procedures, take medicines, follow exercise programs, and observe symptoms. Academic advisers give students information about curricular requirements and administrative processes. Team leaders often inform new members of a work unit about expectations and operating procedures.

Information-Getting Interviews   In this type of interview, the interviewer asks questions to learn about the interviewee's opinions, knowledge, attitudes, experience, and so forth. Public opinion polls, census taking, and research surveys are common examples of **information-getting interviews**. Physicians also use these to gain insight into patients' medical histories and current conditions (Farnill, Hayes, & Todisco, 1997). Journalists devote a great deal of time to information-getting interviews to obtain background material for stories they are writing and to learn about experts' opinions on newsworthy topics.

Persuasive Interviews   Interviews designed to influence attitudes or actions are **persuasive interviews**. We're all familiar with the sales interview, in which a salesperson attempts to persuade a customer to buy a product or service. Persuasive interviews can sell more than products. They may also promote people (political candidates) and ideas (persuading an administrator to act on your team's report, convincing a company to implement environmental regulations).

Problem-Solving Interviews   When people need to address a dilemma, they may engage in **problem-solving interviews**. Perhaps you have met with a professor to discuss difficulties in a course. The two of you may have collaborated to identify ways to improve your note taking, study habits, and writing. Supervisors sometimes hold problem-solving interviews with employees to discover and resolve impediments to maximally effective work.

Counseling Interviews   Like problem-solving interviews, **counseling interviews** focus on a problem. In counseling interviews, however, the problem is not mutual. A client has a problem, such as stress, depression, or compulsiveness, that she or he wants to overcome. The counselor attempts to help the client understand the problem more fully and collaborates with the client to develop strategies for coping with or overcoming the difficulty (Evans, Coman, & Goss, 1996). Counseling interviews also occur outside the therapeutic setting: We may seek counseling from attorneys to address (or avoid) legal problems, from accountants to get help with financial matters, and from religious leaders to deal with spiritual issues.

Employment Interviews   The purpose of **employment interviews** is to allow employers and job candidates to assess each other and decide whether there is a good fit between them. Typically, employment interviews include periods of information giving and information getting as well as persuasive efforts on the part of both participants. The prospective employer wants to convince the job candidate of the quality of the company, and the candidate wants to convince the prospective employer of the quality of his or her qualifications. Ideally, both participants gain enough information to make a sound judgment of the fit between the candidate and the job.

Complaint Interviews   **Complaint interviews** allow people to register complaints about a product, service, or person. Many firms have departments whose sole purpose is to accept and respond to complaints. Of primary importance is showing the people who complain that they are heard and that they matter. The interviewer (company representative) attempts to gain information about the customer's dissatisfaction: What was defective or disappointing about the product? Was service inadequate? What would it take to satisfy the customer now? The person conducting complaint interviews should call recurring complaints to the attention of those who can diagnose and solve underlying problems.

Performance Reviews   Most organizations require **performance reviews**, or performance appraisals, at regular intervals. By building performance appraisals into work life, organizations continually monitor employees' performance and foster their professional growth. The performance review is an occasion on which a supervisor comments on a subordinate's achievements and professional development, identifies any weaknesses or problems, and collaborates to develop goals for future performance. During the interview, subordinates should offer their perceptions of their strengths and weaknesses and participate actively in developing goals for professional development (Kikoski, 1998).

Reprimand Interviews   When a person's work is unsatisfactory, a supervisor may conduct a **reprimand interview**. The goals are to identify lapses in professional conduct, determine sources of problems, and establish a plan for improving future performance. Because reprimands tend to evoke defensiveness, developing a constructive, supportive climate for these interviews is especially important. Supervisors may foster a good climate by opening the interview with assurances that the goal is to solve a problem together, not to punish the subordinate. Supervisors should also invite subordinates to express their perceptions and feelings fully.

Stress Interviews   **Stress interviews** are designed to create anxiety in respondents or interviewees. Stress interviews are unique in their deliberate intent to apply pressure. Frequently used communication techniques for inducing stress are rapid-fire questions, intentional misinterpretations and distortions of the interviewee's responses, and hostile or skeptical nonverbal expressions.

Why, you might ask, would anyone deliberately create a high-stress interview situation? Actually, stress interviews may be useful in several contexts. Attorneys may intentionally intimidate reluctant or hostile witnesses or people whose honesty is suspect. Similarly, prison administrators and police officers may communicate aggressively with people they think are withholding important information. This kind of interview also may be used in hiring people for high-stress jobs. By deliberately trying to rattle job candidates, interviewers can assess how well they manage and respond to stress.

Exit Interviews   In academic and professional life, **exit interviews** have become increasingly popular. The goal of this type of interview is to gain information, insights, and perceptions about a place of work or education from a person who is leaving. While people are in a job or learning environment, they may be reluctant to mention dissatisfactions or to speak against those who have power over them. When people are leaving an organization or school, however, they can offer honest insights and perceptions with little fear of reprisal. Thus, exit interviews can be especially valuable in providing information about policies, personnel, and organizational culture.

The Structure of Interviews

To be effective, interviews should follow a structure that builds a good communication climate and allows the interviewer and the interviewee to deal with substantive matters. Experienced interviewers, even those without professional training, tend to organize interview communication into a three-stage sequence. Interviewees who understand the purpose of each stage in the sequence increase their ability to participate effectively.

The Opening Stage   The initial stage of an interview tends to be brief and aims to create an effective climate for interaction, clarify the purpose, and preview issues to be discussed (Wilson & Goodall, 1991). Typically, opening small talk encourages a friendly climate:

- "I see you're from Buffalo. Are the winters there still as harsh as they used to be?"

- "It's been 6 months since our last performance review. Any new developments in your life?"

- "I noticed you got your B.A. from State University. I graduated from there, too. Did you ever take any courses with Doctor Barnette in anthropology?"

After opening small talk, effective interviewers state the purpose of the interview and how they plan to accomplish that purpose:

- "As you know, I'm on campus today to talk with liberal arts majors who are interested in joining Hodgeson Marketing. I'd like to ask you some questions about yourself and your background, and then I want to give you an opportunity to ask me anything you want about Hodgeson."

- "Pat, the reason I asked you to meet with me today is that there have been some complaints about your attitude from others on your work team. I know you are good at your job and have a fine history with the firm, so I want us to put our heads together to resolve this matter. Let's begin with me telling you what I've heard, and then I'd like to hear your perceptions of what's happening."

The Substantive Stage The second stage of an interview, which generally consumes the bulk of time, deals with substance or content relevant to the purpose of the interview. For example, in reprimand interviews, the substantive stage would zero in on identifying problem behaviors and devising solutions. In a hiring interview, the substantive stage might concentrate on the job candidate's background, experience, and qualifications.

Because the goal of the substantive stage is to exchange information, it takes careful planning and thought. Most interviewers prepare lists of topics or specific questions and use their notes to make sure they cover all the important topics. During the interview, they may also take notes of responses. Communication during this phase tends to progress from broad topic areas to increasingly specific questions within each topic. After introducing a topic, the interviewer may ask some initial general questions and then follow up with more detailed probes. Because the pattern of communication moves from broad to narrow, it has been called the **funnel sequence** (Cannell & Kahn, 1968; Moffatt, 1979). The interviewer may repeat the funnel sequence for each new topic area in an interview.

During the substantive stage, an interviewer may invite the interviewee to take the lead in communication, either by posing questions or by volunteering perceptions and ideas in response to what has been covered thus far. To be an effective interviewee, you should be prepared with questions and topics that you want to introduce. This portrays you as someone who prepares and takes initiative. It is also important to monitor your nonverbal communication. Interviewers tend to be most impressed with interviewees whose paralanguage and kinesics convey enthusiasm, confidence, and an outgoing personality (Mino, 1996).

The Closing Stage Like the opening stage, the closing stage tends to be brief. Its purposes are to summarize what has been discussed, state what follow-up will occur, if any, and create good will in parting. Summarizing the content of the interview increases the likelihood that an accurate and complete record of the interview will survive. If the interviewer overlooks any topics, the interviewee may appropriately offer a reminder. Interviewees also may ask about follow-up if interviewers fail to mention this.

Most interviews follow the three-step sequence we've discussed, but not all do. Some interviewers are ineffective because they are disorganized, unprepared, and inadequately trained in effective interviewing. They may ramble for 15 minutes or more and fail to provide any closing other than "Gee, our time is up." In other instances, interviewers may deliberately violate the standard pattern to achieve their goals. For example, in stress interviews designed to test how well a person responds to pressure, the interviewer may skip opening comments and jump immediately into tough substantive questions. This allows the interviewer to assess how well the respondent copes with unexpected pressure.

Styles of Interviewing

Interviews may be more or less formal. In highly formal interviews, participants tend to stay within social and professional roles. The content of highly formal interviews tends to follow a standard format, often one that the interviewer has written to structure the interaction. Nonverbal communication provides further clues to formality: clothes, a formal meeting room, stilted postures, and a stiff handshake are all signs of formality.

In contrast, informal interviews are more relaxed, personal, and flexible. The interviewer attempts to engage the interviewee as an individual, not just a person in a general role. Typically, informal interviews aren't as rigidly structured as formal interviews. The interviewer may have a list of standard topics (either memorized or written down), but these provide only guidelines, not a straitjacket for communication. Informal interviews often include nonverbal cues such as smiling, relaxed postures, casual surroundings, and informal dress.

Most interviews fall between the extremes of formality and informality. Also, interviews may become more or less formal as a result of communication between participants. A person who communicates in a stilted manner is likely to encourage formality in the other person. Conversely, a person who communicates casually promotes a relaxed style of response.

Another influence on the communication climate in interviews is the balance of power between interviewer and interviewee. Power may be evenly balanced between participants or skewed toward the interviewer or the interviewee.

Interviewees have the greatest power to direct communication in **mirror interviews**, in which the interviewer consistently reflects the interviewee's comments to the interviewee. This may be done by restating verbatim what an interviewee says, paraphrasing an interviewee's comments, or making limited inferences about an interviewee's thoughts and feelings based on the communication. Skillful listening is essential for effectively using the mirror style (Banville, 1978). Consider this sample excerpt from a mirror interview:

> INTERVIEWER: Tell me about your studies.
>
> INTERVIEWEE: I'm a communication major.
>
> INTERVIEWER: So you've studied communication?
>
> INTERVIEWEE: Yes, especially organizational communication and leadership.
>
> INTERVIEWER: Then you're particularly interested in leadership in organizations?
>
> INTERVIEWEE: Yes. I think communication is the heart of effective leadership, so majoring in communication prepares me to lead.
>
> INTERVIEWER: So you see communication as the heart of effective leadership?
>
> INTERVIEWEE: Well, I see leadership as motivating others and empowering them to achieve their goals. A person who knows how to communicate clearly, listen well, and establish rapport with others is most able to motivate them.

In this exchange, the interviewer lets the interviewee to lead. What the interviewee says is the basis for the interviewer's subsequent questions and probes. Astute interviewees realize that mirror interviews give them significant opportunity to highlight their strengths and introduce topics they wish to discuss.

Distributive Interviews   In **distributive interviews**, power is equally divided (or distributed) between participants. Both ask and answer questions, listen and speak, and contribute to shaping the direction and content of communication. The distributive style of interviewing is generally used when participants are equal in professional or social standing. Distributive interviews may also be used between people with unequal power if the interviewer wants to create a relaxed exchange. Recruiters often use distributive styles to put job candidates at ease.

Authoritarian Interviews   In **authoritarian interviews**, the interviewer exercises primary control over interaction. The interviewer may avoid or quickly cut off discussion of any topics not on the list and may give the interviewee little or no opportunity to ask questions or initiate topics. Efficiency is the primary strength of the authoritarian style of interviewing: Many topics can be covered quickly. But the authoritarian style of interviewing can be frustrating to interviewees, and the interviewer may miss relevant information by failing to specifically seek it and by not giving the interviewee an opportunity to initiate topics.

In stress interviews, which we discussed previously in this appendix, the interviewer has primary control, as in authoritarian interviews. Unlike authoritarian interviews, however, stress interviews are a deliberate attempt to create anxiety in the interviewee. Thus, the interviewer controls not only the pace and content of interaction but also the psychological agenda.

Interviewees have even less control than in authoritarian interviews because stress interviews often rely on trick questions, surprise turns in topic, and unsettling responses to interviewees. If you find yourself in a stress interview, recognize that it is probably a deliberate attempt to test your ability to cope with pressure. Stay alert and flexible to deal with unpredictable communication from the interviewer.

Forms of Questions in Interviews

Most interviews follow a question–answer pattern in which each person speaks only briefly before the other person speaks. Consequently, skill in asking and responding to questions is central to effectiveness. Skillful interviewers understand that different kinds of questions shape responses, and effective interviewees recognize the opportunities and constraints of distinct forms of questions. We'll consider eight of the most common types of questions and discuss the responses invited by each.

Open Questions   Open questions are general queries that invite expansive responses: "What can you tell me about yourself?" "What is your work experience?" Because open questions are broad, they give interviewees opportunities to steer communication toward topics that interest or reflect well on them.

Closed Questions   Unlike open questions, closed questions do not invite broad answers. Instead, they ask for a concrete, narrow reply, often in the form of "yes" or "no." Closed questions are often used to follow up on general replies to open questions. "How many business courses have you taken?" "What was your position at the summer camp?" "Do you prefer working individually or on teams?" Closed questions call for short, direct answers, and an interviewer may interpret more broad responses negatively.

Mirror Questions   Mirror questions paraphrase or reflect the previous communication. If an interviewee says, "I have worked in a lot of stressful jobs," the interviewer might respond reflectively by saying, "So you can handle pressure, right?" At the content level of meaning, a mirror question seems pointless because it merely repeats what preceded it. At the relationship level of meaning, however, mirror questions say, "Elaborate; tell me more." Thus, they represent opportunities to expand on ideas.

Hypothetical Questions   Hypothetical questions ask a person to speculate. Recruiters often pose hypothetical questions to see how well candidates can think on their feet. A student of mine provided the following example of a hypothetical question she was asked in a job interview: "Assume you are supervising an employee who is consistently late to work and sometimes leaves early. What would you do?" My student responded that her first course of action would be to talk with the employee to determine the reason for his or her tardiness and early departures. Next, she said, she would work with the employee to eliminate the source or, if company policies allowed it, to rearrange the schedule to accommodate the employee's circumstances.

This response showed that the job candidate was collaborative and supportive—precisely the qualities the recruiter wanted to assess. Hypothetical questions are designed to find out how you grasp and approach complex situations (Gladwell, 2000).

Probing Questions   When we probe something, we go beneath its surface to find out more about it. During interviews, probing questions go beneath the surface of a response to gather additional information and insight. Consider this example of several probing questions that follow an open question and a broad response:

INTERVIEWER: Tell me about your work history.

INTERVIEWEE: I've held 10 jobs while I've been attending college.

INTERVIEWER: Why have you held so many different jobs instead of sticking with one of them?

INTERVIEWEE: I kept switching in the hope of finding one that would be really interesting.

INTERVIEWER: What makes a job interesting to you?

INTERVIEWEE: It would have to be challenging and have enough variety not to bore me.

INTERVIEWER: Are you easily bored?

Note how the interviewer probes to learn more about the interviewee's responses. Each probe seeks more details about the interviewee's attitudes toward work.

Leading Questions Leading questions predispose a certain response. For example, "You believe in teamwork, don't you?" encourages "Yes" as a response, whereas "You don't drink on a regular basis, do you?" encourages "No" as a response. Leading questions generally are not a good way to get candid responses because they suggest how you want a person to respond (Stewart & Cash, 1991). Leading questions can be useful, however, if an interviewer wants to test an interviewee's commitment to an idea. An acquaintance of mine who recruits employees for sales positions that require a lot of travel often poses this leading question: "After a year or two of travel, the novelty wears off. I assume you expect a permanent location after a year or so with us, right?" Applicants who answer "yes" do not get job offers because travel is an ongoing part of the sales positions.

Loaded Questions Loaded questions are worded to reflect the emotions or judgments of the person asking the question. The language in the question is laden with emotion and may cause an interviewee to respond emotionally. "How do you feel about slackers who expect to leave work at 5 p.m. every day?" In this question, the word *slackers* suggests the interviewer's negative judgment of employees who expect to quit at 5 p.m. each day. An interviewee is likely to pick up on the bias in the question and reply, "I think an employee should work until the job is done, not until the clock strikes 5 p.m." But this may not reflect the interviewee's actual views, so the question isn't effective in probing the interviewee's attitudes.

Another version of the loaded question involves baiting an interviewee. The classic example of a loaded question is, "When did you stop beating your dog?" The question presumes something (in this case, that the interviewee at some point did beat his or her dog) that hasn't been established. This kind of loaded question is likely to foster defensiveness in an interviewee and to limit what an interviewer learns about the interviewee.

Summary Questions A final kind of question is the summary question, which covers what has been discussed. Although summary questions often are phrased as statements, they function as questions. For example, "I believe we've covered everything" should be perceived as, "Do we need to discuss anything else?" "It seems we've agreed on expectations for your performance during the next quarter" should be perceived as, "Do you feel we have a common understanding of what's expected of you?" Communication that summarizes topics in an interview provides an opportunity for participants to check whether they agree about what they've discussed and what will follow.

What we've discussed gives us a foundation for discussing two important challenges for communicating in interviews.

CHALLENGES WHEN COMMUNICATING IN INTERVIEWS

Like all other kinds of interaction, interviewing presents challenges that require communication skills. We will discuss two specific challenges: preparing to be interviewed and dealing with illegal questions. We will use the hiring interview to illustrate these challenges, but the ideas we'll discuss pertain to other kinds of interviews as well.

Preparing to Interview Effectively

My students sometimes tell me that they can't prepare for interviews because they don't know what the interviewer will ask. Even without knowing exactly what questions will arise, you can do a great deal to prepare yourself for a successful interview. First, prepare a résumé that is concise, accurate in content and style (proofread carefully!), and professional in appearance. Your résumé is your first chance to "advertise yourself" to potential employers (Krannich & Banis, 1990).

Conduct Research Every type of interview benefits from advance research, although the appropriate research varies according to the interview's purpose. Before performance appraisals, both the supervisor and the subordinate should review any previous performance appraisals. In addition, both participants should think about what has happened since the last appraisal: Have goals that were set been met? Have there been notable achievements, such as development of new skills or receipt of awards? It's also appropriate to talk with others to learn what is expected of employees at various stages in their careers.

Research is critical for effective employment interviewing. To learn about an organization, you'll want information about its products and services, self-image, history, benefits, organizational culture, and so forth. If you know someone who works for the company, ask that person to share perceptions and information with you. If you aren't personally acquainted with employees at the company, check for materials in your library or placement office or an online service. Standard references such as *Moody's Manuals* and *Standard & Poor's Index* provide information about the size, locations, salary levels, structure, employee benefits, and financial condition of many organizations.

The Internet is an additional source of information. Many companies have Web pages that allow you to learn such things as how the company thinks of itself, the image it wants to project, and its size and geographic scope. Because Websites are updated regularly, visiting a company's Website is a good way to get the current information about a company that interests you.

Research enhances your effectiveness in two ways. First, the information you gather provides a basis for questions that show you have done your homework and understand the company. Second, when you know something about a company's or program's priorities, image, and goals, you can adapt your communication to acknowledge the expectations and norms of the company.

Engage in Person-Centered Communication   In Chapter 2, we discussed person-centered communication, in which one person recognizes and respects the perspective of another person. To prepare for an interview, ask yourself, "What would I want to know if I were interviewing me for this position?" Don't ask what you want to tell the interviewer about yourself or what you think is most important about your record. Instead, take the perspective of the interviewer as you anticipate the interaction.

You are not likely to know the interviewer personally, so you can't realistically expect to understand him or her as a unique individual. What matters is to recognize that in the interview situation the recruiter is a representative of a particular company with distinct goals, history, expectations, and culture. If you have researched the company, you will be able to adapt your communication to the interviewer's frame of reference.

Person-centered communication also requires sensitivity to cultural differences. For instance, people who were raised in some Asian cultures tend to be modest about personal achievements and abilities. Viewed from a Western perspective, such modesty might be misinterpreted as lack of confidence (Kikoski, 1998; U.S. Department of Labor, 1992).

Practice Responding   One of the most common complaints of employment recruiters is that candidates are unprepared for interviews (DeVito, 1994). Examples of appearing unprepared include not bringing a résumé to the interview, not knowing about the company, and not recalling specific information, such as names of former supervisors and dates of employment. Ability to recall specific information shows you are prepared and knowledgeable. Yet many people fumble when asked about specifics. Why? Because they assume they know about themselves—after all, it's their life—so they don't bother to review details and practice responses.

You can avoid appearing unprepared by taking time before an interview to review your experiences and accomplishments and to remind yourself of key names, places, and dates. It's also a good idea to practice responding aloud to questions. You want your communication to reflect what employers look for—attentiveness, positive attitude, preparation, clarity, and motivation (Anderson & Killenberg, 1998; Farnill et al., 1997; Peterson, 1997; Ramsay, Gallois, & Callan, 1997). Figure B.1 lists questions commonly asked during employment interviews.

Conducting research, engaging in person-centered communication, and practicing responses will not prepare you for everything that can happen in an interview. However, they will make you better prepared and more impressive than candidates who don't follow the guidelines we've discussed.

Managing Illegal Questions in Interviews

Just a couple of years ago, a student who was completing a professional degree was asked this question by a job recruiter: "What methods of birth control do you use?" Fortunately, this student knew the question was discriminatory, so she refused to answer and reported the interviewer to the campus placement service.

1. Why did you decide to attend this school?
2. Why did you choose _____ as your major?
3. Tell me about yourself.
4. Why are you interested in our company (firm)?
5. How does your academic background pertain to this job?
6. What do you consider your most serious weakness?
7. What are your long-term professional goals?
8. Which of the jobs you've held has been most satisfying to you? Why?
9. What is the most difficult situation you have ever been in? How did you handle it?
10. Who has been the biggest influence in your life?
11. What are your hobbies? How do you spend spare time?
12. How do you define success in sales (marketing, management, training, etc.)?
13. Why should we hire you instead of another person?
14. What kind of people do you prefer to work with? Why?
15. Are you willing to travel?
16. What do you expect your employer to do for you?
17. What do you think of the president's budget proposal (or another current national issue)?
18. Describe your closest friend.
19. How long would you expect to remain with our company?
20. Define *teamwork*. Give me an example of a team on which you worked.

Know the Law   The Equal Employment Opportunity Commission (EEOC) is a federally created entity that monitors various kinds of discrimination in hiring decisions. In 1970, the EEOC issued initial guidelines pertinent to employment interviews, and these have been updated periodically. EEOC guidelines also apply to tests, application forms, and other devices used to screen job applicants.

EEOC regulations prohibit discrimination on the basis of criteria that are legally irrelevant to job qualifications. Because the EEOC is an arm of the federal government, it protects interviewees in all states from intrusive questions about race, ethnicity, marital status, age, sex, disability, and arrests. Individual states and institutions may impose additional limits on information about candidates that may be used in hiring decisions. For instance, my school has a policy against discrimination based on military service or sexual orientation.

An illegal question reflects either an interviewer's ignorance of the law or his or her willful disregard of it. People who conduct interviews should review restrictions on questions in a good source such as Arthur Bell's 1989 book *The Complete Manager's Guide to Interviewing*. Whether interviewers intend to ask illegal questions or not, it's important for interviewees to know what questions are not legally permissible in employment interviews. If you don't understand the legal boundaries on questions, you cannot protect your rights.

Respond Deliberately to Illegal Questions   Knowing which questions are out of bounds doesn't tell us what to do if we are asked an inappropriate question. You may choose to respond if it doesn't bother you. You also have the right to object and to point out to an interviewer that a question is inappropriate. If you don't care about the job, this is a reasonable way to respond. But realize that even if you exercise your rights diplomatically, doing so may lessen an interviewer's interest in hiring you.

One effective way to respond to unlawful questions is to provide only information that may be sought legally. This strategy preserves a supportive climate in the interview by not directly reprimanding the interviewer. For instance, if an employer asks whether you are a native Chinese speaker, you might respond, "I am fluent in both English and Chinese." If you are asked whether you belong to any political organizations, be wary because this is often an effort to determine your religion or political affiliation. You might answer, "The only organizations to which I belong that are relevant to this job are the Training and Development Association and the National Communication Association." If a diplomatic response, such as a partial answer, doesn't satisfy the interviewer, it is appropriate for you to be more assertive. You might ask, "How does your question pertain to qualifications for this job?" This more direct response can be effective in protecting your rights without harming the climate. It is possible to be both assertive and cordial, and this is generally advisable. Figure B.2 lists some questions that can and cannot legally be asked by employment interviewers.

Figure B.2
Legal and Illegal Questions

It's legal to ask:
1. Are you a law-abiding person?
2. Do you have the physical strength to do this job?
3. Are you fluent in any languages other than English?
4. Could you provide proof that you are old enough to meet the age requirements for this job?
5. Your transcript shows you took a course in socialism. Did you find it valuable?

But illegal to ask:
1. Are you physically disabled?
2. Are you a native speaker of English?
3. How old are you?
4. Are you a socialist?
5a. Would you be willing to live in a town without a temple/church/synagogue?
5b. Does your religion allow to work on Saturdays?
6. May I have a picture to put with your file?
7. Do you have (plan to have) children?
8. Are you married?
9. Do you have reliable child care?
10. Do you own a car or a house?
11. What is your political affiliation?

CHAPTER SUMMARY

In this appendix, we have gained insight into the structure and processes involved in interviewing. We have learned that most interviews follow a three-part sequence and that different styles and forms of questions are used to achieve different objectives in interview situations.

In the second section of this appendix, we focused on three guidelines for effective communication when interviewing, especially in the context of job seeking. The first guideline is to prepare by researching the company and the interviewer, by reviewing your qualifications

and experience, and by practicing dealing with questions, including difficult ones. A second guideline for effectiveness in interviews is to be person-centered in your communication. Adapting the content and style of your communication to the person with whom you are interacting is important. A final suggestion is to become familiar with legal issues relevant to interviewing. Whether you are an interviewer or an interviewee, you should know and abide by laws governing what can and cannot be asked in interviews.

COMMUNICATION IN OUR LIVES ONLINE

The key concepts, For Further Reflection and Discussion questions, and Experiencing Communication in Our Lives case study that follow will help you review, reflect on, and extend the information and ideas presented in this appendix. These resources, and a diverse selection of additional study tools, are also available online at

the Premium Website for *Communication in Our Lives*. Your Premium Website includes a student workbook, interactive video activities, a book companion Website, Speech Builder Express, and InfoTrac College Edition. For more information or to access this book's online resources, visit **www.cengage.com/login**.

KEY CONCEPTS

authoritarian interviews An interviewing style in which the interviewer has and exerts greater power than the interviewee.

complaint interviews Interviews conducted for the purpose of allowing someone to register a complaint about a product, service, person, or company.

counseling interviews Interviews in which one person with expertise helps another to understand a problem and develop strategies to overcome the difficulty or cope more effectively with it.

distributive interviews A style of interviewing in which roughly equal power is held by interviewer and interviewee.

employment interviews Interviews in which employer and job candidate assess each other and decide whether there is a good fit between them.

exit interviews Interviews designed to gain information, insights, and perceptions about a place of work or education from a person who is leaving.

funnel sequence A pattern of communication in interviews that moves from broad, general questions to progressively narrower, more probing questions.

information-getting interviews Interviews in which the interviewer asks questions to learn about the interviewee's qualifications, background, experience, opinions, knowledge, attitudes, or behaviors.

information-giving interviews Interviews in which the interviewer provides information to the interviewee.

interview A communication transaction that emphasizes questions and answers.

mirror interviews A style of interviewing in which an interviewer's questions reflect previous responses and comments of the interviewee. Mirror interviews allow interviewees substantial power.

performance reviews Interviews in which a supervisor comments on a subordinate's achievements and professional development, identifies any weaknesses or problems, and collaborates with the subordinate to develop goals for future performance. Subordinates should offer perceptions of their strengths and weaknesses and participate actively in developing goals for professional development. Also known as a *performance appraisal.*

persuasive interviews Interviews designed to influence attitudes, beliefs, values, or actions.

problem-solving interviews Interviews in which people collaborate to identify sources of a mutual problem and to develop ways to address or resolve it.

reprimand interview An interview conducted by a supervisor with a subordinate to identify lapses in the subordinate's professional conduct, determine sources of problems, and establish a plan for improving future performance.

stress interviews A style of interviewing in which an interviewer deliberately attempts to create anxiety in the interviewee.

FOR FURTHER REFLECTION AND DISCUSSION

1. Arrange an information-seeking interview with a person in the field you hope to enter. Ask the person to tell you about the job—its advantages and disadvantages and the skills it requires.

2. Schedule an interview with a peer on a topic of mutual interest. During the interview, experiment with different forms of questions (e.g., open, closed, mirror, probing, hypothetical). How do the different types of questions affect the interviewee's comfort and responses?

3. Think about the ethical issues in choosing how to respond to illegal questions if the questions are not personally offensive or bothersome. For instance, Christians might think they have nothing to lose by responding honestly to the question, "Can you work on Saturdays?" If only members of minority religions refuse to answer questions about religion, how effective are the legal protections provided by EEOC guidelines? If all Protestants answer questions about religion honestly, are members of other religions jeopardized?

4. Identify a company that is of interest to you for future employment. Visit the company's Website and record what is presented there. How does information on the Website help you prepare for an effective job interview? Compare what you find on the Website with what is available in printed materials (brochures, annual reports, etc.) about the company.

5. If you would like tips for how to be effective in a virtual interview, use your Premium Website for *Communication in Our Lives* to access **WebLink B.1**.

6. Watch one television program that features interviews of newsmakers. *Face the Nation*, *Meet the Press*, and *60 Minutes* are programs that feature news interviews. Also watch one television program that features interviews with celebrities or people in the limelight. The talk show of Oprah Winfrey is an example of this genre. Identify the form of each question posed (i.e., open, extended, closed) and the response it generates. Do the different kinds of interviews rely on distinct types of questions? Why? What do you conclude about how the style of question affects responses?

EXPERIENCING COMMUNICATION IN OUR LIVES

CASE STUDY: *Tough Questions*

A video of the following conversation is featured in your Appendix B Online Resources for *Communication in Our Lives*. Select "Tough Questions" to watch the video. Improve your own interviewing skills by reading, watching, and evaluating this speech.

Elliott Miller is a second-semester senior who has double-majored in business and communication. Today, he is interviewing with Community Savings and Loan, which is recruiting managerial trainees. Elliott has dressed carefully. He is wearing his good suit, a light blue shirt, a conservative necktie, and wingtips. At 10 a.m. sharp, he knocks on the office door of Karen Bourne, the person with whom he will interview. She is in her mid-30s and is dressed in a conservative navy blue suit. She opens the door and offers her hand to Elliott.

BOURNE: Mr. Miller, I see you're right on time. That's a good start. (*They shake hands.*)

MILLER: Thank you for inviting me to interview today.

BOURNE: Sit down. (*He sits in the chair in front of her desk; she sits behind the desk.*) So, you're about to finish college, are you? I remember that time in my own life—exciting and scary!

MILLER: It's definitely both for me. I'm particularly excited about the job here at Community Savings and Loan.

BOURNE: (*smiles*) Then there's a mutual interest. We had a lot of applications, but we're interviewing only eight of them. What I'd like to do is get a sense of your interests and tell you about our managerial trainee program here, so that we can see if the fit between us is as good as it looks on paper. Sound good to you?

MILLER: Great.

BOURNE: Let me start by telling you about a rather common problem we've had with our past managerial trainees. Many of them run into a problem—something they have trouble learning or doing right. That's normal enough—we expect that. But a lot of the trainees seem to get derailed when that happens. Instead of finding another way to approach the problem, they get discouraged and give up. So I'm very interested in hearing what you've done when you've encountered problems or roadblocks in your life.

MILLER: Well, I can remember one time when I hit a real roadblock. I was taking an advanced chemistry course, and I just couldn't seem to understand the material. I failed the first exam, even though I'd studied hard.

BOURNE: Good example of a problem. What did you do?

MILLER: I started going to all the tutorial sessions that grad assistants offer. That helped a little, but I still wasn't getting the material the way I should. So, I organized a study team and offered to pay for pizzas so that the students who were on top of the class would have a reason to come.

BOURNE: (*nodding with admiration*) That shows a lot of initiative and creativity. Did the study team work?

MILLER: (*smiling*) It sure did. I wound up getting a B in the course, and so did several other members of the study team who had been in the same boat I was in early in the semester.

BOURNE: So you don't mind asking for help if you need it?

MILLER: I'd rather do that than flounder, but I'm usually pretty able to operate independently.

BOURNE: So you prefer working on your own to working with others?

MILLER: That depends on the situation or project. If I have all that I need to do something on my own, I'm comfortable working solo. But there are other cases in which I don't have everything I need to do something well—maybe I don't have experience in some aspect of the job or I don't have a particular skill or I don't understand some perspectives on the issues. In cases like that, I think teams are more effective than individuals.

BOURNE: Good. Banking management requires the ability to be self-initiating and also the ability to work with others. Let me ask another question. As I was looking over your transcript and résumé, I noticed that you changed your major several times. Does that indicate you have difficulty making a commitment and sticking with it?

MILLER: I guess you could think that, but it really shows that I was willing to explore a lot of alternatives before making a firm commitment.

BOURNE: But don't you think that you wasted a lot of time and courses getting to that commitment?

MILLER: I don't think so. I learned something in all of the courses I took. For instance, when I was a philosophy major, I learned about logical thinking and careful reasoning. That's going to be useful to me in management. When I was majoring in English, I learned how to write well and how to read others' writing critically. That's going to serve me well in management too.

BOURNE: So what led you to your final decision to double-major in business and communication? That's kind of an unusual combination.

MILLER: It seems a very natural one to me. I wanted to learn about business because I want to be a manager in an organization. I need to know how organizations work, and I need to understand different management philosophies and styles. At the same time, managers work with people, and that means I have to have strong communication skills.

Glossary

abstract Removed from concrete reality. Symbols are abstract because they are inferences and generalizations derived from a total reality.

***ad hominem* argument** Latin for "to the man," an argument that attacks the integrity of the person instead of the person's ideas.

agenda setting Mass media's ability to select and call to the public's attention ideas, events, and people.

ambiguous Subject to more than one interpretation. Symbols are ambiguous because their meanings vary from person to person and context to context.

ambushing Listening carefully in order to attack a speaker.

arbitrary Random; not determined by necessity. Symbols are arbitrary because there is no particular reason for any one symbol to stand for a certain referent.

artifacts Personal objects we use to announce our identities and personalize our environments.

assimilation The giving up of one's own culture's ways for those of another culture.

attachment style Any of several patterns of attachment that result from particular parenting styles that teach children who they are, who others are, and how to approach relationships.

attribution A causal account that explains why a thing happened or why someone acted a certain way.

authoritarian interview An interviewing style in which the interviewer has and exerts greater power than the interviewee.

authoritarian leadership A leadership style in which a leader provides direction, exerts authority, and confers rewards and punishments on group members.

bandwagon appeal The fallacious argument that because many people believe or act in a certain way, everyone should.

chronemics A type of nonverbal communication concerned with how we perceive and use time to define identities and interaction.

claim An assertion. A claim advanced in speaking requires grounds (evidence) and warrants (links between evidence and claims).

climate communication One of three constructive forms of participation in group decision making. Climate communication focuses on creating and sustaining an open, engaged atmosphere for discussion.

cognitive complexity The number of constructs used, how abstract they are, and how elaborately they interact to create perceptions.

cognitive restructuring A method of reducing communication apprehension that involves teaching people to revise how they think about speaking situations.

cohesion Closeness among members of a group; *esprit de corps.*

commitment A decision to remain with a relationship. One of three dimensions of enduring romantic relationships, commitment has more impact on relational continuity than does love alone. It is also an advanced stage in the process of escalation in romantic relationships.

communication A systemic process in which people interact with and through symbols to create and interpret meanings.

communication apprehension Anxiety associated with real or anticipated communication encounters. Communication apprehension is common and can be constructive.

communication network A set of formal and informal links between members of organizations.

communication rules Shared understandings of what communication means and what behaviors are appropriate in various situations.

comparison A form of evidence that uses associations between two things that are similar in some important way.

complaint interview An interview conducted for the purpose of allowing someone to register a complaint about a product, service, person, or company.

constitutive rules Communication rules that define what communication means by specifying how certain communicative acts are to be counted.

constructivism The theory that we organize and interpret experience by applying cognitive structures, called *schemata*.

content level of meaning One of two levels of meaning in communication. The content level of meaning is the literal, or denotative, information in a message.

convergence The integration of mass media, computers, and telecommunications.

counseling interview An interview in which one person with expertise helps another to understand a problem and develop strategies to overcome the difficulty or cope more effectively with it.

credibility The perception that a person is informed and trustworthy. Listeners confer it, or refuse to confer it, on speakers.

critical listening Attending to communication to analyze and evaluate the content of communication or the person speaking.

critical thinking Examining ideas reflectively and carefully to decide what you should believe, think, or do.

cultivation The cumulative process by which television fosters beliefs about social reality.

cultivation theory The theory that television promotes an inaccurate worldview that viewers nonetheless assume reflects real life.

cultural relativism The idea that cultures vary in how they think, act, and behave as well as in what they believe and value; not the same as moral relativism.

culture Beliefs, understandings, practices, and ways of interpreting experience that are shared by a number of people.

deductive reasoning A form of reasoning in which a general premise followed by a specific claim establishes a conclusion.

defensive listening Perceiving personal attacks, criticisms, or hostility in communication when no offense is intended.

democratic leadership A style of leadership that provides direction without imposing strict authority on a group.

demographic audience analysis A form of audience analysis that seeks information about the general features of a group of listeners.

derived credibility The expertise and trustworthiness that listeners attribute to a speaker as a result of how the speaker communicates during a presentation.

digital divide The gap between people and communities with access to media, especially social media, and people and communities with less or no access.

direct definition Communication that explicitly tells us who we are by specifically labeling us and reacting to our behaviors. Direct definition usually occurs first in families and then in interaction with peers and others.

distributive interview A style of interviewing in which roughly equal power is held by interviewer and interviewee.

dual perspective The ability to understand another person's perspective, beliefs, thoughts, or feelings.

dynamic Evolving and changing over time.

ego boundaries A person's internal sense of where he or she stops and the rest of the world begins.

egocentric communication An unconstructive form of group contribution that blocks others or calls attention to oneself.

either–or logic The fallacy of suggesting or assuming that only two options or courses of action exist when in fact there may be more.

emotional intelligence The ability to recognize which feelings are appropriate in which situations and the ability to communicate those feelings effectively.

empathy The ability to feel with another person or to feel what that person feels in a given situation.

employment interview An interview in which employer and job candidate assess each other and decide whether there is a good fit between them.

environmental factors Elements of settings that affect how we feel and act. Environmental factors are a type of nonverbal communication.

ethnocentrism The tendency to regard ourselves and our way of life as superior to other people and other ways of life.

ethos The perceived personal character of the speaker.

evidence Material used to support claims. Types of evidence are statistics, examples, comparisons, and quotations. Visual aids may be used to represent evidence graphically.

example A form of evidence; a single instance that makes a point, dramatizes an idea, or personalizes information. The four types of examples are undetailed, detailed, hypothetical, and anecdotal.

exit interview An interview designed to gain information, insights, and perceptions about a place of work or education from a person who is leaving.

extemporaneous speaking A presentational style that includes preparation and practice but not memorization of words and nonverbal behaviors.

fallacy An error in reasoning.

feedback Response to a message; may be verbal, nonverbal, or both. In communication theory, the concept of feedback appeared first in interactive models of communication.

formal outline A complete outline of a speech, including the parts of a speech, main points, supporting material, transitions, and citations for sources.

funnel sequence A pattern of communication in interviews that moves from broad, general questions to progressively narrower, more probing questions.

gatekeeper A person or group that decides which messages pass through the gates of media that control information flow to consumers.

grounds Evidence that supports claims in a speech.

group Three or more people who interact over time, are interdependent, and follow shared rules of conduct to reach a common goal. The team is one type of group.

groupthink The cessation of critical, independent thought on the part of a group's members about ideas generated by the group.

halo effect The tendency to assume that an expert in one area is also an expert in other unrelated areas.

haptics Nonverbal communication that involves physical touch.

hasty generalization A broad claim based on too few examples or insufficient evidence.

hearing The physiological activity that occurs when sound waves hit our eardrums. Unlike listening, hearing is a passive process.

high-context communication style The indirect and undetailed communication favored in collectivist cultures.

hypothetical thought Cognitive awareness of experiences and ideas that are not part of the concrete, present situation.

identification The recognition and enlargement of common ground between communicators.

identity script A guide to action based on rules for living and identity. Initially communicated in families, identity scripts define our roles, how we are to play them, and basic elements in the plot of our lives.

impromptu speaking Public speaking that involves little preparation. Speakers think on their feet as they talk about ideas and positions with which they are familiar.

indexing A technique of noting that statements reflect specific times and circumstances and may not apply to other times or circumstances.

individualism/collectivism One of five dimensions of variation among cultures, this refers to the extent to which members of a culture understand themselves as part of, and connected to, their families, groups, and cultures.

inductive reasoning A form of reasoning that begins with specific instances and forms general conclusions based on them.

informational listening Listening to gain and understand information; tends to focus on the content level of meaning.

information-getting interview An interview in which the interviewer asks questions to learn about the interviewee's qualifications, background, experience, opinions, knowledge, attitudes, or behaviors.

information-giving interview An interview in which the interviewer provides information to the interviewee.

informative speech A presentation that aims to increase listeners' knowledge, understanding, or abilities.

initial credibility The expertise and trustworthiness that listeners attribute to a speaker before a presentation begins. Initial credibility is based on the speaker's titles, positions, experiences, or achievements known to listeners before they hear the speech.

inoculation "Immunization" of listeners to opposing ideas and arguments that they may later encounter.

interpersonal communication Communication between people, usually in close relationships such as friendship and romance.

interpretation The subjective process of evaluating and explaining perceptions.

interview A communication transaction that emphasizes questions and answers.

intrapersonal communication Communication with ourselves; self-talk.

investment Something put into a relationship that cannot be recovered should the relationship end. Investments, more than rewards and love, increase commitment.

key word outline An abbreviated speaking outline that includes only key words for each point in a speech. The key words trigger the speaker's memory of the full point.

kinesics Body position and body motions, including those of the face.

***laissez-faire* leadership** From the French for "to allow to do," this style of leadership is nondirective and sometimes leads to unproductive group work.

leadership A set of functions that assists groups in accomplishing tasks efficiently and well while maintaining a good climate.

listening A complex process that consists of being mindful, physically receiving messages, selecting and organizing information, interpreting, responding, and remembering.

literal listening Listening only to the content level of meaning and ignoring the relational level of meaning.

loaded language An extreme form of evaluative language that relies on words that strongly slant perceptions and hence meanings.

logos Rational or logical proofs.

long-term/short-term orientation One of five dimensions of variation among cultures, this refers to the extent to which members of a culture think about long term (history and future) versus short term (present).

low-context communication style The direct, precise, and detailed communication favored in individualistic cultures.

mainstreaming The process by which mass communication stabilizes and homogenizes social perspectives; a concept in cultivation theory.

manuscript speaking A presentational style that involves speaking from the complete manuscript of a speech.

masculinity/femininity One of five dimensions of variation among cultures, this refers to the extent to which a culture values aggressiveness, competitiveness, looking out for yourself, and dominating others and nature (considered masculine orientations) versus gentleness, cooperation, and taking care of others and living in harmony with the natural world (considered feminine orientations).

mass media Channels of mass communication, such as television and radio.

meaning The significance we attach to phenomena such as words, actions, people, objects, and events.

media literacy The ability to understand the influence of mass media and to access, analyze, evaluate, and respond to mass media in informed, critical ways.

memorized speaking A presentational style in which a speech is memorized word for word in advance.

metaphor An implicit comparison of two different things that have something in common.

mindfulness From Buddhism, being fully present in the moment; the first step of listening and the foundation of all other steps.

mind map A holistic record of information on a topic. Mind mapping is a method that can be used to narrow speech topics or to keep track of information gathered during research.

mind reading Assuming that we understand what another person thinks or how another person perceives something.

minimal encouragers Communication that, by expressing interest in hearing more, gently invites another person to elaborate.

mirror interview A style of interviewing in which an interviewer's questions reflect previous responses and comments of the interviewee. Mirror interviews allow interviewees substantial power.

monopolizing Continually focusing communication on oneself instead of on the person who is talking.

motivated sequence pattern A pattern for organizing persuasive speeches that consists of five steps: attention, need, satisfaction, visualization, and action.

multilingual Able to speak and think in more than one language.

neutralization One of four responses to relational dialectics; involves balancing or finding a compromise between two dialectical poles.

noise Anything that has potential to interfere with intended communication.

nonverbal communication All forms of communication other than words themselves; includes inflection and other vocal qualities as well as several other behaviors.

norm An informal rule that guides how members of a group or culture think, feel, act, and interact. Norms define what is normal or appropriate in various situations.

oral style The visual, vocal, and verbal aspects of the delivery of a public speech.

organizational culture Ways of thinking, acting, and understanding work that are shared by members of an organization and that reflect an organization's distinct identity.

paralanguage Vocal communication that does not include actual words; for example, sounds, vocal qualities, accents, and inflection.

paraphrasing A method of clarifying others' meaning by restating their communication.

participation A response to cultural diversity in which people incorporate some practices, customs, and traditions of other groups into their own lives.

particular others One source of social perspectives that people use to define themselves and guide how they think, act, and feel. The perspectives of particular others are the viewpoints of people who are significant to the self.

passion Intensely positive feelings and desires for another person. Passion is based on the rewards of involvement and is not equivalent to commitment.

pathos Emotional proofs for claims.

perception The process of actively selecting, organizing, and interpreting people, objects, events, situations, and activities.

performance review An interview in which a supervisor comments on a subordinate's achievements and professional development, identifies any weaknesses or problems, and collaborates with the subordinate to develop goals for future performance. Subordinates should offer perceptions of their strengths and weaknesses and participate actively in developing goals for professional development. Also known as a *performance appraisal*.

personal construct A bipolar mental yardstick that allows us to measure people and situations along specific dimensions of judgment.

personal relationship A relationship defined by uniqueness, rules, relational dialectics, and commitment and affected by contexts. Personal relationships, unlike social ones, are irreplaceable.

person-centered perception The ability to perceive another as a unique and distinct individual apart from social roles and generalizations.

perspective of the generalized other Viewpoint based on the rules, roles, and attitudes endorsed by the whole social community in which we live.

persuasive interview An interview designed to influence attitudes, beliefs, values, or actions.

persuasive speech A presentation that aims to change listeners by prompting them to think, feel, or act differently.

physical appearance Physical features of people and the values attached to those features; a type of nonverbal communication.

policy A formal statement of an organizational practice. An organization's policies reflect and uphold the overall culture of the organization.

positive visualization A technique of reducing speaking anxiety; a person visualizes herself or himself communicating effectively in progressively challenging speaking situations.

post hoc, ergo propter hoc Latin phrase meaning "After this, therefore because of this." The fallacy of suggesting or assuming that because event B follows event A, event A has therefore caused event B.

power The ability to influence others; a feature of small groups that affects participation.

power distance One of five dimensions of variation among cultures, this refers to the size of the gap between people with high and low power and the extent to which that gap is regarded as normal.

power over The ability to help or harm others. Power over others usually is communicated in ways that highlight the status and influence of the person using the power.

power to The ability to empower others to reach their goals. People who use power to help others generally do not highlight their own status and influence.

problem-solving interview An interview in which people collaborate to identify sources of a mutual problem and to develop ways to address or resolve it.

procedural communication One of three constructive ways of participating in group decision making. Procedural communication orders ideas and coordinates the contributions of members.

process Something that is ongoing and continuously in motion, the beginnings and endings of which are difficult to identify. Communication is a process.

prototype A knowledge structure that defines the clearest or most representative example of some category.

proxemics A type of nonverbal communication that includes space and how we use it.

pseudolistening Pretending to listen.

psychological responsibility The responsibility for remembering, planning, and coordinating domestic work and child care. In general, women assume the psychological responsibility for child care and housework even if both partners share in the actual tasks.

puffery In advertising, superlative claims for a product that seem factual but are actually meaningless.

punctuation Defining the beginning and ending of interaction or interaction episodes.

qualifier A word or phrase that limits the scope of a claim. Common qualifiers are most, usually, and in general.

quotation A form of evidence that uses exact citations of statements made by others. Also called *testimony*.

rebuttal A response to listeners' reservations about a claim made by a speaker.

red herring argument An argument that is irrelevant to the topic; an attempt to divert attention from something the arguer can't or doesn't want to address.

reflected appraisal Our perceptions of others' views of us.

reframing One of four responses to relational dialectics. The reframing response transcends the apparent contradiction between two dialectical poles and reinterprets them as not in tension.

regulative rules Communication rules that regulate interaction by specifying when, how, where, and with whom to talk about certain things.

relational culture A private world of rules, understandings, and patterns of acting and interpreting that partners create to give meaning to their relationship; the nucleus of intimacy.

relational dialectics Opposing forces or tensions that are normal parts of all relationships. The three relational dialectics are autonomy/connectedness, novelty/predictability, and openness/closedness.

relational listening Listening to support another person or to understand another person's feelings and perceptions; focuses on the relational level of meaning as much as on the content level of meaning.

relationship level of meaning One of two levels of meaning in communication; expresses the relationship between communicators.

reprimand interview An interview conducted by a supervisor with a subordinate to identify lapses in the subordinate's professional conduct, determine sources of problems, and establish a plan for improving future performance.

resistance A response to cultural diversity in which the cultural practices of others are attacked or the superiority of one's own cultural traditions is proclaimed.

resonance The extent to which media representations are congruent with personal experience.

respect A response to cultural diversity in which one values others' customs, traditions, and values, even if one does not actively incorporate them into one's own life.

rite A dramatic, planned set of activities that brings together aspects of an organization's culture in a single event.

ritual A form of communication that occurs regularly and that members of an organization perceive as a familiar and routine part of organizational life.

rules Patterned ways of behaving and interpreting behavior; all relationships develop rules.

role The collection of responsibilities and behaviors associated with and expected of a specific position in an organization.

schemata (singular: *schema*) Cognitive structures we use to organize and interpret experiences. Four types of schemata are prototypes, personal constructs, stereotypes, and scripts.

script One of four cognitive schemata. A script defines an expected or appropriate sequence of action in a particular setting.

segmentation One of four responses to relational dialectics. Segmentation responses meet one dialectical need while ignoring or not satisfying the contradictory dialectical need.

selective listening Focusing on only selected parts of communication. We listen selectively when we screen out parts of a message that don't interest us or with which we disagree and also when we rivet attention on parts of communication that do interest us or with which we agree.

self A multidimensional process in which the individual forms and acts from social perspectives that arise and evolve in communication.

self-disclosure Revelation of information about ourselves that others are unlikely to discover on their own.

self-fulfilling prophecy An expectation or judgment of ourselves brought about by our own actions.

self-sabotage Self-talk that communicates that we're no good, we can't do something, we can't change, and so forth. Undermines belief in ourselves and motivation to change and grow.

self-serving bias The tendency to attribute our positive actions and successes to stable, global, internal influences that we control and to attribute negative actions and failures to unstable, specific, external influences beyond our control.

separation One of four responses to relational dialectics, in which friends or romantic partners assign one pole of a dialectic to certain spheres of activities or topics and the contradictory dialectical pole to distinct spheres of activities or topics.

silence The lack of verbal communication or paralanguage. Silence is a type of nonverbal communication that can express powerful messages.

simile A direct comparison that typically uses the words *like* or *as* to link two things.

situational audience analysis A method of audience analysis that seeks information about specific listeners that relates directly to a topic, speaker, and occasion.

skills training A method of reducing communication apprehension that assumes that anxiety is a result of lack of speaking skills and therefore can be reduced by learning skills.

slippery slope The fallacy of suggesting or assuming that once a certain step is taken, other steps will inevitably follow that will lead to some unacceptable consequence.

social climbing The attempt to increase personal status in a group by winning the approval of high-status members.

social community A group of people who live within a dominant culture yet who also have common distinctive experiences and patterns of communicating.

social comparison Comparing ourselves with others to form judgments of our own talents, abilities, qualities, and so forth.

social loafing Exists when members of a group exert less effort than they would if they worked alone.

social media Electronic tools that allow people to connect and to interact actively.

specific purpose A behavioral objective or observable response that a speaker specifies as a gauge of effectiveness; reinforces a speaker's more general speaking goals.

speech to entertain A speech the primary goal of which is to amuse, interest, or engage listeners.

speech to inform A speech the primary goal of which is to increase listeners' understanding, awareness, or knowledge of some topic.

speech to persuade A speech the primary goal of which is to change listeners' attitudes, beliefs, or behaviors or to motivate listeners to action.

standpoint theory The theory that a culture includes a number of social groups that differently shape the knowledge, identities, and opportunities of members of those groups.

static evaluation Assessments that suggest something is unchanging or static. "Bob is impatient" is a static evaluation.

statistics A form of evidence that uses numbers to summarize a great many individual cases or to demonstrate relationships between phenomena.

stonewalling Refusal to discuss issues that are creating tension in a relationship. Stonewalling is especially corrosive in relationships because it blocks the possibility of resolving conflicts.

stereotype A predictive generalization about people and situations.

stress interview A style of interviewing in which an interviewer deliberately attempts to create anxiety in the interviewee.

structure In an organization, the set of procedures, relationships, and practices that provides predictability for members so that they understand roles, procedures, and expectations and so that work gets done.

survey research Research that involves asking a number of people about their opinions, preferences, actions, or beliefs relevant to a speaking topic.

symbol An arbitrary, ambiguous, and abstract representation of a phenomenon. Symbols are the basis of language, much nonverbal behavior, and human thought.

system A group of interrelated elements that affect one another. Communication is systemic.

systematic desensitization A method of reducing communication apprehension that teaches people how to relax physiologically and then helps them practice feeling relaxed as they imagine themselves in progressively difficult communication situations.

task communication One of three constructive forms of participation in group decision making; focuses on giving and analyzing information and ideas.

team A special kind of group characterized by different and complementary resources of members and a strong sense of collective identity. All teams are groups, but not all groups are teams.

terminal credibility The cumulative expertise and trustworthiness listeners attribute to a speaker as a result of the speaker's initial and derived credibility; may be greater or less than initial credibility, depending on how effectively a speaker communicates.

thesis statement The main idea of an entire speech. It should capture the key message in a concise sentence that listeners can remember easily.

tolerance A response to diversity in which one accepts differences even though one may not approve of or even understand them.

totalizing Responding to people as if one aspect of them were the sum total of who they are.

Toulmin model of reasoning A representation of effective reasoning that includes five components: claim, grounds (evidence), warrant (link between grounds and claim), qualifier, and rebuttal.

transitions Words and sentences that connect ideas and main points in a speech so that listeners can follow a speaker.

uncertainty avoidance One of five dimensions of variation among cultures, this refers to the extent to which people try to avoid ambiguity and vagueness.

understanding A response to cultural diversity in which it is assumed that differences are rooted in cultural teachings and that no traditions, customs, and behaviors are intrinsically more valuable than others.

uses and gratification theory The theory that people choose to attend to mass communication in order to fulfill personal needs and preferences.

visual aids Presentation of evidence by such visual means as charts, graphs, photographs, and physical objects to reinforce ideas presented verbally or to provide information.

warrant A justification for grounds (evidence) and claims in persuasive speaking.

working outline A sketch of main ideas and their relationships; used by and intended only for the speaker.

works cited A list of sources used in preparing a speech.

References

Acitelli, L. (1988). When spouses talk to each other about their relationship. *Journal of Social and Personal Relationships, 5,* 185–199.

Adams, K., & Galanes, G. (2011). *Communicating in groups.* New York: McGraw-Hill.

Adler, J. (2007, March 12). The great sorority purge. *Newsweek,* p. 47.

Adler, R., Hirsch, S., & Mordaunt, M. (Eds.). (2012). *Voice and communication therapy for the transgender/transsexual client: A comprehensive clinical guide* (2nd ed.). San Diego, CA: Plural Publications.

Adler, R., Towne, N., & Proctor, R., II. (2010). *Looking out/looking in* (13th ed.). Belmont, CA: Wadsworth/Cengage.

Agee, W., Ault, P., & Emery, E. (1996). *Introduction to mass communications* (12th ed.). Reading, MA: Addison-Wesley.

Aires, E. (1996). *Men and women in interaction: Reconsidering differences.* New York: Oxford University Press.

Alberts, J., Tracy, S., & Trethewey, A. (2011). An integrative theory of the division of domestic labor: Threshold level, social organizing and sensemaking. *Journal of Family Communication, 11,* 21–28.

Alcoff, L. (1991, Winter). The problem of speaking for others. *Cultural Critique, 5*–32.

Allen, B. J. (2006). Communicating race at WeighCo. In J. T. Wood & S. W. Duck (Eds.), *Composing relationships: Communication in everyday life* (pp. 146–155). Belmont, CA: Thomson Wadsworth.

Allen, M., Hale, J., Mongeau, P., Berkowitz-Stafford, S., Stafford, S., Shanahan, W., et al. (1990). Testing a model of message sidedness: Three replications. *Communication Monographs, 37,* 275–291.

Allen, M., Hunter, J., & Donahue, W. (1989). Meta-analysis of self-report data on the effectiveness of public speaking anxiety treatment techniques. *Communication Education, 38,* 54–76.

Amodio, D., & Showers, C. (2006). "Similarity breeds liking" revisited: The moderating role of commitment. *Journal of Social and Personal Relationships, 22,* 817–836.

Andersen, M. L., & Collins, P. H. (Eds.). (2006). *Race, class, and gender: An anthology* (6th ed.). Belmont, CA: Wadsworth.

Andersen, P. (1993). Cognitive schemata in personal relationships. In S. W. Duck (Ed.), *Understanding relationship processes, Vol. 1: Individuals in relationships* (pp. 1–29). Newbury Park, CA: Sage.

Andersen, P. (1999). *Nonverbal communication: Forms and functions.* Mountain View, CA: Mayfield.

Anderson, C., & Martin, M. (1995). The effects of communication motives, interaction, involvement, and loneliness on satisfaction: A model of small groups. *Small Group Research, 16,* 118–137.

Anderson, K., & Leaper, C. (1998). Meta-analyses of gender effects on conversational interruption: Who, when, where, and how? *Sex Roles, 39,* 225–252.

Anderson, R., & Killenberg, G. (1998). *Interviewing: Speaking, listening, and learning for professional life.* Mountain View, CA: Mayfield.

Angelou, M. (1990). *I shall not be moved.* New York: Random House.

Aratani, L. (2007, February 27). Teens aren't studying at 100%. *Raleigh News & Observer,* p. 4A.

Argyle, M., & Henderson, M. (1984). The rules of friendship. *Journal of Social and Personal Relationships, 1,* 211–237.

Ashcraft, K. L. (2006). Back to work: Sights/sites of difference in gender and organizational communication studies. In B. J. Dow & J. T. Wood (Eds.), *The handbook of gender and communication* (pp. 97–122). Thousand Oaks, CA: Sage.

Ashcraft, K. L., & Mumby, D. K. (2004). *Reworking gender: A feminist communicology of organization.* Thousand Oaks, CA: Sage.

Axtell, R. (1990a). *Dos and taboos around the world* (2nd ed.). New York: Wiley.

Axtell, R. (1990b). *Dos and taboos of hosting international visitors*. New York: Wiley.

Axtell, R. (2007). *Essential do's and taboos: The complete guide to international business and leisure travel*. New York: Wiley.

Ayres, J., & Hopf, T. S. (1990). The long-term effect of visualization in the classroom: A brief research report. *Communication Education, 39*, 75–78.

Babbie, E. (2009). *The practice of social research* (11th ed.). Belmont, CA: Wadsworth.

Bachen, C., & Illouz, F. (1996). Imagining romance: Young people's cultural modes of romance and love. *Critical Studies in Mass Communication, 13*, 279–308.

Badiou, A. (2012). *In praise of love*. London: Serpent's Tail.

Bailey, A. (1998, February 29). Daily bread. *Durham Herald-Sun*, p. C5.

Bakalar, N. (2012, July 24). Fitness products come mostly filled with fiction. *New York Times*, p. D5.

Balcetis, E., & Dunning, D. (2010). Wishful seeing: Desirable objects are seen as closer. *Psychological Science, 21*, 147–152.

Banse, R. (2004). Adult attachment and marital satisfaction: Evidence for dyadic configuration effects. *Journal of Social and Personal Relationships, 21*, 273–282.

Banville, T. (1978). *How to listen: How to be heard*. Chicago: Nelson-Hall.

Barash, S. (2006). *Tripping the prom queen*. New York: St. Martin's Griffin.

Barge, K. (2009). Social groups, workgroups, and teams. In W. F. Eadie (Ed.), *21st century communication: A reference handbook* (pp. 340–348). Thousand Oaks, CA: Sage.

Bargh, J. (1997). *The automaticity of everyday life*. Mahwah, NJ: Erlbaum.

Bargh, J. (1999, January 29). The most powerful manipulative messages are hiding in plain sight. *Chronicle of Higher Education*, p. B6.

Baron, N. (2010). *Always on: Language in an online and mobile world*. New York: Oxford University Press.

Baron, R. A., & Berne, D. (1994). *Social psychology* (7th ed.). Boston: Allyn & Bacon.

Barry, B. (2001). *Culture and equality: An egalitarian critique of multiculturalism*. New Haven, CT: Harvard University Press.

Bartlett, T. (2003, March 7). Take my chair (please). *Chronicle of Higher Education*, pp. A36–A38.

Baxter, L. A. (1987). Symbols of relationship identity in relationship cultures. *Journal of Social and Personal Relationships, 4*, 261–279.

Baxter, L. A. (1990). Dialectical contradictions in relational development. *Journal of Social and Personal Relationships, 7*, 69–88.

Baxter, L. A. (1993). The social side of personal relationships: A dialectical perspective. In S. Duck (Ed.), *Understanding relationship processes, Vol. 3: Social context and relationships* (pp. 139–165). Newbury Park, CA: Sage.

Baxter, L. A., & Montgomery, B. (1996). *Relating: Dialogues and dialectics*. New York: Guilford Press.

Bazar, E. (2007, April 24). Stalking "definitely a problem" for women at college. *USA Today*, p. 5A.

Beatty, M. J., & Behnke, R. R. (1991). Effects of public speaking trait anxiety and intensity of speaking task on heart rate during performance. *Human Communication Research, 18*, 147–176.

Beatty, M. J., Plax, T., & Kearney, P. (1985). Reinforcement vs. modeling theory in the development of communication apprehension: A retrospective analysis. *Communication Research Reports, 12*, 80–95.

Beck, A. (1988). *Love is never enough*. New York: Harper & Row.

Beckman, H. (2003). Difficult patients. In M. Feldman & J. Christensen (Eds.), *Behavioral medicine in primary care* (pp. 23–32). New York: McGraw-Hill.

Beebe, S., & Masterson, J. (2011). *Communication in small groups: Principles and practices*. New York: Allyn & Bacon.

Begley, S. (2009, February 16). Will the BlackBerry sink the presidency? *Newsweek*, pp. 36–39.

Beil, L. (2011, November 29). The certainty of memory has its day in court. *New York Times*, pp. D1, D6.

Bell, A. (1989). *The complete manager's guide to interviewing*. Homewood, IL: Dow Jones-Irwin.

Bellamy, L. (1996, December 18). Kwanzaa cultivates cultural and culinary connections. *Raleigh News & Observer*, pp. 1F, 9F.

Benenson, J., Gordon, A., & Roy, R. (2000). Children's evaluative appraisals in competition in tetrads versus dyads. *Small Group Research, 31*, 635–652.

Bergen, K., & Braithwaite, D. O. (2009). Identity as constituted in communication. In W. F. Eadie (Ed.),

21st century communication: A reference handbook (pp. 166–173). Thousand Oaks, CA: Sage.

Berger, A. (2011). *Ads, fads, and consumer culture.* Lanham, MD: Rowman.

Bergner, R. M., & Bergner, L. L. (1990). Sexual misunderstanding: A descriptive and pragmatic formulation. *Psychotherapy, 27,* 464–467.

Berne, E. (1964). *Games people play.* New York: Grove Press.

Berrett, D. (2011, November 18). What spurs students to stay in college and learn? Good teaching and diversity. *Chronicle of Higher Education,* p. A27.

Berrett, D. (2012, February 3). "Adrift" in adulthood: Students who struggled in college find life harsher after graduation. *Chronicle of Higher Education,* p. A20.

Bertman, S. (1998). *Hyperculture: The human cost of speed.* Westport, CT: Praeger.

Birdwhistell, R. (1970). *Kinesics and context.* Philadelphia: University of Pennsylvania Press.

Blow, C. M. (2009, February 21). A nation of cowards? *New York Times,* p. A17.

Bodey, K., & Wood, J. T. (2009). Grrrlpower: What counts as voice and who does the counting? *Southern Journal of Communication, 74,* 325–337.

Bohill, C., Owen, C., Jeong, E., Alicea, B., & Bocca, F. (2009). Virtual reality. In W. F. Eadie (Ed.), *21st century communication: A reference handbook* (pp. 534–542). Thousand Oaks, CA: Sage.

Borchers, T. (2006). *Rhetorical theory: An introduction.* Belmont, CA: Thomson Wadsworth.

Bornstein, M., & Bradley, R. (Eds.). (2003). *Socioeconomic status, parenting, and child development.* Mahwah, NJ: Earlbaum.

Bornstein, R., & Languirand, M. (2003). *Healthy dependency.* New York: Newmarket Press.

Bostrom, R. N. (1988). *Communicating in public: Speaking and listening.* Santa Rosa, CA: Burgess.

Bourhis, J., & Allen, M. (1992). Meta-analysis of the relationship between communication apprehension and cognitive performance. *Communication Education, 41,* 68–76.

Bowlby, J. (1973). *Separation: Attachment and loss* (Vol. 2). New York: Basic Books.

Bowlby, J. (1988). *A secure base: Parent-child attachment and healthy human development.* New York: Basic Books.

Braithwaite, D., & Braithwaite, C. (1997). Viewing persons with disabilities as a culture. In L. Samovar & R. Porter (Eds.), *Intercultural communication: A reader* (8th ed., pp. 154–164). Belmont, CA: Wadsworth.

Braithwaite, D., & Kellas, J. K. (2006). Shopping for and with friends: Everyday communication at the shopping mall. In J. T. Wood & S. W. Duck (Eds.), *Composing relationships: Communication in everyday life* (pp. 86–95). Belmont, CA: Thomson Wadsworth.

Braithwaite, S. R., Delevi, R., & Fincham, F. D. (2010). Romantic relationships and the physical and mental health of college students. *Personal Relationships, 17,* 1–12.

Brenning, K., Soenens, B., Braet, C., & Bosmans, G. (2011). An adaptation of the experiences in close relationships scale-revised for use with children and adolescents. *Journal of Personal and Social Relationships, 28,* 1048–1072.

Bruess, C., & Hoefs, A. (2006). The cat puzzle recovered: Composing relationships through family ritual. In J. T. Wood & S. W. Duck (Eds.), *Composing relationships: Communication in everyday life* (pp. 65–75). Belmont, CA: Thomson Wadsworth.

Bryant, J., & Oliver, M. B. (Eds.). (2008). *Media effects* (3rd ed.). New York: Routledge.

Buber, M. (1957). Distance and relation. *Psychiatry, 20,* 97–104.

Buber, M. (1970). *I and thou* (Walter Kaufmann, Trans.). New York: Scribner.

Burgoon, J. K., & Le Poire, B. (1999). Nonverbal cues and interpersonal judgments: Participant and observer perceptions of intimacy, dominance, and composure. *Communication Monographs, 66,* 105–124.

Burke, K. (1950). *A rhetoric of motives.* Englewood Cliffs, NJ: Prentice Hall.

Burleson, B. R., & Rack, J. (2008). Constructivism theory. In L. A. Baxter & D. O. Braithwaite (Eds.), *Engaging theories in interpersonal communication: Multiple perspectives* (pp. 51–63). Thousand Oaks, CA: Sage.

Business bulletin. (1996, July 18). *Wall Street Journal,* p. A1.

Buzzanell, P. M., & Lucas, K. (2006). Gendered stories of career: Unfolding discourses of time, space, and identity. In B. J. Dow & J. T. Wood (Eds.), *The handbook of gender and communication* (pp. 161–178). Thousand Oaks, CA: Sage.

Calero, H. (2005). *The power of nonverbal communication: What you do is more important than what you say.* Los Angeles: Silver Lake.

Canary, D., & Stafford, L. (Eds.). (1994). *Communication and relational maintenance.* New York: Academic Press.

Cancian, F. (1987). *Love in America.* Cambridge, UK: Cambridge University Press.

Cannell, C., & Kahn, R. (1968). Interviewing. In G. Lindzey & E. Aronson (Eds.), *The handbook of social psychology* (2nd ed., Vol. 2, pp. 569–584). Reading, MA: Addison-Wesley.

Carnegie, D. (1936). *How to win friends and influence people.* New York: Simon & Schuster.

Carr, N. (2011). *The shallows: What the Internet is doing to our brains.* New York: Norton.

Cassirer, E. (1944). *An essay on man.* New Haven, CT: Yale University Press.

Caughlin, J., & Vangelisti, A. (2000). An individual difference explanation of why married couples engage in the demand/withdraw pattern of conflict. *Journal of Social and Personal Relationships, 17,* 523–551.

Center for Health Communication. (2012). *Harvard alcohol project.* Retrieved June 13, 2012, from http://www.hsph.harvard.edu/research/chc/harvard-alcohol-project/index.html

Centers for Disease Control and Prevention. (2009). *STD surveillance 2009.* Retrieved July 1, 2011, from http://www.cdc.gov/std/stats09/chlamydia.htm

Centers for Disease Control and Prevention. (2011). *HIV/AIDS.* Retrieved June 27, 2011, from http://www.cdc.gov/hiv/default.htm

Chan, Y. (1999). Density, crowding, and factors intervening in their relationship: Evidence from a hyper-dense metropolis. *Social Indicators Research, 48,* 103–124.

Chen, H., Luo, S., Yue, G., Xu, D., & Zhaoyang, R. (2009). Do birds of a feather flock together in china? *Personal Relationships, 16,* 167–186.

Chen, P. (2012, June 5). The trouble with "doctor knows best." *Raleigh News & Observer,* p. D5.

Christensen, A. (2004). *Patient adherence to medical treatment regiments: Bridging the gap between behavioral science and biomedicine.* New Haven, CT: Yale University Press.

Ciarrochi, J., & Mayer, J. (2007). *Applying emotional intelligence.* Florence, KY: Psychology Press.

Clancy, C. M. (2011, May 3). *Safety culture creates better care for patients.* U.S. Department of Health and Human Services: Agency for Healthcare Research. Retrieved from http://www.ahrq.gov/consumer/cc/cc050311.htm

Clark, R., & Delia, J. (1997). Individuals' preferences for friends' approaches to providing support in distressing situations. *Communication Reports, 10,* 115–121.

Clydesdale, T. (2009, January 23). Wake up and smell the new epistemology. *Chronicle of Higher Education,* pp. B7–B9.

Cockburn-Wootten, C., & Zorn, T. (2006). Cabbages and headache cures: Work stories within the family. In J. T. Wood & S. W. Duck (Eds.), *Composing relationships: Communication in everyday life* (pp. 137–145). Belmont, CA: Thomson Wadsworth.

Cole, T., & Leets, L. (1999). Attachment styles and intimate television viewing: Insecurely forming relationships in a parasocial way. *Journal of Social and Personal Relationships, 16,* 495–511.

Collins, F. S., & Fauci, A. S. (2010, May 23). AIDS in 2010: How we're living with HIV. *Parade,* pp. 10–12.

Collins, P. (1998). *Fighting words: Black women and the search for justice.* Minneapolis: University of Minnesota Press.

Conley, D. (2009). *Elsewhere, U.S.A.* New York: Pantheon.

Connerley, M. L., & Pedersen, P. B. (2005). *Leadership in a diverse and multicultural environment.* Thousand Oaks, CA: Sage.

Cooley, C. H. (1912). *Human nature and the social order.* New York: Scribner.

Cooper, L. (1997). Listening competency in the workplace: A model for training. *Business Communication Quarterly, 60,* 75–84.

Coopman, S., & Lull, J. (2013). *Public speaking: The evolving art.* Belmont, CA: Wadsworth.

Cox, J. R. (1989). The fulfillment of time: King's "I Have a Dream" speech (August 28, 1963). In M. C. Leff & F. J. Kaufeld (Eds.), *Texts in context: Critical dialogues on significant episodes in American rhetoric* (pp. 181–204). Davis, CA: Hermagoras Press.

Cox, J. R. (2013). Personal communication.

Cronen, V., Pearce, W. B., & Snavely, L. (1979). A theory of rule-structure and types of episodes and a study of perceived enmeshment in undesired repetitive patterns ("URPs"). In D. Nimmo (Ed.), *Communication yearbook* (Vol. 3, pp. 225–240). New Brunswick, NJ: Transaction Books.

Cross, G. (2008). *Men to boys: The making of modern immaturity.* New York: Columbia University Press.

Crossen, C. (1997, July 10). Blah, blah, blah. *Wall Street Journal*, pp. 1A, 6A.

Crowley, G. (1998, March 16). Healer of hearts. *Newsweek*, pp. 50–55.

Cummings, M. (1993). Teaching the African American rhetoric course. In J. Ward (Ed.), *African American communication: An anthology in traditional and contemporary studies* (pp. 239–248). Dubuque, IA: Kendall/Hunt.

Dainton, M. (2006). Cat walk conversations: Everyday communication in dating relationships. In J. T. Wood & S. W. Duck (Eds.), *Composing relationships: Communication in everyday life* (pp. 36–45). Belmont, CA: Thomson Wadsworth.

Daly, J., & McCroskey, J. (Eds.). (1984). *Avoiding communication: Shyness, reticence, and communication apprehension.* Beverly Hills, CA: Sage.

Darling, A., & Dannels, D. (2003). Practicing engineers talk about the importance of talk: A report on the role of oral communication in the workplace. *Communication Education, 52,* 1–16.

Davies-Popelka, W. (2011). Mirror, mirror on the wall: Weight, identity, and selrf-talk. In D. O. Braithwaite & J. T. Wood (Eds.), *Casing interpersonal communication* (pp. 25–32). Dubuque, IA: Kendall Hunt.

Davis, S., & Kieffer, J. (1998). Restaurant servers influence tipping behaviors. *Psychological Reports, 83,* 223–236.

Deal, T., & Kennedy, A. (1999). *The new corporate cultures: Revitalizing the workplace after downsizing, mergers, and reengineering.* Reading, MA: Pereus Books.

DeFleur, M. L., & Ball-Rokeach, S. (1989). *Theories of mass communication* (5th ed.). White Plains, NY: Longman.

Delia, J., Clark, R. A., & Switzer, D. (1974). Cognitive complexity and impression formation in informal social interaction. *Speech Monographs, 41,* 299–308.

DeMaris, A. (2007). The role of relationship inequity in marital disruption. *Journal of Social and Personal Relationships, 24,* 177–195.

Demographics. (2009, January 26). *Newsweek*, p. 70.

Devereux, E. (Ed.). (2007). *Media studies: Key issues and debates.* Thousand Oaks, CA: Sage.

DeVito, J. (1994). *Human communication: The basic course* (6th ed.). New York: HarperCollins.

Dickson, F. (1995). The best is yet to be: Research on long-lasting marriages. In J. T. Wood & S. W. Duck (Eds.), *Understanding relationship processes, 6: Understudied relationships: Off the beaten track* (pp. 22–50). Thousand Oaks, CA: Sage.

van Dijk, J. (2005). *The deepening divide: Inequality in the information society.* Thousand Oaks, CA: Sage.

Dixon, T. L. (2006). Psychological reactions to crime news portrayals of Black criminals: Understanding the moderating roles of prior news view and stereotype endorsement. *Communication Monographs, 73,* 162–187.

Dixson, M., & Duck, S. W. (1993). Understanding relationship processes: Uncovering the human search for meaning. In S. W. Duck (Ed.), *Understanding relationship processes, Vol. 1: Individuals in relationships* (pp. 175–206). Newbury Park, CA: Sage.

Domrose, C. (2010, August 23). *The time is now: "Culture of safety" key to preventing errors.* Retrieved from Nurse.com: http://news.nurse.com/article/20100823/NATIONAL01/108230030/-1/frontpage

Downing, J., & Garmon, C. (2001). Teaching students in the basic course how to use presentation software. *Communication Education, 50,* 218–229.

Doyle, G. (2008). *Understanding media economics* (2nd ed.). Thousand Oaks, CA: Sage.

Duck, S. W. (2006). The play, playfulness, and the players: Everyday interaction as improvised rehearsal of relationships. In J. T. Wood & S. W. Duck (Eds.), *Composing relationships: Communication in everyday life* (pp. 15–23). Belmont, CA: Thomson Wadsworth.

Duck, S. W. (2007). *Human relationships* (4th ed.). Thousand Oaks, CA: Sage.

Duck, S. W., & McMahan, D. (2012). *Basics of communication* (2nd ed.). Thousand Oaks, CA: Sage.

Duck, S. W., & Wood, J. T. (2006). What goes up may come down: Gendered patterns in relational dissolution. In M. Fine & J. Harvey (Eds.), *The handbook of divorce and dissolution of romantic relationships* (pp. 169–187). Mahwah, NJ: Erlbaum.

Dunbar, R. (2012). *The science of love and betrayal.* London: Faber & Faber.

Einhorn, L. (2000). *The Native American oral tradition: Voices of the spirit and soul.* Westport, CT: Praeger.

Ekins, R., & King, D. (2006). *The transgender phenomenon.* Thousand Oaks, CA: Sage.

Ellis, A. (1988). *How to stubbornly refuse to make yourself miserable about anything—yes, anything.* New York: Lyle Stuart.

Emmons, S. (1998, February 3). The look on his face: Yes, it was culture shock. *Raleigh News & Observer*, p. 5E.

Erbert, L. (2000). Conflict and dialectics: Perceptions of dialectical contradictions in marital conflict. *Journal of Social and Personal Relationships, 17,* 638–659.

Evans, B., Coman, G., & Goss, B. (1996). Consulting skills training and medical students' interviewing efficiency. *Medical Education, 30,* 121–128.

Eytan, T., Benabio, J., Golla, V., Parikh, V., & Stein, S. (2011, Winter). Social media and the health system. *Permanente Journal, 15,* 71–74.

Fackelmann, K. (2006, March 6). Arguing hurts the heart in more ways than one. *USA Today*, p. 10D.

Faigley, L., & Selzer, J. (2000). *Good reasons.* Needham Heights, MA: Allyn & Bacon.

Fanning, L., Brewer, D., Parker, G., Reyna, K., & Weigel, C. (2007). Apprehension among hospital nurses providing end-of-life care. *Journal of Hospice and Palliative Nursing, 9,* 86–91.

Farnill, D., Hayes, S., & Todisco, J. (1997). Interviewing skills: Self-evaluation by medical students. *Medical Education, 31,* 122–127.

Fehr, B. (1993). How do I love thee: Let me consult my prototype. In S. W. Duck (Ed.), *Understanding relationship processes, 1: Individuals in relationships* (pp. 87–122). Newbury Park, CA: Sage.

Fehr, B., & Russell, J. A. (1991). Concept of love viewed from a prototype perspective. *Journal of Personality and Social Psychology, 60,* 425–438.

Ferguson, S. D. (2008). *Public speaking: Building competency in stages.* New York: Oxford University Press.

Ferrante, J. (2009). *Sociology: A global perspective* (7th ed.). Belmont, CA: Thomson Wadsworth.

Fincham, F. D., & Bradbury, T. N. (1987). The impact of attributions in marriage: A longitudinal analysis. *Journal of Personality and Social Psychology, 53,* 510–517.

Fitch, N. (Ed.). (2000). *How sweet the sound: The spirit of African American history.* New York: Harcourt College.

Fogg, P. (2008, July 25). Thinking in black and white. *Chronicle of Higher Education*, p. B19.

Foley, M. (2006). Locating "difficulty": A multi-site model of intimate terrorism. In C. D. Kirpatrick, S. W. Duck, & M. K. Foley (Eds.), *Relating difficulty: The processes of constructing and managing difficult interaction* (pp. 43–59). Mahwah, NJ: Erlbaum.

Ford Foundation. (1998, October 6). *Americans see many benefits to diversity in higher education, finds first ever national poll on topic.* Press release via Business Wire.

Forsyth, D. (2009). *Group dynamics* (5th ed.). Belmont, CA: Wadsworth Cengage.

Fox, S. (2011, January 21). *Americans living with disabilities and their technology profile.* Washington, DC: Pew Research Center.

France, D. (2006, January & February). Domestic violence. *AARP Magazine*, pp. 84–85, 112–118.

Freeman, J. (2009). *The tyranny of e-mail.* New York: Simon & Schuster/Scribner.

Gabric, D., & McFadden, K. (2001). Student and employer perceptions of desirable entry-level operations management skills. *Mid-American Journal of Business, 16,* 51–59.

Galanti, G. (2000). An introduction to cultural differences. *Western Journal of Medicine, 172,* 335–336.

Galvin, K. (2006). Gender and family interaction: Dress rehearsal for an improvisation? In B. Dow & J. T. Wood (Eds.), *Handbook of gender and communication research* (pp. 41–55). Thousand Oaks, CA: Sage.

Galvin, K., Dickson, F., & Marrow, S. (2006). Systems theory: Patterns and (w)holes in family communication. In D. O. Braithwaite & L. A. Baxter (Eds.), *Engaging theories in family communication: Multiple perspectives* (pp. 308–324). Thousand Oaks, CA: Sage.

Garner, T. (1994). Oral rhetorical practice in African American culture. In M. Houston & V. Chen (Eds.), *Our voices: Essays in culture, ethnicity, and communication* (pp. 81–91). Los Angeles: Roxbury Press.

Gass, R. (1999). *Fallacy list: SpCom 335. Advanced argumentation.* California State University, Fullerton. Retrieved October 27, 2007, from http://comm-faculty.fullerton.edu/rgass/fallacy31.htm

Gentner, D., & Boroditsky, L. (2009). Early acquisition of nouns and verbs: Evidence from the Navajo. In V. Gathercole (Ed.), *Routes to language* (pp. 5–86). New York: Taylor & Francis.

George, L. (1995, December 26). Holiday's traditions are being formed. *Raleigh News & Observer*, pp. C1, C3.

Gerbner, G. (1990). Epilogue: Advancing on the path of righteousness (maybe). In N. Signorielli & M. Morgan (Eds.), *Cultivation analysis: New directions in media effects research* (pp. 250–261). Thousand Oaks, CA: Sage.

Gibb, C. (1969). Leadership. In G. Lindsey & E. Aronson (Eds.), *The handbook of social psychology* (2nd ed., pp. 205–282). Reading, MA: Addison-Wesley.

Gladwell, M. (2000, May 29). The new-boy network: What do job interviews really tell us? *New Yorker*, pp. 68–72, 84–86.

Golberg, A. E., & Perry-Jenkins, M. (2007). The division of labor and perceptions of parental roles: Lesbian couples across the transition to parenthood. *Journal of Social and Personal Relationships, 24*, 297–318.

Goldstein, S. (2011). Relational aggression in young adults' friendships and romantic relationships. *Journal of Personal Relationships, 18*, 645–656.

Goleman, D. (1995). *Emotional intelligence.* New York: Bantam.

Goleman, D. (1998). *Working with emotional intelligence.* New York: Bantam.

Goleman, D. (2007). *Social intelligence: The new science of human relationships.* New York: Bantam.

Goleman, D. (2011). *The brain and emotional intelligence.* Florence, MA: More than Sound.

Goleman, D., McKee, A., & Boyatzis, R. (2002). *Primal leadership: Realizing the power of emotional intelligence.* Cambridge, MA: Harvard Business School Press.

González, A., Houston, M., & Chen, V. (Eds.). (2012). *Our voices: Essays in culture, ethnicity, and communication.* New York: Oxford University Press.

Goodall, H., & Trethewey, A. (2009). *Organizational communication: Balancing creativity and constraint.* Boston: Bedford/St. Martin's.

Gottman, J. (1993). The roles of conflict engagement, escalation, or avoidance in marital interaction: A longitudinal view of five types of couples. *Journal of Consulting and Clinical Psychology, 61*, 6–15.

Gottman, J. (1994a). *What predicts divorce? The relationship between marital processes and marital outcomes.* Hilllsdale, NJ: Erlbaum.

Gottman, J. (1994b). Why marriages fail. *Family Therapy Newsletter*, pp. 41–48.

Gottman, J. (1999). *Seven principles for making marriages work.* New York: Crown.

Gottman, J., & Carrère, S. (1994). Why can't men and women get along? Developmental roots and marital inequities. In D. Canary & L. Stafford (Eds.), *Communication and relational maintenance* (pp. 203–229). New York: Academic Press.

Gregory, G., Healy, R., & Mazierkska, E. (2007). *The essential guide to careers in media and film.* Thousand Oaks, CA: Sage.

Gregory, T. (2012, March 5). Young adults in an age of "hyper-connectivity." *Raleigh News & Observer*, p. D1.

Griffin, C. (2004). *An invitation to public speaking* (2nd ed.). Belmont, CA: Wadsworth.

Griffin, C. (2012). *An invitation to public speaking* (4th ed.). Belmont, CA: Wadsworth.

Gronbeck, B. E., McKerrow, R., Ehninger, D., & Monroe, A. H. (1994). *Principles and types of speech communication* (12th ed.). Glenview, IL: Scott, Foresman.

Groopman, J. (2007). *How doctors think.* Boston, MA: Houghton Mifflin.

Gueguen, N., & De Gail, M. (2003). The effect of smiling on helping behavior: Smiling and good Samaritan behavior. *Communication Reports, 16*, 133–140.

Guerrero, L. (1996). Attachment style differences in intimacy and involvement: A test of the four-category model. *Communication Monographs, 63*, 269–292.

Guerrero, L., Andersen, P., & Afifi, W. (2008). *Close encounters: Communication in relationships* (2nd ed.). Thousand Oaks, CA: Sage.

Guerrero, L., & Floyd, K. (2006). *Nonverbal communication in close relationships.* Mahwah, NJ: Erlbaum.

Guerrero, L., Jones, S., & Boburka, R. (2006). Sex differences in emotional communication. In K. Dindia & D. Canary (Eds.), *Sex differences and similarities in communication* (pp. 242–261). Mahwah, MJ: Erlbaum.

Guerrero, L., La Valley, A., & Farinelli, L. (2008). The experience and expression of anger, guilt, and sadness in marriage: An equity theory explanation. *Journal of Social and Personal Relationships, 25,* 699–724.

Gunns, R., Johnson, L., & Hudson, S. (2002). Victim selection and kinematics: A point-light investigation of vulnerability to attack. *Journal of Nonverbal Behavior, 26,* 129–158.

Gupta, S. (2012, August 1). More treatment, more mistakes. *New York Times,* p. A21.

Hacker, K., Goss, B., & Townley, C. (1998). Employee attitudes regarding electronic mail policies: A case study. *Management Communication Quarterly, 11,* 422–432.

Hager, M., & Springen, K. (1998, March 16). Is love the best drug? *Newsweek,* pp. 54–56.

Hall, E. T. (1966). *The hidden dimension.* New York: Anchor.

Hall, E. T. (1977). *Beyond culture.* New York: Doubleday.

Hall, J. (2006). How big are nonverbal sex differences? The case of smiling and nonverbal sensitivity. In K. Dindia & D. Canary (Eds.), *Sex differences and similarities in communication* (pp. 59–82). Mahwah, NJ: Lawrence Erlbaum.

Hall, J. A. (1987). On explaining gender differences: The case of nonverbal communication. In P. Shaver & C. Hendricks (Eds.), *Sex and gender* (pp. 177–200). Newbury Park, CA: Sage.

Hall, J. A., Coats, E., & Smith-LeBeau, L. (2004). Nonverbal behavior and the vertical dimension of social relations: A meta-analysis. *Psychological Bulletin, 131,* 898–924. (Cited in M. L. Knapp & J. A. Hall (2006), *Nonverbal communication in human interaction.* Belmont, CA: Thomson Wadsworth.)

Hamachek, D. (1992). *Encounters with the self* (3rd ed.). Fort Worth: Harcourt Brace Jovanovich.

Hamilton, C. (2005). *Essentials of public speaking* (4th ed.). Belmont, CA: Wadsworth.

Hamilton, C. (2008). *Essentials of public speaking* (8th ed.). Belmont, CA: Cengage Wadsworth.

Hamermesh, D. (2011). *Beauty pays: Why attractive people are more successful.* Princeton, NJ: Princeton University Press.

Haraway, D. (1988). Situated knowledges: The science question in feminism and the privilege of partial perspective. *Signs, 14,* 575–599.

Harding, S. (1991). *Whose science? Whose knowledge? Thinking from women's lives.* Ithaca, NY: Cornell University Press.

Hargie, O. (Ed.). (2006). *The handbook of communication skills.* Florence, KY: Psychology Press.

Harmon, A. (2002). Talk, type, read e-mail: The trials of multitasking. In E. Bucy (Ed.), *Living in the information age* (pp. 79–81). Belmont, CA: Thomson Wadsworth.

Harris, G. (2011, July 11). For aspiring doctors, the people skills test. *New York Times,* pp. A1, A12.

Harris, T., & Sherblom, J. (2010). *Small group and team communication.* Boston: Allyn & Bacon.

Harris, T. J. (1969). *I'm OK, you're OK.* New York: Harper & Row.

Heider, F. (1958). *The psychology of interpersonal relations.* New York: Wiley.

Hendrick, C., & Hendrick, S. (1996). Gender and the experience of heterosexual love. In J. T. Wood (Ed.), *Gendered relationships* (pp. 131–148). Mountain View, CA: Mayfield.

Hendrick, C., Hendrick, S., Foote, F. H., & Slapion-Foote, M. J. (1984). Do men and women love differently? *Journal of Social and Personal Relationships, 2,* 177–196.

Hendrick, S., & Hendrick, C. (2006). Measuring respect in close relationships. *Journal of Social and Personal Relationships, 23,* 881–899.

Hendrix, K. (2012). Home as respite for the working-class academic. In A. González, M. Houston, & V. Chen (Eds.), *Our voices: Essays in culture, ethnicity, and communication* (pp. 240–246). New York: Oxford University Press.

Herbert, B. (2009, August 8). Women at risk. *New York Times,* p. A17.

Hesmondhaigh, D. (2007). *The cultural industries* (2nd ed.). Thousand Oaks, CA: Sage.

Hewes, D. (Ed.). (1995). *The cognitive bases of interpersonal perception.* Mahwah, NJ: Erlbaum.

Hickson, M., III, Stacks, D., & Moore, N. (2003). *Nonverbal communication: Studies and applications* (4th ed.). Los Angeles: Roxbury.

Hillis, K. (2006). A space for the trace: Memorable eBay and narrative effect. *Space and Culture, 9,* 140–156.

Hillis, K., Petit, M., & Jarrett, K. (2012). *Google and the culture of search.* New York: Routledge.

Hobson, K. (2010, July 2). Health care workers behaving badly. *Wall Street Journal Health Blog.* Retrieved June 14, 2012, from http://blogs.wsj.com/health/2010/07/02/health-care-workers-behaving-badly/

Hobson, K. (2011, March 11). Report: Communication breakdown leads to hospital errors. *Wall Street Journal Health Blog*. Retrieved June 14, 2012, from http://blogs.wsj.com/health/2011/03/22/report-communication-break-down-leads-to-hospital-errors/

Hochschild, A., & Machung, A. (2003). *The second shift* (Rev. ed.). New York: Viking.

Hodson, R., & Sullivan, T. A. (2002). *The social organization of work* (3rd ed.). Belmont, CA: Wadsworth.

Hoffman, J. (2012, June 4). A warning to teenagers before they start dating. *New York Times*, pp. A12, A13.

Hofstede, G. (1980). *Cultural consequences: International differences in work-related values*. Beverly Hills, CA: Sage.

Hofstede, G. (1991). *Culture and organizations: Software of the mind*. New York: McGraw-Hill.

Hofstede, G. (2001). *Cultures' consequences: Comparing values, behaviors, institutions, and organizations across nations*. Thousand Oaks, CA: Sage.

Hofstede, G., Hofstede, G. J., & Minkov, M. (2010). *Cultures and organizations: Software of the mind* (3rd ed.). New York: McGraw-Hill.

Holt-Lunstad, J., Smith, T. B., & Layton, J. B. (2010). Social relationships and mortality risk: A meta-analytic review. *PLoS Med, 7*, 1–20.

Honoré, C. (2005). *In praise of slowness*. San Francisco: Harper.

Hoon, H., & Tan, M. (2008). Organizational citizenship behavior and social loafing: The role of personality, motives, and contextual factors". *Journal of Psychology, 142*, 89–108.

Hoover, E. (2010, January 29). An immigrant learns 2 new languages. *Chronicle of Higher Education*, p. A22.

Houston, M., & Wood, J. T. (1996). Difficult dialogues, expanded horizons: Communicating across race and class. In J. T. Wood (Ed.), *Gendered relationships* (pp. 39–56). Mountain View, CA: Mayfield.

Huesmann, L. R., Moise-Titus, J., Podolski, C., & Eron, L. D. (2003). Longitudinal relations between children's exposure to TV violence and their aggressive and violent behavior in young adulthood: 1977-1992. *Developmental Psychology, 39*, 201–221.

Huston, M., & Schwartz, P. (1996). Gendered dynamics in the romantic relationships of lesbians and gay men. In J. T. Wood (Ed.), *Gendered relationships* (pp. 163–176). Mountain View, CA: Mayfield.

Inman, C. C. (1996). Friendships among men: Closeness in the doing. In J. T. Wood (Ed.), *Gendered relationships* (pp. 95–110). Mountain View, CA: Mayfield.

International Listening Association. (1995, April). An ILA definition of listening. *ILA Listening Post, 53*, 4.

Irvine, M. (2012, June 4). Does texting ruin the art of conversation? *Raleigh News & Observer*, p. 3A.

Jackson, M. (2008). *Distracted: The erosion of attention and the coming dark age*. New York: Prometheus.

Jackson, S., & Allen, J. (1990). *Meta-analysis of the effectiveness of one-sided and two-sided argumentation*. Paper presented at the International Communication Association, Montreal, Canada.

Jaffe, C. (2013). *Public speaking: Concepts and skills for a diverse society* (7th ed.). Belmont, CA: Wadsworth.

Jaffe, E. (2004, October). Peace in the Middle East may be impossible: Lee D. Ross on naïve realism and conflict resolution. *American Psychological Society Observer, 17*, 9–11.

James, D., & Clarke, S. (1993). Women, men, and interruptions: A critical review. In D. Tannen (Ed.), *Gender and conversational interaction* (pp. 281–312). New York: Oxford University Press.

James, N. (2000). When Miss America was always white. In A. González, M. Houston, & V. Chen (Eds.), *Our voices: Essays in culture, ethnicity, and communication* (pp. 42–46). Los Angeles: Roxbury.

Jandt, F. E. (2009). Culture. In W. F. Eadie (Ed.), *21st century communication: A reference handbook* (pp. 396–404). Thousand Oaks, CA: Sage.

Janis, I. L. (1989). *Crucial decisions: Leadership in policymaking and crisis management*. New York: Free Press.

Jenkins, H. (2006). *Convergence culture: Where old and new media collide*. New York: NYU Press.

Jenkins, H. (2007, February 16). From YouTube to YouNiversity. *Chronicle of Higher Education*, pp. B9–B10.

Jhally, S., & Katz, J. (2001, Winter). Big trouble, little pond. *UMass*, pp. 26–31.

Johnson, F. (2000). *Speaking culturally: Language diversity in the United States.* Thousand Oaks, CA: Sage.

Johnson, F. L. (1989). Women's culture and communication: An analytic perspective. In C. M. Lont & S. A. Friedley (Eds.), *Beyond the boundaries: Sex and gender diversity in communication* (pp. 301–316). Fairfax, VA: George Mason University Press.

Johnson, F. L. (1996). Friendships among women: Closeness in dialogue. In J. T. Wood (Ed.), *Gendered relationships* (pp. 79–94). Mountain View, CA: Mayfield.

Johnson, M. P. (2006). Gendered communication and intimate partner violence. In B. Dow & J. T. Wood (Eds.), *Handbook of gender and communication research* (pp. 71–87). Thousand Oaks, CA: Sage.

Johnson, M. P. (2008). *A typology of domestic violence.* Boston: Northeastern University Press.

Jones, D. (2007, March 30). Do foreign executives balk at sports jargon? *USA Today*, pp. 1B–2B.

Jordan, M. (2012, February 17). More marriages cross race, ethnicity lines. *Wall Street Journal*, p. A2.

June, A. (2012, March 23). Work-life balance is out of reach for many scientists, and not just women. *Chronicle of Higher Education*, p. A29.

Kaufman, M., & Kimmel, M. (2011). *The guy's guide to feminism.* Berkeley, CA: Seal Press.

Keizer, G. (2010). *The unwanted sound of everything we want: A book about noise.* New York: Perseus-Public Affairs.

Kellerman, K. (2011, November). From communication professor to trial consultant. *Spectra*, pp. 11–15.

Kelley, H. H. (1967). Attribution theory in social psychology. In D. Levine (Ed.), *Nebraska symposium on motivation* (Vol. 15, pp. 192–238). Lincoln: University of Nebraska Press.

Kendall, D. (2011). *Framing class.* Lanham, MD: Rowman.

Kennedy, G. (Ed. & Trans.). (1991). *Aristotle on rhetoric.* London: Oxford University Press.

Kiesler, C. A., & Kiesler, S. B. (1971). Role of forewarning in persuasive communications. *Journal of Abnormal and Social Psychology, 18,* 210–221.

Kikoski, J. (1998). Effective communication in the performance appraisal interview: Face-to-face communication for public managers in the culturally diverse workplace. *Public Personnel Management, 27,* 491–513.

Kilbourne, J. (2004). The more you subtract, the more you add: Cutting girls down to size. In J. Spade & K. Valentine (Eds.), *The kaleidoscope of gender* (pp. 234–244). Belmont, CA: Thomson Wadsworth.

Kimmel, M. (2008). *Guyland: The perilous world where boys become men.* New York: Macmillan.

Klass, P. (2012, January 10). Seeing social media more as portal than pitfall. *New York Times*, p. D5.

Knapp, M., & Hall, J. A. (2006). *Nonverbal communication in human interaction.* Belmont, CA: Thomson Wadsworth.

Kohlberg, L. (1958). *The development of modes of thinking and moral choice in the years 10 to 16.* Unpublished doctoral dissertation, University of Chicago.

Korzybski, A. (1948). *Science and sanity* (4th ed.). Lakeville, CT: International Non-Aristotelian Library.

Krannich, R., & Banis, W. (1990). *High-impact résumés and letters* (4th ed.). Woodridge, VA: Impact Publications.

Kreps, G. L. (2010). *Health communication.* Thousand Oaks, CA: Sage.

Kupfer, D., First, M., & Regier, D. (2002). *A research agenda for SSM-V.* Washington, DC: American Psychiatric Press.

LaFasto, F., & Larson, C. (2001). *When teams work best: 6,000 team members and leaders tell what it takes to succeed.* Thousand Oaks, CA: Sage.

Lamb, S., & Brown, L. (2006). *Packaging girlhood: Rescuing our daughters from marketers' schemes.* New York: St. Martin's Press.

Landrum, R., & Harrold, R. (2003). What employers want from psychology graduates. *Teaching of Psychology, 30,* 131–133.

Lane, R. (2000). *The loss of happiness in market democracies.* New Haven, CT: Yale University Press.

Langer, S. (1953). *Feeling and form: A theory of art.* New York: Scribner.

Langer, S. (1979). *Philosophy in a new key: A study in the symbolism of reason, rite, and art* (3rd ed.). Cambridge, MA: Harvard University Press.

Lasch, C. (1990, Spring). Journalism, publicity and the lost art of argument. *Gannett Center Journal*, pp. 1–11.

Laswell, H. D. (1948). The structure and function of communication in society. In L. Bryson (Ed.), *The communication of ideas* (pp. 37–51). New York: Harper & Row.

Lau, B. (1989). Imagining your path to success. *Management Quarterly*, 30, 30–41.

Lawless, B. (2012). More than white: Locating an invisible class identity. In A. González, M. Houston, & V. Chen (Eds.), *Our voices: Essays in culture, ethnicity, and communication* (pp. 247–253). New York: Oxford University Press.

Le, B., & Agnew, C. (2003). Commitment and its theorized determinants: A meta-analysis of the investment model. *Personal Relationships*, 10, 37–57.

Leaper, N. (1999). How communicators lead at the best global companies. *Communication World*, 16, 33–36.

Lee, J. A. (1973). *The colours of love: An exploration of the ways of loving*. Don Mills, Ontario, Canada: New Press.

Lee, J. A. (1988). Love-styles. In R. J. Sternberg & M. L. Barnes (Eds.), *The psychology of love* (pp. 38–67). New Haven, CT: Yale University Press.

Lee, W. (1994). On not missing the boat: A processual method for intercultural understandings of idioms and lifeworld. *Journal of Applied Communication Research*, 22, 141–161.

Lee, W. (2000). That's Greek to me: Between a rock and a hard place in intercultural encounters. In L. Samovar & R. Porter (Eds.), *Intercultural communication: A reader* (9th ed., pp. 217–224). Belmont, CA: Wadsworth.

Lefkowitz, J. (2003). *Ethics and values in industrial-organizational psychology*. Mahwah, NJ: Erlbaum.

Lehman, C., & DuFrene, D. (1999). *Business communication* (12th ed.). Cincinnati, OH: South-Western.

Levin, D., & Kilbourne, J. (2008). *So sexy, so soon*. New York: Ballantine.

Levine, M. (2004, June 1). Tell the doc all your problems, but keep it to less than a minute. *New York Times*, p. D6.

Levy, D., Nardick, D., Turner, J., & McWatters, L. (2011, May 13). No cellphone? No internet? So much less stress. *Chronicle of Higher Education*, pp. B27–B28.

Levy, S. (2006, March 27). (Some) attention must be paid! *Newsweek*, p. 16.

Lewin, K., Lippitt, R., & White, R. K. (1939). Patterns of aggressive behavior in experimentally created "social climates." *Journal of Social Psychology*, 10, 271–299.

Lister, K. (2009). *Undress for success: The naked truth about making money at home*. New York: John Wiley and Sons.

Lubrana, A. (2012). Lack of computer access a major hurdle for the poor. *Raleigh News & Observer*, p. 2D.

Lumsden, G., & Lumsden, D. (2004). *Communicating in groups and teams* (4th ed.). Belmont, CA: Wadsworth.

Lumsden, G., & Lumsden, D. (2009). *Communicating in groups and teams* (6th ed.). Belmont, CA: Wadsworth.

Lund, M. (1985). The development of investment and commitment scales for predicting continuity of personal relationships. *Journal of Social and Personal Relationships*, 2, 3–23.

Lustig, M., & Koester, J. (1999). *Intercultural competence: Interpersonal communication across cultures*. New York: Longman.

Lutz-Zois, C., Bradley, A., Mihalik, J., & Moorman-Eavers, E. (2006). Perceived similarity and relationship success among dating couples: An idiographic approach. *Journal of Social and Personal Relationships*, 23, 865–880.

Lyles, J., Dwamena, F., Levin, C., & Smith, R. (2001). Evidence-based patient-centered interviewing. *JCOM*, 8, 28–34.

Major, B., Schmidlin, A. M., & Williams, L. (1990). Gender patterns in social touch: The impact of setting and age. In C. Mayo & N. M. Henley (Eds.), *Gender and nonverbal behavior* (pp. 3–37). New York: Springer-Verlag.

Manusov, V., & Harvey, J. (2001). *Attribution, communication behavior, and close relationships*. Port Chester, New York: Cambridge University Press.

Manusov, V., & Patterson, M. L. (2006). *The Sage handbook of nonverbal communication*. Thousand Oaks, CA: Sage.

Manusov, V., & Spitzberg, B. (2008). Attribution theory. In L. A. Baxter & D. O. Braithwaite (Eds.), *Engaging theories in interpersonal communication: Multiple perspectives* (pp. 37–49). Thousand Oaks, CA: Sage.

Martin, H., & Finn, S. (2010). *Masculinity and femininity*. Minneapolis: University of Minnesota Press.

Matsumoto, D., Franklin, B., Choi, J., Rogers, D., & Tatani, H. (2002). Cultural influences on the expression and perception of emotion. In W. Gudykunst & B. Mody (Eds.), *The handbook of international and intercultural communication* (2nd ed., pp. 107–126). Thousand Oaks, CA: Sage.

McCombs, M., Ghanem, S., & Chernov, G. (2009). Agenda setting and framing. In W. F. Eadie (Ed.),

21st century communication: A reference handbook (pp. 516–524). Thousand Oaks, CA: Sage.

McCroskey, J., & Teven, J. (1999). Goodwill: A reexamination of the construct and its measurement. *Communication Monographs, 66*, 90–103.

McGee, M. (2005). *Self-Help, Inc.: Makeover culture in American life*. New York: Oxford University Press.

McGrane, S. (2000, September 4). Absence makes the typing skills grow stronger. *Raleigh News & Observer*, p. 5D.

McGuire, W. J. (1989). Theoretical foundations of campaigns. In R. E. Rice & C. K. Atkin (Eds.), *Public communication campaigns* (2nd ed., pp. 43–65). Newbury Park, CA: Sage.

McKinney, M. (2006, October). Communication among top-10 fields of study. *Spectra*, p. 8.

McMurtrie, B. (2011, November 18). International enrollments at U.S. colleges grow but still rely on China. *Chronicle of Higher Education*, pp. A16–A20.

Mead, G. H. (1934). *Mind, self, and society*. Chicago: University of Chicago Press.

Meeks, B., Hendrick, S., & Hendrick, C. (1998). Communication, love, and satisfaction. *Journal of Social and Personal Relationships, 15*, 755–773.

Mehrabian, A. (1981). *Silent messages: Implicit communication of emotion and attitudes* (2nd ed.). Belmont, CA: Wadsworth.

Mernissi, F. (2004). Size 6: The Western woman's harem. In J. Spade & C. Valentine (Eds.), *The kaleidoscope of gender: Prisms, patterns, and possibilities* (pp. 297–301). Belmont, CA: Wadsworth.

Metts, S. (2006a). Hanging out and doing lunch: Enacting friendship closeness. In J. T. Wood & S. W. Duck (Eds.), *Composing relationships: Communication in everyday life* (pp. 76–85). Belmont, CA: Thomson Wadsworth.

Metts, S. (2006b). Gendered communication in dating relationships. In B. Dow & J. T. Wood (Eds.), *Handbook of gender and communication research* (pp. 25–40). Thousand Oaks, CA: Sage.

Meyers, D. G. (1993). *Social psychology* (4th ed.). New York: McGraw-Hill.

Meyers, M. (1994). News of battering. *Journal of Communication, 44*, 47–62.

Meyers, M. (1997). *News coverage of violence against women: Engendering blame*. Thousand Oaks, CA: Sage.

Milia, T. (2003). *Doctor, you're not listening*. Philadelphia: Xlibris.

Miller, C. (2012). *Organizational communication: Approaches and processes* (7th ed.). Belmont, CA: Wadsworth/Cengage.

Mino, M. (1996). The relative effects of content and vocal delivery during a simulated employment interview. *Communication Research Reports, 13*, 225–238.

Modaff, D., Butler, J., & DeWine, S. (2011). *Organizational communication: Foundations, challenges, and misunderstandings* (3rd ed.). Boston: Allyn & Bacon.

Moffatt, T. (1979). *Selection interviewing for managers*. New York: Harper & Row.

Mokros, H. (2006). Composing relationships at work. In J. T. Wood & S. W. Duck (Eds.), *Composing relationships: Communication in everyday life* (pp. 175–185). Belmont, CA: Thomson Wadsworth.

Monastersky, R. (2002, March 29). Speak before you think. *Chronicle of Higher Education*, pp. A17–A18.

Monroe, A. H. (1935). *Principles and types of speech*. Glenview, IL: Scott, Foresman.

Monsour, M. (2006). Communication and gender among adult friends. In B. Dow & J. T. Wood (Eds.), *Handbook of gender and communication research* (pp. 57–69). Thousand Oaks, CA: Sage.

Morning, A. (2011). *The nature of race: How scientists think and teach about human difference*. Berkeley, CA: University of California Press.

Morreale, S. (2003, September). Importance of communication. *Spectra*, p. 14.

Morreale, S., Osborn, M., & Pearson, J. (2000). Why communication is important: A rationale for the centrality of the study of communication. *Journal of the Association for Communication Administration, 29*, 1–25.

Motley, M. (1990). Public speaking anxiety qua performance anxiety: A revised model and an alternative therapy. *Journal of Social Behavior and Personality, 5*, 85–104.

Motley, M., & Molloy, J. (1994). An efficacy test of a new therapy ("communication-orientation motivation") for public speaking anxiety. *Journal of Applied Communication Research, 22*, 48–58.

Muehlhoff, T. (2006). "He started it": Everyday communication in parenting. In J. T. Wood & S. W. Duck (Eds.), *Composing relationships:*

Communication in everyday life (pp. 46–54). Belmont, CA: Thomson Wadsworth.

Mumby, D. K. (1993). *Narratives and social control: Critical perspectives*. Newbury Park, CA: Sage.

Mumby, D. K. (2006a). Constructing working-class masculinity in the workplace. In J. T. Wood & S. W. Duck (Eds.), *Composing relationships: Communication in everyday life* (pp. 166–174). Belmont, CA: Thomson Wadsworth.

Mumby, D. K. (2006b). Introduction to Part II. In B. J. Dow & J. T. Wood (Eds.), *The handbook of gender and communication* (pp. 89–95). Thousand Oaks, CA: Sage.

Nagourney, E. (2006, May 9). Surgical teams found lacking, in teamwork. *New York Times*, p. D6.

Nass, C. (2012, May/June). The keyboard and the damage done. *Pacific Standard*, pp. 22–25.

Newsbeast. (2012, January 30). *Newsweek*, p. 12.

Nichols, M. (2009). *The lost art of listening: How learning to listen can improve relationships*. New York: Guilford Press.

Nicotera, A., Clinkscales, M., & Walker, F. (2002). *Understanding organization through culture and structure*. Thousand Oaks, CA: Sage.

Nie, N. (2004). *Better off: Flipping the switch on technology*. New York: HarperCollins.

Niedenthal, P. M., Krauth-Gruber, S., & Ric, F. (2006). *Psychology of emotion*. Thousand Oaks, CA: Sage.

Northouse, P. (2006). *Leadership: Theory and practice* (4th ed.). Thousand Oaks, CA: Sage.

Nunes, M. (2006). *Cyberspaces of everyday life*. Minneapolis: University of Minnesota Press.

O'Hair, D., & Eadie, W. F. (2009). In W. F. Eadie (Ed.), *21st century communication: A reference handbook* (pp. 3–11). Thousand Oaks, CA: Sage.

Ohanian, H. (2009). *Einstein's mistakes*. New York: W.W. Norton.

Olson, D., & Windish, D. (2010). Communication discrepancies between physicians and hospitalized patients. *Archives of Internal Medicine, 170*, 1302–1307.

Olson, J. M., & Cal, A. V. (1984). Source credibility, attitudes, and the recall of past behaviors. *European Journal of Social Psychology, 14*, 203–210.

OMG!!!!! ♥ OED LOL!!!!! (2011, April 5). *New York Times*, p. A20.

One in Four Girls. (2008, March 17). *New York Times*, p. A22.

Opfer, C. (2011, November/December). Disappearing ink: The burgeoning business of tattoo removal. *Miller-McCune*, pp. 20–21.

Orbe, M., & Harris, T. (2001). *Interracial communication: Theory into practice*. Belmont, CA: Wadsworth.

Ornish, D. (1998). *Love and survival: The scientific basis for the healing power of intimacy*. New York: HarperCollins.

Ornish, D. (1999). *Love and survival: 8 pathways to intimacy and health*. New York: HarperCollins.

Pacanowsky, M. (1989). Creating and narrating organizational realities. In B. Dervin, L. Grossberg, B. O'Keefe, & E. Wartella (Eds.), *Rethinking communication: Paradigm exemplars* (pp. 250–257). Thousand Oaks, CA: Sage.

Pacanowsky, M., & O'Donnell-Trujillo, N. (1983). Organizational communication as cultural performance. *Communication Monographs, 30*, 126–147.

Palmieri, P., Peterson, L., Pesta, B., Flit, M., & Saettone, D. (2010). Safety culture as a contemporary healthcare construct: Theoretical review, research assessment, and translation to human resource management. *Advances in Health Care Management, 9*, 97–133.

Papadakos, P. (2011). Electronic distraction: An unmeasured variable in modern medicine. *Anesthesiology News, 37*, 11.

Parker-Pope, T. (2009a, January 13). A problem of the brain, not the hands: Group urges phone ban for drivers. *New York Times*, p. D5.

Parker-Pope, T. (2009b, January 20). Your nest is empty? Enjoy each other. *New York Times*, p. D5.

Parker-Pope, T. (2010, April 14). Is marriage good for your health? *New York Times*, p. MM46.

Pearce, W. B., Cronen, V. E., & Conklin, F. (1979). On what to look at when analyzing communication: A hierarchical model of actors' meanings. *Communication, 4*, 195–220.

Peterson, M. (1997). Personnel interviewers' perceptions of the importance and adequacy of applicants' communication skills. *Communication Education, 46*, 287–291.

Petronio, S., & Caughlin, J. (2006). Communication privacy management theory: Understanding families. In D. O. Braithwaite & L. A. Baxter (Eds.), *Engaging theories in family communication: Multiple perspectives* (pp. 35–49). Thousand Oaks, CA: Sage.

Piaget, J. (1932/1965). *The moral judgment of the child.* New York: Free Press.

Potter, J. (2002). *The 11 myths of media violence.* Thousand Oaks, CA: Sage.

Potter, J. (2009). *Media literacy* (4th ed.). Thousand Oaks, CA: Sage.

Rae-Dupree, J. (2008, December 7). Teamwork, the true mother of invention. *New York Times*, p. B3.

Ramsay, S., Gallois, C., & Callan, V. (1997). Social rules and attributions in the personnel selection interview. *Journal of Occupational and Organizational Psychology, 70,* 189–203.

Rawlins, W. K. (1981). *Friendship as a communicative achievement: A theory and an interpretive analysis of verbal reports.* Unpublished doctoral dissertation, Temple University, Philadelphia.

Rawlins, W. K. (1994). Being there and growing apart: Sustaining friendships during adulthood. In D. Canary & L. Stafford (Eds.), *Communication and relational maintenance* (pp. 275–294). New York: Academic Press.

Reinhard, C. D., & Dervin, B. J. (2009). Media uses and gratifications. In W. F. Eadie (Ed.), *21st century communication: A reference handbook* (pp. 506–515). Thousand Oaks, CA: Sage.

Reis, H. T., Clark, M. S., & Holmes, J. G. (2004). Perceived partner responsiveness as an organizing construct in the study of intimacy and closeness. In D. J. Mashek & A. P. Aron (Eds.), *Handbook of closeness and intimacy* (pp. 201–225). Mahwah, NJ: Erlbaum.

Remland, M. (2000). *Nonverbal communication in everyday life.* Boston: Houghton Mifflin.

Rhodes, T. (2010, November). Learning across the curriculum. *Spectra*, pp. 12–15.

Rhodewalt, F. (Ed.). (2007). *Personality and social behavior.* Florence, KY: Psychology Press.

Rice, A. (2011, November 25). Bleary-eyed students can't stop texting, even to sleep, a researcher finds. *Chronicle of Higher Education*, p. A13.

Richmond, V. P., & McCroskey, J. C. (1992). *Communication: Apprehension, avoidance, and effectiveness* (3rd ed.). Scottsdale, AZ: Gorsuch Scarisbrick.

Richmond, V. P., & McCroskey, J. C. (1995a). *Communication: Apprehension, avoidance, and effectiveness.* Scottsdale, AZ: Gorsuch Scarisbrick.

Richmond, V. P., & McCroskey, J. C. (1995b). *Nonverbal communication in interpersonal relations* (3rd ed.). Boston: Allyn & Bacon.

Richtel, M. (2011, December 15). As doctors use more devices, potential for distraction grows. *New York Times*, pp. A1, A4.

Roberts, S. (2008, August 14). A generation away, minorities may be the majority. *New York Times*, pp. A1, A18.

Robinson, G. (2001, March 4). Sometimes a thank you is enough. *New York Times*, pp. 16, 18.

Robinson, J. D. (2009). Media portrayals and representations. In W. F. Eadie (Ed.), *21st century communication: A reference handbook* (pp. 497–505). Thousand Oaks, CA: Sage.

Rodriguez, R. (2003, September 12) "Blaxicans" and other reinvented Americans. *Chronicle of Higher Education*, pp. B10–B11.

Rosenbaum, L. (2011, November 22). The doctor feels your pain. *Raleigh News & Observer*, pp. 1D–2D.

Rothenberg, P. (2006). *Race, class, and gender in the United States* (7th ed.). New York: Worth.

Rothwell, J. D. (2009). *In mixed company: Small group communication* (7th ed.). Belmont, CA: Wadsworth.

Rowe, A. C., & Carnelley, K. B. (2005). Preliminary support for the use of a hierarchical mapping technique to examine attachment networks. *Personal Relationships, 12,* 499–519.

Salas, E., & Frush, K. (2012). *Improving patient safety through teamwork and team training.* New York: Oxford University Press.

Salerno, S. (2005). *Sham: How the self-help movement made America helpless.* New York: Three Rivers Press.

Samovar, L., & Porter, R. (2009). *Communication between cultures* (6th ed.). Belmont, CA: Wadsworth.

Samovar, L., Porter, R., & McDaniel, E. R. (Eds.). (2011). *Intercultural communication: A reader* (13th ed.). Belmont, CA: Wadsworth.

Samp, J. A., & Palevitz, C. E. (2009). Dating and romantic partners. In W. F. Eadie (Ed.), *21st century communication: A reference handbook* (pp. 322–330). Thousand Oaks, CA: Sage.

Sawyer, K. (2008). *Group genius: The power of creative collaboration.* New York: Basic.

Scarf, M. (2008). *September song: The good news about marriage in the later years.* New York: Riverhead.

Schiavo, R. (2007). *Health communication: From theory to practice.* San Francisco: Jossey-Bass.

Schmidt, J., & Uecker, D. (2007). Increasing understanding of routine/everyday interaction in relationships. *Communication Teacher, 21*, 111–116.

Scholz, M. (2005, June). A "simple" way to improve adherence. *RN, 68*, 82.

Schooler, D., Ward, M., Merriwether, A., & Caruthers, A. (2004). Who's that girl: Television's role in the body image of young white and black women. *Psychology of Women Quarterly, 28*, 38–47.

Schram, P., & Schwartz, H. (2000). *Stories within stories: From the Jewish oral tradition.* Leonia, NJ: Jason Aronson.

Schramm, W. (1955). *The process and effects of mass communication.* Urbana: University of Illinois Press.

Schumpeter. (2011, December 31). *Economist,* p. 50.

Schütz, A. (1999). It was your fault! Self-serving bias in autobiographical accounts of conflicts in married couples. *Journal of Social and Personal Relationships, 16*, 193–208.

Scott, C., & Myers, K. (2005). The socialization of emotion: Learning emotion management at the fire station. *Journal of Applied Communication Research, 33*, 67–92.

Segrin, C. (1998). Interpersonal communication problems associated with depression and loneliness. In P. Andersen & L. Guerrero (Eds.), *Communication and emotion: Theory, research, and applications* (pp. 215–242). San Diego: Academic Press.

Segrin, C., Hanzal, A., & Domschke, T. (2009). Accuracy and bias in newlywed couples' perceptions of conflict styles and the association with marital satisfaction. *Communication Monographs, 76*, 207–233.

Seligman, M. E. P. (1990). *Learned optimism.* New York: Simon & Schuster/Pocket Books.

Seligman, M. E. P. (2002). *Authentic happiness.* New York: Free Press.

Servaty-Seib, H., & Burleson, B. (2007). Bereaved adolescents' evaluations of the helpfulness of support-intended statements: Associations with person centeredness and demographic, personality, and contextual factors. *Journal of Social and Personal Relationships, 24*, 207–223.

Shanahan, J., & Jones, V. (1999). Cultivation and social control. In D. Demers & K. Viswanath (Eds.), *Mass media, social control, and social change* (pp. 89–116). Ames: Iowa State University Press.

Shannon, C., & Weaver, W. (1949). *The mathematical theory of communication.* Urbana: University of Illinois Press.

Shapiro, J., & Kroeger, L. (1991). Is life just a romantic novel? The relationship between attitudes about intimate relationships and the popular media. *American Journal of Family Therapy, 19*, 226–236.

Shattuck, T. R. (1980). *The forbidden experiment: The story of the wild boy of Aveyron.* New York: Farrar, Straus & Giroux.

Shimanoff, S. B. (1980). *Communication rules: Theory and research.* Beverly Hills: Sage.

Sias, P., Heath, R., Perry, T., Silva, D., & Fix, B. (2004). Narratives of workplace friendship deterioration. *Journal of Social and Personal Relationships, 21*, 321–340.

Signorelli, N. (2009). Cultivation and media exposure. In W. F. Eadie (Ed.), *21st century communication: A reference handbook* (pp. 525–567). Thousand Oaks, CA: Sage.

Smiles, S. (1859). *Self-help.* London: John Murray.

Smith, R. (1998, December 1). *Civility without censorship: The ethics of the Internet cyberhate.* Speech delivered at the Simon Wiesenthal Center/Museum of Tolerance, Los Angeles.

Snider, M. (2012, February 24). Study details digital lives by age, sex, and race. *USA Today,* p. 4A.

Sonnentag, S. (2001). High performance and meeting participation: An observational study in software design teams. *Group Dynamics: Theory, Research, and Practice, 5*, 3–18.

Spaeth, M. (1996, July 1). "Prop" up your speaking skills. *Wall Street Journal,* p. A15.

Spencer, T. (1994). Transforming personal relationships through ordinary talk. In S. W. Duck (Ed.), *Understanding relationship processes, 4: Dynamics of relationships* (pp. 58–85). Thousand Oaks, CA: Sage.

Spenser, L., & Pahl, R. (2006). *Rethinking friendship: Hidden solidarities today.* Princeton, NJ: Princeton University Press.

Spitzberg, B., & Cupach, W. (2009). Unwanted communication, aggression and abuse. In W. F. Eadie (Ed.), *21st century communication: A reference handbook* (pp. 444–453). Thousand Oaks, CA: Sage.

Stafford, D. (2012, July 22). Business world is awash in buzzwords. *Raleigh News & Observer*, pp. 1E, 3E.

Stafford, L. (2005). *Maintaining long-distance and cross-residential relationships*. Mahwah, NJ: Erlbaum.

Stafford, L. (2009). Spouses and other intimate partnerships. In W. F. Eadie (Ed.), *21st century communication: A reference handbook* (pp. 296–302). Thousand Oaks, CA: Sage.

Stafford, L., & Merolla, A. (2007). Idealization, reunions, and stability in long-distance dating relationships. *Journal of Social and Personal Relationships, 24*, 37–54.

Stafford, L., Merolla, A., & Castle, J. (2006). When long-distance dating partners become geographically close. *Journal of Social and Personal Relationships, 23*, 901–919.

Stanton, E. C., Anthony, S. B., & Gage, M. J. (1881/1969 reprint). *History of woman suffrage, Vol. I*. New York: Arno and *New York Times*.

Stapel, D. A., & Blanton, H. (Eds.). (2006). *Social comparison theories: Key readings*. Florence, KY: Psychology Press.

Steil, L. (1997). Listening training: The key to success in today's organizations. In M. Purdy & D. Borisoff (Eds.), *Listening in everyday life: A personal and professional approach* (2nd ed., pp. 213–237). Lanham, MD: University Press of America.

Stewart, C., & Cash, W. (1991). *Interviewing: Principles and practices* (6th ed.). Dubuque, IA: Wm. C. Brown.

Stiff, J. B. (1994). *Persuasive communication*. New York: Guilford Press.

Stobbe, M. (2012, March 22). Move-in before marriage no longer predicts divorce. *Raleigh News & Observer*, p. 4A.

Stolberg, S. (2009, January 29). From the top, the White House unbuttons formal dress code. *New York Times*, pp. A1, A14.

Strasser, M. (1997). *Legally wed: Same-sex marriage and the constitution*. Ithaca, New York: Cornell University Press.

Straus, S., Glasziou, P., Richardson, W. S., & Haynes, B. (2010). *Evidence-based medicine* (4th ed.). Philadelphia: Churchill Livingstone.

Styer, J. (2012). *Talking back to Facebook*. New York: Scribner.

Swain, S. (1989). Covert intimacy: Closeness in men's friendships. In B. Risman & P. Schwartz (Eds.), *Gender and intimate relationships* (pp. 71–86). Belmont, CA: Wadsworth.

Swidler, A. (2001). *Talk of love: How culture matters*. Chicago: University of Chicago Press.

Swiss, T. (Ed.). (2001). *Unspun: Key concepts for understanding the World Wide Web*. New York: New York University Press.

Sypher, B., Bostrom, R., & Siebert, J. (1989). Listening, communication abilities, and success at work. *Journal of Business Communication, 26*, 293–303.

Tabuchi, H. (2012, May 30). Educated, but not fitting in. *New York Times*, pp. B1, B2.

Tashiro, T., & Frazier, P. (2003). "I'll never be in a relationship like that again": Personal growth following romantic relationship breakups. *Personal Relationships, 10*, 113–128.

Tavris, C., & Aronson, E. (2007). *Mistakes were made (but not by me): Why we justify foolish beliefs, bad decisions, and hurtful acts*. New York: Harcourt.

Taylor, A., Wiley, A., Kuo, F., & Sullivan, W. (1998). Growing up in the inner city: Green spaces as places to grow. *Environment and Behavior, 30*, 3–27.

Telework. (2010). Retrieved from http://www.telework.gov/Reports_and_Studies/Annual_Reports/2010teleworkreport.pdf

Thomas, J. (1999). Do you hear what I hear? *Women in Business, 51*, 1–14.

Thompson, F., & Grundgenett, D. (1999). Helping disadvantaged learners build effective learning skills. *Education, 120*, 130–135.

Thrun, S. (2011, December 6). Leave the driving to the car, and reap benefits in safety and mobility. *New York Times*, p. D4.

Tilsley, A. (2010, July 2). New policies accommodate transgender students. *Chronicle of Higher Education*, pp. A19–A20.

Ting-Toomey, S. (2005). The matrix of face: An updated face-negotiation theory. In W. B. Gudykunst (Ed.), *Theorizing about intercultural communication* (pp. 71–92). Thousand Oaks, CA: Sage.

Toulmin, S. (1958). *The uses of argument*. Cambridge, MA: Cambridge University Press.

Toulmin, S., Rieke, R., & Janik, A. (1984). *An introduction to reasoning* (2nd ed.). New York: Macmillan.

Trenholm, S. (1991). *Human communication theory* (2nd ed.). Englewood Cliffs, NJ: Prentice Hall.

Trice, H., & Beyer, J. (1984). Studying organizational cultures through rites and ceremonials. *Academy of Management Review, 9,* 653–669.

Tsai, F., & Reis, H. (2009). Perceptions by and of lonely people in social networks. *Personal Relationships, 16,* 221–238.

Tugend, A. (2011, July 2). Comparing yourself to others: It's not all bad. *New York Times,* p. B6.

Turkle, S. (2011). *Alone together: Why we expect more of technology and less of each other.* New York: Basic.

Turow, J. (2008). *Media today* (3rd ed.). New York: Routledge.

Tusing, K., & Dillard, J. (2000). The sounds of dominance: Vocal precursors of perceived dominance during interpersonal influence. *Human Communication Research, 26,* 148–171.

Underwood, A., & Adler, J. (2005, April 25). When cultures clash. *Newsweek,* pp. 68–72.

Urgo, J. (2000). *The age of distraction.* Jackson: Mississippi University Press.

U.S. Department of Labor. (1992). *Cultural diversity in the workplace.* Washington, DC: Government Printing Office.

Van Styke, E. (1999). *Listening to conflict: Finding constructive solutions to workplace disputes.* New York: AMA Communications.

Walker, M. B., & Trimboli, A. (1989). Communicating affect: The role of verbal and nonverbal content. *Journal of Language and Social Psychology, 8,* 229–248.

Walker, S. (2007). *Style and status: Selling beauty to African American women.* Lexington: University of Kentucky Press.

Watzlawick, P., Beavin, J., & Jackson, D. D. (1967). *Pragmatics of human communication.* New York: W. W. Norton.

Wayne, T. (2010, December 12). *Digital divide is a matter of income.* Retrieved from Pew Center for Research: http://www.nytimes.com/2010/12/13/business/media/13drill.html

Weed, J. (2012, June 12). The app as health aide. *New York Times,* p. B6.

Wegner, H., Jr. (2005). Disconfirming communication and self-verification in marriage: Associations among the demand/withdraw interaction pattern, feeling understood, and marital satisfaction. *Journal of Social and Personal Relationships, 22,* 19–31.

Weimann, G. (2000). *Communicating unreality: Modern media and the reconstruction of reality.* Newbury Park, CA: Sage.

Werner, C., Altman, I., & Oxley, D. (1985). Temporal aspects of homes: A transactional perspective. In I. Altman & C. M. Werner (Eds.), *Home environments, 8. Human behavior and environment: Advances in theory and research* (pp. 1–32). Beverly Hills: Sage.

West, C., & Zimmerman, D. H. (1987). Doing gender. *Gender and Society, 1,* 125–151.

Whitman, T., White, R., O'Mara, K., & Goeke-Morey, M. (1999). Environmental aspects of infant health and illness. In T. Whitman & T. Merluzzi (Eds.), *Life-span perspectives on health and illness* (pp. 105–124). Mahwah, NJ: Erlbaum.

Whorf, B. (1956). *Language, thought, and reality.* New York: MIT Press/Wiley.

Williams, G. (1995). *Life on the color line: The true story of a white boy who discovered he was black.* New York: Plume.

Williams, R. (1994). *The non-designer's design book: Design and typographic principles for the visual novice.* Berkeley, CA: Peachpit Press.

Wilson, G., & Goodall, H., Jr. (1991). *Interviewing in context.* New York: McGraw-Hill.

Wilson, J. F., & Arnold, C. C. (1974). *Public speaking as a liberal art* (4th ed.). Boston: Allyn & Bacon.

Winans, J. A. (1938). *Speechmaking.* New York: Appleton-Century-Crofts.

Winbush, G. (2000). African American women. In M. Julia (Ed.), *Constructing gender: Multicultural perspectives in working with women* (pp. 11–34). Belmont, CA: Wadsworth.

Wines, M. (2011, November 12). Picking the pitch-perfect brand name in China. *New York Times,* p. A4.

Wolvin, A. (2009). Listening, understanding and misunderstanding. In W. F. Eadie (Ed.), *21st century communication: A reference handbook* (pp. 137–146). Thousand Oaks, CA: Sage.

Wong, K. (2012). Working through identity: Understanding class in the context of race, ethnicity, and gender. In A. González, M. Houston, & V. Chen (Eds.), *Our voices: Essays in culture, ethnicity, and communication* (pp. 254–260). New York: Oxford University Press.

Wood, A., & Smith, M. (2001). *Online communication: Linking technology, identity, and culture.* Mahwah, NJ: Erlbaum.

Wood, J. T. (1982). Communication and relational culture: Bases for the study of human relationships. *Communication Quarterly, 30,* 75–84.

Wood, J. T. (1992). Telling our stories: Narratives as a basis for theorizing sexual harassment. *Journal of Applied Communication Research, 4,* 349–363.

Wood, J. T. (1993). Engendered relations: Interaction, caring, power, and responsibility in intimacy. In S. W. Duck (Ed.), *Understanding relationship processes, 3: Social context and relationships* (pp. 26–54). Newbury Park, CA: Sage.

Wood, J. T. (1994a). Engendered identities: Shaping voice and mind through gender. In D. Vocate (Ed.), *Intrapersonal communication: Different voices, different minds* (pp. 145–167). Hillsdale, NJ: Erlbaum.

Wood, J. T. (1994b). Saying it makes it so: The discursive construction of sexual harassment. In S. Bingham (Ed.), *Conceptualizing sexual harassment as discursive practice* (pp. 17–30). Westport, CT: Praeger.

Wood, J. T. (1994c). *Who cares? Women, care, and culture.* Carbondale: Southern Illinois University Press.

Wood, J. T. (1995a). Feminist scholarship and research on personal relationships. *Journal of Social and Personal Relationships, 12,* 103–120.

Wood, J. T. (1995b). The part is not the whole. *Journal of Social and Personal Relationships, 12,* 563–567.

Wood, J. T. (Ed.). (1996). *Gendered relationships.* Mountain View, CA: Mayfield.

Wood, J. T. (2001). The normalization of violence in heterosexual romantic relationships: Women's narratives of love and violence. *Journal of Social and Personal Relationships, 18,* 239–261.

Wood, J. T. (2002). Gendered speech communities. In L. Samovar & R. Porter (Eds.), *Intercultural Communication: A Reader* (10th ed. pp. 218–229). Belmont, CA: Wadsworth.

Wood, J. T. (2004). *Interpersonal communication: Everyday encounters* (4th ed.). Belmont, CA: Wadsworth.

Wood, J. T. (2005). Feminist standpoint theory and muted group theory: Commonalities and divergences. *Women & Language, 28,* 61–64.

Wood, J. T. (2006a). Chopping the carrots: Creating intimacy moment by moment. In J. T. Wood & S. W. Duck (Eds.), *Composing relationships: Communication in everyday life* (pp. 15–23). Belmont, CA: Thomson Wadsworth.

Wood, J. T. (2006b). Monsters and victims: Male felons' accounts of intimate partner violence. *Journal of Social and Personal Relationships, 21,* 555–576.

Wood, J. T. (2007a). *Gendered lives* (7th ed.). Belmont, CA: Wadsworth.

Wood, J. T. (2007b). *Interpersonal communication: Everyday encounters* (5th ed.). Belmont, CA: Wadsworth.

Wood, J. T. (2010). The can-do discourse and young women's anticipations of future. *Women & Language, 33,* 103–107.

Wood, J. T. (2011). Which ruler do we use? Theorizing the division of domestic labor. *Family Communication Journal, 11,* 39–49.

Wood, J. T. (2013). *Gendered lives: Communication, gender and culture* (10th ed.). Belmont, CA: Wadsworth.

Wood, J. T., Dendy, L., Dordek, E., Germany, M., & Varallo, S. (1994). Dialectic of difference: A thematic analysis of intimates' meanings for differences. In K. Carter & M. Presnell (Eds.), *Interpretive approaches to interpersonal communication* (pp. 115–136). New York: State University of New York Press.

Wood, J. T., & Dow, B. (2010). The invisible politics of "choice" in the workplace. In S. Hayden & L. Hallstein (Eds.), *Contemplating Maternity in an Era of Choice* (pp. 203–225). New York: Lexington.

Wood, J. T., & Duck, S. (2006). Introduction. In J. T. Wood & S. Ducks (Eds.), *Composing relationships: Communication in everyday life* (pp. 1–13). Belmont, CA: Thomson Wadsworth.

Wood, J. T., & Inman, C. C. (1993). In a different mode: Masculine styles of communicating closeness. *Journal of Applied Communication Research, 21,* 279–295.

Wood, J. T., & Phillips, G. M. (1990). The pedagogy of group decision making: Teaching alternative strategies. In G. M. Phillips (Ed.), *Small group communication: Theory and pedagogy* (pp. 101–118). Norwood, NJ: Ablex.

Woolfolk, A. E. (1987). *Educational psychology.* Englewood Cliffs, NJ: Prentice Hall.

Wu, C., & Shaffer, D. R. (1988). Susceptibility to persuasive appeals as a function of source credibility and prior experience with attitude object. *Journal of Personal and Social Psychology, 52,* 677–688.

Yen, H. (2012, May 17). Minority birthrate now surpasses whites in US, Census shows. *Huffington Post.* Retrieved May 28, 2012, from http://www.huffingtonpost.com/2012/05/17/minorities-birth-rate-now-surpass-whites-in-us-census_n_1523230.html

Young, S., Wood, J., Phillips, G., & Pedersen, D. (2001). *Group discussion* (3rd ed.). Prospect Heights, IL: Waveland.

Yum, J. (2000). The impact of Confucianism on interpersonal relationships and communication patterns in East Asia. In L. Samovar & R. Porter (Eds.), *Intercultural communication: A reader* (9th ed., pp. 63–73). Belmont, CA: Wadsworth.

Zediker, K. (1993, February). *Rediscovering the tradition: Women's history with a relational approach to the basic public speaking course.* Albuquerque: Western States Communication Association.

Zukerman, L. (1999, April 17). Words go right to the brain, but can they stir the heart? *New York Times,* p. 9.

Index